Rich and Poor States
in the Middle East

D0075339

About the Book and Editors

Rich and Poor States in the Middle East:
Egypt and the New Arab Order
edited by Malcolm H. Kerr and El Sayed Yassin

While oil wealth has enriched some Middle East Arab nations, others that lack oil resources have remained poor and are looking now to their oil-rich neighbors for development assistance. This collection of studies on the economic, social, and political relationships between the haves and the have-nots in the Middle East focuses on Egypt — the largest state in the region — and on its prospects for change based on financial assistance from other Arab countries.

The authors have many disagreements about the future of both rich and poor nations in the Middle East and considerable skepticism about the possibility of transforming Egypt, but they do agree that the future must be projected in the framework of a new regional order in which oil wealth, labor migration, and liberalized national economies are fundamental realities.

Malcolm H. Kerr is professor of political science, University of California, Los Angeles, and director of the University of California Study Center in Cairo. He was visiting professor at the American University in Cairo from 1979 to 1981 and director of the Von Grunebaum Center for Near Eastern Studies, UCLA, 1977–1979. Among his publications are *The Arab Cold War* (1971) and *Islamic Reform* (1965). **El Sayed Yassin** is director of the Center for Political and Strategic Studies, Al Ahram, Cairo.

Westview Press

Rich and Poor States in the Middle East

Egypt and the New Arab Order

edited by Malcolm H. Kerr and El Sayed Yassin

Westview Press • Boulder, Colorado

The American University in Cairo Press • Egypt

Library
I.U.P.
Indiana, Pa.

338.0956 R371i
c.1

This volume is included in Westview's Special Studies on the Middle East.

All rights reserved. No part of this publication may be reproduced or transmitted in any form or by any means, electronic or mechanical, including photocopy, recording, or any information storage and retrieval system, without permission in writing from the publisher.

Copyright © 1982 by The Regents of the University of California

Published in 1982 in the United States of America by
  Westview Press, Inc.
  5500 Central Avenue
  Boulder, Colorado 80301
  Frederick A. Praeger, President and Publisher

Published in 1982 in Egypt by
  The American University in Cairo Press
  111 Sharia Qasr El Aini, Cairo

Library of Congress Catalog Card Number: 820126
ISBN: 0-86531-275-3
ISBN: 0-86531-276-1 pbk

Composition for this book was provided by the editors.
Printed and bound in the United States of America.

Contents

Preface

This book is the fruit of a collaborative enterprise undertaken by the Gustave E. Von Grunebaum Center for Near Eastern Studies of the University of California, Los Angeles, and the Centre for Political and Strategic Studies of Al-Ahram Foundation, Cairo, with the generous financial support of the Ford Foundation. The participants in the project include three permanent members of the UCLA faculty, four members of the research staff of the Ahram Centre, and other American and Egyptian scholars. Five of the Egyptian participants spent periods of six months or more at UCLA on visiting professorial appointments while they prepared their chapters for this volume. A workshop was held at UCLA in July 1980 and was attended by nine of the participants; on this occasion the first drafts of chapters underwent intensive critical review by all members of the group.

The following four chapters draw upon work initially undertaken under other auspices. A previous unpublished Arabic-language draft of Essam Montasser's paper, "The Arab Economy and Its Developing Strategy: A New Arab Economic Order", was presented at a meeting of the Association of Arab Economists in Baghdad in 1978. The chapter by Gouda Abdel-Khalek, "The Open Door Economic Policy in Egypt: Its Contribution to Investment and Its Equity Implications," is adapted in part from his paper, "The Open Door Economic Policy in Egypt: A Search for Meaning, Interpretation, and Implication," in Herbert M. Thompson, editor, *Studies in Egyptian Political Economy* (Cairo Papers in Social Science, Vol. 2, Monograph 3, March 1979, American University in Cairo). Jeswald Salacuse's chapter, "Arab Capital and Trilateral Ventures in the Middle East: Is Three a Crowd?" is derived from a larger study he prepared with the support of the Ford Foundation on "Arab Capital in the Development of Egypt and the Sudan". Other portions of this study are contained in his article "The Arab Authority for Agricultural Investment and Development: A New Model for Capital Transfer in the Middle East", *Journal of World Trade*, Vol. XII (1978), pp. 55–66. The chapter by Naiem Sherbiny and Ismail Serageldin, "Expatriate Labor and Economic Growth: Saudi Demand for Egyptian Labor", captures highlights of work they have undertaken in the course of their duties at the World Bank. Several passages from the first and last chapters of this volume, by Malcolm H. Kerr, appear also in his article "Rich and Poor in the New Arab Order," *Journal of Arab Affairs* (Fresno, Calif.), vol. 1, no. 1 (Fall 1981).

Saad Eddin Ibrahim, author of the chapter "Oil, Migration and the New Arab Social Order", has also prepared a considerably magnified version of the material, to be published in book form under the title *The New Arab Social Order*.

Most of the planning and editorial work for this volume was done by Malcolm H. Kerr, with the frequent advice and assistance of El Sayed Yassin. Our roles will be reversed in the preparation of a revised version of the text to be published in Arabic by Al-Ahram in Cairo, edited primarily by El Sayed Yassin.

The contents of all chapters in this volume are the sole responsibility of their individual authors. No opinions expressed therein should be attributed to the editors of the volume or the authors of other chapters, nor to any institution with which the authors have been affiliated, the Ford Foundation, the University of California, Al-Ahram Foundation, or the World Bank.

Finally, we wish to express our warmest thanks to the following persons whose efforts and encouragement have been of particular help to us in preparing this volume: Messrs. Robert Edwards and Guillaume de Spoelberch and Dr. Ann Lesch of the Ford Foundation; Professor Speros Vryonis, Director of the Von Grunebaum Center for Near Eastern Studies at UCLA, Mrs. Teresa Joseph, Editorial Assistant, and Ms. Nina Bertelsen, Administrative Assistant at the Center; Mrs. Mervyn Adams Seldon of Westview Press; and Mrs. Lindy Ayubi, who retyped and copy-edited the entire manuscript and prepared the Index.

Cairo   *Malcolm H. Kerr*
                                               El Sayed Yassin

I
Introduction:
Egypt in the Shadow of the Gulf

Malcolm H. Kerr

The revolution in oil prices in the 1970s has had profound effects throughout the world, nowhere more dramatically than in the Arab states. These countries, though widely different from one another in population, resources, and stages of development, are traditionally grouped together by ties of culture, geography, history, and political sentiment. Thanks to the presence of great concentrations of oil and money in their midst, and thus to their potential for both progress and conflict, they now find themselves the objects of intense world attention for which they are quite unprepared.

The oil being located mainly in the most thinly populated and, until recently, backward and remote of the Arab states, while the financial requirements of the others grow apace, the overall prospects for regional progress are complicated and problematical. What is certain is that despite the differences among them, the societies of all the Arab states, oil-producing and non-producing alike, have been engaged in a common process of structural change. Both among and within these states it has become possible to speak of a new Arab order, socially, economically and politically. This does not mean that life among the Arabs has become more orderly, but rather that the patterns of interaction among them have become more intensive and have undergone important changes in character.

On the social level the engine of change is the massive migration of manpower to the oil states, a phenomenon with consequences of fundamental importance to the sending and receiving countries alike. On the economic level it is the accumulation of financial assets in the oil states and their availability for circulation throughout the region. On the political level it is the new belief that power grows, not out of the barrel of a gun nor out of the appeal of a revolutionary leader or movement, but out of an ample state treasury.

All of these changes give rise to a host of consequences, described at length in the various chapters of this volume. And in all three spheres of change — social, economic and political — the "new order" has meant new mechanisms binding the Arab world to the West: a flood of persons travelling in both directions for work, business or study; a great upsurge in commercial and financial transactions as petrodollars are recycled; and a new perception by Western governments, for good or ill, of their vital stake in the existing political arrangements in the Gulf and a new determination to protect it.

As for the implications of the oil boom for public policy in the Arab states, perhaps the most important are the steps that may be taken towards regional economic integration. This is by no means a new idea, but the sudden accumulation of revenues in several Arab states has made it possible for the first time to consider many development schemes that once seemed beyond reach. In many other respects, government planners and private entrepreneurs are now reminding themselves of all the ways in which the potential for regional cooperation had already been present but has not been implemented. And for many Arabs, economic unity looks like a possible short cut to the long-elusive goal of political unity, as well as an historic opportunity for the Arab nation to act in concert to raise the living standards of all of its 140 million people.

Despite the existence of various formal agreements and a good many years of verbal commitment to the idea of economic integration, the level of implementation has remained disappointingly low. Part of the problem has been political, with regimes sharply divided on grounds of ideology, personal rivalry, and foreign affiliation. Part of it has been economic, as the underdeveloped economies of the Arab states have not been naturally complementary in many respects. The institutional framework for cooperation is inadequate. The conflict with Israel drains several states of resources for development and also impedes interaction by imposing a geographic barrier between the African and Asian Arab countries.

Still, in principle the long-range potential for development in the Arab world is very good indeed, provided that the separate resources of labor, capital, land, water and mineral wealth — which tend to be found in different countries — can be brought together. The chapter in this volume by Essam Montasser projects some of the possibilities. While the recent focussing of attention on petroleum and petrodollars has encouraged much preoccupation with the industrial potential of the region, agriculture also remains a target area for development of prime importance. According to one (rather optimistic) estimate, for instance, in the Sudan alone, the pooling of Egyptian manpower and expertise, Gulf capital, and Sudanese land and water could produce as many as 100 million acres of reclaimed farmland. According to the same source, adequate investment and organization could also increase annual grain production in Egypt from seven million to 16.8 million tons; in Iraq from six to 24 million tons; and in Syria from 1.7 to seven million tons.[1]

Yet the recent political history of the Arab world has made it clear that calculations of this sort are of no practical importance in an atmosphere in which inter-governmental confidence is lacking. If economic unity could become a short cut to political unity, the fact remains that economic unity will not impose itself by any natural process outside a political context. Just how much money, from whom to whom, for what purpose, and with what conditions, will the money flow? And particularly, what are the implications of the flow for individual Arab states, and for the pattern of political relationships among governments in the region as a whole?

To an important extent, conflicts and uncertainties among governments can be minimized by means of imaginative efforts to establish appropriate institutional mechanisms designed to capitalize on common economic or other interests. The Arab Agricultural Authority, the Arab Fund for Economic and Social Development, and the Kuwait Fund for Arab Economic Development (the pioneer institution for inter-Arab developmental cooperation) are obvious examples. How such institutions have come into existence, what combinations of Arab interests they serve, and what kind of potential they represent is the subject of the chapter by Jeswald Salacuse.

But beyond the point of cooperation reached in such operations, the dimension of uncontrolled political maneuvering still remains. As Ali E. Hillal Dessouki reminds us in his contribution to this volume, the overall pattern of political relationships in the Arab world underwent fundamental changes in the 1970s. Hence the government of each state, whether a prospective dispenser or receiver of oil funds, must face basic choices as to how to play its part in the game.

The oil producers have naturally had an easier range of practical options from which to select, with less at stake. Libya, Kuwait, Saudi Arabia and Iraq, in accordance with their circumstances and the whims of their leaders, have each made distinctive decisions. Libya has cultivated a high profile as a radical populist society at home and a patron of revolution abroad, using her money as a sort of guerilla weapon. Kuwait has sought the lowest possible profile, while also reducing her production and channelling much of her surplus into non-political foreign investment. Saudi Arabia, while hardly less cautious by instinct than Kuwait, has carefully built up her role as a conservative regional manipulator in the interests of Arab stability and solidarity. Iraq seemed for a time to try to avoid the role of a surplus producer in order to avoid an entangling regional role, concentrating instead on internal development while masking her isolationism by verbal extremism on international issues.

These policies did not always produce the desired results. Libya has found that to exert strong influence over time, neither the dispensing of money nor the preaching of ideology is really enough. As Hazem Beblawi suggests in his chapter, neither Kuwait nor others have grasped — or acted upon — the truth that their own Arab and Third World community offers them the only ultimately productive outlet for the investment of their surplus funds. Saudi Arabia has found that even when the lines of patronage seem firmly established, as they did in her relationship with Egypt, the client may be capable of surprisingly independent behavior. Iraq has found that the temptation to seek regional hegemony — expressed in her invasion of Iran in 1980 — was too great to allow her to persevere in her self-imposed isolation.

Yet whatever the miscalculations of the oil-rich, they can generally expect to survive them. For their capital-poor Arab brothers, the stakes in the choices they make are much greater, for the prospect of financing truly effective development programs presents itself to them as a once-in-a-lifetime opportunity that they cannot afford to miss.

Most significantly has this been the case for Egypt, not only because her population (43 million in 1980) is by far the largest in the Arab world, but because more than once in the past Egypt has been in the forefront of movements of modernization and development in the area, all of which have eventually led to disappointment. The reasons for disappointment are surrounded with much controversy which we need not consider here. Let us instead just ask whether there is now another path by which Egypt, and perhaps others with her, can now hope to organize human progress. This is a question of great historic drama.

Thus we see that the prospective recipients of oil funds in the Arab world face policy choices that are portentous yet unpredictable. For better or for worse, almost all of them, including Egypt, Syria, Jordan, the Sudan, North Yemen and Tunisia, have followed economic policies in the 1970s pointing in a basically similar direction: that of liberalization or, in Arabic, *al-infitah* ("the opening up"). Despite considerable variations of detail from one country to another, *infitah* has everywhere included measures to relax central controls over the economy so as to facilitate the entrance of foreign capital, the productive investment of domestic capital, and the movement of domestic labor out to the oil-producing neighbors.

Meanwhile, the economic liberalization has been accompanied in most cases with a political counterpart: the revival of certain conservative interests at home, closer and more deferential relations with the oil states (especially Saudi Arabia), and similar relations with the OECD countries (especially the United States).

Together, the economic and political liberalizations have been the means by which the capital-poor have adapted themselves to the oil boom. While some analysts seeking to explain these changes, such as Nazih Ayubi in this volume, have concentrated mainly on the interplay of domestic social forces that has produced *infitah,* remarking on the fragility of the previous era of socialist-oriented reform in countries such as Egypt, Syria and Tunisia, these domestic factors may not have been so significant as the pressure generated by the proximity of the oil wealth, and its close connection with the industrial and financial system of Europe and the United States. The Western states have seen the shift in the politics and economics of Egypt and other Arab states both as a strategic instrument to wean them away from past ties with the Soviet Union, and as a commercial device to enlarge their own fields of trade and investment. Thus Galal Amin in his chapter suggests that external pressure was much the most important factor of all in explaining the chances of economic policy in both the oil and the non-oil states in the Middle East. The relative importance — and interrelationships — of internal and external factors of change will doubtless remain a matter of debate for many years. In any event, the combination of factors was strong enough to sweep aside all sorts of institutional and ideological obstacles.

It is true that in several of the capital-poor states before 1973, certain domestic changes had already occurred which served to prepare their governments to react effectively to the sudden quadrupling of oil prices. In Egypt, Gamal ʿAbd al-Nasir and his more leftist associates had gone; in Syria the ideological militants of the Salah Jadid faction of the Baʿth Party had been ousted by Hafiz al-Asad; in Tunisia, Habib Bourguiba had deposed Ahmad Ben Salah from his position as economic czar and cut short his collectivist experiments. In each of these countries there was a new readiness to loosen some of the controls, attract foreign capital, and allow the underemployed domestic labor force to migrate to the oil fields in Libya and the Gulf.

Yet these budding changes prior to 1973 were nothing compared to what followed, for the boom in oil revenues offered the governments of the poor states far more than they had previously dreamed of. The most important of these changes and the one destined to have the most profound impact on the society of the entire region, is the subject of Saad Ibrahim's chapter: a quantum increase in the number of migrant workers and skilled professionals employed in the oil states and in the volume of the wages they remitted to their home economies. Other benefits of the post-1973 era included a lavish scale of private investment by citizens of the oil states in the non-oil ones, and the flow of inter-governmental aid and investment in amounts far exceeding previous receipts in foreign aid from the great powers. In fact, one would not be a substitute but a supplement to the other, for an Egypt or a Tunisia lubricated with Arab petrodollars would become a much more eligible trading partner and field for investment for the Western countries (if not the Soviet Union) than before.

These changes were also occurring at a critical moment for the national economies of several of the poorer countries. Egypt and Syria had been hard hit by the effects of the 1967 and 1973 wars and by the continuous military mobilization in the years between; Yemen was struggling to recover from the devastation of eight years of civil war. In 1973 a spectacular increase in world grain prices added several hundred million dollars to the foreign exchange burden of Egypt, and imposed comparable burdens on others. The détente between the superpowers made it look less and less plausible that the consumption and investment needs of these countries would be met by great-power aid, at least not by the sort of competitive bidding that Nasir had once managed to encourage between Moscow and Washington. In these circumstances, one should hardly wonder that the fund of capital that suddenly began to accumulate within the Arab family itself should have appeared to hard-pressed governments as a heaven-sent opportunity.

Despite Egypt's political decline and despite the quarantine imposed on the regime of Anwar al-Sadat by other Arab governments in retaliation for the Egyptian-Israeli peace treaty, Egypt continues to play a central role in the new Arab order, primarily within an unspoken bilateral relationship with Saudi Arabia. The pairing of these two—of which much is discussed in Paul Jabber's chapter—is particularly interesting not only because it has survived the rupture of diplomatic relations between them but also because of the almost total contrast in their characteristics, a contrast that might prove fruitful because of the elements of complementarity. Egypt possesses the largest population in the region, and one of the lowest levels of per capita income; but she also boasts the Arab world's most extensive industrial base, its most elaborate educational and cultural network, and by far the largest pool of skilled and unskilled manpower. Saudi Arabia, on the other hand, enjoys a fabulous income but has only a sparse population, and only recently has made a beginning in building the physical, social and institutional elements of a modern society. As Naiem Sherbiny and Ismail Serageldin show in their chapter, even with a sustained effort to restrict oil production and/or public expenditure in the coming years there is no prospect that Saudi Arabia will be able to do without the migrant Arab manpower on which it has come to depend so heavily. Saudi Arabia's situation is shared by the other Gulf states and by Libya, while that of Egypt is more or less representative of the other non-oil-exporting Arab states such as Syria, Jordan, Lebanon, and Tunisia. In this respect, the bilateral Saudi-Egyptian connection reflects the new Arab order at large.

As each possesses what the other needs, the basis for partnership is obvious. The rapid rise of oil revenues has meant a great explosion of economic activity of all kinds, which has served to attract the massive migration of manpower from the non-oil states. This has led to the heavy flow of remittances of earnings from laborers back to their countries of origin, and these in turn have become the mainstays of several Arab economies. Other aspects of *infitah* — tourism and foreign investment for example — bring added revenues into the economy. Egypt, Tunisia, Syria and other states experienced a rapid rise in their Gross National Product during the second half of the 1970s, reaching in the case of Egypt some nine percent annually.

All this is indeed impressive, and is certainly to the benefit of large numbers of people: especially to the migrant workers but also to certain of their compatriots left at home to fill in the gap and whose services are now in greater demand — an important mechanism of social mobility analyzed by Georges Sabagh in his chapter — as well as to contractors, importers, retailers and others. As Professor Sabagh indicates, however, it remains an open question as to just how rapidly the loss of skills from emigration can be replaced in the home market; there is bound to be a time lag and thus some loss. A casual visitor to Cairo, Damascus, Tunis, Amman or Sanaa becomes quickly aware, from the congested traffic and incessant building construction, that plenty of money is circulating within the economy, much of it spent on luxuries to which Egyptians and others have grown accustomed while working in the oil countries. All of this helps to explain the phenomenon of inflation, which in turn explains why it was that in a supposedly prospering Egypt, bloody riots against the government erupted in January 1977, duplicated in equally prosperous Tunisia just a year later.

Inflation, partly imported into the liberalized economies along with consumer products and workers' remittances, has meant mounting hardship for the majority of the population of the non-oil states who are in no position to market their labor or their products on advantageous terms: government employees, most agricultural workers, public sector industrial and commercial employees, and the mass of under-employed people performing half-needed petty personal services in the cities. At the government level, inflation means mounting pressure to subsidize commodities and public services, thereby adding to the deficit in the budget and in the balance of payments: a sure rule of thumb is that the rise in public expenditure occasioned by the liberalization outstrips any rise in public revenues generated by expanded commercial activity. For the population as a whole, the rule of thumb is that while some gain and many do not, the net result is a sharp increase in inequality and in mass hardship. This is to some extent offset by the fact that labor migration is a process drawing in a sprinkling of members of all social classes.

In the long run the liberalization may be justified if it leads to a real expansion in the productive capacity of the economy, through the stimulation of investment in the right areas. But the short-term results are discouraging, and it is hard to see why the longer term is likely to bring anything much better. As the chapters in this volume by Gouda Abdel-Khalek, Galal Amin and Nazih Ayubi confirm, up to the end of 1980 investment capital has found its way in Egypt primarily into commercial rather than into agricultural or industrial expansion: luxury housing, luxury consumer imports, banking, tourist facilities. These are areas in which both the remittances from abroad and the advent of large numbers of foreigners pump plenty of demand into the economy, and add to the pressures for inflation without generating more than limited increases in employment: all in all, apparently, "hardly a useful arrangement" as Gouda Abdel-Khalek has remarked in his chapter on *infitah*. The large investments in manufacturing enterprises hoped for by the planners of the liberalization policy have failed to materialize—partly because of inadequate infrastructure and facilities, partly because the socialist-oriented bureaucratic restrictions and procedures of an earlier era have not been sufficiently dismantled. These and other shortcomings are examined in Nazih Ayubi's chapter, as are also some of the related political and social incentives that stimulated *infitah* in Egypt in the first place.

Thus the overall effect of *infitah* in several Arab states has included an accentuated maldistribution of income, governmental financial squeeze, labor shortages, agricultural decline, and an overall distortion of development priorities. Public services—low-cost housing, education, transport—have suffered.

All of this seems bizarre, when we remember that the starting point in these events was the increased supply of money in the Arab community, presumably available both for development and for improved levels of mass consumption. After all, as some welfare experts in the United States have remarked, what the poor most conspicuously lack is money. One would have thought in a country as well endowed with talent and as short of money as Egypt, the advent of an extra three or four billion dollars a year would serve to put the country on its feet. But this presumption overlooks the possibility that shortage of money may not be the chief deficiency in Arab development and that, as our colleague Galal Amin shrewdly observed many years ago,[2] priorities are perhaps more likely to be misplaced when easy money is on hand than when it is not. The downfall of the Iranian monarchy in 1978–1979, evidently fuelled in part by inflation and governmental corruption and waste, may be highly instructive for a poor state such as Egypt whose leaders might be tempted to suppose that petrodollars will solve their problems. I have speculated on this and other points of comparison between the Shah's Iran and Sadat's Egypt in my chapter at the end of this volume.

Nonetheless, there is no doubt that in all the non-oil countries the need for infusions of capital is real enough. In the Egyptian case, indeed, this is an old story, for Egypt has faced balance-of-payments problems ever since the exhaustion of her sterling reserves in the 1950s. In the 1950s and 1960s Nasir conducted an incessant campaign to muster contributions from the Soviet Union, the United States and others to finance his ambitious development programs. After the defeat by Israel in 1967 he was obliged to negotiate for aid from the Arab oil monarchs to compensate for the loss of the Suez Canal revenues and to re-equip his armed forces.

But the access to Arab oil money in the 1970s (and prospectively in the 1980s) has had much more dramatic implications. The amount of money potentially available is unimaginably greater than anything received in the past, and because it comes from within the Arab family there is some reason to imagine that the donors may prove more responsive to Egypt's particular needs and requests than others have been. Moreover, with their need for Egyptian manpower and, in some instances, Egypt's political cooperation, the relationship has an aspect of healthy mutuality.

The mutuality, however, is less than complete, and so is the goodwill. On the Egyptian side there has been a pointed conviction that the oil states bore Egypt a heavy moral obligation because of her sacrifices in the wars against Israel. In fact, during the four years that followed the 1973 war, assistance committed to Egypt by the Gulf states of Saudi Arabia, Kuwait, the United Arab Emirates and Qatar, totalled no less than $6.5 billion, conservatively estimated.[3] This was a large sum, though it fell far short of what the "Arab Marshall Plan" sometimes spoken of in Egyptian official circles might have entailed. More than a few Egyptians expressed the belief that the intention of the Gulf states was to give Egypt just enough to keep her and the Sadat regime alive, but not enough to restore her previous strength and potential for Arab leadership.

Meanwhile, on the part of the Gulf states there has been a widespread feeling that no amount of aid would satisfy Egypt or rescue her crumbling economy; and there has also been plenty of anger at Sadat and his government for abandoning the struggle against the Arabs' common enemy.

Egypt's readiness to cultivate the Saudi connection carries a number of crucial implications. Saudi Arabia is not just another Arab country: it is the citadel of Islamic orthodoxy, and it is governed by men whose political outlook is highly conservative. Moreover, the Saudis' constant preoccupation in Arab affairs has been a defensive one: how to fend off threats and challenges from other parties who are more sophisticated, better armed, better manned and better organized than themselves, and who are jealous of their wealth. Beyond this, they are well aware of the extent to which their security, finance and growing infrastructure depend on the preservation of a cooperative relationship with the United States and Europe—a condition not always compatible with the requirements of inter-Arab politics.

How the Saudi leaders deal with Egypt, therefore, how ready they are to meet her needs, or to rely on her to meet theirs, must depend on their calculation of Egyptian intentions and of the practical long-term consequences of a closely cooperative relationship. How strong do they really want Egypt to become? How economically healthy and independent? To what extent are they willing to see Egypt regain political influence in the Arab world? How confident are they that, with their own recent accumulation of wealth, they can hold their own in inter-Arab politics and control the political consequences of their distribution of aid?

The answers to these questions have been considerably complicated by two events of recent years: the Egyptian-Israeli peace treaty of 1979, and the Iraqi invasion of Iran in 1980. Both of these events illustrated the ambiguity as well as the vulnerability of Saudi Arabia's political, strategic and economic interests.

Sadat's initiative and the Saudi response to it suggested that some of the new images of petrodollar politics in the mid-1970s were in need of correction. It had become fashionable to point to the growing diplomatic ascendancy of Saudi Arabia, and to the helplessness of Egypt. Not only had the Saudis come into the possession of enormous financial assets, but they seemed to show considerable skill at using them in the international arena, building up their credit, their reputation for probity, and their leadership in a discreet way—with the industrialized world, the Third World, and in the Middle East. If money talks, as surely it must when it exists in billions, the Saudi leaders seemed to have the knack of making it speak authoritatively in a whisper. Egypt, it was said, was Saudi Arabia's completely dependent client, and Riyadh held a clear veto over Cairo's foreign and domestic policies. The same held for Jordan, Sudan and North Yemen. Syria may have been somewhat less beholden, but was still considered very responsive. Even Southern Yemen and Somalia had been (more or less) bought off.

Sadat showed that all this was a faulty view of the situation. His trips to Jerusalem and Camp David, and his negotiation of a virtually undisguised separate peace with Israel, took no account whatever of Saudi interests. Angry as the Saudis undoubtedly were with Sadat for presenting them and the other Arab states with a *fait accompli*, it was not to their advantage to seek Sadat's overthrow and replacement by unknown elements, or to deal destructive blows at the Egyptian economy. Their relationship with Egypt passed from that of a close partnership to that of a divorced couple who keep in touch and are "still friends". Egypt might be officially quarantined from the Arab system, but her weight and her interests were not altogether excluded from the Arab states' calculations.

While the Saudi government joined in the general Arab political boycott of Egypt, and in the cancellation of governmental aid and investment programs, they nevertheless took the lead in seeing to it that transport and communication links were kept open, that the employment of Egyptian workers in other Arab countries continued, and that the large deposits of Arab oil-rich governments in Egyptian banks were left intact.

Was this the old story, familiar everywhere between patrons and clients, of the tail wagging the dog? Or was this an indication that Sadat sensed an alternative to Saudi handouts: a new commercial and political connection with the United States and Israel, plus a spectrum of private investors from the Middle East and elsewhere? The lesson emerges, in any case, that the hegemony of mere money, unsupported by manpower, cultural attainments, military strength or industrial development, may be something of a mirage.

The Iraqi-Iranian war added something further to this lesson, for it served to remind the Saudis of their vulnerability in the face of ambitious and militarily more powerful neighbors, and therefore of the need for something other than Iraqi good will and forbearance to protect them. To defend their interests in the long run, they would need support from other Arab parties capable to some extent of offsetting Iraq's bid for military and political predominance in the region. Logic dictated, therefore, that somehow a way should be found to restore the bonds of legitimate partnership with Egypt, without offending Iraq or other Arab parties in the process.

Thus the new order of inter-Arab alignments appears not to be one in which the old Egyptian hegemony is replaced with Saudi or Iraqi leadership, but one in which all states in the region find themselves in flux, groping somewhat inconclusively for stable positions within a multi-polar equilibrium. In this new system, as Ali Dessouki tells us, we may expect an increasing tendency of governments to separate economic and political considerations in their relations with each other, following a new pragmatism in place of mercurial sentiment or inflexible ideology; and we may expect that in spite of the great need of the non-oil-exporting countries for aid and investment from their neighbors, the reciprocal nature of the ties will be better recognized.

Whatever the course of events between Egypt and Israel or in other conflict situations in the Middle East in coming years, the drama of Egypt's bid to prosper in the shadow of the Gulf states will continue to be poignant. This bid promises to be a test case for many other Third World countries whose developmental processes until now have been blocked. The enrichment of the OPEC countries can be greatly to their benefit or it can be at their expense, depending on the policies the oil producers decide to follow. Used positively, the oil income can become a collective Third World resource of enormous potential, while if the OPEC members miss their chance at statesmanship they may wind up simply driving the economies of the have-not nations into pauperism. While Egypt herself is a modest net exporter of oil, she remains nevertheless in urgent need of investment capital which the Arab oil states are in a unique position to supply. If they do not meet her needs, what help will there be for other less developed countries outside the Arab fold, such as Turkey, Pakistan or Zaire, whose financial problems are much more critical?

Furthermore, what is the future of Arab nationalism if the oil boom fails to salvage the largest of the Arab states? Even if it should be said that Egypt forfeited her eligibility for Arab aid by making peace with Israel, an obvious retort is that the prospects of relying on the Arabs for aid were insufficiently attractive to deter the president of Egypt from making his peace initiative. Matters might have been different had the proposal of massive aid to Egypt at the Baghdad conference in the fall of 1978 been made seriously at an earlier time, not as a political bribe but as an expression of Arab solidarity in meeting national development prob-lems.

Under whatever combination of regimes, the Arab world in the coming ten to twenty years faces an opportunity to develop the potential of its society that may not recur if it is missed. Among the many re-quisites for success, three general ones seem to be worth noting.

First is the need to generate mechanisms of progress indigenous to the society rather than imported from abroad. This means that technology needs not only to be "transferred" and "appropriate" but, in order to possess these qualities fully, it must be adapted and even *generated* locally. It means that imported capital, public or private, is no substitute for domestic savings and domestic entrepreneurial initiative. And it means that it matters a great deal for the development process to what extent the demand being met in the local market is *culturally* appropriate.

Like appropriate technology, appropriate demand signifies a genuine correspondence between what the inherited cultural patterns of members of a society lead them to use effectively in their lives, and what they consciously think they want: for what is consciously desired, as a response, for example, to the propagation of international fashions of consumption, may well go hand in hand with the expansion of national economies without contributing anything to national productive capacities to meet basic needs. In short, cultural alienation is bad for economic development, while development oriented towards basically alien modes of living may not really be development.[5]

Secondly, given the scattered distribution of resources in the Arab world — land, water, mineral wealth, manpower and capital — it is clear that organized progress requires an emphasis on coordinated multilateral projects which, in turn, require a solid institutional grounding. With or without political unity, it is vital that incentives among multiple Arab governments and enterprises be systematically guided in the direction of rationality and progress, and not left to their own devices to pursue ephemeral and anti-social objectives. Common planning among regimes, whether through the Arab League or less comprehensive state agencies, is essential in order to avoid duplication, to choose high priority investment targets, and to impart confidence to those putting up the money, as well as to those in whose territory the projects are to be carried out. The chances for development of Sudanese agriculture or of Egyptian industry, on the success of which the livelihood of millions in coming generations will depend, are closely tied up with the creation and nurturing of strong multilateral institutions.

Third and last is the political sphere. No other region of the globe presents the same baffling spectacle as the Arab world, with its perennial combination of an obsession with the ideal of unity and the practice of rivalry and mistrust. Between governments that do not trust each other, the ideal of unity can even be a destructive instrument, as it encourages each to interfere in the affairs of the other. The shape of relationships among Arab regimes has shifted constantly, as moments of harmony alternate with periods of bitter conflict; and the history of the past thirty years, during which most of the Arab states achieved independence, provides no very clear indication of the inner workings of this pattern or of the direction in which it may evolve in the future, whether towards greater harmony, greater conflict, or, for that matter, a lessening of public interest in the issues of pan-Arabism altogether.

Whatever the answer, however, it is clear that the first two requirements of development just mentioned — the indigenous generation of productive forces and the institutional framework for technical cooperation — cannot take shape in the absence of a steady minimum level of political harmony: something much less than pan-Arab union, perhaps, but something much more positive than the mercurial relationships of the past.

NOTES

1. Magdi Hifni, *Mustaqbal al-tanmiya wa al-taᶜawun al-iqtisadi alᶜarabi* [The Future of Development and Arab Economic Cooperation], (Cairo: Haiᵓat al-Kitab, 1975), pp. 121–123.

2. Galal Amin, *The Modernization of Poverty* (Leiden: Brill, 1974).

3. This includes bilateral aid commitments of $4.7 billion from the Gulf Organization for the Development of Egypt, but excludes loans from the various development funds, unannounced *ad hoc* gifts arranged between rulers, and deposits by Gulf governments in Egyptian banks. See United Nations Conference on Trade and Development (UNCTAD), "Financial Solidarity for Development: Efforts and Institutions of the Members of OPEC", (January 1979), and *Al-Nahar Arab Report and Memo,* (23 April 1979), both cited in Jake Wien, *Saudi-Egyptian Relations: the Political and Military Dimensions of Saudi Financial Flows to Egypt* (Santa Monica, Calif.: The Rand Corporation, P-6327, 1980), pp. 47–60.

4. See Galal Ahmad Amin, "Baᶜd qadaya al-infitah al-iqtisadi fi misr" [Some Issues of Infitah. . .] in Société Egyptienne d'Economie Politique, de Statistique et de Legislation, *Al-Iqtisad al-Misri fi rubᶜ qarn. . .* [The Egyptian Economy in a Quarter of a Century, 1952–1977: Papers and Discussions of the Third Conference of Egyptian Economists], ed. by Ismaᶜil Sabri ᶜAbdallah et al. (Cairo: Haiᶜ at al-Kitab, 1977), pp. 424–426. Amin offers as a definition of progress an expression borrowed from H. Merrill Jackson, "the increasing attainment of one's own cultural values."

Part One

The New Arab Social Order

II
Oil, Migration and the New Arab Social Order

Saad Eddin Ibrahim

I. INTRODUCTION

Social orders reproduce themselves with every new generation. But with each reproduction, varying degrees of alteration or even mutation take place. The Arab social order is no exception. Since the traumatic rediscovery of the West by the Arabs at the end of the 18th century and the subsequent penetration by the West into the Arab homeland, four big waves of social change have left their profound impacts on the Arab social structure. The colonial experience, modern science and technology, the national struggle for emancipation, and oil are the hallmarks of the four tidal waves and their chain reactions in the transformation of Arab society.[1] Every Arab generation since the 1800s has experienced the collapse of one or more aspects of the pre-modern social order, and the gestation, difficult labor and occasional caesarian birth of a new one. There have been many false pregnancies and several miscarriages. But through it all the old structures never disappeared — they continued to coexist, albeit in a crumpled or twisted form, with new or caricaturized modern structures. The continuous interplay between elements of the old and the new has given the Arab world a permanent state of "transition" for the last two centuries. Every generation believed it was the bearer of the burdens of transition, and occasionally felt trapped or victimized by it.

The Arab social order in the 1980s is a product of previous orders intersecting with regional and global events of the previous two decades. The symbolic point of its emergence may date back to the Arab defeat of 1967, to the death of Nasir in 1970, or to the Arab sense of triumph in their fourth war with Israel in 1973.[2] But whatever the hypothetical conception point of the new order, oil has been its underlying factor. As a

17

salient substructural force, oil has not only altered the global relation between the Arabs and the rest of the world, but has also triggered manifest as well as latent forces of change in the inter-Arab equation, within each Arab society, and inside most men and women of the Arab world. To be sure, oil has been affecting the social landscape in a score of producing countries for the previous three decades. But it is in the last ten years that the oil-related social changes have been phenomenally accelerated within those countries and have spilled over dramatically into neighboring countries. In this sense, it is justifiable to speak of one Arab social order—the chain of causation begins in some countries and ends up in others, and vice versa.

It would be an oversimplification to attribute all features of the new Arab social order to oil. But it is not an exaggeration to contend that oil is one of the most important factors in giving this order its unique characteristics. In this sense, we submit that oil in its own right has triggered as many qualitative and quantitative changes as did each of the three previous waves—colonialism, the introduction of science and technology, and the national struggle for liberation.

The new Arab social order, of which we propose to analyze one aspect in this chapter, is still emerging; that is, it is in a continuous state of flux. Thus the word "order" should not imply "orderliness", "congruency" or "harmony". If anything, early indications point to marked tension, conflict, and inconsistencies in the new Arab social order. It is an "order", nevertheless, insofar as its elements are linked to and affect one another. This new order may be held together by fear or trust, love or hate, national unifiers or subcultural diversifiers, or by a combination of them all. But it is held together with constant internal motion even if it seems to outsiders to be immobile.

When we assert that oil has been a major determinant of the new social order it should of course be realized that we are talking not simply about oil as a raw material. It is all the multi-facets of this strategic substance— i.e., as an energy source, technology, money, geopolitics, and manpower. The interaction among all these facets on one hand, and the existing social structures on the other, has produced a host of socio-cultural changes which we are subsuming under the label "new order". It includes the emergence of new social formations (e.g., classes, status groups), new demographic allocations and dislocations, new values and normative systems, new behavioral patterns, and new lines of conflict.

The major societal dynamics to which these new socio-cultural products are traceable may be summed up in one phrase: movement of manpower and money across country borders caused by oil. The volume, pattern, causes and consequences of this movement are analyzed in this chapter.

Egypt and Saudi Arabia will be our focal points of reference. They epitomize the salient features of the new Arab social order. One, Egypt, is overpopulated, poor, with surplus labor, tremendous capacity to absorb capital of which she possesses very little, and with fairly well-developed manpower and social institutions. The other, Saudi Arabia, is underpopulated, with a shortage of labor, limited capacity to absorb capital of which there is plenty, and with underdeveloped manpower and only the embryonic genesis of modern institutions. The two countries, in many ways, represent opposite ends of one bi-polar social order in the Arab world at present.

The Arab world has had several revolutions in this century. Some have been loud with sounds of fury. Others have been silent. Loud or silent, a revolution is primarily defined by its impact. Oil and movement of manpower and money across country lines are one of the Arab world's silent revolutions. Its impact is the birth of a new Arab social order.

II.   INTER-ARAB LABOR MIGRATION: AN OVERVIEW

The new Arab social order has been shaped by the intersection of oil wealth and the already existing demographic and socio-economic structures of various countries of the Arab world. Manpower movement among the Arab countries in recent years is a manifestation, a product, and a reinforcer of the new social order. Through an investigation of inter-Arab labor migration (henceforth ALM), many of the inputs, dynamics, and outputs of the new order become apparent. We propose to present an overview of this migratory phenomenon, and then to focus on Egypt and Saudi Arabia as representative of the two ends of the migration stream.

To put ALM into its full demographic context, we present in Table I some basic population indicators of the Arab world. Briefly described, the total number of Arabs in the mid-1970s was over 136 million, most of whom are under-age children (below 15 years of age), with high birth rate and high, but declining, death rate. As such, Arab population has been experiencing high rates of natural growth (about 3.0 percent annually). Yet both economic participation and literacy rates were fairly low (about 30 percent). This overall profile, of course, conceals some very significant quantitative and qualitative variations, which are reflected in Table I, and in fact, it is these variations which have made an inter-Arab migratory system possible.

Movement of Arab individuals, families, and tribes throughout the

TABLE I
The Arab World: Basic Demographic Indicators, Mid-1970s

Countries Ranked by Population Size	Population Size in millions (nationals only)	Area in sq. km. (000)	Density per km²	Crude Birth Rate %	Crude Death Rate %	Natural Growth Rate %	Literacy Rate of Pop. 15 & over %
Egypt	38.2 (1976)	1,001	38	3.5	1.2	2.3	40
Morocco	18.4 (1977)	447	44	4.6	1.5	3.1	26
Algeria	16.9 (1977)	2,382	7	4.4	1.4	3.0	35
Sudan	14.1 (1973)	2,506	7	5.1	1.9	3.2	15
Iraq	11.1 (1975)	435	26	4.2	1.1	3.1	26
Syria	7.3 (1975)	185	41	4.8	1.5	3.3	53
Tunisia	5.6 (1975)	164	36	3.6	0.9	2.7	55
Yemen	5.3 (1975)	195	27	4.9	2.5	2.4	10
Saudi Arabia	4.6 (1975)	2,150	2	5.0	2.0	3.0	15
Somalia	3.2 (1975)	393	8	n.a.	n.a.	n.a.	50
Jordan	2.6 (1975)	98	27	4.7	1.6	3.1	62
Lebanon	2.6 (1975)	10	260	n.a.	n.a.	n.a.	68
Libya	2.3 (1975)	1,760	2	4.7	1.6	3.1	—
Democratic Yemen	1.7 (1975)	288	6	n.a.	n.a.	n.a.	10
Mauritania	1.3 (1975)	670	2	n.a.	n.a.	n.a.	10
Oman	0.6 (1975)	213	3	n.a.	n.a.	n.a.	20
Kuwait	0.5 (1975)	18	31	5.1	0.6	4.5	55
Bahrain	0.3 (1976)	1	437	n.a.	n.a.	n.a.	47
U.A.E.	0.2 (1975)	84	3	5.0	1.9	3.1	14
Qatar	0.1 (1975)	11	5	5.0	2.0	3.0	33
TOTAL	136.9	13,011	10				32

SOURCES: Compiled from The World Bank's *World Development Report 1978*, Tables 1–18, pp.76–111; United Nations Economic Commission for West Asia (UNECWA) *Demographic and Related Socio-Economic Data Sheets*, (Beirut), No.2; *The Arab World in the Year 2000* (Beirut: Inst. of Arab Projects and Development, 1975), p.22; UNESCO's Regional Office for Education in Arab Countries, *Education and Development in Arab Countries*, (Cairo, 1976), p.2.

area extending from Iraq to Morocco had been a common occurrence over centuries (from the 7th to the beginning of the 20th). Cultural affinities of language, religion and life styles facilitated such movement and subsequent adjustment in a new residence; and the absence of rigid national state borders made it all possible. However, with the exception of brief large-scale migrations, namely in the early Arab-Islamic conquest of the 7th and 8th centuries, the human movement remained small, though frequent. The Pilgrimage to Mecca from all over the Arab Muslim world has kept at least a minimum of human movement in the area at all times.

The advent of Western colonialism, the Balkanization of the Arab homeland, the rigid border demarcation and subsequent creation of country-states slowed inter-Arab movement during the first part of the 20th century. However, the discovery and exploitation of oil in countries of the Arabian Peninsula in the middle of this century made it possible for inter-Arab labor migration (ALM) to pick up again in the 1950s and 1960s. It was in the 1970s, though, that the scale of ALM assumed a dimension unprecedented since the Arab Conquest of the 7th century. Noteworthy are the reverse directions of the historical and the present human movements. The early Arab migration of the 7th century and the Hilaliyya movement of the 11th century were all from the Arabian Peninsula outwards. The present waves are from the outside inward into the Peninsula.

The Arab-Israeli war of 1973, the Arab oil embargo, and the quadrupling of oil prices resulted in an astronomical increase in state revenues of the Arab oil producers. As Table II shows, these revenues rose from $2.3 billion in 1965 to $12.7 billion in 1973, and from $53.6 billion in 1974 to $77.5 billion in 1977. At present (1980) these revenues are estimated at more than $100 billion. Thus if we take 1970 as a benchmark, major Arab producers would have raised their oil revenues from less than $5.0 billion to $100.0 billion in one decade—that is, a twentyfold increase (2000 percent).

With this kind of money, the oil-rich or "capital-rich"[3] countries launched ambitious socio-economic development plans. Their aim has been (i) to complete the building of basic infrastructures (roads, airports, water desalination plants, power stations. . . etc.); (ii) to expand and consolidate social service institutions (schools, hospitals, housing, community centers, and the appropriate bureaucracies for their maintenance and operation); (iii) to diversify their respective economic bases in anticipation of the post-oil era; and (iv) to step up and modernize their defence capabilities.

The vast oil revenues put some Arab countries in a category by themselves as the capital-rich—namely Saudi Arabia, Kuwait, Qatar, the United Arab Emirates (UAE), Bahrain, Oman, and Libya. Iraq and Algeria, though also having substantial oil resources and corresponding revenues, do have large populations, more diverse economic bases and a high absorptive capacity. The rest of the Arab countries are, by comparison, quite poor in terms of capital, although most of them are substantially populated (e.g. Egypt, Yemen, Tunisia and Sudan) and with diverse economic bases (e.g. Egypt, Syria and Lebanon).

With the exception of Iraq and Algeria, all capital-oil-rich Arab countries are underpopulated. With a small demographic base their pool of

TABLE II
Evolution of Oil Revenues for Major Arab Producers, 1965-1977
(In $ Millions)

Years Major Producers	1965	1970	1971	1972	1973	1974	1975	1976	1977
Saudi Arabia	655	1214	1885	2745	4340	22574	25676	37809	36900
Kuwait	761	899	1407	1634	1980	8645	7706	8063	6800
Iraq	375	521	840	575	1843	5700	7500	8500	8800
United Arab Emirates	33	233	431	551	900	5536	6000	7000	8000
Qatar	69	122	200	255	464	1802	1700	2090	2100
Libya	371	1351	1674	1563	2223	5999	5101	7500	8600
Algeria	102	272	321	613	988	3299	3262	3699	3984
TOTAL	2366	4612	6758	7936	12738	53555	56945	74661	75184

SOURCE: Up to 1974 compiled by Mahmud ʿAbd al-Fadil, *Al-naft wal-wihda al-ʿarabiyya* [Oil and Arab Unity], (Beirut: Centre for Arab Unity Studies, 1979) p. 10. The following years are from various other sources.

labor supply would be naturally limited; and in fact it had been all along, even before the 1973 oil boom. These countries had been net labor importers since the 1950s. Now, however, with an even greater labor demand at all levels to carry out their new ambitious plans, the importation of labor has intensified enormously, and with a supply of labor in nearby countries and substantial wage differentials, it is not surprising that a migration system which had already started two decades earlier has expanded by leaps and bounds.

A. THE SIZE OF INTER-ARAB LABOR MIGRATION

No one knows exactly the size of inter-Arab labor movement. Neither sending or receiving countries have been in the habit of keeping reliable or retrievable statistical records. It is however possible to piece together an approximate picture from diverse sources, including some gallant scholarly efforts by a score of pioneers.[4]

Tables III and IV show the estimated size of inter-Arab labor migration before and after the October War and the oil boom of 1973. The figures indicate that it jumped from less than 680,000 to about 1.3 million — that is, it nearly doubled in three years. The only decisive factor that can account for this phenomenal rise is, naturally, oil revenues. Saudi Arabia, for instance, increased its share of imported labor from 345,000 to 700,000 in the short interim, which represents more than a 100 percent increase. Libya nearly tripled its importation of Arab labor in two years, from 107,000 in 1973 to 310,000 in 1975.

Nevertheless, the leading Arab labor importers have remained the same. Saudi Arabia, Libya and Kuwait topped the list of labor importers before and after 1973. By the same token, Egypt, Yemen and Jordan/Palestine topped the list of labor exporters. The only noticeable change among the exporters is the trading off of first and second place between Egypt and Yemen in 1970 and 1975. Egypt's share of labor export jumped from less than 100,000 to 398,000, thus nearly quadrupling, while that of Yemen rose from 234,000 to 290,000 which represented a 24 percent increase.

By the late 1970s, the size of ALM had, no doubt, increased even more but once again it is difficult to obtain exact figures. Table V gives three estimates, two of which are by international agencies and one of which is based on Arab sources. The study by the International Labor Organization (ILO) and Durham University puts the figure at around 1.3 million in 1975. The study by the International Monetary Fund (IMF) two years later gives the figure of 1.4 million on the basis of official data from labor-exporting states, and the figure of 1.6 million based on data from labor-importing states. In the third study, M.A. Fadil of the Arab Planning Institute in Kuwait discusses the under-reporting bias in these figures, which usually do not take into account illegal migrants, nor the fact that some countries do not require entry visas or registration of citizens from other Arab countries. For example, until recently Saudi Arabia did not require either formality from Yemenis, while Iraq is another country which treats Arab migrants as its own citizens so that they often do not appear in official statistics or in estimates of ALM made by international agencies. Relying on various Arab sources in the exporting countries, Fadil comes up with a figure of 2.1 million. In supplementing Fadil's estimate with figures from official sources in labor-importing countries, the present author came up with the figure of 2.2 million for 1977.[5]

In 1980, the size of inter-Arab migration was probably in the

TABLE III

Inter-Arab Labor Migration Before the 1973 Oil Boom*

Labor Importing Countries	Year of Ref.	Yemen	Egypt	Syria	Palestine**	Jordan**	Lebanon	Oman	Other Arab countr.	TOTAL
Saudi Arabia	1970	225000	n.a.	40000	50000	n.a.	30000	n.a.	n.a.	345000
Kuwait	1970	7000	18000	13000	n.a.	41000	8000	10000	24000	121000
Libya	1973	n.a.	61000	6000	4000	4000	8000	–	24000	107000
Lebanon	1970	n.a.	5000	34000	8000	n.a.	–	n.a.	n.a.	47000

Library,
I.U.P.
Indiana, Pa.

338.0956 R37i
c.1

Country	Year									Total
U.A.E.	1968	7000	11000	7000	7000	7000	n.a.	7000	4000	43000
Qatar	1970	n.a.	n.a.	n.a.	n.a.	n.a.	n.a.	n.a.	n.a.	(24000)
Bahrain	1971	2000	n.a.	2000	2000	2000	n.a.	6000	4000	16000
Oman	1973	n.a.	n.a.	n.a.	n.a.	n.a.	n.a.	n.a.	n.a.	(2000)
TOTAL	Before Oct. 1973	234000	95000	100000	71000	54000	46000	23000	56000	679000

* The reference in this and other tables is to gainfully employed migrants and not their dependents.
** Palestine and Jordan are used interchangeably by many official Arab agencies.
n.a. is not available: figures in parentheses denote rough estimates.

SOURCE: Based on A. Farrag, "Migration Between Arab Countries," in *Manpower and Employment in Arab Countries*, (Geneva: International Labor Office), 1976.

TABLE IV
Inter-Arab Labor Migration in 1975
(after the Oil-Price boom of 1973-74)

Labor Exporting Countries / Labor Importing Countries	Egypt %	Yemen %	Jordan Palestine %	Democratic Yemen %	Syria %
Saudi Arabia	95,000(23.9)	28,000(96.6)	175,000(66.1)	55,000(77.9)	15,000(21.3)
Libya	229,500(57.7)	———	14,150(5.3)	———	13,000(18.5)
Kuwait	37,558(9.4)	2,757(1.0)	47,653(18.0)	8658(12.2)	16,547(23.4)
United Arab Emirates	12,500(3.1)	4,500(1.6)	14,500(5.5)	4,500(6.4)	4,500(6.4)
Jordan (East Bank)	5,300(1.3)	———	———	———	20,000(28.4)
Iraq	7,000(1.8)	———	5000(1.9)	———	———
Qatar	2,850(0.7)	1,250(0.4)	6000(2.3)	1250(1.8)	750(1.1)
Oman	4,600(1.2)	100(0.0)	1600(0.6)	100(0.1)	400(0.6)
Bahrain	1,237(0.3)	1,121(0.4)	614(0.2)	1122(1.6)	68(0.1)
Yemen	2,000(0.5)	———	200(0.1)	———	150(0.2)
Total	397,545(100.0)	290,128(100.0)	264,717(100.0)	70,630(100.0)	70,415(100)
%	(30.7)	(22.4)	(20.4)	(5.5)	(5.4)

Sources: J.S. Birks and C.A. Sinclair, *International Migration and Development in the Arab Region* (Geneva: ILO, 1980), pp. 134-135.

Lebanon %	Sudan %	Tunisia %	Oman %	Iraq %	Somalia %	Algeria Morocco %	TOTAL
20,000(40.3)	35,000(76.3)	_____	17,500(45.6)	2,000(9.7)	5000(76.4)	_____	699,900
5,700(11.5)	7,000(15.3)	38,500(99.6)	_____	_____	_____	2,500(98.2)	310,350
7,232(14.6)	873(1.9)	49(0.1)	3,660(9.5)	17,999(87.3)	247(3.8)	47(1.8)	143,280
4,500(9.0)	1,500(3.2)	_____	14,000(36.4)	500(2.4)	1,000(15.2)	_____	62,000
7,500(15.1)	_____	_____	_____	_____	_____	_____	32,800
3,000(6.0)	200(0.4)	_____	_____	_____	_____	_____	15,200
500(1.1)	400(0.9)	_____	1,870(4.9)	_____	_____	_____	14,870
1,100(2.2)	500(1.1)	100(0.3)	_____	_____	300(4.6)	_____	8,800
129(0.3)	400(0.9)	_____	1,383(3.6)	126(0.6)	_____	_____	6,200
_____	_____	_____	_____	_____	_____	_____	2,350
49,661(100)	45,873(100)	38,649(100)	38,413(100)	20,625(100)	6,547(100)	2547(100)	1,295,750
(3.8)	(3.5)	(3.0)	(3.0)	(1.6)	(0.5)	(0.2)	(100.0)

TABLE V
Comparisons of Various Estimates of Arab Labor Migration
(1975-1977)

Countries	Estimates by	A ILO - Durham Univ. (Birks & Sinclair) (1975)	B International Monetary Fund (1977)	C Arab Sources (M.A.Fadil) (1977)
A.Major Arab Labor Exporters				
Egypt		398,000	350,000	600,000
Arab Yemen		290,000	500,000	600,000
Democratic Yemen		70,000	300,000	300,000
Jordan/Palestine		265,000	150,000	225,000
Sudan		46,000	50,000	174,000
Syria		70,000	n.a.	70,000 (1975)
Lebanon		50,000	n.a.	50,000 "
Tunisia		39,000	n.a.	39,000 "
Others		68,000	n.a.	68,000 "
TOTAL		1,296,000	1,350,000	2,126,000
B.Major Arab Labor Importers				(our estimates)
Saudi Arabia		700,000	900,000	1,170,000
Libya		310,000	325,000	420,000
Kuwait		143,000	276,000	350,000
U.A.E.		62,000	96,000	115,000
Qatar		15,000	19,000	26,000
Oman		9,000	12,000	16,000
Bahrain		6,000	7,000	9,000
Iraq		15,000	n.a.	100,000
TOTAL		1,260,000	1,635,000	2,206,000

SOURCES: A: J. S. Birks and C. A. Sinclair, *International Migration...*,
op.cit., pp. 134-135.
B: IMF *Survey*, (Washington D.C., 1978), pp. 260-262.
C: M. A. Fadil, *Oil and Arab Unity*, op.cit., p. 30.
Estimates by the author are based on a wide range of official sources.

neighborhood of 3 million. This steady increase is due to more of the same factors operating since 1973; greater increase in oil revenues, more ambitious developmental plans, greater demands on labor than can be supplied by the indigenous pool in capital-rich countries, a greater supply of labor in capital-poor countries than could be absorbed by or enticed to stay in those countries.

The labor shortage in most capital-rich countries is not due only to their under-population and small demographic base. Additional socio-cultural factors have limited the annual flow of manpower into the active labor market. Most important among these are the social mores barring women from participation in non-household employment, especially in Saudi Arabia.[6] There is also the fact that the demographic pyramids of these countries are quite inflated with a broad base of under-age children, thus reducing the proportion of males deployable as an active labor force.[7] Finally, the presence of a sizeable nomadic population[8] in all capital-rich countries means at least some 10 percent potential loss of the indigenous deployable labor force in modern sectors. As a result, the crude participation rate in these countries is quite low by both international and regional standards. As Table VIA shows, these ratios for the capital-rich oil countries range between 18.4 percent in Qatar and 24.9 percent in Oman, with an overall average for the whole group of 21.7 percent. In most labor-exporting capital-poor countries, the comparable ratio ranges between 20.4 percent (Jordan) and 33.5 percent (Egypt), with the average for the group as a whole close to 30 percent as shown in Table VIB.

In mid-1970, therefore, we find migrant labor contributing nearly half (48.7 percent) of all the actively-employed labor in capital-rich Arab countries, as Table VII illustrates. In some of these countries, the share of migrant labor is as high as 85 percent of the work force, as for example in the United Arab Emirates. This heavy reliance on migrant Arab labor is one of the salient features of the new social order in the Arab world, and its full consequences will be explored later in this chapter.

B. COMPOSITION OF ARAB LABOR MIGRANTS

Available data on occupational and educational background of Arab labor migrants indicate that the process is quite selective. As Table VIII shows, migrants in Kuwait, Saudi Arabia, Libya and Oman seem to dominate the construction and building sectors as well as that of services (education, health, banking, insurance, the civil service...etc.), and these tend to be the largest sectors of the economy. In three of the four oil-rich countries shown in this Table, migrant labor makes up more than 60 percent of the construction workforce—65 percent in Libya, 67 percent in

TABLE VI
Capital-Rich and Capital-Poor Arab States: National
Populations and Workforces Ranked by Size, 1975

State	Population (thousands)	Workforce (thousands)	Crude parti-cipation rate (%)
A. Capital-Rich			
Saudi Arabia	4,592.5	1,026.5	22.4
Libya	2,223.7	449.2	20.2
Oman	550.1	137.0	24.9
Kuwait	472.1	91.8	19.4
Bahrain	214.0	45.8	21.4
U.A.E.	200.0	45.0	22.5
Qatar	67.9	12.5	18.4
Sub-total of Capital-Rich	8,320.2	1,807.8	21.7
B. Capital-Poor			
Egypt	37,364.9	12,522.2	33.5
Sudan	15,031.3	3,700.0	24.6
Syria	7,335.0	1,838.9	25.1
Yemen	5,037.0	1,425.8	28.3
Jordan	2,616.7	532.8	20.4
Democratic Yemen	1,660.0	430.5	25.9
Sub-total of Capital-Poor	69,044.9	20,450.2	29.6
TOTAL	77,365.1	22,258.0	28.6

SOURCES: Compiled by J.S. Birks, & C.A. Sinclair, *International Migration and Development...* op.cit., pp.131-132

Oman, and 95 percent in Kuwait. But even in manufacturing and processing, the percentage of migrant labor is quite substantial in Kuwait (86 percent) and in Saudi Arabia (62 percent).

One sector on which we have no data is that of defence. In three of the four selected capital-rich countries there is no data on the percentage of non-nationals in their armed forces and defence establishments generally. It is not a secret that most capital-rich Gulf states recruit non-nationals.

The occupational characteristics of Arab migrant labor seem to have

TABLE VII
Capital-Rich States: Employment by Nationality, 1975

State	Nationals		NonNationals		Total Employment
	No.	%	No.	%	
Saudi Arabia	1,026,500	57.0	773,400	43.0	1,799,900
Libya	449,200	57.5	332,400	42.5	781,600
Kuwait	91,800	30.6	208,000	69.4	299,800
U.A.E.	45,000	15.2	251,500	84.8	296,500
Oman	137,000	66.0	70,700	34.0	207,700
Bahrain	45,800	60.4	30,000	39.6	75,800
Qatar	12,500	18.9	53,700	81.1	66,200
TOTAL	1,807,800	51.3	1,719,700	48.7	3,527,500

SOURCE: Birks and Sinclair, ibid., p. 132.

evolved in the last ten years to include all levels of manpower. In the fifties and early sixties most Egyptians working in oil countries were professionals: doctors, teachers, engineers. With the expansion of economic activities following the oil price "mutation" of the 1970s, the need for all sorts of occupations is reflected in recent data.

Kuwait, which keeps the best statistical records among capital-rich countries, mirrors the present situation, as Table IX illustrates. Thus, while the percentage of migrant labor in the two top occupational categories remains high (89.6 and 46 percent, compared with 10.4 and 53.9 percent of the Kuwaitis respectively), the share of migrant labor in the lower categories is also high. Of all skilled and semi-skilled manual workers, for example, migrants make up nearly 86 percent and Kuwaitis only 14 percent. Even in the lower level of manpower (i.e. unskilled manual occupation) non-Kuwaitis account for nearly two-thirds of the total (65.0 percent). Incidentally, the Arab migrant groups which are over-represented in this low-level manpower are the North Yemenis (68 percent), South Yemenis (53 percent), Iraqis (39 percent) and Egyptians (35 percent). Among non-Arab immigrant labor in Kuwait, Indians and Iranians were also heavily represented in unskilled manual occupations, as is shown in Table IX. The Palestinians were, in contrast, under-represented in this category (13 percent) and over-represented in the top professional category (11 percent). Egyptians followed in this top

TABLE VIII
Sectoral Distribution of Local and Imported Labor Force
in Selected Oil-Rich Countries (1973-1975)
(percentages)

Country	S.Arabia(1973)		Libya (1973)		Kuwait (1975)		Oman (1975)	
Economic sector	local	migrant	local	migrant	local	migrant	local	migrant
Agriculture	37.1	62.9	89.5	10.5	53.0	47.0	n.a.	n.a.
Manufacturing & Processing	38.2	61.8	65.5	34.5	13.6	86.4	64.1	35.9
Construction	52.4	47.6	35.4	64.6	5.5	94.5	33.4	66.6
Gas, water, & Electricity	78.3	21.7	84.3	15.7	28.0	72.0	80.5	19.5
Commerce	47.2	52.8	90.3	9.7	16.0	84.0	54.0	46.0
Transport & Communication	53.9	46.1	95.6	4.4	29.1	70.9	81.4	18.6
Civil Service & Defence	n.a.	n.a.	96.1	3.9	n.a.	n.a.	n.a.	n.a.
Services (education, health, banking, etc.)	43.7	56.3	81.3	18.7	38.5	61.5	36.0	64.0
TOTAL	57.0	43.0	78.0	22.0	29.1	70.9	66.0	34.0

SOURCES: Saudi Arabia's *Labor Survey for the Private Sector, 1973*; Libyan Arab Jamahiriya's *Preliminary Population Census Results of 1973*; Kuwait's *Population Census of 1975*; Oman's *Labor Survey of Private Sector Establishments Employing Ten or More Persons* (Dec. 1974–Aug. 1975); M. A. Fadil, *Oil and Arab Unity*, op. cit., p. 38

category, with 7 percent: in other words, Egyptian migrants were heavily represented in both the very top and the very low levels of manpower in Kuwait.

The situation in Kuwait seems to be typical of the capital-rich countries. In a study by M. A. Faris of the Arab Labor Organization, it was also revealed that Arab migrant labor occupied 75 percent of all top professional and administrative jobs in Saudi Arabia, 56 percent in Libya, and 85 percent in Oman in the mid-seventies.[10] Commenting on this

TABLE IX

Kuwait: Occupational Distribution of Kuwaitis and Selected Migrant Communities by Skill Level, 1975

(percentages)

Occupational category	migrant communities from:												% of the total	
	Kuwaitis	Palestine	Egypt	Jordan	Lebanon	India	Syria	Iraq	Pakistan	Yemen	Democ. Yemen	Iran	Kuwait	non-Kuwait
A1	1.2	10.8	7.2	6.5	4.0	3.6	1.7	1.9	2.1	0.3	0.2	0.1	10.4	89.6
A2	5.8	3.3	3.3	2.8	3.8	1.0	1.6	1.2	1.0	1.3	0.5	0.2	53.9	46.1
B	12.0	35.9	21.1	17.6	17.5	9.0	8.8	4.1	5.5	1.3	0.7	2.7	28.6	71.4
C1	24.4	22.7	7.9	26.1	26.5	21.7	21.1	12.7	11.7	16.2	40.9	13.9	35.6	64.4
C2	12.1	14.2	25.6	25.8	27.8	12.9	39.7	40.8	59.5	12.6	4.7	48.3	14.3	85.7
D	44.5	13.1	34.9	21.2	20.4	51.8	27.1	39.3	20.2	68.2	53.0	34.8	35.0	65.0
Total	100	100	100	100	100	100	100	100	100	100	100	100	29.1	70.9
TOTAL NO. of WORKFORCE	86621	8200	37500	38900	7200	2400	16500	17800	11000	2700	8600	27500	–	–

A1: professional jobs usually requiring science or math. based univ. degree; A2: professional & sub-professional jobs usually requiring univ. arts degree; B: technicians & others usually requiring 1-3 yrs. post-secondary education/training; C1: skilled & semi-skilled office & clerical occupations; C2: skilled & semi-skilled manual occupations; D: unskilled occupations.

SOURCE: *Kuwait Census of 1975* (Kuwait: Central Dept. of Statistics, Min. of Planning, 1976), p.105.

situation, Fadil notes that "...the migration stream in the new oil era has become more diversified. The new era made it possible for greater numbers of production and ordinary service workers to migrate to the oil countries. These categories were never used to large-scale migration before."[11]

The case of Egyptians is, again, quite typical of other capital-poor countries. In 1965, of all Egyptians working in Kuwait, over 52 percent were professionals and highly specialized. By 1975, however, the share of this high level manpower dropped to 29.5 percent. In contrast, Egyptian migrant labor in low level manpower jumped from 21.8 to 38.3 percent during the same period.[12] Of course, the absolute number of Egyptians in both levels continued to rise, but the increase in middle and low levels was significantly much greater. This is a point worth remembering, since we begin to note some strategic labor shortages even in capital-poor countries like Egypt in the late seventies — an issue that will be dealt with in due course.

C. LABOR MIGRANT REPLACEMENT AND CIRCULATION

Two important characteristics of inter-Arab migration are worth noting here. First is the migration replacement in some Arab countries — i.e., the same country is both a labor exporter and a labor importer. If we refer back to Table IV it can be observed that Jordan, Iraq, Oman and Yemen fall into this category. In the case of Jordan and Yemen, the balance is still heavily tipped on the side of labor export, as is shown in Table X. But in the case of Iraq and Oman, both of which are rich oil producers in their own right, the difference is not as large. The main source of labor migrant replacement for the four countries appearing in Table IV is Egypt, Syria and Lebanon. Out of the nearly 33,000 non-Jordanian labor force in that country in 1975, 20,000 were Syrians, 7,500 were Lebanese and 5,300 were Egyptians. In Iraq, Oman and Yemen combined, out of their 26,000 imported Arab labor, 14,000 were Egyptians (i.e. 54 percent), 7,000 were Jordanians/Palestinians (i.e. 27 percent) and 4,000 were Lebanese. It is believed that this kind of replacement labor had increased even more by the late 1970s. Thus as a labor-exporter country begins to experience a shortage in its own domestic labor market as a result of the inability to control out-migration, it resorts to importing replacement labor to fill the gap. This applies especially to Jordan, where it is believed that Syrians and Egyptians are simply replacing medium and low level manpower Jordanians/Palestinians who out-migrate to oil-rich countries. The replacement labor obviously receives wages markedly higher than those prevail-

TABLE X
Labor Exporter Importer Arab Countries, 1975

Country	Size of Labor Export	Size of Labor Import	Net
Jordan	264,717	32,000	232,717
Iraq	20,625	15,200	5,425
Oman	38,413	8,800	29,613
Yemen	290,128	2,350	287,778

SOURCE: Birks and Sinclair, op.cit.

ing in its country of origin — for example, Egypt and Syria — but not as high as those prevailing in the oil-rich countries.

The situation with Oman and Yemen is different in the sense that the three-way labor movement is not mechanical replacement. Most likely, the Arab labor imported into Yemen and Oman is of higher level occupationally, while that exported is of middle and lower levels.

The second phenomenon is migrant Arab labor circulation. Most treatments of the subject analyze ALM statistically and cross-sectionally. The concepts of "stock" and "annual flow" do not take into account the fact that most migrant labor is temporary.[13] In 1970, the average work sojourn for an Egyptian in Kuwait, for example, was about 3.6 years and that of Yemenis was 4.7 years, while that of Palestinians was about 6.3 years. As these migrants return home, however, other fellow countrymen replace them in capital-rich countries. In other words there is a constant circulation of Arab migrant labor, which means that the process touches many more than the "stock" and "flow" statistics suggest. Thus 1.7 million Egyptians became labor migrants every 10 years — not counting their dependents.[14] According to this view of migrant circulation a total of nearly 4 million Arabs moves across state borders for employment purposes every ten years. If each is a member of an average family of 5 persons, then a total of 20 million Arabs is directly affected by Arab labor migration every decade, not counting future incremental growth of labor migrants and their dependents.

D. NON-ARAB MIGRANT LABOR

Although ALM constitutes the bulk of the workforce in capital-rich countries, there is an increasing presence of non-Arab labor in these countries. Pulled and pushed by the same structural factors in their own and in the oil-rich countries as are Arab migrants, non-Arab migrants from Asian countries have been trickling in for two decades. However, the trickle was turning into a significant stream during the 1970s, with non-Arab migrants coming mainly from India, Pakistan, Iran and Afghanistan. More recently Koreans and Filipinos have made their appearance on the Arabian landscape as well.

As Table XI shows, the number of non-Arab migrants in the Gulf states has increased in both absolute and relative terms. The Asians (i.e. Indians, Pakistanis and Orientals) have increased from about 84,000 in 1970 to about 248,000 by mid-decade — that is by about 300 percent in five years. While the Asians constituted only 26 percent of the migrant workforce in 1970 they grew to make up nearly 46 percent of it by 1975. At that point non-Arab exceeded Arab labor migrants in the Gulf States. The latter, though growing in absolute numbers from 166,000 in 1970 to 226,000 in 1975, slipped in relative terms from 51 percent to 42 percent in the same period. Given the fact that the indigenous populations of the Gulf states are quite modest in size (about one million in 1975), the growing presence of non-Arab communities could radically change the ethnic make-up of these states. Some voices have been raised in alarm at the process of de-Arabization of the Gulf.[15] But the temptation of cheap labor is too strong to stop the flow of non-Arab migrants.

E.   PROSPECT OF FUTURE LABOR MIGRATION

The migratory system set in motion with the 1970s will continue throughout the 1980s — that is, the labor movement from over-populated capital-poor countries will continue to flow to under-populated capital-rich Arab countries. In a recent study by the World Bank[16] manpower requirements for the oil-rich Arab countries are projected to rise from the 1975 level of 6.2 million to about 10.3 million by 1985, which is a net increase of 4 million and a relative growth of 66 percent. The sectoral composition of total manpower requirements indicates a greater relative demand for labor in manufacturing (131 percent), in utilities (107 percent), in trade and finance (97 percent) and in services (95 percent). The lowest growth demand for labor is projected to be in the agricultural sector, at around 20 percent. In terms of absolute volume of demand, however, the services sector will appropriate over one third of the net increase, followed by construction (17 percent), trade and finance (15 percent), and manufacturing (13 percent). The relative share in agriculture of the labor force will decline from its 1975 level of 37 percent to 27 percent in 1985; while the share in manufacturing will grow from 6 to 9 percent during the same period.

Another projected trend in labor requirements until the mid-1980s is the relatively greater demand on high level manpower. Professional-

TABLE XI
Bahrain, Kuwait, Qatar & U.A.E. Workforce by Ethnic Origin, 1970 & 1975

Ethnic Origin	1970		1975	
	No.	%	No.	%
Arab (non-nat.s)	165,900	51.0	226,400	41.7
Asian	83,900	25.8	247,700	45.7
Iranian, European & other	75,300	23.2	68,400	12.6
Subtotal	325,100	100.0	542,500	100.0
National	147,600	31.2*	195,100	26.5*
TOTAL	472,700	100.0	737,600	100.0

* = percentage of total

SOURCE: Birks & Sinclair, op.cit.

technical occupations are projected to increase by 170 percent followed by technical (150 percent) and sub-professional occupations (125 percent). Manual occupations will have only a modest growth in the period from 1975 to 1985, ranging between 53 percent for semi-skilled and 48 percent for unskilled labor. In absolute volume, however, the last two categories will still account for most of the net growth of manpower requirements during the ten year period ending in 1985.

The question most relevant to the new Arab social order is the extent to which these manpower requirements will be supplied from indigenous sources and also to what extent they will have to come from outside, especially from neighboring Arab countries. The same World Bank study, on the basis of an elaborate model, estimated that the demographic base and educational system outputs of the eight capital-rich Arab countries would only cover the labor required for the lowest occupational level—i.e. semi-skilled and manual occupations.[17] As a matter of fact, there will be an indigenous over-supply in these two categories, of 16 percent in the semi-skilled and 127 percent in the unskilled groups.

It is, however, in the middle and high level manpower that the capital-rich countries will still be in dire need until the mid-1980s. Between 64 and 77 percent of manpower requirements in four of the top five occupational levels will have to be filled by expatriates. The volume of the latter is projected to increase in each of the Arab capital-rich countries, and the net growth of manpower requirements of expatriates at all levels is projected at about 2 million by 1985. That of course is in addition to the 1.7 to 2.0 million who were already working in these countries in 1975. All in all, then, the size of migrant labor in the oil-rich Arab countries would amount to nearly 4 million out of the 10.3 million total manpower requirements in 1985.

The above projected evolution of migrant labor indicates clearly that it is going to grow more professional, technical, and highly educated, and this profile of expatriate manpower will, without doubt, have serious consequences for the capital-poor labor-exporting countries. As the World Bank study states,

> More than ever, the demand for manpower is likely to drain the labor exporting countries of the better qualified workers. Already, in 1975, high proportions of vacancies in professional, technical, and clerical occupations in labor importers were constrained by a requirement of Arabic and English language competence. Consequently it is reasonable to assume that high and middle level manpower in Arab labor exporting countries will be increasingly sought after by public and private employers in the labor importing countries. The wider recruiting areas of South and Southeast Asia, which have supplied increasingly large shares of additional expatriate manpower since the mid-1970's, may not be appropriate as sources of labor in the future as the structure of expatriate manpower requirements shifts from unskilled and semi-skilled production and service occupations to more highly skilled and professional occupations.[18]

Nothing illustrates the dynamics of the inter-Arab labor migratory system implied in the conclusion above better than Egypt and Saudi Arabia. In the next two sections we shall focus on some of the consequences of labor migration in each of these two countries.

III. SOME CONSEQUENCES OF LABOR
EXPORTATION: EGYPT

Like most large-scale societal processes, the consequences of Egyptian migration are quite complex. The positive and the negative are so entangled that it is hard to assess their relative weights or trade-offs for the society at large in both the short and the long run. The consequences for individuals seem, on the surface at least, to be mostly positive, since many of them do indeed solve their immediate economic and financial problems. A utilitarian approach may argue that what is good for most individuals must be good for their society. But it is now axiomatic in social science that society is a product, and not just a simple sum, of its individuals or their actions.

A.   REMITTANCES OF EGYPTIANS ABROAD AND MULTIPLIER EFFECTS

The most concrete outcome of Egyptian labor abroad is its remittances in hard currencies. Like most other migrant national groups, Egyptians increased the size of their remittances — from $189 million in 1974 to $1,425 million in 1977, which represents an increase of nearly 400 percent in four years. The phenomenal growth is even more staggering if we take, let us say, 1970 as a base year. At that point remittances did not exceed $10 million. According to official Egyptian sources, by 1979 the level had reached, or exceeded, the $2.0 billion mark.[19] Thus in one decade Egyptians abroad raised their monetary transfers from $10 million to $2000 million — that is, two hundred-fold. This amount equals, or exceeds, the combined returns of Egypt's cotton export, the Suez Canal revenues, tourism, and the value added from the Aswan High Dam.[20] Proponents of the Open Door policy may well argue that Nasir's Egypt waged battles and spilled blood for the Suez Canal and the Aswan Dam, yet the silent outcome of one measure of *infitah* is bringing much more hard currency to Egypt.

Theoretically, these growing remittances should help Egypt's balance of payments and stimulate the process of capital formation. The remittances represented 11 percent of all Egypt's exports in 1974; but by 1977 the percentage had risen to 66 percent, a six-fold relative increase. As a percentage of Egypt's imports it rose from five to 27 in the same four years.[21] By any measure this is indeed quite impressive. Of course other countries benefitted as much. Yemen especially seems to have reaped greater relative increases in its remittances from its labor abroad — from $159 million to $1,013 million between 1974 and 1977.[22] The value of these remittances represented over 1,300 percent of its export in the former year and over 5,000 percent of its export in the latter. All in all by the end of the seventies, remittances from Arab workers in capital-rich Arab countries totalled about $4.0 billion annually.[23]

In terms of bank deposits — as one indicator of savings — these were estimated at $3.4 billion in 1978 and rose to $4.7 billion in 1979, at a growth rate of 33 percent in one year. This is a far cry from the early 1970s when Egypt's savings rates fell to their lowest in several decades.[24] However, some economists still argue that the levels of remittances and savings should have been much higher, had there been effective channels for attracting and utilizing the immense financial resources of Egyptians working abroad.[25]

Recent figures for investments under both Law No. 43 for 1974 and Law No. 32 for 1977 (the foundation stones of the policy of *infitah*) indicate that most investment has been made by Egyptians. At the end of 1977, of all investments in the preceding five years, foreigners contributed 17 percent, Arabs 25 percent, while the share of Egyptians amounted to 57 percent.[26] While it is hard to pin down the sources of these Egyptian investments, it is assumed that a substantial part comes from Egyptian workers abroad. It is known, for example, that at least a number of sizeable ventures (such as banks, real estate development and industrial firms) were initiated by Egyptians in the Gulf.[27]

Another effect is the contribution made by wages earned abroad to the improvement of the standard of living of a sizeable sector of Egyptian society. Even if we take the conservative estimate of 500,000 Egyptians in the workforce abroad in the late 1970s, and assuming that each is a member of an average household of five people, then the migratory process would have a direct impact on some 2.5 million Egyptians—that is, six percent of the total population. It may even be argued that given the extended kinship system in Egypt, at least twice as many would reap some material benefit from migrant relatives, either in monetary benefits or in kind (i.e. in gifts).

B.   THE FEMINIZATION OF THE EGYPTIAN FAMILY

One curious effect of labor migration is the feminization of Egyptian households. It is estimated that as many as half the married Egyptian migrants to Arab countries leave their wives and children behind. The result is that the wife often takes upon herself the total management of the household, including the exclusive bringing up of children in their most formative years. A whole new generation of Egyptian youngsters is now growing up in one-parent families, with the other parent no more than a periodic visitor. It is hard to label this effect as positive or negative, nor is it possible to gauge its long-term repercussions. Feminists may hail the phenomenon as giving women greater sexual power and self-assertion.[28] Others may think it merely makes explicit what usually takes place anyhow, even with the fathers around—that is that women have undertaken most of the socialization process all along.

Another related phenomenon is the increasing number of female labor migrants to the capital-rich countries. These tend to be mostly professional, sub-professional and white collar workers. Some are domestic workers (e.g. maids and nannies). Nothing in this process is problematic if the female is accompanied by a spouse who is equally employed. But in several cases, these women are either unmarried or married but without their spouses accompanying them. The latter situation may be dictated by the same factors which may lead the husband to migrate alone—e.g. saving, the schooling of children...etc. Often it is because the husband either cannot obtain a job in the host country or cannot or does not want to leave his job at home. Whatever the cause, this phenomenon is rather novel on the Egyptian social scene. The splitting of females from their families of origin or families of orientation may be hailed again as another step in the emancipation of women; that is, the fact that they are on their own and earning money in another country. But it may also be perceived as yet another step in the decadent vulgarization of the Egyptian family by oil money.

Probably the hardest situation for a married couple is when the wife has a job and the husband does not, in a country like Saudi Arabia which requires that employed females must be accompanied by a *mahram*—a husband or an older male relative. This happens especially when the wife has an employable skill with a salary far exceeding the couple's combined income in Egypt. No systematic research has been done on this phenomenon regarding Egypt. But cases with which the author is familiar were quite stressful and distressing. The role-reversal for an Egyptian husband is still very hard to take, and the boredom of staying at home and the feeling of worthlessness is emasculating for many of them.

C. SECTORAL LABOR SHORTAGES AND THEIR MULTIPLIER EFFECTS

The initial euphoria surrounding mass labor migration from Egypt gave way recently to a more sober assessment of its implications for the development of Egypt itself. As it turned out it has not been surplus labor or surplus population which was tapped by migration to capital-rich countries. Rather it has been the high level manpower, the trained and the most skilled of Egypt's labor force. To be sure, some of the un-skilled manage to filter through the borders of the oil-rich countries. But by and large the bulk of Egypt's migrants are Egypt's best labor. In essence, therefore, most of Egypt's unemployed at home were unemploy-able abroad. They have remained in Egypt. Migration has not reduced the rate of unemployment which, as shown in Table XII, stood at 11.5 percent in 1976. It has been hovering around 11.0 percent since the late 1960s, at which period Egypt's development plans were halted. In other words, migration did not do what it was "supposed" to do for Egypt. It did not reduce unemployment and population pressure but has, in effect, deprived Egypt of its most valuable brains and hands.

The negative effect of this loss is now acknowledged by most

TABLE XII
Estimate of Employment in Egypt by Sector, 1976

Sector	Number	Percentage
Agriculture*	6,490,000	50.7
Government**	1,740,000	13.6
Public Sector**	1,210,000	9.4
Private Sector**	950,000	7.4
Armed Forces***	342,000	2.7
Workers Abroad****	600,000	4.7
Unemployed*	1,479,000	11.5
TOTAL	12,811,000	100.0

*   Estimate by Birks and Sinclair of employment in agriculture;
**   Ministry of Planning, *Five Year Plan 1978-82*, Vol. I, table 4, p. 31;
***   International Inst. for Strategic Studies, *The Military Balance 1977-78*, table 3, p. 85;
**** Ministry of Planning, op.cit., Vol. II, p. 184.

SOURCE: J. S. Birks and C. A. Sinclair, "Egypt, Frustrated Labor Exporter", *Middle East Journal*, Vol. 31 (Summer 1979), pp. 288-303 and p. 290.

observers, but it is hard to assess its real economic and social cost. One argument may contend that even the best brains are not properly utilized in Egypt under the present regime anyhow. The Cairo University-Massachusetts Institute of Technology (MIT) research team, which has so far investigated two important migrant groups, would argue differently. Egypt's construction workers are one of the most sought-after groups all over the region. This is understandable in view of all the infrastructure prerequisites for any subsequent development. Choucri, Eckaus and Mohie-Eldin noted that employment in Egypt's construction sector is symptomatic of Egypt's economy in the past two decades.[29] It grew rapidly between 1960 and 1966 (31 percent at an annual rate of 4.5 percent increase), then it slowed down between 1966 and 1974 (with a modest increase of 14 percent in 8 years). That period was characterized by declining levels of investment. Then came the 1973 boom and mounting demand on Egypt's construction labor. The instant response created a domestic shortage leading to an increase of money and real wages of construction workers, as Table XIII illustrates. Some construction labor categories registered wage increases of over 480 percent between 1970 and 1977 (such as assistant builders). Most other categories have at least doubled their wages. Much of that rise, it should be noted, occurred from 1973 on.

TABLE XIII
Average Wage Per Worker 1959/60 — 1978 in Egypt
(in Egyptian pounds)

Year	Construction	Agriculture	Services	Mining & Industry
1960	161.6	30.2	164.5	147.6
1961	164.4	27.5	162.5	147.7
1962	159.3	32.5	161.7	153.3
1963	150.1	34.8	185.5	172.2
1964	156.2	37.9	190.2	174.8
1965	155.6	44.6	208.4	181.3
1966	170.4	50.8	209.3	183.4
1967	180.4	53.3	213.5	183.3
1968	182.8	51.7	208.7	181.9
1969	182.8	53.1	223.4	184.3
1970	184.6	53.9	238.6	187.6
1971	184.2	55.0	241.0	190.0
1972	190.4	55.4	251.0	255.2
1973	233.3	60.5	266.0	287.1
1974	233.2	70.8	295.0	297.0
1975	376.2	106.5	314.8	292.4
1976	378.7	107.0	327.1	305.9
1977*	328.3	107.6	340.0	320.0
1978*	354.7	108.0	353.4	334.7
Increase:	119%	258%	115%	127%
Average Annual Increase:	4.4%	7.1%	4.2%	4.5%
Increase from 1974-78:	52.1%	52.5%	19.8%	12.7%

*Projections

SOURCE: Ministry of Planning, *Followup Report*, (Cairo: 1977).

Table XIII also gives average wages from 1960 to 1978 for construction workers as well as those in three other sectors. All of them registered impressive increases, but it should be noted that wages in agriculture especially have increased at the highest rate over the eighteen year period (258 percent). Part of this exceptional rate of increase is due to the very low base in 1960, but most of it, especially since 1974, is due to sectoral replacement in construction. In other words, with domestic shortage resulting from migration, some agricultural labor was drawn and enticed into construction by higher wages. That in turn created some shortages in agricultural labor — a condition which usually sends up wages.

It should be noted that these wage increases were not matched by any increase in labor productivity, and possibly the latter declined because of under-trained replacement. In other words, the wage rise is due mainly to shortage created by migration. This means a higher corresponding construction labor cost for the consumer. Phrased differently, this is one way of creating inflationary pressures within the economy. The rising wages are no doubt beneficial to the workers involved (300,000 in construction) and to other groups whose incomes rose at the same or higher rates. But this has not been the case for 3.2 million government and public sector employees on fixed incomes and their dependents (another 6.0 million). The income per capita in Egypt as a whole, estimated at between $200 and $240 in the mid-1970s, could not have risen at the same rate (52 percent in four years). The closest indication of the rate of increase for government employees is by examining the "services" column in Table XIII, since most civil servants would fall there. The service sector wages rose by only 19.8 percent in the same four year period—that is by less than half the rate of those in construction and agriculture.

The sectoral shortages and their inflationary consequences could, of course, have been avoided or at least minimized had there been a rational labor training and labor exporting policy. As it exists now, Egypt's labor market does not have the flexibility which makes quick adjustments and inter-sectoral replacements possible. Birks and Sinclair describe Egypt's labor market as highly segmented with relatively little occupational mobility between segments.[30] On the basis of available data they conclude that the Egyptian labor market is characterized by extraordinary immobility between even relatively similar occupations.[31] This occupational rigidity has made it not only difficult to offset shortages inside Egypt, but also, they feel, has limited Egypt's ability to capture more of the Arab market. Obviously the two Arab labor authorities think that Egyptian labor migration is something valuable for Egypt—only there is little of it because of this occupational immobility.[32] Most Egyptian critics, on the other hand, contend at present that there is too much of Egypt's best labor force abroad and that strategic sectoral shortages are beginning to take their toll.[33] Construction workers are cited as a case in point.

Some categories within that sector which are simply skilled workers (such as bricklayers) had by 1977 topped architects and civil engineers in terms of daily wages. This is an exceptional phenomenon since engineers, especially, were the highest-paid category even among high level manpower during the heydays of Nasir's industrialization in the late 1950s and the 1960s. Indeed, so valuable and scarce were the engineers then that a law was issued by presidential decree to draft them upon graduation from college to serve in various public and state functions. This was, incidentally, the year that Egypt's Ministry of Labor was established,[34] and the first industrialization plan was enacted soon after. The point here is that by the late 1970s, engineers — still undoubtedly needed — were being out-paid by certain skilled manual workers who suddenly were in short supply because of migration to neighboring countries.

If the shortage of construction workers has caused inflationary havoc in the building industry, hurting those on fixed incomes in particular — i.e. the majority of Egyptians — shortages in other sectors have caused an alarming decline in quality of service. One such case is that of university professors. The pioneering work of Mohie-Eldin and A. Omar on their migration is quite enlightening.[35] They first show that the total registered academic staff in Egypt's three largest universities (Cairo, Ein Shams and Alexandria) grew from 3,177 in 1970 to 4,081 in 1975, an increase of 904, or 28.4 percent, in five years. However, by 1976 the number which had "brain-drained" to the West was 1,058 — i.e. more than 25 percent of the total staff of the three universities in that year, and more than the net increase in staff in the previous five years. As for those seconded to Arab countries (temporary migration), their number grew steadily from 388 in 1970/71 to 605 in 1974/75 — a 63 percent increase in five years. Thus while the growth rate of the total academic staff was 6.3 percent per annum between 1970 and 1975, the emigration rate to Arab countries increased at over 12.0 percent, and the brain-drain rate to the West was 5 percent per annum during the same period. Table XIV illustrates the case of Cairo University in recording the emigration of academics by field of specialization between 1967 and 1975. In some fields as many as 30 percent of the total faculty were out of their institutions and teaching somewhere else in the region.

Now, does Egypt have a surplus of university professors that it can allow them to go abroad on such a scale? The answer is: hardly. The ratio of students to faculty in most American universities is 20 to 1. In Egypt in 1970 it was five times as high in social sciences and the humanities; that is, 100 students to each faculty member — if all the faculty members were there. With nearly 25 percent of them on secondment to Arab countries, the ratio in 1970/71 was 123 to 1. The following year the ratio jumped from 111 to 1 before emigration of the staff and to 144 to 1 after their emigration. Table XV shows the same trend in detail for Cairo University. If the ratio in physical sciences has not worsened as rapidly as it has in the humanities and social sciences, it is only a matter of time. Most rich Arab countries found it easier, in their rush to open new universities, to start with social sciences and the humanities (including law and business) which did not require setting up of laboratories

TABLE XIV
Average Number of Staff and of Emigration From Cairo University (1967/68-1974/75)

Field of Specialization	Academic Staff		Emigration		Emigration/ Academic Staff %
	Avg.	%	Avg.	%	
Literature & Human Studies	164	11.48	33	17.76	20.12
Legal Studies	51	3.57	13	6.99	25.49
Commercial Studies	28	1.96	8	4.30	28.57
Economics & Statistics	48	3.36	14	7.53	29.17
Basic Sciences	168	11.75	25	13.44	14.88
Medical Sciences	457	31.97	24	12.91	5.25
Pharmaceutical Science	60	4.20	3	1.61	5.00
Veterinary Science	85	5.95	11	5.91	12.94
Engineering Science	189	13.23	31	16.67	6.88
Agricultural Science	179	19.53	24	12.90	13.02
TOTAL	1429	100.00	186	100.00	13.02

SOURCE: Amr Mohie-Eldin and Ahmad Omar, *The Emigration of Universities' Academic Staff* (Cairo University-MIT Technology Adaptation Program, 1980), p. 29.

TABLE XV
The Ratio of Students to Each Staff Member Before and After Migration for Cairo University

Year	Human Sciences		Change	Physical Sciences		Change
	Before Emigration	After Emigration		Before Emigration	After Emigration	
1967/68	76 to 1	89 to 1	17%	24 to 1	28 to 1	17%
1968/69	76 to 1	103 to 1	36%	24 to 1	28 to 1	17%
1969/70	77 to 1	111 to 1	44%	23 to 1	28 to 1	22%
1970/71	79 to 1	100 to 1	27%	23 to 1	28 to 1	22%
1971/72	90 to 1	118 to 1	31%	23 to 1	26 to 1	13%
1972/73	107 to 1	146 to 1	36%	22 to 1	25 to 1	14%
1973/74	122 to 1	172 to 1	41%	22 to 1	26 to 1	18%

SOURCE: Mohie-Eldin and Omar, op.cit., Table 9, p. 46 and sources cited therein.

and complicated equipment. However, by the end of the 1970s they were beginning to open engineering and medical schools. No doubt there will be a similar run on Egyptian professors in these fields as well.

The point made here is that even in sectors in which Egypt had shortages to begin with, a similar exodus and an "oil run" has taken place. This has caused the quality of service, low to begin with, to deteriorate still further. The case of university professors is illustrative of the immense social costs to Egypt, despite whatever material gain to the migrants themselves. And here, as in the case of doctors and engineers, even the misgivings of Birks and Sinclair on the rigidity of Egypt's labor force hardly apply. No easy or quick replacement from one sector to any of the above can be effected in Egypt (or in any society for that matter). It takes nearly twenty years to train a professor. As much lead time would be required to effect any substantial replacement. This is not like the construction worker who may take no more than one or two years to train. It has been pointed out that more than 95 percent of Egyptians working abroad have between four to eight years of work experience.[36] Thus they are already well-trained and are not seeking employment for the first time.

D.   DOWN-GRADING OF EGYPT'S LABOR FORCE

Since most Egyptian labor to capital-rich countries is not simply seeking employment but is also looking for higher wages, a number of essentially negative effects have been observed. For one thing it is noted that most of the labor has been transferred from sectors with highly productive activities in Egypt. This is unlike Turkish, North African and Southern European workers who migrated in the fifties and sixties to Western and Northern Europe.[37] In the latter, workers were essentially moving from low-productive activities to high-production ones in the host employing countries. Therefore the migratory process entailed for them a labor up-grading — i.e. they acquired new skills and experiences.[38]

In the case of Egypt, the situation is almost the opposite. The wages in the capital-rich countries being so high, it bears little direct correlation to productivity or performance when compared to the standards at home. This has led, among other things, to many Egyptians accepting jobs far below their level of skill, provided the pay is so much higher than anything they can get in Egypt. This is quite detrimental to the skilled workers, to Egypt, and to the entire Arab world in the long run, since over time these workers simply lose their skills. At best they stop learning and improving.[39] Even in cases where the job description formally matches the qualification level of the migrant, it often turns out that so little is required of him in the way of performance that his productivity indeed deteriorates. This applies, for example, in the case of university professors. While the capital-rich countries may recruit the best academics from Egypt, Lebanon or from among the Palestinians, little is required of them apart from six to nine hours of teaching each week — much less than they would do at home, but for ten times the salary. Some Egyptian professors who were quite prolific in Egypt published very little during their four years' secondment in Kuwait or Saudi Arabia.[40]

As one writer has put it, the tenure of Egyptian laborers abroad "seems to involve an element of 'rent' which has nothing to do whatsoever with productive efficiency compared to their respective fields back home. Thus one of the most negative effects of the oil era is a widening gap between productivity of labor and cost of labor in the Arab world at large."[41]

E.   THE SPREAD OF CONSPICUOUS CONSUMPTION

The rapid increase of money-wealth for Egyptians working abroad has naturally led to new consumption patterns. This was made all the easier in the host countries by the endless demonstration of the latest products from the industrial machine of the First World. For those Egyptians who had never owned standard durable goods (e.g. refrigerators, washing machines, cooking stoves, televisions...etc.) these would be the first items to acquire — either from the capital-rich countries and shipped to Egypt, or from the numerous "duty-free" shops in Egypt itself (which, however, sell only in hard currency). For Egyptians who had already acquired these standard durables while still in Egypt, the items to aim for would be cars, color television sets, air conditioners...etc. For those who had both before leaving Egypt, the consumption pattern usually becomes of a higher order altogether — either a second set of everything (e.g. two cars) or more sophisticated items such as videotape equipment, stereo systems, expensive carpets, expensive imported clothes...etc. These consumption patterns are confirmed by the results of two surveys on school teachers and university professors respectively.[42]

The point is that Egyptians working abroad do achieve much higher living standards. Aside from creating shortages and an unstable labor force in certain sectors, as we have already seen, the standard of living and consumption patterns enjoyed by these individuals create a demonstration effect, so that even those who may not have quite the same kind of income or savings from their work abroad begin to crave similar luxuries and to develop similar consumption tendencies, going beyond basics and even average luxuries to the conspicuous. Those who cannot afford to consume at the same level but who belong to the same reference group (e.g. other university professors) would thus soon develop an irresistable urge to be seconded.

Even for the returnees there are adjustment problems to their pre-migration employment, earnings, and expenditure patterns. People can adjust quickly to a higher standard of living, but not vice versa. Thus it is difficult for a returnee to live on his modest Egyptian salary any longer after having spent lavishly for the previous four years or so. So he begins to dip into his savings until they are nearly exhausted, at which point, if not before, he and his family will be caught up in the struggle for a new secondment. Work and productivity become quite marginal or secondary to a returnee's existence in either case—a point we take up next.

Thus the indivdual expenditure pattern among citizens of the oil-rich countries spreads down to migrant laborers in these countries and through the usual demonstration effect it spreads to the capital-poor countries. The only difference, of course, is that the latter cannot afford it: or more accurately, they could put whatever money resources they might have to much more productive use in their own society. Material expectations have by far outdistanced any possible earning level in Egypt for various elements of the population. Finding employment in a capital-rich country has therefore become the dream of many Egyptians—spanning the entire class and age structures of the society. The quick money and the dazzling consumer goods it can buy has become part of the "Egyptian national imagination".

The role of the state in all this is far from being neutral. For one thing, the leadership at the highest level feeds these high material expectations. The model projected to the Egyptian people by President Sadat is not just limited to his own behavior and consumption patterns, but more by his verbal assertion that the goal of every Egyptian should be to have a car and a villa. While no one should object to that in principle, the ability to fulfill this material aspiration does not exist inside Egypt for the vast majority of Egyptians. The only way to make the dream come true is to work in an oil country. In essence, then, the state is, in the person of the President, selling a dream that can only be fulfilled if the majority leave their country on a temporary labor migration The state has also pampered those who work abroad. It has done away with the law that required them to transfer a minimum of 10 percent of their earnings to Egypt at the official exchange rate.[43] More than that, it has exempted them from paying any taxes, even in Egyptian currency, on their earnings abroad.[44] In other words, there is no attempt on the part of the state to check the conspicuous consumption by resorting to some of the conventional fiscal policies at its command.

Worse still is the state's reinforcement of conspicuous consumption by its own deliberate policies. By allowing "own-import", and general import of all kinds of luxury items, the markets of Cairo and Port Said are now full of a dazzling array of goods which only a few Egyptians can easily afford. Not counting what Egyptians abroad bring back with them, Egypt's imports of consumer goods have steadily grown, from LE36 million in 1970 to LE133 million in 1975 and to LE1,224 in 1979 — and projected to reach LE1,331 million in 1980. Simply stated, Egypt's imports of consumer goods in one decade have increased by 3600 percent (compared with only 2000 percent increase in capital goods).[45] Granted some of this is due to a rise in the importation of wheat and other basic food stuffs, but neither population growth nor the rate of inflation in one decade would justify this steep rise in the importation of consumer goods. The major factor which explains it is real increase in the levels of consumption of luxury goods.

Thus we are faced with an emerging breed of Egyptians who are earning a lot, consuming conspicuously, and who are quite hostile to any notion of paying taxes or transferring money at the official exchange rate. Their behavior is reinforced by the state, and the demonstration effect is taking hold of an increasing number of Egyptians. This is accompanied by state policies disposed to import more consumer goods to satisfy the consumers' insatiable appetite. The trade deficit, as a result, has grown from less than LE200 million in 1970 to over LE2,000 million in 1977. In 1960, consumer goods accounted for 19 percent of Egypt's total imports — in 1975 it was over 45 percent. The state has financed the annual deficits by relying increasingly on foreign aid or borrowing.[46] In brief, the state's behavior and that of the new Egyptian breed are alike in many ways.

F. DECLINE OF WORK ETHICS

Probably the most devastating negative effect of the oil wealth and its chain reaction has been the near collapse of work ethics in the Arab world. Easily earned and easily spent money undermines the value of productive work. This, of course, applies anywhere; and the Arabs are no exception. Here we shall examine the manifestation of this proposition as it applies to Egyptians working in the capital-rich countries.

We have already alluded to the fact that the huge wage differentials between the poor and the rich Arab states have led to a gradual downgrading of work skills. This operates, as we saw, when a worker accepts a job far below his skill level so long as there is significantly higher pay than anything he could earn at home. But aside from this, there is a subtle and yet damaging change of attitudes towards work, regardless of the skill level required. The belief that hard work and achievement are the essential means of professional and financial success is no longer supported by empirical facts in Egypt or in the rest of the Arab world. The persistent and accumulated perceptions of "others", especially of those who "made it" financially, are beginning to strike root in the psyche of an increasing number of Egyptians. The code words now for success are *hazz* (luck), *Essuᶜudiyya* (Saudi Arabia). *Ekkuwait* (Kuwait), *intidab* (secondment), *ᶜaqd* (a contract), and *fursah* (opportunity). Rarely does an average Egyptian ask how much work is involved, what skill is required or what the working conditions are. Not that he does not entirely care; but these are now secondary matters, removed to the periphery of his consciousness. Rarely does one hear a returnee describing his work in any professional detail, or conveying an impression that he enjoyed what he was doing or derived any intrinsic gratification from occupational achievement. The rare occasions when "work" is mentioned at all by a vacationer or a returnee are in the context of competition for a renewal of a contract or of the obtaining of a contract for a friend; or of a conflict with other national groups (like Palestinians or Syrians or Pakistanis) to get to the ear of the native boss or to get rid of one another in the host country. In brief, just "being there" means success, with a minimum of, or no work. Money means consumption of things, which "significant others"—i.e. one's reference group—cannot obtain on their incomes at home.

Another devastating effect on work attitudes pertains to those who are still in Egypt. Most of the latter are waiting for their turn (*al-dour*) to be seconded, if they are government employees; or waiting for a "contract" from a relative, a friend, an agent, or a *kafil* (a sponsor). And since "getting there" is not contingent on anything exceptional in the way of work performance in Egypt, the work itself suffers in the process. People are either anticipating a secondment, waiting for a contract, preparing to leave, or otherwise lamenting their "luck" and feeling demoralized. In all these mental states, performance on the job in Egypt itself becomes as marginal as it is for the lucky ones who are "there".

In other words, healthy attitudes towards work have been undermined both in the capital-rich and the capital-poor countries.[47] In neither case is hard work proportionately rewarded or poor work proportionately penalized. What matters now, in most cases in the Arab world, is really where one is geographically situated—i.e. on which side of the wealth divide.

Thus a new attitudinal syndrome is developing towards "success", "work" and "consumption". All these conventional attitudinal objects are redefined in the Arab societal context. The usual instrumental links among them are being supplemented or altogether replaced by new ones which bear very little on productivity or creativity. Among these links in the new syndrome are "luck", "opportunity", "secondment", "contract" and "being there". This layer of attitudinal qualities is to be added to the ones already sketched when we discussed conspicuous consumption.

G. DEVALUATION OF AUTHENTICITY

Related to the new oil syndrome is a steady decline of pride in authentic objects and values. Thus, for example, consuming Egyptian-made products is no longer a source of national pride or statement of conscience. For the majority it is because they cannot afford to consume foreign ones. They do not have the money—they have not "been there".

Even if one has money for certain items, it has to be of a special kind, non-Egyptian—i.e. hard currency. This degrading attitude towards authentic objects, including the country's own products and its own national currency, may have begun with those working abroad. But by the late 1970s the attitude had become so widespread that the government itself had adopted it. In 1979, the Egyptian Minister of National Economy issued Decree No. 600 which stipulated that customs and tariffs on imported goods must be paid for in hard currency. And for several years now, government agencies and private companies have given priority to applicants and customers for the purchase of housing, real estate and durable goods (even when made in Egypt) if they pay in hard currency. Even the release of tenders by some state organizations for Egyptian contractors and suppliers has become conditional on the payment of the required fee in American dollars.[48]

This phenomenon is both a cause and an effect at the same time. It is a symptom created by a glut of money in the hands of a substantial minority who "made it" in the capital-rich countries. Given the scarcity of goods and services in a still ailing Egyptian economy, having such money acquires an added exaggerated dimension which depresses the value of local currency even more. The symptomatic, however, has become a moving cause in its own right; that is, people now compete to obtain foreign jobs to be able to obtain foreign goods (and even some of the local but scarce goods such as housing).

Initially triggered off by Egyptian labor migrants, this phenomenon has been further reinforced by other components of the Open Door policy. The opening up of branches of foreign banks and companies (both by Arabs and Westerners) has fuelled the trend of devaluing things Egyptian. Since the mid-seventies another way of striking it rich is to associate with foreign institutions in Egypt. Working for national institutions is no longer rewarding; people seem to be doing it only because they have not yet managed or are not able either to go to an oil-rich country or to join a foreign institution in Cairo itself. A recent graduate of the American University in Cairo (AUC) working for a foreign institution usually receives a starting salary that is at least ten times the size of his counterpart's who has graduated from a national university and is working for a national institute in Egypt. Little wonder that the AUC, a private institution which in the late 1950s and 1960s admitted those who were unable to enter the national universities because of low grades, is now the ultimate dream for many young Egyptians.

It should be obvious by now that the consequences of Egyptian labor migration to capital-rich Arab countries are quite mixed. The positive and the negative are intertwined both for individuals and for the society. On balance, the negatives at this point may seem to exceed by far the positives for Egypt as a labor exporter, as a developing country and as the former pace-setter for the entire Arab nation. But in any dialectical social process the negatives of today may turn into tomorrow's positives. And of course there is no "one Egypt" in the abstract. In reality there are several; and what may seem positive for one may very well be negative for another. It is this very fact that sets the stage parameters for social conflict, with all its creative as well as its destructive functions, a point discussed in a later section of this chapter. In concluding this section, we may also note that several of the consequences discussed above apply for other Arab labor-exporting countries — Tunisia, Sudan, Jordan and the Palestinians, and Yemen.

IV. SOME CONSEQUENCES OF LABOR IMPORTATION: SAUDI ARABIA

Saudi Arabia is the largest Arab oil producer with around 9.5 million barrels a day. In 1979 it accounted for nearly half of total Arab oil production. Saudi oil revenues increased from $0.6 billion in 1965 to $1.2 billion in 1970 and to $4.3 billion in 1973. But in 1974 revenues jumped to $22.5 billion as a result of price quadrupling in the aftermath of the October War. In 1977 they hit the $37 billion mark and nearly doubled again to about $70 billion in 1979 in the aftermath of the Iranian revolution. Middle Eastern crises, so far, seem to result in quantum leaps in oil revenues (see Table II above).

Being the leader in production and in revenues, Saudi Arabia has naturally embarked on the most ambitious public expenditure programs in the Arab world. Its Five Year Plan for the period 1975 to 1980 called for an expenditure of $145 billion, while the Plan for 1980 to 1985 nearly doubles this amount to $285 billion. This in turn has set in motion an accelerated labor importation process. Of the total volume of 700,000 inter-Arab migrants in 1970, Saudi Arabia appropriated one half (see Table III above) while the other seven labor importers shared the remaining half. The same trend continued into the post-1973 years; thus in 1977 Saudi Arabia's share of 2.2 million Arab migrants was about 1.2 million.

The consequences of labor importation are as mixed and complicated for Saudi Arabia as those of labor exportation are for Egypt. The question of which of these consequences are positive and which negative is a value-loaded one. For example, would the breakdown of certain indigenous values and practices—such as slavery and the seclusion of women—as the result of massive contact with outsiders be viewed as positive or negative? While the abolition of slavery may be universally endorsed even within the most conservative quarters of Saudi society, the same would not apply to attitudes towards women; the argument for their continued seclusion and veiling is still quite strong, to the extent that many non-Saudi females coming to work in the country find it both expedient and necessary to veil. By the same token, it is hard to evaluate the impact of the vast numbers of expatriate labor on the political vulnerability or the stability of the regime. Although we can identify several consequences—the erosion of traditional culture, new social formation, growing social discontent, mounting pressure on services...etc.—we shall discuss here only the issue of growth versus security, which is in the nature of a dilemma for Saudi Arabia at the present time.

The predicament facing the Saudi political elites derives from the hard choices confronting them and the price tag attached to each choice. We can identify several paradoxes in which choices may work at cross purposes. That of security versus growth is directly related to labor importation. The vast oil and financial resources of Saudi Arabia have placed equally large obligations on the ruling elite to modernize the country, to create new and viable institutions, to build an elaborate infrastructure, raise the standard of living, and diversify the economic base in anticipation of the post-oil era. By the same token, these vast resources with their regional and global geopolitical implications thrust the Kingdom into a sudden position of importance and vulnerability at the same time. This has made the ruling elite quite sensitive to questions of national security. The latter has resulted in an augmenting of the country's defence capabilities in terms both of manpower in the armed forces and of weapon systems. But national security also means for the Saudis internal stability, which, among other things, calls for reducing dependence on expatriate labor. At present Saudi Arabia is so dependent on expatriates that if they were to leave, the whole Kingdom, in the opinion of experts, "would grind to a halt".[49]

In brief, the equation of growth and security is quite tenuous. The Saudis' defence spending rose from $171 million in 1968 to $13,170 million in 1978—i.e. by more than 770 percent in one decade.[50] The per capita defence expenditure is $1,704, compared to Algeria's $25, Egypt's $112, Iraq's $141, Iran's $224 and Israel's $887.[51] With a population of less than one fifth of Egypt's, the Saudi defence budget in 1978 was three times the size of the Egyptian defence budget, which, no doubt, reflects the over-concern of the ruling elite with questions of security. And if there is any doubt about the internal component of security one has only to look at the allocations to and the strengthening of the Saudi National Guard (sometimes called the White Guard) whose exclusive concern is the protection of the regime of the Al-Sa'ud Royal Family.[52] It has grown from less than 10,000 in the 1960s to a force of 41,000 in 1978.[53] Designed to quell any internal disturbances or military coups d'état, the National Guard is a match for the Saudi regular army (45,000), air force (12,000), and the navy (1,500). While these regular armed forces are dispersed along the Saudi frontiers, the National Guard has its concentrations and installations near most of the important cities.[54] Until the early 1970s it had lighter arms than the regular ground forces, but has been undergoing a process of total modernization, due for completion in 1980, which will give it armored vehicles, mechanized infantry battalions, air defence weapons and anti-tank capabilities.[55]

The concern with internal security must have seemed more than justified in view of repeated attempts to stage coups d'état, the latest and most spectacular of which was the one which involved the seizing of the Grand Mosque, which houses the Ka'ba shrine, by a group of Saudi and non-Saudi dissidents in 1979. The counter-attack and the liberation of the shrine was carried out by the National Guard.

Thus the goal of rapid socio-economic development works, in some ways, at cross-purposes with the goal of internal security and the political stability of the regime. The solution of the leadership for this difficult equation has been to increase investments on both sides. As defence- and security-related expenditures skyrocketed during the past ten years, so too did development expenditures. The first Five Year Plan (1970–1975) earmarked about $12 billion (SR41.3 billion) for development projects, at an annual rate of $2.5 billion. The second Five Year Plan (1975–1980) was pegged at $145 billion, averaging about $30 billion annually. The third Five Year Plan (1980–1985) announced in June 1980 would invest $285 billion, at an average annual rate of $57 billion.[56] In other words, the annual expenditure on development has jumped from $2.5 billion in 1970 to $57 billion in 1980, an increase of 2200 percent in one decade. This kind of huge investment in a country with a very modest demographic base has, as we have seen, dictated the need for the massive importation of labor on all levels. The influx of such a large and heterogeneous population into a fragile and basically conservative social structure was bound to create all sorts of stresses and strains. The participation by expatriates from other Arab and Muslim countries in the seizing of the Grand Mosque is evidence of just one of these strains – that of "security".

The financial ability of the Saudis to deal with the apparent contradiction of the goals of security and development by escalating expenditure on both sides does not ensure a "desirable" outcome. Iran under the Shah is a glaring case in point: there, because of the miniscule number of expatriates there was even less cause for alarm.

Their awareness of the potential danger from the huge number of foreign migrants has made the Saudi leadership resort to a number of protective measures and policies, which range from prohibiting any form of labor organization, to swiftly and ruthlessly dealing with the slightest labor unrest. The wholesale deportation of expatriates at a few hours' notice is not at all uncommon. One way of containing the flood of expatriates – or at least neutralizing their existence in the country – is through what may be called "expatriate labor camps". Both Saudi Arabia and Kuwait have recently encouraged this new approach, the most notorious example of which is the South Korean contractors. Each contractor brings his entire workforce with him and then takes it away again upon completing the job; thus the Koreans have very little, if any, contact with the native population,[57] although the number of Koreans in Saudi Arabia at the end of 1977 was estimated at about 80,000.[58] These Korean style labor camps are, however, suitable only for construction programs – of which there were plenty in the first two Five Year Plans. The 1980–1985 Plan, while still containing a substantial component of infrastructure projects, concentrates on services, social welfare, institution-building, and human development, and for achieving these targets there is no major substitute for Arab manpower.[59]

A variant of the same practice of insulating expatriates from the natives is "enclave development projects". This is another compromise chosen by political leaders and technocrats for the difficult equation of security versus development. Here the concept is physically to separate from existing urban centers the new industrial areas on which future growth will be based. It is hoped that this will minimize any close or prolonged contacts between expatriates and indigenous Saudis. It also reduces the economic cost of supporting migrant labor, since standard social services like education and health are not readily available to them, and this in turn discourages them from bringing their dependents to join them. Examples of such industrial enclaves are the multi-billion dollar projects at Yanbu and Jubail. Other capital-rich Arab states have done the same[60] — Ruwais in Abu Dhabi, Shuaiba in Kuwait, Jebel Ali in Dubai and Urum Said in Qatar. The optimistic assumption is, of course, that by the time these projects have been completed, indigenous manpower will have been trained and will be available to operate and to maintain them.

The sociological naiveté inherent in all this is astounding, though we will not elaborate upon it here. Suffice it to say that the Saudi elite and the entire system along with the élite wants to have its cake and eat it too. This is not confined to the dilemma of security versus growth but applies to many other aspects of contemporary Saudi society.

One such paradox is equating growth with development and confusing one for the other. Thus while the expanding of education is commendable, one wonders why it is necessary in such a thinly populated country to build the world's largest university campus in Riyadh where there are already two universities functioning (in addition to three others elsewhere in the Kingdom, at Jeddah, Mecca and Dhahran), or why such an effort is being made at a cost of billions of dollars when the government has signally failed to motivate sufficient numbers of Saudis to enroll in the several vocational training centers, most of which stand empty and are hard-pressed for recruits. The same mistaken sense of priorities and of scale applies to the issue of economic diversification. Again we are told that the industrial complex now under construction at Yanbu is the world's largest. It will include refineries and petrochemical industries. While the concept of processing oil products instead of exporting crude petroleum is no doubt very sound and long overdue, under present manpower realities the Saudis will have to rely heavily on expatriates for several years for running and maintaining the complex. It would have made more sense, given the present Saudi population policy, to have smaller-scale projects spread more evenly along the Jubail-Yanbu axis. Alternatively, if they wish to maintain the projected colossal scale, they should seriously entertain a new population policy which would allow expatriates to settle and to be eligible for citizenship after a certain number of years of residence. The fear that such a course might alter the demographic-cultural composition of the country is really an academic point, since this is *de facto* the case. By adding a *de jure* component, expatriates would have a stake in the developmental process and would possess a deeper commitment to their new country. Not only would this reduce the security risk but it would also help broaden the demographic base of an otherwise underpopulated country, and would also gradually eliminate the present pecuniary or mercenary mentality that prevails among most expatriates. The Saudi leadership continues instead to follow a course bristling with the seeds of destabilization, including quantitative growth confused with development and a self-fulfilling distrustful population policy.

Many of the paradoxes of the Saudi society may be attributed to its unique developmental experience: a quasi-capitalist mode of development juxtaposed on a semi-tribal society, with the state playing the major economic role, with abundant financial resources, a small population, but with little of anything else, and presided over by a theocratically-based autocratic monarchy. This hodge-podge has proved amazingly tenacious so far, thanks to the *esprit de corps* and the inner solidarity of the large clan of Al-Sa'ud and their minor partners the Al-Sheikh. But again, with Iran at the back of one's mind, it may well prove to be a house of steel built on quicksand, and the Khaldunian cycle of Arab dynasties may be entering its final phase. The same paradoxes exist in other opulent oil sheikhdoms on the Gulf where most of the same structural forces are at work; the differences between them and Saudi Arabia are merely in order of magnitude.

V. GROWING ARAB INTERDEPENDENCE

It should be clear by now how closely linked the Arab countries have become as a result of oil and its multitudinous "spill-overs". Of course, cultural, religious and political links had always existed, long before the appearance of oil. What the oil has done is to turn the stratification of the Arab world nearly upside down. Many of the formerly poverty-stricken countries with small populations, tribal formations and undifferentiated social structures have emerged almost overnight as financial giants by both regional and world standards. Several of the formerly well-to-do countries have become, in relative terms, the poor relations of the Arab world.[61] Tables XVI and XVII show respectively the stratification of Arab states by income and other indicators. There are glaring disparities in the former—a fact that by itself is socially and regionally destabilizing. Further incongruencies between income on one hand and other indicators of socio-economic development on the other make the new Arab order potentially explosive. Nevertheless, replete as it may be with actual and potential tension, this new order has developed various mechanisms of interdependence.

The links among the rich, the well-to-do, the middle and the poor Arab countries have locked the Arab world into a new social order with a sharp division not only of wealth but also of socio-economic labor. This

TABLE XVI
Inter-Arab Stratification by Income

Country	GNP ($ Million)	Indigenous Population (000)	Per Capita GNP ($)
	Stratum I (The Rich)		
1. Kuwait	7,478	0,472	15,840
2. U.A.E.	2,798	0,200	13,990
3. Libya	17,368	2,600	6,680
4. Qatar	429	0,068	6,310
5. Saudi Arabia	27,784	4,600	6,040
Sub-Total	55,857 (38.7%)	7,940 (5.6%)	7,035
	Stratum II (The Well-to-do)		
6. Oman	1,474	0,550	2,680
7. Bahrain	482	0,225	2,140
8. Iraq	18,290	11,800	1,550
9. Lebanon	3,480	2,900	1,200
10. Algeria	18,803	16,940	1,110
Sub-Total	42,529 (29.5%)	32,415 (22.7%)	1,312
	Stratum III (The Struggling Middle)		
11. Syria	7,098	7,800	910
12. Tunisia	5,074	5,900	860
13. Jordan	2,059	2,900	710
14. Morocco	10,120	18,400	550
Sub-Total	24,351 (16.9%)	35,000 (24.6%)	696
	Stratum IV (The Poor)		
15. Yemen (A)	2,166	5,037	430
16. Yemen (D)	578	1,700	340
17. Egypt	12,998	38,328	320
18. Sudan	4,901	16,900	290
19. Mauritania	405	1,500	270
20. Somalia	407	3,700	110
Sub-Total	21,455 (14.9%)	67,165 (47.1%)	319
GRAND TOTAL	144,192 (100.0%)	142,520 (100.0%)	1,011

SOURCE: The World Bank, *The World Development Report* (Washington, D.C.: August 1979), pp. 126–127, and author's estimates. Per capita GNP is calculated for the indigenous population only (i.e. total population *less* migration population).

TABLE XVII

Inter-Arab Stratification: Selected Indicators of Status, 1977

	1	2	3	4	5	6
Country	Per Capita GNP (Ranked)	Labor Participation Rate % (Rank)	Literacy Rate % (Rank)	Death Rate % (Rank)	Life Expectancy (Rank)	Armed Forces (000) (Rank)
Stratum I (The Rich)						
Kuwait	(1)	19.4 (16)	60 (2)	0.5 (1)	69 (1)	10 (17)
U.A.E.	(2)	22.5 (11)	18 (14)	1.9 (7)	49 (9)	26 (12)
Libya	(3)	20.2 (15)	45 (7)	1.4 (5)	55 (6)	29 (11)
Qatar	(4)	18.4 (17)	35 (9)	2.0 (8)	50 (8)	4 (18)
Saudi Arabia	(5)	22.4 (12)	18 (14)	1.8 (6)	48 (10)	62 (7)
Combined Ranking	(1)	(4)	(3)	(3)	(3)	131 (4)
Stratum II (The Well-to-Do)						
Oman	(6)	24.9 (8)	20 (13)	2.0 (8)	49 (9)	13 (16)
Bahrain	(7)	21.4 (13)	50 (6)	1.3 (4)	55 (6)	2 (19)
Iraq	(8)	24.0 (10)	26 (12)	1.3 (4)	55 (6)	188 (3)

Lebanon	(9)	28.0 (3)	88 (1)	0.8 (2)	65 (2)	17 (14)
Algeria	(10)	25.0 (7)	35 (9)	1.3 (4)	56 (5)	76 (5)
Combined Ranking	(2)	(3)	(2)	(2)	(2)	296 (3)
Stratum III (The Struggling Middle)						
Syria	(11)	25.1 (6)	53 (5)	1.3 (4)	57 (4)	228 (2)
Tunisia	(12)	26.0 (4)	55 (4)	1.2 (3)	58 (3)	30 (10)
Jordan	(13)	20.4 (14)	59 (3)	1.3 (4)	56 (5)	68 (6)
Morocco	(14)	25.0 (7)	28 (10)	1.3 (4)	55 (6)	85 (4)
Combined Ranking	(3)	(2)	(1)	(1)	(1)	411 (2)
Stratum IV (The Poor)						
Arab Yemen	(15)	28.3 (2)	23 (16)	1.9 (7)	47 (11)	40 (9)
Democratic Yemen	(16)	25.9 (5)	27 (11)	1.9 (7)	50 (8)	22 (13)
Egypt	(17)	33.5 (1)	44 (8)	1.3 (4)	54 (7)	345 (1)
Sudan	(18)	24.6 (9)	20 (13)	1.9 (7)	46 (12)	52 (8)
Mauritania	(19)	24.0 (10)	17 (15)	2.2 (9)	46 (12)	15 (15)
Somalia	(20)	25.0 (7)	50 (6)	2.0 (8)	43 (13)	40 (9)
Combined Ranking	(4)	(1)	(1)	(4)	(4)	514 (1)

SOURCE: The World Bank, *World Development Report* (Washington D.C.: 1979), pp. 128-171; Institute for Strategic Studies, *The Military Balance 1977-1978* (London: 1978), pp. 33-42; and other scattered Arab and foreign sources.

is expressed diagrammatically in the following Chart which shows some of the salient features of direction of "inputs" in the new order.

Some Arab nationalists have recently been lamenting the lack of progress in Arab economic integration, a step deemed necessary by them for ultimate political unification. Several have even pointed at regression in this respect over the last decade, as indicated by the diminishing percentage of, for example, inter-Arab trade or by the diverse, contradictory and competitive economic policies of Arab states.[62] Using these indicators the lamentation is, of course, quite warranted. There is a conceptual problem, however, in these assessments. They are based on an idealized vision of what Arab socio-economic integration ought to be. Such an idealized vision was written about extensively in the 1950s and 1960s, and its literature is still flowing in popular as well as in academic texts. The vision was even articulated and formalized in numerous inter-Arab treatises and charters of all varieties: bilaterally, multilaterally, under the auspices of the League of Arab States, and outside the League.[63] But little has come out of all this intellectual, ideological and institutional commotion.

Nevertheless, we submit that the Arab world is more closely linked socio-economically at present than at any time in its modern history. The linkage, as we have tried to substantiate throughout this chapter, is dramatically manifested in the flow of manpower and money (in opposite directions) across the borders of the Arab states and at levels and of magnitudes unprecedented in previous centuries. With this two-way flow are more subtle flows of ideas, attitudes, new consumption patterns, attempts at inter-governmental political influence, as well as the flow of fears, potential military threats, upheavals and socio-political destabilization. Again these latter subtle input flows are at levels and magnitudes never before encountered in modern Arab history. Observers may debate what is negative and what is positive in these intense interactions within the new Arab order. But they can deny neither its reality nor its magnitude.

We call this reality a new Arab social order, and we assess its magnitude as a growing Arab interdependence. Both the reality and the magnitude are gradually assuming a self-propelling power to an extent that renders the whims of political leaders increasingly unreliable. Two major examples may illustrate our contention.

In the summer of 1977, relations between the Egyptian and Libyan regimes reached an all-time low. The spiral of deterioration had been punctuated by an escalation of mass media attacks and acts of sabotage on both sides. Threats and counter-threats were heatedly exchanged. Then a border war broke out between the two neighbors in July. Army,

THE GROWING ARAB INTERDEPENDENCE

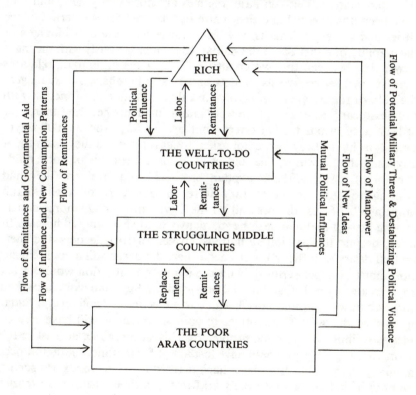

navy and air forces were used by both sides in that brief but intense war.[64] Arab blood was spilled between the two regimes which, only six years earlier, had signed a political unity agreement. In fact, "unity with Libya" was President Sadat's rallying cry in his showdown with his rivals (the ʿAli Sabri-Shaʿrawi Gumʿa-Sami Sharaf group) in May 1971. At that time Sadat accused them of turning their backs on "sister" Libya and of betraying the cause of Arab Unity for which the late President Nasir had worked so hard.[65] But by July 1977 much had changed and Sadat's new battle cry was to punish the "madman of Libya". These ups and downs of the inter-relations between Arab regimes are not exactly new, and they have been documented and their patterns analyzed for the period of the fifties and sixties.[66] What is new here, however, is the unwillingness or the inability of either Sadat or Qaddafi to tamper seriously with the man-power link between the two countries. Thus while diplomatic relations were severed, angry words, bullets and finally bombs were exchanged, the bulk of the Egyptian workforce in Libya continued to function with business nearly as usual. There were minor incidents here and there – or at least accusations to that effect – but by and large the 400,000 Egyptians working in Libya were not asked to leave; nor did they want to. If anything, the Libyan regime, out of idealism, expediency or both, made a point of assuring the "Egyptian brothers" in Libya that they had nothing to fear and that they were in one part of their "Arab homeland".[67] Sadat did not call on the Egyptians to come home either, and we suspect that had he done so, many would have ignored his call. In brief, despite the passionate hatred between the two leaders and their mutual desire to inflict pain on each other, there was still a cool realiza-tion that to tamper seriously with the manpower question would inflict even greater pain. If Qaddafi had deported the Egyptian workforce then (or even now) he would have been courting economic collapse; if Sadat had asked the 400,000 Egyptians to come home he would have created just as serious an economic problem for his own regime, at least in the short run, since Egypt would have lost about $500 million in remittances annually, and would have been hard-pressed to try to re-absorb such a number of individuals into the workforce at a time when it had frozen the public sector and when the private sector had opted for capital-intensive (rather than labor-intensive) schemes.

The second example of the growing Arab interdependence also in-volves Egypt and its rich sister Arab states. This time the occasion was Sadat's peace initiative towards Israel, his subsequent trip to Jerusalem in November 1977, the signing of the Camp David accords (September 1978), and the peace treaty between Egypt and Israel (March 1979). Most of the Arab regimes, including those of the oil-rich states, deplored

Sadat's actions and denounced his agreements with Israel as betrayals of the Arab nation and the Palestinian cause. Several official Arab meetings, including three summits, were held to deliberate over Sadat's move and to design appropriate policy responses.[68] The latter involved a carrot-and-stick approach. The amount of Arab aid to Egypt was to be raised substantially and sustained for five years (totalling $15 billion at $3 billion annually) if Sadat's moves towards Israel were stopped.[69] When that failed to entice him back to the fold, severe penalties were to be imposed, including severing diplomatic relations, cutting off all bilateral and multilateral aid (averaging at the time about $1.5 billion a year), withdrawing the deposits of Arab governments from Egyptian banks, and a total ban on trade with Egypt.[70] These and other measures were thought to be severe deterrents to the Egyptian regime. As events unfolded, many of the penalty measures were indeed enforced, and while they may in fact have hurt Sadat's regime and isolated it morally and diplomatically in Arab, Islamic and Third World circles, Egypt under Sadat has so far managed to muddle its way through them. The one thing which could have had a much greater damaging effect on Egypt and the Sadat regime would have been a manpower boycott. This may have been contemplated by both sides, but obviously neither has dared so far to tamper with it. Even Iraq's regime, one of the most vehement in the Arab crusade against Sadat, which sits in a country more endowed with diverse human and natural resources and which is therefore relatively less dependent on Egyptian imported labor, has steadily increased rather than reduced its importation of Egyptian manpower since Camp David.

In brief, the Arab states are no longer willing to "cut off their noses to spite their faces" as they often did in the 1950s and 1960s. In the 1970s — and into the 1980s too — such action would involve more than the deforming of a "face". It would be more likely to deform, if not to destroy, the whole "body-economic". Nor does this apply just to the relationship between Egypt and the rich Arab states: it applies equally to the relationship between the rich Arab states and the Palestinian workforce as well. As much as some rulers in the Gulf may toy with the idea of reducing the Palestinian presence in their Sheikhdoms as a way of reducing the potential for internal unrest, they must also have realized that the socio-economic — and the political — risks are much greater.

Gone are the days when one Arab ruler could send home the citizens of another ruler wholesale, or when the other could withdraw his citizens wholesale in retaliation. The Saudi regime could do so in the early sixties as a protest against Egypt's involvement in Yemen, and the Nasir regime could afford to repatriate its workforce in Saudi Arabia by absorbing them into an expanding public sector and an ambitious developmental program. The order of magnitude was different then. Nowadays, regimes at loggerheads with each other may go all the way to war before acting seriously on any form of manpower boycott.

This is the new calculus of Arab interdependence. It may be full of all kinds of unequal exchanges between the rich and the poor Arab states—the labor importers and the labor exporters. It may entail distortions in the evolution of Arab socio-economic structures, and it may generate and spread new but undesirable values, attitudes and behavioral patterns. And it is definitely a far cry from the kind of Arab interdependence idealistically envisioned by the romantics and the practitioners of Arab political unification, But it is an interdependence woven by millions of individuals who make up the labor force, and their millions more dependents, on both sides of the wealth divide in the Arab world. It is also an interdependence that far exceeds in magnitude and levels—if not in quality —anything that the several thousand Arab nationalist intellectuals and practitioners were able to produce between the birth of the Arab League in 1945 and the October War in 1973, an event which accelerated the birth of the new Arab order.

NOTES

1. For an elaboration on these great waves of social change see S. Ibrahim and N. Hopkins, eds., *Arab Society in Transition* (Cairo: AUC Press, 1977), pp. 179–182, 299–322, 409–417, 615–687. See also Frantz Fanon, *A Dying Colonialism* (New York: Monthly Review Press, 1965), and Michael Hudson, *Arab Politics: The Search for Legitimacy* (New Haven: Yale University Press, 1977), pp. 107–162.

2. Some social scientists have noticed a corresponding emergence of new regional and political orders in the area. See Gamil Matar and ʿAli al-Din Hilal, *Al-nizam al-iqlimi al-ʿarabi...* [The Arab Regional System: A Study of Arab Political Relations], (Beirut: Centre for Arab Unity Studies, 1979), and John Waterbury and Ragei El Mallakh, *The Middle East in the Coming Decades: From Well-head to Well-being?* (New York: McGraw Hill, 1978); Michael Hudson, *Arab Politics...,* op.cit., pp. 389–404.

3. This label was coined by J. S. Birks and C. A. Sinclair in their pioneering work *International Migration and Development in the Arab Region* (Geneva: ILO, 1980), which is the culmination of a series of studies undertaken by Durham University under the auspices of the International Labor Office (ILO) since 1976. We find the term capital-rich particularly appropriate not only because it states the most salient fact about these countries but also because this is about the only aspect of richness that they have at present. As the text argues, these countries have a shortage (i.e. poverty) in almost all other resources (such as manpower, agriculture...etc.).

4. These include Birks and Sinclair, op.cit.; Nazli Choucri, Richard N. Eckaus, and A. Mohie-Eldin, *Migration and Employment in the Construction Sector: Critical Factors in Egyptian Development* (Cairo University-MIT Technology Adaptation Program, 1978); N. Choucri, "Migration Among Developing Countries: the Middle East", paper at the American Political Science Association meeting, Washington D.C., September 1977; Joan

Clarke, "Jordan: A Labor Receiver — A Labor Supplier", paper at the AID/Near East Bureau Seminar on Labor Migration in the Middle East, Washington D.C., 1977. Another paper by the same author, presented at the same seminar is "Yemen in Profile". See also Muhammad Amin Faris, "Imkaniyyat tanaqul al-aydi al-ᶜamila..." [Movement of Arab Labor Force among Arab States], paper at the National Conference on Strategy for Joint Arab Economic Action, Baghdad, 2–5 May 1978; Mahmud ᶜAbd al-Fadil, *Al-naft wa al-wihda al-ᶜarabiyya* [Oil and Arab Unity], (Beirut: Centre for Arab Unity Studies, 1979); and Naᶜim al-Sherbini, "Tadaffuqat al-ᶜummal wa raʾs al-mal..." [Flow of Labor and Capital in the Arab world] in *Al-naft wal-taᶜawun al-ᶜarabi* [Oil and Arab Cooperation], Vol. 3–4, 1977, pp. 44–64.

5. Our main sources included Central Agency for Public Mobilization and Statistics (CAPMAS), *Preliminary Results of Egypt's 1976 Census* [Arabic] (Cairo, 1977); M. A. Faris, "Imkaniyyat tanaqul al-aydi al-ᶜamila..." [Movement of Arab Agricultural Labor Force During 1975–85 Period], unpublished research for the Arab Labor Organization, 1977; Lee Ann Ross, "Yemen, Migration: Blessing or Dilemma", paper at the AID/Near East Bureau Seminar on Labor and Migration in the Middle East, Washington D.C., 1977; and Joan Clarke, "Jordan...", op.cit., in which she relied on reports published by Jordan's Ministry of Labor.

6. See Birks and Sinclair, *International Migration...,* op.cit., pp. 20–21.

7. See Saad E. Ibrahim, "Population of the Arab World; An Overview" in Ibrahim and Hopkins, *Arab Society in Transition,* op.cit.

8. For more on this point see Saad E. Ibrahim and Donald Cole, *Saudi Arabian Bedouin,* The Cairo Papers in Social Science, Vol. One, Monograph Five, April 1978.

9. It is believed that the actual participation ratio is even higher in labor-exporting countries like Egypt and Yemen where a sizeable number of women are often engaged in agricultural labor on family farms but are not counted as gainfully employed, when in fact they are.

10. M. A. Faris, "Regional Cooperation and Integration of Arab Manpower Resources: A Migration Strategy", paper at the Seminar on Population, Labor and Migration in the Arab Gulf States, Kuwait, 16–18 December, 1978.

11. M. A. Fadil, *Oil and Arab Unity,* op.cit., p. 40.

12. M.A. Ramadan, paper in Arabic on "The Status of Egyptians in Kuwait" cited in M. A. Fadil, ibid., p. 41.

13. M. A. Fadil, ibid., p. 33.

14. Ibid.

15. See for example Muhammad al-Rumaihi, "Al-hijra al-ᶜarabiyya ila al-khalij", [Arab Migration to the Gulf: Economic Causes and Social Consequences], *Al-ᶜArabi,* no. 244 (March 1979).

16. The World Bank, *Research Project on Labor Migration and Manpower in The Middle East and North Africa: Interim Report* (Washington D.C., 1977), memo.

17. Ibid., pp. 35–38.

18. Ibid.

19. *Al-Ahram al-Iqtisadi* [Al-Ahram Economist], special supplement on "Financial and Economic Policy" [Arabic], (1 January 1980).

20. Fadil, *Oil and Arab Unity,* op.cit., p. 51.

21. Declaration by the Egyptian Minister of the Economy (Dr. Hamed al-Sayih) in *Al-Ahram al-Iqtisadi,* op.cit., p. 94.

22. *Al-Ahram al-Iqtisadi,* op.cit., pp. 83–84.

23. Ibid.

24. Ibid.

25. Fadil, op.cit., and Galal Amin's chapter in the present volume on the new Arab economic order.

26. *Al-Ahram al-Iqtisadi* (15 January 1980).

27. Ibid.

28. This point was in fact stated by the Turkish sociologist Deniz Kondioyoti in a public lecture on "Rural Transformation and Sex Roles in Turkey" at the University of California, Los Angeles on 2 June 1980.

29. Choucri, Eckaus and Mohie-Eldin, *Migration and Development...*, op.cit.

30. Birks and Sinclair, *International Migration...*, op.cit., p. 94. For a fuller discussion of Egypt as a labor exporter see the chapter in this volume by Sherbiny and Serageldin, on expatriate labor and economic growth.

31. Birks and Sinclair, ibid.

32. See their argument in "Egypt: A Frustrated Labor Exporter", op.cit. pp. 288–303.

33. See Ibrahim Saʿad al-Din, "Al-athar al-salbiyya lil furuq al-dakhiliyya bain al-aqtar al-ʿarabiyya" [Negative Effects of Income Differentials Among Arab Countries on the Lower Income Countries: the Case of Egypt], *Al-Naft wa al-taʿawun al-ʿarabi* [Oil and Arab Cooperation], Vol. III, no. 4 (1977), pp. 22, 40; ʿAdil Husain, "Al-mal al-nafti ʿaʾiq lil tawhid...[Oil Money: an Obstacle for Integration and Unification] in *Al-Mustaqbal al-ʿArabi* [Arab Future], Vol. II, no. 5 (January 1979), pp. 16, 31; and M. A. Fadil, *Oil and Arab Unity,* op.cit., pp. 53–58.

34. See Ali E. Hillal Dessouki, "Development of Egypt's Migration Policy, 1952–1978," mimeo, paper for Egyptian Labor Migration Project (Cairo University-MIT Technology Adaptation Program, Cairo, 1976).

35. Amr Mohie-Eldin and Ahmad Omar, *The Emigration of Universities' Academic Staff* (Cairo: Cairo University-MIT Technology Adaptation Program, 1980).

36. ʿAbd al-Fattah Qandil, "Raʾs al-mal al-ʿarabi..." [Commitment of Arab Capital Towards the Arab Region], paper at the Fifth Congress of Arab Economists, Baghdad, 12–15 April 1975, p. 26.

37. Isam Muntasir, "Al-nizam al-iqtisadi al-ʿarabi..." [The Arab Economic Order and Strategy of Development], paper at the National Conference for Strategic Joint Economic Arab Action, Baghdad, 6–12 May 1978, pp. 7–8.

38. For more on this point see Suzanne Paine, *Exporting Workers: The Turkish Case* (Cambridge: Cambridge University Press, 1974).

39. M. A. Fadil, *Oil and Arab Unity,* op.cit.

40. This observation was made to the author by the Egyptian sociologist Muhammad al-Gawhari while the latter was on secondment in Saudi Arabia (1974–1979). He was describing himself and others like him.

41. M. A. Fadil, *Oil and Arab Unity,* op.cit., p. 58.

42. Suzanne Messiha, *Export of Egyptian School teachers,* The Cairo Papers in Social Science, Volume Three, Monograph Four, April 1980; and Amr Mohie-Eldin and A. Omar, op.cit.

43. See Ali Dessouki, "Development of Egypt's Migration Policy", op.cit. pp. 17–25.

44. This is the law which allows citizens to use their hard currency in importing goods from abroad without obtaining the usual 'import permit' which was formerly required. For more details see the chapter in this volume by Gouda Abdel-Khalek.

45. Up to 1975 the figures are from the *UN Yearbook of International Trade Statistics,* Vol. I. The figure for 1979 is from the Minister of the Economy's report to the People's Assembly, quoted in *Al-Ahram* (1 January 1980).

46. See the Minister of the Economy's report, ibid.

47. For a discussion of the impact of oil wealth on work attitudes, see ʿAdil Husain, "Oil Money, an Obstacle...", op.cit., pp. 27–28.

48. An announcement to this effect was placed in all daily newspapers by the Egyptian Electric Distribution Company, a public sector state corporation, and reproduced in *Al-Ahram al-Iqtisadi* (15 January 1980), p. 30.

49. See the article "Saudi Arabia: Slowdown in Development Eases Social Pressure", in *The Arab Economist,* Vol. XI, no. 117 (June 1979), pp. 22–25.

50. A. Cottrell and F. Bray, *Military Forces in the Persian Gulf* (Beverly Hills, Calif.: Sage Publications, 1978), p. 18; and Ali Mahmud, "Arms Purchases Outpace Reconstruction and Economic Development", *The Arab Economist,* Vol. XI, no. 113 (February 1979), p. 22.

51. Ali Mahmud, ibid.

52. Cottrell and Bray, op.cit., p. 16.

53. Ibid., p. 19.

54. Ibid., p. 21.

55. D. R. Tahtinen, *National Security Challenge to Saudi Arabia* (Washington, D.C.: American Enterprise Institute for Public Policy Research, 1978), p. 17.

56. See the article "285 Billion Saudi Arabia Third Five-Year Development Plan Spending" in *Mid-East Business Exchange,* June 1980, p. 34. See also the discussion by Sherbiny and Serageldin in this volume.

57. Birks and Sinclair, *International Migration...,* op.cit., pp. 110–111.

58. See the article "Kuwait: Expatriate Workers Outnumber Nationals", in *The Arab Economist,* Vol. XI, no. 115, p. 32.

59. This assessment is confirmed by the World Bank, *Research Project on Labor Migration...,* op.cit.

60. Birks and Sinclair, ibid.

61. For a view over time of the distribution of several socio-economic indicators on Arab countries, see M. al-Himsey, *Arab Development Plans: Convergence and Divergence* [Arabic], (Beirut: Centre for Arab Unity Studies, 1980), pp. 195–215, which presents valuable statistical data on the period between 1960 and 1977.

62. See, for example, ibid, pp. 216–243; M. A. Fadil, *Oil and Arab Unity,* op.cit., pp. 143–165; ʿAdil Husain, "Arab Oil...", op.cit.; and Yusef Sayigh, "Al-indimaj al-iqtisadi al-ʿarabi..." [Arab Economic Integration and the Pretext of State Sovereignty], *Al-Mustaqbal al-ʿArabi* no. 6 (March 1979), pp. 23–41.

63. See, for example, Nadim al-Bitar, *Al-nazariyya al-iqtisadiyya...* [Economic Theory and the Road to Arab Unity] (Beirut: Arab Development Institute, 1978); Samir al-Tanir, *Al-takamul al-iqtisadi al-ʿarabi...* [Economic Integration and the Issue of Arab Unity], (Beirut: Arab Development Institute, 1978); ʿAbd al-Hadi Yamut, *Al-taʿawun al-iqtisadi al-ʿarabi...* [Arab Economic Cooperation and the Necessity of Integration for Development], (Beirut: Arab Development Institute, 1976); Matar and al-Din Hilal, *Arab Regional System...,* op.cit. The last three sources contain appendices of various inter-Arab treaties on socio-economic cooperation, as well as lists of various pan-Arab agencies within and outside the framework of the League of Arab States.

64. For a detailed account of the events of this border war see *Arab Report and Record* (henceforth *ARR*), the issues for 1–15 July, 16–31 July and 1–15 August 1977.

65. *ARR* 1–15 May 1971.

66. Malcolm Kerr, *The Arab Cold War* (London: Oxford University Press, 1971).

67. *ARR* 16–31 July 1977.

68. For an account of various Arab reactions to President Sadat's peace initiative see

ARR, issues for 15–30 November 1977; 16–30 September, 1–15 October 1978; 1–15 April and 16–30 April 1979.

   69. *ARR* 16–31 October 1978.

   70. An account of these penalties and the broader economic issues of Sadat's peace initiative are disucussed in Fuʾad Mursi, "Al-nataʾij al-ʾqtisadiyya..." [Economic Consequences of the Egyptian-Israeli Treaty] in *Al-Mustaqbal al-ʿArabi,* Vol. III, no. 18 (August 1980), pp. 28–53.

III
Migration and
Social Mobility in Egypt

Georges Sabagh

I. INTRODUCTION[1]

The massive labor migration from capital-poor Arab countries such as Egypt, Jordan and Yemen to the capital-rich Arab oil states in the 1970s has ushered in a new "demographic order" to the Arab world. While there was a sizeable migration of Moroccans, Algerians and Tunisians to France and Western Europe after the Second World War, the large-scale movement of workers from one Arab country to another is a very recent phenomenon.[2] It represents a new "demographic order" in the sense that it has resulted in a noticeable population redistribution *between* poor and rich Arab countries. A few receiving countries such as Kuwait and the United Arab Emirates have substantial proportions of Arab non-nationals, while some sending countries such as Yemen have a significant segment of their labor force abroad.

In view of its importance, the Arab regional migration needs to be studied extensively in terms of the following perspectives: (i) its effects on the political, economic and social relationships between Arab countries, as described in the chapters by Professors Nazih Ayubi, Galal Amin and Ali Dessouki; (ii) its social-psychological and socio-structural impact on the receiving countries; and (iii) its social-psychological and socio-structural causes and consequences in the sending countries. The chapter by Professor Saad Eddin Ibrahim contains not only a detailed description of the volume and characteristics of Arab regional migration but also a comprehensive analysis of its consequences for Egypt. The focus of the present chapter is on those consequences that have an implication for the process of development in Egypt. More specifically, geographic and social mobility were selected for such an analysis. Both constitute an integral part of the process of socio-economic transformation of Egypt. Social mobility reflects the occupational and educational

upgrading of the labor force that is necessary for successful industrialization and modernization, and migration from rural areas is needed for an
expanding labor force. To the extent that external migration has an impact on internal migration or social mobility, it could facilitate or hinder
the development of Egypt.

In view of the increasingly large numbers of Egyptians who have
sought their fortunes elsewhere during the 1970s, particularly in rich
Arab countries, there should be an observable influence on internal
migration in Egypt during this period. But the nature of this link depends
on the regional origins of external migrants. If all or nearly all of them
were city dwellers, this would create labor shortages in cities that would
provide an additional "pull" for villagers. The rural-urban stream could
also swell with all those involved in two-step moves from village to urban
areas and from urban areas to a foreign country. On the other hand, if
all or most external migrants originate *directly* from villages, the rural-
urban flow would be slowed down markedly. What complicates the
analysis is that there is an unknown mix of emigrants from villages and
cities. Nevertheless, some indication will be given of the impact of external on internal migration.

There are two competing hypotheses about the effect of external
migration on social mobility in a sending country such as Egypt. One
argument is that the job vacancies created in various communities
stimulate upward mobility among the stayers. This assumes that there
are no rigidities in social structure in Egypt, that there are no great
obstacles to the redistribution of social and economic opportunities, and
that there is wide "access to training".[3] The opposite argument puts forward the hypothesis that such rigidities and obstacles do exist, and that,
consequently, external migration does *not* lead to any appreciable social
mobility. Instead serious shortages of labor are created. Birks and
Sinclair have argued that the first hypothesis applies to Jordan and the
second describes the situation in Egypt. They express their argument as
follows:[4]

> Because of the more rigid structure of the Egyptian labor market, Cairo
> and the country as a whole have experienced critical labor shortages... *Few
> data are available to substantiate the following analysis,* which must
> therefore be in the nature of a *hypothesis*... Besides the usual barriers to oc-
> cupational mobility... the Egyptian labor market appears to be character-
> ized by extraordinary immobility between even relatively similar occupa-
> tions... Because of the very limited occupational mobility there is very little
> internal readjustment within the labor market to minimize the selective ex-
> ports of certain types of manpower... Despite the much discussed Egyptian
> rural-urban migration, it is suggested that in proportional and real terms,

there is relatively little transfer of labor from the traditional to the modern sector. (My emphasis).

The general lack of "upward occupational mobility" in Egypt is also noted by Findlay who attributes it to the "highly segmented character of the Egyptian labor market" and to "government domination of the economy".[5] Since neither Birks and Sinclair nor Findlay present any systematic evidence to support their argument, some data will be given in this chapter to verify their assertion about Egypt's social structure. This is best accomplished not only by assessing the degree of occupational mobility, but also by studying the relationship between geographic and social mobility. The closer this relationship, the more open are the avenues of social mobility in cities. Those who move from villages to cities or from one city to another do so in order to maximize their opportunities for higher achievement. If they fail in this endeavor, then it could be argued that this is a further indication of the rigidity and barriers of the occupational structure of urban areas. It would also suggest that external migration could not have any appreciable effect on occupational mobility in these areas.

II.   SOURCES OF DATA AND METHODOLOGY

The following information was used in the present analysis:

1. published tabulations from Egyptian censuses from 1947 to 1976 and from labor force surveys;[6]
2. published results of a small survey of occupational mobility in Cairo in 1979;
3. data files from a survey carried out in 1978 by the Research Department of the Egyptian Family Planning Board in selected smaller towns and villages.

Descriptions of the design of the 1979 Cairo survey and the 1978 survey of smaller towns and villages are given in this section

A.   1979 CAIRO SURVEY[7]

This survey consists of an area probability sample of 232 heads of households drawn from nine wards (*shiyakhas*) in Cairo which are considered to be representative of the city as a whole. Ibrahim cautions as follows about the limitations of his sample:[8]

Extreme caution must be exercised in generalizing the findings with regard to urban Egypt. For one thing the sample size is too small for a city of over six million. Second, Cairo is hardly representative of urban Egypt.

To some extent the availability of the 1978 survey for smaller towns provides the additional data needed.

B.   1978 SURVEY OF SMALLER TOWNS AND VILLAGES[9]

The 1978 survey was carried out by the Research Department of the Egyptian Population and Family Planning Board as part of a study of the relationship between industrialization and population. Out of the 120 *marakiz* (regional subdivisions of governorates) of Egypt, exclusive of Cairo and Alexandria, *six* were selected to represent different levels and types of industrialization. These *marakiz* are as follows:

Upper Egypt: Mahalla al-Kubra, Gharbiyya governorate
              Kafr al-Dawwar, Beheira governorate
              Damietta, Damietta governorate
              Al-Khanka, Qalyubiyya governorate
Lower Egypt: Nagᶜ Hammadi, Qena governorate
              Saqulta, Suhag governorate

Loza and El-Khorazati give the following description of the characteristics of these *marakiz:*[10]

...Mahalla al-Kubra and Kafr al-Dawwar are similar in level and type of industry: spinning and weaving industry. They rank fourth and sixth in terms of level of industrialization for all Egypt. Mahalla, however, has a longer industrial history and a greater number of small size industrial establishments specializing in spinning and weaving and related industries. The industry in Damietta is also consumer industry but smaller and more diversified than Mahalla al-Kubra or Kafr al-Dawwar. It ranks third in industrialization. Damietta is known for its cottage industry, speciality industry, spinning and weaving, food products, leather products, etc...
Al-Khanka's industrial pattern differs from the other *marakiz*. Its industries are intermediate ones such as pharmaceutical and chemical industries. It is located near Cairo.
Nagᶜ Hammadi is one of the highest *marakiz* in Upper Egypt in terms of industrialization. It is distinguished by consumer food industries. Sugar cane is the dominant agricultural crop and Nagᶜ Hammadi has a seasonal sugar cane factory. A large new aluminium plant was built and started production in 1975.
Saqulta is a non-industrial *markaz* to be used as a control region. It has very few industrial activities.

In each *markaz* a probability sample of households was chosen from randomly selected two villages, districts within each administrative city of the *markaz,* and industrial workers' residential areas. The selection was done in such a way as to yield an equal number of heads of

TABLE I
Sample Size and Total Population 1976, Localities in Egypt, 1978 Sample

Localities in Samples	Sample Size	Total Population 1976
Damietta	433	93,546
Ezbet al-Borg	157	22,916
Al-Anania	109	6,245
Mahalla al-Kubra	926	292,853
Manshiet al-Omara	69	6,731
Meet al-Leeth	78	5,541
Industrial workers' residences	199	–
Kafr el-Dawwar	437	160,554
Kafr Abou Kir	226	18,318
Manshiet Bouline	120	9,341
Industrial workers' residences	207	–
Al-Khanka	494	32,381
Abu Za'bal	286	20,070
Kafr Hamza	81	5,832
Nag' Hammadi	299	19,791
Howe	392	22,126
Abu Amouri	152	5,883
Saqulta	177	10,866
Fawjulie	95	4,471
Gramta Sharq	46	2,011

SOURCE: Sarah Loza, "Socio-spatial and Fertility Differentials in Egypt", (Cairo: Population and Family Planning Board, December 1980), p.10.

households with industrial and non-industrial occupations. The sampled sites, their populations in 1976, and the number of heads of households interviewed, are given in Table I. The total sample size was nearly 5,000. Interviews were conducted with both the household heads and their spouses. While this sample can hardly be considered representative of rural areas and small towns in Egypt, it should give some indication of the patterns of occupational mobility in an important segment of the Egyptian population. It shoud be noted, however, that unmarried males who are mostly younger and in the early stages of their occupational careers are excluded from the sample.

III.   EXTERNAL AND INTERNAL MIGRATION

The rapid expansion of external migration from Egypt during the 1970s is documented in Table II. The number of Egyptians seconded and on contract abroad increased from 9,280 in 1970 to 101,464 in 1978. During the same period, the estimated total number of departures from Egypt rose spectacularly from 58,000 to almost one and half million. These figures, as high as they are in the late 1970s, may still represent an underestimate of the actual volume of external migration.[11] It would be surprising, therefore, if this trend did not have a noticeable impact on rural-urban and inter-regional migration *within* Egypt. To measure this impact in an unambiguous way would require data on the regional origins of the *total* stream of external migration. Since these data were not available at the time this chapter was prepared, the effects of external on internal migration have to be inferred from growth patterns of various regions or from estimates of net migration.

Exponential rates of population growth for Egypt and its various regions in the periods 1947 to 1960, 1960 to 1966, and 1966 to 1976, are given in Table III. The regional figures prior to 1966 represent the combined effects of natural increase, internal migration, and changing administrative boundaries of regions. After 1966, the effects of external migration have to be added.

Considering first the figures for urban and metropolitan Egypt, there was a marked decrease in the rate of urban population growth from 3.8 to 2.7 percent between 1960–1966 and 1966–1976. By contrast, there was an increase in this rate prior to 1966. The estimated annual rate of *in-migration* of .49 percent in 1966–1976 was about *half* the comparable figure of .89 percent in the previous period.[12] This decline represents an unknown combination of a reduction in net rural-urban migration and an increase in net external migration. On the other hand, the rate of net rural *out-migration* decreased only slightly from .9 to .7 percent in the same period. There are two different interpretations of this new trend. According to one interpretation, Egyptian villagers were increasingly opting for migration to the rich Arab states rather than to Egyptian cities. Thus a noticeable decrease in rural-urban migration would account for the pattern observed in Egyptian urban areas between 1966 and 1976. Another hypotheses would be that a large number of villagers were engaged in two-step migration from rural to urban areas and then to the rich Arab states.[13] In other words, Egyptian cities were receiving the same or nearly the same volume of rural in-migrants, but these were mostly on their way abroad. Whichever hypothesis is correct, there is no doubt that external migration had a marked impact on internal migration in the 1970s.

TABLE II

Total Number of Egyptians Seconded and on Contract Abroad, 1970-1978, Total Number of Departures, 1972 and 1974, and Estimated Number of Departures, 1970, 1971, 1973, 1975-1978.

Year	Total Number of Egyptians Seconded and on Contract Abroad	Total Number of Departures from Egypt
1970	9,280	58,000*
1971	16,231	102,000*
1972	32,917	206,763
1973	36,980	528,000**
1974	35,355	505,071
1975	40,399	577,000**
1976	59,195	845,000**
1977	89,957	1,285,000**
1978	101,464	1,449,000**

*: Estimated by using the observed ratio of $\dfrac{206,763}{32,917} = 6.28$ in 1972.

**: Estimated by using the observed ratio of $\dfrac{505,071}{35,355} = 14.28$ in 1974.

SOURCE: "Temporary Emigration of Egyptians for Working Abroad Particularly in Arab Countries", *Economic Bulletin* (Cairo: National Bank of Egypt, 1979), p. 276.

The population growth rates for Lower and Upper Egypt and the various metropolitan areas suggest that the impact of external on internal migration was not the same in all parts of Egypt. In interpreting the trends in these rates, however, one should be careful to note the influence of other factors. For example, the construction of the High Dam starting in 1960 undoubtedly accounts for the high rate of growth of urban Upper Egypt from 1960 to 1966. The sharp reversal in population trends in the Port Said and Suez governorates is partly a consequence of the 1967 war.

One striking feature of the 1960–1966 period is that urban Upper Egypt, smaller towns and cities outside of the Cairo urban region, and Alexandria had the highest rate of growth of any urban or metropolitan area. It is true that some of this growth could be attributed to the expansion of Alexandria into the Beheira governorate and the influx of persons displaced by the 1967 war. But even if we were to exclude the Beheira and Sharqiyya governorates, the smaller cities of Lower Egypt still had a very high rate of population growth of 2.5 percent in the period 1966 to 1976. Comparisons between urban Lower Egypt and Cairo in this period suggest an interesting hypothesis about the differential effects of external migration. First of all, it is likely that villagers who went to smaller towns and cities in Lower Egypt originated in that region. But, unlike villagers

TABLE III
Annual Exponential Rates of Population Change, Metropolitan, Urban and Rural Areas
of Egypt, 1947-1960, 1960-1966, 1966-1976

Areas	Annual Per Cent Population Change		
	1947-1960	1960-1966	1966-1976
Cairo "urban" region[1]	3.8	4.6	2.9
Alexandria	3.5	3.0	2.4
Port Said and Suez			
Governorates	3.7	3.5	−1.7
Lower Egypt			
Urban[1]	2.8	2.8	3.1
Rural	2.0	2.1	1.5
Upper Egypt			
Urban[1]	2.2	4.3	2.6
Rural	1.6	1.1	1.2
Frontier Governorates	2.0	.6	1.7
Egypt			
Urban and			
Metropolitan	3.2	3.8	2.7
Rural	1.8	1.7	1.4
Total	2.4	2.5	1.9[2]

[1] The urban parts of the Qalyubiyya Governorate included in the Cairo "urban" region and excluded from Lower Egypt urban. The urban parts of the Giza Governorate included in the Cairo "urban" region and excluded from Upper Egypt urban.
[2] Excludes an estimated number of 1,425,000 abroad and 147,000 in the occupied zones of Suez and Sinai.

SOURCES: CAPMAS, *Statistical Yearbooks*, 1968 and 1979.

who went to Cairo they stayed in their communities of destination. On the other hand, if the two-step hypothesis is correct, villagers who went to Cairo were more likely to use this city as a transfer point to the rich Arab states. This does not exclude the possibility of a three step migration from village to small town or city, small town or city to Cairo, and Cairo to some foreign country.

IV. PATTERNS OF OCCUPATIONAL CHANGES, OCCUPATIONAL MOBILITY AND OCCUPATIONAL ACHIEVEMENT

New policies aimed at a radical transformation of Egyptian society were adopted under the leadership of Nasir during the years that followed the revolution of 1952. They are best exemplified by the socialist laws that were initiated in the period from 1960 to 1965. The aims of these policies were to reduce the hold of the old bourgeoisie on Egyptian society, to achieve a rapid rate of modernization and industrialization within the framework of state-owned or -directed enterprises, and to redistribute income and opportunities in favor of the lower and middle strata. There is no doubt that there was a noticeable alteration in Egypt's social structure after the mid-fifties. On the basis of available evidence on the distribution of income, occupation, and education, Saad Ibrahim has concluded that the "socialist" transformation of the 1960s resulted in "probably the biggest change in Egypt's stratification system in this century."[14] El-Saaty argues that the policies of the new regime created two new classes which he describes as follows:[15]

> The aristocratized class consists of different groups [created] by the new regime... By decree various and numerous posts were filled in the cabinet, which was greatly extended, in the diplomatic corps, in the public economic sector, in local government, and in some scientific organizations – with the supporters of the regime and their followers, the climbers. Later on, opportunists began to emerge and were able to pursue their illicit economic activities.
>
> The bourgeoisized class [consists of] that section of the lower class which the new regime, through its measures favoring social justice and full employment in a planned economy, made bourgeoisistic by giving them access to free education, thus making them mobile and ready to move from their rural areas, to live in big towns and cities and get good jobs.

El-Saaty estimates that the aristocratized and bourgeoisized classes comprise 3.4 and 14.3 percent respectively of the total population of Egypt.[16] The figure for the "bourgeoisized" class suggests an appreciable amount of social mobility, at least for the first years after the revolution. On the other hand, a number of studies have documented the continued upper and upper-middle class bias in the recruitment of political and bureaucratic elites and the most prestigious occupations.[17] This pattern is documented in the following figures from four such studies[18] which show the percent distribution of occupations of fathers of the bureaucratic elite and engineers.

Father's occupation	Bureaucratic elite			Engineers
	Berger sample 1953/54 (N = 242)	Qassem sample 1966/67 (N = 180)	Akeel sample 1973 (N = 96)	Moore sample (N = 351)
A. Urban aristocracy and bourgeoisie (landlord, army officer and independent professionals)	33	28	31	40

B. White collar civil servants or employees	42	47	44	38
C. Small merchants (traditional entrepreneurs)	9	15	11	10
D. Others	16	10	14	12

There was little change between 1953/54 and 1973 in the markedly high social origin of the bureaucratic elite. Also the tiny upper class contributed a noticeably disproportionate number of its sons and daughters to the engineering profession. Since the highest class in the 1978 survey of small towns and villages was made up of "professionals and high administrators", it is of some interest to compare its social origins to those of the groups that were studied by Berger, Qassem, Ayubi, Akeel and Moore. The results obtained are illustrated in the following tabulation of the percent distribution of occupation of the fathers of "professionals and high administrators" in a sample taken in 1978 of small towns (Damietta, Mahalla al-Kubra and Kafr al-Dawwar):

Father's occupation	Professionals and high administrators 1978 (N = 99)	Total sample 1978 (N = 172)
A. Professionals and high administrators	14	1
B. Intermediate technicians and administrators, clerical jobs	22	10
C. Private owners and entrepreneurs	32	25
D. Other:		
i. Farm landlords and tenants	11	15
ii. Production workers, service workers, agricultural workers and fishermen	21	49

While it is clear that professionals and high administrators in Damietta, Mahalla al-Kubra and Kafr al-Dawwar were much more likely to have higher class origins than the general population, this tendency was much less marked than in the samples of elites studied by Berger, Qassem, Akeel and Moore. This difference may reflect both the less restrictive definition of "elite" in the 1978 sample, and the contrasts in elite recruitment between small towns and the metropolitan centers of Cairo and Alexandria. It should however be noted that the openness of an occupational structure should be measured in terms of mobility at all levels of this structure rather than just at the top. It is not sufficient to study the social origin of elites; we have also to consider the social origin of other groups in the society.

The picture of the Egyptian occupational structure that emerges from available studies is not quite consistent with that delineated by Birks and

Sinclair and Findlay. This structure seems to be characterized by *both* rigidities and some degree of openness. It is problematic, however, as to whether this openness is decreasing or increasing, and the aim of the present analysis is to explore this question further.

To test the hypothesis of the rigidity of the Egyptian occupational structure we need information not only on job changes between generations but also on such changes during a person's own life history. Of particular significance would be the changes that occurred during the 1970s. Both the 1978 sample of smaller towns and villages and the 1979 Cairo survey provide data on occupations of heads of households and their fathers. In addition, the 1978 sample included questions on the job held prior to migration and the first one held after migration. It did not, however, have questions on previous occupations for non-migrants. Nevertheless, information on occupational distributions in Egypt at various points in time in the 1970s and the 1960s could provide some clues on the extent of current mobility.

A. Trends in Occupational Distribution

The data given in Table IV indicate that there was some upgrading of the Egyptian occupational structure between 1960 and 1976. If we consider only men, who constituted about 94 percent of the labor force, the changes are generally not spectacular and suggest only a moderate amount of job mobility. The share of the white-collar class among men in the labor force increased slowly from 16.1 per cent in 1960 to 20.1 percent in 1976. Within this class, however, there was a rapid increase in the relative importance of the professional and technical occupations. In view of the numerical importance of the emigration of professional and technical workers, it is likely that there would have been an even higher rate of growth of this class in the absence of emigration.

While this trend may, in part, reflect the renewed popularity of the "free" professions such as doctors and lawyers in the 1970s, it may more plausibly be attributed to the phenomenal growth of university enrollments and university graduates in Egypt. The number of these graduates increased from about 15,000 in 1972/73 to about 40,000 in 1976/77.[19] The professional and technical class provides the main employment for these university students and graduates. Thus, in Cairo in 1976, 67 percent of all males who had a job and university education could be found in this class.[20] Or to put it another way, 65 percent of members of this class had a university education. The next class of administrators and managers also had a high percent of college-educated persons. But there is a sharp drop in the percentage of college-educated as we move to the group of clerical workers. These workers have mainly

TABLE IV

Per Cent Distribution by Occupations, Males and Females, Egypt 1947, 1960, 1966, and 1976

Occupations	Males				Females			
	Censuses				Censuses			
	1947[1]	1960[2]	1966[2]	1976[2]	1947[1]	1960[2]	1966[2]	1976[2]
Professional and Technical	2.7	3.2[3]	3.9	6.0	3.1	12.7	17.5	25.9
Administrative and Managerial	1.0	1.1	1.8	1.1	.2	1.0	1.2	1.7
Clerical and Related Workers	2.2	3.7	5.2	6.3	.5	3.2	8.5	19.3
Sales Workers	6.8	8.1	6.3	6.7	6.5	7.9	6.3	4.7
Service Workers	7.6	7.9[3]	7.0	8.4	19.6	24.2	15.7	9.1
Craftsmen, Production, Processing, and Transportation Workers	16.8	19.8	22.1	22.4	6.9	18.2	8.8	8.3
Farmers and Related Workers	60.5	54.3	52.3	44.4	60.0	32.6	25.3	11.6
Not Specified	2.4	1.8	1.4	4.7	3.2	8.0	17.0	19.4
Total	100.0	100.0	100.0	100.0	100.0	100.0	100.0	100.0
Number in millions	(6.2)	(6.5)	(7.7)	(8.9)	(.7)	(.4)	(.6)	(.7)

[1]Population in ages 5 and over   [2]Population in ages 15 and over
[3]The group of "Muslim clergy, mosque servants, and other employees of religious places," and "musicians and related workers" were transferred from "Service Workers" to "Professional and Technical". See Abdel-Fattah Nassef, *The Egyptian Labor Force: Its Dimensions and Changing Structure, 1907-1960*, p. 194.

SOURCES: Abdel-Fattah Nassef, *The Egyptian Labor Force: Its Dimensions and Changing Structure, 1907-1960* (Philadelphia: Population Studies Center, University of Pennsylvania, 1970); International Labour Office, *Yearbook 1965* (Geneva, 1965); Central Agency for Public Mobilization and Statistics, (CAPMAS), *Al-taʿdad al-ʿamm li al-sukkan wa al-iskan 1976* [The Population and Housing Census...], (Cairo, 1978).

a primary and preparatory education. A real education gulf separates these three top occupational classes from the others, most of whom did not have a formal education. While there is no doubt that education is the fastest avenue of social mobility, those who do not have sufficient education have a very difficult time climbing the educational ladder. The most formidable barrier is between manual and sales workers and the higher white-collar group. Only a small minority of the former have the formal education that is a prerequisite for upward mobility.

The relative importance of craftsmen and industrial workers remained relatively constant during the 1970s. This lack of change reflects both changing policies of modernization and industrialization and the impact of external migration. In view of the sharp drop in the percentage of men in farm work from 54.3 in 1960 to 44.4 in 1976, one would have expected increased mobility from this occupation to craftsmen and industrial jobs. That it did not occur to any noticeable amount demonstrates both the rigidities of the manual labor market and the greater pull of jobs in the rich Arab countries. It also provides further support for the hypothesis of one or two-step emigration of villagers to these countries.

B. INTER-GENERATIONAL OCCUPATIONAL MOBILITY

Data on inter-generational occupational mobility are presented in Table V for 4,530 male heads of households in the 1978 sample of small towns and villages. For each of eight occupational categories of fathers, this Table shows the percentage distribution of sons for the same categories. For example, 34.5 percent of fathers who were professionals and high administrators had sons with the same occupation. The cases off the main diagonal in the Table represent the upward or downward mobility, and they comprise 67.1 percent of the total sample. While this index of *gross mobility* is high, it reflects in part *structural mobility* or the percentage of sons who are forced to have different occupations from their fathers because of changes in occupational distribution between fathers and sons. *Circulation* mobility which represents the difference between gross and structural mobility is not affected by these changes. For the 1978 sample, it was equal to 32 percent, thus suggesting fairly open avenues of mobility between fathers and sons.

In order to compare the 1978 survey with the 1979 Cairo survey, it was necessary to combine occupational groups to obtain the three categories of white collar, manual, and farming (Table VI). Birks and Sinclair's assertion that there is a boundary between manual and non-manual classes that is difficult to cross is supported by data from both surveys. Thus, according to the 1978 sample, only 18 percent of respondents with a manual class background were able to secure white-collar jobs. The

TABLE V
Per Cent Distribution of Respondents' Occupations in 1978 by the Occupation of
Their Fathers, Egypt, 1978 Sample.

Respondents' Fathers' Occupation	Respondents' Occupations									
	1	2	3	4	5	6	7	8	Total	N
1. Professional and High Administrators	34.5	10.3	20.7	10.3	13.8	6.9	3.4	0	.6	(29)
2. Intermediate Technicians and Administrators	7.5	31.1	11.8	3.7	12.4	26.7	3.1	3.7	3.6	(161)
3. Clerical Jobs	3.5	24.8	23.5	4.4	12.8	29.6	.9	.4	5.0	(226)
4. Private Owners and Entrepreneurs	3.4	12.6	9.0	23.1	18.3	32.1	1.3	.3	16.4	(745)
5. Production Workers	.9	5.2	4.4	4.9	38.7	41.7	1.7	2.5	18.6	(844)
6. Service Workers	1.6	7.5	4.4	6.4	16.6	61.5	.7	1.5	16.7	(755)
7. Farm Landowners and Tenants	1.9	9.7	5.7	3.8	18.7	31.7	22.6	5.8	26.3	(1,190)
8. Agricultural Workers and Fishermen	.3	1.0	2.8	2.8	33.3	30.9	3.6	25.3	12.8	(580)
Total	2.2	9.4	6.6	7.5	23.3	38.0	7.2	5.7	100.0	
N	(100)	(426)	(299)	(341)	(1,057)	(1,723)	(327)	(257)		(4,530)

Ch-square = 2,168.9   p = .00   Gamma = .34

SOURCE: Sample Survey carried out by the Research Department of the Population and Family Planning Board.

TABLE VI

Comparisons of Inter-Generational Occupational Mobility Matrices, Cairo 1979 Sample and
Sample of Selected Urban and Semi-Urban Places and Industrial Workers Residences,
Egypt, 1978

Sample and Respondents' Fathers' Occupations	Respondents' Occupations in 1978			
	White collar	Manual	Farming	Total
Cairo, 1979[1]				
White collar	76.5	23.4	–	39.9
Manual	34.8	65.2	–	30.9
Farming	58.3	41.7	–	29.2
Total	58.3	41.7	–	100.0
Egypt, 1978[2]				
White collar	51.2	46.5	2.3	25.6
Manual	17.5	79.3	3.2	35.3
Farmer	16.5	54.9	28.5	39.1
Total	25.7	61.4	12.9	100.0

[1]SOURCE: Saad Eddin Ibrahim, "Social Mobility and Income Distribution" forthcoming in
Robert Tignor et al., eds., *The Political Economy of Income Distribution in Egypt* (New York:
Holmes and Meier). Total sample excluding 24 housewives was 288.
  White collar: professional, executive, clerical, and sales
  Manual: production, services

[2]SOURCE: See Table V.
  White collar: professional or higher administrators, intermediate technicians or administrators,
  clerical jobs, private owners and entrepreneurs
  Manual: service, production
  Farming: farm owners or tenants and agricultural workers

comparable figure for Cairo was 35 percent, thus suggesting more
permeability between white-collar and manual groups in this metropolis
than in smaller towns and villages in Egypt. But because there were no
respondents in Cairo in farming, a combination of the two classes of
manual and farming would be more appropriate. When this is done there
appears to be very little difference in inter-generational mobility between
the two surveys. The index of *circulation* mobility is .19 for Cairo and
.25 for smaller towns and villages.

The other barrier described by Birks and Sinclair pertains to the
agricultural and non-agricultural occupations. Unfortunately, they fail
to make a distinction between the more and less prosperous farmers.
About 21 percent of sons of farm landowners and tenants had white-
collar occupations in 1978 as compared to 6 percent of sons of
agricultural workers. While the data for Cairo in 1979 show that about

58 percent of farmers' sons had white collar occupations, this could be a consequence of both small samples and the particular farm background of the farmers.

It is clear that the data presented in this section only partially support the assertion of Birks and Sinclair and Findlay. There are undoubtedly some barriers to occupational mobility in Egypt, particularly between manual and non-manual jobs. But these barriers are not insurmountable.

C. OCCUPATIONAL ACHIEVEMENT

Another way to assess the extent of openness of the occupational structure of a country is to consider the determinants of occupational achievement. A relatively closed structure would be one in which occupational status is mainly inherited, and hence predominantly dependent on social origin. On the other hand, in a relatively open structure, social origin is less important than a person's own achievement as measured by his education and his occupational career. But in a country such as Egypt which is experiencing marked economic changes, there is substantial exchange mobility, and consequently there is a limit to occupational inheritance.

The net impact of social origin as compared to other factors such as education and migration status was measured by a multiple regression analysis carried out for the total 1978 sample of small towns and villages. Husband's occupational status was the dependent variable, and the independent variables consisted of his age, education, migration status, and the education and occupation of his father. The following net regression weights were obtained:

Education:	.64
Age:	.11
Father's Occupation:	.10
Migration status:	.06
Father's education:	.05

With the exception of father's education, all other variables had a statistically significant net effect on husband's occupational status.[21] Together these variables account for a high proportion of the variance ($R^2 = .50$) in the dependent variable. In view of the close relationship between education and occupation that was described earlier on the basis of census data for Cairo in 1976, it should come as no surprise to find that education has the greatest net effect on occupational achievement. While social origin (father's education and occupation) is important, it trailed far behind. Surprisingly, migration is much more important than father's education in its impact on occupational status. It is in the expected direction with migrants achieving higher status than non-migrants.

It could be argued, however, that the importance of education reflects in an indirect way the impact of social origin. Notwithstanding the democratization of education in Egypt since 1952, it may well be that rich parents could better afford a higher education for their sons and daughters. The widespread system of private tutoring by teachers would certainly reinforce greater access to education among the children of the rich.[22] Another multiple regression was carried out to measure the net effects of social origin on husband's education. The following net regression weights were obtained:

Father's education:	.27
Age:	− .22
Father's occupation:	.19
Migration status:	.16

It is clear from these figures that social origin had an appreciable impact on educational achievement. At the same time, however, the net negative association between age and education suggests an equally important effect of the democratization of education. The net effect of migration status measures in part the fact that migration is often necessary to obtain a higher education. This process, however, is relatively independent of social origin. It should be noted that all these variables taken together account for only 24 percent of the variance in the dependent variable. There is much that remains to be explained in the process of educational achievement in the sample studied.

Occupational career is one important dimension that was left out of the preceding analysis. Unfortunately, information on previous occupations was only available for the sub-sample of migrants. Nevertheless, their experience should throw some light on the impact of occupational career. The variables that have a statistically significant net effect on the occupational achievement of migrants are given below with their net regression weights;

First occupation after migration:	.57
Education:	.22
Occupation prior to migration:	.12
Years of residence:	.07

Together these four variables account for a large share of the variance ($R^2 = .69$) in the occupational achievement of migrants. What is striking about these results is that neither father's occupation nor his education have any statistically significant effect on the occupational success of their sons. Migrants appear to be "self-made" men.

While higher occupational status undoubtedly carries higher prestige, it does not imply commensurate economic returns in Egypt. This is clearly documented by the findings from the Cairo 1979 survey and the 1978 sample of smaller towns and villages. In Cairo in 1979, the median monthly income in Egyptian pounds (one Egyptian pound = $1.40 at the official rate of exchange) ranged from about LE90 for professionals and executives, to LE50 for clerical workers, and to around LE40 for manual workers.[23] The 1978 sample reported the following average monthly income in Egyptian pounds according to husbands' ages and their occupations:

	Men under 40 years of age	Men 40 years of age and older
Professional and high administrators	LE53	LE94
Intermediate technicians and administrators	LE42	LE65
Clerical occupations	LE33	LE44
Private owners and entrepreneurs	LE49	LE50
Service workers	LE23	LE29
Production workers	LE30	LE42
Farm landowners and tenants	LE33	LE40
Agricultural workers and fishermen	LE20	LE22

Among younger men, with the exception of agricultural and service workers, there is little variation of income by occupational status. Indeed, those in private business do almost as well as men with the most prestigious occupations. Partly because of promotions policies of the government bureaucracy, there is a somewhat more marked gradient of income by occupation among older men. Still, top professionals and executives have an income which is only slightly more than double that of clerical and production workers, Because of the close association between occupation and education, the economic returns to education are also very limited. Thus, a national sample survey of Egypt in 1974 revealed that the median monthly family income increased slowly from LE31 among those with a primary education to LE38 for those in the category "above intermediate certificate." It is only when we reach the college educated that there is a marked jump to about LE70 for those with a university certificate and LE100 for those with a post-graduate degree.[24] The glaring discrepancy between educational and occupational achievement and income is undoubtedly one factor that accounts for the corruption documented by Professor Nazih Ayubi's chapter in this volume. It is also one of the main motivations for the emigration of professionals and the highly educated to the rich Arab oil states.[25]

Notwithstanding the lack of appropriate economic return to education and occupation, the preceding analysis suggests a fairly open and dynamic occupational structure where achievement is more a function of one's action than of social origin. The social and economic policies of the revolution have undoubtedly played an important role in mitigating the impact of social origin and providing new opportunities for those oriented towards achievement.

V. INTERNAL MIGRATION AND OCCUPATIONAL MOBILITY ACHIEVEMENT

Since the observed relationship between migration status and occupational achievement may provide additional clues about the possible impact of external migration on social mobility among stayers, it is important to study this relationship in greater detail.

While there have been numerous studies of internal migration in Egypt and other Middle Eastern countries, only a few have focused on social mobility among migrants. The few studies that are available show that this process depends in part on the type of community of origin. For example, in Ankara, Cairo, and Shiraz, migrants from urban communities achieved higher socio-economic status than metropolitan natives or rural migrants.[26] This is a point that was neglected by Birks and Sinclair in their argument about the consequences of internal migration. It could be argued, however, that the higher mobility of urban-to-urban migrants may simply reflect their greater preparedness to experience such mobility. But a multiple regression analysis for Ankara showed that the differences in achievement between various migrant groups remained even after effects of education and other relevant variables were taken into account.[27] A distinction will, therefore, be made between migrants from urban communities and those from rural areas.

In order to have some measure of the effects of external migration on the occupational mobility of migrants, a distinction needs to be made between internal migration before and after the late 1960s. Unfortunately, because of the small numbers involved, the only distinction that could be made was between moves before 1960 and in 1960 and after. The following four types of migrants were identified:

1. recent rural migrants (1960 and after)
2. less recent rural migrants (before 1960)
3. recent urban migrants (1960 and after)
4. less recent urban migrants (before 1960).

There were altogether 1,280 migrants, or persons born elsewhere, distributed as follows in the four categories: 16.5, 39.7, 13.0, and 30.8

percents. Thus, about 27 percent of male heads of households in the sample were migrants. But this percent varied greatly between villages, towns, and industrial workers' residences. These peculiarities of the sample design mean that the results to be presented have to be interpreted with some caution.

It is clear from Table VII that non-migrants in the older ages were noticeably less upwardly mobile than most migrant groups. The differences in younger ages are somewhat less marked, but they tend to favor migrants. What is surprising is that, for each period and each age group, rural migrants experienced more upward mobility than urban migrants. These results partly reflect the fact that farming occupations are rated lower than urban ones and that rural-urban migrants are more likely to have fathers who were farmers.

Since in a relatively open occupational structure migrants should experience more upward mobility than natives, the results of this analysis show that the barriers to occupational mobility that appear to exist in Egypt can be surmounted by migrants. The data in Table VII also suggest that external migration may have contributed to some upward mobility in Egypt. In general, those migrants who moved after 1960 tended to have a higher rate of upward mobility than those who moved before 1960.

While the comparisons in occupational distribution between migrant groups and non-migrants are biased by the characteristics of the sample, it is of some interest to examine what they reveal. If we limit the analysis to the two highest occupational strata of "professional and high administrators" and "intermediate technicians and administrators" there are noticeable differences between the five groups, particularly for the older men. Recent urban migrants had the highest percent in the top occupations, a pattern that was most pronounced for older men (Table VIII). For older men, non-migrants had a much lower occupational achievement than any of the migrants. If we include the next occupational level (clerical jobs, private owners, and entrepreneurs) this is also true for the younger men. In general, rural migrants tend to have the lowest percent in the top occupations. These results are comparable to the findings in Ankara and Shiraz, although they do suggest the need to take the timing of migration into account. What is interesting, is that the relationship between migration and occupational achievement in smaller Egyptian communities would be similar to that in a large metropolitan center such as Ankara. But, as was done in the Ankara study, it is essential to assess the effects of migration on occupational status irrespective of such variables as education, etc. This is the objective of a multiple regression analysis.

The data presented earlier indicated that migration status had a small

TABLE VII

Inter-Generational Occupational Mobility by Migration Status and Age, Egypt, 1978 Sample

Age and Inter-generational mobility	Migrants from Villages		Migrants from Urban Areas		Non-Migrants
	After 1960	1960 and before	After 1960	1960 and before	
Under 40 years of age					
Downward mobility	15.1	29.8	24.4	21.0	22.2
No mobility	26.9	23.9	20.7	38.6	33.7
Upward mobility	58.0	46.3	54.9	40.4	44.1
Total	100.0	100.0	100.0	100.0	100.0
N	(119)	(67)	(82)	(57)	(1.416)
40 years of age and older					
Downward mobility	18.9	25.1	21.2	30.7	24.7
No Mobility	16.7	18.3	27.0	26.5	39.1
Upward Mobility	64.4	56.6	51.8	42.8	36.2
Total	100.0	100.0	100.0	100.0	100.0
N	(90)	(442)	(85)	(332)	(1,840)

SOURCE: See Table V.

but significant effect on occupational achievement in the 1978 sample of villages and towns. The findings for migrants were even more striking. For this group of men, current occupational success was almost entirely a consequence of education and previous occupational achievement. The objective now is consider how this relationship is affected by the origin and timing of the migration.

For each category of migrants, the net regression weights for the variables included in the multiple regression analyses and R^2 are given below (weights which are significant at the 5 per cent level are starred):

	Migration from rural areas		Migration from urban areas	
	After 1960	1960 and earlier	After 1960	1960 and earlier
First occupation after migration	.62**	.45**	.60**	.59**
Education	.24**	.31**	.12**	.22**
Occupation prior to migration	.04	.11	.31**	.05
Years of residence	.06	.01	.00	.07
Age	.09	.05	.05	-.06
Father's occupation	-.01	.03	.00	-.02
Father's education	.00	.03	-.05	.11**
R^2	.71	.55	.90	.66

TABLE VIII

Occupational Distribution by Migration Status and Age, Selected Urban and
Semi-Urban Places and Industrial Workers' Residences, Egypt, 1978.

Age and occupation[1]	Migration Status				
	Migrants from rural areas		Migrants from urban areas		Non-migrants
	1960 and after	Before 1960	1960 and after	Before 1960	
Under 40 years of Age					
(A)	18.2	12.1	33.7	27.8	13.6
(B)	18.2	15.5	13.2	22.2	13.4
(C)	67.7	72.4	53.0	50.0	66.8
(D)	.9	0	0	0	6.3
Total	100.0	100.0	100.0	100.0	100.0
40 years of age and over					
(A)	12.6	16.6	28.1	11.4	3.4
(B)	26.4	14.2	25.6	38.4	29.5
(C)	59.8	67.9	45.2	31.1	43.0
(D)	1.1	1.4	1.2	19.5	23.9
Total	100.0	100.0	100.0	100.0	100.0

(¹) (A): Professional and high administrators; intermediate technicians and administrators
(B): Clerical jobs; private owners and entrepreneurs
(C): Production and service workers
(D): Farm landowners or tenants; agricultural workers and fishermen
SOURCE: See Table V.

As for all migrants, and with the exception of urban migrants who moved in 1960 and earlier, social origin has no perceptible impact on current occupational achievement. The case of the urban migrants is interesting, since it suggests a decrease in the impact of social origin as measured by father's education between the earlier and later period. This suggests an increasing openness in the urban occupational structure of smaller Egyptian cities. This tentative conclusion is further supported by the trends in the R^2. For both urban and rural migrants, the R^2 increase between the earlier and later period. It is thus possible that Egyptian men who moved within the country after 1960 could better translate their education and training into higher occupational status than those who moved before 1960. Since the years after 1960 witnessed the rapid growth of external migration, it would not seem farfetched to infer that this migration had a beneficial effect on those who remained in Egypt.[28]

VI. CONCLUSION

Analysis of available data for Egypt as a whole and for some communities suggests that Birks and Sinclair underestimated the possible effects of external migration on geographical and social mobility within Egypt. As could be expected from its importance, the emigration of Egyptians to the rich Arab states had a marked impact not only on the volume of internal migration but also on its direction. While it is somewhat more difficult to trace the effect of emigration on social mobility among the stayers, the results of this analysis are partly contrary to what was hypothesized by Birks and Sinclair and Findlay. Even though inter-generational mobility between manual and non-manual occupations is not large, Egypt does not have a particularly rigid occupational structure. This may be partly attributed to the crucial role of education in the process of social mobility. The lack of formal education represents the most formidable obstacle to movement between lower and higher occupational levels. At the same time, however, even a secondary school education opens the doors to the top occupations. Partly as a result of governmental policies adopted early in the revolution, almost all college-educated persons are in the highest occupational classes. Since current occupational achievement is influenced more by a person's own educational accomplishments, it is clear that there is less occupational inheritance in Egypt than one might have anticipated.

The results for migrants are even more striking than for the total sample. Again, education emerges as the most important variable. But it is clear that for migrants social origin has a very small net effect on their occupational achievement. These results suggest that if migrants have the requisite training and education, they can achieve a higher occupational status than they had before migration. This success can occur as early as their first occupation after migration. It may be inferred that external migration is likely to have its greatest effects on educated Egyptians. It should be noted, however, that within Egypt the economic returns to higher education and to occupational success are relatively modest. Clearly, those who wished higher status could achieve it within Egypt, given that they had a higher education. But those who preferred a high income emigrated to the rich Arab oil states.

NOTES

1. The author is grateful to Mr. Robert Latowsky for his help in the gathering and processing of data for this research, and is indebted to Dr. Aziz Bindary, Director, and Dr. Sarah Loza, Consultant, of the Population and Family Planning Board, for making available the data from the Survey of Population and Industrialization.

2. Larbi Talha, "L'évolution du mouvement migratoire entre le Maghreb et la France", *Maghreb-Machrek,* no. 61 (January-February 1974), pp. 17–34.

3. Charles B. Keely, "Managing Migration for Development" in *Report of the Study on Worker Migration* (Amman, December 1978 and Cairo, the Population Council, 1979).

4. J. S. Birks and C. A. Sinclair, *International Migration and Development in the Arab Region* (Geneva: International Labour Office, 1980), p. 94.

5. A. M. Findlay, "Migration in Space: Immobility in Society" in G. H. Blake and R. I. Lawless, eds., *The Changing Middle Eastern City* (New York: Barnes and Noble, 1980), p. 69.

6. Abdel-Fattah Nassef, *The Egyptian Labor Force: Its Dimensions and Changing Structure, 1907–1960* (Philadelphia: University of Pennsylvania, Population Studies Center, 1970); Central Agency for Public Mobilization and Statistics (CAPMAS), *Al-taᶜdad al-ᶜamm li al-sukkan wa al-iskan 1976* [The Population and Housing Census...], (Cairo, 1978).

7. Saad Eddin Ibrahim, "Social Mobility and Income Distribution", mimeo, November 1979, forthcoming in Robert Tignor et al., eds., *The Political Economy of Income Distribution in Egypt* (New York: Holmes and Meier).

8. Ibid., p. 4.

9. Sarah Loza, "Socio-Spatial and Fertility Differentials in Egypt" (Cairo: Population and Family Planning Board, 1980), and her "Differential Concern for Children's Education in Egypt and its Effects on Fertility", *Dirasat Sukkaniyya,* Vol. 6, no. 51 (October-December 1979), pp. 9–29.

10. Ibid., pp. 5–7.

11. See Birks and Sinclair, op.cit.; the chapter by Saad Eddin Ibrahim in this volume; and Nazli Choucri, Richard S. Eckaus and Amr Mohie-Eldin, *Migration and Employment in the Construction Sector: Critical Factors in Egyptian Development* (Cairo University-MIT Technology Transfer Program, 1978).

12. Widad S. Morcos, "Trends and Patterns of Urbanization in Egypt During the 1966-1976 Intercensal Period", *Dirasat Sukkaniyya,* Vol. 7, no. 52, (January-March 1980), pp. 1–17.

13. Since the demographic effects of external migration would be in terms of *net* interna-

tional migration, a third hypothesis to account for the observed trends would be that the rate of return of international migration is greater for rural than for urban areas.

14. Ibrahim, op.cit., p. 10.

15. H. El-Saaty, "Egypt", in C. A. Van Nieuwenhuijze, ed., *Commoners, Climbers and Notables* (Leiden: E.J. Brill, 1977), pp. 196–198.

16. Ibid., pp. 198, 200.

17. Clement Henry Moore, *Images of Development: Egyptian Engineers in Search of Industry* (Cambridge, Mass.: MIT Press, 1980); and H.A. Akeel and C. H. Moore, "Class Origins of Egyptian Engineer-Technocrats" in C. A. Van Nieuwenhuijze, ed., *Commoners, Climbers and Notables,* op.cit.; also Nazih N. M. Ayubi, *Bureaucracy and Politics in Contemporary Egypt* (London: Ithaca Press, 1980), especially Chapter 5; and Leonard Binder, *In a Moment of Enthusiasm* (Chicago: University of Chicago Press, 1978).

18. Ayubi, op.cit., p. 362; Moore, op.cit., p. 115; and Akeel and Moore, op.cit., p. 282.

19. CAPMAS, *Statistical Yearbook* (Cairo, July 1979), p. 176.

20. CAPMAS, *Population and Housing Census...,*op.cit., Table 36.

21. In the regression analysis each of the eight occupational groups was assigned weights proportional to the mean educational level and mean income of each group. It would, of course, have been preferable to carry out the analysis with a much more detailed occupational breakdown, but such a breakdown was not available.

22. See John Waterbury, "Corruption, Political Stability, and Development: Comparative Evidence from Egypt and Morocco", *Government and Opposition,* Vol. 11, no. 4 (Autumn 1976), p. 429; and Mona Hammam, "Women and Industrial Work in Egypt: The Choubra el-Kheima Case", *Arab Studies Quarterly,* Vol. 2, no. 1 (Winter 1980), p. 64; and Ayubi, op.cit., p. 415. Ayubi mentions other factors such as the growth of private education as contributing to the greater access to education among the children of the upper and upper middle classes. Messiha's sample of Egyptian school teachers reported that they earned the equivalent of 60 percent of their official salaries by giving private lessons. Suzanne Messiha, *Export of Egyptian School Teachers,* The Cairo Papers in Social Science, Volume Three, Monograph Four, April 1980, p. 58.

23. Ibrahim, op.cit., p. 61.

24. Ibid., p. 65.

25. The number of seconded emigrants with at least a BA degree or the equivalent increased from 6,851 in 1970 to close to 40,000 in 1977–78. See the article "Temporary Emigration of Egyptians for Working Abroad Particularly in Arab Countries", *Economic Bulletin* (Cairo: National Bank of Egypt, 1979), pp. 265, 276 and 278. For data on the occupational characteristics of migrants from Egypt during the period from 1968 to 1973 see Choucri, Eckaus and Mohie-Eldin, op.cit., p. 62. The income of such people is noticeably higher outside Egypt; in the four years that they spent in Kuwait or Saudi Arabia, Egyptian school teachers had earnings whose net present value far exceeded the lifetime earnings they could expect in Egypt. Messiha, op.cit., pp. 61 and 77.

26. Baron L. Moots, "Migration, Community of Origin, and Status Achievement: A Comparison of Two Metropolitan Communities in Developing Societies", *Social Forces,* Vol. 54, no. 4 (June 1976), pp. 816–832; and A. A. Paydarfar, "Differential Life Styles Between Migrants and Nonmigrants: A Case Study of the City of Shiraz", *Demography,* Vol. 11, no. 3, 1974, pp. 509–520.

27. Moots, ibid.

28. Choucri, Eckaus and Mohie-Eldin conclude from their analysis of the emigration of construction labor from Egypt that "the construction labor which emigrates is replaced in part by labor which would otherwise be less than fully employed and that generates additional welfare." (p. 135). They also point to other more negative consequences of the emigration of construction labor.

Part Two

The New Arab Economic Order

IV
The Arab Economy and Its Developing Strategy: A New Arab Economic Order

Essam Montasser

I. INTRODUCTION

In the last few years, traditional Arab cooperation mechanisms and channels have been subjected to heavy stress. Global changes in economic, geopolitical and other power balances — especially subsequent to the 1973 War and its aftermath — compounded by local changes, brought about substantial upheavals in the prevailing pattern of Arab regional inter-relations. These changes created a superficial impression of a reverse movement towards Arab regional disintegration, politically and, naturally, economically.

This, in fact, prompted some to go so far as to interpret such a short- to medium-term trend of events as tantamount to the demise of Arab nationalism which has been the rallying point of Arab cooperation in the recent past. If this were the case, it would be both presumptuous and superficial to speak about an "Arab Economy" which is neither expected nor extant.

The argument here is in the opposite direction. Arab nationalism is alive and well. The currently observed disarray in Arab relations is transitory, and is likely to lead to a higher stage of organic relations in the Arab region rather than otherwise. The Arabs are probing towards a new order consistent with their internal developmental needs and concomitant external relations. Until the new equilibrating order is achieved, there will naturally be a great deal of intra-Arab friction and positioning. A brief word of explanation is in order.

In the 1960s the spearhead of Arab integration was Arab socialism, as an Arab politico-economic movement with regional dimensions and objectives. While it focused attention on the need for Arab integration and

brought the issue to the forefront as a pan-Arab national objective—indeed a major achievement—its contribution to the actual accomplishment of economic cooperation was, in fact, minimal.

This could be explained in the light of a number of factors. First were
the disparate phases of development in the Arab countries, the non-
complementarity of their production structures, patterns of specialization, and international economic relations. Secondly there was the
heterogeneity of their political and economic systems and external
alliances. Thirdly there was the lack of any adequate soft infrastructure
for regional economic coordination in the form of functional market
and/or planning mechanisms.

Accordingly, while there has been a consensus among the Arab countries as to the objective of economic integration, the means of achieving
this goal have been lacking. Therefore, the main instrument became intergovernmental (bilateral or multilateral) coordination and administration of economic relations.

But given the rapid pace of political change in most countries of the
region, intergovernmental coordination constituted a highly unstable
mechanism for sustained and systematic growth in regional economic
cooperation. Furthermore, given the dynamics of expectations, economic entities other than governments became reluctant to undertake
any major investment in other Arab countries because of their anticipation of unstable political interrelations. In other words, while the desire
for economic integration among Arab people and governments existed,
its economic foundation and the vehicles for its implementation were
lacking.

At present, however, this situation has changed in at least two substantive areas. The first was triggered by the October War in 1973 and the
subsequent accumulation of oil revenue surpluses by the major Arab oil-
exporting countries. Taken as a whole, the Arab countries now have
enough financial surpluses to finance aggregate investment levels exceeding 50 percent of their aggregate regional product—that is, of
course, if and when they can absorb such levels of investment.

This new situation constitutes a reversal of the established historical
and cross-sectional associations between development levels, savings,
and sources of financing investment. The established world pattern is
that less developed countries suffer from low savings rates and are
therefore dependent on net financial resource inflows to finance their accelerating rates of investment. This established historical pattern of international capital movement has contributed to the tendency of many
developing countries to become producers of mono crops, impeding a
more balanced pattern of output growth and specialization.

This constraint on the pattern of growth and specialization of the Arab region, which in the past has been a major impediment to integration efforts, is no longer binding. Changing the pattern of growth of output and trade towards closer intra-regional relations is tantamount to changing the pattern of regional growth and specialization in a global context. The financial surpluses of the oil-rich countries allow the Arab countries to be self-reliant with regard to their financial needs, thus enhancing their freedom of choice in their future pattern of growth and specialization and allowing them to move towards greater regional integration.

Financial autonomy and mobility in the Arab region permit the mobility and utilization of other regional features of production. Capital movement creates demand for labor, and finances its movement from labor-surplus to labor-scarce countries. It also provides the requisite overhead capital for better utilization of agricultural production capacity. A rational pattern of capital allocation within the region creates a new production structure conducive to regional integration via commodity and services trade. In other words, as things stand now, factor movement constitutes the engine of integration in the Arab region, which flies in the face of traditional Ricardian trade theory.

A potential large-scale factor movement within the Arab region will not be a systematic or a smooth process. It has myriad prerequisites and will have far-reaching consequences, both economic and non-economic. Therefore, one should not be discouraged by possible temporary setbacks in the process.

The second major change has been the fact that many Arab countries have made enormous strides along the road to industrialization. In most cases, however, industrial growth via the domestic markets of individual countries has already reached its limits, thus necessitating a centrifugal, outward orientation in industrial policies. More than ever, these countries feel the need for regional cooperation. In fact one is warranted in saying that such cooperation has become an essential ingredient for sustaining the previously achieved rates of industrial growth, not to speak of accelerating that growth. More will be said about this later, in our outline of the Arab region's long-term economic strategy.

It is in the light of such factors that we conclude that Arab economic cooperation is in transition towards a higher stage. The above-described organic economic relations and their anticipated future expansion and intensification, are likely to bring about more congenial relations in the political and other non-economic spheres.

To sum up; with the massive factor movement that took place after the October War, a solid foundation for an Arab economy has been laid. This movement could be expanded, rationalized and built upon in order to achieve economic integration, and it is in this light that we speak here of an Arab economy. The strategy prescribed below will illustrate how the Arab economy could achieve integration and structural balance between now and the end of this century.

At present, the Arab regional economy is the product of certain internal and external factors and organic relations which are mostly exogenous to it. It reflects the organic relations of its individual components (the Arab states) with the world economy; it likewise mirrors the internal imbalances characterizing these national economies; and last but not least, it reveals its deficient infrastructure and mechanisms. In spite of this, the Arab economy's integration with its national components has been increasing at an accelerated pace in recent years, thus creating an autonomous force. The outcome of such a process is that its needs and pattern of development have become—more than ever before— parameters for national planners and policy-makers. We should therefore look at the Arab economy, its structure, problems and balances, from a regional as well as from a national point of view. We should also analyze the causal relations between the pattern of growth and strategic objectives of the regional Arab economy on the one hand, and the pattern and strategies of national economies on the other.

Our analysis of the Arab economy starts with a definition of its dimensions and a diagnosis of its interrelations with its national tributaries. In the light of this diagnostic analysis, we shall propose a regional Arab strategy for economic development. The present study differs in this regard from other studies which focus on Arab economic objectives and pay scant attention to the means or constraints dictated by the organic balances and development phases of Arab states.

The essay is divided into three parts. The first offers a definition of the characteristics of Arab economic cooperation, a diagnosis of its problems, and the identification of its interrelations with national economies. The second part looks at some basic dimensions of a regional strategy for development and forecasts a development pattern which secures the objectives and balances of the proposed strategy. We then examine some organizational aspects of the Arab economy.

II.   THE ARAB ECONOMY: MACRO BALANCES
AND ORGANIC RELATIONS

A. EMERGENCE OF THE ARAB ECONOMY

During the past twenty-five years, several attempts were made to increase Arab economic cooperation, mostly following the traditional modes of free trade agreements and common markets between groups of Arab states. This pattern failed to achieve its objectives for well-known reasons, these being mainly the lack of an effective market mechanism and its requisite organizational structure, and an efficient and consistent demand management and the like. This approach also relied on the movement of goods and services. But the productive structures of Arab states are similar and, in most cases, do not yield an industrial exportable surplus (with the exception of some primary commodities). This is why this approach failed to increase inter-Arab trade.

Arab economic cooperation showed a sharp increase only after the 1973 War, as a result of the sudden rise in oil surpluses. The successive rises in oil prices brought about a greater change in international terms of trade which, in turn, significantly altered the distribution of world income in favor of oil-exporting countries. Export receipts of oil-exporting countries increased at an exponential rate.

Changes in external terms of trade had a direct negative effect on the income of non-oil-exporting countries because of the rising costs of their oil imports. Moreover, as a result of the inflationary price rises in markets of Western industrialized nations — which soared following the increase in oil prices — and of policies used to absorb the negative effect of inflation on the income of these nations, the price of food and producer goods rose. Consequently, the negative effect of the changing external terms of trade was most acutely felt by those non-oil-exporting Arab states that relied heavily on imports to meet their needs for consumer and producer goods, and which showed a great deficit in the balance of their external trade. This, in particular, was the case with Egypt.

Egypt's deficit in the external balance of trade rose from LE200 million in 1973 to LE500 million in 1975, and to over LE1000 million in subsequent years. Furthermore, price subsidies granted by the government rose from LE80 million in 1973 to LE440 million in 1974 and to LE1000 million in 1975. The increase in the external trade deficit did not result from a rise in production and income and related requirements, for the real growth rate during these two years averaged less than 5 percent per annum.

The disequilibrium in the balance of trade was the outcome of rising import prices. Furthermore, attempts by the government to protect domestic production costs as well as consumption levels against sudden increases in import prices raised price subsidies as indicated above.

In other words, the change in external terms of trade had the effect of lowering the income and production of the non-oil-exporting states. In order to maintain their standard of living, these states had to contract external loans to offset their declining income. Government price subsidies were the means whereby the domestic economy was protected against external price changes. However, such methods can only be a temporary remedy and cannot be sustained at their current level.

Thus, economic changes ensuing from the October War brought about a substantial increase in the oil and balance of trade surpluses of oil-exporting countries and, in a reverse process, a drop in the income of non-oil countries and a deficit in their balance of payments. As a result of the steep rise in their income and surplus, oil countries spent increasingly on consumption and investment. Higher investment rates generated a growing demand for labor from labor-surplus Arab states, thus sharply escalating labor outflow rates among Egyptians, Palestinians and Tunisians to underpopulated oil states such as Saudi Arabia, the Gulf States and Libya.

On the other hand, non-oil countries had to obtain external loans to meet the deficit in their government budgets and balance of payments. Most of these loans were granted by oil countries, which also provided the non-oil countries with other forms of financial assistance such as the Arab subsidy to the front line states, or public and private investments. Accordingly, major financial assistance flowed in the reverse direction of labor outflow. Labor and financial outflows contributed to an unprecedented organic linkage of the Arab economy. It could even be said that such outflows brought into being what can, for the first time, be termed an "Arab economy".

We should also add that the movement of millions of workers and their dependents as well as of billions of dollars within the Arab region had important indirect effects on inter-Arab economic linkages and external relations. The revenues of Arab factors of production invested in other Arab states represent one such indirect effect. The income earned by expatriate labor working in other Arab states and the surplus funds transferred by them to their home countries have become a major source of foreign currency to these countries. Moreover, rising incomes all over the Arab world led to a greater demand for intra-Arab tourism, which in turn made for greater direct contact among Arab people, resulting in increased social and cultural interaction. Such interaction on as massive a scale as has recently been witnessed will, no doubt, have long-term effects on Arab relations.[1]

It must be pointed out, however, that the increasing intra-Arab economic relations following the October War, resulting from direct and indirect effects of intra-Arab factor movements, were not at the expense of interrelations with the world economy. While some of the Arab oil surpluses went to non-oil Arab countries, the great bulk of these surpluses were invested in international financial markets and in the Western economy at large. To that extent, the links between the Arab economy and its components on the one hand, and the international economy on the other, have been greatly solidified as a result of these recent developments. Furthermore, the faster growth in income and in output in the Arab economy and the import demand it generated for Western consumer and producer goods, constituted a rapidly growing source of demand and growth for Western countries. In other words, this Arab import demand is increasingly acting as a "mini" engine of growth for Western countries.[2] Such a factor must be kept in mind in the design and assessment of any Arab regional strategy.

B. MACRO BALANCES

Having briefly outlined the state of affairs of the Arab economy and its internal and external linkages, we move to a diagnosis of some of the major imbalances characterizing this economy. This could represent an initial step in the process of suggesting some long-term policy prescriptions that would aim at achieving greater balance and integration in the Arab economy, and these prescriptions would constitute the building blocks for the proposed Arab development strategy.

1. Wages and productivity

An attempt to diagnose current conditions of the Arab economy from the viewpoint of its future growth prospects yields the following results. The Arab economy is affected at present by two main factors which have a negative impact on its macro balances and potential development: (a) a large and growing gap between aggregate labor productivity and cost and (b) an excess of Arab savings over investments that creates a surplus amounting to 30 percent of the gross domestic product of the Arab region. This is naturally invested outside the region, mainly in a few American and European financial markets. The perpetuation of these two factors will certainly have serious negative effects on the future development rates and patterns of the Arab economy.

As regards relations between wages and productivity and the wide gap dividing them, their evolution may be summed up as follows. Until 1973, relations between wages and productivity and their rates of change were never balanced in any Arab state. This imbalance was to a great extent linked to the development phases of these states and to their structural balances, but it was limited and could easily have been adjusted. After 1973 the imbalance was accentuated in most Arab states. The sudden rise in income of the oil countries led to higher expenditure rates, including capital formation rates. As a result of their limited domestic labor force and its slow growth rate as compared with capital formation growth rates, oil countries needed to import a larger labor force from other Arab states; moreover, in view of their difficult working conditions, they had to pay higher wages to attract the labor they needed, particularly skilled labor and technicians.

This sudden increase in income and expenditure was not limited to the oil-rich, underpopulated countries, but also extended to countries such as Iraq which did not rely exclusively on oil. Their economic activities also increased as a result of higher oil revenues on the one hand, and of development policies adopted in recent years on the other. Investment rates far exceeding their labor force growth rates led them to compete with other oil countries for Arab labor, and raised their average money wages.

Non-oil countries labored under the same problem. Inflow of Arab capital accelerated their development rates, particularly capital formation rates: this was notably the case in Egypt. Labor requirements for national development (particularly skilled labor) ran counter to their policy of exporting labor to oil and semi-oil countries, but these competing demands for Arab labor were settled, given their higher wage levels, in favor of the oil producers. As a result we note — for example in Egypt — that the average wage in the construction sector (a labor-intensive sector) quadrupled from 1973 to 1975, while agricultural wage rates also multiplied several times.

In this connection, one should point out that in Egypt the labor market has some specific characteristics. First, a large proportion of what seems to be surplus labor is, in fact, low productivity labor. Withdrawal of this low productivity (underemployed) labor necessitates higher productivity from the labor remaining, through an increased average capital labor ratio; that is, by substituting capital for labor. Secondly, the rise in money wages results not only from an imbalance between labor supply and demand, but also from other structural causes, prominent amongst which is rising food costs.

The above-described overall substantial increase in average money wage, witnessed in all Arab states as a result of the demand for labor exceeding its supply, was not accompanied by an increase in average productivity. On the contrary, for various reasons labor productivity dropped in some sectors and in some Arab states. For example, the higher labor demand and employment in many Arab countries did not bring about a change in the production structure; nor did it lead to a shift from low labor productivity and less capital-intensive sectors, such as agriculture, to other sectors with higher labor productivity, such as manufacturing industries. Furthermore, a large proportion of the marginal additions to employed labor was of the unskilled type which, naturally, had a very low productivity. One can also add the mushrooming bottlenecks at all levels, which interrupted work and lowered productivity in general.

At present, the gap separating the current average labor productivity and cost and their marginal rates of change does not greatly affect Arab economic development, despite its negative effects on savings, investment and economic development. The reason for this is the existence of a surplus. This surplus makes up for the lack of, or negative, savings of other business sectors whose high labor cost is cutting into their profits.

However in the long run, when the importance of large oil revenues dwindles, such an imbalance will seriously affect economic development. In view of its structural nature and because of the impossibility of the non-oil-exporting countries — particularly Egypt — being able to solve this problem in the short or medium run, the warning is opportune, and corrective measures should not be delayed. In these countries, particular attention must be given to production cost and competitiveness since the growth of production and exports of manufactured goods is a *sine qua non* for their overall growth.

2. Savings and investment

The great increase in the income of oil countries resulted in a similar increase in savings. And since the oil sector is both owned and controlled by government, its surplus naturally goes to government. However, time is needed to transfer a portion of this government-owned oil surplus to the household sector and thus to affect its consumption pattern. The household sector in these states (excluding Iraq and Algeria) is of limited size; in 1975 their population did not exceed 9 million. Hence, no matter how high their income rose, the absolute increase in consumption expenditure was still limited in comparison with the soaring oil revenues. Furthermore, the limited capacity of the production, import and distribution sectors was not conducive to a rapid increase in the domestic supply of goods and services and therefore constituted a constraint on the growth of consumption rates in the short and medium term.

Furthermore the capacity of the government and business sectors to raise their investment rates in the short and medium run was limited by the absorptive capacity of these states, and in particular the capacity of the construction sector (which is a home industry). Construction represents 50 to 60 percent of total fixed investments, and thus higher investments are translated into additional construction works. Further, a rise in investment requires large imports of capital goods (machines and equipment) which account for 35 percent of investment costs. Because of the limited capacity of port, transportation and storage sectors, etc, which cannot be improved to any great extent in the short and medium term, speedy delivery of imported capital goods was hindered by various bottlenecks and delays. Moreover, there is need for other services both in advance of and concomitant with investments — such as engineering and economic consultancy firms — and time is therefore needed to translate a rising income into higher consumption or investment rates. That is why the soaring income of oil-producing countries is mostly turned into financial savings.

Part of these savings went to finance current deficits in the balance of payments of the non-oil countries in the form of aid, but it is an insignificant part (perhaps less than 3 percent of the total oil surplus). The balance of these financial surpluses is mostly invested in the international financial markets of Europe and America.

The larger surplus resulting from the difference between savings and investment at the overall Arab level (that is, after covering the deficits of the non-oil countries), which amounted to 40 billion dollars in 1975 and which has probably multiplied by now, represents a serious imbalance in the structure and macro balances of the Arab economy. This is due to the absolute and relative size of this surplus on the one hand, and, on the other, to its escalating growth rates and high level of regional concentration. The continued investment of such huge Arab financial surpluses in world markets currently constitutes an element of instability and imbalance in world financial markets. Sooner or later these nations will have to protect their markets against the present and potential negative effects of the destabilizing and highly volatile movements of Arab capital.

3. Inflation

All Arab states suffer from a high inflationary rise in prices. Causes might differ from one country to another, or from one group of countries to another, but some are common to them all.

As regards oil countries, and to a lesser extent semi-oil countries, the source of their inflationary trend is the sudden and rapid growth in levels of economic activities in recent years. In the face of rigid economic structures and numerous bottlenecks, rising domestic demand is mostly translated into higher prices rather than into higher production, because production cannot possibly keep pace with the sudden rise in demand, especially in the short run.

Attempts to accelerate production of goods and services have brought about a rise in cost factors, the most serious being that of labor and construction costs. Annually increasing construction costs resulted in a parallel increase in investment costs, to which one should add the inflationary rise in international prices of capital goods, which amounted on average to 25 percent per annum in recent years. Needless to say, import prices of consumer goods — particularly food — were not much different. In other words, the inflationary trend in these countries resulted from a sudden rise in demand and an ensuing excess demand, i.e., demand-pull inflation. The latter led to a rise in production cost, i.e., cost-push inflation which fed the inflationary spiral.

It must be pointed out, however, that an additional offshoot of the rising cost of production has been one of a structural nature, namely the inflexible production structure and the numerous constraints characterizing it. As for the role of money supply, it has been mainly, and on the whole, a dependent rather than an autonomous factor contributing to inflation. This is a natural outcome of the lack of active monetary and demand management policies in most, if not all, Arab countries. As far as non-oil countries, and particularly Egypt, are concerned, there are some additional dimensions to the problem.[3] Rising foodstuff prices and increasing external and internal labor demand tangibly raised the subsistence wage level and with it the general wage structure. Increase in the cost of imports of producer goods, as well as construction, considerably raised production costs generally, as has been mentioned earlier. This overall rise in production cost elements, with no parallel rise in prices of public goods, cut into the surpluses of public enterprises, thus reducing their capacity to finance their investments.

Attempts by government to absorb the increase in import and local production costs led to a sharp rise in expenditures without generating a similar increase in receipts. Rising current government expenditure and government-financed investments led to an increasing resort to deficit financing. This had an adverse effect on the inflationary trend of the Egyptian economy.

We can therefore conclude that there have been three major factors underlying the inflationary trend in the Arab economy: (i) changes in the external terms of trade of the Arab countries, the ensuing changes in income distribution, and their consequential changes in the Arab region's aggregate demand and supply and their structures; (ii) rising labor wages and costs on an Arab regional scale, and (iii) international inflation.

4. Regional income distribution

Average per capita income in oil countries rose from $900 in 1970 to $6000 in 1975, whereas in non-oil countries it rose from $220 in 1970 to

$400 in 1975.[4] The disparity would be even greater if we were to compare the more affluent oil countries with the less endowed among the non-oil countries.

The recent widening gap in income distribution among Arab states was fortunately not accompanied by as wide a gap in average consumption levels. As previously mentioned, a sizeable share of the income of oil countries was directed to savings rather than to consumption. Furthermore, the negative effect of the changes in the external terms of trade on the income and, accordingly, on the consumption levels of non-oil countries was greatly offset by government price subsidies. Needless to say, the latter were partially financed through intra-Arab trade, and as a result, average per capita consumption in oil countries rose from $350 in 1970 to $840 in 1975, whereas corresponding figures for non-oil countries were $140 and $280 respectively. Although differences in average consumption rates are less disparate than those in average income rates, rising consumption rates ought to be a matter of great concern, both for economic and non-economic reasons.

On the non-economic side, one can mention the absolute low level of consumption among certain income brackets in some major Arab countries, including Egypt. This should be a cause for welfare, social and political concern. On the economic side, the lopsided Arab regional income distribution constitutes a major constraint on the region's market size as well as a source of distortion in its commodity structure. If the Arab region is to achieve its hoped-for rapid growth, some measures aiming at a gradual levelling of regional income distribution in the course of economic development and cooperation must be sought.

C. ORGANIC AND STRUCTURAL RELATIONS

National Arab economic problems, their causes, remedies and future trends, vary according to the country's development phase and economic resources. An analytical study must therefore start from this premise.

Analytically, Arab states can be divided into three groups. First are those states that are still in their first development phase and engaged in primary production (agriculture and extracting industries). All oil-rich countries come into this category: Saudi Arabia, the Gulf States and Libya, in addition to other agricultural states such as Sudan, North and South Yemen, and Mauritania. Second are the states where industrialization is of recent date and industries are at the early stages of import substitution. This group comprises the remaining Arab states, with the exception of Egypt. Two types of countries fall into this group: (i) countries which export oil but do not rely on it exclusively (namely Iraq and Algeria) and (ii) the Arab Mashriq states (Syria, Jordan, Lebanon), and the remaining Maghreb countries (Tunisia and Morocco). The third category comprises only Egypt, whose industrialization process, which started with import substitution, began at a much earlier period and has now come to an end. Its industrial development strategy should therefore focus on a more advanced stage of import substitution, that is to establish capital goods industries to substitute for imports, since its needs for consumer goods — other than foodstuffs — are mostly satisfied locally. Furthermore, the export coefficient of its industries should be raised. It must also emphasize, and gradually move into the export of, manufactured goods.

1. Primary-producing Arab states: pattern of sectoral growth

The basic factor which at present determines the income growth of the first group is the rise in oil prices. But as far as non-oil countries within the group are concerned — as is the case with Sudan, for example — their engine of growth is agricultural production and, to a lesser extent, mining production apart from oil. Growth of other sectors depends on the domestic demand generated by the growth of income and surplus of the primary sectors.

Continued development of these primary sectors in this group of Arab states — even at an accelerated rate — is of vital importance to, and a basic objective of, development at both local and pan-Arab levels, as will later be explained. In this regard, two factors have to be taken into account: first that the development of primary sectors (whether agriculture or mining) is limited by their production capacity which, in turn, is restricted by their natural endowments and supplies. Our present knowledge indicates that oil is an exhaustible resource, the lifespan of which may not extend beyond half a century, given the current mining rates, and the same applies also to agricultural resources, in particular arable land resources. Second, if this is so, there is therefore a need to create new alternative sources and capacities for production and income growth, namely an industrial base.

There is a basic interlinkage of primary sector development and industrial development which is explained in textbooks and economic writings and which need not be discussed here. Let us only add that the relation between development and industry is not limited to industry's contribution to national production and income, but extends to far-reaching social and economic effects. It is also a basic link in the development chain, instrumental in the evolution of any autonomous economic system.

Egypt's experience might be useful in this regard. The modern development of Egypt began in the previous century with the development of the agricultural sector. During the early years of the present century, before the outbreak of the First World War, Egypt had exhausted its potential for agricultural expansion, having reached the intensive and extensive margin of agricultural production capacity. But agricultural growth did not lead to a parallel industrial growth, and this might well be at the heart of the difficulties and complexities which now plague the industrialization process in Egypt. Industrial growth and the ensuing rise in income increased the demand for foodstuffs, industrial products and agricultural surplus which, because it had long before exhausted its production capacity, the agricultural sector could not satisfy. To increase agricultural production there is a need for new capacities, modern techniques and up-to-date practices which require both time and large investments.

Arab states still in their first development phases should benefit greatly from Egypt's experience, especially since their conditions differ greatly. In the first place, the surpluses of primary sectors are appropriated by the governments and people of these countries, particularly by the former, whereas in the Egypt of the nineteenth century, the agricultural surplus was taken over by tradesmen and financiers (largely foreign-dominated), leaving for the Egyptian producers only a pittance which was barely sufficient for their subsistence. Moreover, Egypt was under foreign occupation and its government could not encourage industrialization attempts, whereas the current primary-producing Arab states are politically independent and have the power to boost industrial growth by channelling a major share of their available resources and surpluses into industrial projects.[5]

We have indicated above that the mono crop pattern of growth that until recently characterized the historical experience of the primary-producing Arab states needs to be changed in favor of a greater diversification in the commodity composition of their production. We have also proposed the need for encouraging industrial growth, both directly and indirectly, whether on the national, sub-regional or regional level. However, industrial development prospects in these states are not very promising for two main reasons, one being the small size of the national domestic market and the other being labor shortages and high cost. With regard to the former, it must be noted that in 1975, average per capita consumption amounted to $400 per annum. Significantly, less than 20 percent of this was spent on industrial consumer goods other than foodstuffs. Moreover, this trifling sum was largely spent on imported goods. In some Arab states, per capita expenditure may perhaps be a multiple of this average per capita consumption, but this increase in consumption is offset by the small number of consumers.

In these states, domestic demand for industrial goods constitutes the basis for industrial growth. The establishment of domestic consumer industries generates a secondary demand for other industrial goods such as intermediate and capital goods, lays the pyramidal base, and provides the expertise needed to expand the more advanced capital goods industries.

The domestic market for industrial goods must therefore be expanded on a regional or national basis. In this connection, the first step is to protect the domestic market and the demand for such goods, while expanding their production and encouraging foreign exporters to participate in the establishment of such industries locally. In other words, the next development stage—namely that of consumer goods import substitution—should be started before the depletion of the primary sector development sources.

Some oil states side-stepped the import substitution stage and directly established export industries, such as petrochemicals. While such projects are satisfactory and opportune, it should nevertheless be emphasized that they are extremely capital-intensive, and are complementary to world markets. Therefore, from the point of view of the national economies they constitute enclaves with limited or virtually no forward-, backward- or final-demand linkages, and accordingly will have very limited effects on the stimulation of industrial growth in the national economies.

The limited size of the domestic market is not the sole problem that confronts industry in these countries; there is also the lack of domestic labor, the need to import labor, and the high cost of labor as compared with its productivity. Rising labor costs pose no problem at this stage, neither will they pose any in the short or medium terms because such industries start as domestic industries. But in the long run they will become a major liability for industrial growth.

Labor imports from Arab states with labor surpluses represent a basic mechanism for the promotion of the Arab economy and the consolidation of its organic linkage and, as such, should be encouraged. But labor imports should be regulated because labor movements within the Arab region started at random, and the time has now come to create an Arab labor market that would make Arab labor migration an orderly and economically efficient process.

However, this solution will not suffice, and new policies should be evolved to regulate and encourage migration—not only of labor—among Arab states. Temporary labor migration is only a provisional solution. It is in the interest of labor-importing countries to create their own permanent industrial labor base as indicated above: this necessitates a permanent and stable population base. Industrial investment relies not only on analysis of short-term conditions prevailing on the market but also on its medium- and long-term prospects. Without a wide and permanent urban population base, and in the absence of an agricultural rural population base, the development process of oil countries will be dependent on their oil or other mineral resources, and will falter when these resources are depleted. Once again, a reason for this is the absence of the population and labor bases required for industrial growth other than extraction industries.

The case of the United States might be a useful example in this regard. Emigration to the United States was instrumental in the achievement of the growth rates secured in the 18th and 19th centuries. In 1770 America had a population of 2.5 million when those of England and France were 9 and 24 million respectively. By 1910, the population of the United States had risen to 92 million, twice the populations of England and France at the same period, both of whom had 40 million each. In 1975 the United States' population had reached 214 million, representing a multiplier coefficient of 84 in the two previous centuries, against a multiplier coefficient of 4 for Europe (with the exception of the Soviet Union), immigration accounting for 50 percent of that increase in the United States during that period. Without such high immigration rates the United States could not have achieved its present development.[6]

The psychological effect of temporary labor migration on economic efficiency must also be considered. In such cases, relations between labor and host country are not really economic but basically commercial. Each party tries to secure maximum benefits in minimum time in total disregard of more lasting economic factors.

Countries still at the primary production stage should therefore reconsider their immigration policies, but this exercise should be carried out within a regional Arab framework that seeks regional economic and strategic objectives with a view to securing both national and pan-Arab objectives.

2. Import-substituting industrializing states

The second group of Arab states has only recently tackled the industrialization process and is still in the early phases of the import substitution strategy. Basic problems confronting their industrial development also include (a) shortage of factors of production (either labor or capital or both); (b) increasing production costs, low profit rates and weak competitive capacity abroad, and (c) the limited size of the domestic market and its low growth rates.

The population base in countries which do not rely exclusively on oil, such as Iraq and Algeria, is medium-sized and so is their labor force base, but in view of their domestic market size, average per capita expenditure on industrial consumer goods is low. Attempts at achieving a balanced development in several sectors concurrently — investment needed being supplied by oil revenues — has created a demand for labor exceeding locally available supply. Iraq, for example, has come close to what might be called full employment in the light of its present technological level and social framework.

The inevitable outcome of a shortage in labor in domestic industries is rising wages (which once again is financed from the oil sector's surplus). If we add to this the drop in economic efficiency and productivity as a result of numerous bottlenecks and other shortages which accompany the rapid growth of these countries, we find that local industries are confronting a situation of rising costs and declining productivity and economic profitability. This problem can now be overcome through the oil sector surpluses, but in the future, when substitution for imported industrial consumer goods is exhausted, growth rates of industrial domestic product in these Arab states will slow down in line with the growth in domestic demand. A superior alternative is to move towards a higher stage of industrial growth, namely exports. This stage calls for a wider market, a higher efficiency and, consequently, some specialization. In other words, it calls for Arab industrial coordination and an efficient Arab labor market to provide these states with their requisite labor inputs.

The problem of other Arab states within this group is more complex because they lack oil surpluses. Their short-term problems have been solved by loans, in particular those granted by oil countries. But these loans were contracted to meet deficits in the balance of payments and not to create new production capacities. The solution of their industrial problems lies therefore within a regional Arab framework. Prime examples of such states are Syria, Morocco and Tunisia.

3. Post-import substitution industrialization: Egypt

As far as Egypt is concerned, its main development source is the industrial sector because the agricultural sector has long since exhausted its capacity for expansion and its annual growth rate does not currently exceed 1 percent. Raising the agricultural production growth rate to 3 percent requires substantial investments in land reclamation, irrigation and drainage; hence, in order to raise real income by 5 percent per annum, industrial production must be developed by at least 8 percent per annum.

As for the contribution of the services sector to overall growth, it is tied to the rate of growth of the commodity sectors. Cross-sectional international experience as well as historical evidence indicate an income and growth elasticity of services of around 1.1.

Demand growth resulting from consumer goods import substitution has been exhausted and, as a result of a more liberal import policy in recent years, a negative substitution has actually taken place. Domestic demand is linked to an increase in income but the income growth rate is far lower than that of industrial production because of a slow agricultural development rate. Furthermore, part of the increase in income is eroded because of unfavorable external terms of trade. If one also adds the burden of debt servicing, we find that income available for expenditure grows at a rate only half that of industrial production.

Increase in oil output and in revenue yielded by the Suez Canal has raised the income growth rate in recent years; monetary transfers from Egyptians working abroad have constituted another income source. But such additional sources of income and, accordingly, expenditure, cannot strike a balance between supply and demand for domestically produced manufactured goods in domestic markets. To circumvent this problem, the government has resorted to such economic policies as price subsidies and wage increases at rates exceeding those of productivity. These are, however, provisional solutions. Both subsidy and wage policies are unbalanced and do not help to lower the costs of industrial production or to raise its efficiency to the extent of its becoming competitive on external markets. Furthermore, it has led to excess demand for other scarce commodities, particularly food, thus fuelling inflation. Such provisional solutions should therefore be replaced by more lasting measures, such as (a) the establishment of domestic capital goods industries to replace imports, thus opening new markets for local industries, and (b) an expansion in local production for exports.

In order to fulfill these two objectives, bases should be laid for a high efficiency national economic management, in particular within the context of the "open door" economic policy *(infitah)*. There is also a need for increased Arab economic cooperation.

This analysis corroborates our earlier statements and provides an analytical basis for the existence of a sound material foundation for Arab economic cooperation, and for a new regional Arab economic order. This material basis is provided by organic national balance requirements which can be secured only through cooperation among Arab states. These requirements include not only organized intra-Arab factor movement but also a need for coordinated regional commodity production and growth.

III. AN ARAB ECONOMIC STRATEGY: LONG-TERM PRESCRIPTIONS

The above diagnosis of Arab economic problems and of constraints upon Arab economic development lays the foundation for a long-term Arab economic development strategy. The analysis has indicated that regional and national objectives are similar and complementary. The components of the Arab regional strategy are therefore determined by the objectives of overall Arab economic balance and development, and the means whereby these objectives can be achieved.

Long-term economic balance calls first for a balance between labor productivity and costs and their respective growth rates. Secondly it calls for a balance between savings and investment and their respective growth rates, and thirdly for an organic balance between sectoral development rates, that is to say, a regionally consistent sectoral growth pattern. We shall outline below some overall policies likely to secure such balances. Note, however, that the remedies to be prescribed for each of the above-mentioned imbalances take into consideration the fact that these imbalances are not mutually exclusive; rather they are interdependent. Thus the direct and indirect effects of these prescriptions are designed in such a way as to be consistent with one another and with the overall development strategy for the region.

A. THE LABOR MARKET

We have indicated that in the light of the existing social organizations of the Arab states, their labor sectoral distribution, production technological levels, demographic growth rates, labor force and capital formation, there exists a gap between the supply and demand of labor, particularly of skilled labor. This gap will widen in the future unless a radical change occurs in economic policies at both the national and regional levels. The existing and growing shortages in the Arab national and regional balance between labor supply and demand has brought about rising wage levels that far exceed those of productivity, and has also affected industrial development and economic surplus. It must be noted here that labor shortages are not restricted to the rapidly growing oil and semi-oil Arab states, but that they actually constitute an overall characteristic of recent growth in the Arab economy. For example, even in traditionally labor-surplus states like Egypt, the country's recently accelerated growth (made partially possible through Arab aid) on the one hand and labor emigration to other Arab states on the other, have created labor shortages in a number of sectors as well as of skills.

In order to rectify this situation, the following long-term policies should be applied. The first should be an attempt to raise labor supply growth rate, taking into account demographic behavioral patterns and their eventual change. The second would be to ensure a rational labor redistribution among economic sectors, and third would be an attempt to raise labor productivity and economic efficiency directly by securing a higher average capital labor ratio (not only material capital but also non-material capital such as education, health . . . etc.) and, indirectly, by removing bottlenecks and securing a sound organization. The fourth would be to create an Arab labor market to facilitate labor distribution and its movement among Arab states.

At present, demographic growth in Arab states ranges between 2.5 percent and 3 percent per annum; these are high growth rates and are therefore not likely to be exceeded in the future. Death rates will probably drop as a result of higher income and better standards of living but in other states—particularly Egypt—birth rates will also drop because the end of the demographic explosion stage has been reached. Given the importance of the relative weight of the Egyptian population in relation to the overall Arab population (26 percent), the decrease in its demographic growth rate is expected to offset the possible demographic increase of some other Arab states.

Despite an average Arab population growth rate of 3 percent per annum, the labor force is expected to grow at a far higher rate due to a rising labor force participation rate. At present this rate varies between 15 percent and 25 percent in most Arab states, whereas it rises to over 60 percent in some developed nations. An increase in this rate will depend on the social and economic policies applied by Arab states. However, in the light of available historical and cross-sectional patterns, it is possible to foresee a labor force growth rate varying between 4 percent and 5 percent on the average. If we aim at a rate of growth of gross regional product of 6 percent to 7 percent per annum, this would require a rate of growth of capital formation of no less than 10 percent per annum, in real terms. This rate can be achieved only if a change is brought about in production methods and in the labor sectoral distribution pattern.

The main labor source in all Arab states is the agricultural sector which accounts for 50 percent to 90 percent of the total labor force. To create a labor surplus in the agricultural sector while trying to raise agricultural production both vertically and horizontally, there is a need for radical changes in agricultural methods: greater mechanization and modern techniques at all stages of agricultural production as well as in irrigation. Egypt has, in fact, started to follow such practices. It will not be possible to increase agricultural production in Sudan, Iraq, and Somalia—mainstays of agricultural expansion in the Arab world—without modernizing their agricultural techniques. But changing production techniques through capital-intensive means will require considerable investments, in addition to investments in land reclamation, in prospecting for water resources, and in irrigation and drainage networks. Improving agricultural production will therefore require an inflow of Arab investments in agriculture, particularly in those states with an agricultural surplus and a financial deficit such as the Sudan and Somalia.

One should, however, emphasize that there will be no inflow of Arab capital unless drastic measures are taken to put the organization of the agricultural sector in a form appropriate enough to entitle it to receive the requisite external capital and finance needed for its development. External capital is not invested in the agricultural sector because of the primitive management of family farms which yield neither a surplus nor profitable returns from the invested capital. If capital is to be attracted to the agricultural sector, its production should be reorganized, in particular regarding the management along corporate or cooperative lines of new and reclaimed lands. Whether the corporate capital is publicly, privately or jointly owned is immaterial here; the important thing is the fact that it would be capable of creating an after-wage surplus to pay for the borrowed capital.

Higher investments in the agricultural sector would not only increase labor productivity in agriculture and create a labor surplus in it, but would also raise the production growth rates of this sector which in most Arab states are under 1.5 percent per annum. A higher agricultural production and income are essential to generate an agricultural surplus whose volume will determine the size of rural demand for industrial goods and, hence, the size of the market for industrial goods. It will also increase food production, bringing about a drop in the region's dependence on food imports. There is also a need to raise labor productivity and to substitute capital for labor—wherever possible—in all economic sectors. A labor market is also essential to strike a balance between labor supply and demand, and to secure a national and sectoral Arab labor distribution with a view to regulating productivity. Rational relations should be maintained between the existing structures and patterns of growth on the one hand and those of inter-sectoral and cross-national productivity on the other.

To sum up: achieving an Arab regional balance between demand and supply of labor on one hand, and between the rates of growth of wages and productivity on the other, requires a great deal of intra-Arab capital movement. The flow of capital from the capital-rich Arab states to the capital-short ones would, at this stage, be mainly allocated to agricultural capacity, production, and farm surpluses. While this is in itself an objective, it would also indirectly serve other objectives, mainly industrial growth, food security and low living costs. Furthermore, and as far as labor supply for employment in sectors other than agriculture is concerned, intra-Arab capital movement must also go to substitute for labor in the traditional labor-intensive Arab agriculture. This would not only increase labor productivity and income in agriculture, but would also allow for the transfer of labor from agriculture to other sectors, thus gradually filling in the gap between labor supply and demand, whether at the national or at the regional level.

B. SAVINGS AND INVESTMENT

As previously stated, over two-thirds of regional Arab savings are invested outside the Arab world, a factor which greatly contributes to a disequilibrium, not only in the Arab economy but also in the world economy. According to neo-classical theory (as modified by Keynes), this disequilibrium can be adjusted as follows: surpluses in the balance of payments lead to an increase in monetary reserves, resulting in an increased money supply. This in turn lowers interest rates which, assuming a sustained capital productivity, brings about a rise in investment demand. The increase in investments and income in countries with surplus balance of payments leads to an increase in imports, thus eliminating the surplus in the external balance. This mechanism, which aims at restoring the external and internal balance, is complemented by the price mechanism.

However, Arab circumstances do not lend themselves to such a process. The increase in exports — particularly of oil — and in savings (mainly in the form of oil surpluses), was sudden and sharp. A balance between the rates of growth of exports and savings on one hand, and imports and investments on the other, cannot be struck in the short or even medium run. This is particularly so given the nature and size of the oil-rich surplus Arab states. In these states (as well as in the rest of the Arab region) the main impediment to a real and substantial increase in investment rates is the weak Arab absorptive capacity, which is determined by several factors, prominent among which is the capacity of the construction sector to increase its production and the prevailing infrastructure in the form of ports, roads, communications, utilities, etc. One can also mention the almost total lack of such soft infrastructure as financial markets and economic consulting and engineering firms which are needed for the evaluation and implementation of investment.

One can safely conclude, therefore, that rectifying the external imbalance between imports and exports on the one hand, and the internal imbalance on the other in most Arab states, is neither likely, nor even possible, in the short or medium run. While investment rates in the oil countries could be accelerated through the gradual elimination of either soft or hard infrastructural bottlenecks, their growth would still be considerably limited by the small size of their domestic markets. As for the oil-poor Arab states, infrastructural limitations and the lack of capital to finance their development constitutes the most binding constraint on growth.

Intra-Arab capital movement plays a pivotal role in achieving the internal and external balance of the Arab economy in the long run, as it would allow for the elimination of the capital constraint on the development of the non-oil countries. If this latter growth is coordinated with the oil countries' own patterns of growth, it would widen the market and allow for a faster growth of the oil countries themselves via a regionally integrated market. The rapid growth of both oil and non-oil countries would bring about the desired internal and external balance and, furthermore, this balance would take place *pari passu* with an accelerated development in the Arab region as a whole, rather than at its own expense. Needless to say, such an objective could be achieved only gradually and in the long term.

As for the relation between the Arab economy and the world economy, the former's accelerated development generates input demand from the latter which would, as mentioned earlier, act as an engine of growth for it. There would therefore be a consistency between the patterns of financial and commodity flows. So far, outflows of Arab financial surpluses to the world economy, unaccompanied by real growth, have proved to be inflationary. Accordingly, the balancing mechanism has been inflation and not growth. The balance of payments surpluses of the Arab oil countries, resulting from the initial price rises after the October War in 1973 had, by the end of 1977 and as a result of world-wide inflation, largely been exhausted. In the absence of real growth along the lines prescribed above, such a balancing mechanism will continue to function in the future. It must also be pointed out that capital movement would partially allow for the substitution of capital for labor, creating an exportable labor surplus and thus reinforcing labor movement and an accelerated Arab-wide growth and integration.

C. The Pattern of Growth

The above analysis has outlined the Arab development pattern which can best serve objectives of Arab economic balance and development. In this connection, a few comments are in order. First, the largest share of Arab capital flows will go to finance the agricultural and infrastructural sectors as well as urban development. The capital requirements of these sectors are extremely high. If the percentage of Arab urban-to-total population currently amounts to 25 percent — a low rate by international standards, given their income levels — and if population growth amounts to 3 percent per annum, then one should expect urban growth rates to exceed by far the rate of population growth. The exact rate of urban growth depends, of course, on a number of social and economic factors, particularly the rate of growth of arable land area and the agricultural product surplus. If we know that the incremental capital output ratio is over 20 for the infrastructural, housing and other overheads, we can imagine the sizeable investments needed to cater for the potential development of this sector: investments beyond the means of most non-oil Arab states.

Moreover, as regards the industrial sector, Arab economic cooperation should focus on implementing joint projects, widening the scope of the market, and increasing specialization within the region. This applies in particular to capital goods industries which, being practically non-existent in most Arab states, could easily be established on a regional rather than on a national Arab basis. Another important candidate, given its standardized nature, would be the construction materials and housing components industry.

The following Table outlines a long-term development pattern until the year 2000 on the basis of a simple simulation model to ensure macro and sectoral consistency. This development pattern puts in concrete form — in terms of figures — our prescribed Arab economic strategy.

As the Table indicates, real investment rises at double the rate of labor force growth which, in turn, doubles the capital/labor ratio. This pattern also secures a balance between savings and investments on the one hand and imports and exports on the other, thus realizing the objective of an internally as well as an externally balanced Arab economy. It also provides a pattern of sectoral growth which is consistent at both macro and structural levels. This development pattern secures an annual income increase of 6 percent. It is a reasonable rate but an ambitious objective too, since it means increasing investment absorptive capacity, and this calls for immediate and intensive efforts.

D. INCOME DISTRIBUTION

Finally one should point out that the above-prescribed patterns of growth and factor movements provide a number of mechanisms leading to a more equitable distribution of Arab regional income. The most important of these mechanisms is the intra-regional movement of factors of production — whether labor or capital — from surplus to deficit countries. This will lead to a rise in income in all Arab states, particularly in the

TABLE I
Regional Arab Product and Expenditure, 1975-2000
(at 1975 fixed prices: in $US million)

	1975	1980	1990	2000	Annual growth rate 1975 – 2000
Agriculture	12411	13502	17204	24268	2.7
Extracting industries	69842	88919	144440	213550	4.5
Oil	68571	87516	142554	211015	4.5
Others	1271	1403	1886	2535	
Manufacturing industries	10171	12981	25536	55129	6.8
Electricity & water	1194	1524	2998	6472	
Construction	7674	10270	22199	61687	8.3
Services	37009	51463	114035	277492	8.1
Trade	10017	14049	33260	86268	
Transport & communications	6890	9220	19906	47125	
Other services	20102	28194	60869	144099	
Gross Regional Domestic Product (at factor cost)	138301	178659	326412	638598	6.1
Net Current Transfers from Abroad	9181				
Total Consumption	73219	102693	214729	431115	7.1
private consumption	50812	71266	146881	275777	6.8
public consumption	22407	31427	67848	155338	7.7
Total Investment	26659	37391	90072	249242	8.9
Exports (goods & services)	84058	107282	174751	258674	4.5
Imports (goods & services)	44178	64912	140140	258674	7.1
Gross Regional Expenditure	139758	182454	339412	680357	6.3
Total Domestic Savings	66539	79761	124683	249242	5.3
Population	138	158	209	275	

	PERCENTAGES	
	1975	2000
Agriculture: Gross regional domestic product (at factor cost)	8.9	3.8
Oil: Gross regional domestic product (at factor cost)	49.6	33.0
Manufacturing industry: Gross regional domestic product (at factor cost)	7.4	8.6
Services: Gross regional domestic product (at factor cost)	26.8	43.5
Private consumption: Gross regional domestic product (at market price)	36.4	40.5
Public consumption: Gross regional domestic product (at market price)	16.0	22.8
Gross Investment: Gross regional domestic product (at market price)	19.1	36.6
Gross Savings: Gross regional product (at market price)	47.6	36.6

SOURCE: Data collected by the Council for Arab Economic Unity from official publications in various Arab states.

low-income, capital-short countries, in addition to increasing the productivity of capital and labor by assuring their complementary supplies. Needless to say, the rise in levels of employment and labor productivity in labor-surplus countries will contribute to the rise in income of those countries. However, these will not be the sole source of income increase in these countries. Another source will be in the form of transfers from the labor they have exported to the oil-rich countries.

Another important mechanism is the raising of investment rates in agriculture. Since, because of their low productivity, rural populations and labor traditionally represent the poorest brackets among Arab peoples, a greater emphasis on the agricultural sector, substantial agricultural investment and higher agricultural productivity would, *ipso facto,* lead to an improvement in income distribution, not only among Arab countries but also within each one of them. Moreover, absorption of surplus agricultural labor will certainly raise the average rural income.

Last but not least, a levelling of income distribution within and among Arab countries would not only represent an objective in itself, but would also have other indirect but positive effects. It would lead mainly to a widening of national and regional domestic markets, thus easing the domestic market size constraint on industrial growth.

IV. A REGIONAL ORGANIZATIONAL STRUCTURE

It would be a purely academic exercise to draw up an Arab economic strategy without determining the organizational framework within which it can be studied, highlighted and translated into well-defined short- and medium-term policies, and in due course implemented. Therefore the existing Arab organizational framework will be briefly described, and followed by proposals for specific modifications and additions that can turn this framework into a regional economic management system.

The nucleus of Arab economic management lies in the economic and sectoral organizations of the Arab League which, up till now, have adopted the development pattern of United Nations agencies and which at present have a similar structure. Although the development pattern of Arab organizations and the establishment of additional institutions along the same lines are positive assets for Arab joint action, and lay sound organizational foundations for the long-sought Arab economy, this structure should nevertheless be streamlined and turned into an economic management system. Present relations between Arab economic and sectoral organizations are mainly horizontal, and there is virtually no formal vertical relationship amongst them. In other words, they are not structured along hierarchical lines.

At the overall regional level, there is the Arab League's Economic and Social Council and the Council for Arab Economic Unity, apart from which there are also the Arab sectoral organizations such as the Agricultural Development Organization, the Industrial Development Center, the Arab Labor Organization . . . etc. Furthermore there are financial organizations such as the Arab Development Fund and the Arab Monetary Fund, among others. All these organizations have been established on a horizontal basis, and each operates in its own sphere of activity. But each one of them deals with only one organ of an inter-related regional economic body whose interlinked components should follow an organically balanced development pattern. Hence there is need for coordination among these organizations if they are to function harmoniously and to achieve a unified set of regional objectives.

Had there been a stable and efficient Arab regional price system at the country level of a sufficiently integrated character (at the national or regional levels), these could have functioned as a coordinating mechanism for the different Arab regional organizations. Each economic, sectoral or financial Arab organization could have determined its policies and strategies in the light of the existing regional or national Arab price systems, which reflect market scarcities and balances. But because of the current development level of the Arab states, their markets and price systems show structural imbalances and their market size does not allow for competitive prices. In most cases, for the reasons stated above and as a result of haphazard governmental intervention in market prices, Arab price systems are not in any way related to real economic scarcities.

Let us therefore not indulge in romantic reveries such as "pure economic freedom" and "laissez faire". Such systems exist only in textbooks, and Keynes said so forty years ago. The real competition in our contemporary world is among systems that are all centrally managed or directed in some fashion or another. For example, in countries like the United States, the economy is centrally directed through macro management; in socialist countries, the central control mechanism is that of national comprehensive planning. That is to say that competition exists between German, French, Japanese, American, Russian, Chinese and Indian economic systems with their different economic management and control mechanisms. Moreover, in recent years there has been a rising trend among Western countries to adopt indicative planning: France and Japan are examples, and even the United States is currently contemplating a similar move. The main reasons underlying such trends have been the rise of problems of a global nature, such as scarcities of energy, food and other raw materials and of environmental pollution.

The world market price system has not been able to cope satisfactorily with these problems. Perhaps the recently witnessed shifts in international prices of certain commodities and their consequential changes in external terms of trade and international income distribution are a living example of the above phenomenon.

Coordination among the Arab economic and sectoral organizations cannot be achieved through a planning mechanism either. None of the Arab countries has a meaningful, operational planning mechanism. This is mainly due to the total lack of the social organizations of modes of production and other types of material and non-material overheads needed for an effective national comprehensive planning mechanism. Most of the prevailing Arab plans for the 1980s are closer to being aspirations than objectives with specific means for their realization. Thus it is not practicable to rely on coordination of Arab plans to achieve a balanced regional Arab development; nor is it feasible to use Arab plan targets as guidelines on the basis of which the Arab League could draw up its sectoral policies and overall strategies. Such an approach would be unrealistic and of a very limited operational value. The Arab economies are, on the whole, governmment-administered, with basically short-term national objectives, and accordingly these are not amenable to regional coordination.

Hence, the best approach is gradually to turn the structure of Arab League organizations into a system for regional (rather than national) Arab economic orientation and management. This could be achieved by vertically structuring the various Arab League organizations to constitute a pyramidal hierarchical structure. One can perhaps go one step further by designing the links that would be needed between this regional organizational structure and its country counterparts, at both aggregate and component levels. However, the latter is not attempted here.

The prescribed regional hierarchical structure could be visualized as follows. There would be an Arab Summit Council at the top of the organizational structure, followed by general, then sectoral, organizations. The latter would prepare long-term alternative growth projections and strategies at the sectoral levels which would be submitted to the overall Arab organizations for coordination and consistency tests, thus resulting in an overall development strategy. This strategy would then be submitted to an economic summit for approval and directives. The overall sectoral organizations would then carry out the function of translating the strategy into programs and assigning roles. Such programs would then constitute a medium-term regional indicative plan (or program) which would serve as a guide to policy-makers at both national and regional levels. This is as far as an Arab economic management system is concerned, but there is also a need for a regional Arab business sector, independent of national business and government sectors. Joint Arab projects constitute the basic mechanism needed to expand this proposed regional Arab business sector.

Within the context of the organization proposed above, Arab sectoral organizations could identify feasible regional projects or country projects with regional dimensions, then prepare the relevant economic feasibility studies and submit such projects for financing to Arab financing organizations. A specific body would then be set up to supervise implementation and follow-up of projects that had been approved. Sectoral organizations could then act as holding or trust companies for these regional projects and, in this capacity, perform the function of coordinator amongst them.

According to the above design, the Arab regional business sector would be both owned and controlled regionally, and would in fact be a regionally integrated business sector forming an island in the larger pool of its country counterparts. However, it must be added here that to endow this regional business sector with structural flexibility to allow it to grow faster, it becomes imperative to establish a regional finanancial Arab market. Such a market could be used to finance this budding regional business sector and allow for a larger participation of Arab governments, businesses and individuals in its capital ownership.

This chapter has proposed a long-term Arab development model with specific characteristics that set it apart from prototypical theoretical models such as the classical and neo-classical types. The classical model envisages a development pattern based on low wages and labor costs with consequences for profit rates, factor income distribution and capital accumulation, whereas the neo-classical model is founded on equilibrium growth, the equilibrating and allocative mechanism being an efficient and flexible market price system. The proposed model is based on the premise of an imbalance between wages and productivity on the one hand and, on the other, between savings and investment, its balanced mechanism being Arab intra-regional factor movement. Here, sectoral balance is secured through regional indicative planning and orientation.

In fact, in putting the pieces together, the strategy outlined above—along with its complementary organizational structure—spells out the rudiments of a new Arab economic order. And, as we have attempted to show in this chapter, there is every reason to believe that this can be more than just an impossible dream.

NOTES

1. See the chapters by Saad Ibrahim and by Naiem Sherbiny and Ismail Serageldin in this volume.

2. Accordingly, one can safely say that Arab regional integration as envisaged in this paper and looked at from a dynamic perspective would be a "trade-creating" rather than a "trade diverting" one, if one may use Jacob Viner's static concept for evaluating types of integration normatively. Cf. e.g., J. Viner, *The Customs Union Issue* (Washington: A. Kramer, 1961).

3. See also the chapter by Nazih Ayubi in the present volume.

4. Figures throughout this chapter are based on data collected by the Council for Arab Economic Unity from official publications in various Arab states.

5. Of course, the encouragement of industrial growth prescribed here must be a balanced and economic process abiding by organic relations, dynamic comparative advantage and economic efficiency criteria, and must not overlook the dictates of such economic laws if it is not to be self-abortive.

6. See S. Kuznets, "Two Centuries of Economic Growth: Reflections on the United States' Experience", *The American Economic Review,* Vol. 67, no. 1 (February 1977) pp. 1–14.

V

Arab Capital and Trilateral Ventures in the Middle East: Is Three a Crowd?

Jeswald W. Salacuse

I. INTRODUCTION

The rise in oil prices during the last decade has enabled a few Arab states to accumulate large capital surpluses as a result of a dramatic increase in revenues and the limited absorptive capacity of their domestic economies.[1] At the same time, developing countries without petroleum resources have experienced severe shortages of investment funds and growing balance of payment deficits.[2] At the global level the specter of huge petrodollar surpluses on the one hand and staggering Third World debt on the other has evoked alarm at the impending collapse of the international monetary system and despair at the futility of attempting to alleviate the poverty of most of the world's population.

Within the Middle East itself, however, this co-existence of a great supply of and a great demand for capital within the same region has prompted a certain optimism in that it appears to offer significant potential for financing the development of the Arab world as a whole. And in fact, over the past ten years, a variety of mechanisms has emerged to facilitate the transfer of funds from the rich to the poor countries of the Middle East. The oil-producing countries have provided substantial direct aid on a bilateral basis to developing countries in general and to the Arab world in particular,[3] and they have created several specialized institutions to carry out this task. In addition, they have organized and participated in various multi-lateral mechanisms whose purpose is to channel surplus capital to the countries in need of investment funds. Yet

Author's Note: Material in this chapter has been drawn from a Ford Foundation-sponsored study by the author on "Arab Capital in the Development of Egypt and the Sudan." The views expressed herein are those of the author and are not to be attributed to any organization with which he has been affiliated.

another mechanism has been "petrodollar recycling", the process by which the major depositories of Arab surplus funds — private international banks — have lent significant amounts of their holdings to developing country governments and their public enterprises, among others, primarily through the "Eurodollar market".[4] Here the banks, rather than their Arab depositors, bear the risks of lending to developing countries; consequently the primary beneficiaries of petrodollar recycling through the Eurodollar market have been those countries such as Mexico and Argentina, whose development is relatively advanced, rather than those such as Egypt and the Sudan, which rank among the poorest and where the lending risks are presumably the greatest.[5]

Yet another proposed device for transferring capital from the rich to the poor is the "trilateral venture" which would unite Arab capital, Western technology, and local manpower and resources in productive enterprises within developing countries and particularly those located in the Middle East.[6] But while both direct OPEC aid and petrodollar cycling by banks have resulted in the transfer of relatively significant amounts of capital to developing countries, trilateral investment projects have been few and have yet to make an impact on the development of the Middle East. Proponents of the trilateral concept nonetheless assert that it represents a "non-zero-sum-game",[7] a means to achieve useful projects that neither Arab investor, Western firm, nor developing country government would be able or willing to undertake alone.

The effective mobilization of Arab capital for investment in the poor countries of the Middle East has been and will continue to be severely constrained by the absence within either rich or poor Arab states of sources of appropriate technology and of widespread managerial and financial skills. The industrialized countries of the West, as well as Japan, possess these attributes; consequently the trilateral investment project, it is argued, enables Arabs to obtain the know-how and management skills necessary for investment projects. Trilateralism would therefore appear crucial in any attempt to diversify their foreign holdings outside the West and to create enterprises capable of satisfying certain of their agricultural and industrial needs.

For Western firms, the trilateral concept offers the prospect in developing countries of increased sales of technology and expanded markets for their products without the political and financial risks inherent in a large direct investment. Moreover, through their association with Arab capital partners, they may also forge useful links to the lucrative markets and sources of finance on the Arabian Peninsula itself. And to the extent that trilateral projects result in purchases from Western countries and a reduction in Arab petrodollar surpluses, one could also expect Western governments to view them with favor.

For developing countries too, the trilateral venture would appear to be a desirable investment form since it permits them to acquire the necessary capital and technology without giving Western multi-national firms a large equity ownership interest which might threaten national sovereignty and generate internal political problems.

Despite the above-mentioned theoretical advantages, as well as significant efforts by Western firms and international banks to mobilize Arab funds for such ventures, the trilateral project has not become a reality as the model investment form in poor countries of the Middle East. While certain trilateral projects have indeed been organized, the great influx of Arab capital coupled with Western technology that was originally contemplated, has yet to come to pass. Indeed a review of the results of the past few years might lead the skeptic to conclude that in the art of joint venture, as in the art of love, two is company but three is a crowd.

The aim of this chapter is to explore the problems and prospects of trilateral ventures in the poor nations of the Middle East, particularly in Egypt and the Sudan, two countries which would appear especially suitable for investments of this type and in which Arab investors have shown special interest. With a combined population of some 60 million people, amounting to nearly one half of the Arab world, Egypt and the Sudan hold major political, economic and cultural attraction for the oil producers of the Arabian Peninsula. Indeed, until Egypt's peace treaty with Israel in 1979, these two countries had been the principal beneficiaries of Arab development and investment funds in the Middle East.

Analysis of the problems and prospects of trilateral ventures as a means to mobilize Arab funds for Egypt and the Sudan will focus on three fundamental dimensions—the conceptual and policy dimensions, the institutional dimensions, and the operational dimensions—and attention throughout will be devoted to the newly emerging Arab financial institutions upon which the success of the trilateral concept will ultimately depend.

II. THE CONCEPTUAL AND POLICY DIMENSIONS

A. GENERAL COMMENTS

Despite extensive discussion of the trilateral venture during the past few years, the underlying concept remains vague and highly abstract.[8] Advocates of the idea, for example, usually identify the parties in the most general fashion as "Arab capital", "Western technology sources" and "developing country partners", and few commentators have endeavoured to define concretely the nature of the relationship which is to exist among the participants in the venture. As a result of this vagueness, both as to parties and relationships, individuals interested in pursuing trilateral ventures have often tended to define the concept to fit their own particular needs — a factor which has often contributed to considerable disagreement accompanying attempts to organize specific investment projects.

For many Western firms, any project in a developing country to which they have supplied technology or know-how and which is financed by Arab capital is a trilateral project. According to this view, the construction by an American firm of an earth satellite communications system in the Sudan financed by a loan from the Arab Fund for Economic and Social Development would be a trilateral venture. For Arabs on the other hand, such a broad definition really leaves the concept empty of any significance. Since Arab countries have no technology of their own and must therefore seek it from non-Arab sources, primarily in the West or Japan, virtually any project financed with Arab capital in a developing country would qualify as a trilateral project.[9]

Rejecting such an approach, most Arab investors believe that a true trilateral venture requires the Western technology partner to have some continuing stake in the success of the venture and to be more than a supplier or contractor. In practical terms, this usually means that the technology partner must share risks and make some equity investment in the enterprise in addition to the management contract, licensing agreement or other arrangement by which it is paid for its know-how. If nothing else, such equity participation serves to give Arab partners confidence in the quality of the know-how being provided. On the whole, Western firms have been reluctant to venture their own funds and have taken the position that their prospective Arab financial partners should contribute virtually all of the capital. Disputes on this point have resulted in the abandonment of more than one proposed trilateral project.[10]

In view of the lack of a generally accepted operational definition of a trilateral venture, it may be useful to enquire into the nature and relevant policies of the three potential partners in interest to determine the extent to which the concept offers a realistic means of using Arab capital to develop the poor countries of the region, particularly Egypt and the Sudan.

B. ARAB CAPITAL

Its Nature

For all practical purposes, the sources of Arab capital available for significant investment in Egypt and Sudan are limited to just four countries: Saudi Arabia, Kuwait, the United Arab Emirates and Qatar.[11] With an estimated accumulated surplus of over $65 billion as of 1977, Saudi Arabia clearly dominates the entire group. Although all four states have devoted large amounts of their earnings to their own development, the absorptive capacity of their economies remains limited because of small populations, rudimentary infrastructure, lack of trained manpower, and inadequacy of financial and economic institutions.[12] In view of the difficulties in overcoming these constraints in the near future, the oil producers of the Arabian Peninsula will continue to accumulate surplus funds until well into the 1980s.[13]

Since it is the state rather than private individuals or institutions which is the recipient of oil revenues, the bulk of this surplus is controlled by Arab governments and public entities, such as the Saudi Arabian Monetary Authority and the Kuwaiti Ministry of Finance. With limited domestic investment prospects, the governments of the oil-producing states have tended to hold their surplus abroad — primarily in the United States, Europe and Japan[14] — in the form of safe, relatively liquid securities such as certificates of deposit and short-term government obligations.[15] Such holdings do not appear to constitute investments in the true sense of the word but rather a temporary "storing of value" until such time as the Arab governments have determined a more permanent use for their surplus funds. On the other hand there is evidence that Arab funds held abroad are gradually and cautiously moving into equity securities and obligations of a more long-term nature.[16] The significance of this fact is, of course, that a reduction in liquidity may adversely affect the availability of such funds for investment in the poor countries of the Middle East.[17]

Despite the overwhelming amount of surplus capital controlled by Arab governments and public institutions, private Arab capital is nonetheless also a potentially significant source of finance for trilateral investments. Unfortunately one finds little reliable information on its nature, amount and form.[18] Moreover, it is often difficult to delineate clearly between public and private sources of capital. In Kuwait, for example, the primary "private investment company" with interests in Africa and the developing world is the Kuwait Foreign Trading Contracting and Investment Company, 80 percent of whose shares are owned by the Kuwaiti government. Generally speaking, private capital in the Arabian Peninsula appears to be held largely by three groups: members of ruling families; merchants who have amassed large sums of money as agents for foreign firms; and (to a lesser extent) selected government officials. Here too, one must rely on conjecture and anecdotes for information.

In considering the size and nature of the pool of Arab capital potentially available for investment in Egypt, the Sudan and the other poor countries of the region, one should also take into account the funds held "off-shore" in foreign banks by the nationals of those countries who have worked or who are now working in the Arabian Peninsula. For example, since approximately 1.2 million Egyptians alone were residing in the oil states as of 1978, bankers in Cairo estimated that the total amount of funds held off-shore by such individuals was between $1.5 billion and $3 billion.[19]

On the basis of the foregoing, it can be seen that Arab capital as a potential source of investment finance differs in several respects from capital originating in the West. Whereas Western capital is controlled primarily by numerous privately-owned multi-national companies and institutions based in a variety of countries, Arab capital is highly concentrated in a few Arab countries (primarily Saudi Arabia, Kuwait and the United Arab Emirates), is controlled for the most part by governments and public institutions, and is held abroad in liquid form. While privately-held Arab funds may also constitute a potentially important source of finance, their mobilization for investment in the poor countries, as will be seen, raises special problems. Moreover, all Arab capital, whether public or private, is generally not accompanied by the technology, management systems, and access to world markets that characterize the usual Western investment in a developing country. Indeed, due to the lack of financial and technical skills within the Arabian Peninsula, the oil-producing countries are dependent, in varying degrees, on foreign individuals and institutions in the management and investment of their funds.[20] It was the absence of technology and know-how, of course, which gave rise to the very idea of trilateralism whereby Western firms would supply this vital ingredient.

An appraisal of Egyptian and Sudanese prospects for attracting a portion of this surplus capital to finance their development leads one to examine the investment motivations and policies of the oil states towards the poor countries of the region. Indeed, in view of the special political and economic risks inherent in an investment in either Egypt or the Sudan, why should managers of the Arab funds consider these two countries at all?

Investment Motivations and Policies

Various motivations — economic, political, cultural, humanitarian and religious — condition the use of surplus capital by the governments and citizens of the oil states. The factors influencing investment choices differ, of course, from country to country, and indeed from person to person. Nonetheless, one can discern certain common trends and policies throughout the Arabian Peninsula.[21]

The governments of the oil states quite naturally give first priority in the use of surplus funds to the development of their own domestic economies. In this context "development" means above all lessening their dependence on oil as a source of wealth and replacing this dwindling asset with stable, income-producing investments. Throughout the Arabian Peninsula, government officials and private financiers alike, afflicted with what one informant has called a "last-drop-of-oil mentality", are acutely conscious of the need to find economic alternatives to petroleum. While this attitude varies in intensity from Kuwait where the foreseeable end of oil makes it acute, to Saudi Arabia where extensive reserves render it less stringent, it nevertheless conditions the investment policies of all the oil-producing states. Above all, it argues strongly for stable investments and places a high priority on conservation of the value of the capital.

Recognizing that their small population and limited resource bases may never absorb their surplus entirely or offer domestic investments fully capable of replacing revenues derived from oil, the surplus states are forced to look outside their borders to find other uses for their funds. With respect to investments abroad, the declared policy of their governments is to give priority to other Arab countries and then to the developing world generally.[22] Until they are able to identify and develop productive long-term investments, the oil producers have chosen to hold the bulk of their surplus in the currencies and short-term obligations of Western countries; however, this method of storing value has proved to be less than satisfactory due to substantial losses in purchasing power resulting from inflation and monetary devaluation.[23]

While a shift to longer-term investments in the West may be one way of confronting the monetary risks — a trend which seems to be developing in fact — Arab governments are at the same time aware that such a course also has its risks, since dependence on the West as a place of investment makes them vulnerable to Western political pressure, a point that was underlined by the American freezing of Iranian assets in the United States in 1979. Nor are they comfortable with their reliance on Western countries as a source of food and manufactured goods. As net importers of food and without an agricultural base to speak of, they are becoming increasingly sensitive to what they choose to call their "food security problem", which renders them vulnerable to increases in commodity prices and Western political influence.[24]

The desire to diversify their investments geographically and to develop alternative, close sources of food and manufactured goods is a strong motivation to invest a portion of their surplus capital in the Arab world and in other non-Western countries. In this respect, of course, the Sudan with its great agricultural potential and Egypt with its industrial base and large pool of skilled manpower constitute near and potentially attractive sites for investment. A further economic motivation for such investments is that Egypt and the Sudan may in turn become major markets for products — such as petrochemicals and fertilizers — which the oil states hope one day to supply.

The above-mentioned factors, of course, are those that primarily motivate governments, rather than private capitalists, in making investment decisions. Nonetheless, a link would appear to exist between Arab governmental aid and investment, which has tended to emphasize infrastructure in Egypt and Sudan, and commercial investments to be undertaken by private Arab capital, since construction of highways, power plants and other infrastructure elements serves to pave the way for and create a climate conducive to private commercial investments.

Both with respect to investment in and aid to the deficit states, an overriding consideration is monetary stability and protection of capital against the ravages of inflation and monetary devaluation. Private Arab capital has, as a result, tended to concentrate heavily in real estate development and projects such as hotels, where land is a major component. And the fact that various development funds denominate their loans in their own currencies, rather than in dollars, is not merely an expression of national sovereignty, but also a means to protect the value of the debt against erosion by inflation and monetary fluctuation.[25]

On at least one occasion, the drive for investment stability encountered opposition in a host country and resulted in the abandonment of a large project. In 1976 the Kuwait Real Estate Investment Consortium, a syndicate financed by both public and private Kuwaiti capital and enjoying a virtual monopoly over Kuwaiti real estate investments in the Arab world, made an agreement with the Sudanese government to purchase in freehold a plot of prime Nile-front land in which the Consortium committed itself to invest approximately $100 million. The Sudanese People's Assembly refused, however, to approve the agreement on the grounds that while the grant of a freehold interest in Sudanese land to a foreigner was not specifically illegal, it was against established public policy. The best interest which a foreigner might obtain in Sudanese land was a longterm leasehold. When renegotiation of the agreement took place, the Kuwaitis, motivated by a desire for stable, sure investments, insisted upon freehold ownership of the land in question and ultimately withdrew from discussions when the Sudanese refused to yield on the point.

Political considerations also motivate the transfer and investment of Arab funds to the less fortunate countries of the region. Since the surplus states have small populations and little military power, they seek to achieve diplomatic strength and to preserve their independence by securing the goodwill of other countries of the region through the use of surplus funds. Kuwait, of course, has represented the clearest example of this tendency. In order to counter Iraq's threat to its sovereignty, Kuwait, with a population of less than one million persons, has employed its surplus capital liberally through aid and investment to gain the support of the other countries in the region and thereby to legitimize its existence as an independent state.[26] With this end in mind, the Kuwait government in 1961, a few months after attaining independence, established the Kuwait Fund for Arab Economic Development, which was to become a model to other oil states of a regional development bank offering concessional loans to finance the development projects of the region's deficit states.

Governed by conservative regimes, the oil states of the Arabian Peninsula have a major interest in increasing the political stability of the Middle East, and they have shown a disposition to finance endeavors that will contribute to the economic development and integration of the region and to the reduction of tensions caused by great disparities in wealth within the Arab world. At the same time, in the name of Arab and Islamic solidarity, they have strongly supported the confrontation states—Egypt, Syria and Jordan—in their conflict with Israel, and have provided them with mammoth amounts of aid for military purposes, the single most important form of inter-Arab capital transfer to date.

The fact that the surplus and deficit states share a common religion, culture and language also to some extent encourages Arab aid to and investment in Egypt and the Sudan. Throughout the Arabian Peninsula one encounters the belief that the more fortunate members of the Islamic community have an obligation to help the less fortunate, and that it is natural to employ surplus funds for this purpose. Moreover, certain quarters advance the notion that Arab surplus capital should be used to establish a new economic order based on Islamic principles, including the Shari'a's prohibition on *riba* or the taking of interest. The clearest expression of this tendency was the creation in 1974 of the Islamic Development Bank in Jeddah and more recently, at the local level, the spread of private Islamic banks, such as the Faisal Islamic Bank, recently established in Egypt and the Sudan under the auspices of the son of the late King Faisal of Saudi Arabia.

A history of human contact and interaction between the people of the Arabian Peninsula on the one hand and the people of Egypt and the Sudan on the other has also contributed towards a certain predisposition on the part of the surplus states to devote a portion of their capital to aid and investment on the other side of the Red Sea. Numerous Saudi and Kuwaiti officials and businessmen have received their education in

Egypt, have resided in Cairo and have married Egyptians. Then too, over a million Egyptians and Sudanese are now living in the countries of the Arabian Peninsula. Because of this contact, Arab investors have a certain familiarity with prevailing conditions in Egypt and the Sudan, and many believe that they will enjoy greater receptivity there than they would in the West where the idea of "Arab investment" has engendered public hostility.

The relative weight which each of the above-mentioned factors has in effecting a given capital transfer varies from case to case. As will be seen in the sections which follow, one cannot assume that economic motivations always prevail in investment decisions, nor that political and cultural factors invariably determine the provision of aid.

The Nature of Past Arab Capital Transfers to Egypt and the Sudan

Prior to the 1973 oil price rise, most inter-Arab capital transfers consisted of aid under the 1967 Khartoum Agreement by which Saudi Arabia, Kuwait and Libya made balance of payments grants to Egypt, Syria and Jordan to assist them in their struggle with Israel. These payments amounted to approximately $400 million a year during the period from 1970 to 1973. On the other hand, assistance for economic development, provided mainly by Kuwait, was considerably less and ranged between $40 million and $50 million annually during the same period.[27] At that time, the oil states, with the exception of Kuwait, enjoyed little surplus capital, but a number of other factors also served to constrain inter-Arab capital flows to the deficit states of the region. They included the unstable political climate and hostility to foreign capital prevailing in certain capital-deficit states, the dearth of information on investment prospects in such countries, the inexperience and conservatism of many Arab investors, and the lack of a suitable institutional and legal framework for facilitating and channelling inter-Arab investments and capital flows.

Since 1973 this situation has begun to change markedly, as increasing though still relatively small amounts of Arab capital have found their way to Egypt and the Sudan. The nature and form of such capital transfers have demonstrated a significant degree of diversity; consequently, at this point, it may be useful to categorize them.

One can divide capital transfers between the Arabian Peninsula on the one hand and Egypt and the Sudan on the other into two basic groups—direct transfers and indirect transfers. Each group contains a number of sub-categories.

a. *Direct Capital Transfers.* Direct capital transfers are those which emanate from a particular oil-producing state and flow directly to Egypt or the Sudan. They include:

i. Grants for Military Purposes. While hard data on this type of transfer is naturally difficult to obtain, aid to assist the front-line states in their struggle with Israel appears to constitute the single largest type of inter-Arab capital flow. One study[28] estimates that between 1973 and 1975 total assistance for military purposes amounted to approximately $1.248 billion. Egypt has been the primary beneficiary of such aid. The Sudan, which is not a front-line state, has received relatively little of this type of assistance, except for the occasional equipment grant, such as the one made by Saudi Arabia in 1977 to finance the purchase of six C-130 aircraft at an estimated cost of $65 million.

ii. Official Development Assistance. "Official development assistance", as that term is defined by the OECD, refers to "flows from the official sector that are concessional in nature—grants, and loans with a grant element of at least 25% — and which are undertaken primarily for the purpose of assisting development."[29] According to information gathered by the OECD,[30] total official *bilateral* development assistance from Saudi Arabia, Kuwait, the United Arab Emirates and Qatar to Egypt and the Sudan from 1973 to 1975 amounted to $1665.26 million. In both Egypt and the Sudan disbursements have generally lagged far behind the level of commitments. For example, with respect to Egypt, out of the total soft loan commitments by the various Arab development funds of $695 million as of 31 October 1977, only $275 million had actually been disbursed.[31] While the wide discrepancy between commitments and disbursements may lead certain observers to raise questions about the quality or firmness of Arab aid, in reality the slowness in disbursing funds is due primarily to bottlenecks and constraints *within* the recipient country in the planning and execution of development projects. For purposes of comparison, it is worth noting that out of a total loan commitment of $967 million by the World Bank to Egypt as of October 1977, only $239 million had actually been spent.[32]

Official development assistance takes a variety of forms and may include the following:

- Cash grants for budgetary support, balance of payments assistance, and relief in cases of emergency such as the resettlement of refugees in southern Sudan. Usually these transfers are arranged at the very highest levels of government, often between heads of state, and generally little information is available on them. At present, the surplus states demonstrate a strong tendency to shift their aid away from general support grants towards concessional loans for specific projects.
- Concessional loans without interest or at interest rates significantly below market levels for balance of payments support or general program purposes. Similar to these are bank deposits at

little or no interest by an oil state with the central bank of a deficit state, thereby providing balance of payments support. For example, in 1976 the Saudi Arabian Monetary Authority afforded such support to the Sudan by depositing $150 million with the Bank of Sudan at 5 percent interest.

*   Project loans at concessional rates of interest. An increasingly prevalent type of developmental assistance between Arab countries is the "soft loan" to finance a specific project such as a road, power plant or agricultural scheme. Unlike cash grants and general budgetary support which are often concluded on an *ad hoc* personalized basis, project loans represent an institutionalized form of assistance and are usually accomplished through the development fund of the donor country. Unlike similar loans from the industrialized countries, Arab concessional loans are not generally tied to any particular source of procurement.

iii. Non-concessional Financing with Public Capital. In addition to development assistance of the traditional variety, the oil states, through government departments, central banks, and government-controlled companies, have provided financing to Egypt and the Sudan on a more or less commercial basis during the past few years. Such capital transfers have included loans at prevailing rates of interest (such as the loan of KD. 2.5 million at 9 percent to the Sudan by the Kuwait Foreign Trading, Contracting and Investment Company to finance the purchase of Boeing 737's for Sudan Airways); deposits with banks of the deficit states at prevailing interest rates (such as the deposit by Kuwait of KD. 6.82 million at 7 percent annual interest with the Bank of Sudan); and equity investments in specific enterprises (such as the SUMED Pipeline Project in Egypt or the Kenana Sugar Company in the Sudan).

Precise figures on the nature and magnitude of such capital flows are fragmentary and hard to verify. Moreover, it is sometimes difficult to determine whether such financings are to be considered public or private. According to estimates by the OECD, commitments of bilateral, non-concessional public capital to Egypt and the Sudan during the period from 1973 to 1975 amounted to approximately $2880.26 million.

iv. Private Financing and Equity Investments. While the bulk of capital transfers to Egypt and the Sudan have been public in origin, private capital has also financed certain investment projects of a commercial nature. Such financings take the form of both debt and equity investments in projects, although precise figures on their nature and magnitude are not available.

v. Remittances by Egyptian and Sudanese Nationals Working in the Arabian Peninsula. The numerous Egyptian and Sudanese nationals working in the Arabian Peninsula have accumulated a sizeable pool of capital. In 1978 private bankers in Cairo estimated that this pool of funds, exclusive of remittances, held offshore by Egyptians probably approximated three billion dollars. Through such devices as special incentive exchange rates for nationals, the governments of Egypt and the Sudan have encouraged the remittance of a portion of these funds, some of which has been invested in real estate and small businesses in the home countries. The remainder of such capital remains offshore; however, a few banks offering foreign currency accounts, such as Cairo Barclays International, have devoted a portion of these funds to finance projects within Egypt itself. In addition public offerings of securities in particular projects, such as one conducted by the Misr-Iran Development Bank for a Cairo hotel, have also tapped a portion of this pool of savings.

b. *Indirect Capital Transfers.* Indirect capital transfers are those which do not proceed directly from a surplus state to a deficit state, but instead pass to or through some intermediate institution before reaching the capital-importing country. Here too one can identify several different forms, including the following:

i. *Capital Transfers to Multi-Lateral Development Assistance Organizations.* The surplus states have made sizeable capital contributions to multi-lateral institutions which in turn provide soft loans and technical assistance for developmental purposes to the deficit states. These institutions may have a world-wide scope of activities, such as the United Nations or the International Development Association, or they may have a more limited mandate such as the Arab Fund for Economic and Social Development or the Islamic Development Bank. For example, according to the OECD[33] disbursements by Saudi Arabia, Kuwait, the United Arab Emirates and Qatar to the Arab Fund and to the Islamic Development Bank — the two principal multilateral institutions benefitting Egypt and the Sudan — amounted to $136 million in 1975.

ii. *Equity Investments in Inter-Arab Enterprises and Joint Ventures.* Within the past few years, the Arab world has witnessed the appearance of numerous multi-lateral institutions and joint ventures, often created by international treaty, to undertake certain operations, investments, and activities on a commercial basis. They, in turn, have financed specific projects in Egypt and the Sudan. Deriving their capital from the sale of shares to individual Arab states, these institutions include the Arab Investment Company, the Arab Authority for Agricultural Investment and Development, the Arab Mining Company, and the Arab Company for the Development of Animal Resources.

iii. *Loans, Deposits and Investments in Private Institutions Based in Third Countries.* The surplus states have transferred significant amounts of capital, in the form of deposits, loans, or equity investments to private institutions in third countries. In certain instances, these institutions, often through the Eurodollar market, have financed projects in Egypt and the Sudan. The Union des Banques Arabes et Françaises (UBAF) and the Banque Arabe et Internationale des Investissements (BAII), both based in Paris, are examples of such institutions in which Arabs also have a substantial interest.

iv. Loan Guarantees Issued to Non-Arab Lenders. Increased financial flows to Egypt and the Sudan have also resulted from the issuance of guarantees by Arab governments or financial institutions to induce Western intermediaries to make loans to deficit states. In 1974, for example, the Sudanese government, with the aid of a guarantee from the Saudi Arabian Monetary Authority, was able to borrow $200 million on the Eurodollar market to establish the capital of the Sudan Development Corporation, a sum which the Sudan had no hope of obtaining by itself. Similarly in 1977, the Gulf Organization for the Development of Egypt (GODE), a creation of four oil states, guaranteed a loan of $250 million to Egypt by a syndicate of Western and Japanese banks.

The foregoing would seem to indicate that the Arab oil states, for a variety of reasons in their own self-interest, have demonstrated a certain disposition to devote a portion of their surplus funds to finance the development of Egypt and the Sudan. Motivated in large part by political considerations and controlled primarily by governments, such financial flows have shown themselves to be extremely sensitive to the political vagaries of the Middle East, a phenomenon most recently illustrated by the cutting off of Arab assistance to Egypt, and its expulsion from most Arab financial organizations as a result of its peace treaty with Israel.[34]

C. THE POLICIES OF EGYPT AND THE SUDAN

The policies of Egypt and the Sudan towards Arab capital and trilateral investments are also important factors affecting their ability to mobilize Arab funds for their own development. Policies of both countries towards Arab capital, with or without Western technology, have been shaped by a variety of factors including their domestic economic situations, prevailing attitudes of officials, past experience with foreign investment as well as the shifting political dynamics of the Middle East itself.

Both suffer from extensive poverty and neither is able at the present time to generate internally the resources necessary to finance development. They have therefore chosen to seek the necessary investment capital from abroad. For example, the Sudan's Six Year Plan, adopted in June 1977, calls for a total investment of $6.5 billion and assumes that 52 percent of that amount will be obtained from external sources. At the same time, both countries suffer from acute balance of payments deficits, staggering foreign indebtedness, and severe shortages of foreign exchange—factors which seriously inhibit their ability to secure the necessary funds on the international capital markets and from Western financial institutions. As a result, for both Egypt and the Sudan the capital surplus of the Arabian Peninsula has been a critically important source of finance, one which many of their officials have tended to assume would be available in greater quantity and on easier terms than would capital from Western financial institutions or governments.

Officials in the capital-deficit states appear to have based their expectations of significant Arab capital flows upon a variety of considerations. First, in the case of Egypt, the fact that it had borne the brunt of the conflict with Israel on behalf of all the Arab states had given it reason to expect that the wealthy Arab states, having been spared the military role, would compensate it for the loss of resources and retardation of development due to the war which Egypt waged on their behalf.

Secondly, sentiments of Arabism and of those arising out of a shared culture and religion have led both countries to consider Arab capital as somehow less foreign than that emanating from the West. This idea is expressed quite clearly in various Egyptian policy statements and laws which refer to "Arab *and* foreign capital". The implications flowing from such designations are not precisely defined but it may reflect a view that Arab capital is less dangerous than foreign capital and ought to be treated as domestic investment. Then too, Arab investment in Egypt and the Sudan is seen as contributing to regional integration, one of the goals of Arab solidarity.

Both capital-deficit countries have received assistance from the Arabian Peninsula on generous terms in the past—a factor which gives them reason to believe that Arab aid will increase and commercial investment will come in large quantities and on favorable terms now that Arab financial surpluses have grown so dramatically. While both Egypt and the Sudan have shown hostility to foreign capital in the recent past and, indeed, have effected sweeping nationalizations, they now demonstrate greater receptivity to foreign and particularly Arab investments. In this connection, some individuals have argued that Arab capital is different from other foreign capital and that it presents fewer dangers to national sovereignty and the domestic political order, since it emanates from small, militarily weak countries and is not generally associated with large multi-national enterprises.

While the realities of this argument remain to be tested, it is worth asking at this point whether a large Arab investment, regardless of the small size of its country of origin, is nonetheless capable of generating in a developing country the same kind of influence and power relationships for which large Western investors are criticized. Moreover, it should also be pointed out that Arab capital will be required to form associations with large multi-national enterprises in order to obtain the necessary technology, management skills and access to world markets. Regardless of the foregoing, it does appear that officials in Egypt and the Sudan generally see less to fear from Arab investments than from those coming from the West.

On the other hand, sentiments of Arab solidarity occasionally lead the deficit states to expect greater generosity from Arab financial institutions than they would from comparable Western organizations.

The case of the Arab Fund loan of 10 million Kuwaiti Dinars ($35 million) in 1977 to finance the extension of Egypt's Kafr al-Dawwar textile mill is perhaps illustrative in this respect.[35] The loan agreement provided for 4 percent interest and also imposed certain conditions concerning financial management. One would have thought that such a loan at concessional rates of interest would have been readily accepted; however, when the agreement reached the Egyptian People's Assembly for approval, a vigorous debate ensued and several members urged that it be rejected on the grounds that "there should be no interest between brothers" and that the imposed conditions constituted a violation of Egyptian national sovereignty. In the end, the People's Assembly approved the loan but the debate reflected a certain sentiment that the terms of Arab capital flows were more severe than was expected.

Sentiments and attitudes such as those indicated above do not, of course, constitute policy although they may have an important role in shaping it. Formal statements of policy on the question of trilateral investments and Arab capital are to be found primarily in the foreign investment legislation and international agreements of the two countries concerned.

Investment Legislation

Coincidental with the growth of Arab capital surplus has been the adoption by both Egypt and the Sudan of investment promotion laws which, by offering incentives and guarantees, have sought to attract Arab capital specifically or foreign investment in general. For both, such new measures represented a marked departure from earlier policies that had limited private and foreign capital and had stressed the development of government planning and public sector enterprises.

Beginning in 1971, Egypt tentatively and somewhat hesitantly took a step in this direction with the adoption of Law No. 65 concerning the Investment of Arab Funds and the Free Zones.[36] As its title indicates, the law generally favored Arab investment over other forms of foreign capital and in addition specifically reserved to Arab capital alone the area of real estate investment, a field to which Arabs are particularly attracted but one not normally stressed in the usual investment promotion laws of most developing countries. Eventually Egypt would formulate a generalized policy of *infitah*; this policy was to open the door to all foreign investors, Arab and non-Arab alike, replacing Law No. 65 for 1971 with Law No. 43 for 1974[37] (itself subsequently revised by Law No. 32 for 1977)[38] as the legal framework for the policy.[39] One factor among many which may have contributed to this result was the recognition that virtually any Arab investment project in Egypt would require the participation of a non-Arab technology partner. Nonetheless, Arab investors continued to have a special advantage in housing projects.[40]

To induce Arab and foreign capital to enter the country, Egyptian legislation, like that of other developing nations, offered certain guarantees and incentives such as tax holidays. In addition, however, it exempted approved projects from various restrictive laws and regulations designed to control such matters as foreign exchange, labor relations and internal corporate management. In short, one of the effects of the investment promotion law was to release to private economic ordering various matters which until then had been within the exclusive domain of goverment control. Like the capitulations of old, the laws created legal enclaves of special rights and privileges for approved investment projects.[41]

The Sudan followed a pattern similar to that of Egypt. After undertaking a sweeping series of nationalizations in 1970 that failed to produce desired results, the Sudanese government also began to formulate a policy of attracting foreign investment. Accordingly it enacted the Organization of Investment in Economic Services Act in 1973, revised its existing industrial investment law in 1974, and passed the Development and Encouragement of Agricultural Investment Act in 1976, thus giving the country three separate investment promotion laws administered by three separate ministries.[42] While none of this legislation gave a special place to Arab capital as the Egyptian law had purported to do, there seems little doubt that after 1972 the accumulating pool of capital on the other side of the Red Sea was an important factor in shaping Sudanese policy and legislation on foreign investment. For example, in view of the Sudan's expressed goal of becoming "the breadbasket of the Middle East" and the oil-producers' need for a close and reliable source of food, the Sudanese Agricultural Investment Act of 1976 can be seen as aimed especially at Arab investors.

International Agreements

Egypt and the Sudan, as members of the Arab world, have over the years entered into a series of bilateral and multi-lateral agreements with various oil-producing states to facilitate investment and the transfer of capital. Beginning as early as 1973, such agreements contained little more than general statements by the deficit states of a desire to receive Arab investments as well as willingness to grant them vaguely defined privileges. Without provision for enforcement mechanisms and by virtue of their vague terms and numerous escape clauses, these agreements did not really set down any definite policy on investment in either country, and as a result did little to foster inter-Arab capital flows.

One treaty worthy of note, however, is the Agreement on the Investment and Movement of Capital Among the Arab States,[43] a multi-lateral convention concluded in 1970 to which Egypt, the Sudan, and Kuwait are parties, and which attempts to set down certain basic principles governing inter-Arab investments.

The Agreement recognizes "Arab investments" and "Arab capital" as distinct from other forms of foreign capital and investment and sets down the basic principle that Arab investments are to receive priority in treatment. In addition to granting Arab investors the right to repatriate capital and profits and to reside in the country in which the investment is made, it provides that the host country shall offer Arab investments the same treatment as domestic investments without discrimination and shall offer them a treatment not less advantageous than that granted to foreign investments.

The Agreement's provisions on protection against nationalization have experienced an interesting evolution. Originally Article VI recognized the right of the host country to nationalize an investment on grounds of public interest, provided that adequate, effective and prompt compensation was made. In December 1973, however, in an effort to implement a resolution of the Sixth Arab Summit Conference, it was amended to prohibit altogether nationalizations of most Arab investments:

> The host states shall be bound not to nationalize or confiscate Arab investments made in their territories at their request or in the fields open to Arab investments in accordance with the basis set out in Article III of this Agreement.

At first glance the terms of the Agreement would appear to run counter to the current ambivalence and sometimes hostile attitude of many developing countries towards foreign investments, particularly as expressed in such documents as the Charter of Economic Rights and

Duties of States, adopted by the United Nations General Assembly in December 1974 at the insistence of its Third World members.

The Agreement on the Investment and the Movement of Capital Among Arab States, however, provides no mechanism for enforcement of its rules on investment, nor does it lay down sanctions for violation or non-compliance. Instead, the member states, bearing in mind the principles of the Agreement, are each to devise the special rules governing Arab investments and then communicate them to other Arab states as well as to the General Secretariat of the Council of Arab Economic Unity. Such communication is deemed, for purposes of the above-quoted Article on nationalization, a request for investments.

Despite its lack of enforcement provisions, the Agreement may reflect an emerging consensus by the capital-deficit Arab states, such as Egypt and the Sudan, on the special status and privileges of Arab investments. While these principles do not yet form a definite inter-Arab investment code they constitute an important part of the framework within which the new Arab financial investment institutions are operating. Indeed, the charters establishing many inter-Arab institutions, such as the Arab Authority for Agricultural Investment and Development, specifically incorporated many of the principles enunciated by the Agreement.

Individually Egypt and the Sudan have also indicated their willingness to receive Arab capital by concluding with specific oil states various bilateral and multi-lateral agreements whose purpose is to undertake investments within their territories. Here one may cite agreements setting up the Kuwaiti-Egyptian Investment Company, the Sudanese-Kuwaiti Investment Company, the United Arab Emirates-Sudan Investment Company, and the Arab Authority for Agricultural Investment and Development.

Since the capital-surplus states do not themselves possess the technology and know-how necessary to undertake specific investment projects, both Egypt and the Sudan recognize that Arab investments, to be productive, must have some association with non-Arab sources of technology and that in most instances Western or Japanese companies will supply these elements. Thus, implicitly, the trilateral project would appear to be contemplated as a model form of investment, although the term itself is nowhere specifically mentioned in either legislation or international treaties.

Despite declarations of policy in laws and treaties, Egypt and the Sudan have not thrown the door open wide to any and all projects originating from the Arabian Peninsula. Both countries have established procedures requiring approval by a governmental agency before an investment may actually be undertaken. Nor do they appear to apply different standards or methods of evaluation to projects which include Arab capital than to those which do not. Indeed, instances have occurred when a host country, in an effort to protect what it considered legitimate national interests, became embroiled in severe conflict with a prospective source of Arab finance. Sometimes the reason for the problem was that the deficit states expected easier terms from Arab capital institutions than from those outside the region. Conversely, Arab investors sometimes expect to receive better treatment than would be accorded to investors from the West. In either event disappointed expectations may make agreement on investment proposals difficult.

The types of investments favored by Arabs may also tend to generate conflict with host country governments. On the one hand, the drive for investment stability and protection of capital against inflation and monetary devaluation has led Arabs to concentrate heavily in real estate development and projects where land is a major component. On the other hand, deficit countries with a heightened desire to preserve sovereignty over their land and natural resources felt a growing need to regulate strictly the entry by foreign investors, Arab or otherwise, into this domain of economic activity. In Egypt, for example, urban land has become a major attraction for Arab investors. As a result, the price of real estate and the cost of housing have increased phenomenally, leading to much discontent among Egyptians, some of whom are beginning to question the wisdom of having opened Egypt to Arab capital in the first place. As indicated above, the Sudan also entered into conflict with Arab investors in the negotiations relating to the attempted acquisition by the Kuwait Real Estate Investment Consortium of a freehold interest in land in Khartoum.

D. POLICIES OF NON-ARAB PARTICIPANTS

Generalizations about the policies and attitudes of Western and Japanese firms towards trilateral ventures are extremely difficult to make due to the great diversity of such firms and their differing approaches to foreign investment in general. Nonetheless, one can say that many, if not most Western firms with an interest in the Middle East have tended to give verbal support to the trilateral investment concept; however, they have viewed it primarily as a vehicle to sell to developing countries technology that will be paid for by the oil-producing states. By and large, with certain exceptions Western firms have not found either Egypt or the Sudan to be attractive sites in which to invest their own capital. Because of political risks, poor infrastructure, inadequate foreign exchange reserves, and high construction and operating costs, neither country, generally speaking, holds out the prospect of adequately high rates of return to justify a capital investment by a Western firm. On the other hand, such companies are willing, indeed eager, to participate in Egyptian and Sudanese projects which are financed by Arab capital and in which their own participation is confined to management contracts, licensing agreements or other forms of technology transfer. Where they are willing to advance some capital it is usually small in amount and recovered quickly through management fees and sales charged to the investment project.

The Western policy of minimum capital commitment tends to conflict with the Arab desire that a technology partner invest a sufficient amount of its own funds to assure the quality of the technology supplied and thereby the ultimate success of the project. For many Arab investors, the minimum amount of capital necessary ranges between 10 percent and 33 percent of the total project investment.[44] Most Western firms consider such amounts prohibitively high so as to preclude their participation.

Another area of policy controversy between Western and Arab partners concerns control over the project: specifically the rights and powers with respect to management and control attributed to Arab capital on the one hand and Western technology on the other in the project package. Arab capital partners have usually felt that their contribution of the major part of the capital should give them the right to exercise control. Indeed, even when they are in the minority, Arab investors, in the opinion of Western observers, have a tendency to seek veto power over major project decisions. On the other hand, many potential Western technology partners appear to have adopted a policy of demanding control of projects in which they were involved and of assuring their dominance through such mechanisms as non-amendable "founders' agreements" and long-term management contracts.[45] Conflict on this issue has led to the abandonment of more than one investment project.

III. THE INSTITUTIONAL DIMENSIONS

A. GENERAL COMMENTS

The trilateral concept presupposes the participation not just of "Arab capital", but of Arab capital *institutions*, since it is institutions which bring to the investment process the indispensible functions of capital mobilization, risk spreading, and project formulation and management, among others. The lack of appropriate financial institutions both in the surplus and the deficit states has until recently constituted a severe constraint not only upon the creation of trilateral projects but also upon the mobilization in any form of Arab funds for development in the Middle

East. While capital surpluses as a result of large and rapid increases in oil prices have grown rapidly and dramatically, the development of financial institutions capable of managing and investing that surplus has taken place much more slowly and painstakingly.

As Raymond Goldsmith has suggested, financial institutions "facilitate the migration of funds to the best user, i.e., to the place in the economic system where the funds will yield the highest social return."[46] Without appropriate financial institutions of their own, the Arab states had little choice other than to deposit their surplus funds with foreign banks and organizations, for they themselves did not have the means to invest those funds directly and efficiently. Although significant direct transfers have taken place between governments of the surplus states and the governments of the deficit states, most of such payments have been for military purposes, balance of payments support, or general welfare assistance, rather than for investments in economic development. Ministries of finance, as traditionally organized, have not proved to be highly effective at facilitating the migration of funds to the best user for development purposes.

Since 1973 Arab capital has undergone a significant degree of institutionalization. The accumulation of surplus funds by oil-producing states has stimulated the growth of a variety of new specialized institutions to facilitate and channel the flow of Arab capital to the deficit states of the Middle East in particular and to a lesser extent to the developing world in general. Together, these institutions constitute an emerging but as yet incomplete framework for financing Middle Eastern development, a framework which is being constructed on three basic levels: (i) within the capital-surplus states; (ii) within the capital-deficit states; and (iii) at the transnational level.

B. THE EMERGING INSTITUTIONAL FRAMEWORK OF THE SURPLUS STATES

As one might expect, the first financial institutions to emerge in the oil states were concerned with domestic investment (largely in the area of foreign trade financing and land development) and with the transfer of surplus funds to the West for placement. In recent years, however, the Middle East has witnessed the creation, both at the national and the international levels, of a broad variety of institutions whose primary purpose is to invest surplus funds in the non-oil producing states of the region. While they display a broad variety of forms, objectives and states of development, they tend to share certain common characteristics: first, their capital is derived primarily from public funds; secondly they are, by and large, subject to the control of one or more Arab governments; thirdly, with few exceptions, their effectiveness has been hampered by the lack of sufficient manpower with the requisite financial and managerial skills; fourthly, Egypt and the Sudan have constituted countries of major concern for them; and fifthly, many of these new organisms have taken the form of international organizations whose membership includes not only the oil-producing states but also Egypt and the Sudan, as well as other poor states of the region. One may briefly categorize them as follows:

1. The Arab Monetary Fund: established in April 1976, the Arab Monetary Fund, with a paid-in capital of over $250 million as of January 1979, includes all Arab states and exists primarily to provide short- and medium-term balance of payments assistance to member states. Both Egypt and the Sudan have received loans from the Fund.

2. Development Funds: while most of the aid from the oil states to developing countries has been dispensed, often for political purposes, in the form of grants or general purpose loans by political leaders or government ministries, the principal oil-producing states have also created more or less autonomous "development funds" to institutionalize part of the aid-giving process and to base it more solidly on economic and technical grounds.[47] Influenced in varying degrees by the World Bank and its affiliates as models, the development funds provide long-term "soft loans" on concessional terms to finance specific projects, often of an infrastructural nature, in other Arab countries or throughout the developing world. Basically they are of two types: (i) national development funds, such as those in Kuwait, Saudi Arabia and Abu Dhabi, which are essentially creatures of national law and policy; and (ii) multi-national funds, such as the Arab Fund for Economic and Social Development and the Islamic Development Bank, institutions created and financed by several sovereign states pursuant to a treaty and subject to an international form of administration.

The Kuwait Fund for Arab Economic Development, established in 1961, is the oldest of the Arab development funds, and by virtue of its experience, the professionalism of its staff and the efficiency of its management, it ranks almost certainly as the premier development finance institution in the Arab world.

The position of the development funds with respect to trilateral projects is not altogether clear. On the one hand, they have financed the purchase by developing countries of hundreds of millions of dollars worth of equipment and technology derived from the West. Moreover, their policy of stressing infrastructure can be seen as paving the way for and creating a climate conducive to subsequent commercial investment, particularly by Arab interests. On the other hand, the funds have adopted a policy of dealing primarily with developing country governments and are reluctant to enter into participation directly with Western firms or private interests generally. Certain proposals by Western banks of project cooperation, whereby the banks would assume short and medium term lending while the funds would assume the long-term loans, have been declined by the funds apparently on grounds that such proposals represent an effort to use the cheap fund loans to sell the more costly commercial loans to developing country governments. Cooperation between the funds and comparable development finance institutions such as the World Bank, has however been close. The Bank and the funds co-finance many projects, and the funds often rely on the Bank's expertise in project preparation and appraisal.

3. Institutions of Commercial Investment and Finance: the development funds have tended to restrict their activities to long-term loans for financing infrastructure and other public sector projects. With one or two exceptions, they have avoided equity and debt financing of commercially profitable enterprises. Arab institutions devoted to commercial investment and finance in the Third World have evolved slowly and cautiously. It is, of course, precisely this type of institution which is best suited to join with Western technological firms in the execution of trilateral projects in Egypt and the Sudan.

While a few wealthy Arab individuals have made direct investments (often in areas of land development and tourism), Arab governments, generally speaking, have been the primary stimulus for the creation of investment companies. Within the Arab world, institutions of commercial investment and finance can be divided into two groups: national and multi-national. With regard to the national institutions, the State of Kuwait appears to lead the way with such investment organizations as the Kuwait Foreign Trading, Contracting and Investment Company (80 percent owned by the Kuwait government), the Kuwait Investment Company (50 percent government-owned), and the Kuwait Real Estate Consortium (over 20 percent government-owned). In addition, on a bilateral and multi-lateral basis, the governments of the Arab states created, usually by treaty, a variety of international institutions devoted to commercial investment and finance. They include the Arab Investment Company and the Arab African Bank, as well as various bilateral firms, such as the Egyptian-Kuwaiti Investment Company, the Kuwaiti-Sudanese Investment Company, and the Emirates and Sudan Investment Company.

On the whole, the principal constraint on the activities of these institutions has been the lack of experienced manpower capable of identifying, preparing and executing development projects. As a result, one finds that many of these investment companies have devoted a considerable portion of their resources to short-term loans and foreign trade financing, rather than to project development.

4. Arab Joint Ventures: many of the agreements and documents relating to inter-Arab investments have stressed the importance of and have urged priority for "Arab joint ventures" primarily because they are seen as a means to further the economic integration of the Arab world. They are also a useful device for bringing together investors from the rich and poor countries in a single project, thus facilitating the flow of funds between the capital-exporting and the capital-importing states of the region. Moreover they permit the development of projects which require large amounts of capital or extensive multi-country markets.

Since private Arab capital, with certain exceptions, has been reluctant to invest in the poorer countries of the region, Arab governments themselves have played an important role in this area, either by participating with private capital or by forming "state joint ventures", enterprises created by treaty among individual Arab states who contribute the necessary capital and become shareholders. Among the types of Arab joint ventures, one may cite (i) project joint ventures, such as the Kenana Sugar Company in the Sudan and the SUMED Pipeline in Egypt; (ii) "sectoral joint ventures" which seek to promote and develop projects in a particular field and then to act as holding companies for the enterprises actually established, examples being the Arab Company for Mining and the Arab Company for Development of Animal Resources; and (iii) "geographic joint ventures" where governments of two or more Arab countries form a company to identify, develop and manage investments and enterprises within the geographic limits of one or both of the states concerned. Egypt and the Sudan have been sites for activities of all three types of joint ventures.

5. Investment Authorities: most recently the Arab states have been experimenting with the creation of a new type of institution which can be called an "investment authority". Like the multi-lateral development funds and investment companies, it takes the form of an international public corporation whose shareholders are individual Arab states. But unlike the usual development fund or investment bank, whose portfolios consist of loans to or shares in numerous unrelated projects in many different countries, the investment authority seeks to finance in a given country a large-scale, integrated program of investments, which may include both infrastructure requiring concessional loans, and enterprises of a commercial nature. Thus far, the most significant example of this type of institution is the Arab Authority for Agricultural Investment and Development,[48] a multi-national agency capitalized at over $500 million, which will seek to finance a long-range plan to realize the food production potential of the Sudan. A second example, which now appears dormant, especially in view of the deterioration of diplomatic relations between Egypt and the oil states, is the Gulf Organization for the Development of Egypt (GODE) created in 1976 to assist in financing Egypt's five-year development plan. Despite the declared intent of GODE, its initial capital of $2 billion was not used to finance specific projects, but for general balance of payments support to the Egyptian government.

6. *Facilitating Institutions*: various institutions have also assumed the function of facilitating and encouraging the investment of surplus capital in other parts of the Arab world. Some, such as the Arab Fund and the Kuwait Fund, while transferring large amounts themselves, have also sought to encourage investment through the identification of potential projects and the dissemination of information about investment prospects in the non-oil producing countries of the Middle East. Others, such as the Council for Arab Economic Unity, have attempted to encourage investment through the conclusion of treaties on the avoidance of double taxation and the settlement of investment disputes. Probably the most innovative of such institutions, however, is the Inter-Arab Investment Guarantee Corporation,[49] an international organization whose members consist of both the capital-exporting and capital-importing states (including Egypt and the Sudan) and whose purpose is to provide insurance against non-commercial risks (nationalization, currency non-convertibility and civil disturbances) of investments by the nationals of one member state in the territory of another member state. It is thus far the only functioning example of a multi-lateral investment insurance scheme in the world. Since the corporation can issue insurance to legal persons whose shares are substantially (but not necessarily totally) owned by an Arab national, it would be possible for a trilateral project to obtain insurance coverage under this scheme.

While numerous financial institutions have thus emerged in a relatively short time through the conclusion of treaties or the enactment of laws, their effectiveness in the investment process and their willingness and ability to participate in trilateral ventures have been constrained by a number of factors. First, virtually all have suffered from the lack of manpower skilled in investment and finance. Secondly, their newness has required them to take time to determine their investment plans and to formulate their policies with regard to Western firms. In addition, because governments have played the primary role in their development, many of these institutions have, in varying degrees, taken on the style and outlook of public sector institutions, and indeed many of their officials and employees have come from government service or public corporations in individual Arab countries. As a result, certain of these organizations may reflect some of the suspicion traditional to the public sector in its dealings with private capital, particularly multi-national companies and banks. Moreover, they are sensitive to political considerations and pressure in conducting their operations, a phenomenon aptly illustrated by the expulsion of Egypt from many of these same institutions as a result of its peace treaty with Israel.

Although private Arab capital expresses a somewhat greater acceptance of association with Western firms, it is not as highly institutionalized as public Arab capital, nor as well endowed in the requisite financial and managerial skills. Moreover, it has been much less visible than public organizations and has clung to anonymity, a factor which inhibited Western efforts initially in finding appropriate Arab capital partners.

C. Western Firms and the Deficit States

Western firms seeking Arab financing for trilateral ventures have faced an initial and difficult task merely in identifying potential Arab capital partners amenable to participating in projects in Egypt or the Sudan. Because of lack of information and established institutional channels, the search for Arab capital has been a time-consuming, empirical, and basically entrepreneurial activity. Most Western firms have also found it a frustrating experience and have received little help in the process from international commercial banks and similar intermediaries. Having begun their search with some ill-defined notion of "Arab capital", experience soon taught them the necessity of making distinctions between Saudis and Kuwaitis, between public and private institutions, between merchants and middlemen, and between national and international agencies.

In view of the difficulties in making a direct approach to Arab capital, many firms have tried an indirect approach by securing the assistance of local partners, governments or other agencies within the developing country where the project is to take place. The success of this approach has varied. Generally, governmental agencies and ministries, such as the Egyptian General Authority on Investment and Free Zones or the appropriate Sudanese Ministry have provided little help, either because they themselves do not have useful knowledge of or strong links to Arab capital sources, or because they do not conceive of their role as one of assisting in the search for capital. It may also be that developing country governments wish to preserve their "credit" with the oil producers for essential major public undertakings and for emergency assistance such as balance of payments support, rather than to squander it in helping Western firms secure financing. On the other hand, in several ventures, local Egyptian and Sudanese private sector partners have proved themselves to have useful links to private Arab capital and have been instrumental in securing private finance. In addition, certain Western firms have found that their agents and customers in the Arabian Peninsula constitute a potential source of finance for investment in Egypt and the Sudan. And just as Western firms face problems in identifying sources of Arab financing, Arab partners encounter difficulties in locating appropriate sources of Western technology for specific projects.

The effective mobilization of Arab capital and trilateral ventures has also been constrained by the lack of appropriate institutions within Egypt and the Sudan themselves. To remedy this situation, Egypt created the General Authority for Foreign Investment to publicize the new investment policy, to pass on investment applications, promote foreign investment in Egypt, and generally to administer the investment law. In addition, both countries have evolved institutions to finance and participate in projects with domestic and foreign capital. Towards this end, Egypt in 1971 founded the Egyptian International Bank for Foreign Trade and Development with a capital of 10 million pounds sterling, and the Sudan in 1974 created the Sudan Development Corporation with the aid of a Saudi Arabian Monetary Authority guarantee which enabled it to secure a $200 million Eurodollar loan to use as capital for investment in commercially viable projects within the country.

Despite the emergence of these new national institutions, Arab and Western investors continue to perceive within Egypt and the Sudan a variety of institutional constraints on the flow of Arab and foreign capital, including policy and decisional instability, bureaucratic obstructionism and insensitivity, insufficient indigenous managerial skills and sources of technology, and lack of project formulation and promotion. In the opinion of many Arab financial managers, this last-mentioned factor is a particularly severe constraint. They argue that effective investment promotion must include more than goodwill visits to the Arabian Peninsula and the adoption of favorable foreign investment laws. They believe that the most significant form of investment promotion which the capital-deficit states can undertake is the preparation of specific project proposals and their subsequent presentation for financing to Arab capital institutions. This insistence upon prepared project proposals, which appears to be particularly strong among Arab investors, is probably a reflection of their own lack of capacity in this area.

In response to criticism on this point, officials in Egypt and the Sudan argue that project preparation is costly and that they simply do not have the human and material resources to prepare a "shelf" of project proposals whose financing is not assured. Moreover, they point out that feasibility studies have a very limited "shelf life" and can rapidly diminish in value with the passage of time. And finally, they argue that project preparation is the normal function of the firm making the investment. While the two sides may differ on who should have the responsibility for project formulation, both agree that this capacity needs strengthening in both countries.

IV. THE OPERATIONAL DIMENSIONS

The trilateral project faces a number of operational problems both in substance and in form. A preliminary question concerns which of the three sides — Western, Arab or local — should take the lead in promoting the project and putting together the financial package in the first place. There is no uniform answer to this question, and different projects have been promoted by different parties. Generally speaking, however, because both Arab capital sources and developing countries lack extensive capability in project identification and preparation, one finds that Western firms have been the most active in this respect. On the other hand, there is some evidence to suggest that local interests have been successful in identifying and advancing projects most suited to the needs and conditions of the developing country.

The lengthy task of merely identifying a potential capital partner is followed by an even more time-consuming process of working out the project agreement. Generally, because the parties are strangers to one another and are not negotiating against a shared background and experience, negotiations for trilateral projects tend to be lengthy, and much time is devoted to familiarizing the parties with one another. Moreover, because the parties have usually had no previous dealings and therefore have little basis for mutual confidence, they often seek special protective devices, such as veto powers over certain questions, in order to protect themselves against possible unfavorable actions by the other partners during the course of the project. Arab investors fear particularly a drain on project income through excessive prices for technology and equipment, exorbitant management fees, and costly licensing arrangements. Without technical expertise of their own, they are at a disadvantage to protect themselves from abuses in these areas. In the case of the Kenana Sugar Company in the Sudan, the Kuwait Foreign Trading, Contracting and Investment Company, one of the principal Arab investors in the project, was able to define its interest and lay the basis for the eventual cancellation of Lonhro's management contract by hiring an American sugar firm as its own consultant.

Differences in the parties' investment strategies and objectives may further complicate the organization of a trilateral project. The Western firm may be seeking primarily to sell technology, expand a market or acquire a commodity supply at low cost, while the Arabs' objective is to develop a stable investment which will maintain its value against inflation and at the same time provide a high return for a long period of time. This type of conflict may arise, for example, over the project's dividend policy. The Arab investor, accustomed to a rapid return on investments, may wish a large portion of project earnings to be paid out in dividends, while the Western firm, desirous of expanding its position in the market and in any event deriving its income from management licensing fees, may wish to retain earnings for expansion and development.

Alliances among the three parties may shift depending on the issue in question. For example, in negotiations with the government of the host country, the Arab partner might be adamant about obtaining a freehold interest in land while the Western partner, whose capital stake may be slight, would find a long-term lease acceptable. On questions relating to the choice of technology, one often finds that Arab and Western firms agree in seeking the most advanced form while the local partner may wish for one that uses more local managerial skills or more local raw materials. In one case in the Sudan, the suggestion by the Sudanese partner that local materials be used in roofing a proposed housing development was summarily dismissed by Kuwaiti investors. In another case conflict arose because the local Sudanese partners felt that they would supply certain managerial skills to an agricultural project, while the Saudi investor insisted that all the management be entrusted to an American firm.

Matters of form and style also affect the operation of a trilateral venture. Arab partners, for example, are particularly sensitive to cavalier Western attitudes which suggest that trilateralism is a matter of "your money and our brains". On the other hand, Western managers find that the business style of Arab investors often complicates day-to-day management of the project. Arab financiers often travel much, do not maintain permanent well-staffed offices, and are reluctant to delegate responsibility to subordinates. Consequently Western firms often find that it is difficult to communicate at a given moment with their Arab partners, to arrange for meetings, or to be assured of rapid responses to telexes and letters.

V. CONCLUSION: THE PROSPECTS OF TRILATERALISM

Trilateralism is clearly not a magic formula that will obliterate the constraints and bottlenecks impeding the mobilization and investment of Arab capital in Egypt and the Sudan. Indeed, those constraints will probably limit severely the flow of Arab funds across the Red Sea for some time to come.

Trilateralism merely expresses the truism that effective investment of Arab funds requires an input of know-how from the industrialized countries because in most cases (but not all), the Arab world itself is unable to supply all the technological and managerial requirements of investment and development projects in the two countries. Beyond that, relationships among partners to a trilateral venture have to be worked out through experience and the process of negotiation. Some of the inhibitions to those relationships are weakening as Western firms gain more knowledge and information about Arab capital sources, and as the institutionalization of Arab capital progresses with its concomitant development of professional skills, particularly with respect to project identification, preparation, analysis and management.

Knowledge hopefully will result in each of the three sides adopting a more realistic appraisal of one another. Through increased knowledge and interaction, the three potential sides in trilateral projects may gain a more accurate and realistic understanding of each other's objectives and capabilities and thereby lay a more solid foundation for trilateralism in the Middle East. The governments of Egypt and the Sudan, it would seem, can do much to advance this process. Having adopted the trilateral venture as the model investment project which each especially wishes to attract, the two countries ought not merely to sit back and wait for them to materialize as is now the case, but should instead actively seek to promote their formulation and execution. As an initial step, the Egyptian and Sudanese agencies responsible for encouraging foreign investment should endeavor to become more knowledgeable about the sources of Arab capital, both public and private, and should seek to establish definite links to them. Where sound project proposals are in need of Arab financing, responsible agencies in Egypt and the Sudan should take an active role in seeking out the necessary funds and in promoting such projects among the financial institutions across the Red Sea. If a project has the active endorsement of the host country, it is likely to receive a far better hearing by Arab capital institutions than where a Western firm appears to be its sole sponsor.

Arab and Western governments and institutions might also consider the possibility of improving opportunities for trilateralism through cooperative programs aimed at easing some of the bottlenecks and constraints now inhibiting Arab capital investment in productive projects in both Egypt and the Sudan. For example, Arab funds or investment companies, in association with Western banks and financial institutions, might create an organization to undertake feasibility studies and prepare projects for execution in Egypt and the Sudan. The Arab institutions might provide the capital necessary for the venture while the contribution of the Western banks might take the form of skilled manpower. The resulting organization, as compensation for its work, might receive a participation in the projects it prepared, and through this process eventually become self-sustaining.

Arab and Western governments and institutions together might also seek to organize training institutions and programs aimed at increasing the level of Egyptian and Sudanese skills, as well as those of the oil countries themselves, with respect to investment planning, analysis, negotiation and management.

The possibilities of trilateral cooperative action are numerous; however, an indispensible condition precedent to their realization is an effective means of dialogue among the three sides. At present, occasional meetings on this subject, such as the 1977 OECD Conference on Trilateral Co-operation with Arab Involvement, often assume an atmosphere of confrontation and consequently achieve little. It would seem that the likelihood of fruitful discussion would be much improved if Egypt and the Sudan themselves took the lead in trying to establish and promote such dialogue. As an initial step towards this end, each might consider the possibility of organizing a series of meetings or conferences in Egypt and the Sudan at which the three sides might explore means for trilateral cooperation in such areas as project planning, preparation and management.

NOTES

1. As of 1977, the combined surplus of the Arab petroleum producers was estimated to exceed $100 million. *The Financial Times* (London), (26 September 1977), p. 18. More recently, a Rand Corporation study estimated that by 1985 total accumulation of foreign assets of Saudi Arabia and Kuwait would amount to $84 billion and $63 billion respectively, assuming a 2 percent annual increase in export income, and $127.5 billion and $114.6 billion respectively, assuming a 5 percent annual increase in export income. Arthur Smithies, *The Economic Potential of the Arab Countries* (Santa Monica, Calif.: The Rand Corporation, 1978), p. 91.

2. See generally for example, Paul M. Watson, *Debt and the Developing Countries: New Problems and Actors*, Development Paper No. 29, (Overseas Development Council, 1978).

3. According to OECD's *Development Co-operation: 1977 Review* (Paris: OECD, 1978), pp. 83-86, total net flows to all developing countries during the period 1973 to 1976 by Saudi Arabia, Kuwait and the United Arab Emirates (the three leading OPEC donors) were respectively $7.299 billion, $5.386 billion and $3.338 billion.

The states of the Middle East—especially those (Egypt, Syria and Jordan) directly involved in the confrontation with Israel—have been the primary recipients of Arab aid. Among the "non-confrontation" Arab states, the Sudan has been one of the more significant beneficiaries. See OECD, *Development Co-operation: 1978 Review* (Paris: OECD, 1978), pp. 268-269.

4. According to the figures of the Morgan Guaranty Trust Company, reported in *The New York Times* (3 December 1978), section F, pp. 3-4, total Eurocredits issued to non-OPEC developing countries during the period from 1 January 1976 to 30 November 1978 amounted to $60.1 billion. In 1977, the total flows of net resources to developing countries amounted to $64 billion, of which nearly two thirds came from private sources. The private banking sector provided $18 billion, primarily in the form of Eurocurrency lending. In the same year, total OPEC aid disbursements to developing countries exceeded $5.5 billion. OECD, *Development Co-operation: 1978 Review*, op.cit.

5. For example, in 1979 net deposits with international banks by OPEC countries amounted to $30 billion, while net bank credits to non-oil developing countries totalled $24 billion. Argentina, Brazil and Mexico accounted for two thirds of the net borrowing. *Wall Street Journal* (2 June 1980), p. 29.

6. Discussion of the concept has been fragmentary. Probably the most comprehensive treatment is to be found in the two-volume OECD publication entitled *Trilateral Co-operation* (Paris, 1978), of which the first volume, edited by Traute Scharf, is subtitled *Arab Development Funds and Banks: Approaches to Trilateral Co-operation*. This volume is concerned primarily with the role of public Arab capital institutions in undertaking trilateral cooperation.

7. Scharf, op.cit., p. 88.

8. For example, as Scharf, op.cit., p. 83, comments, "Trilateral co-operation means the factor input of finance, technology, and other resources by developing countries, oil-exporting countries and industrialized nations into any development project, programme or scheme in the field of infrastructure, agriculture, industry or services located in a non-oil exporting, developing country. The type and mix of contributions as well as conditions will basically depend upon the balance of interest of the three groups involved in the specific development task: it will be the result of a negotiating process among the three parties involved."

9. See Zacharia Nasr, *The Kuwait Fund and Trilateral Cooperation* (The Kuwait Fund, 1977), p. 6.

10. The material in this and subsequent sections of the essay is based on interviews conducted by the author in Europe, Kuwait, Egypt and the Sudan with bankers, financial experts and entrepreneurs, during the period 8 November to 12 December 1977.

11. The US Central Intelligence Agency in a short "research aid" indicated that these four countries in 1975 accounted for 90 percent of the total accumulated by all OPEC countries, Arab and non-Arab alike. *OPEC Countries: Current Account Trends 1975-76* (June 1976, Er-76-1037Q), p. 2.

12. R. El Mallakh and M. Kadhim, "Capital Surpluses and Deficits in the Arab Middle East: A Regional Perspective", *International Journal of Middle East Studies,* Vol. 8 (1978), pp. 183-186. See also Ragei El Mallakh, Mihssen Kadhim and Barry Poulson, *Capital Investment in the Arab Middle East: The Use of Surplus Funds for Regional Development* (New York: Praeger, 1977), pp. 14-17, and hereafter cited as El Mallakh *et al.*).

13. One study estimated that the average annual surplus for the oil producers as a group during the period 1975 to 1980 would amount to $30.5 billion and that as late as 1985 they may realize an annual surplus of nearly $30 billion. El Mallakh *et al.*, op.cit., pp. 68, 91-92. For projected figures to 1985 see F.N. 1 above and the reference to Smithies, *The Economic Potential of the Arab Countries*, as cited.

14. For example, *The New York Times* (9 January 1978), Section D, p.1, estimated total overseas investments, gold and foreign currency holdings of the Saudi Arabian Monetary Authority to be approximately $55 billion, one third of which was invested in the United States, one third in Europe and a significant portion of the remainder in Japan.

15. In April 1978, for instance, the United States Treasury Department estimated that Arab countries held $29 billion in the United States, of which $13.3 billion was in US Treasury bills, bonds and notes; $5.3 billion in bonds of Federal agencies or American corporations; about $5 billion in commercial bank obligations; and $5.2 billion in stocks. Youssef M. Ibrahim, "Arabs Vary Investing—Warily", *The New York Times* (15 June 1978), Section D, p. 64.

16. See ibid.

17. For an extensive discussion of these matters see the chapter by Hazem Beblawi in this volume.

18. *The Middle East* (December 1977), p. 80, claimed that in 1977 Kuwaiti private investment abroad totalled $3 billion, but such figures represent little more than an educated guess.

19. Based on interviews conducted by the author in Cairo, December 1977.

20. The degree of reliance varies among the oil-producing countries. Kuwait, for example, appears to demonstrate more financial sophistication and to be less dependent on foreign assistance than is Saudi Arabia.

21. Much of the information in this and succeeding sections was obtained by the author in approximately 60 interviews conducted in the Middle East, Europe and the United States with bankers, financial managers, lawyers, government officials, and others having knowledge of and experience with Arab investments.

22. See for example R. El Mallakh and M. Kadhim, "Capital Surpluses and Deficits...", op.cit., and J. Hoaglund and J. P. Smith, "The U.S. Saudi $35-billion Secret", *The Boston Globe* (27 December 1977), p. 2.

23. Again see Hazem Beblawi, Chapter VI in this volume, for a discussion of these points.

24. A major motivation in the creating of the Arab Authority for Agricultural Investment and Development was to find a solution to the "food security problem". This is an inter-Arab institution which is to mobilize and invest large amounts of capital to realize the Sudan's agricultural potential. See Jeswald W. Salacuse, "The Arab Authority for Agricultural Investment and Development", *Journal of World Trade Law*, Vol. XII (1978), pp. 56-66.

25. See Ragei El Mallakh and Mihssen Kadhim, "Arab Institutionalized Aid: An Evaluation", *The Middle East Journal,* Vol. XXX, (Autumn 1976), pp. 471–484.

26. Soliman Demir, *The Kuwait Fund and the Political Economy of Arab Regional Development* (New York: Praeger, 1976), pp. 5-6.

27. See Maurice J. Williams, *Development Co-operation: 1976 Review* (Paris: OECD, 1976), p. 99.

28. El Mallakh *et al.*, *Capital Investment in the Arab Middle East...*, op.cit., p. 65.

29. Maurice J. Williams, *Development Co-operation: 1975 Review* (Paris: OECD, 1975), pp. 14-15.

30. See generally Maurice J. Williams, *Development Co-operation: 1975* and *1976 Review*, op.cit.

31. Unofficial figures supplied to the writer by the Egyptian Ministry of the Economy and Economic Cooperation.

32. Unoffical figures supplied to the writer by the Egyptian Ministry of the Economy and Economic Cooperation.

33. Maurice J. Williams, *Development Co-operation: 1976 Review*, op.cit., p. 120.

34. Meeting in Baghdad, the foreign ministers of 18 Arab states adopted a series of resolutions on 31 March 1979 aimed at isolating Egypt diplomatically and economically. These measures included cutting off all loans, deposits, guarantees, bonds, and contributions — financial, material or technical — to the Egyptian government, and banning economic aid to Egypt by Arab funds, banks and financial institutions. See *The Economist* (7 April 1979), p. 64.

35. For a discussion of Egyptian reactions to the Kafr al-Dawwar loan, see *Al-Ahram al-Iqtisadi,* no. 523 (1 June 1977), pp. 4–14.

36. Issued by President Sadat on 23 September 1971. Published officially in *Al-Jarida al-Rasmiyya* [The Official Gazette], no. 39 (30 September 1971). One of the main advantages which the law granted to Arab, as opposed to other foreign investments, was procedural in nature. Whereas an Arab investment needed only to obtain the approval of the General

Authority for the Investment of Arab Funds and Free Zones, the administrative agency charged with administering the law, a non-Arab investment had first to be approved by the Council of Ministers and then sanctioned by the President.

37. Published officially in *Al-Jarida al-Rasmiyya*, no. 26 (27 June 1974). See generally, Jeswald W. Salacuse, "Egypt's New Law on Foreign Investment: The Framework for Economic Openness", *The International Lawyer*, Vol. IX (1975), pp. 647–660.

38. Published officially in *Al-Jarida al-Rasmiyya*, no. 23 (bis) (9 June 1977). See generally J.W. Salacuse and T. Parnall, "Foreign Investment and Economic Openness in Egypt: Legal Problems and Legislative Adjustments of the First Three Years", *The International Lawyer*, Vol. XII (1978), pp. 759-777.

39. For a detailed discussion of the legislative provisions of the "open door" policy see the chapters in the present volume by Gouda Abdel-Khalek and Nazih N.M. Ayubi.

40. Law No. 43 for 1974, as amended by Law No. 32 for 1977, provides that "Housing projects constructed for the purpose of investment may be undertaken only by Arab capital; foreign capital may not undertake housing projects even in participation with Egyptian capital."

41. See Jeswald W. Salacuse, "Back to Contract: Implications of Peace and Openness for Egypt's Legal System", *American Journal of Comparative Law*, Vol. XXVIII (1980), pp. 315, 325-326.

42. In 1980, the Sudanese government unified its investment legislation by enacting a single investment law, The Encouragement of Investment Act, 1980.

43. The original text is published by The Council for Arab Economic Unity, *The Idea, the Application, the Achievements* (in Arabic), (Cairo, 1975), p. 80. An English translation of the agreement has been published by the Sudanese government as Law No. 32 for 1971, appearing in the Legislative Supplement to the Democratic Republic of the Sudan Gazette.

44. Based on interviews with Arab financial managers conducted by the author.

45. Such was the case with Lonrho which was able to control the development of the Kenana Sugar Company in the Sudan during the first few years, although it held only a 12.5 percent equity investment in the enterprise.

46. Raymond W. Goldsmith, *Financial Structure and Development* (New Haven: Yale University Press, 1969), p. 400.

47. For a comparative study of the Kuwait, Abu Dhabi and Arab Development Funds, see generally Soliman Demir, *Cooperation for Development: Arab Development Funds in the Middle East* (New York: UNITAR, 1978). See also Traute Scharf, *Arab Development Funds...*, op.cit.

48. For a detailed discussion of the AAAID see Jeswald W. Salacuse, "The Arab Authority for Agricultural Investment and Development: A New Model for Capital Transfer in the Middle East", *Journal of World Trade Law*, Vol. XII, (1978), pp. 56-66.

49. For background on the investment guarantee program see generally Ibrahim F. Shihata, "Arab Investment Guarantee Program; a Regional Investment Insurance Project", *Journal of World Trade Law*, Vol. VI (1972), pp. 185-202. See also Abdelaziz Mathari, "The Philosophy of the Inter-Arab Investment Guarantee Corporation" in OECD, *Trilateral Co-operation*, Vol. II (Proceedings and Background Papers of the Conference on Special Approaches to Trilateral Co-operation, 26-27 January 1977), (Paris, 1978), pp. 201-214. As of January 1978 the corporation had insured a total of six investments.

VI
The Predicament of the Arab Gulf Oil States: Individual Gains and Collective Losses

Hazem El-Beblawi

I. INTRODUCTION

It is no longer a matter for debate that the international economic order, inherited from the Second World War, is becoming more and more obsolete. The issue to be considered here is the extent to which the new order can be related to an emerging new Arab order.

The increase in oil prices in the wake of the war of October 1973 was acclaimed by most of the Third World as a turning point in international economic relations, and this has even been seen as the first major change undertaken by small countries since the age of Vasco da Gama.[1] Indeed, the Organization of Oil-Exporting Countries (hereafter OPEC)—a group of mostly small countries—has successfully imposed on the industrial West a redistribution of world income to the benefit of its members. Thus it is not surprising that in the minds of many developing countries a new era has started and the long-ignored "have not" nations have at last found a place in the sun. To some extent this view has also been shared by OPEC countries; the seventh Special Session of the United Nations General Assembly was, in fact, convened on the initiative of the late President Boumedienne of Algeria to discuss the establishment of a new international economic order.

Now, only a few years after what is probably "the largest shock per unit of time that the world economy has ever seen",[2] observers in the Third World and elsewhere are less exuberant, and euphoria has given way to a more sober assessment. The OPEC countries too, no less than the others, have discovered that behind a treacherously simple facade, reality is far more complex and involved. Almost everyone but OPEC has been studying the new situation thoroughly. Members of the

Organization for Economic Cooperation and Development (hereafter OECD) were particularly interested in recycling oil funds with minimum disruption of economic activity and short of reversing the trend of oil price increases.[3] The Third World was—and still is—preoccupied with the increased external debt. OPEC countries alone seemed to be quite content with their action on prices, as if other problems were not their business or else could be settled in a matter-of-fact fashion. Later experience showed that the investing of oil funds is anything but a matter-of-fact business; what appears to be conventional common sense may turn out to be utter nonsense. Things are by no means clear.

My intention in this chapter is to discuss the problem of the investment of oil funds from the perspective of OPEC's self-interest. An explicit formulation of the problem and of the underlying assumptions is, nevertheless, expedient in clarifying OPEC relationships with developed and developing countries.

The Problem

As a first approximation OPEC surplus countries face two problems in their relations with the rest of the world; these may be called, respectively, the energy problem and the financial problem. Although they are intimately related, it is useful to look at them separately.

The level and the value of oil production are major policy issues facing OPEC countries. Financial considerations are no doubt prominent among those influencing the level of oil production. There are, however, other important factors—technical, political, economic...etc.—that affect OPEC countries in their production and price policies, and these include among others production-reserve ratios, availability of energy substitutes (actual and potential), domestic absorptive needs, world demand, and political stability in producing and consuming countries.

In the prevailing circumstances, given any realistic level of production, some OPEC countries will realize balance of payments surpluses. With small populations, very limited domestic absorption, large reserves and oil production capacity, some OPEC countries are unable to spend their oil earnings domestically with any degree of efficiency. The largest share of the oil revenues goes to three small countries in the Peninsula and the Gulf—Saudi Arabia, the United Arab Emirates (UAE) and Qatar—and also to Libya. These countries are "far too small to absorb more than a fraction of the money pouring into their treasuries"[4] and will always have a financial problem, namely the proper use of their financial surpluses.

My analysis will be confined to this financial problem, assuming that the energy problem has been settled one way or the other. This is, by and large, a problem for the Arab Gulf states. In the following discussion I shall use "OPEC surplus countries" and "Arab Gulf states" interchangeably.

It has been suggested that economic analysis would gain increased insight, once the emphasis is laid on the assets as the central analytical concept.[5] This is more so in the case of the oil producing countries. What is usually referred to as the huge income of OPEC is a misnomer. From OPEC's viewpoint there is no income earned; there is only an exchange of assets. OPEC countries are, in fact, transforming their real asset (oil) into foreign exchange. Broadly speaking, assets are of two types. First we have the real or tangible assets which consist of producers' and consumers' goods of all kinds. Secondly there are the financial assets, which are certificates, ownership shares, and promises to pay.[6] Since every financial asset creates liabilities of equal value, it is the real assets which are the ultimate wealth. Financial assets are in fact nothing but claims on the real assets. The value of any financial asset resides, in the final analysis, in its ability to be converted into a real asset. Financial assets then are deferred real assets.

From the foregoing it is easy to define a guiding principle for the asset management of the Gulf states. These countries should follow a conservation policy, understood in the larger sense, for their various assets. Applying this to the management of the financial problem, the criterion for the foreign investment of the Arab Gulf states should, then, be the maintenance of, if not the increase in, the value of their financial assets. This can be done only if the financial assets maintain their value in terms of real assets; that is, if financial assets are hedged somehow against inflation. From the economic point of view, what matters is not the accumulation of financial assets *per se,* but the implicit deferred transfer of real assets involved. This is a problem similar to the one known to students of international economics as the "transfer problem".[7]

We can now define the "self-interest" of the Arab Gulf states in the context of the financial problem. It is ultimately to sustain the long-run economic viability of these states, given the transient nature of the oil. This can be accomplished by preserving for the future the value of the accumulated financial assets in terms of real assets. To define any country's self-interest by one objective is oversimplified, if not simplistic. Nonetheless I think that the relevance of this narrow definition remains quite valid. In spite of the fabulous affluence observed in certain circles in the Gulf states, everyone, without exception, is haunted by the fear of the post-oil era. The viability of these states after the oil is perhaps the most legitimate and pervasive concern of the population in the area. The "defective telescopic faculty" defined by Pigou is probably reversed in the Gulf area. Under the tranquil surface there is a panic for survival.

Having defined the scope of the problem (that is, the financial problem of the Arab Gulf states), and the criterion for their self-interest (that
is, the maintenance of the real value of the financial assets), we now need
to identify the possible options available to them in relation to this
problem.

I shall not investigate every possible alternative. Rather, I shall limit
myself to a high level of aggregation, namely the option between investing oil funds in developed or in developing countries. In real life
things are never presented in this simplistic manner of "either/or", but
there exist many possible combinations. Also there are practical limits, at
least in the short run, which make this option academic rather than real.
Less developed countries (hereafter LDCs) are simply not prepared, in
the short run, to absorb the totality of the oil funds. Much ink has been
poured into the pinpointing of various bottlenecks in developing countries. Many bottlenecks, real as they are, could be alleviated in the
medium term — as I shall explain later — with proper development effort.
They are no more than "quasi-bottlenecks". [8]

OPEC has, of course, many political, cultural and moral affinities
with developing countries. If OPEC countries were isolated politically
from the developing countries, they would be extremely vulnerable in a
world composed predominantly of oil-importing countries. [9] My purpose
in this study is, however, to see if there is also an economic case for
OPEC solidarity with the LDCs. It is not only from an enlightened moral
concern, but from an enlightened self-interest that I approach the problem. The quest for a new international economic order is intimately
related to the consolidation of the new oil order.

The Magnitude of the Problem

In a subject such as the new Arab wealth, loaded with political emo-
tions and involving the mass media, nothing is easier than exaggeration.
A proper assessment of the real impact of oil funds has a direct bearing
on the method of analysis. In fact the validity of the whole macro
analysis is based on the premise that some variables are significant in affecting the behavior of the economy; that is, it is based on the faith that
there exist few strategic variables that cannot be dealt with by the traditional marginalist method. The absolute value of any economic aggregate has no meaning *per se*. It is only through comparison with other
relevant aggregates that we can form an idea of its significance. The
choice of comparison-aggregates is not an arbitrary act.

There are two concepts of oil funds which need to be kept separated in
our minds: a "stock" concept and a "flow" concept. Both are important

and they are, moreover, interdependent, since the "stock" concept is nothing other than the cumulative value of previous "flows". It is always useful, however, to keep the two concepts distinct for the purpose of proper analysis.

Oil funds have been compared with the accumulated financial capital in the United States. "The total financial capital of the Arab oil countries at that time [1980] should thus be about 3-4 percent of that of the United States".[10] And accordingly, "the Arab oil funds will be large, but the United States is financially larger".[11] That the Arab oil funds are only a negligible fraction of the financial assets of the United States, much less of the total tangible wealth, is a fact that no one, I think, would dare to challenge. After all, this is a comparison between a "stock" accumulated over two centuries with another "stock" piled up in less than a decade. The Arab oil-producing countries are in fact extremely poor in their resource endowment, except for oil, and even this is only for the time being. It could never be claimed that the Arab wealth could compare in a meaningful sense with the wealth of any OECD country, let alone that of the United States. The comparison is nevertheless useful for other purposes. It refutes all allegations of an eventual risk of Arab money controlling the host OECD countries. In this respect, 3 to 4 percent is really insignificant even if we do not take into account the lack of Arab know-how to make such control effective.

But to conclude from the foregoing that oil funds are only marginal to the functioning of the world economy is equally misleading. The functioning of the economy depends to a large extent on flow aggregates. It is much to the point here to compare oil funds with the major annual flows. Although Bent Hansen, for example, concedes that the gross private savings in the United States were "about $250 billion in 1974" and oil surplus funds in the same year "about $60 billion", he concludes that such a "comparison with annual flows also dwarfs the oil-fund accumulation".[12] This is almost one quarter of the savings of the biggest economy in the world. A change of this order in American savings cannot leave either the American economy or the world economy unaffected. In fact world economic stability would suffer from much smaller changes.

Oil surplus funds are additions to world savings in the form of foreign financial assets, a fact about which I shall have much to say later. But for the time being, this is sufficient to suggest a comparison with aggregate flows like savings (or investment) and exports. Being an addition to world savings it is natural to compare these oil funds with savings (or investment) aggregates in major countries. But they are savings of a particular form; that is, they are foreign financial assets. Therefore they should be transformed in the future, through exports, into real assets. Thus investment and exports are appropriate aggregates for comparison. Table I shows American exports and private investment during the seventies.

The choice of American aggregates for comparison is based not only on the fact that the United States is the leading economy in the world, but also because there existed strong reasons to believe that it might become "the major intermediary in the process of investing the Arab oil funds",[13] an assumption confirmed to a great extent by subsequent experience.[14]

In 1974 the annual flow of oil surplus funds (some $60 billion) represented more than 50 percent of American exports and Arab funds alone represented more than 40 percent. The oil funds were some 30 percent of American private investment in the same year. These are not small quantities. Any change of such magnitude is bound to have a substantial effect on the world economy. It is true that the oil surplus funds tended to decrease in subsequent years from their peak of $60 to $65 billion in 1974, and their downward trend continued to some $5 billion in 1978. With the Iranian revolution and the subsequent oil price increases in 1979, a second round of the oil shock took place, with oil surpluses boosted to about $45 to $50 billion in 1979 and projected surpluses of $110 to $120 billion for 1980.[15]

The continuous decrease in oil surplus funds in the first round (1974 to 1978) was in fact the result of economic forces that were caused, at least partly, by policies of oil fund investment. Without a different strategy for oil fund investment for this second round, inaugurated in 1979, there is no reason why the final outcome should be any different from that of the previous round.

TABLE I
United States Exports and Private Investment During the 1970s
(in $ billion)

	1970	1971	1972	1973	1974	1975	1976	1977	1978	1979
Exports	53.9	56.0	62.5	87.5	113.0	129.0	141.7	150.6	175.9	214.3
Private Gross Fixed Capital Formation	137.0	156.3	178.8	202.1	205.7	201.6	233.0	281.3	329.1	369.0

SOURCE: International Monetary Fund (IMF), *International Financial Statistics*, December 1977; April 1980.

In the following pages I propose to study the basic option of oil fund investment in developed or in less developed countries in two stages. To begin with I shall depart briefly from major constraints to make an economic case for investing these funds in the LDCs. Following a method cherished by most economists, that of "partial analysis", I assume other things to be equal and take it, in the first part, that the long-run economic interests of oil surplus countries are paramount. This will help us fix our ideas. It is much easier to proceed by successive approximations. In the second stage I can relax this single-minded approach by introducing more realism. This part will consist of a discussion of major social and political constraints on the optimization of the problem facing the Arab Gulf states.

II.   AN ECONOMIC CASE: INVESTMENT IN THE LESS DEVELOPED COUNTRIES (LDCs)

A.   THE CONVENTIONAL WISDOM

Accumulating financial assets for a limited period, no matter how long, while being terribly lacking in other resources and know-how, suggests that the Arab surplus states have essentially to be conservative investors. This seems to be the only rational investment policy and the least troublesome. What is needed is simply to maintain the *status quo* with the minimum possible disruption to the system. This is the conventional wisdom.

OPEC and OECD Complementarity

On the face of it, OECD countries seem to offer OPEC surplus countries a wide spectrum of advantages that LDCs are unable to match. The complementarity of OPEC and OECD countries has in fact been pointed out by several authors[16] and various levels of complementarity have been distinguished.

> There is a mutual dependence based upon oil trade: the two sides now represent respectively more than 90% of all imports and exports....There is a mutual dependence based on trade outside of oil: the OECD countries are the major suppliers of food, consumer goods, capital goods, arms and modern technology, and the OPEC countries provide important export markets for OECD countries....There is a mutual financial dependence: the OECD countries are dependent on the recycling of OPEC financial surpluses and several of the most important OPEC countries have increasing financial interests in OECD countries....There is a mutual political dependence created by the situation in the Middle East.[17]

The implications of this approach are clear. OPEC countries gain enormous economic benefits by investing their surplus funds in OECD countries as opportunities there for investment are greater, technology is available, credit-worthiness is much higher and more secure, and markets are highly organized. The situation in the LDCs is almost the opposite. The various inadequacies of the economies of the LDCs are too well-known to need any further elaboration. It is, then, only fair to say "that any large scale recycling scheme....to less developed countries soon would be faced with demands for lower interest rates, moratoria and so forth that would challenge the very principle on which all these schemes are based, i.e., loans at commercial rates."[18]

There is of course no denying the great and badly needed political leverage that OPEC countries can obtain from investment in the LDCs. However, this political advantage should be weighed against the economic advantage that OPEC countries obtain from their investment in OECD countries. The trade-off between these considerations would in all probability indicate some mix of oil fund investment in both OECD and LDCs with the OECD getting the oil funds primarily for economic reasons, the LDCs for political reasons.

In broad lines, this is the commonsense reasoning and, to a great extent, it represents the dominant attitude to the financial problem in OPEC surplus countries. Of course, there is a general recognition of the need for greater efforts for development in the LDCs. But it is recognized also that the development of LDCs is a very long, hazardous process. It is a task that OPEC cannot handle, and the safest investment opportunities remain in the OECD countries. In other words, sound investments for OPEC countries are somewhat different from development aid for the LDCs. Aid for development is a meritorious undertaking, and there has been genuine aid-giving by OPEC countries to LDCs. But as a senior American government official has remarked, OPEC's attitude towards developmental investments in the LDCs is seen by them "in a somewhat different category than their investment funds. They see [it as] a contribution to the development process, to political stability in their part of the world — and I am referring to Arab countries — in that light[sic], rather than as part of their funds on which they are going to have to draw in the late 1970s and 1980s, as they develop."[19]

The rationale behind this conventional wisdom rests with the implicit famous assumption of *ceteris paribus*. In particular it is assumed that oil funds cannot change the economic situation; that they are mere additions to the world economy and make no qualitative change. Hence OPEC surplus countries face pre-established options to choose from, and these options themselves are independent of the pattern of investment given to these oil funds. In other words, the conventional wisdom deals with OPEC financial problems in a marginalistic fashion, in the same way as an individual behaves under perfect conditions: a "price taker" rather than a "price maker". The irony of the situation is that while OPEC countries have understood the limits of "price taker" behavior in the area of oil *pricing* they have been led—or rather misled—by the same price taker behavior in the *financial* arena. What makes a great deal of sense from the viewpoint of an individual engaged in prudent financial mangagement may prove to be extremely harmful in the aggregate. This has a name in logic: the "fallacy of composition". I shall discuss at greater length the conflict of common and private interests in the second part of this study.

To enforce the argument let us pursue this kind of calculus to see how far it can lead us astray. It was the fashion among economists in the aftermath of the oil shock in 1974 to come up with projections for future oil funds. More often than not these were based on the assumption of "other things being equal". It was an exercise in futility, a fallacy of arithmetics. Financial institutions and professional economists in the West—the World Bank, United Nations agencies, the OECD, banks, governmental offices, investment companies…etc.—came up with their projections for future oil funds and their recommended policy in this regard.[20] The degree of sophistication varies from one study to another but all were more or less based on the assumption that everything could be handled by the partial analysis of supply and demand. The underlying world economic structure, it was assumed, remained basically the same.

The Fallacy of Arithmetics

Without the hindsight of later developments, let us imagine the process that OPEC surplus countries would follow in trying to work out their own projection with the benefit of the conventional wisdom.

We are in 1975. The OPEC countries, particularly in the Gulf area, have realized unprecedented financial surpluses. Aware of the seriousness of the problem, let us imagine that the governments of these countries have asked a "dummy" group of experts to work out a probable scenario for their future financial surpluses. Being good economists, well trained in the profession, our distinguished imaginary team would, in all probability, start by making the obvious—though unrealistic—assumption of "other things being equal", in particular by conducting the whole exercise in real terms, in 1974 prices.[21] The inflation factor could be introduced later, and the necessary adjustments would be easy to calculate. Thus, the team has cleared its conscience. After making this devastating assumption, our team would proceed confidently to make reasonable assumptions about the relevant variables to our problem. The techniques used for the projection could be quite sophisticated, such as the use of various elasticities and regression analysis in econometric micro-models, or crude and simple methods. The results alter very little with the refinement of techniques used; it is the reasonableness of the assumptions that matters.

The purpose of the whole exercise is to show the futility of the conclusion no matter what reasonable assumptions are made, once inflation is eliminated. This is similar to demonstrations known to mathematicians as *reductio ad absurdum*. In these circumstances it is no use refining too much the technique of projection once the fundamentals are inadequate. I shall assume that the team uses very simple methods, and we shall now see what "reasonable" assumptions could be made:

   a.   Accumulation of financial assets. In 1973 oil surpluses amounted to some $5 billion. In 1974 they were $60 billion. At the beginning of 1975, what would be the reasonable assumptions about the yearly addition to financial assets? It might look reasonable *at the time* to assume that OPEC countries would be able to add annually some $40 billion to their financial assets.[22] As a matter of fact, in retrospect, the OPEC countries realized in the following two years surpluses ranging between $35 and $45 billion, in spite of the tremendous increase in public spending and the magnitude of their aid to the Third World.

The OPEC surpluses are the difference between total receipts and total expenditures. Many factors affect the development of receipts and expenditures. Receipts are primarily determined by oil prices and production levels. More refined methods would work out different cases for demand elasticities for oil in consuming countries. However, increased refinement is not always synonymous with increased realism. Given the structure of the oil market (a seller's market for OPEC) and the tendency for exhaustible resource prices to increase over time[23] it is not altogether unreasonable to assume that the OPEC receipts will continue to increase. On the expenditure side, it is important to note that a large part of investment expenditure in the Gulf area was made in large infrastructure projects which, in most cases, are expensive import-intensive and — at least in the medium term — once-for-all projects. Thus it is not inconceivable that domestic expenditure would, after the initial increase, tend to stabilize at a lower level.[24]

With these considerations in mind the figure of $40 billion as an annual average financial surplus would seem easily justifiable. To assume constant equal annual financial surpluses is no doubt unrealistic; however, for the sake of the simplicity of exposition let us assume that this is a reasonably approximate average.

   b.   The time horizon for financial surpluses. To estimate the life cycle of oil is a difficult task. Available estimates for the Gulf states vary from 30 to 100 years. Let us assume that our team would take the conservative estimate of 15 years. It is absurd to think that output would continue steadily on the same level during the whole period and then stop suddenly. But since it is more likely that oil will still be flowing after 1990, it is simple to limit the time horizon to 1990 with constant output to that date. So it is assumed that oil will be forthcoming during the whole period to end completely by 1990.

c. *Investing oil funds in OECD countries.* Following the conventional wisdom, our team would recommend that, as conservative investors, OPEC countries should place their financial assets in secure investment opportunities in the Western industrial countries and preferably in the United States. It is maintained that the American financial market is a huge one and that the oil funds can accordingly "be accommodated completely in the American financial system without serious upheavals."[25] Later experience, in fact, confirmed this assumption, with the OPEC surplus countries — particularly the Saudis — showing a striking preference for the American market.[26] Hence it is perfectly in order to emphasize the American market.

Since OPEC investments in the United States, or more generally in OECD countries, are motivated by the vast investment opportunities available it is natural that our team would expect to realize a handsome return on these investments, which we can assume would be at around 6 percent.

d. *Repatriation of the OPEC yields after 1990.* As rentiers, OPEC countries are accumulating financial wealth to draw upon when the oil runs out. Since our hypothetical team has set 15 years for financial surplus accumulation let us assume that OPEC surplus countries will start to consume 8 percent annually of their accumulated wealth; that is, they will be living on their yields rather than eating up their capital. This means that these countries would become *rentier* economies, living on the fruits of their past accumulations.

These are the assumptions of the imaginary scenario undertaken by a dummy group of experts in 1975. On these assumptions, OPEC countries would be accumulating some $1140 billion by 1990. This is a huge amount of money. But such a reputable institution as the World Bank in one of its estimates advanced the figure of $1206 billion for 1985, not for 1990.[28] The figure of $500 billion was very much quoted in the wake of oil price increases for 1980[29] and it is not very much out of tune to expect it to have doubled in a decade.

The transfer of only a reasonable annual yield on this accumulated wealth (8 percent) would amount to something like $91 billion annually in the early nineties. This is a kind of debt service of which host countries, particularly OECD countries, should assume the burden. With the assumption that American exports increase from 1974 onward by 6 percent annually in *real* terms, this means that the debt service for OPEC financial wealth would represent the equivalent of 30 percent of American exports in the early nineties. This is hardly an acceptable burden. A substantial reverse capital outflow to OPEC surplus countries should, then, take place precisely at the end of the oil era. The recipients of oil funds in the seventies and eighties would, beginning in the nineties, have to maintain a persistent surplus current account to service OPEC financial assets.

Fundamentally it is a country's overall level of savings relative to investment that determines its current account. Underlying the sustainability of current accounts surpluses is an assessment of the sustainability of the consumption patterns.[30] Servicing previously accumulated OPEC financial assets without increasing the future potential for savings would amount to a reduction of real consumption. This is supposed to take place after the cessation of oil flows from OPEC to oil importing countries. The higher the financial burden, the more difficult it is to enforce it. In fact, a going concern is the most effective guarantee for enforcing one's financial claims. If the oil consuming countries cannot decrease their *real* consumption to pay for the oil imports and add to their future wealth while the oil is still forthcoming, it will be extremely difficult for them to do so after the oil depletion. The future needs of the present oil surplus countries do not seem to offer sufficient motivation for the oil importing countries to reduce their real consumption in the future, precisely when there is no longer any going concern among them. The heavier the financial burden, the less likely that it will be honored. Only through increasing the world's future propensity to save by adding to its wealth could OPEC financial assets be serviced without reduction of future consumption.

The moral of the imaginary exercise above does not lie in any particular figure or assumption. In fact there is ample room for changes in these assumptions. But even then the result will remain the same. What is wrong is the belief that oil funds are just more finance looking for investment. Investment opportunities are not given before and independently of the use of the oil funds; on the contrary, they depend on the way oil funds are used. Oil funds being major additions to world savings, it is only by analyzing the underlying forces of investment and consumption that we can draw any meaningful conclusions. The basic flaw in the preceding scenario is not with figures but with the mode of thinking. Oil funds are not simply arithmetics of quantities to be added, multiplied, compounded... and so forth. Oil funds represent a structural change in the world economy, and without analyzing this structural change, any attempt at understanding it is as doomed to absurdity as is our imaginary exercise.

B. The Dilemma of OPEC Savings

Increased World Propensity to Save

Sparsely populated and already enjoying high per capita income before the oil price increases in 1973–1974, OPEC surplus countries have a very high propensity to save.[31] The oil price increase is, in fact, nothing more than a redistribution of world income in favor of OPEC countries, brought about by the changes in their terms of trade. This means an increase in the world propensity to save.[32] The fact that the increase in world savings is related to income redistribution is of paramount importance to the understanding of the new situation created by the oil price increases.

The standard practice in macro-analysis, following Keynes, is to relate savings to the level of income. It is maintained that savings are a function of the level of income. Many refinements to the savings/consumption function are available, such as introducing the permanent rather than the actual income,[33] or the relative alongside the absolute income, among independent variables.[34] Even the "distribution of income" factor is used, but it is also affirmed that "these distributional effects are commonly exaggerated by observers."[35] In any case, these refinements are very often relegated to the background, and we are left again with savings and the level of income. A notable exception to this practice is to be found in the Cambridge School (England),[36] in whose models distribution of income has always played a prominent part. The Cambridge School is, however, concerned with long-run growth models:[37] the relationship of distribution of income (as between profits and wages) and the growth of the economy. In the OPEC case we are witnessing an immediate (and rather abrupt) change in income distribution with the result of an increase in savings without a corresponding increase in income (it actually declined). This would call for a new line of thought for the problem.

Savings-Investment Equality

I shall analyze the new situation by using the Keynsian technique of the identity of *ex post* savings and investment. Keynsian economics might be greeted now with more protest than acclaim. This is one thing, but the use of the specifically Keynsian apparatus of thought is another. It has in fact embraced the modern system of national income accounts, and has, accordingly, a general applicability.[38] Keynes himself used it to account for income (employment) changes (through the multiplier), while Kaldor, for example, accommodated it for a theory of income distribution in a growth model.

Whatever determines the *ex ante* savings and investment, there must be *ex post* equality between realized savings and investment. This is an accounting identity. In a closed economy there must be equality between realized savings and investment. International relations complicate the picture without altering any of its essentials. Taken as a whole, the world economy is nothing more than a closed economy.

It has been shown that oil funds add substantial flows to the world economy aggregates. They are, moreover, injected into the world economy and not confined within the political boundaries of their initial owners. It may therefore be best to deal with these funds through a macro framework for the world economy as a whole. This macro-analysis gives a spurious air of neatness and simplicity to a real situation far more intricate and complex. It has, nonethless, the merit of bringing to light the whole situation and allowing us to see the whole wood rather than just the single trees.

Possible Responses to Increased OPEC Savings

If the savings-investment equality must hold *ex post* in all cases, theorists differ among themselves as to the way the economy would respond to an *ex ante* change in either of them. There is no doubt that OPEC countries have increased their savings after the oil price increases in 1973 and 1974. Yet every saving is matched, *ex post,* by a parallel investment. Three logical scenarios can then take place in the face of the OPEC savings increase:

  i. there could be a parallel increase in the rate of real investment in the world;
  ii. there could be dis-savings elsewhere in the world to offset the increase in OPEC savings: i.e. no change in the net position of the world;
  iii. there could be neither increase in real investment nor dis-savings, but only increase in financial assets, with real investment remaining unchanged.

Let us call the first scenario "the investment case", the second "the distribution of wealth case" and the third "the placement case". These labels need little explanation — for this purpose we need only to understand the French term *placement,* as distinguished from "investment". By placement I mean the purchase of titles to debts or shares; that is, the purchase of financial assets. The term "investment" can then be confined to the use of finance to add to capital goods.[39] Whereas investment adds to the productive capacity of the economy, placement adds only to the financial assets.

It is not necessary that only one of the above scenarios should take place as a result of OPEC's new savings. A combination of elements from different scenarios is always possible, and is even more likely to happen. It is useful, however, to analyze each case separately in order to emphasize the different outcome from each.

Scenario I: The Investment Case. This is a very interesting case, since it represents the ideal outcome for OPEC countries and the world at large. It implies some temporary sacrifices during a transitional period for resource allocation. There will be a real response to the increase in the world propensity to save. The allocation of resources between consumption and investment will be shifted in favor of investment. Thus the immediate effect of the oil price increase would be a reduction in consumption equal to the increase in OPEC's savings. However, there is no reason why the decrease in consumption would be distributed equally among various countries. It is likely, though not necessarily so, that this would be distributed somewhat in relation to oil imports.

This is the true meaning of the assertion that oil price increases imply the transfer of real resources. The issue is not the transfer of real resources from oil importing countries to OPEC as is usually maintained:[40] rather it is the reallocation of resources from consumption to investment. What is important is not who foregoes resources and to whom they go; rather it is to what uses resources are allocated. It is natural, nonetheless, that the oil exporters would have substantial claims on the additional investment (in ownership and/or debt).

The reduction of real consumption in this case need not be permanent. With a higher rate of capital formation the world would grow richer, and previous consumption levels would accordingly be resumed and even surpassed in time. The world economy would move to a higher growth path.[41] The transition to this new path would inevitably imply some distortions in prices, employment, and so forth, before full adjustment could be accomplished. The important aspect about this case is not to visualize the final outcome but to identify the mechanism for bringing it about. Here we find that economists would differ in their appreciation of the economic forces capable of achieving this result.

Interest rates versus effective demand. The neo-classical versus neo-Keynsian debate is a longstanding one and it is easy to recognize its traces in almost every policy issue. In our specific problem the neo-classical could only be brought about by a change in relative capital price, the rate of interest. Economists nurtured in the Keynsian tradition would claim that only a change in effective demand could enhance the real investment.

Bent Hansen, otherwise a Keynsian, seems to think that the neo-classical mechanism would do the trick as regards problems of our kind. He argues that investing oil funds in OECD countries and in particular in the United States would, under reasonable assumptions, affect the credit market in such a way that it "would generally tend to be easier. *Real investment* would tend to increase because the desired long-term real capital stocks tend to increase with *lower interest rates* [emphasis mine]."[42] Thus the increase in world savings following the emergence of OPEC surpluses would mean that "interests would fall just sufficiently to induce that amount of real investment."[43]

This argument assumes that the rate of interest is not a monetary phenomenon dependent on the policies of monetary authorities. To put it differently, it is assumed that "the monetary system operates in such wise as to interpret and not to distort the influence of real forces", that is "the rate of interest depends on the demand for and supply of investable funds; behind the former stand the forces of productivity, behind the latter those of thrift."[44] More serious is the implication in this approach that investment is a demand for capital, itself a productive factor employable in the economy according to its relative price as compared with the prices of other factors of production.[45] If one accepts this representation, the traditional thesis which assumes the dependence of investment on the rate of interest naturally follows.

The second approach, in a Keynsian vein, would portray investment as independent of the propensity to save. It is the effective demand, with all the structural ingredients that it embodies, that determines the investment function. A shift in effective demand towards more capital formation would be necessary to bring about an increase in real investment. Here it is worth emphasizing that underlying the apparent difference between the neo-classical and the neo-Keynsian approaches is a deeper policy recommendation. In the neo-classical approach no structural change is needed; financial markets with their ordinary instruments (interest rates) would be sufficient. Hence OECD countries with their highly organized financial markets would be the proper place to invest oil funds. Following the neo-Keynsian approach there is no guarantee that the market forces would bring about the necessary changes in effective demand. Hence, OECD countries by the simple fact that they have better financial markets are not necessarily the best market; LDCs with vast potential investment opportunities might be the answer to the required change in effective demand.

In any case, following this scenario, there would be a parallel increase in real investment to match the increase in OPEC savings. Real consumption has to be curtailed, at least in the early stages. Financial assets would in all probability increase proportionately to the increase in real investment. "With real investments running at a higher level, a continued inflow of oil exporters' funds might thus take place without further increase in the price of financial assets."[46] It is by no means necessary, according to this scenario, that general prices should increase if the curtailment of real consumption is brought about by appropriate policy measures. There might be one-time changes in prices to bring about the necessary reallocation of resources, but there would not be any inherent need for continuous price increases.

Scenario II: The Distribution of Wealth Case. In this case there will be no net change in the global situation; there will be only a redistribution of wealth. This scenario corresponds to a great extent to the general popular feeling in the wake of the oil price increases. The mass media at this time cried wolf, and exaggerated stories about an eventual Arab takeover of the Western economy made headlines. This was a time when one could read articles about how many years or months it would take Saudi Arabia to purchase General Motors or even all the Fortune 500 corporations. A minority share in Krupp purchased by Iran, a Kuwaiti purchase of some real estate in South Carolina, Libya's investment in Italy's Fiat, and similar transactions gave support to such fears.

In any case this scenario assumes that the increased wealth of OPEC countries will be accomplished by the impoverishment of the oil importing countries. The former will save more and the latter less; that is, the increased OPEC savings will be offset by the other's dis-savings. The allocation of resources between investment and consumption will remain, by and large, unaffected; only the holders of claims on wealth will change. OPEC surplus countries will have more financial assets, the rest of the world less. But to assume that there would be no real change, and that only the holders of financial assets would alter, is an extreme simplification. Some alterations in industrial allocations are conceivable and even likely with the change in holders of assets. There is no reason to suppose that the latter would necessarily perpetuate the "old" demand. However, the main feature of this case is that the overall allocation of resources between investment and consumption will remain unchanged regardless of the change within each of them. The world as a whole would be neither richer nor poorer; only the distribution of wealth would change.

If real consumption, savings and investment aggregates remain unchanged as suggested by this scenario, so would the volume of financial assets. There is no reason why the rate of flow of financial assets would increase in this case, neither is there any inherent reason why general prices should change. There is only a change in the holders of the financial assets.

Although the outcome of this scenario is simple to conceive, it is difficult to think of a mechanism that would bring it about. What is needed is a mechanism whereby oil importing countries would finance their oil deficit by handing over financial claims on their domestic wealth to OPEC surplus countries; that is, liquidating part of their wealth in favor of OPEC countries. A similar mechanism was at work in the fifties and sixties in the relationship between the American economy and the rest of the world. During most of that period the United States had a favorable trade balance, though the overall balance of payments was in deficit. The American dollar was — and still is — the principal international reserve currency: these two factors account for the ability of the United States to finance its major overseas investments, i.e. the transfer of wealth to the United States.

There are, however, at least two basic differences between this American example and the OPEC case. First, American foreign investments were carried out gradually over a long period, while the OPEC phenomenon is an abrupt one. A difficulty with the OPEC situation stems to a large extent from the suddenness of its appearance.[47] Had the increase in OPEC wealth taken place gradually over the last 25 years (at 3 percent annually for example), the world accommodation to this transfer of wealth would have been smooth. Second, and more important, American foreign investments usually took the form of a technology-management-finance package, whereas the OPEC savings are pure finance without any element of technology. This accounts partly for the hostile reaction to OPEC finance in most host countries, particularly the OECD countries.

In view of these features of the new OPEC riches, it is hard to conceive of a situation where a substantial sellout of existing securities and/or of newly issued ones to OPEC countries could take place without creating a major disruption in financial markets and affecting the underlying confidence in it. This is a situation that most oil importing countries would resist. OPEC countries, for their part, would be extremely reluctant to accept it either. They have shown a great deal of discretion in these matters. Therefore we believe that this scenario is very unlikely to take place, not only because it is difficult to think of a smooth mechanism for bringing it about but particularly because all interested parties are opposed to it for various reasons. Thus the most publicized scenario for the aftermath of oil price increases is, in fact, the least likely to occur.

Scenario III: The Placement Case. In the previous two cases financial assets were introduced in the system only indirectly. The world economy adjusted to the new situation of increased propensity to save through changes in *real aggregates;* in the first case the increase in real investment, and in the second the redistribution of wealth. Financial assets *followed* the real adjustments. They increased proportionately to the increase in real investment in Scenario I, and remained constant — if in new hands — in Scenario II. The basic fact in these two scenarios is that there exists a direct relationship between real investment and the flow of financial assets, which remains constant in both.

The characteristic feature of the new scenario is that this relationship is broken. Financial assets would increase independently of real investment and would set the economy in motion. Financial assets are therefore introduced directly into the picture as a result of the increased OPEC savings, and other adjustments would follow. Thus in this scenario the reactions to OPEC savings are mainly financial rather than real. Here we assume that the overall allocation of resources between investment and consumption remains by and large unchanged after the oil price increases, and that there is no apparent dis-saving in other parts of the world following the OPEC savings increase.

This opens a new chain of reactions through the behavior of financial assets. In the face of increases in the oil import bill and the emergence of a trade deficit on one hand, and the reluctance of all parties to transfer wealth to OPEC or to change consumption patterns on the other hand, the deficit countries would issue new financial assets. OPEC countries on the other side would be desirous of holding the new forms of wealth that were credit-worthy and did not create political animosity. Hence the supply of new financial assets would be matched by a new demand from OPEC to hold them.

Now everything seems in order. OPEC countries would increase their savings and hold a preferred form of wealth. The deficit countries would minimize the *real transfer of resources* (from consumption to investment, or from oil-consuming to OPEC) and finance their deficit by issuing new paper. But this cannot be the end of the story — there must be something missing. OPEC's savings seem to be increasing without a corresponding increase in investment or an off-setting by dis-savings. This is impossible. What is left out is the behavior of costs and prices in the new situation.

The increase of financial assets held by OPEC countries means a corresponding increase in the financial liabilities of deficit countries. If OPEC countries choose to increase their savings in the form of new financial assets this means that they intend to own them, i.e. to receive a reasonable return on them.[48] Since we assume that the real capital stock has not undergone any change with the issuance of new financial assets, capital is now owned (directly and indirectly, in equity and debt) by a wider class of owners. The new claimants on wealth are entitled to a nominal return on their assets equivalent to that of the "old" owners of wealth. In a smooth, frictionless, certain world, the increase in loanable funds would bid up prices for financial assets and hence reduce the interest rate. This is the neo-classical world. But one of the best-known lessons of monetary history is that any disturbance in economic activity leads to a crisis of confidence and to a rise rather than a fall in interest rates.[49] The banking system would be induced in all probability to generate the necessary increase in liquidity. With the oil price increase under the shadow of bombs and shells in the Middle East and the effects of the oil embargo, one is hardly dealing with a tranquil neo-classical world. Rates of interest are necessarily increasing. The new financial assets will produce the same nominal yields as the "old" ones. In order to be able to pay the same capital returns to the new owners, prices and costs must be pushed up. In other words, with increased financial liabilities, the capital cost for production is increased.

In fact empirical investigations have shown a remarkable historical constancy in the rate of profit, capital/output ratio and the share of profit in the Gross Domestic Product (GDP) of advanced industrial countries.[50] It follows that the nominal increase in the value of capital would lead to a corresponding increase in the nominal value of output. If it is assumed then, that the rate of profit and the capital/output ratio remain constant, the value of output must go up with every increase in capital cost. A general price increase movement is set in motion. Now prices are introduced into the picture. With the increase in OPEC savings in the form of new financial assets the capital cost would increase. A general movement of price increase would be triggered off and nominal investment would be increased. Hence, in reaction to the increase in OPEC's savings there would take place a nominal increase in investment and our sacred identity between savings and investment would be rescued.

Here we find that inflation is built into the scenario. It is necessary in order to bring about the equality of savings and investment. Failing to increase real investment or to effect parallel dis-savings leaves open only the possibility of increasing nominal investment. And inflation is part and parcel of the story; it is the villain of the drama, but without it there would be no drama at all.

This is a very different approach from the much-publicized allegation that oil price increases are responsible for world inflation. It is not the oil price increase *per se* that is responsible for inflation; rather it is a particular mode of investment of oil surpluses that gives rise to the price increase. It has been found that only 2.4 percent of the increase in prices in the United States in 1974 could be explained by oil price increases. And this should be only a one time increase. Similar conclusions have been found for other OECD countries. In other words, ours is a macro interpretation of inflation based on the need to increase nominal—short of real—investment to match OPEC increased savings. This is different from the micro cost-push approach to inflation which attributes the increase in general prices to the increase in energy cost. The difference between the two approaches does not stop at the diagnosis but extends to the cure. If inflation were the villain it could be controlled according to the micro approach simply by reducing oil prices, and according to the macro approach by increasing investment in the world.

Before proceeding any further in developing this inflation argument a word of warning is necessary. It would be a great mistake to lose a sense of proportion in discussing inflation. This is a world problem to which various factors contribute. Since I am dealing here with oil funds and the mode of their investment, it is natural to focus on their impact on inflation. Their role should not be exaggerated, however; they are not the unique cause but are merely an aggravating factor. In most industrial countries inflation has deep-rooted causes in the social, political and economic situation. We will not discuss here the hanging sterling balances or bargains between the government and the trade unions in Britain, the unsettled political situation in Italy with its continuous strikes and the flight of capital, or the monetary acquiescence (or recklessness some would say) of the Federal Reserve Board in the United States...etc. This scenario simply says that among so many factors responsible for world inflation, the placing of oil funds to increase financial assets without a parallel increase in real investment could be inflationary.

Insufficient Investment and Inflation
What I am trying to convey in Scenario III seems to be at odds with established post-Keynsian economics. Official Keynsian doctrine maintains that an increase in *ex ante* savings over investment is deflationary rather than inflationary. On the contrary, Scenario III suggests that the increase in OPEC savings, if not matched by an increase in real investment, is inflationary when we might have expected it to be demand-deflationary.[52] This is a very serious point. However, I think that the clue to this apparent contradiction lies in the origins of OPEC savings, which are realized through income redistribution and forced to some ex-

tent on the system. I have alluded earlier to this fact: I will now make use of it.

Since there has not been any major change in the distribution of income in industrial countries over short periods, the official doctrine, though recognizing the importance of income distribution, would postulate savings as a function of the level of income. This is also, more or less, a stable relation. In a nutshell we may say that Keynsian economics maintain that investment – or more precisely the ratio of investment to output – is an independent variable, invariant with respect to changes in savings.[53] Since savings depend on the level of income, if investment were then to fall short of savings, income would have to decline to reduce savings. The equality of investment-savings is maintained. The decline in income (deflation) is necessary to undo the excess savings over investment. So far so good.

But if the increase in savings is the result of a redistribution of income and not of a rise in its level, a change in the level of income would not be absolutely necessary. By analogy, one would expect that if investment fell short of savings, a reverse distribution of income would take place and so reduce the excess savings. This could be done by means of a general increase in prices, the valuation of financial assets being the triggering mechanism in this process. This price increase would eventually start to erode the new savings and a new mechanism to reverse the income distribution is set up. In a comparable argument (a neo-Pasinetti theorem) Kaldor has shown that net savings depend not only on the propensity to save but also on the investment policy.[54] The revaluation of the financial assets will be instrumental in bringing about the identity of savings and investment.

From all this it seems easy to agree with the general conclusion of the Cambridge neo-Keynsian school that "within certain limits, there is a redistribution of income at which the system produces the required amount of savings."[55] *An isolated policy of income distribution to increase OPEC savings is bound to fail if it is not accompanied by a proper investment policy.*

Having emphasized the different sources of OPEC increased savings, it remains true that savings are also a function of the level of income. The traditional Keynsian diagnosis is not altogether inaccurate. The excess of savings over investment is also deflationary. The fact that OPEC's increased savings are due to income redistribution does not deny the dependence of the savings on the level of income also. The "income distribution" variable supplements, but does not supplant, the "level of income" variable. This in fact accounts for the ambivalent impact of OPEC increased savings which are mainly inflationary but also partly deflationary. Undoing OPEC excess savings would require a reverse action on the distribution of income but also a decline in the level of income. The inflationary effects of OPEC savings remain prominent in this scenario.

Different Scenarios and OPEC's Interests

Before proceeding any further it might be advisable to see to what extent the various outcomes of the scenarios outlined above correspond to OPEC interests. If we accept the definition of OPEC self-interest given earlier, it seems that from the OPEC point of view, Scenario I provides the best result. "The investment case" would in fact ensure the maintenance of the real value of OPEC assets. The oil funds would contribute to the increase in the world investment rate; the world as a whole would get richer thanks to oil funds while the probability of converting OPEC's financial assets into real assets would be greater; and in the end everybody would be better off.

"The transfer of wealth case" has an intermediate position in this order. While the real value of OPEC's accumulated assets would be maintained in this scenario, the outcome would be politically dangerous. The transfer of wealth to OPEC is real, it is true, but the world as a whole is possibly poorer, not richer. What OPEC gained under these conditions would be a loss for the others: it is a zero-sum game. Moreover, risks of the convertibility in the future of OPEC financial assets into real assets would become greater in the post-oil period.

The worst case is in fact "the placement case", since OPEC financial assets would be losing their real value continuously through inflation. The gains accrued to OPEC through oil price increases would be eroded by general price increases and a reverse income distribution would be set in motion.

The World Economy and OPEC's Savings

In the light of observations during the past few years, world economic developments seem to suggest that the third scenario is probably the best description of the actual situation. Data on worldwide real investment rates, general prices, financial asset flows and OPEC surpluses provide ample evidence that the world response to OPEC savings best fits the placement case.

In the 1970s, after more than two decades of unprecedented growth, the world economy faced its most serious setback for some years. At that time the world plunged into its deepest recession for a quarter of a century, which started late in 1973 and reached its low point in the first half of 1975.[56] Economic activity picked up again late in 1975 but compared to past standards the recovery was mild and growth rates remained modest. Real investment did not show any marked increase following the increase of OPEC savings, but was on the contrary disappointingly slow. It became almost a ritual with the International Monetary Fund (IMF) in its annual reports to lament the low rate of fixed investments, particularly in OECD countries.[57] As it became a world problem, inflation captured public attention and made headline news. Two-digit inflation became universal and not just the prerogative of the Latin American economies. From less than 7 percent in 1973 — which was already high by the standards of the day — the rate of inflation averaged 13.5 percent in the industrial countries in 1974[58] and if it dropped in the following year, it still remained at twice the annual average prevailing in the sixties.[59] There were, of course, great disparities in inflation rates among nations: the Swiss did best with an inflation rate of only 2 percent (at the cost, however, of a low growth rate); the Germans scored second with about 3.5 percent. In the United Kingdom the rate was 13.5 percent in 1977 and in Italy 21 percent in the same year.[60] The United States, long accustomed to price stability, had to accommodate itself to an annual rate of inflation of 13 to 15 percent and higher rates were recorded in 1979/1980.

It is worth noting the behavior of interest rates here. In the face of the huge OPEC funds looking for placement opportunities, interest rates have risen substantially instead of going down as a neo-classical approach would expect. The United States, which was the major beneficiary of OPEC funds, set the pace for interest rate increases. In the spring of 1974 that country's rates rose to a record level, for that time, of 8 percent for the discount rate, 13.5 percent for Federal funds, about 12.5 percent for deposits, and around 13 percent for the bankers' prime lending rate.[61] Prime rates of 19 percent became quite common early in 1980. As for the share of profit in total income, available data seem to suggest that they have recently tended to increase too.[62]

Against the sluggish growth in GNP and the slackness of real investment, financial assets flows have increased enormously. The spectrum of financial assets is very broad indeed. They include the all-liquid money and quasi-money, less liquid securities, and still more illiquid claims and debts. It is sufficient here to refer to simple indicators for the increase in the world's financial assets: the Euro-currency market and the indebtedness of countries. These are incidentally related directly to OPEC surplus funds and in both cases financial claims have been soaring following the increase in OPEC savings.

Statistics on the size of the Euro-currency market differ greatly, depending on the different definitions retained. It is estimated that the

gross size of this market had surpassed the $1 trillion mark sometime be-
tween June and September 1979;[63] since then the annual average growth
has been about 22 percent. It is ironic to reflect that when the IMF met in
Nairobi in the autumn of 1973 it was widely believed that the Euro-
currencies would soon disappear,[64] while in fact the Euro-market was at
the time preparing its giant forward step.

The increase in public foreign debt, particularly of the LDCs, has
become one of the major concerns of international organizations such as
the IMF, the International Bank for Reconstruction and Development
(IBRD) and the United Nations Conference for Trade and Development
(UNCTAD), and has reached such alarming proportions as to need no
further comment. The total debt of the LDCs increased from less than
$75 billion in 1970 to over $240 billion in 1977,[65] and was projected to
reach some $300 billion in 1980. The LDCs' debt represented more than
27 percent of their GNP in 1978.[66] Given the unequal concentration of
this debt among LDCs, these percentages have reached critical thresholds
in some countries.

If we look now into OPEC surpluses during the past few years we
come to the same conclusion. From the high figure of $60 to $65 billion
in 1974, OPEC's current account balance continued to decline steadily.
OPEC's surplus in 1978 was estimated at $18 billion before official
transfers and at only $5 billion after these transfers.[67] This continuous
decline is not only the result of real import increase, but is indeed the
result of the downward trend in the real oil price.[68] In fact the dramatic
changes in world income distribution brought about by the oil price increases in 1974 have been reversed by a continuous deterioration in the
terms of trade of the OPEC countries since then. They have lost almost a
quarter of their oil purchasing power in the last five years as Table II
shows.

From this evidence it seems that in spite of OPEC's new savings there
has been no parallel increase in real investment nor in real dis-savings.
The emergence of OPEC's savings increased the flow of financial assets,
rates of interest went up, and a general increase in prices followed.
Nominal investment increased with the general price increase and a
reverse process of income distribution came into play. OPEC surpluses
are continuously being eroded. This seems to be accepted as a foregone
conclusion. Distinguished economists seemed to take it for granted that
oil fund debts would continue to erode with inflation and that "under
current and prospective conditions, such debts will actually involve a
transfer of real resources, properly measured, from the lenders to the
borrowers",[69] that is, with actual and prospective inflation there would
be a "kind of subsidy on borrowing". To continue the present mode of

TABLE II
OPEC Terms of Trade
(1974 = 100)

Year	Oil Prices	Import Prices	Terms of Trade
1970-1973	20.8	70.3	29.5
1974	100.0	100.0	100.0
1975	98.4	112.8	87.2
1976	105.7	114.6	92.2
1977	113.9	125.2	91.0
1978	116.6	144.0	81.0
1979Q_1	116.6	151.5	77.0

SOURCE: *World Financial Markets*, December 1978.

placing of oil funds is not in the long term interest of OPEC countries but against them, and this is in broad terms "the placement case" referred to earlier.

The situation was partially corrected in 1979 with a second major price increase and the prospects for another wave of substantial surpluses are open again. However, without a different strategy for oil funds investment there is no reason why the final outcome of the next round should be different from the previous one.

Developed and Developing Countries.

The emergence from among the possible outcomes of "the placement case" is not fortuitous. Its realization is related to the way in which economic forces have acted on the oil funds and particularly to the way they have been used. Whether the oil funds are placed in developing or in developed countries is not irrelevant to the final outcome. By and large, oil surplus funds were, and still are, placed in OECD countries. Probably no more than 20 percent of the total funds were allocated by OPEC to the LDCs, in which they are, in fact, following the conventional wisdom.

The accumulated surpluses of OPEC are not exactly known, but there seems to be general agreement that they stood at about $180 billion at the end of 1978.[78] Of this amount only $30 billion — which is not even 20 percent — was allocated either directly or indirectly through the World Bank and other multilateral lending institutions by OPEC to the LDCs.[71] The rest of their surpluses were channelled to the OECD countries, and it is this mode of placing oil funds that to a great extent determined the actual outcome of OPEC savings. It must be emphasized that this outcome is not due to any deliberate policy on the part of the OECD countries to set economic forces in motion with the intention of eroding OPEC financial assets. Everyone is suffering from inflation. In fact the economic structure of the OECD forbade the increase of real investment in response to the increase in OPEC savings. Unless there is a shift in effective demand towards capital goods industries it will be impossible to increase the rate of investment. The inability of OECD countries to increase their real investment triggered off inflation in response to the increased savings funds of OPEC. This is a matter of structure rather than of policy.

The situation in the LDCs is diametrically opposite in this respect to that of OECD countries. The LDCs are capital-hungry; many investment projects in the LDCs are held back for lack of finance. This does not mean, of course, that development in the LDCs is dependent only on the availability of finance. It has been shown that development is a complex process involving institutional, cultural and political changes as well as economic ones; however, it remains true that possibilities of increasing real investment in the LDCs are enormous and require finance if they are to proceed. Of course increased investment in LDCs would inevitably lead to enhanced demand for the capital goods of OECD countries. Thus it is not unrealistic that, given enough time for adjustments, capital goods industries in OECD countries would expand under the expected new demand from the LDCs.

C. The Surplus-Deficit Game

No conclusion can, however, be drawn from the previous section before discussing the impact of the financial institutions on the recycling process. The basic function of the financial institutions is to act as financial intermediaries.[72] OPEC surpluses placed initially in the OECD financial markets could be — and in fact are — used to finance deficits of the LDCs, thus introducing a new complicating factor that requires separate consideration. The intermediary role of the financial institutions makes it difficult to identify who lends to whom. It may well be that funds first placed in OECD financial institutions are then rechannelled to other developing countries. OPEC oil funds would then be financing the deficits of the LDCs, albeit in an indirect way.

If this is the case, then one can doubt the validity of the provisional conclusions reached in the previous section. It was argued that placing OPEC funds in developed rather than in less developed countries resulted in general price increases instead of increasing real investment in the world; or in our terminology, "the placement case" instead of "the investment case". If it is proved that oil funds were after all channelled to the LDCs, the argument would, if it did not collapse, suffer seriously.

Thus "the placement case" would seem independent of whether oil funds are placed in developed or less developed countries, and this would restore the conventional wisdom. If inflation is inevitable anyway, it is better for OPEC countries to place their financial assets with the more credit-worthy OECD countries and their financial institutions and let the latter assume the risks of the LDCs.

This is a very serious criticism of the whole approach used in this study. Let us first look at the facts.

Increasing Deficits of the LDCs

It seems that before the oil shock in 1973–1974 there existed a relatively constant structure of trade relations. The OECD countries as a group were realizing a favorable current account, non-oil developing countries incurred a comparable deficit, and OPEC countries had an almost balanced account with a slight surplus. In 1970, OPEC countries ran a small deficit in their current account and in 1973 they had a surplus of about $5 billion. The OECD countries' surplus averaged $10 billion in the five years preceding the oil price increase, and non-oil developing countries incurred a deficit of almost the same magnitude as the OECD's surplus.

This situation was suddenly disrupted in the aftermath of the oil price increases in 1973 and 1974. The OECD countries, being the major oil importers, shifted from a surplus position of about $9.5 billion in 1973 to a deficit on current account of $28 billion in 1974. The non-oil developing countries doubled their deficit from $10 billion in 1973 to $20 billion in 1974.[73] OPEC countries were of course the beneficiaries of this new situation, with their current surplus jumping to some $60 billion in 1974.

All these figures are subject to the familiar shortcomings: errors and omissions on one hand and different definitions of surplus and deficit on the other help to explain discrepancies between figures issued by different data sources. However, it remains important that these figures trace the direction of the development in the international current account.

The immediate effect on current account observed in world trade in 1973–1974 was only the first step in a long process, and subsequently evolved to a new structure. Less than five years after the initial oil price increase, OECD countries had readjusted their economies to the new situation in such a way that their combined current account reached a virtual balance in 1978.[74] The non-oil developing countries were the losers in this readjustment process. OECD countries still account for more than three quarters of world oil imports while maintaining an almost balanced account; the LDCs — without increasing their share in oil imports — ran a deficit on current account of $34 billion in 1978.[75]

In 1979 a new oil price shock not unlike that of 1973–1974 occurred. After its virtual balance in 1978, the balance of payments of the OECD countries is expected to worsen. However, as with the first round, we cannot exclude the possibility that the same process will start again and that OECD countries will eventually redress their global balance of payments. It is therefore more revealing to focus our attention on the first round of oil price increases, as outlined in Table III below.

After the full adjustment of the first round of oil price increases, the new structure of the world's current accounts seemed to settle at a more or less balanced account for OECD countries, at a more manageable OPEC surplus and a corresponding deficit for the LDCs.[76] Under these conditions it was only natural that financial flows would be forthcoming to the LDCs and this in fact happened. It is estimated that during 1974 and 1975 commercial banks in OECD countries (either mainland or off-shore) financed about 45 percent of the current deficit of the LDCs. Since 1975 the annual amount of the financing by the new banks of the LDCs has not fallen from its 1974–1975 level.[77] Of OPEC's total net deposits of $30 billion in the international banking system in 1979, some $24 billion were rechannelled to the LDCs.[78]

It is clear then that OPEC surpluses are to a great extent used to offset the deficits of the LDCs and that OPEC funds initially placed in OECD's financial institutions are probably partly channelled to the LDCs. To what extent does this affect the argument about oil funds investment in developed or less developed countries?

The Economic System

In economics, no less than in other social sciences, it is difficult to distinguish between cause and effect. Relations between them are so interconnected with continuous feedbacks that it is not uncommon to confuse them. In the particular case of oil funds investment we need to keep two concepts about the economic system in mind. The first is that of process. Economic activity proceeds as a sequence of actions and reactions; every action calls for a specific set of economic forces out of which will emerge the final outcome. The second is that of a circuit; different parts or sectors are linked together through the interaction in the economy. This is the old *tableau économique*. Injecting OPEC oil funds into the world economy would necessarily call forth different economic forces and involve other parts of the world economy. The path of the economy would be different according to the economic forces involved, nor can it be indifferent to actions taken in the first place.

Scenario I ("the investment case") showed that injecting oil funds into the LDCs in the first place would enhance world demand for capital goods; this would bring about a reallocation of world resources between

TABLE III
Shifts in Global Structure of Current Account Balance
($ billion)

| | 1967-72 Average | | 1977 |
	Actual current Account Balance	Rescaled to 1977 Prices and Output	
Major oil exporting countries	0.7	3	42
Industrial countries	10.2	30	–
Other non-oil countries			
more developed	– 1.7	– 6	– 12
less developed	– 8.1	– 27	– 27
TOTAL	1.1	–	3

SOURCE: International Monetary Fund, *IMF Survey*, 16 May 1977.

consumption and investment. The world would be moving along a new path with increased rates of real investment and an increase in the imports by the LDCs of capital goods would be involved, with the OECD countries being affected by oil funds indirectly through increasing capital goods trade with the LDCs. This is different from the path that would result from the initial placing of the oil funds with the OECD. Scenario III ("the placement case") showed that this would aggravate and fuel inflationary forces and pressures, with the increase in financial assets (liabilities) producing a corresponding increase in capital costs. The world would be moving along a different path with inflation *en route*. The LDCs would be affected by oil funds indirectly through imported inflation and deterioration of their current accounts, and oil funds would be rechannelled to the LDCs to finance their balance of payments deficit, not their increased investment.

It is then fair to conclude that the mere fact that oil funds are ultimately financing the LDCs does not affect our previous conclusions.

Surplus-Deficit Relations

It is always easy to overlook simple facts. The surplus-deficit situation is, after all, a zero-sum game. The surplus exists as far as the deficit is permitted to exist. This may seem a trivial fact but it is very important. OPEC surplus countries not only have a vital interest in preserving the value of their financial assets in the future, but they need also to maintain their surplus status for as long as they are unable to undertake productive domestic investment. The maintenance of the surplus status hinges upon the persistence of a corresponding deficit status. In a way, surplus and deficit countries are in the same boat.

We have seen that the initial OPEC surplus in 1974, as was to be expected, was matched with an OECD deficit. This situation could not last. Five years later, though still consuming more than three quarters of oil imports, the OECD had reached virtual current balance in 1978. The deficit of the LDCs continued to increase, in fact counterbalancing the OPEC surplus, a situation that seems to represent a new structure for world current account balances. The LDCs' deficit as a counterbalance to the OPEC surplus does not seem to be an ephemeral event but is there to stay. This is not a coincidence. It is the "normal" outcome of economic forces ("normal" being understood in a positivistic sense), which would help bring this about.

Oil funds are not only an addition to world savings; they are also savings realized through a disequilibrium in the balance of payments. Economic forces related to disequilibria are very much in action here. Economic theory usually distinguishes between a stable and an unstable equilibrium. We need not go far to see whether or not the oil funds disequilibria are stable. It is important to keep in mind that not only can there never be a deficit without finance, but also that the ability of various economies for readjustment is different.

Broadly speaking, developed countries are in a better position than developing ones to correct any imbalances in their external accounts. In a classic article Hla Myint distinguished between two kinds of external vulnerability. The first stems from what he called "the productivity theory of trade" where a country "has adapted and reshaped its productive structure to meet the requirements of the export market through a genuine process of specialization." The second is related to his theory of "the vent for surplus" where a country "happens to possess a sizeable surplus productive capacity which it cannot use for domestic production" and which implies "an inelastic domestic demand for the exportable commodity and/or a considerable degree of international immobility and specificness of resources."[79] In general developed countries exhibit the first kind of vulnerability, while the developing countries suffer from the second. The increased productivity in the first case and the high rigidity in the second explain, to a great extent, the ability of the OECD countries to adjust their external accounts in due course to the oil price shock, and the failure of the LDCs to cope with it.

In this readjustment effort, the OECD countries have greater flexibility in their relationships with other non-oil developing countries than they have with OPEC countries. Their ability to redress their external accounts with OPEC is very limited, while they maintain a tremendous economic superiority over other developing countries. The low price elasticity of the demand for oil, the limited absorptive capacity of key oil-producing countries and the meager prospects, at least in the short term, for substantially increased energy production outside OPEC, are all factors that account for the very narrow scope for the readjustment of OECD's external account with OPEC through changes in the quantities of commodities traded. Moreover, the use of foreign exchange alterations is almost denied to OECD countries in adjusting their relations with OPEC. National OPEC currencies are not in fact independent of major OECD currencies. In most cases, particularly in the Gulf area, they belong to the same currency area of major OECD importing countries. In this case the only available variable would be general price increases which normally hit more at other non-oil developing countries. This will be manifested in the increasing deterioration of the terms of trade of the non-oil LDCs. As the managing director of the IMF has noted:

> ...On a terms of trade basis, the cumulative loss incurred in the seven-year period 1973–79 was of the order of $80 billion. Although much stress has rightly been laid on the effect of oil price increases on the import bills of developing countries, it should be borne in mind that oil still accounts for only about one fifth of the current account deficit of the LDCs. Thus the current account deficits of LDCs have also been raised considerably by the general inflation in countries which export manufactures.[80]

It seems therefore, that given the actual world economic structure and the dominant economic status of the OECD, it is the LDCs that are bound, in the final analysis, to incur the counter deficit of the OPEC surplus. The acknowledgement of this fact is bound to be of the utmost importance to the OPEC investment policy. "It is the poorest industrial countries and the LDCs which have had to carry the largest share of the importing countries' deficit."[81]

The LDCs are, in fact, the ultimate debtors of OPEC's financial claims on the world economy and the real value of these claims cannot be separated from the credit-worthiness of the LDCs. OPEC countries have a definite economic interest in the prosperity of the LDCs who are the last resort guarantors for their claims. Financial institutions are so closely interwoven that any default or failure of substantial magnitude by the LDCs will undoubtedly affect OPEC financial assets. The financial institutions that receive the bulk of OPEC surplus funds are those which extend loans to the LDCs. Any disruption of the international financial market will set forth a chain reaction, similar to that known in political theory as the "domino effect". Indeed, OPEC countries have a direct stake in the economic health of the LDCs.

Moreover, it is likely that the OPEC countries will be called upon to assist the LDCs in case of any serious failure on their part to honor their obligations, since the world cannot afford a serious upheaval in international economic affairs. One of the possible reasons behind the so-called "Witteveen facility" was the increase in the borrowing by some LDCs (e.g. Zaire) from the international capital market to an extent that could have affected some major international and American banks. The OPEC countries are of course *en tête* with countries contributing to this facility. Thus it is probably an illusion to think that OPEC's risks are reduced by the intermediate role played by the financial institutions in the OECD countries.

III.   SOCIO-POLITICAL CONSTRAINTS

A.   OPENING REMARKS

Part II of this chapter attempted to show that there exists an economic case for oil surplus countries to *invest* their oil funds in the LDCs rather than to *place* them in the developed countries. This conclusion was, however, reached according to certain assumptions. It was postulated that the long-run economic interests in preserving the real value of OPEC financial assets are paramount. Oil surplus countries were treated implicitly, moreover, as one homogeneous block entertaining convergent and even coordinated objectives. This is only a device to fix ideas, a first step in an analysis by successive approximations. Further steps are needed to relax these simplifications by introducing more realism into the analysis.

Oil surplus countries are no more *Homo Economicus* than any other entity. The socio-political context of oil surplus countries, particularly in the Gulf area, is overwhelming and cannot be ignored. It is not possible to tackle the so-called financial problem dealt with earlier in terms of abstract economic analysis; there is no such thing as an "economic rationality" — there is only rationality *tout court*.

It is my intention here to introduce other factors which affect the behavior of the oil surplus countries. What looks like an aberration from economic rationality is perfectly justifiable, given the constraints on the oil surplus countries in the Gulf area. It should be noted here, however, that my treatment of these constraints cannot be comprehensive or complete since this would require a complete study of the political sociology of the Gulf, the international politics of oil and finance, and the problems of the absorptive capacity of the LDCs, a task beyond the scope of this work and, indeed, a forbidding area for research.

I shall limit myself to constraints within the oil surplus countries; that is, to those factors in the Gulf area which contribute to the divergence of the present investment policy from that advocated in the first part of this study. It follows that even if these constraints were removed, nothing would guarantee that oil funds would be invested in the LDCs. The international politics of oil and finance on one hand and the situation in the LDCs on the other may still hinder such a flow. It is important, nevertheless, to show that oil surplus countries are constrained from within and that the apparently economically irrational placing of oil funds is, in their own context, justifiable after all. Moreover, external factors, particularly the international politics of oil and finance, normally exert their influence through an internal mechanism. Internal factors themselves are partly the reflection of external factors.

Two sets of problems will be considered. The first concerns the particular situation *of* the oil Gulf states; the second, the situation *in* these states. The former corresponds to the morphology of these states as small, fragmented, mono-resource entities; the latter refers to the texture of the decision-making process within these countries. The one is more concerned with an outside view, the other with an inside view. However, these problems will not be treated equally. The socio-political factors affecting decision-making are so complex and intricate that only a bird's eye view can be attempted in the following section.

OPEC Financial Flows to the LDCs

Before considering these constraints we should first look at the magnitude of oil surplus funds channelled from the Gulf area to finance the LDCs. It would be a grave mistake and an unfair conclusion to overlook or to underestimate the considerable contribution which they make. After 1973/74 OPEC members emerged as a major source of finance to be reckoned with. There is, however, considerable disparity among them in their effort to finance the LDCs. The Arab Gulf states — Saudi Arabia, Kuwait, the United Arab Emirates and Qatar — are obviously the major contributors.[82] Data on financial flows to developing countries leave much to be desired but UNCTAD and the OECD are among a number of international organizations which are currently involved in the collection of information on them.

A comparison between the Development Assistance Committee (DAC) countries and OPEC flows to the LDCs is subject to a number of reservations which bias the final picture against the contributions of the OPEC members;[83] for example, private transfers are not included in the OPEC flows, contrary to DAC flows; equity capital provided by DAC countries to investment in the LDCs is included in their Official Development Assistance (ODA) while the same is not applied to OPEC, and so on.

However, regardless of these reservations, the record of OPEC and particularly the Arab Gulf states is by all standards impressive. After a fourfold increase from 1973 to 1974, total commitments of OPEC donors increased by another 22 percent in 1975 to reach a figure in excess of $15 billion, corresponding to 7.5 percent of the combined GNP of these countries. The volume of total disbursement from OPEC countries to other developing countries increased from about $1.6 billion in 1973 to $11.5 billion and $9.2 billion in 1975 and 1976 respectively, corresponding to 5.6 percent and 3.8 percent of the donors' GNP.[84] It is reported, however, that aid from the OPEC countries declined substantially in 1979. About $4.7 billion only were disbursed that year. Not only does this compare badly with the current account surplus of about $55 billion for that year but it also comprises the lowest percentage of OPEC's total GNP at any time since the 1973 oil price rise.[85]

Compared with DAC countries, the commitment of the ten OPEC donors amounted to 60 percent of the estimated total of the DACs, although the GNP of the latter was almost 16 times the size of the former group.[86] Though it is believed that the total *concessional* net disbursements from OPEC countries in 1978 fell from the 1977 level of $5.9 billion to some $3.7 billion, the Gulf states (Saudi Arabia, Kuwait and the Emirates) continued to allocate a very high proportion of their GNP to these flows as compared with DAC countries.[87] The decline in concessional flows is largely due to the sharp decrease of bilateral flows from the Arab Gulf states to Egypt after the exceptionally high disbursement of the Gulf Organization for the Development of Egypt (GODE) in 1977. The net disbursement of ODA by major groups of donor countries is shown in Table IV.

The non-concessional flows from OPEC members are channelled largely through multilateral institutions such as the World Bank and the IMF. An emerging sector of bilateral non-concessional flows, dominated by Kuwait, is also gaining more ground in the relationships between oil surplus countries and the LDCs. In 1976 Kuwaiti non-concessional flows to the LDCs accounted for fully three quarters of all OPEC non-concessional flows, as compared with 64 percent and 47 percent in the two preceding years respectively. Kuwait's pre-eminence is explained by the existence of several publicly controlled investment companies willing and able to tap investment opportunities in the LDCs. The Kuwait Foreign Trade, Contracting and Investment Company (KFTCIC) is a case in point in this respect. Established in the early sixties with more than 80 percent of public-held shares, KFTCIC is the Kuwaiti government's arm for commercial investment in the LDCs. The complementarity of KFTCIC with the Kuwait Fund for Arab Economic Develop-

TABLE IV

Overseas Development Aid Disbursement by Major Groups of Donor Countries

Donor Group or Country	$ billion			Percentage of Total			Percentage of GNP		
	1973	1977	1978p	1973	1977	1978p	1973	1977	1978p
DAC	9.7	14.7	19.9	78.3	68.7	81.5	0.30	0.31	0.35
OPEC	1.3	5.9	3.7	10.8	27.5	15.2	1.41	1.96	1.11
of which:									
Kuwait	0.3	1.4	0.9	2.5	6.6	3.7	5.7	10.1	4.5
Saudi Arabia	0.3	2.4	1.5	2.5	11.3	6.1	4.0	4.3	2.3
UAE	0.3	1.2	0.6	2.5	5.6	2.5	16.0	10.7	5.4
CPE*	1.3	0.8	0.8	10.8	3.7	3.2	0.09	0.04	0.04
TOTAL**	12.0	21.4	24.4	(100)	(100)	(100)	(not applicable)		

* CPE = Centrally Planned Economies
** excludes amounts provided by donors outside groups: $0.3 billion in 1978.

SOURCE: OECD, *Review; Development Cooperation, 1979*, p. 85.

ment (KFAED) established in 1961 is unmistakeable; the KFAED is the main Kuwaiti instrument for aid to the LDCs.

Huge as they are, OPEC financial flows to the LDCs are only a fraction of the oil surpluses. By and large, oil surplus funds are placed in the developed countries, in spite of the spectacular increase in their financial flows to the LDCs. I intend next to deal with some factors in the Gulf oil states which are constraints on massive investment in the LDCs in general and in the Arab countries in particular.

B. FRAGMENTATION AND MARGINALITY

It has been shown that the Arab Gulf oil countries have a common economic interest in investing their surpluses in the LDCs. This is not, however, the same thing as saying that *each* Gulf oil country has the same interest. There is a gap between the common and the individual interests that is not always easy to bridge. The theory of public or collective goods has helped dissipate some confusion in the matter. Moreover, though raised to world economic — or rather financial — prominence the Gulf oil states are too dependent on oil and in the long run are, after all, only peripheral economies. Fragmentation and marginality plague their investment policy and partly account for the divergence of actual oil funds placement from the otherwise collectively desirable pattern of investment.

Fragmentation of Oil Surplus Countries

We have perhaps been so much indoctrinated in recent years by the OPEC role in oil pricing that we have come to believe that OPEC really exists outside the oil pricing process. With all the fanfare that accompanies the ritual annual ministerial OPEC meetings for deciding the next round of oil price increases, nothing is easier than to lose sight of the basic facts. Outside oil pricing there is, in fact, very little indeed of OPEC concern. The investment of oil surplus funds in particular is decidedly each individual country's affair. What we have called "the financial problem" has never been an OPEC problem, nor an Arab Gulf states' problem. Rather it is a Saudi, a Kuwaiti or a Qatari problem. One would even hesitate to speak of a UAE financial problem, since the ruler of each state in the Federation, with the possible exception of Abu Dhabi, jealously preserves his autonomy in managing his oil funds portfolio. In addition to preserving their independence in their portfolio management, the individual Gulf states even insist on making the confidentiality of their financial placement in the recipient country a *sine qua non* for the continuation of their investment in these countries.[88] Except probably for Kuwait, published information on the Gulf states' surpluses is evasive, if it exists at all. This reflects an utterly individualistic — one could even say personal — attitude towards oil funds investment that is hardly compatible with any collective investment policy for these funds.

Looked at from this angle, the problem of oil funds investment takes on completely different dimensions. The funds no longer appear as a major structural change in the world economy. Rather they are the sum of individual surpluses, each of them more or less marginal. Some countries still enjoy quite substantial surpluses. Saudi Arabia alone accounts for about half of the annual oil surpluses and Kuwait comes second. The rest of the Gulf states, though very wealthy, add only a trifle to world aggregate economic flows, each country being but an atom in the world's financial flows. Of course some countries are bigger atoms than others; the fact remains however that oil surpluses, though important in their totality, are nevertheless marginal and without economic significance once fragmented among many decision makers. In these conditions, investment in the LDCs would appear to be an extremely costly venture for each surplus country behaving independently.

Common Interest and Individual Behavior

It is often suggested that groups of individuals, or for that matter of states, with common interests usually attempt to further them. This opinion is not only held in popular discussions but is also maintained in many scholarly writings. However, nothing seems to support this view, either logically or in practice.[89] Common interest is a necessary condition for collective action but by itself it is not sufficient to bring this about. In many cases, rational, self-interested members of a group will not act to achieve their common or group interest. Rather, rational individual behavior can be contrary to the common interest. This is a classic problem in welfare economics, and a whole literature is devoted to the issue. It is even more central to the theory of development and industrialization of underdeveloped areas.[90]

A public or collective good is defined as one in which the consumption by one member of a group does not reduce its utility to other members of the group.[91] The distinguishing feature of a collective good is that, once provided to one member of the group it can be made available to other members at no extra cost (Samuelson's joint supply principle),[92] and/or the rest of the group cannot be excluded from benefitting from it (Musgrave's exclusion principle).[93]

A correct assessment of the nature of the costs of the collective goods is fundamental to the understanding of the principle. To be sure, they are not free goods since the production of collective goods requires the use of scarce resources and implies risks. However, once provided, a collective good appears to other members of the group as costless and they can enjoy it as free riders. In most cases the indivisibility of costs appears to reside at the heart of the collective goods problem. Whereas costs are indivisible and have to be incurred all at once, benefits can be divided among members of the group. A member of a group may not be able to incur the cost of the collective good because the initial cost exceeds its benefit to him. It is no consolation to know that the total benefit to the group could outmatch the total cost. What matters to each member is the fraction of benefit that he gains from the collective good regardless of the benefits accruing to other members of the group. Without coercion and/or coordination collective goods cannot be provided, no matter how useful they may be.

Investment in the LDCs as a Collective Good

A vast literature on development has emphasized the need for a substantial investment effort to break the vicious circles in the LDCs and hence to make the effort worthwhile. Whether it is called the "big push", "balanced growth" or "takeoff"[94], the message is always the same. Investment in the LDCs cannot be made profitable unless undertaken on a massive scale. While this scale could be within the reach of the oil surplus countries as a group, it is not necessarily attainable by any one country alone. Massive investment in infrastructure as well as in productive projects is, in fact, the condition to secure the profitability of investment in the LDCs. The costs of investment in the LDCs are in a way indivisible. To overcome this limitation and short of coercion being exerted by a supra-national authority, coordination among countries is needed.

The situation is, to some extent, similar to that of the marketplace where structure matters a great deal. The power of, and the benefit for each participant differs with the types of market structure. Under atomistic competition they are "price takers", whereas they are "price makers" with more coordinated types of organization. The analogy with the market structure is very suggestive. Not only is it useful for a better understanding of the actual situation, but it can also shed some light on potential developments. After all, the same countries have experienced a similar situation in oil pricing. Whereas they were all losing under competitive conditions, the establishment of OPEC in 1960 and later its role in oil pricing since 1970, proved to be extremely effective in that respect.

In questioning the extent to which fragmented oil surplus countries can coordinate their investment policy, a brief review of OPEC — itself an instructive example — may be useful.

The OPEC Example

OPEC is a vivid example of the need for, and the success of, a collective action to bring about a common interest to a group of countries, and its history reveals both the potential and the limitations of such a collective action. What has proved to be beneficial in oil pricing matters can be equally important in oil funds investment policy.

The success of OPEC can be ascribed to a great extent to the simplicity of the problem facing its members, who confine themselves to the relatively simple task of agreeing on oil prices. In fact OPEC "does not perform all the functions normally associated with an export cartel which usually has rigid agreements on prices, production control and market shares. Rather, OPEC ministers, during their periodic conferences, merely agree on the price of OPEC marker crude oil."[95] There are two points to be noted here. The first concerns the perception of the need for coordinated action. It seems that, in the perception of the common interest, it is much easier to recognize losses incurred than to grasp profits foregone. The second point is that by failing to establish a collective action, the cost inflicted on the individual member who tries to act for the common good would be very high. There is something here too in the nature of a collective good.

The timing of the establishment of OPEC illustrates the first point. In spite of the advocacy of Sheikh ʿAbdallah Tariqi, former Saudi oil minister, of the tremendous benefits for oil exporting countries in coordinating their oil policy, and his repeated pleas for collective action, OPEC was set up only in 1960, the "oil consciousness" of the producing countries having been aroused by the 1959 and 1960 price cuts, unilaterally imposed by the oil companies without informing, much less consulting, the governments involved.[96] Historically OPEC was created to halt oil price cuts: it was a defensive mechanism against real losses incurred. Later on it became a powerful instrument to increase oil prices; that is, to recoup foregone profits.

Early attempts by member countries to establish their national control over the oil, which would eventually benefit all oil producing countries, were thwarted by actions from other producers. The attempt by the Mossadeq government to nationalize the Anglo-Iranian Oil Company in 1950 and 1951, and later the move by Prime Minister Qassem in 1959 to restrict severely the concession granted to the Iraq Petroleum Company, were both made pointless by the increase in oil production in other oil producing countries who competed for more markets, more production and more revenues.[97] The Iranian and Iraqi examples illustrate the high cost of an individual's failure to act for the common interest without coordinating with other members of the group. It is also true that the role of oil companies was predominant at that time and the governments concerned had little control over their oil production.

Although the first oil price increase by OPEC took place in Teheran in 1971, it was through the Libyan effort that the breakthrough was possible. The road to Teheran passed by way of Tripoli: with the advent of the Libyan revolution in 1969, a new exogeneous factor was introduced to OPEC. The new Libyan government, whether acting from naiveté or shrewdness, was an outsider to the rules of the game in the oil market. A puritan revolutionary regime, the new government was prepared in the early days—perhaps without being fully aware of the consequences—to forego some of the oil revenues and thus to incur for others, if need be, the initial cost of disrupting the prevailing situation of the oil companies working in Libya. The new military junta was obviously helped in its risk-assuming enterprise by having to deal with the weakest link in the chain of oil companies. Occidental Petroleum, the Los Angeles independent, depended almost totally on its Libyan operations with 96 percent of its world investment concentrated there. Bunker-Hunt was in a similar situation, and these two companies were particularly vulnerable to the Libyan decisions.[98] In addition, the American Administration at the time seemed to have concluded that it could not openly assist the oil industry.[99] The success of the Libyan government paved the way for OPEC to move into the new role of collectively fixing oil prices in Teheran.

The relevance of external factors can hardly be overestimated in the two subsequent major oil price increases that followed the Teheran agreement. The October War in 1973 with the concomitant oil embargo on the one hand, and the Iranian revolution and the overthrowing of the Shah in 1979 on the other, gave OPEC valuable opportunities to increase oil prices almost with impunity. In between these two events, oil prices either increased mildly or there was a failure to reach the desired consensus (for example, the two-tier price system resulting from the OPEC meeting in Doha in December 1976). Even with OPEC, the stimulus to oil price increases was more external than internal.

It would be a grave mistake, however, to think that the growing role of OPEC in oil pricing is due only to external factors. The underlying economic and political conditions have seen dramatic changes. The role of the companies has been continuously reduced. The economics of the oil industry have also changed with the passage from easily accessible to less accessible oil fields. A parallel change took place in oil pricing principles. In a first phase, the cost of production was the main point of reference in oil prices. In a second phase, with less accessible oil fields, the cost of substitution became more relevant in oil pricing.[100]

The difficulties of achieving the common interest are obvious, but there are promising indications of a change in attitudes: new factors are emerging which call for a more coordinated investment policy by oil surplus countries.

New Prospects

New developments which are affecting the international scene could lead to a reconsideration of, and eventually to more coordination in, the investment policies of the oil surplus countries. First and foremost was the American decision to freeze the Iranian government's assets in the wake of developments that followed the seizing of American Embassy personnel in Teheran by a group of Iranian militants in November 1979. Though the American President's action under the International Emergency Act of 1977 was nothing novel—similar measures were in fact applied extensively during the Second World War—the American decision came as a revelation, or more accurately as a psychological shock, to oil surplus governments. The illusion of security was cruelly shattered. The disconcerted public statements made by OPEC officials at the time reflected their disarray and confusion. A case in point is the immediate comment of the Saudi Foreign Minister who asserted—and his assertion should not be taken literally—that the American decision "gives us no ground for concern whatsoever, because it could never happen to us. No one could *ever* seize the American Embassy in Riyadh."[101]

Fundamentalist Muslim rebels were apparently not interested in the American Embassy in Riyadh, but they did seize the Grand Mosque in Mecca, the holiest of all Muslim shrines, only five days after the Minister's statement.

Moreover, the Saudi Minister could not have failed to observe that the American decision to freeze Iranian assets was taken ten days *after* the seizing of the Embassy and within hours of the Iranian Finance Minister's threat to move Iran's funds out of American banks.[102] The American Secretary of the Treasury was categorical in affirming that "the President acted to protect American claims against Iran and not to increase pressure on Teheran to release the U.S. hostages."[103] The Oil Minister of the United Arab Emirates perhaps reflected better the state of mind in the area when he described the American measure as "creating doubt and anxiety in investment circles and setting a precedent for other countries to do the same whenever they have a problem."[104]

Oil surplus countries have discovered, to their dismay, that the political risks of investment are as serious in developed as in developing countries. By way of analogy, the American "freeze" can be compared with the oil companies' price cuts in 1959. In both cases OPEC countries stood to incur realized losses and not only foregone profits. Price cuts in 1959 and in 1960 triggered a process to coordinate oil price policies, while the fear of further freezes may lead to a corresponding coordination in investment policies. The Arab Monetary Fund took the initiative in discussing "...the serious and dangerous precedent created by the United States' decision to freeze the deposits and assets of a particular country."[105] This could be only a first step.

Secondly, the increasing concern among the members of the international community over the fate of the oil surpluses might eventually oblige oil surplus states to come up with something constructive. In the early days after the first oil price shock in 1973–1974, the world was faced with the problem of the recycling of the oil funds. At the time the IMF came up with the Oil Facilities in 1974 and 1975, and another supplementary Facility known as the Witteveen Facility was agreed upon in late 1978. The bulk of the burden was, however, taken up by the private international commercial banks. It is recognized that although the international capital market succeeded in absorbing and rechannelling oil funds fairly efficiently, the costs to the world, and particularly to the Third World, are quite high. There is now an increasing demand for oil funds to be used for a kind of global Marshall Plan. In 1977 the Scandinavian countries proposed a scheme to the United Nations General

Assembly which involved the massive transfer of resources on a scale resembling that of the Marshall Plan. It would allow for the possibility of directing the demand created in the developing countries towards industries with excess capacity in developed counties. A similar proposal put forward by Mexico is being studied by the World Bank and the OECD is looking at a co-financing program with OPEC to the LDCs, while similar resolutions have been submitted to the United States Congress.[106] These proposals would not necessarily take the interests of the oil surplus countries as their focal point.

More imminent is the proposal to create a substitution account within the IMF. It is true (at the time of writing) that the proposal seems for the moment to be shelved, but the message is clear enough. In their first statement, the Consultative Group on International Economic and Monetary Affairs — known as the Group of Thirty — declared that there was urgent need to reach agreement on the proposal for the establishment of a substitution account in the International Monetary Fund to issue claims denominated in Special Drawing Rights (SDRs) in exchange for official dollar reserve assets. Although the principal objective of such an account was to alleviate the pressure on the dollar, its implication for the liberty of disposal of oil surplus funds cannot be mistaken. This was explicitly stated: "...the need to establish this account has been lent added urgency by the prospects that members of OPEC are likely to run a substantial aggregate current account surplus for a number of years."[107] Oil surplus countries cannot remain insensitive to these developments indefinitely.

Peripheral Economies

In a very real sense, the Gulf oil states are in the long run peripheral economies. The notion of the center (or the core) and of the periphery has gained increasing recognition in economic and political writings. Recent literature on economic development emphasizes the notion of center and periphery as a tool of analysis for the development of modern capitalism.[108] Domination and dependence are the salient ingredients in that notion. Political scientists are using similar notions to account for the difference in impact and influence.[109]

We are using the term "periphery" here in a very special sense, meaning the limited potential role of oil surplus states in the post-oil era. Though promoted to world financial prominence, these countries are too dependent on oil to represent any economic significance in a post-oil period. Economically as well as culturally, they are marginal to the mainstream. No one can doubt the influence of oil and finance in present-day life. Fabulous petroleum wealth has transformed these states and their relations with other countries, yet they remain mono-resource economies, terribly lacking in endowments other than oil. In particular they lack the human resources necessary to play a real, as opposed to a financial, role. Not only is their population base very limited, but their labor policies in particular do not seem to encourage definitive settlement and assimilation of expatriate labor.

In a different context Malcolm Kerr described Egypt's failure to assume the role of Prussia, and Nasir that of Bismarck, to bring about Arab unity in the sixties.[110] It seems less plausible that the Gulf oil states, individually or collectively, can assume this sort of role in the eighties or nineties, much less maintain their leadership in the post-oil period. The role of an oil surplus country as a financier is bound to be self-liquidating after the oil era. Economic power can be expected eventually to move from financial centers to more productive centers in the future. With the depletion and/or decline in the importance of oil, this will be more than a possibility; it is virtually a certainty.

The economic marginality — in the long run — of oil surplus countries, if it does not explain the present investment policies in these countries, accounts for the lack of incentive to invest in the LDCs in general and the Arab countries in particular. Without pushing the analogy too far, nor attributing to it more of a very controversial farsightedness than really existed,[111] it could be said that the success of the Marshall Plan owed a great deal to the fact that its financial sponsor — the United States — was not only a surplus country in the financial sense, but stood particularly to assume a central, not a peripheral, place in a reconstructed Europe. With the success of the Marshall Plan, the United States consolidated rather than liquidated that position. It is very doubtful if any Gulf state envisages itself in such a role.

We will have more to say about the core and the periphery in the next section of this chapter.

C. DOMESTIC ENVIRONMENT

Non-economic aspects of domestic environment can induce as well as constrain financial flows to the LDCs. A comprehensive catalogue of the domestic factors affecting decision-making in the Gulf goes beyond the scope of this essay, and I shall merely make a brief general mention of a few of the salient features which can influence the Gulf states in their handling of the financial problem, since it definitely takes more than an economist to deal with them.

Pan-Arabism

It might appear paradoxical to include pan-Arabism as a domestic factor in the Gulf area. It is, however, indisputable, irrespective of the ideological leanings of the observer, that particularly in the Gulf area Arab politics is not foreign policy.

Writers disagree as to the relative weight and the direction of the tide of pan-Arabism.[112] For some, the Arab states system is first and foremost a "pan" system. It postulates the existence of a single Arab nation behind the façade of a multiplicity of sovereign states. For others, pan-Arabism is near its end, if not already a thing of the past. Still others see a continuous struggle for predominance between a "Middle Eastern system" and an "Arab system" or between *"raison d'état"* and "pan-Arabism". However all will agree that some Arab component is always present in domestic affairs.[112]

This is not an essay on pan-Arabism; we are interested in it only as it affects the Gulf states in their decisions on the financial problem. Our understanding of the problem will be enhanced if it is related to another concept to which I alluded earlier, namely the core and the periphery. For all practical purposes we can identify the Arab Gulf states with the periphery and most of the Arab recipient states with the core. It is not a coincidence that the champions of pan-Arabism came from the Arab core, while Saudi Arabia "...has long been a foe of pan-Arabism and has traditionally seen itself as a guardian of the *turath,* the heritage or Islam to be more precise....Muslim universalism is a safer doctrine than the geographically more limited but politically more troublesome idea of pan-Arabism."[113]

The relations between the core and the periphery are not simple. If the core proclaims pan-Arabism and confers super-legitimacy over individual countries, the periphery has the power of oil wealth. Pan-Arabism and Arab money are the stick and the carrot, but in different hands, to bring about a very subtle equilibrium. The stick is in the hands of the advocates of pan-Arabism and the carrot in those of the partisans of *raison d'état*. Arab finance is not a complement to pan-Arabism; rather, it is a counterpart to it. Arab money will be forthcoming to other Arab countries in the name of Arabism, but only to a certain limit.

It is no wonder then that Arab financial flows to Arab brothers coincided with the retreat of the pan-Arab system after the war of 1967, which "marked the Waterloo of pan-Arabism". Far from being a triumph for pan-Arabism the Khartoum Agreement in August 1967 marked a shift of power in favor of oil wealth. "The radical regime in Cairo would capitulate to the will of the oil states led by Saudi Arabia, but the oil states would not press their victory too far or too hard....Slowly and grimly, with a great deal of anguish and outright violence, a normal state system is becoming a fact of life."[114] In the wake of the war of October 1973, it was Sadat and Assad—"revisionists" or "correctionists" of the pan-Arab doctrine—who obtained the Arab finance. "The logic that triumphed in October 1973 was not the pan-Arabist one held up by Nasser and the Baath, it was the more limited notion of solidarity preferred by those states that had long opposed pan-Arabism".

Even the Baghdad Summit in April 1979 was not a break with this very subtle game. It is a game between pan-Arabism and *raison d'état,* between radicals and moderates, between the core and the periphery, or else between Arab legitimacy and Arab money. It is true that "the oil states have wanted from Egypt an abandonment of pan-Arabist ideology and acceptance of the logic of the state system, and they got that."[115] However, Sadat went further than his financial sponsors could accept. "The Egyptians' urge to break out and do things on their own was precisely what Saudi Arabia did not want." Saudi Arabia understands the political fragility that lies beneath its prosperity. "Above and beyond particular foreign policy decisions, the oil states will continue to experience the difficulties of living in a militarized, impoverished part of the world."[116]

Moreover, as in Khartoum where the oil money was a check to radicalism, in the final analysis the Baghdad Summit rallied the most radical Arab states to the idea of a peaceful settlement of the Arab-Israeli conflict based on the famous United Nations Resolution 242. After grooming the Sadat regime and consolidating Egypt's de-Nasirization, conservative Arab money had to appease and even to buy the more radical elements.

Institutionalization and Family Rule

The Gulf states are still largely governed along traditional lines.[117] Though oil wealth has transformed them into advanced welfare states they still remain patriarchal in a distinctly familial way.[118] The Saʿuds, the Sabahs, the Al Thanis, the Qasimis, the Al Nahyans, the Al Maktums, the Al Khalifas, are not only the ruling families: they embody the legitimacy of the existing regimes.

There are of course differences in degree among these states. Kuwait is a case in point. A more institutionalized legitimacy is obviously ingrained in Kuwait's political setting alongside, but not in place of, the traditional legitimacy. For more than two centuries this small country has been ruled by the Sabah family, generally renowned for moderation and wisdom. A long tradition of consultation between rulers and ruled (mainly the merchant community) has paved the way for the only (relatively long-lived) parliamentary experience. Traditional kinship, however, remains the basis of social life.

In varying degrees the ruling families are not only providing heads of state and political élites in the Gulf; they are also well represented in leading managerial, administrative and economic activities. In Saudi Arabia the numbers of the royal family of approximately 4,000 male members—almost a class apart—makes the House of Saʿud the world's largest family enterprise, and causes the Rothschild banking octopus or Rockefeller's Standard Oil Complex to look like small town enterprises.[119] The same is true, though numbers are less impressive, of the rest of the Gulf oil states. Family connections loom equally in other Gulf states where the core of the political and business élite always consists of members of the ruling families. Other members of the élite are almost without exception drawn from other wealthy aristocratic families.[120]

We have seen that the pan-Arab system is retreating before the *raison d'état* system. In reality, *raison d'état* is largely quite indiscriminately mixed with *raison de famille*. Though institutionalization is progressing, *raison d'état* is, at least partially, perceived through *raison de famille,* and this perception cannot remain without effect. First a family, whatever its identification with the state, remains a collection of specific individuals with limited time horizons. This is in contrast with the metaphysical, immortal entity which is the nation. Second, family rule in the area is weighed down with a long history of family feuds. These two facts account for the more personalized outlook of the future than the otherwise more abstract *raison d'état* on the one hand, and the personal frictions—and hence limits of coordination—on the other.

In these conditions, as a high-ranking American official once observed, "it is not possible to draw a meaningful line in the abstract between 'private' and 'government' investment."[121] It seems that there is a general inclination in the Gulf area to leave the investment decisions to advisers. Very often the same individual is managing the personal investment portfolio of the ruler and that of the government. Names such as Mahdi Tajir, Faraʿun (father and son) and Kamal Adham are too well-known to need any further mention; they are both public and private figures in the world of business affairs. Khalid Abu Saʿud, investment and financial adviser to the Amir of Kuwait,[122] has long been in charge of Kuwait's investment within the Ministry of Finance. "Usually operating behind closed doors in London, New York or a mid-East capital, the petrodollar manager can bring cheer or gloom to the foreign exchange market."[123] It would indeed be curious if these same advisers used different approaches to the investment of "public" and "private" funds. A private outlook would more likely be prevalent in these conditions.

It is interesting to note here that Kuwait's relative advance and sophistication in investment policies are not altogether unrelated to its more institutionalized system. Kuwait was not only the first Gulf state to have a parliamentary system, but also the first to have published records of its financial transactions (budgets, closing accounts), and the first to introduce the concept of a reserve fund. Compared to other ruling families, the share of the Sabah family in government public revenues is the lowest in the Gulf. During the period from 1952 to 1970/1971 the family's share was only about 2.7 percent in Kuwait compared with 32.4 percent in Bahrain, 40.6 percent in Qatar and 25 percent in the Emirates.[124] Even in its investment policy, Kuwait is the largest OPEC surplus country to invest on *commercial* terms in the LDCs, which it views not only as recipients of aid for political considerations, but also as untapped opportunities for productive investment. "There is no doubt that the increase in real investment subsequent to the availability of oil funds would have necessitated a change in world demand to make these investments profitable...the Third World with its untapped resources and unsatisfied needs....could be made the locomotive for the world increase in real investment....for matching available resources with investment opportunities."[125] It is no wonder then that the more institutionalized Kuwait is the leading OPEC surplus country in non-concessional financial flows to the LDCs along with its high contribution to the concessional flows. Long-term state interests are clearer with more institutionalization.

The United Arab Emirates present yet another striking example. The contrast between Sheikh Zaid Al Nahyan, the Head of the State, and Sheikh Rashid Al Maktum, his deputy, typifies two different concepts of a non-institutionalized system. To some extent this is a contrast between *raison d'état* and *raison de famille;* Sheikh Rashid is a shrewd merchant while Sheikh Zaid is more politically minded. The *raison d'état* of Abu Dhabi in its relations to other LDCs is, however, of a pre-institutionalized era. It is the largesse of an Arab ruler rather than a commitment to restructure the world economy.

The personalized nature of family rule also accounts for the continuous rivalry among the Gulf states which, in turn, puts limits to coordination among them. Political history in the area, when it is not the action of foreign powers, is a long history of feuding and disputes between ruling families.[126] Abu Dhabi was in continuous conflict with the Qawasims of Sharjah and Ras al-Khaima for the leadership of the area,[127] while the long dispute between Al Khalifa of Bahrain and Al Thani of Qatar prevented the constitution of an enlarged United Arab Emirates which would include both of them with the other seven Sheikhdoms.[128] Frontier conflicts are a constant part of life in the Gulf area. There are — or were — frontier problems between Saudi Arabia and Abu Dhabi (Buraimi), Abu Dhabi and Dubai, Dubai and Sharjah, Ras al-Khaima and Oman, Bahrain and Qatar, and many more.[129]

The uncertainty over the Gulf area has, however, encouraged its rulers to strengthen coordination on political, economic, oil and security matters among themselves.[130] It is not unlikely that with more awareness of the risks involved in oil funds investment, coordination among the oil Gulf States may also extend to policies of foreign investment.

The Second Stratum: Merchants and Technocrats

The second stratum, it must be remembered, is not the ruling class, but although it does not rule, it is the stratum without which the rulers cannot rule.[131] It is not our purpose here to delineate a complete social stratification of the Gulf states. It can, however, be fairly agreed that merchants and an emerging technocratic élite together constitute what could be regarded as the second stratum in the Gulf states.

In the Gulf states other than Saudi Arabia, the leading social function has been won by trading traditions. These states emerged as sedentary trading centers, although folklore and the general perception would have them only as nomadic tribes. Because of its vast territory the situation in Saudi Arabia is more complex. Since the early days of Islam trade has been highly esteemed. The society in which Islam was born — that of Mecca — was after all a center of capitalist trade.[132] The trading traditions have accompanied most of the later history of the Arabian Peninsula, particularly the coastal states. Pearl-diving industries, sea-faring, commercial entrepots and/or smuggling all added to the increasing influence of the merchant families which grew up as trading dynasties. The merchant, or better the middleman, is a king in the Gulf area.

With the oil money, the middleman mentality was given a pronounced *rentier* content. Trade is mixed with speculation. Profits — and incomes in general — are not always related to risk-bearing or merit. Rather they are privileges of position and status. Citizenry and social status are of paramount importance here. Productivity is to a great extent an alien concept and hardly fits with an oil economy.

The situation in the Gulf oil states is so peculiar that they are in many ways economies in reverse. For them generating income is less of a problem than spending it. Everywhere else, governments are not on the whole "income earners" and have therefore to concentrate on being tax collectors: by contrast governments in the Gulf are in fact able to distribute benefits and favors. *L'Etat Providence* if it existed at all is probably best represented in the Gulf area. As the oil sector — virtually the sole productive sector — is owned by the government, it is imperative to devise ways and means of enabling some of the oil earnings to percolate down. To the tribal tradition of buying loyalty is now added the need for the redistribution of part of these earnings to the population. As welfare states, in which the unprecedented provision of free services is second to none, the Gulf states provide their populations with a complex array of services and benefits: free education, free health care, soft (sometimes free) loans, grants, subsidies...etc. In a very real sense, this is a negative tax system whereby citizens levy various forms of impositions on governments.

The practices of the governments of the Gulf states in redistributing benefits to the population not only increased the sense of windfall profits and *rentier* mentality but also enhanced speculation. An early method of redistributing part of the oil revenues was through land purchases by the government. Beginning in Kuwait in the early fifties, land was bought from individuals at prices hardly related to the market value. Inversely, the government's price would set the market at exceedingly high levels. Huge fortunes were made through this mechanism. With the excessive availability of liquidity on one hand and the very thin spectrum of productive assets offered on the other, real estate prices continued to skyrocket. Governments stood to back this trend by their active role as regular purchasers in the market. In these circumstances it is quite normal to speak of a "real estate mentality", which spread all over the Gulf area. The speculation has not, however, been confined to real estate: the stock market experienced a similar phenomenon, also with the backing of governments.[133]

We are not interested here in an in-depth analysis of the outlook and/or behavior of the merchants. This is only relevant to our study insofar as it may affect their perception of investment opportunities outside the local market. Understandably they are attracted by easy profit-making ventures, with a marked inclination to real estate. The flourishing inter-Arab real estate investment companies illustrate this point. This does not, however, preclude a genuine businesslike attitude by the Gulf private sector towards the LDCs. Hotel building, contracting and trade are particularly favorite sectors for private investment in other Arab and developing countries. However these sectors remain limited and fall short of the investment needs of the LDCs.

Besides the merchant stratum, an emerging technocratic élite is increasingly participating in the public life of the Gulf states. The education and training of the inhabitants and the vast opportunities open to them paved the way for a growing role for the intelligentsia. Most rulers in the area have been willing to satisfy their demands for participation, and the role of the new élite has, in fact, steadily increased. While ideals of pan-Arabism are still powerful among the intelligentsia, new factors are diverting their interests towards Europe and the United States. More impressed by the technological advance of the West on one hand, but also on the other affected by the general retreat of the whole pan-Arab ideology, the new technocratic élite is more oriented to the West. Rather than Beirut or Cairo, it is London, Denver, Los Angeles or Houston which moves their memories.

Among the intelligentsia a generation gap separates those who were educated in the forties, fifties and early sixties from those of the late sixties and seventies. Not only are the latter mainly trained in Western universities but their outlook is also different. Equipped with better techniques from more prestigious universities in engineering, financial analysis and management, the new élite lacks the political perspective and commitment of the earlier generation. The new élite rests its claim for allegiance almost exclusively on the balance sheet preferring favorable facts and figures to emotional commitments.[134] The earlier generations may be at a loss with the new jargon of the Euromarket, financial analysis and/or computerized programs, but they are more at home with political discussions and major historical trends. In other words, what they lack in technical proficiency they make up in broader perspective. With greater self-confidence, the new generation, on the other hand, is gaining in sophistication in the small what they fail to see in the large. Fluent in foreign languages, regular passengers at international airports and hotels, sharp observers of interest rate differentials, spreads and margins in the Euro-market, and expert in foreign exchange rates, spot and forward rates, etc., the new élite is very active in international business. For this new breed of technocrats, dealing with Western institutions is more professionally rewarding and also more prestigious, if not more fun. In fact, unless basically committed to Third World finance, there is a built-in bias to do business with the industrial developed countries rather than with the LDCs.

It is no wonder then that a casual look at the balance sheets of the financial institutions in the area would show the major role of foreign assets — almost exclusively assets in Western countries — among their total assets. In Kuwait, for instance, the investment companies hold as much as 60 percent of their total assets in foreign assets: the specialized banks which have a specific domestic mandate, hold a quarter of the total in foreign assets; and this figure reaches around 50 percent in the commercial banks.[135] The situation in other Gulf states is similar. Even development funds whose charters stipulate that their unique role is to finance projects in developing countries show the same predilection for portfolio management in Western capital markets, rather than for a committing of all their resources for financing projects in the LDCs. It was found that the share of the total assets of the Kuwait Fund for Arab Development and the Saudi Fund for Development for project finance in the LDCs never exceeded 35 percent, the balance being invested in bank deposits or other financial securities in the international capital market.[136] It is interesting to note that the corresponding percentage for project finance in the Arab Fund for Economic and Social Development (an Arab regional institution) exceeds 70 percent, leaving less than 30 percent to be placed in the capital market.

The charm of the West for the new élite is not confined to the more professional and prestigious types of business but is related to another phenomenon which always accompanies situations of sudden prospects of money-making. The sudden wealth accruing to governments cannot bear the strains of uncontrolled venality. The rapacity of certain elements of a new civil service entirely devoid of anything which can seriously be regarded as public spirit can hardly be overlooked. Huge development projects, joint venture partnerships, agents, tenders and awards of million – and sometimes billion – dollar contracts have provided opportunities for those in public office to use their positions for private gain.[137] Some countries are more conspicuous than others in that respect. Philby's observation in the fifties of the emergence in Saudi Arabia of "a new bureaucracy, whose thin veneer of education has done in a couple of decades more harm to the reputation of a great country than the wild man of the desert has done in thousands of years"[138] is probably more topical now than it was a quarter of a century ago. Stories about excessive corruption in some Gulf states are attracting more attention outside the area as they arouse intense resentment inside it.[139] This can hardly be reconciled with a developmental mentality.

IV. CONCLUSION

OPEC surplus countries, particularly in the Arab peninsula, emerged in 1973–1974 as a world financial power. The oil price increases have introduced far-reaching financial and monetary rearrangements worldwide. There is no doubt that money and finance are powerful instruments for affecting real resources, which alone are the ultimate wealth. However, without bringing about a parallel rearrangement in real resources they risk remaining sterile.

More than two hundred years ago Adam Smith warned against the fallacy of identifying money and wealth. This was his battle with the Mercantilists. The example of Spain and England is very instructive in this regard. In the sixteenth century Spain found new riches with the influx of gold and silver from her colonies in the New World. England, with no colonies at that time, had to labor to restructure her real economy. Two different approaches are contrasted: the financial versus the real. Needless to say, it was England and not Spain that became the first world economic and sea power. Not only was the Armada defeated in a battle between the two concepts of warfare, but the defeat also represented the precursor of the triumph of the real over the monetary approach. OPEC surplus countries in the last quarter of the twentieth century are facing the same old problem of confusing finance and wealth. Smith's teaching seems to be as topical as ever.

Developed countries can only perpetuate the financial character of OPEC financial wealth. The easy façade of investing the oil funds in the rich, credit-worthy and secure OECD countries conceals the eventual erosion of the same funds. Motivated by self-interest, the placing of oil funds in the OECD countries can only be self-defeating. Developing countries, with all their shortcomings, can offer OPEC surplus countries a chance of transforming the *financial phenomenon* of oil into a *real phenomenon*. What seems to be a disinterested act of moral commitment towards brotherly poor countries is probably the only way OPEC has to preserve the value of its financial wealth.

This is not all. Regardless of what they do with their surplus funds, OPEC surplus countries will anyway be left with developing countries as the ultimate debtors of their surplus. The fate of the one depends then on the prosperity of the other.

Keynes once introduced the "widow's cruse" and the "Danaid jar" legends[140] into economic literature to depict situations in which entrepreneurs would stand to gain what they spent and to lose what they withheld. OPEC surplus countries seem to be in a similar situation. They gain what they "give" to the poor and lose what they "invest" commercially. Only an imaginative and unconventional policy for oil funds investment — to bring about a real as opposed to a financial restructuring of the economy — can promote the interests of both OPEC and the LDCs.

The new international economic order is not only the fight of non-oil developing countries; it is also the condition for the consolidation of OPEC gains in oil prices. A new oil order is not separated from it: OPEC surplus countries can in fact play a leading role in bringing about this new order. If they do not, others will do it. There is now an increasing concern in the world that oil funds should be used for a kind of global Marshall Plan that would not necessarily take OPEC interests as the focal point.

Developing countries are not, however, the promised land for oil funds investment. The development record of the LDCs—quite impressive in the sixties but less so in the seventies—leaves much to be desired. The odds against secure and successful investments in the LDCs are substantial. Not only inadequacy of infrastructure and qualified manpower, but particularly inefficient management and political instability, impede any sustained development effort in the LDCs. One country alone—even an oil rich one—cannot assume all the hazards of investment in the LDCs.

As we have shown, the oil surplus countries, led by the Arab Gulf states, are allocating unprecedented programs of aid to the LDCs. However, this is not sufficient to bring about a restructuring of the world economic order. It would be unrealistic in fact to leave this difficult task to the oil surplus countries. They are burdened by heavy limitations of size, potential and political constraint.

It is heartening nonetheless that there is an increasing awareness of the seriousness of continuing the actual pattern of oil funds investment. Inflation, political risks and other factors in the developed countries are opening the eyes of the oil surplus countries to the dangers they are incurring by continuing the actual investment policy. The need for a reconsideration of and more coordination in investment policies by oil surplus countries is more and more felt in all these countries. The newly established Gulf Council for Cooperation, which includes Saudi Arabia, Kuwait, Qatar, Oman, Bahrain and the United Arab Emirates, should be looked at as a step in this direction. A more prominent role for the LDCs as recipients of investment funds cannot fail to show itself in the near future.

NOTES

1. Dag Hammarskjold Foundation, *What Now: Another Development* (Uppsala, (1975), p. 6.

2. From a statement by Richard Cooper, Under Secretary of State for Economic Affairs before International Economic Policy and Trade, and International Development subcommittees, House of Representatives, *The Bonn Summit: Its Aftermath and New International Economic Initiatives,* (Washington D.C.: US Government Printing Office, 1978).

3. We note here that a new global approach to the oil funds in the OECD countries emphasizing world interdependence has recently gained more ground. We shall refer later to some proposals to that effect.

4. US Senate Committee on Foreign Relations, *International Debt, The Banks and the U.S. Foreign Policy,* Sub-Committee on Foreign Economic Policy Staff Report, Washington D.C., 1977, p. 4.

5. Kenneth E. Boulding, *A Reconstruction of Economics* (New York: John Wiley, 1950).

6. Tibor Scitovsky, *Money and the Balance of Payments* (Chicago: Rand McNally, 1969).

7. Jan Tumlir, "Oil Payments and the Oil Debt and the Problem of Adjustment", in T. M. Rybcznski, ed., *The Economics of Oil Crisis* (New York: Holmes and Meier, 1976).

8. Arthur Lewis, "Economic Development with Unlimited Supply of Labour..." in A. N. Agrawala and S. P. Singh, eds., *The Economics of Underdevelopment* (London: Oxford University Press, 1958), p. 406.

9. Oystein Noreng, *Oil Politics in the 1980's* (New York: McGraw Hill, 1978), p. 130.

10. Bent Hansen, "The Accumulation of Financial Capital by the Middle East Oil Exporters: Problems and Policies", in A. L. Udovitch, ed., *The Middle East: Oil, Conflict and Hope* (Lexington, Mass.: Lexington Books, 1976).

11. Ibid.

12. Ibid.

13. Bent Hansen, op. cit.; also Thomas D. Willett, *The Oil Transfer Problem and International Stability,* Princeton University, Essays in International Finance No. 113 (1975), p. 15.

14. Saudi Arabia has chosen to invest around 85 percent of its funds (the bulk of which are in dollars) in the United States and in deposits in Eurobanking markets. See Fred Bergsten, *U.S.-Saudi Economic Interests* (New York: American Association for Commerce and Industry Inc, 1980).

15. *World Financial Markets,* March 1980; *IMF Survey,* 5 May 1980.

16. See for example Aninda K. Bhattacharya, *The Myth of Petropower* (Lexington, Mass.: Lexington Books, 1977); Noreng, op.cit.; Eric Davis, "The Political Economy of the Arab Oil Producing Nations; Convergence with Western Interests", *Studies in International Comparative Development,* Summer 1979.

17. Noreng, op.cit.

18. Bent Hansen, op.cit., p. 47.

19. From a statement by Richard Cooper, op.cit., p. 33.

20. For a survey of different oil funds estimates see Bhattacharya, op.cit, p. 13; Thomas D. Willett, *The Oil Transfer Problem...,* op.cit., p. 6.

21. See for instance Farid Abolfath et al., *The OPEC Market to 1985* (Lexington, Mass.: Lexington Books, 1977), p. 329. Willett used constant 1974 prices for future oil prices but allowing inflation to erode accumulated surpluses; op.cit., p. 31.

22. The figure of $40 billion annually for OPEC surpluses was quoted by Senator J. Javits in a speech "Danger on the International Economic Front", on 8 February 1978, in *The Bonn Summit: Its Aftermath...,* op.cit., p. 141. This was also the conclusion reached by the US Treasury. See *International Debt, the Banks and the U.S. Foreign Policy,* op.cit., p. 33.

23. Robert Sollow, "The Economics of Resources or the Resources of Economics", *The American Economic Review,* May 1974; H. Hotelling, "The Economics of Exhaustible Resources", *Journal of Political Economy,* April 1931.

24. Later experience confirmed this assumption. The value of exports of the industrial countries to members of OPEC, which had represented the most rapidly expanding market since 1973, actually declined in 1979 with a 5 percent decline in value implying a much more substantial fall in volume. General Agreement on Tariff and Trades (GATT), *International Trade in 1979 and Present Prospects,* 1980.

25. Bent Hansen, op.cit., p. 104.

26. Fred Bergsten, op.cit.

27. Hansen, op.cit., p. 113.

28. Gerald A. Pollack, *Are the Oil Payments-Deficits Manageable?*, Princeton University, Essays in International Finance No. 111 (June 1975), p. 9.

29. Arthur Burns, then Chairman of the US Federal Reserve Board, reportedly sug-

gested that OPEC's accumulative surpluses might be as large as $500 billion in 1980. See Pollack, op.cit.

30. Joanne Salop and E. Spitaller, "Why Does Current Account Matter?" in *Staff Papers* (IMF), Vol. 27, no. 1 (March 1980), p. 106.

31. In Kuwait the propensity to save ranged in the fifties and sixties between 40 and 45 percent of the GNP. See Ragei El Mallakh, *Economic Development or Regional Cooperation: Kuwait* (Chicago: Chicago University Press, 1968), p. 81. For the seventies the figure increased to about 60 percent from 1974 to 1976. State of Kuwait, *Annual Statistical Abstract 1978*, p. 195.

32. W. M. Corden and Peter Oppenheimer, "Economic Issues for the Oil Importing Countries" in Rybcznski, *The Economics of Oil Crisis*, op.cit., p. 27; Bent Hansen, op.cit., p. 110.

33. Milton Friedman, *The Theory of Consumption Function* (Princeton: Princeton University Press, 1957).

34. James S. Deusenberry, *Income, Savings and the Theory of Consumer Behavior* (Cambridge: Harvard University Press, 1962).

35. James Tobin, "The Consumption Function", *International Encyclopaedia of Social Science*, Vol. III, 1968.

36. In particular N. Kaldor, J. Robinson, L. Pasinetti and also M. Kalecki.

37. N. Kaldor, "Alternative Theories of Distribution", *Review of Economic Studies*, Vol. XXIII, no. 2, 1955–56, and "Capital Accumulation and Economic Growth" in F. A. Lutz and D. C. Hague, eds., *The Theory of Capital* (London: Macmillan, 1969).

38. W. A. Ellis, *Growth and Distribution* (London: Macmillan, 1973), p. 72.

39. Joan Robinson, *The Accumulation of Capital* (London: Macmillan, 1956), p. 8.

40. Oystein Noreng, op.cit., p. 133.

41. Gerald Pollack, op.cit., p. 12.

42. Bent Hansen, op.cit., p. 112.

43. Ibid.

44. Dennis H. Robertson, "Some Notes on the Theory of Interest" in *Money, Trade and Economic Growth, in honour of John Henry Williams* (New York: Macmillan, 1951), p. 193.

45. P. Garengni, "Notes on Consumption, Investment and Effective Demand; Pt.II", *Cambridge Journal of Economics*, Vol. III, no. 1 (March 1979), p. 29.

46. Bent Hansen, op.cit., p. 112.

47. Hollis B. Chenery, "Restructuring the World Economy", *Foreign Affairs*, January 1975, p. 247.

48. For a comparable argument see Luigi L. Pasinetti, "Growth and Income Distribution" in his *Essays in Economic Theory* (London: Cambridge University Press, 1974), p. 106.

49. Joan Robinson, *Economic Heresies; Some Old-Fashioned Questions in Economic Theory* (New York: Basic Books, 1971), p. 84.

50. It is the merit of the Cambridge Neo-Keynsian school that it draws attention to this fact and develops growth models that account for the constancy of these ratios. See N. Kaldor, "A Model of Economic Growth", *Economic Journal*, 1957; and "Capital Accumulation...", op.cit.; also Pasinetti, op.cit.; and J. Robinson, *Economic Philosophy* (Chicago: Aldine Press, 1963).

51. Helmut A. Merklein and W. Carey Hardy, *Energy Economics* (Texas: Gulf Publishing Co., 1977), p. 53. It has recently been stressed that the petroleum price increase which occurred in several steps between December 1978 and June 1979 did not cause the present resurgence of inflation in industrial countries. GATT, *Press Release*, 4 September 1979.

52. W. M. Corden and Peter Oppenheimer, "Economic Issues....", op.cit., p. 29.

53. Kaldor, "Alternative Theories...", op.cit.; W. A. Ellis, op.cit.

54. N. Kaldor, "Marginal Productivity and Macro Economic Theories and Distribution", *The Review of Economic Studies,* October 1966, p. 316.

55. Pasinetti, op.cit.

56. IMF, *Annual Report 1976,* p. 3.

57. IMF, *Annual Report 1976,* p. 8; *Annual Report 1977,* p. 3; *Annual Report 1978,* p. 3.

58. IMF, *Annual Report 1974,* p. 1.

59. IMF, *Annual Report 1976,* p. 4.

60. IMF, *Annual Report 1977,* p. 2.

61. Bank for International Settlements, *Annual Reports, No. 45,* June 1975.

62. IMF, *Annual Report 1978,* p. 4.

63. The Bank for International Settlement, cited in *International Herald Tribune* (25 February 1980).

64. Denis Healey, "Oil, Money and Recession", *Foreign Affairs,* Winter 1979/80, p. 220.

65. OECD, *Development Cooperation Review 1978.*

66. Address by the Managing Director of the IMF at the Fifth Session of UNCTAD, in *IMF Survey,* 11 May 1979.

67. *World Financial Markets,* May 1979.

68. Thomas D. Willett, "Structure of OPEC and the Outlook for International Oil Prices", *The World Economy,* Vol. 2, no. 1 (January 1979), p.51; it was estimated that OPEC prices declined in real terms by 25 percent in constant dollar terms between 1974 and 1978, and by 40 percent in D-marks and by 50 percent in Yen. W. Brown and H. Kahn, "Why OPEC is Vulnerable", *Fortune,* 14 July 1980.

69. Harry G. Johnson, "Higher Oil Prices and the International Monetary System", in Rybcznski, *The Economics of the Oil Crisis,* op.cit., p. 169.

70. *IMF Survey,* June 1977; *Financial Times Survey: World Banking* (22 May 1978). See also Senator J. Javits in *The Bonn Summit: Its Aftermath...,* op.cit.

71. *World Financial Markets,* July 1979.

72. Johnson, "Higher Oil Prices...", op.cit., p. 168.

73. Chenery, op.cit., p. 258.

74. *The Economist* (17 March 1979).

75. Ibid.

76. Bhattacharya, *The Myth of Petropower,* op.cit. p. 11.

77. *World Financial Markets,* July 1979.

78. Bank for International Settlement, *Annual Report,* No. 50, 1980.

79. Hla Myint, "The 'Classical Theory' of International Trade and Underdeveloped Countries", *Economic Journal,* Vol. LXVIII, No. 270, June 1958.

80. From an address by J. de Larosière, Managing Director of the IMF, before the Economic and Social Council of the United Nations, Geneva, 4 July 1980, and reported in *IMF Survey,* 7 July 1980.

81. See US Senate Committee on Foreign Relations, *International Debt...,* op.cit., p. 33.

82. Hossein Askari and John T. Cummings, *Oil, OECD and the Third World: A Vicious Triangle?* (Austin, Texas: Texas University Center for Middle East Studies, 1978), p. 37.

83. Muhammad W. Khouja, "Some Observations on the Flow of Financial Resources to Developing Countries", *OAPEC News Bulletin,* March 1980, p. 10.

84. UNCTAD, *Financial Solidarity for Development,* 1979, p. 6.

85. *Financial Times* (15 July 1980).

86. UNCTAD, *Financial Solidarity...,* op.cit.

87. OECD, *Development Cooperation Review 1979*, p. 85.

88. The Assistant Secretary of the United States Treasury stated before a Congressional Sub-Committee that "several OPEC countries have repeatedly expressed concern about the confidentiality of their investment in the United States leaving a clear implication that they might be less inclined to invest here in the absence of such confidential treatment." Statement of Fred Bergsten quoted in *Department of Treasury News* (Washington D.C.), 18 July 1979, p. 18. Similar views were held by Kuwait's Minister of Finance on the occasion of the American Treasury Secretary's visit to Kuwait late in 1978.

89. Mancur Olson, *The Logic of Collective Action* (Cambridge, Mass.: Harvard University Press, 1971), p. 1.

90. Tibor Scitovsky, "Two Concepts of External Economies", *The Journal of Political Economy*, April 1954,

91. William Baumol, *Welfare Economics and the Theory of the State*, 2nd ed. (Cambridge: Harvard University Press, 1965), p. 20.

92. P. Samuelson, "The Pure Theory of Public Expenditure", *Review of Economics and Statistics*, November 1954; November 1955; November 1958.

93. R. Musgrave, *The Theory of Public Finance* (New York: McGraw Hill, 1959).

94. See respectively D. N. Rosenstein-Rodan, "Notes on the Theory of the Big Push" in H. Ellis and H. Wallish, eds., *Economic Development for Latin America* (London: St Martins Press, 1966); R. Nurske, *Problems of Capital Formation in Underdeveloped Countries* (Oxford: Blackwell, 1954); W. W. Rostow, *The Stages of Economic Growth* (New York, 1952).

95. General Accounting Office, *Relationship Between Oil Companies and OPEC*, Report to the US Congress, January 1978.

96. Joe Stork, *Middle East Oil and the Energy Crisis* (London: Monthly Review Press, 1975), p. 88; Robert Stobaugh, "After the Peak: the Threat of Imported Oil", in R. Stobaugh and D. Yergin, eds., *Energy Future* (New York: Random, 1979), p. 59.

97. Stork, op.cit., p. 155.

98. J. A. Bill and C. Leiden, *The Politics of the Middle East* (Boston; Little Brown, 1979), p. 375; Stork, *Middle East Oil...*, op.cit., p. 160; C. F. Doran, *Myth, Oil and Politics; Introduction to the Political Economy of Petroleum* (New York: The Free Press, 1977), p. 59.

99. Doran, op.cit., p. 60.

100. Jean-Marie Chevalier, *Le Nouvel Enjeu Petrolier* (Paris: Calmann-Levy, 1973), p. 20.

101. *Los Angeles Times* (15 November 1979).

102. Informed at 05.45 on 14 November 1979 of Iran's intention to withdraw its funds from American banks, the President promptly invoked the International Emergency Economic Powers Act. Reported in the *Los Angeles Times* (15 November 1979).

103. Ibid.

104. *Los Angeles Times* (27 November 1979).

105. *International Currency Review*, Vol 12, no. 1, 1980, p. 20.

106. See *The Bonn Summit, Its Aftermath...*, op.cit.

107. *IMF Survey*, 3 March 1980.

108. A. Emmanuel, *L'Echange Inégale* (Paris, 1969); Samir Amin, *L'Accumulation à l'Echelle Mondiale* (Paris, 1970).

109. Michael Hudson distinguishes between the pan-Arab core states and those of the periphery in his *Arab Politics; the Search for Legitimacy* (New Haven: Yale University Press, 1977).

110. A. S. Becker, B. Hansen and M. Kerr, *The Economics and Politics of the Middle East* (Amsterdam: Elsevier, 1975), p. 55.

111. John Gimbel, *The Origins of the Marshall Plan* (California: Stanford University Press, 1976).

112. For various views on pan-Arabism see Walid Khalidi, "Thinking the Unthinkable: A Sovereign Palestinian State", *Foreign Affairs,* July 1978; Fouad Ajami, "The End of Pan-Arabism", *Foreign Affairs,* Winter 1978/79; Mohamed Heikal, "Egyptian Foreign Policy", *Foreign Affairs,* July 1978.

113. Ajami, op.cit., p. 364. The general resurgence of a more militant Islam encourages a climate conducive, however, to local protest movements expressing religious, nationalist, political or economic grievances. See also Valerie Yorke, *The Gulf in the 1980's* (London: The Royal Institute of International Affairs, 1980), p. 10.

114. Ajami, op.cit.

115. Ajami, op.cit. See also Fred Halliday, *Arabia Without Sultans* (London; Penguin Books, 1974), p. 23.

116. Fouad Ajami, "The Struggle for Egypt's Soul", *Foreign Policy,* No. 35, Summer 1979, p. 17; and "The End of Pan-Arabism", op.cit., p. 372.

117. Hassan Ali Al Ebraheem, "Factors Contributing to the Emergence of the State of Kuwait", PhD dissertation, Indiana University, 1971, p. 199.

118. Bill and Leiden, op.cit.

119. *International Herald Tribune* (Supplement), February 1978. Saudi Arabia is the only state in the world that was named after a single dynasty; F. Halliday, op.cit., p. 49.

120. Bill and Leiden, op.cit., p. 96.

121. *International Currency Review,* Vol. 11, no. 6.

122. The first is a UAE diplomat and businessman, being Ambassador Extraordinary and Plenipotentiary to the United Kingdom; the second are respectively Rashed (father), Saudi royal adviser and Gaith (son), a businessman; the third is a Saudi politician and administrator with wide business interests. The fourth was described as "Kuwait's money man" by the *Wall Street Journal* (9 October 1979).

123. Bill Paul, "Playing it Safe", *Wall Street Journal* (9 May 1978).

124. Ali Al-Kawari, *Oil Revenues in the Gulf Emirates: Patterns of Allocation and Impact on Economic Development* (Durham: University of Durham, 1978), pp. 83, 105, 140, 120.

125. Address by the Kuwaiti Minister of Finance, Mr Al Atiqi on "OPEC Funds and Opportunities for Investment in an Interdependent World" at the Ausbildungszentrum Wolfsberg, October 1979.

126. Muhammad al-Rumaihi, "Al-sira⸢ wa al-ta⸢awun fi al-Khalij al-⸢arabi" [Conflict and Cooperation in the Arab Gulf], *Al-Mustaqbal al-⸢Arabi,* March 1980.

127. Donald Hawley, *The Trucial States* (London: Allen and Unwin, 1970), p. 19.

128. al-Rumaihi, op.cit., p. 85.

129. Buraimi is the name of only one village out of the nine forming the oasis; six belong to the ruler of Abu Dhabi and three to the Sultan of Muscat and Oman. See Hawley, op.cit., p. 186; and al-Rumaihi, op.cit., p. 85.

130. Valerie Yorke, op.cit., p. 48.

131. Leonard Binder, *In A Moment of Enthusiasm* (Chicago: Chicago University Press, 1978), p. 26; Gaetano Mosca, *The Ruling Class* (trans.), (New York: McGraw Hill, 1939).

132. Maxime Rodinson, *Islam and Capitalism* (trans.), (Austin: Texas University Press, 1978), p. 28.

133. After an unprecedented boom in the Kuwaiti share market, many share prices went down by as much as 25 to 40 percent from their 1976 peak levels. In December 1977 the Kuwaiti government was prompted to declare its readiness to buy shares at minimum purchase prices. M. Khouja and P. G. Sadler, *The Economy of Kuwait* (London; Macmillan, 1979), p. 186.

134. Robert Springborg, "On the Rise and Fall of Arab Isms", *Australian Outlook,* April 1977, p. 93.

135. Hazem Beblawi and Erfan Shafey, *Strategic Options of Development for Kuwait* (The IBK Papers), (Kuwait: International Bank of Kuwait, 1980).

136. Mahmud ʿAbd al-Fadil, *Al-Naft wa al-wahda al-ʿarabiyya* [Oil and Arab Unity], (Beirut: Centre for Arab Unity Studies, 1979), p. 84; *Kuwait Fund Annual Report,* No. 17, 1978–79; *Saudi Fund Annual Report IV,* 1978.

137. V. Yorke, op.cit., p. 19.

138. H. St. John Philby, *Saudi Arabia* (London: Ernest Benn, 1955), p. xviii.

139. Very recently, after revealing the scandal of an oil deal between the Saudi Arabian oil company Petromin, and the state-owned Italian energy company ENI in November 1979, rumors of similar deals with excessive "commissions" being made in Liechtenstein continued to appear in the mass media. *Financial Times* (9 April 1980). When interviewed in Washington in April 1980 the Saudi Finance minister implicitly recognizing these practices, revealed the existence of "several laws and royal decrees outlawing payment of *excessive* commissions and limiting the role of the middle man." *International Herald Tribune* (24 April 1980). Prince ʿAbdallah of Saudi Arabia in an interview with the Washington Post promised a crackdown on Arab middlemen who have collected enormous commissions for placing contracts in Saudi Arabia, thereby "presenting a distorted image of the Kingdom to the rest of the world". *International Herald Tribune* (26 May 1980). On the other hand, when an ex-oil marketing adviser to a Gulf oil ministry writes a novel about corruption in oil dealings in that country with accurate descriptions of almost everything else, one cannot totally dismiss the reliability of his account of such illegal dealings. Desmond Meiring, *A Foreign Body* (London: Constable Books, 1979).

140. J. M. Keynes, *A Treatise on Money* Vol. I. (London; The Royal Economic Society ed., 1971), p. 125.

VII
Expatriate Labor
and Economic Growth:
Saudi Demand for Egyptian Labor

Naiem A.Sherbiny
Ismail Serageldin

INTRODUCTION

Saudi Arabia and Egypt have emerged as principal partners in the recent process of international migration in the Middle East. Saudi Arabia began to import substantial numbers of expatriates following the oil-price boom of 1974, and over a short period of time it has become the major importer of labor. Typical of the large-population capital-poor non-oil countries of the Middle East, Egypt began to export increasing numbers of workers abroad during the second half of the 1970s, and in the course of a few years has become the major exporter of labor. A natural complementary relationship developed between the two countries, in which significant international labor flows take place, and their respective labor markets drew closely together. To be sure Saudi Arabia imports labor from sources other than Egypt, such as North and South Yemen and Jordan/Palestine, and it is equally true that Egypt exports labor to oil countries other than Saudi Arabia, such as Libya and the Gulf States. What is noteworthy about the labor markets in Saudi Arabia and Egypt are the rates at which they have become interlinked in the recent past and the enormous implications of this linkage for the future development of the two countries.

To demonstrate this proposition the present chapter analyzes the process of economic growth in Saudi Arabia and focuses especially on the role of expatriate labor, using data from published sources only. Special

Authors' Note: The views and interpretations in this chapter are those of the authors, and should not be attributed to the World Bank, to its affiliated organizations, or to any individual acting on their behalf. The comments made by Stace Birks Nader Fergani, and Richard Herbert are acknowledged with gratitude.

attention is then given to the Kingdom's economic prospects during the 1980s. Meanwhile the case is made for Egypt as an exporter of labor to the oil countries in general and to Saudi Arabia in particular. The Saudi-Egyptian relation faces conflicting challenges and opportunities in the 1980s when Arab sources of labor supply begin to taper off. The chapter aims at showing that the trends established in the late 1970s will most probably continue through the 1980s barring, of course, some major political crisis which would alter many of the assumptions made.

I. THE SAUDI-EGYPTIAN CONNECTION

To place Saudi Arabia in the context of labor importers and Egypt in the context of labor exporters, Table I highlights the two sides of international labor flows in the Arab world. The Table shows that while Saudi Arabia was the largest among the labor-importing countries, Egypt was the largest single labor exporter.

A focus both on the national composition of Saudi Arabia's labor imports and of the destination of Egyptian labor exports reveals the magnitude of the Saudi-Egyptian labor linkage. Table II shows that in 1975 while Egypt accounted for about 12 percent of Saudi Arabia's labor imports, Saudi Arabia absorbed 24 percent of Egypt's labor exports. It may be tempting to conclude that in 1975, so far as labor flows were concerned, Saudi Arabia was relatively more important to Egypt than Egypt

TABLE I
Labor Importers and Exporters in the Arab World
(1975)

	The Importers			The Exporters	
Country	Imported Labor	Percent	Country	Exported Labor	Percent
Saudi Arabia	773,400	42.5	Egypt	397,500	21.8
Libya	332,400	18.3	N. Yemen	290,100	15.9
U.A.E.	251,500	13.8	Jordan/		
			Palestine	264,700	14.5
Kuwait	208,000	11.4			
Others	254,700	14.0	Others	867,700	47.8
TOTAL	1,820,000	100.0	TOTAL	1,820,000	100.0

SOURCE: J. S. Birks and C. A. Sinclair, *International Migration and Development in the Arab Region* (Geneva: International Labor Office, 1980), Tables 10 and 13.

was to Saudi Arabia. However, such interpretation is misleading for two reasons. First, it does not address the quality or skill composition of Egyptian labor by comparison with labor from other sources. Second, and perhaps more significantly, the question of relative importance is especially difficult to assess in situations involving interdependence. The very fact that a link was established between the labor markets of the two countries is a sufficient demonstration that each country derives some benefits from interdependence. As will be argued later, this degree of interdependence seems to have increased significantly over the past few years. The main factor to explain such development is the increased importance both of Saudi Arabia as a labor importer and of Egypt as a labor exporter.

II. SAUDI ARABIA AS A LABOR IMPORTER

This section explores the factors involved in determining the size and dynamics of the labor market in Saudi Arabia. Typical of rapidly growing economies, the Saudi demand for labor expanded quickly. The engine of growth of the Saudi economy has been oil, or more precisely oil revenues. The section shows that the phases of growth of the economy corresponded closely to the phases of growth in oil revenues. The various phases of economic growth, in turn, were associated with differential

TABLE II
The Composition of Labor Imports Into Saudi Arabia
and Labor Exports From Egypt (1975)

Saudi Labor Imports			Egyptian Labor Exports		
Nationality	*Number*	*Percent*	*Country*	*Number*	*Percent*
Yemenis	335,000	43.3	Libya	229,500	57.8
Jordanians/ Palestinians	175,000	22.7	Saudi Arabia	95,000	23.9
Egyptians	95,000	12.3	Kuwait	37,600	9.4
Other Arabs	95,000	12.3	U.A.E.	12,500	3.1
Asians	38,000	4.9	Iraq	7,000	1.8
Other*	35,000	4.5	Other**	15,900	4.0
Total	773,000	100.0	Total	397,500	100.0

* includes Turkey, Iran, Africa, Europe and America
** includes Qatar, Oman, Bahrain, Yemen and Jordan.

SOURCE: As for Table I.

growth in the demand for labor. Expatriate labor comes into the picture in two ways, quantitatively and qualitatively.

The quantitative dimension is determined by the sheer size of *total* demand for labor in comparison with the size of *domestic* supply of labor. Continued expansion of the small-population economy has pushed the demand for labor beyond the confines of domestic supply. In Saudi Arabia, this is a relatively recent phenomenon. The qualitative dimension of expatriate labor, by contrast, is a much more rooted phenomenon; it resulted from the mis-match between the *structures* (in terms of skill profiles) of total demand for labor and domestic supply of labor. Expatriate labor flows continue because the quantitative and qualitative factors in the labor market continue to operate. Thus, demand continues to outpace supply, and the mis-match in their structures seems to widen, rather than to narrow.

A. GROWTH OF THE SAUDI ECONOMY

A review of nearly three decades of economic growth performance shows the central role which oil revenues have played. During the 1950s, the rate of growth of gross domestic product (GDP) in real terms is estimated to have been a little below 6 percent per annum, almost identical to the rate of growth of oil production.[1] During the 1960s, growth of GDP increased to 8 percent per annum in association with the acceleration of oil production at 11.5 percent per annum. During the 1970s, however, it became necessary to distinguish between oil GDP and non-oil GDP. While growth of oil production continued at the same rate as in the 1960s, non-oil GDP accelerated to above 10 percent in the first half of the decade, and still further to about 16 percent in the second half of the decade.

It may persuasively be argued that for the Arab oil-exporters, the era of capital-constrained development has ended early in the 1970s. A new era of labor-constrained development has just begun. For this reason, 1970 serves as a point of departure in reviewing past development in the demand for labor in general and in the demand for expatriate labor in particular.

B. CHANGES IN THE DEMAND FOR LABOR

Corresponding to the accelerated growth of the economy described above are changes in the demand for labor of a quantitative and qualitative nature. The quantitative changes derive from the so-called production function, a stable relationship between output and labor inputs. The qualitative changes, on the other hand, draw upon the relationship between economic growth and structural changes. Thus, growth of per capita GDP is generally associated with changes both in the structure of output (Kuznets)[2] and in the structure of employment (Chenery).[3] These aspects of change in the demand for labor are taken up in this section.

1. The Quantitative Dimension

The production function stipulates some kind of stability in the response of output to changes in labor and capital inputs. Problems of estimating production functions in highly industrialized societies are well known, despite the availability of fine and reliable data on labor inputs. In Saudi Arabia such data are available only sporadically. No attempt can therefore be made to construct a production function for the Saudi economy. However, the logic underlying the production function may be employed to develop a sort of gross measure of the relation between output and labor. To be sure, such a labor-output coefficient must by definition contain statistical bias resulting from the inevitable exclusion of capital inputs for the reasons just stated.

Furthermore, while the standard notion of the production function considers output as a function of labor, what is used here is another version — one which states labor "requirements" for a given level of output. Correspondingly, the emphasis will be on the change in labor input which is necessary to produce specific changes in output. The labor elasticity of output (q) may thus be defined as the relative change in labor input (dL/L) corresponding to a given relative change in output (dX/X). Specifically:

$$q = (dL/L) / (dX/X)$$

Only discontinuous data are available on labor and output for the same periods. The labor elasticity of output thus defined would then be estimated from fragmentary information, and for time intervals only (i.e. no annual observations). The published estimates on employment in Saudi Arabia come from voluminous studies done by various organizations and/or researchers on specific years and are therefore not easily reconcilable. The best estimates the present authors were able to put together from such published sources are as follows: in 1962/63 total employment was about 722,000; in 1969/70 it was 1,187,300; in 1974/75 it was 1,679,200; and in 1978/79 it is estimated at 2,458,000 (see Table IV). These estimates produce annual growth rates of employment for the time intervals indicated as 7.4 percent, 7.2 percent and 10.0 percent, respectively. Combining these estimates with growth of non-oil GDP for the same time intervals computes the labor elasticity of output (q) as shown in Table III.

TABLE III
Estimation of the Labor Elasticity of Output (q)

Period	Growth of Non-oil GDP (dX/X)	Growth of Labor (dL/L)	$q = \dfrac{dL/L}{dX/X}$
1962/63 - 1969/70	8.1%	7.4%	.91
1969/70 - 1974/75	10.4%	7.2%	.69
1974/75 - 1978/79	15.8%	10.0%*	.63

* tentative estimate

SOURCES: Growth of non-oil GDP from several sources including E.Y. Asfour, op.cit.; IMF, *International Financial Statistics* (annual), (Washington D.C.); and Saudi Arabia Monetary Agency (SAMA), *Annual Report*, (Riyadh). Growth of labor from Table IV of this chapter, and its sources.

Table III shows that growth of non-oil GDP during the periods observed was indeed accelerating: from 8.1 percent to 10.4 percent, and then to 15.8 percent. Employment expansion, by contrast, did accelerate too, but not in the same step-wise fashion. It stayed at the 7 percent rate for over 10 years, then shot up to about 10 percent during the second five year plan.

Tentative as the data reported here may be, they give what appear to be plausible results. They suggest that during the 1960s an increase of one percentage point in the growth of the economy was generally associated with 0.9 percent growth in employment. During the first half of the 1970s, the associated expansion in employment was about 0.7 percent. Continued acceleration of economic growth in the second half of the 1970s, however, was associated with about 0.6 percent expansion in employment.

Part of this apparent decline can be explained by the acceleration in the growth of the overall average productivity of labor. Thus, while the growth of average productivity was a mere 0.7 percent per annum during 1962/63 to 1969/70, it accelerated dramatically to 3.2 percent per annum during 1969/70 to 1974/75. This reflects in part the massive increase in investment per worker. Continued acceleration of economic growth during 1974/75 to 1978/79 was accompanied by growth of average productivity at about 5.8 percent per annum. As already noted, the data base for these estimates is rather shaky. Nevertheless, they appear to be compatible with the so-called Verdoorn law, which was developed from a firm data base in a number of industrially-advanced countries. Simply stated, Verdoorn formulated an empirically-based hypothesis which suggests that a significant positive association exists between rates of economic growth and rates of average productivity growth. This relationship holds at the macro- as well as at the sectoral levels.[4]

2. The Qualitative Dimension

Studies of economic growth, whether on developed or developing countries, have established that significant changes in the structure of output and employment usually accompany such growth. Furthermore, these changes have *predictable trends*. Thus, as the economy grows, the relative share of the primary sector (agriculture and mining) in total employment declines, and those of the secondary sector (manufacturing, utilities, transport, and construction) and the tertiary sector (all other) expand. By how much these changes are associated with growth is, of course, a matter which varies between countries and even for the same country over time.

The Saudi economy is no exception. An attempt is made here to trace the structure of employment since 1962/63 to show the extent of changes in that structure which accompanied the accelerated growth of the economy. Table IV shows that this structure has shifted significantly during less than two decades. Indeed, it appears that some of those shifts would have taken generations in other countries. These rapid shifts may therefore be explained by the continued acceleration of growth of the non-oil economy. In no other country has the relative share of the primary sector declined from 66 percent to 26 percent of total employment in less than 20 years. But this is an indication of the accelerated expansion of the demand for labor in the secondary and tertiary sectors to the point literally of pulling out some labor from the primary sector. Not only did the relative share of the primary sector in total employment fall, but the absolute numbers employed in that sector also declined.

Also noteworthy is the rapid expansion in the relative employment shares of the secondary and tertiary sectors. These shifts complement the shifts observed in the share of the primary sector. Together, the figures reported in Table IV are indicative of the diversification efforts which have been sweeping Saudi society.

Accompanying such changes in the structure of employment were equally important and significant changes in the occupational structure of the labor force. Let occupations be tentatively classified by skill level into "high", "medium", and "low". The high-skill category refers to professionals and managers/administrators. The medium-skill category refers to clerical, sales and service workers. The low-skill category refers

TABLE IV
Employment Structure by Aggregated Sectors

Sector	Percent of total employment			
	1962/63	1969/70	1974/75	1978/79
Primary (agriculture and mining)	66.0	47.0	36.0	26.0
Secondary (manufacturing, utilities, transport and construction)	10.0	16.0	23.0	27.5
Tertiary (all others)	24.0	37.0	41.0	46.5
Total	100.0	100.0	100.0	100.0
Total number of persons employed, (000s)	(722.0)	(1,187.3)	(1,679.2)	(2,458.0)

SOURCES: Several sources were consulted to construct this table. For 1962/63, see J. S. Birks and C. A. Sinclair, *The Kingdom of Saudi Arabia and the Libyan Arab Jamahiriya: The Key Countries of Employment*, Provisional Draft Working Paper WEP 2-26/WP39, Migration for Employment Project--World Employment Programme Research (Geneva, Switzerland: International Labor Office, May 1979) Table 5. The table introduces slight modifications to the 1962/63 *Census of Population, Buildings and Establishments*. The breakdown of the figures for secondary and tertiary sectors are based on the present authors' estimates. For 1969/70, see the Kingdom of Saudi Arabia, Ministry of Planning, *Second Development Plan* (1975-80), Table II-1; and U.S. Department of Labor, Bureau of Labor Statistics, *Labor Law and Practice in the Kingdom of Saudi Arabia*, 1972, pp. 26-40. For 1974/75, see Birks and Sinclair, op.cit., Table 32 which reports 1974 Census data corrected and modified by the authors; and World Bank, *International Migration Project* (interim report), December, 1979. The figures for 1978/79 are authors' estimates.

to farmers, fishermen, craftsmen, and laborers. Comparative data for these categories are available only for 1974 and 1978. It is presumed that such a short period could hardly show changes in the occupational structure of the labor force, particularly its Saudi component. The true surprise is that significant shifts do take place, and the changes are compatible with the changes in the structure of employment.

For example, the skill profile of the Saudis for 1974 was 12 percent for high skills, 43 percent for medium skills, and 45 percent for low skills. The 1978 profile shows substantial improvements in skill distribution, undoubtedly the result of concerted efforts at skill formation, and possibly some re-alignment in job-entry requirements for certain occupations. The partial data available seems to indicate that the respective ratios have become 23 percent, 54 percent, and 23 percent for the stated skill levels. Thus, the shares of high and medium skill categories increased at the expense of the low skill categories.

C. DEVELOPMENT OF LABOR IMPORTS

As stated in the opening remarks of Part II, Saudi Arabia imported labor for quantitative as well as qualitative reasons. Quantitatively, the accelerated expansion in the demand for labor exceeded domestically available supplies. Expatriate labor had to make up for the difference between supply and demand. Qualitatively, despite the rapid shifts in the occupational structure of supply, there continued to be a mismatch with the faster changing structure of demand for skills. Once again, expatriate labor had to make up for the mismatch in the structures of total demand and domestic supply of labor. Having established 1970 as, more or less, a year of demarcation between fast growth and accelerated growth, the discussion of labor imports follows along these lines.

Some preliminary evidence of international labor migration became available as the first stirrings of modernization began in Saudi Arabia in the 1950s. For example, traders from Yemen had long played a role in the Saudi economy, especially in the Southwest region. This role was consolidated as the economy began to grow in the later 1950s and 1960s. Other trends were also in evidence at this early period. Nationals of other Arab states played an important role as teachers and doctors in the education and health sectors as early as the 1950s. Non-Arabs, mainly Westerners, filled skilled occupations in the oil sector.

As already noted, accurate data on labor in general and labor imports in particular are not possible to come by easily before the 1960s. Even during the 1960s labor data are imprecise for a number of reasons. These reasons include a lack of record-keeping, ill-defined or ill-monitored frontiers, especially to the south, imprecision regarding migrants who had originally entered for purposes of the *hajj* (pilgrimage), lack of clear ethnic or linguistic or cultural characteristics distinguishing some (Yemeni) migrants from some (Southern) Saudis, etc.

In any event, in 1962/1963, the total employment of some 772,000 persons included about 50,000 expatriates. The expatriate labor ratio was therefore about seven percent. Most of the immigrant labor at that time was concentrated in skilled jobs and of the national origins already described. By 1969/70, however, the total employment of 1,187,300 was made up of 867,300 Saudis and 320,000 non-Saudi expatriates. The expatriate labor ratio has increased to 27 percent. What is significant here are the associated rates of growth: while total employment had grown at 7.4 percent per annum, Saudi labor expanded at 3.7 percent, and expatriate labor had grown by no less that 30.4 percent.

Reflecting accelerated economic growth, the influx of expatriate labor underwent a dramatic upsurge in the capital-surplus conditions of the

1970s. By 1974/75, the total employment figure of 1,679,200 was made up of 1,010,700 Saudis and 668,500 non-Saudis. The expatriate labor ratio has now reached 40 percent. Thus, while total employment expanded by 7.2 percent per annum during the first half of the 1970s, Saudi labor expanded by 3.1 percent, and expatriate labor by 15.9 percent. The continued acceleration of economic growth has pushed total employment to about 2,458,000 persons by 1978/79. This total was made up of about 1,142,000 Saudis and 1,316,000 non-Saudis. The expatriate labor ratio has climbed to about 54 percent. The annual growth rates implied here are 10 percent for the total, 3.1 percent for the Saudis and 18.5 percent for the non-Saudis. It should be noted that the demographic effects of this influx were much less severe than would have been expected, because of the much higher crude participation rate for expatriates (some 50 percent) as opposed to 16 percent for the Saudis. Thus Saudis remain a firm majority in the total population residing within the Kingdom.

These changes were accompanied by changes in the occupational structure of the expatriate labor force. The most significant trend was the increased concentration of expatriates in the lower-skilled occupations by the mid-1970s, followed by a trend towards concentration in higher-level occupations later in the decade, as more projects came to completion and hence needed skilled personnel. Thus, the occupational composition of expatriates in 1974 showed a preponderant share (53 percent) of their total in low level occupations compared with a minor share (14 percent) in high level occupations, and 33 percent in the medium level category. By 1978, however, reflecting the fundamental changes that had occurred in the Kingdom as a result of rapid economic growth in the short intervening period, the occupational composition of expatriate labor shifted dramatically. Thus, high level occupations (56 percent of expatriate total) had become the dominant category, evidently at the expense of the shares of the medium and low categories (which had fallen to 16 and 29 percent respectively). Combining these figures with those reported for the Saudis in Section B.2 above, Table V shows the occupational composition of both segments of the labor force. The table shows that by 1978, the emerging occupational pattern of expatriate labor more fully complemented the developing occupational composition of Saudi labor, by comparison with 1974. The logical inference is that much of the higher level technologies in the production process which accompanied the development of, and structural transformation in, the Saudi economy over the period from 1974 to 1978 required much more highly skilled labor than the Saudi education and training system was able to supply.

TABLE V
Occupational Composition of Saudi and Non-Saudi Labor
(1974, 1978)

Occupational Level	Saudi		Non-Saudi	
	1974	1978	1974	1978
High (professionals, managers/ administrators)	12.2	23.1	13.8	55.5
Medium (clerical, sales, and service workers)	43.3	53.8	33.2	15.8
Low (farmers, fishermen, craftsmen & laborers)	44.5	23.1	53.0	28.7

SOURCE: 1. 1974 data from Saudi Arabia, Ministry of Finance and National Economy, Central Department of Statistics, *Population Census 1974/1394 AH*, Vols. I-XIV (Dammam, Saudi Arabia: 1977), after excluding farmers (see text discussion).
2. 1978 data from the World Bank, *International Migration Project* (interim report), December 1979.

D. Labor Imports in the 1980s

Having witnessed profound changes in the quantity and quality of labor force in Saudi Arabia over a short period of time, a number of policy questions with far-reaching implications for the 1980s arises. As expatriates comprise more than 50 percent of the labor force, a major policy concern is the absolute and relative size of expatriate labor in the Kingdom. A corollary concern is the size of the total expatriate population (labor and dependents). With the majority of expatriate labor hitherto from a limited number of Arab countries, another policy concern is the composition of expatriate labor in the 1980s. In the present section, these issues are addressed in order to explore alternative courses for the 1980s.

1. The Size of Expatriate Labor

In a previous study, one of the authors examined the relationship between expatriate labor and economic growth in Saudi Arabia within a quantitative framework.[5] Using sectoral labor-output coefficients, output growth targets were transformed into "labor requirements". These labor requirements varied directly with future growth targets. Thus, higher labor requirements corresponded to higher growth targets and vice versa. Contrasting the varying labor requirements with a given vector of domestic labor supply produced alternative levels of expatriate labor requirements to make up for the quantitative shortages of domestic labor. For each overall growth target, the ratio of the resultant expatriate labor was calculated in relation to total labor requirements. A positive relationship was found to exist between growth targets and the expatriate labor ratio. Accordingly, it would be possible to plan a steady-state growth level of non-oil GDP above which the expatriate labor ratio would increase and below which it would decrease. Thus, a choice of the size or ratio of expatriate labor implies a choice of the non-oil GDP growth target. This simple proposition is often lost in policy discussions about the warranted size of expatriate labor.

In this regard, three scenarios may be contemplated. Their implications for growth of non-oil GDP are then explored:

Scenario I: The expatriate labor *size* in 1985 is frozen at its 1980 level.
Scenario II: The expatriate labor *ratio* in 1985 is frozen at its 1980 level.
Scenario III: The expatriate labor size expands in accordance with maintaining the 1975-80 trends in government expenditures through 1985.

The starting point is to estimate the 1980 size of total labor employment, and the expatriate labor size. Assuming annual growth of total employment during the Second Plan (1975-80) at the 10 percent estimated in Table IV above, and Saudi employment to grow at about 3.1 percent per annum, the most likely estimate of expatriate labor in 1980 is about 1.73 million persons. Relative to the estimated total employment of about 2.7 million for the same year, the expatriate labor ratio would then be about 64 percent.

Thus Scenario I would imply that the size of expatriate labor in 1985 would still be 1.730 million. Total employment would grow only by the increments of Saudi labor alone. By contrast, Scenario II implies that expatriate labor would grow at the same rate as Saudi labor (3.5 percent per annum), therefore maintaining the expatriate labor ratio at 64 percent. The corresponding size of expatriate labor would then be 2.057 million persons. Finally, Scenario III implies growth in total employment of 6.4 percent computed through an elasticity formula relating employment expansion to growth in government expenditures. Again, using growth of the Saudi labor component at 3.5 percent, the implied size of expatriate labor in 1985 would be 2.53 million. The corresponding expatriate labor ratio would be about 69 percent.

Through using the estimate of the labor elasticity of output in Table III of .6, the implications of the three scenarios for growth in non-oil GDP can then be computed. Thus Scenario I which implies growth in total employment of only 1.5 percent would correspond to only 2.5 percent growth of non-oil GDP. Scenario II implies growth in total employment of 3.5 percent, and non-oil GDP growth of 5.8 percent. Finally, Scenario III implies growth in total employment of 6.4 percent and non-oil GDP growth of 10.7 percent.

2. The Composition of Expatriate Labor

Although decision-makers are understandably concerned about the total magnitude of the expatriate component in the labor force, they are equally attentive to the nationality mix of that imported labor. Different nationalities place different burdens upon the Saudi society and polity, and a delicate balance has to be struck between the host country's socio-cultural concerns and its economic growth needs.

If the criterion for acceptability was limited to ease of social integration only, then Peninsula Arabs would rank highest, followed by other Arabs, then (Muslim) Asians and eventually Europeans and Americans. This simplistic approach, however, has to be tempered with the perceived contribution each of these nationalities tends to bring, in terms of skill attributes, organizational knowhow, and access to technology.

A brief overview of the developments of the distribution of expatriate labor by nationality tends to confirm the view that broad socio-cultural acceptability has indeed been tempered by the needs of economic growth. Thus, the 1975 distribution of expatriate labor in Saudi Arabia[6] was dominated by Arabs (90.6 percent) with about 5 percent Asians and less than 5 percent from the rest of the world. As expected, Peninsula Arabs dominated the Arab group: North Yemenis (36 percent) and South Yemenis (7 percent). The next highest group was Jordanians/Palestinians (23 percent), followed by Egyptians (12 percent).

For comparative purposes, estimates of the distribution in 1980 and 1985 were developed. These are shown in Table VI. The best estimate for total expatriate employment in 1980 is about 1.73 million. If the same nationality mix that existed in 1975 was maintained in 1980 (Alternative A in Table VI), it would result in unreasonably high estimates for Yemenis as well as Jordanians/Palestinians, given the population pool from which they are drawn as well as other evidence from Jordan and Yemen. A calibration of these estimates in favor of Egyptians and other

TABLE VI

Saudi Arabia — Distribution of Expatriates by Nationality Groups, 1980

	1975		1980				1985			
	Number	%	A	%	B	%	II	%	III	%
Yemenis	335,000	43.3	752,000	43.3	600,000	34.7	700,000	34.0	750,000	29.1
Jordanians/ Palestinians	175,000	22.7	393,000	22.7	330,000	19.1	350,000	17.0	370,000	14.3
Egyptians	95,000	12.3	213,000	12.3	280,000	16.2	370,000	18.0	530,000	20.5
Other Arabs	95,000	12.3	213,000	12.3	330,000	19.0	390,000	19.0	595,000	23.1
Total Arabs	700,000	90.6	1,571,000	90.6	1,540,000	89.0	1,810,000	88.0	2,245,000	87.0
Asians	38,000	4.9	85,000	4.9	100,000	5.8	140,000	6.8	195,000	7.6
Other	35,000	4.5	78,000	4.5	90,000	5.2	107,000	5.2	140,000	5.4
GRAND TOTAL	773,000	100.0	1,734,000	100.0	1,730,000	100.0	2,057,000	100.0	2,580,000	100.0

1980 - A Maintaining 1975 relative distribution.
B Modifying 1975 distribution by qualitative information; total expatriate labor in A and B is the same.

1985 II Maintaining 1980 foreign labor ratio; growth of expatriate labor is the same as growth of Saudi labor (3.5).
III Total employment expanding by 6.4% in response to an elasticity-based expansion of government expenditures of 9.8%, equal to the rate experienced in 1975-80.

SOURCES: For 1975, same as table 1; for 1980 and 1985 are author's estimates based on the above assumptions.

Arabs is given (Alternative B in Table VI) which appears more consonant with existing observations as well as with the shifting nature of the skills required by the growing and developing economy.

Scenario I is clearly too restrictive. Whether Scenario II or III is adopted, it is clear that the 1985 composition of expatriates will change further against the Yemenis and Jordanians/Palestinians and in favor of Egyptians and other Arabs. Significantly, the acceleration of economic growth implied between the two scenarios results in strengthening the trends already set in motion. Thus, while the absolute numbers of the Yemenis and the Jordanians/Palestinians may continue to increase somewhat, their relative shares in the work force will probably decline. Egypt and the other Arabs will gain both in the absolute numbers and relative distribution.

The explanation is clear. The economic expansion implied in the Third Plan, placing rising demands for expatriate labor of variant skills, tends to be relatively more skill intensive. Thus, the expansion in the demand for skilled and highly skilled labor in Saudi Arabia during the Third Plan is likely to be faster than the expansion in demand for semi-skilled and unskilled labor. This problem of "labor adaptation" as the economy develops has been treated elsewhere by one of the authors.[7] While low-level skills are more dominant among Yemenis, medium and high level skills are relatively more dominant among Egyptians and other Arabs. The Jordanian/Palestinian share declines simply due to constraints on the availability of supply.

These shifts, however, pose serious problems to decision-makers insofar as there is a dimension of sectoral specialization as well as occupational skill content impacting upon the labor adaptation problem. The complexity of managing a labor policy that caters to so many concerns becomes self-evident. Sophisticated computer models, which are used for that purpose by Saudi planners, cannot alone do full justice to the needs of balancing socio-cultural, economic, political and administrative considerations in enunciating and monitoring a labor policy that is consistent, effective, efficient and equitable. A great deal of human judgment, insight and "feel" must perforce shape the prudent course dictated by practical wisdom. That course provides for two main approaches:

[i] the firm establishment of a framework of consistency to guide the development of investments, national human resource development, and the importation of foreign labor; and

[ii] the promotion of selective turnover among expatriates as a means of achieving structural change in the occupational, sectoral, and nationality mix of the labor force.

This last should undoubtedly be of interest to decision-makers in labor-exporting countries, as it indicates that if they wish to retain (or increase) their share of that labor market, they should be alerted to the changing skill mix required. It is at this point that the chapter turns to examine Egypt as a labor exporter.

III. EGYPT AS A LABOR EXPORTER

Labor migration from Egypt is a fairly recent phenomenon compared, for example, to the experiences of other Arab countries like Syria or Lebanon. An increasing number of studies address this novel phenomenon from the vantage points of various disciplines: social, political, psychological, and economic. Inevitably, labor migration cuts across all these disciplines. No attempt is made here either to review literature or provide an interdisciplinary synthesis. For the most part, the emphasis will be on the socio-economic factors underlying labor migration from Egypt. For this reason, the discussion first sets the background by examining the source of labor migration, i.e., population and labor force. The focus turns next to examine the development of labor exports in quantitative and qualitative terms. Quantitatively, an attempt is made to estimate the size of labor outflows and trace them according to recipient countries. Qualitatively, the chapter examines the educational attainments and occupational profiles of migrant labor. Having outlined the characteristics of expatriate Egyptians, the chapter then turns to analyze labor migration as a dynamic process, the net outcome of push-pull factors operating within Egypt and outside Egypt. Specifically, the push factors pertain to domestic pressures resulting from the excess of labor supply over labor demand: low wage rates, limited opportunities for advancement, low occupational mobility, and possible unemployment. The pull factors, by contrast, pertain to external conditions, particularly in the oil-rich states, of labor shortages and higher wage rates. The stage is then set to assess the future prospects of Egyptian labor exports in general, and to Saudi Arabia in particular.

A. GROWTH OF POPULATION AND LABOR FORCE

Statistics on Egyptian population go back to the turn of the century, providing a broad view of the demographic developments over time. During the last four decades, population growth averaged about 2.3 percent per annum. Statistics on labor force and employment, however, are less reliable. They contain definitional inconsistencies between censuses. This is especially evident between 1947 and 1960. For this reason, the paper focuses on the last two decades, which are directly relevant to the subject at hand (see Table VII).

A comparison between the size of the labor force and the size of employment indicates the existence of unemployment: about 0.9 million in 1960, 0.3 million in 1970, and 1.0 million in 1980. The decline in unemployment in 1970 was the result of rapid absorption of labor during the 1960s, partly due to explicit pro-employment government policies, and partly due to rapid economic growth in the first half of the decade and partly to mobilization after 1967. The 1970s witnessed some novel conditions which may in part explain the phenomenon of labor migration. By comparison with the 1960s, the 1970s showed population growth continuing at a slightly higher rate, labor force at significantly higher rate, and employment at significantly lower rates.

B. Development of Labor Exports

As already noted, the large-scale labor migration from Egypt is a recent phenomenon. As recently as 1960, the total number of Egyptians abroad was estimated at 100,000[8] which was less than 0.4 of one percent of the total population. Using a liberal estimate of the crude participation rate of 0.5, the number of Egyptians working abroad was therefore

TABLE VII
Population and Labor in Egypt, 1960-80

(a) The Estimates (mil)

Year	Population	Labor Force*	Employment	Crude Participation Rates (%)
1960	26.085	6.891	6.006	23.0
1970	32.816	8.655	8.361	25.5
1980	41.700	11.868	10.836**	26.0

(b) Growth Rates, Percent per Annum

1960-70	2.3	2.3	3.4
1970-80	*2.4*	*3.2*	*2.6*

*Estimation of civilian home labor force, which exclude armed forces and workers abroad.
**Authors' estimates

SOURCE: N. Choucri, R. S. Eckaus, A. Mohie-Eldin, "Migration and Employment in the Construction Sector: Critical Factors in Egyptian Development", Cairo University/MIT Technology Adaptation Program, 1978 (mimeo), Table I-1.

about 50,000. Relative to total employment estimates for the same year, this number was only 0.8 of one percent. No data are available on either the skill composition or the national destinations of Egyptians working abroad during that period.

It was not until the mid-1970s that the question of labor exports began to assume special significance. Lack of any migration data for the 1960s or precise data for the present is partly characteristic of the migration process itself. However, part of the ambiguity is due to government policies and/or perceptions on the part of would-be migrants. One may therefore think of Egyptian labor exports prior to 1975 in terms of "official" and "unofficial" figures. The official figures represent those formally approved by government channels to work in other countries, mostly in the Arab world. For the most part, the official figures refer to those seconded on fixed-term assignments abroad. The unofficial figures include *de facto* migrants, some of whom did not explicitly apply for migrant status, and who may or may not have fixed-term contracts. Fragmentary data from Egypt on official secondments, and from census figures in selected recipient countries, suggest that the total number of Egyptians working in the Arab countries was somewhere between 130,000 and 150,000 in the early 1970s.

Profiles of the country destination and skill composition of the "early" migrants are quite revealing. The Central Agency for Public Mobilization and Statistics (CAPMAS) compiled data provided by 34,000 Egyptians intending to seek employment abroad in 1973. Those are presumed to have an "official" migrant status. The results showed that 39 percent of those surveyed were working in Libya, 31 percent in Saudi Arabia, 13 percent in Kuwait, 6 percent in Algeria, 3 percent in the United Arab Emirates, 2 percent in Yemen and Oman each, and the rest in the remaining Arab countries.[9] Thus as early as 1973, during the pre-boom years, Saudi Arabia and Libya attracted 70 percent of Egyptian labor abroad.

In terms of educational attainment, Table VIII shows the distribution of the migrant sample in 1973 by comparison with the distribution of the total work force in Egypt for the same year. While the great majority of the employed in Egypt had less than intermediate education, the highest concentration of migrants was in university and post-university education. Using a four-level classification of educational attainment, Table VIII computes an index for relative educational concentration. The index measures the relative skewness in the distribution of educational attainments for Egyptians working abroad and in Egypt. The index has a critical value of one, above which educational attainments are skewed in favor of the recipient countries, and below which they are in favor of Egypt. Not surprisingly, the first three categories show an index value

TABLE VIII

Educational Composition of Egyptian Workforce in Egypt and Abroad (1973/74)

	In Egypt	Abroad	Educational Concentration Index
Post University	0.1	11.3	113.0
University	3.6	28.3	7.9
Intermediate and Secondary	9.2	52.8	5.7
Less Than Intermediate	87.1	7.6	0.09
	100.0	100.0	

SOURCE: Educational composition of workforce in Egypt from Central Agency for Public Mobilization and Statistics (CAPMAS), "Labor Force Sample Survey", cited in World Bank, *Arab Republic of Egypt: Economic Management in a Period of Transition*, Vol. IV, May 1978, Statistical Appendix, p. 6. The figures for abroad from J. S. Birks and C. A. Sinclair, "Egypt: A Frustrated Labor Exporter", *The Middle East Journal*, Vol. 33, no. 3 (Summer 1979).

significantly above one rising to 113 for post University levels. Only in the below intermediate levels of educational attainment is the index value significantly below one: it is barely 1/10th!

As the neighboring Arab rich states accelerated their economic growth in the second half of the 1970s, greater flows of Egyptian labor crossed the borders. Although no recent data is available on the educational attainment of migrant Egyptian labor, field observations in the recipient countries *as a whole* suggest that the distribution of immigrant labor has not shifted in favor of lower educational attainment.

Another dimension of the outflows of Egyptian labor is the development in their occupational structure over time and in relation to the occupational structure of the labor stock at home. The developments of the occupational structure of the work force inside Egypt reflect the output of the educational/training system. By contrast, developments in the occupational structure of Egyptians abroad reflect the changes in the economic structure of the recipient countries and hence in the demand for labor.

The salient features of the domestic supply of occupations are the definite increase in the share of professionals and the decline in the share of farmers. The shares of all the remaining occupations have, by and large, remained the same, as shown in Table IX.

Among Egyptians working abroad, the share of professionals increased rapidly. The significance of such increase is the short time span during which such changes have taken place. For example, the share of profes-

TABLE IX
Occupational Structure of Egyptian Labor

	In Egypt			Outside Egypt			Concentration Index
	1966	Av. 70-71	Av. 72-73	Av. 68-69	Av. 70-71	Av. 72-73	72-73
Professional	4.8	4.9	5.6	19.9	20.8	28.7	5.1
Administrative	1.8	1.3	1.3	5.2	4.8	4.3	3.3
Clerical	5.5	5.2	5.3	13.3	16.4	14.0	2.6
Sales	6.3	6.9	7.0	4.9	3.4	2.0	0.3
Farmers	50.4	51.2	51.5	1.0	1.9	2.7	0.05
Transport Workers	3.2			4.6	3.6	3.0	
Craftsmen and Pro-	18.0			11.2	12.8	11.0	
duction Workers		19.8	19.8				0.7
Service Workers	7.6	9.5	8.7	6.4	5.2	4.1	0.5
Unclassified	2.4	0.7	0.4	22.0	22.4	19.4	48.5
Other	–	–	–	11.5	8.7	10.8	NA
	100.0	100.0	100.0	100.0	100.0	100.0	NA

SOURCE: N. Choucri, R. S. Eckaus, M. Mohie-Eldin, "Migration and Employment in the Construction Sector: Critical Factors in Egyptian Development", Cairo University/MIT Technology Adaptation Program 1978 (mimeo). Figures for "In Egypt" are computed from Table (2) in the Statistical Appendix; the figures for "Outside Egypt" from Table I-13.

sionals (doctors, engineers, and teachers) has increased sharply from about 20 percent to about 29 percent during a short period of six years. Other discernable, but less spectacular, trends are the decline in the shares of sales workers, transport workers, and service workers. Curiously, the share of farmers also showed a continuous upward trend during the six years of observations. The importation of farm labor by Iraq and Jordan may partly explain this observation.

Contrasting the occupational structures of Egyptian labor inside and outside Egypt shows a decided skewness in favor of the high-skill occupations among those working abroad. There are far more professionals, administrators, and clerical workers among Egyptians abroad than among Egyptians at home. The opposite is also true for the remaining occupational categories.

C. THE PROCESS OF LABOR EXPORTATION

Having examined the quantitative dimension of labor migration from Egypt and outlined its qualitative properties in terms of educational attainment and occupational distribution, the focus turns to the explanation of labor migration as a dynamic process. This process is the outcome of factors operating within Egypt and outside Egypt. The domestic factors produce an excess supply of labor and thus tend to push labor out of Egypt. The external factors, by contrast, generate excess demand for labor and thus tend to pull labor towards the oil-rich states. The net effects of both sets of factors may be shown diagramatically in Figures (1.a) and (1.b) for Egypt, and (2.a) and (2.b) for Saudi Arabia as a prototype of the oil producing countries.

Figures 1.a and 1.b illustrate the labor market mechanism in Egypt with and without labor migration. Given increments in labor demand result in shifts in the demand curves from D_0 to D_1. The shift is identical in the two figures. In the case of no migration, the relative shift in the supply of labor (from S_0 to S_1) is greater than the relative shift in the demand for labor. The result is a downward pressure on the wage rate, from W_0 to W_1. Lured by higher wages and better conditions abroad, the migration of labor reduces the available supply and thus shifts its curves inwardly from S_1 to S_2. In the initial phases of migration, the shifts in supply may not go as far as S_2. In later phases, they may surpass S_2. What is important is that the migration process reduces the excess supply of labor and therefore places slow upward pressures on the wage rate. Eventually, the wage rate does rise, instead of falling in the surplus-labor economy.

The migration of labor which eventually raises the wage rate in Egypt is the same process which slows down the rise in wage rate in Saudi Arabia, as shown in Figures 2.a and 2.b. Given the substantial shifts in the demand for labor by comparison with the limited shifts in the domestic supply of labor, the wage rate would have experienced a huge jump from W'_0 to W'_1. However, the inflows of foreign labor help shift the supply of labor from S'_1 to S'_2. Given the increase in the demand for labor from D'_0 to D'_1, the wage rate would not rise to W'_1, but to the more moderate level of W'_2.

Of course, the above picture is oversimplified. However, it is not distorted. The oversimplification comes in discussing the labor markets in Egypt and Saudi Arabia in general terms as if labor in each and between them is homogeneous. But labor is heterogeneous where various categories simply do not substitute for one another. The diagramatic analysis would perhaps be more applicable to sectors dominated by private enterprise and to labor categories with higher educational attainments and/or high-level occupations (professionals, administrators, etc.). The lower the educational attainment and/or occupational level of the labor force, the less applicable is the preceding analysis. Aggregating

Fig. 1: The Labor Market in Egypt

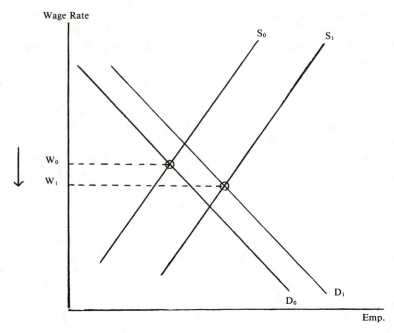

Fig. 1.a: No Labor Migration

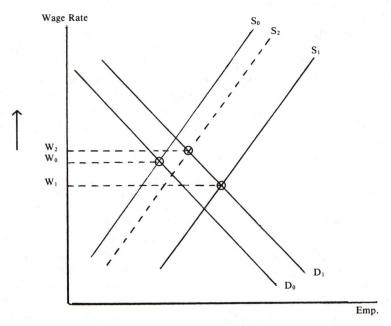

Fig. 1.b: Labor Migration

Fig. 2: The Labor Market in Saudi Arabia

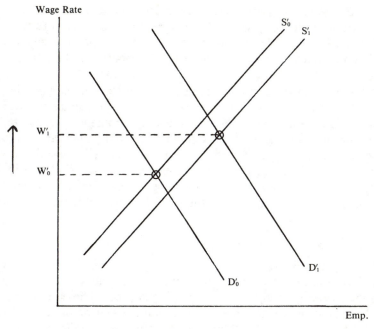

Fig. 2.a: No Labor Imports

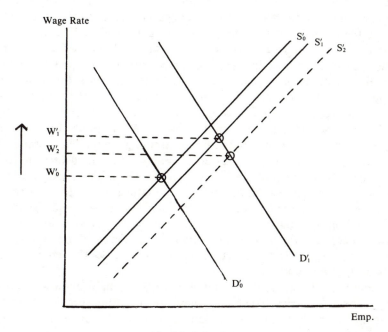

Fig. 2.b: Labor Imports

over the several educational levels or for the various occupational categories as well as between the private and public sectors may introduce great difficulties to the analysis. In fact, it may not be tenable. The intentional oversimplification is intended only to explain the overall picture.

At the heart of the difficulty of any attempt to aggregate public and private employment, as well as across several educational or occupational levels to reach the market at large is the problem of segmentation in the labor market. Segmentation would result in the simultaneous coexistence of excess supply of labor in some segments (the unskilled), and excess demand for labor in other segments (specialized skills). It is this phenomenon which explains the tripartite paradox of chronic unemployment in Egypt, labor shortages in the oil countries, and recent skill shortages in Egypt itself.[10]

D. Prospects of Labor Exports

The prospects of labor exports from Egypt depend on several factors related to the demand for labor from the oil countries and to the supply of labor from Egypt and other competing sources. The case of the demand for labor was made in Section II above, when we discussed Saudi Arabia as a labor importer. This section highlights the labor supply side. It must be noted, however, that the appropriate context to examine labor flows from Egypt to Saudi Arabia is a regional frame of reference, covering all the labor importers and exporters of the Middle East and North Africa. Even though Egypt represents the largest labor pool in the Arab region, there are other suppliers which have hitherto competed effectively with Egyptian labor. Similarly, while Saudi Arabia is the largest importer of labor, there are other oil-rich states which attract labor from various sources including, of course, Egypt. This regional analysis is the subject of a special study undertaken by the World Bank. For the present, this section will be limited to first examining the relative quantitative position of Egypt amongst labor suppliers, then focusing on some qualitative issues which bear on the prospects of labor exports from Egypt. Most recent estimates on labor flows in the Middle East region are only available for the mid 1970s. Table X summarizes this situation by providing data on the total size of the workforce (including military employment) and the number of workers abroad in eight major labor exporting countries: Egypt, North Yemen, Jordan, South Yemen, Syria, Lebanon, Sudan and Oman.

Combined, those countries supply more than one million workers to the recipient countries. To be sure, there are also other suppliers from the Arab world, notably the Palestinians and North Africans. Those addi-

TABLE X
Major Arab Labor Exporters, 1975

Country	Workforce	Workers Abroad	%
Egypt	12,522,200	397,500	3.2
Sudan	3,700,000	45,900	1.2
Syria	1,838,900	70,400	3.8
Lebanon	960,000	49,700	5.2
N. Yemen	1,425,900	290,100	20.3
Jordan*	532,800	150,100	28.1
S. Yemen	430,500	70,600	16.4
Oman	137,000	38,400	28.0
Total	21,547,300	1,112,600	5.2

*For East Bank only; Palestinians are not included.

SOURCE: J. S. Birks and C. A. Sinclair, *International Migration and Development in the Arab Region* (Geneva: ILO, 1980).

tional sources of Arab labor supply another 180,000 persons. Suppliers from outside the Arab world provide another 525,000 persons. The total number of expatriate labor in the recipient countries exceeded 1.8 million workers in 1975.

Focusing on Table X we see a curious breakdown among labor exporters. Countries with a large size workforce export only a small portion of their labor, viz. Egypt, Sudan, and Syria. Meanwhile, countries with a smaller size workforce export a substantial portion of their labor, viz. the two Yemens, Jordan, and Oman. Without going into the reasons for these findings, their implications for the prospects of labor exports from those countries are worthy of closer scrutiny.

Numerically, the figures suggest that countries with large portions of their workforce already placed abroad would be the least able to expand labor exports in the future. By the same token, countries which presently have a small portion of their workers abroad would be the most logical candidates to expand future labor exports; they still have a large reservoir of labor resources from which the oil-rich states can draw. Using the logic of numbers, it is possible to argue that if the small population labor exporters were able to export up to 28 percent of their workforce, then surely the large population exporters should be able to export no less than 10 percent of their workforce. Thus, Egypt could supply an *additional* 800,000 workers, Sudan 320,000, Syria 110,000, and Lebanon another 50,000. This, however, is too simplistic and possibly misleading.

Staying with the quantitative aspects of labor migration a little longer, it is clear that the post 1975 developments in the Arab region have produced further changes in the picture portrayed by Table X. Field observations suggest that workers from various Arab countries must have migrated in large numbers to the recipient oil-rich states. For example, the civil war in Lebanon has forced large numbers of Lebanese to leave and seek employment in the oil states and elsewhere; this created a need to import farm labor from Jordan, Syria, and Egypt. Mobilization of Syrian armed forces to stabilize the political situation in Lebanon has reduced whatever excess supply of labor that has existed in Syria. Jordan in 1975 was already importing farm labor, which seems to have increased in recent years. Greater numbers of Egyptians and Sudanese have migrated further to the oil countries. And recent official statistics in the oil countries are beginning to show the size and extent of these far-reaching changes. However, it is the qualitative factors which tell the more subtle part of the story. The focus turns back to Egypt.

Examining the dynamics of the process of labor exportation, the notion of labor market segmentation was advanced to explain the difficulty in aggregating the sub-markets of various labor categories. Segmentation of the labor market was also proposed as the explanation of the simultaneous coexistence of chronic unemployment and recent skill shortages in Egypt and general labor shortages in the oil countries. In a careful study, Birks and Sinclair addressed this very issue. The thrust of their analysis is that a serious mis-match exists between the structure of labor demand in the importing countries and the structure of labor supply in the exporting countries. The data contained in Tables VII and VIII about differentials in educational attainment and in occupational composition between labor exports and the labor stock at home demonstrate this proposition.

Birks and Sinclair give a penetrating analysis of the Egyptian labor paradox. They explain the low occupational and geographic mobility of Egyptian labor by several reasons. First, they suggest that three-quarters of non-farm civil wage employment is in government sectors for economic security. Secondly, they cite labor market segmentation as the main hurdle for occupational, and hence geographic mobility. Thirdly they contend that the only pool of Egyptian labor from which to draw is urban non-government employment, estimated at about 25 percent of non-farm civil wage employment—about 1.4 million persons in 1975. Those are the urban poor, with low educational attainment, lack of employment and work experience, and often unemployed. Finally Birks and Sinclair identify the institutional constraints working against migration of the poor who are caught in a vicious circle: they are unemployable at home and are too poor to finance their migration abroad.

For these reasons Birks and Sinclair conclude that "the period of marked expansion of exports of Egyptian manpower is over. Egyptians are going to fill a diminishing proportion of jobs held by migrant workers in capital rich countries."[11] And despite the replacement migration of the urban poor and farmers to other labor-exporting countries (for example Jordan) they reach another conclusion, to the effect that "it is most unlikely that there will be one million Egyptians working abroad by 1985, despite a continuing increase in the demand for labor in the industrializing capital-rich states."[12]

While the analysis of past developments by Birks and Sinclair is undoubtedly accurate and insightful, the conclusions they reached concerning prospects for the future are, in the view of the authors, overly pessimistic. This is primarily due to the diminished role of institutional rigidities in stunting further migration than was anticipated by Birks and Sinclair, and also to the fact that they did not place sufficient emphasis on the cumulative impact of the incremental labor supply over the forecast years. Accordingly the authors are more sanguine than Birks and Sinclair concerning the future prospects of Egyptian labor exports in the years to come. Each of the above two factors is discussed in more detail below.

After more than two decades of strong government intervention in practically all facets of Egyptian economic life, it is not surprising that the Egyptian labor market would acquire cumulative institutional rigidities. Looking at labor market data and conditions of the mid-1970s, Birks and Sinclair were correctly alarmed by the extent to which institutional rigidities affected all functions of the labor market: occupational mobility, geographic mobility, and wage determination. The second half of the 1970s brought about far-reaching changes which have at least shaken up many of the assumptions about institutional rigidities. Such changes include the steadily rising role of the private sector, including the increasing presence of international firms, the steadily declining direct government intervention in the labor market, the lifting of restrictions on travel to and from Egypt, the increasing migration of Egyptians with widely varied educational and occupational levels to the Arab countries and beyond, the mushrooming of labor remittances, and so on. These factors, among many others, are restructuring the labor market of the 1980s in ways unanticipated in the mid-1970s. More importantly, these factors are reshaping the expectations of Egyptians about the future. There is hardly an urban family in 1980 which does not have members working abroad. And in rural Egypt, it is no longer extraordinary for village labor to move directly to the international market, thereby skipping the intermediate urban market. Looking at Egypt in 1980, the international migration process appears to have been not only accepted, but more importantly internalized by many Egyptian families. To have expected Birks and Sinclair to foresee such sweeping changes over an incredibly short period would, of course, be unfair. It is therefore quite an accomplishment for the Egyptian labor market to have changed so rapidly that even such experienced and careful observers as Birks and Sinclair did not consider such a development plausible.

There is a second reason to contest their conclusions that "the period of marked expansion of Egyptians manpower is over" and therefore it was "most unlikely that there will be one million Egyptians working abroad by 1985". The present authors believe that the analysis that led to this conclusion did not account for the incremental labor supply in a sufficiently systematic fashion. The Birks and Sinclair anatomy of the Egyptian workforce for 1976 may have been quite correct in pointing out that the existing force could not produce more than 600,000 migrant workers. Nevertheless, the cumulative effects of incremental labor supply over time could change that conclusion. Specifically, the estimated 350,000 new entrants to the labor market every year would add 3.2 million to the workforce by 1985. For the conclusion to hold, a total of no more than 300,000 Egyptian workers can be assumed to migrate over the nine-year period through 1985, or at an annual flow of less than 30,000 workers. The other implicit assumption is that the Egyptian economy would be able to absorb 2.9 million workers over the same period or more than 320,000 per year. Neither assumption is likely. In fact, probably more than 250,000 additional Egyptian workers may have migrated between 1976 and 1980. Precisely because the domestic economy is unlikely to be able to absorb more than 200,000 every year, the remaining 150,000 must somehow seek employment beyond Egypt's borders. This, of course, assumes that the unemployed hardcore remains at its one-million level estimated for the mid-1970s. Should the domestic economy fail to absorb 200,000 per year and migration fall below 150,000, the inevitable result is increasing the army of the unemployed—a burden which Egypt can ill afford, and which explains the government's earnest efforts to liberalize the functioning of the labor market.

Given the increasing concern among government officials for the need to hold the line on public employment, most of the new entrants must be absorbed in the private sector, or simply migrate. Whether the private sector will be allowed to grow to the point of absorbing the better part of the 200,000 annual additional entrants estimated to stay in Egypt remains to be seen. Birks and Sinclair estimated non-farm private-sector employment in 1976 to have been slightly below one million, agriculture 6.5 million, and government employment 3.3 million. The last figure includes employment in public administration, armed forces, and public sector enterprises. Even if the non-farm private sector could not absorb more than 100,000 every year, its employment in 1985 will have doubled by comparison with 1976 — an achievement which requires greater liberalization policies and far greater capital investments. The remaining 250,000 must somehow be distributed among agriculture, government, and migration. Agricultural employment may already have surpassed its limits.[13] And government, through its strong pro-employment policies, has during the past twenty years been the reservoir of disguised unemployment.[14] Together with rising expectations of the urban family, as already mentioned, the most natural channel for the young, educated and aspiring Egyptians will be either the private sector or migration. What, then, is the profile of the new entrants to the labor market?

Three main sources of skill formation exist in Egypt: the formal educational/training system, the informal system of apprenticeship and on-the-job learning, and the vocational training of the military service. The first source had in the mid-1970s the capacity to produce 90,000 university graduates (including technical institute graduates), 40,000 secondary general education graduates, 120,000 secondary technical education graduates, and over 250,000 intermediate school graduates. This capacity will grow during the 1980s in varying degrees, ranging from 1.2 percent for university graduates, 2 percent for secondary general graduates and 7 percent for intermediate graduates, to 15 percent for graduates in technical education.[15]

The second system of skill formation depends on traditional channels, which are deep-rooted in Egyptian labor practices. This is an informal system which over decades produced artisans and craftsmen through apprenticeship and on-the-job training, and which now produces carpenters, electricians, mechanics, masons, blacksmiths, and a wide variety of services and production workers. No recent studies are available on these groups, especially in understanding how to increase their numbers. The supply of these craftsmen and production workers in recent years appears to have accelerated its expansion satisfactorily, from 2.4 percent per annum during the period from 1960 to 1970, to 4.2 percent per annum during the years from 1970 to 1974. Nevertheless, the migration of these workers — lured by rapid expansion in economic activity in the oil-rich states and especially the major construction boom — has produced after 1975 serious dislocations in their specialized sub-markets.[16] Undocumented recent field observations suggest that the rapid expansion in the demand for those labor categories, not only from the Gulf states but also from within Egypt itself, is finally producing a lagged supply response, as increasing numbers of young men seek training and apprenticeship opportunities within this informal system. The triggering mechanism, of course, has been the rapid rise in wage rates to levels well beyond wage rates for university-educated white collar employees. Only time will tell the extent of such supply response. However, the informal system remains a source that cannot and should not be under-estimated, even though the formal sector is increasingly taking over the role of prime trainer of technicians and skilled workers.

While relatively little is known about the informal system of skill formation in Egypt, practically nothing is known about the capacity of the armed forces to generate skills which are usable in civilian economic activity. Yet this is a source which cannot be ignored, precisely because of its role in the past two decades. Within the military establishment, two main branches have generated skills for thousands of young men. The first is the regular operations of the rank and file, where men with little or no previous exposure and education come out of the service as car and truck drivers, assistant builders, masons, and low-level administrators. The second branch is the military industries. Not only do these industries develop the standard industrial skills useable elsewhere, but they also produce a wide range of reasonable quality household appliances at competitive prices for the average urban household. Of course, it is not possible to estimate the cumulative quantitative impact of the military establishment on the skill supplies. But to think it is negligible is to miss the thrust of the preceding discussion.

To conclude the present section, the main points are reiterated. The future of Egyptian labor exports depends on internal and external conditions. The external conditions were reviewed for Saudi Arabia in Section II. The present section reviewed the internal conditions operating in the Egyptian labor market. Quantitatively, the growth of employment was found to lag behind the growth of labor force. The most significant manifestation of this fact was the substantial downward pressures on the average wage rate of the Egyptian worker. Combined with external pull factors, the process of labor migration started with special concentration on high-level and specialized skills. Acceleration of economic growth in the oil-rich states pulled increasing numbers of Egyptians and broadened the variety of migrant skills. However, it failed to alleviate the unemployment problem. Nevertheless, the migration process resulted in increasing the wage rates of the average worker in general, and of specialized skills in particular.

The prospects of Egyptian labor exports have quantitative and qualitative dimensions. Quantitatively, there is no doubt that Egypt can afford to have as many as two million workers abroad by 1985. Qualitatively, the external and domestic demand for skilled workers and technicians will continue to exceed supply. The three sources of skill formation: the formal education/training system, the informal traditional system, and the military establishment have variant capabilities to produce the requisite skills. Combined and appropriately reoriented and expanded, these sources may be able to go some way towards meeting the demand challenges from inside and outside Egypt. However, important qualifications must be met. Special government programs and policies must supplement the operation of the market mechanism, especially in improving training on the supply side. The liberalization policies must be strengthened to give the less skilled workers maximum opportunities to migrate. Some orientation assistance may be provided at labor centers, and initial loans extended to qualified workers. An incentive system for the informal sector may be worked out to expand the base of this important source. In short, the occupational and geographic mobility of Egyptian labor can be improved dramatically without necessarily adding to the government expenditures burden. Imaginative approaches do not necessarily require additional resources, only a better use of existing resources.

IV. THE FUTURE OF SAUDI-EGYPTIAN LABOR RELATIONS

Having first examined the development of the Saudi-Egyptian labor linkage and the dynamics of the Saudi economy as a labor importer, then the case of Egypt as a labor exporter, the stage is set to pull the various parts together in a coherent concluding statement.

It is clear that there is a growing interdependence between the two countries which is being fostered by the interlinkage of their labor markets. It is equally clear, however, that this does not automatically translate into a symbiotic economic relationship which will magically overcome political differences and regional geo-political considerations. Rather, the picture that emerges is one of cautious optimism that, having successfully weathered the worst political storm ever to have clouded Egyptian-Arab relations, the labor relations between the two countries could continue to grow, to the point where both countries clearly perceive the benefits of that continued relationship and are aware of the costs of severing it.

This cautious optimism, however, implies that

i.   the Saudi authorities will continue along the path charted in the Third Development Plan which calls for a modest expansion of foreign labor, with a more deliberate and carefully thought out

foreign policy for the selection and retention of different
segments of the expatriate labor force;

ii. the Egyptian authorities will accelerate their expansion of tech-
     nician training programs, and reinforce the present policies
     towards emigration; and

iii. the liberalization of the Egyptian economy will continue to grow,
     removing the rigidities that have stifled the Egyptian labor market
     in the past and which still continue to do so to a great extent.

The ingredients for a powerful economic relationship are there.
Whether the authorities will effectively make good use of them will be
demonstrated within the next few years, when the key elements of the
Saudi Third Plan will be well on their way to implementation, and when
the role that Egyptian labor can play in that process will have been
clearly delineated.

NOTES

1. E. Y. Asfour, "Aspects and Problems of Economic Development of Saudi Arabia,
Kuwait and the Gulf Principalities", in C. A. Cooper and S. A. Alexander, eds., *Economic
Development and Population Growth in the Middle East* (New York: Elsevier, 1972), pp.
363-396.

2. Simon Kuznets, *Modern Economic Growth* (New Haven, Conn.: Yale University
Press, 1966).

3. H. B. Chenery and M. Syrquin, *Patterns of Development: 1950–1970* (London: Oxford University Press, 1975).

4. N. Kaldor, *Strategic Factors in Economic Development* (Ithaca, N.Y.: Cornell University Press, 1967); R. E. Rowthorn, "A Note on Verdoorn's Law", *The Economic Journal*,
March 1979.

5. N. A. Sherbiny, "Sectoral Employment Projections with Minimum Data Base: The
Case of Saudi Arabia", in N. A. Sherbiny, ed., *Manpower Planning in the Oil Countries*,
Supplement 1 to *Research in Human Capital and Development* (Greenwich: JAI Press Inc.,
1981).

6. J. S. Birks and C. A. Sinclair, *The Kingdom of Saudi Arabia and the Libyan Arab
Jamahiriya: The Key Countries of Employment*, Provisional Draft Working Paper WEP
2-26/WP39, Migration for Employment Project — World Employment Programme
Research (Geneva: International Labour Office, May 1979), from Table 34.

7. I. Serageldin, "The Problem of Labor Adaptation in the Oil Countries" in N. Sherbiny, ed., *Manpower Planning...*, op.cit.

8. ʿAli al-Gritli, *Al-Sukkan wa al-mawarid al-iqtisadiyya...* [Population and Economic
Resources in the United Arab Republic], (Cairo: The Anglo-Egyptian, 1962), p. 12.

9. As reported in J. S. Birks and C. A. Sinclair, "Egypt: A Frustrated Labor Exporter",
The Middle East Journal, Vol. 33, no. 3 (Summer 1979).

10. Ibid.

11. Ibid., p. 303.

12. Ibid., p. 303.

13. A counter argument is articulated by Bent Hansen, "Employment and Wages in Rural Egypt", *American Economic Review,* June 1969.

14. Bent Hansen, "Economic Development of Egypt", in C. A. Cooper and S. S. Alexander, eds., *Economic Development and Population Growth in the Middle East* (New York: Elsevier, 1972).

15. These figures are consistent with the enrollment figures given in Khalid Ikram, *Economic Management in a Period of Transition* (Baltimore and London: The World Bank and Johns Hopkins University Press, 1980), p. 129.

16. N. Choucri, R. S. Eckaus and A. Mohie-Eldin, *Migration and Employment in the Construction Sector: Critical Factors in Egyptian Development,* Cairo University/MIT Technology Adaptation Program, October 1978 (mimeo).

VIII
The Open Door Economic Policy in Egypt: Its Contribution to Investment and Its Equity Implications

Gouda Abdel-Khalek

INTRODUCTION

The shift in Egypt's economic policy which initially manifested itself in the early 1970s in the country's economic relations eventually involved the very basis of its economic system. This shift came to be known, especially after 1974, as the "policy of the opening" (*infitah*) of the economy or, to use a more popular though less accurate term, the "open door" economic policy.

This chapter focuses on the open door economic policy, its meaning, its dimensions and its historical development. It also provides some explanations for the apparently sudden shift from controlled development, based on directives, to development based on private initiative, both local and foreign, and on market forces.

In addition, it puts forth a basic argument which, briefly expressed, says that the shift to the open door economic policy in Egypt is the outcome both of the country's failure to achieve a truly socialist economy, and of external pressure. The policy represents a happy coincidence of the interests of the newly emerging class in Egypt and of the interests of the multinationals.

The chapter further provides an assessment of the impact of *infitah* on social equity and income distribution. In a previous paper[1] the author discussed the contribution which this policy could make towards achieving socio-economic development in Egypt. Our contention in the present

Author's Note: The views expressed in this essay are entirely those of the author and do not represent in any way those of any institution with which he is, or has been, affiliated.

essay is that the policy will be detrimental to income distribution and social equity, in the sense that it will change income distribution against the poor.

In Section I of the chapter we deal with the meaning of *infitah* and in Section II we discuss the interpretation of this policy. Section III offers an examination of the achievements of *infitah* in terms of the size, rate and pattern of investment. The implication of the policy for income distribution and social equity will be discussed in Section IV, and Section V concludes the chapter.

I. THE MEANING OF INFITAH

The term *infitah* is very difficult to define precisely.[2] Needless to say, the Egyptian economy was not closed prior to advocating and adopting the open door economic policy,[3] and we have indicated elsewhere that *infitah* really implies turning north-west, rather than simply looking outside.[4] What it means, in effect, is the re-establishing of the developed market economies as the principal buyers of Egypt's exports and the increasing of their share in the country's imports; that is, the reintegration of the Egyptian economy into the network of the world capitalist market. But hand in hand with trade with the developed market economies must go investment—i.e. direct foreign investment—and from this stems Law No. 43 for 1974 and its amendment through Law No. 32 for 1977.

The document known as the October Paper issued by President Anwar Sadat in 1974 gives us both a definition and a rationale for the policy of *infitah,* which was one of the major objectives to be defined, elaborated and christened in that document.[5] In its diagnosis of Egypt's economic difficulties, the October Paper maintained that due to military expenditure, the rate of the country's growth fell from 6.7 percent to less than 5 percent annually, and that the goal should thus be the restoration of the pre-1965 annual growth rate. It argued further that despite all the domestic resources that could be mobilized, Egypt still badly needed foreign resources. This provides the rationale of the open door policy. "It is based on an assessment of the needs of the Egyptian economy on the one hand, and the opportunities available for external financing on the other."[6]

Infitah thus means, in the conception of the October Paper, opening up the Egyptian economy for direct private investment, both Arab and foreign. Two elements are stressed in offering a rationale for *infitah:* finance and technology. But this "finance and technology" argument involves gross abstractions from social elements in the development process, and virtually equates economic growth with development. In reality, development is a much more fundamental task which involves the eradication of poverty, of unemployment and of inequality.[7]

Finance and technology may be necessary conditions for development but they are not sufficient. First of all, one wonders whether a strong technological base can be sustained in a society with a high illiteracy rate such as Egypt.[8] Moreover, a clear distinction must be made between technology and the products of that technology. Without the provision of basic education for the bulk of the population, only the material products of technology, rather than technology itself, may be obtained.

But the drive towards *infitah* has its own momentum. Thus, corresponding to the restructuring of the international economic relations, there must also be a restructuring of the internal working of the economy. Market forces have to be allowed to function, and private Egyptian investment has to have its share of the cake.

II. THE INTERNAL SOCIAL DYNAMICS OF INFITAH

We maintain in this chapter that the push towards *infitah* was partly endogenously generated; that is, it was partly created by forces emerging from within the system, and because of the very nature of its working. To articulate this point we first examine the nature of the changes which took place during the period from 1952 to 1970 in the institutional framework of the economy. We then examine the actual structural change in the economy over the period from 1960 to 1970, after the changes in the institutional framework had had a chance to work themselves out. It will be clear that it was precisely the very nature of the institutional changes that led to the creation of socio-economic forces; these, in their turn, found the existing framework inadequate for furthering their interests, and it was their push for an alternative framework, coupled with external pressure, which led to the subsequent drive for *infitah.*

A. DEVELOPMENT OF THE INSTITUTIONAL FRAMEWORK OF THE EGYPTIAN ECONOMY, 1952–1970

During the period from 1952 to 1957, there was no substantial institutional change in the economy, apart from the Land Reform Act of 1952, since, outside agriculture, the state played a very limited role in economic activity. In 1957, the Economic Organization was established to function as a holding company for mixed (state-private) companies and Egyptianized foreign property.[9] The main feature of the economic policy during this period of the late fifties and early sixties was that of "directing" the private sector.[10]

With the great nationalization measures from 1960 to 1964, the scope of the public sector expanded dramatically. An early result was the establishment of the Misr Organization and the Nasr Organization in 1961, alongside the Economic Organization. But at the end of 1961 these three organizations were diffused into some forty organizations on the basis of types of activities. Thus, from then onward, the organizational structure in the public sector was based on control by the appropriate Organization as an organism in the middle level between the ministry at the top and the enterprise at the bottom, a structure which continued till the early seventies.

It is our contention that this structure of institutional organization of the public sector was defective, and that the defects therein were really fatal; it led to the frustration of the development effort and created the ideal environment for the appropriation of public surplus by private hands. Although one can speak at length about these defects,[11] it is sufficient here merely to note the confusion about the nature of the economic unit in a socialist society, in contra-distinction to its nature in a capitalist society.[12] The public enterprises were considered the "private" property of the state,[13] and they were manned by individuals who more often than not had no experience in the field, while the organization of the public sector failed to provide enough checks and controls against illicit practices by the management of the public enterprises. This is the nature of the development on the micro level. On the macro level the façade of a socialist society was established, but with very little substance. The Egyptian economy remained a capitalist society run by the state and hence controlled by the state machinery.

Such was the nature of the institutional transformation that took place during the years from 1957 to 1970. It involved a change of ownership of the means of production on a massive scale, but because of the hastily devised organizational structure of the public sector, there was no corresponding change of control to match it. Control merely shifted from capitalists to techno-military elements, with no effective supervision by the public.

Let us now turn to the actual developments in the Egyptian economy in order to substantiate our argument through an examination of the most relevant features of this development during the period from 1960 to 1970. Table I contains data on the distribution of income according to its two main categories; wage income and non-wage income.

Such a distribution of income is a reasonably good indicator of the

TABLE I
The Distribution of National Income in Egypt

Year	Wage Income (%)*	Non-Wage Income (%)*	National Income (%)
1960/61	42.6	57.4	100.0
1961/62	44.0	56.0	100.0
1962/63	46.2	53.8	100.0
1963/64	47.0	53.0	100.0
1964/65	45.7	54.3	100.0
1965/66	43.9	56.1	100.0
1966/67	43.2	56.8	100.0
1967/68	43.7	56.3	100.0
1968/69	43.9	56.1	100.0

* three-year moving averages

SOURCE: Hassan M. Ibrahim, *Al-Taghayyurat al-haikaliyya fi al-iqtisad al-Misri...* [Structural Changes in the Egyptian Economy and Their Impact on Capital Formation During Ten Years of Planned Development (1960-61/1969-70)], (Cairo: Institute for Arab Research and Studies, 1975), p. 15.

degree of social control over the means of production, and the figures in Table I indicate a big jump in the proportion of wage income in 1961/62 and 1962/63, going up from 42.6 percent in 1960/61 to 44.0 percent and 46.2 percent respectively in 1961/62 and 1962/63. The years 1961/62 and 1962/63 saw extensive nationalization measures; thus, as a result of these measures the share of income going to labor increased and, correspondingly, the share of income going to capital decreased. However, this was only temporary and with the mid-sixties we observe a reversal of this trend; by 1968/69 the share of labor had fallen to 43.9 percent and that of capital had risen to 56.1 percent.[14] Thus we have turned full circle.

It therefore appears that the thrust towards a more egalitarian distribution of the benefits of economic growth was only short-lived. Under the mask of socialist transformation, private property and wealth accumulated, with no legal title. Moreover, those put in charge of public enterprise soon made their fortunes and became anxious to find safe and lucrative channels for their wealth.[15] No wonder we find a curious mosaic of public sector leaders and businessmen in support of *infitah*.[16]

B. DEVELOPMENT OF THE EGYPTIAN ECONOMY SINCE 1971

The beginning of the seventies marks the crystallization of group interest advocating *infitah*. It is easy to identify two elements in this group interest: first, commercial and industrial capital[17] and second, bureaucratic and technocratic leadership in the public sector and the government.[18] It is interesting to note that this emerging capitalist class has quite diverse historical origins, including the following:

i.   Activities of national capital in agriculture, industry, trade and commerce, and construction. Such capital expanded tremendously by taking advantage of public spending programs and through contracting and supply.

ii.   State oligarchy in the economic and political spheres. Political and state influence was used to further private interests.

iii.   Big capitalists who continued to dominate contracting, wholesale trade and export trade. It is estimated that in the mid sixties, only 219 traders controlled all wholesale trade, amounting in value to some LE600 million. Private contractors also assumed 70 percent of all construction activities in the First Five Year Plan, with a total value of LE705 million.[19]

iv.   Adventurists, crooks and outcasts, many of whom acquired their initial training in Beirut in the pre-civil war period.

As this group interest gathered momentum, state capitalism was no longer a convenient environment within which to work. It had reached the limit through the "privatization of public surplus". These groups started to push for a change in the existing institutional framework; they wanted a new framework within which they were fully recognized. What they required was the dismantling of the elaborate system of controls that had developed, particularly during the sixties, and they were setting for themselves a real change in the rules of the economic game. This was also the type of change that growing Arab and foreign capital interests relentlessly sought. A commonality of interests gradually developed.

Thus in 1971, Law No. 65, known as the Law for Investing Arab Capital and Free Zones, was passed. It opened the Egyptian economy to Arab private investment. Three years later, Law No. 43 for 1974 was enacted, allowing foreign private investment, and providing both Arab and foreign investment with guarantees and privileges. Three years later in 1977, Law No. 43 was amended by Law No. 32, which increased these guarantees and privileges and extended them to private Egyptian capital.

Although the period since 1971 — or 1974, the date of the manifest shift to *infitah* — is relatively short, it has witnessed a staggering number of institutional changes on two levels. Numerous measures were taken to restructure the country's international economic relations and, concomitantly, many changes were made in the internal workings of the Egyptian economy. The following is an illustrative rather than an exhaustive list of some of these changes.

a. Law No. 43 for 1974 and its amendment through Law No. 32 for 1977

It is no exaggeration to say that Law No. 43 for 1974 and its amendment through Law No. 32 for 1977, was the most important step on the road to *infitah*. The main stipulations of this law are:

- provision for opening the Egyptian economy to foreign and Arab direct investment in almost every field: industrialization, mining, energy, tourism, transportation, reclamation and cultivation of desert and barren lands, housing and urban development, investment companies, banking and insurance, reconstruction, contracting and consultancy firms (Article 3). This list of areas open for foreign investment exhausts virtually all conceivable fields, and leaves no sanctuary for genuine national investment.
- provision against nationalization and confiscation (Article 7).
- tax exemption that lasts for five years, and which may extend to eight years "if warranted by public interest": and a 10 year tax exemption, which may extend to 15 years, for reconstruction projects (Article 16).
- companies established under this Law are considered private companies, regardless of the legal nature of local share capital. Such companies are not subject to legislation and regulation governing public sector enterprises or their employees (Article 9).

It can be noted here that Law No. 43 for 1974 was the successor of Law No. 65 for 1971 and the predecessor of Law No. 32 for 1977. Thus it would appear that every foreign investment law has a brief life cycle of only three years. In every round of changes, additional incentives are added to attract foreign investment; since it was felt that the existing Laws did not provide sufficient incentive for foreign investment, this was the motive behind the replacement of law No. 65 by Law No. 43, and for the replacement of the latter by Law No. 32. As many will argue, this attitude towards foreign investment is self-defeating and counterproductive. Foreign investment will simply ask for more and more incentives.

Let us ponder the implications of the extant Law governing foreign investment. First, the doors of the Egyptian economy are now, after a series of amendments, wide open for foreign investment. Foreign investment in Egypt is dominated by the multinational corporations, and thus their control of the Egyptian economy is likely to be enhanced.[20] In this context, any development that may take place in Egypt will definitely be "dependent development", and given time, this may even endanger the country's political independence.

Second, although it is a constitutional principle in Egypt that the public sector controls the strategic branches of the economy, the law does not define a particular domain for the public sector; almost every activity can be open to private investment.

Third, since companies established under the Law are considered to be private enterprises, the now dominant position of the public sector will gradually be eroded as the private sector expands more rapidly.

It is therefore feared that the foreign investment law will function in such a way that it will be possible for foreign enterprise and the multi-nationals to infiltrate the Egyptian market, drain away the surplus, and establish and perpetuate a pattern of extroverted "development".

b. The new import-export law of 1975

Another step on the road to *infitah* was the promulgation of law No. 118 for 1975 for imports and exports. This Law provides for the importation of certain goods to be open to the private sector as well as to the public sector, and also includes provisions that entitle individuals to import directly some items for private use. The Law also abolishes the import and export laws of 1959 (Law No. 9 and Law No. 203 respectively) and Law No. 95 for 1963 for the regulation of importation, thus in effect dismantling state monopoly and control of foreign trade. Decree No. 1058, issued by the Minister of Trade and Commerce in October 1975, entitled individuals, both Egyptian and foreign, to import everything except for eighteen commodities that were to be imported by public sector companies. These included wheat and flour, maize, beans, sesame, tea, sugar, edible oil, animal and vegetable fats, tobacco, cotton and cotton yarn, jute, coal, petroleum and petroleum products, chemical fertilizers, insecticides, and military production requirements and arms.

With the exception of these basic food items, power and energy items, agricultural production requirements and strategic items, everything else may be imported by the private sector. In particular, machinery and equipment and raw materials—the basic items for any serious investment program or development plan—are now imported by the private sector. Not only that, but there is also the possibility of foreign control over the importation of intermediate and capital goods. These measures really complement the basic laws of *infitah* (Law No. 43 and Law No. 32) since, as already noted, these laws stipulate that any project established under their prerogatives shall be a private enterprise even if the public sector is a major partner.

One may argue that Law No. 118 for 1975 will have fundamental —and detrimental—consequences for the long-term growth and development of the Egyptian economy. Its effects will be fundamental because the Law creates basic changes in the regulation of Egypt's foreign trade by making room for the private (Egyptian and foreign) sector. That the foreign trade of Egypt plays a very important role in the growth of the economy becomes clear through an examination of the data in Table II, which reveal a close correlation between the current deficit in the balance of payments and the rate of investment. High levels of investment, generally speaking, are associated with high levels of the current deficit in the balance of payments. (The correlation coefficient is 0.81). Moreover, high levels of investment are associated with high rates of economic growth.[21] Therefore if trade (and especially the import trade) is important for investment and hence for economic growth, any change in the regulation of trade should reflect on growth.

But the Law's effects are more likely to be detrimental, the reason being that since importation will be carried on in large part by the private sector, it will be determined in terms of quantity and quality by the profit motive only. Since consumption goods are easier to handle and to market than either intermediate or capital goods, the regulations introduced by Law No. 118 for 1975 are likely to result in a change in the commodity composition of Egypt's imports. Such a change will involve increasing the importance of consumer goods imports, and this is probably going to have the effect of inhibiting the economic growth of the country in the future.

Moreover, in view of the pattern of income distribution in Egypt, consumer goods imports will be more of the luxury than of the necessary type. Such goods carry a very strong demonstration effect and will assuredly create pressures on different socio-economic groups for emulation. Thus the propensity to consume may increase with no matching increase in the society's capacity to produce. The result of all this will be either increased dependence on the rest of the world or increased individual frustration and social tension internally — or both. All this looks more pronounced if we view Law No. 118 for 1975 as a complementary measure to other laws such as the own-import system which we will take up later.

c. Foreign Exchange Law No. 97 for 1976

With the outbreak of the Second World War in 1939, Egypt was under a *de facto* exchange control system by virtue of its membership in the sterling area. Such a situation was made *de jure* by the promulgation of Law No. 80 for 1947,[22] and continued for thirty years until it was changed by Law No. 97 for 1976. This latter Law was intended to liberalize foreign exchange transactions outside Egypt. It asserts the freedom of every legal entity — except for government bodies, public authorities and public enterprises — to keep the foreign exchange ac-

TABLE II

The Current Deficit in the Balance of Payments and the
Rate of Growth in the Economy of Egypt, 1960/61-1969/70
(in LE million at current prices)

Year	Current Deficit in Balance of Payments	Investment as a Proportion of Income %	Rate of Growth of Income %
1960/61	15.5	16.5	6.1
1961/62	86.4	17.8	3.5
1962/63	104.0	19.5	8.9
1963/64	135.6	22.3	8.7
1964/65	75.9	20.7	5.5
1965/66	137.0	18.7	4.5
1966/67	56.7	16.0	5.7
1967/68	36.4	11.6	− 2.7
1968/69	− 22.8	12.5	5.8
1969/70	21.1	12.0	6.9
Average 60/61-64/65	83.5	19.4	6.5
Average 65/66-69/70	45.6	14.2	3.0

SOURCE: Gouda Abdel-Khalek, "Namat al-tanmiya wa al-iʿtimad al-mutazayid ʿala al-kharij"
[Pattern of Development and Increasing Dependence on the Outside World: A Study of the Egyptian Experience 1960-1974], in Société Egyptienne d'Economie Politique..., *Al-tanmiya wa al-ʿilaqat al-iqtisadiyya al-dawliyya*... [Development and International Economic Relations: Papers and Proceedings of the First Conference of Egyptian Economists], (Cairo; 1977), p. 627.

quired from any source whatever (except from merchandise exports and tourism) and to make transactions in foreign exchange through the officially authorized banks; these banks include nationalized Egyptian banks, the Chase National Bank, the Egypt International Bank, and the Egyptian American Bank.[23]

It is to be noted that the three latter banks are (according to Law No. 32 for 1977 which amended the 1974 Law No. 43) private banks with some foreign control. Thus private banks are competing with public banks and are acquiring an increasing proportion of foreign currency deposits.[24] Such deposits are recycled to the world financial centers, and sometimes back to Egyptian borrowers.

In foreign exchange transactions Law No. 97 for 1976 provides some flexibility, and such flexibility may, of course, have its merits. But at the same time it undermines the control over foreign exchange derived from certain important sources such as the incomes of Egyptians working abroad.[25] In view of the absence of any effective control by the Central Bank of Egypt over the operations of foreign banks (such as the three authorized under this Law), it immediately become obvious that designing a foreign exchange policy becomes meaningless and implementing it becomes impossible. Thus the whole question of planning, its meaning and its possibilities, becomes an open one.

d. The own-import system

One of the supporting measures of *infitah* taken in 1974 was the so-called "own-import" system. According to this system, anybody who has foreign exchange resources can use them to import directly, without having to go to the banking system. This is another blatant example of the surrender of the power of control that is necessary for planning. Since, in effect, this policy means exchanging the labor of Egyptians working abroad for various fancy foreign goods which are mainly consumer items, it is hardly a useful arrangement.

Further, such a system goes directly against the often-declared objective of strengthening the position of the Egyptian Pound. Because there is so far no control over the local prices of items imported under this system[26] the profit rate is often extremely high (over 100 percent). Hence the exchange rate implicit in such transactions entails a very low value for the Egyptian Pound, which in turn creates increasing pressures to lower the value of the pound in the parallel market.[27]

e. Phasing out of bilateral trade agreements

Another supporting measure for the policy of *infitah* is the phasing out of existing bilateral trade agreements. Trade agreements are a prerequisite for planning, so that phasing them out will result in a failure to plan foreign trade and allow brute market forces to dominate in shaping the country's overall foreign trade picture. Needless to say, the conducting of foreign trade on the basis of market forces is an integral part of the more comprehensive process of re-integrating the Egyptian economy into the world capitalist market, and is likely to have important ramifications for the internal development of the Egyptian economy.

f. Restructuring the public sector

Hand in hand with the many measures of *infitah* goes the restructuring of the public sector. This process started with Law No. 111 for 1975, which abolished public organizations and concentrated power in the hands of the management boards of the companies. As we mentioned earlier, these organizations were not without their defects, but they had nevertheless performed the task of coordinating, sometimes planning, and of following up on the activities of their affiliate companies. One would have liked to see the change towards improving such organizations and rectifying their defects. Simply abolishing them without creating viable substitutes simply opened the way for the management of such companies to revert to capitalistic principles and practices.

On top of that, the government is at present considering selling off part of the capital of the public sector companies to the public.[28] If this measure is taken, state capitalism will be converted to the more genuine private enterprise capitalism. But this process, of course, carries its own limits; only those public sector enterprises making a profit will be "entrusted" to private ownership, while those making losses will either be liquidated or will remain a public "liability".

III.   THE OUTCOME SO FAR: IMPLICATIONS FOR SIZE, RATE AND PATTERN OF INVESTMENT

Let us now examine the impact of *infitah* measures. We limit our discussion to some of the more important aspects, examining first the effect on the encouragement of private investment, both local and foreign. How effective has *infitah* been so far in augmenting investment resources in the country? Emphasis in this context should be placed on *real additional* investment. By real investment we mean investment in building up productive capacity. By additional investment is meant investment that would not otherwise have been forthcoming.

Table III shows both capital and total investment (capital plus loans) for inland investment projects approved by the General Authority for Investment and Free Zones (GAIFZ) until the end of 1979.

Total investment amounts to about LE4190 million, of which equity capital represents 54.4 percent. It is significant to note that for industrial projects the ratio of equity capital to total investment is much lower, making up about one third only. The above figure of total investment is indicative only of the level of investment that could be achieved. But most of this is yet to be implemented, and some may never be so,[29] so that a more significant figure is therefore that of total investment in projects which have already started production. This is put at LE804 million, or slightly less than one fifth of the total investment approved (see Table III). If we exclude investment in financial sectors (LE372.6 million), that gives an annual rate of some LE86 million, which represents only 7.6 percent of average annual gross fixed investment for the period from 1975 to 1979.[30] In relation to planned annual investment over the period from 1980 to 1984, it represents only a meager 4 percent.[31]

TABLE III
Inland Investment Projects Approved Till End 1979
(in LE million)

Projects	Equity Capital	%	Total Investment	%
I.*Approved*	*2277.6*	*100.0*	*4188.9*	*100.0*
A.Non-industrial	(1624.6)	(71.3)	(2384.5)	(56.9)
B.Industrial	(653.0)	(28.7)	(1804.4)	(43.1)
II.*Started*				
Production	*614.4*	*27.0*	*804.2*	*19.2*
A.Non-industrial	(492.0)	(21.6)	(628.3)	(15.0)
B.Industrial	(122.4)	(5.4)	(175.9)	(4.2)
III.*Under*				
Implementation	*874.1*	*38.4*	*2032.8*	*48.5*
A.Non-industrial	(598.1)	(26.3)	(965.2)	(23.0)
B.Industrial	(276.0)	(12.1)	(1067.6)	(25.5)
IV.*Recently*				
Approved	*789.1*	*34.6*	*1351.8*	*32.3*
A.Non-industrial	(534.5)	(23.4)	(791.0)	(18.9)
B.Industrial	(254.6)	(11.2)	(560.8)	(13.4)

SOURCE: General Authority for Investment and Free Zones, *Statistical Statement of Inland Projects Approved According to Investment Law Until 31/12/1979*, (Cairo: 1980).

The sectoral breakdown of investment is shown in Table IV. Of all investment projects that have already started production, investment companies top the list, accounting for exactly one third. Next come industrial projects, accounting for just over one fifth, while agriculture and animal wealth have attracted projects whose share in total investment is 14.8 percent. Banking projects occupy fourth place, accounting for 13 percent of realized investment. Tourism projects account for about 8 percent, and the remaining 9.3 percent represents investment projects in contracting, transport and communications, services, consultancy, housing, health and hospitals.

It is clear that financial investment (investment companies plus banks) is dominant. Banks and investment companies together account for 46.4 percent of total realized investment. Although the private rate of return on such projects is extremely high (at least 25 percent on capital according to publicly stated figures), the social rate of return need not necessarily be so high. The latter will depend on the success of such financial in-

TABLE IV
Sectoral Allocation of Investment Undertaken Until End 1979

Sector	Total Investment	
	LE million	%
1. Investment Companies	267.4	33.3
2. Industry	175.9	21.9
3. Agriculture & Animal Wealth	119.2	14.8
4. Banking	105.2	13.1
5. Tourism	62.0	7.7
6. Contracting	33.0	4.1
7. Transport & Communications	32.0	4.0
8. Services	5.3	0.7
9. Consultancy	3.1	0.4
10. Housing, Health & Hospitals	1.1	0.1
TOTAL	804.2	100.0

SOURCE: General Authority for Investment and Free Zones, *Statistical Statement of Investment Projects Approved Until 31/12/79*, (Cairo: 1980).

stitutions in mobilizing resources for productive investment. Analysis of activities of *infitah* banks shows that the bulk of their business is in financing foreign trade and deposits abroad, which does not really serve the cause of developing the Egyptian economy; in fact it helps to drain away the economic surplus and raises the propensity to consume and distort national priorities. This can only make the development of the Egyptian economy less likely.

At the other end, the truly productive activities, especially industry, agriculture and animal wealth, have received much less attention under *infitah*; their combined share in total realized investment amounted only to 36.7 percent. It can hardly be overstated that the Egyptian economy badly needs investment in these areas because of the country's need for more food production, more industrial exports and more job opportunities for its growing labor force.

A very interesting feature of investment under *infitah* is also revealed in Table IV. The weight of the sectors which are likely to have stronger outside linkages is higher than that of sectors which are oriented towards the local economy. Banks and investment companies, tourism, transport and communications, services, and consultancy projects are more likely to have stronger outside linkages. Industry and agriculture, on the other hand, are more likely to be geared to the domestic economy. Thus, the larger weight given to the former type of projects symbolizes the process of integrating Egypt into the international capitalist system.[32]

This disproportionate emphasis in *infitah* projects has come under fire even from official quarters. Thus a recent report by the Ministry of Economy, Foreign Trade and Economic Cooperation on New Investment Policies (Law 43 for 1974) has the following comments on investment in banking:

> ....what has become crystal clear to us, to start with, is that the number of banks authorized under Investment Law [43], whether it be joint commercial banks, investment banks or branches of foreign banks, *definitely* exceeds the needs of the Egyptian market. [Public] interest necessitates withholding authorization of any new bank in excess of the thirty-six banks authorized so far. *Illegal competition which exists among some of the banks assures that any increase in the number of new banks will intensify such competition and will endanger the banking structure of the country.* Intense competition among them has led some to follow illicit banking practices, and some have exceeded the safety margin in attempting to lure customers. *Therefore there is no place for a new bank*; danger to the banking system will increase with any increase in the number of banking units...[33]

Thus there is no doubt that the Egyptian economy is "over-banked".[34] But such over-banking can be tolerated if it brings *additional* investment into the country. Let us therefore examine this by looking at the consolidated budget of banks established under the Investment Law of *infitah*. Table V indicates that such banks derive more than 50 percent of their resources from local customers (through managing to attract the largest customers of the nationalized Egyptian banks, including public sector companies), and shows that over 50 percent of their assets represent deposits with banks abroad. Most of the loans given by these banks are for the finance of foreign trade rather than for investment.[35]

IV. THE OUTCOME SO FAR: IMPLICATIONS OF INFITAH FOR INCOME DISTRIBUTION

Among the most important ways in which *infitah* affects income distribution are the following:

i. *Infitah* results in public expenditure growing faster than public revenues. This leads to foreign borrowing and/or money creation. In the case of money creation it will have a negative effect on income distribution.

ii. *Infitah* results in a decline in the share of wages in national income.

iii. It results, following International Monetary Fund advice, in

TABLE V

Main Items of Consolidated Budget of Banks
Established Under Investment Law, 1976-1978

	End of 1976		End of 1977		End of 1978	
	LE million	%	LE million	%	LE million	%
I. Liabilities	340	100.0	505	100.0	1326	100.0
1. Deposits	197	57.9	277	54.9	698	52.6
2. Debits to local banks	59	17.1	75	14.9	261	19.7
3. Debits to banks abroad	28	8.2	71	14.1	177	13.3
4. Capital & reserves	38	11.2	34	6.7	96	7.2
5. Other liabilities	19	5.6	48	9.5	94	7.1
II. Assets	340	100.0	505	100.0	1326	100.0
1. Balance with Central Bank of Egypt	26	7.6	28	5.5	55*	4.1
2. Deposits with local banks	35	10.3	63	12.5	187	14.1
3. Deposits with banks abroad	208	61.2	269	53.3	663	50.0
4. Investments & securities	4	1.2	7	1.4	21**	1.6
5. Loans	45	13.2	114	22.6	328	24.7
6. Other assets	22	6.5	24	4.8	72	5.4

*includes Egyptian Pound cash reserve with the Central Bank of Egypt plus loans in foreign currencies for pre-financing of cotton.

**mostly Development Bonds 8% in dollars and equity participation in subsidiaries.

SOURCE: Ministry of Economy, Foreign Trade and Economic Cooperation, Economic Studies Unit, *Report on New Investment Policies (Law 43 for 1974)* [in Arabic], (Cairo: December 1979), p. 73.

devaluation and raising the interest rate, reducing subsidies, and re-instituting market forces.

iv.   Tax exemptions for *infitah* projects under Law No. 43 and its amendments by Law No. 32 are not broadly shared by the public at large, but rather are enjoyed by a limited number of families.

The outcome of all these factors is a worsening distribution of income. Unfortunately, data are not readily available to prove this rigorously; however, partial evidence can be marshalled to substantiate the argument.

A.   INFITAH AND PUBLIC FINANCE

One of the basic instruments used to attract private investment, in the context of *infitah,* is the provision of exemptions from taxes and customs duties. Such exemptions are usually temporary, but for the entire stream of *infitah* projects there will always be new projects enjoying such exemptions. Tax revenues will therefore lag behind economic activity. On the other hand, *infitah* projects require investment in infrastructure (power, roads and telecommunications networks) which is usually financed from the public purse (the 1980–84 Plan stipulates investment allocations of LE5950 million, or close to 30 percent, to these areas).[36]

Vigorous pursuit of the *infitah* policy will therefore cause public expenditure to run ahead of public revenue, resulting in an increasing budget deficit; such deficit has been increasingly financed by borrowing from the banking system (mainly from the Central Bank), thus contributing to inflation. The end result is a worsening income distribution, with wage earners suffering to the benefit of profit makers. The data in Table VI give evidence in support of this argument, indicating that the budget deficit doubled in the three year period from 1976 to 1979, and that financing through the banking system more than tripled, reaching 44.5 percent of the deficit in 1979.

One reason behind the increase in budget deficit in 1979 was the application of the (devalued) unified exchange rate on all imports and payments starting from January 1979,[37] which is another measure of *infitah* taken under pressure from the International Monetary Fund. Consequently, currency issued rose at an annual rate of 25 percent over the period from 1976 to 1978[38] and the resulting inflation is borne out by the data on the consumer price index. The rate of inflation indicated is an underestimation because the index relates to the urban sector only (prices have risen faster in the rural sector), and because it relies on official prices to which only part of expenditures is related. Thus the rate of inflation is much higher than revealed by the consumer price index. It may be in the range of 25 to 30 percent per annum. Note also that prices of necessities (food and clothing) are rising faster than the general price index. Thus the poor and those on fixed incomes are hardest hit.

A new pattern of income distribution is thus revealing itself, with the share of the poor falling and that of the rich rising. Such a change in income distribution is required for the system of *infitah* to continue to function, since most of the additional goods and services produced by *infitah* projects are of the luxury type, and cater to the needs of the well-to-do.[39] The process of redistribution (via inflation) thus adjusts aggregate

TABLE VI
Budget Deficit, Borrowing From Banking System and Inflation
(LE million)

	1975	1976	1977	1978	1979
Budget Deficit		1337.0	1481.0	2097.6	2688.1
Borrowing from Banking System		308.7*	523.0	350.0	1197.0
Borrowing from Banking System as % of Deficit		23%	35%	16.6%	44.5%
Consumer Price Index (urban)	148.9	164.2	185.1	205.6	219.2**
Food Price Index	171.5	196.8	225.0	246.6	256.0**
Clothing Price Index	136.7	145.3	172.6	225.2	242.8**

* includes loans and credit facilities
**average for first quarter only

SOURCE: Budget deficit and borrowing; Central Bank of Egypt, *Annual Report 1977* and *1978*, p. 4 and p. 17 respectively. Consumer, food and clothing price indices; Central Bank of Egypt, *Economic Review*, Vol. 19, No. 1 (1979), p. 146.

and sectoral demands to the level of supply as determined by profitability (and hence the ability to pay), and not by need.

It is to be noted that this process of income redistribution is not always smooth and orderly. It can result — and indeed has resulted — in social tension and political eruption counteracted by repression. This is the lesson of the uprising of January 1977, which was sparked off by the attempt of the government, following the advice of the International Monetary Fund, to force the economic adjustment down the throats of the poor by announcing price increases on various items of basic consumption.

B.   INFITAH AND THE SHARE OF WAGES IN NATIONAL INCOME

The process of inflation caused by *infitah* and analyzed above will result in a reduction in the share of wages expressed in constant prices. But *infitah* may also result in a fall in the share of wages expressed in current prices, an effect that may be related to a number of factors associated with *infitah*. Increased demand for assets in fixed or inelastic supply will tend to raise their prices. In particular, because of emphasis on capital-intensive agro-industrial complexes, the share of profits in agriculture will go up, and that of wages will correspondingly go down. Also, in view of the surge in tertiary activities under *infitah,* urban land prices will go up dramatically. In any production process involving such assets the share of value added going to labor (i.e. wages) must go down. Moreover, *infitah* will undermine the public sector enterprises, given the fierce competition of foreign or locally made substitutes (produced at lower costs thanks to the liberalization of imports, and tax and tariff exemption for *infitah* projects). Public sector enterprises were an essential means of creating job opportunities. On the other hand, *infitah* projects tend to be more capital-intensive; investment per job opportunity for inland projects which have started production exceeds LE15,000, compared to an overall average of less than half that level for the entire economy.[40] In a labor-abundant, capital-scarce economy such as that of Egypt, that should lead to a fall in the share of wages. Thus this share (in current prices) dropped from 46.3 percent in 1973–74 to 42.0 percent in 1976–77.[41]

C. INFITAH AND MARKET PRICES

In the course of *infitah,* the Egyptian economy has been consistently subjected to pressure by the Internatonal Monetary Fund to devalue the Pound, to reduce subsidies, and to raise interest rates. The rationale behind devaluation is to encourage exports and to discourage imports, and hence to achieve equilibrium in the trade balance. In the process, Pound prices of imported goods rise, increasing the cost of living for the consumers and the cost of production for the producers.[42] A similar effect will result from raising interest rates. Low and fixed income classes will lose to businessmen and traders. In fact, one immediate effect of raising interest rates was to raise the cost of new housing by 50 percent, through increasing the cost of borrowing for housing.

D. INFITAH AND INEQUALITY

Infitah will result in skewing the distribution of national income between nationals and foreigners in favor of the latter. Average wages for foreigners in *infitah* projects are seven to ten times higher than the average wage of Egyptians in these projects.

The tax and customs exemptions stipulated under Law No. 43 and Law No. 32 will result in a greater concentration in wealth. The reason is that participation by the Egyptian private sector in *infitah* projects is often based on family ties. Reading through the Presidential and Ministerial decrees establishing these projects, one frequently comes across family names such as ʿUthman Ahmad ʿUthman, Muhammad Mahmud, Hamid Mahmud, Marʿi, ʿAbd al Wahhab, Hamad al-Basil, and al-Ahwal.[43] Some of these families have established their own firms but in many cases teaming up, as junior partners, with foreign investors.

The "family nature" of many *infitah* projects makes the privileges stipulated in the Foreign Investment Law disproportionately distributed, and this naturally leads to more concentration of wealth.

Moreover, *infitah* projects provide highly paid job opportunities to graduates of foreign-language schools, who usually come from well-to-do families. The chances of the offspring of poorer families getting into such projects are very much lower. This can only worsen the distribution of income and inhibit social mobility.

Infitah will change the socio-political matrix. New classes will rise to power and status, and others, at the other end, will suffer. Specifically, it is the landowners, traders and businessmen who will gain in strength, while the peasants, workers, bureaucrats and even the productive segment of national capital will be weakened. Egypt is facing a process of social stratification similar to the one it experienced with the breakdown of Muhammad ʿAli's system in the nineteenth century.[44]

V. CONCLUSION

There has been a definite shift in Egypt's economic policy. Some writers refer to this as economic liberalization; others call it a retreat from economic nationalism.[45] But although there is some truth in both of these characterizations, the first seems to underplay the fundamentality of the change, while the second may give the impression that the shift has been voluntary. This chapter has offered a historical perspective within which interaction between domestic development and the international environment throws more light on the nature of the change. Within this perspective, what is happening in Egypt is more fundamental than "economic liberalization". It is a total restructuring of the economic system. The country seems to be heading now towards a free enterprise system, and the change does not simply represent a "retreat" from economic nationalism, but rather a process of reabsorption of the Egyptian economy into the world capitalist system. This process has its analogy in the second half of the nineteenth century.[46]

The purpose of this essay was to assess the impact of *infitah* on economic growth and social equity. Our conclusion is that there is some addition to real fixed investment but that it is at too low a level to make a significant positive contribution to growth. Moreover, in some cases it is being channelled mainly to sectors which do not contribute to meeting the needs of the majority of the Egyptian population. In other cases, such as banks, it provides a channel for draining away the economic surplus. It is really doubtful whether this policy has availed Egypt of *net* additional resources. More important, the pursuit of this policy is forced on the country by Egypt's lenders, represented by the International Monetary Fund, through the use of the mechanism of the Consultative Group.[47]

It is significant to note that Western economic circles are hailing the Egyptian experiment in economic reform, as it is often called. The rapid growth of the Egyptian economy in recent years, which is often referred to in the Western press, is in fact mainly due to extraneous factors, such as the rise in oil prices, the increase in revenues from the Suez Canal, and remittances from Egyptians working abroad.[48] It cannot be seriously attributed to *infitah*.

Analysis has shown that a change in the entire social pyramid is now in progress, thanks to *infitah*. Comprador elements are riding high in the new environment, and to this group now belong many of the leading figures of the post-1952 regime[49] in addition to the old families which are making a comeback (such as the Abul-Futuh and al-Basil families). Even the heirs of David Adès and Baron Empin (foreign entrepreneurs with previous investment links in the country) are returning to Egypt to investigate the re-establishment of their broken business links.

The analysis in this chapter has also indicated that *infitah* is detrimental to social equity and that it may generate destabilizing social forces. It is at least partly in response to this that a whole arsenal of laws restricting personal freedom has been prepared, ready for deployment.[50] Among other things, it is interesting and revealing to observe that procedures for economic liberalization are in fact going hand in hand with political processes of an entirely opposite nature. The results of these contradictory types of development will undoubtedly be far-reaching in the fabric of Egyptian society.

NOTES

1. Cf. Gouda Abdel-Khalek, "Ahamm dalalat al-infitah..." [The Most Important Implications of Infitah with Regard to the Structural Transformations in the Egyptian Economy, 1971-1977] in Société Egyptienne d'Economie Politique, de Statistique et de Législation, *Al-Iqtisad al-Misri fi rub* qarn... [The Egyptian Economy in a Quarter of a Century: Papers and Discussions of the Third Conference of Egyptian Economists], edited by Isma'il Sabri 'Abdallah et al., (Cairo: Hai'at al-Kitab, 1978), pp. 363-403. Some of the material in the present essay also appears in the author's contribution to Herbert M. Thompson, ed., *Studies in Egyptian Political Economy*, The Cairo Papers in Social Science, Vol. Two, Monograph Three, March 1979.

2. For a detailed and official account of the meaning of *infitah* see Arab Republic of Egypt, Ministry of Planning, *Draft of the Five Year Plan 1978-1982* [in Arabic], Vol. 3, Chap. 1, August 1977.

3. In fact there is evidence that the Egyptian economy has grown more dependent on the outside world over the period 1960-1974. See Gouda Abdel-Khalek, "Namat al-tanmiya wa

al-iʿtimad al-mutazayyid ʿala al-kharij" [Development Pattern and Increasing Dependence on the Outside World; A Study of the Egyptian Experience 1960–1974] in *Al-tanmiya wa al-ʿilaqat al-iqtisadiyya al-Dawliyya...* [Development and International Economic Relations: Papers and Proceedings of the First Conference of Egyptian Economists], (Cairo, 1977).

4. See Gouda Abdel-Khalek, "Looking Outside or Turning Northwest? On the Meaning and External Dimensions of Egypt's Infitah, 1971–1980", forthcoming in a special issue of *Journal of Social Problems* (published by the Society for the Study of Social Problems).

5. Arab Republic of Egypt, *Waraqat ʾUktubar* [The October Paper, presented by Anwar al-Sadat], (Cairo: Maslahat al-Istiʿlamat, April 1974), p. 62.

6. Ibid.

7. Dudley Seers, "What are We Trying to Measure?" in Nancy Baster, ed., *Measuring Development; the Role and Adequacy of Development Indicators* (London: Frank Cass, 1972).

8. For 1975, the adult illiteracy rate is estimated at 56 percent. This compares with only 31 percent average for the group of middle income countries to which Egypt belongs. See The World Bank, *World Development Report, 1979: Annex; World Development Indicators*, p. 170.

9. By the end of 1958, the Organization held control capital in 52 companies covering a wide range of activities such as chemicals, engineering and metallurgy, petroleum, transport and communications, banking and insurance, etc. See Muhammad Duwaidar, *Fi iqtisadiyyat al-takhtit al-ishtiraki...* [On the Economics of Socialist Planning: A Study of the Main Problems of Planning Economic Development in Egypt], (Alexandria: 1967), p. 168 and references cited therein.

10. Ismaʿil Sabri ʿAbdallah, *Tanzim al-qitaʿ al-ʿam...* [Organization of the Public Sector: the Theoretical Principles and Important Applied Problems], (Cairo: Dar El-Maʿrif, 1969), p. 265.

11. See the authoritative study by Ismaʿil Sabri ʿAbdallah referred to above.

12. Duwaidar, op.cit., pp. 232–233.

13. Ibid., p. 233.

14. There is no ready explanation for the decline after 1974 in the share of wages, except perhaps that employment growth had been slowing down after 1965.

15. Fuʾad Mursi, *Hadha al-infitah al-iqtisadi* [This Economic 'Opening'!] (Cairo: Dar al-Thaqafa al-Jadida, 1976), p. 134.

16. Mustafa Kamil Murad, a chairman of a public sector company, remarked in discussing Law No. 43 for 1974, "...the economic system must be changed to take a new form...the government must move to achieve a comprehensive change in the laws governing the economic structure (sic)", in People's Assembly, *Mahdar al-ijtimaʿ* ... [Deliberations on the Law for Investment of Arab and Foreign Capital and for Free Zones], (Cairo, 21 and 22 May 1974), pp. 84–85. This is a very important document for an understanding of the opponents and the proponents of *infitah*. See also citations from it in the chapter by Nazih Ayubi in this volume.

17. Fuʾad Mursi, op.cit., pp. 136–137.

18. Ibid., pp. 250–255.

19. United Arab Republic, Southern Region, *Itar al-khitta al-ʿamma li al-tanmiya...* [Framework of General Plan for Economic and Social Development for the Five Years July 1960 to June 1965], (Cairo: 1960), p. 27.

20. An increasing number of multinationals is setting up joint ventures, often with public sector companies in the same business. Examples include Coca Cola Co., Pepsi Cola Co., Canada Dry, Brown Transworld, Dinacom International, Wilkinson Match AG,

American International Group of New York, Chemitex Fibers, Continental Marine and Power, Taber Metals, Thomas Cook, Dynaspectron Corp., HRI Engineering, Reynolds International, Union Carbide Middle East Ltd., Intergulf Holdings and Investments, IDL, Colgate Palmolive, Craven Investments, Xerox Holdings (Bermuda), Siemens AG, Total International Inc., Brown Hotel Corp., Mineral and Metal Investments Ltd., S. S. Johnson, Arthur D. Little International, Chloride Group Ltd., Economic Company for International Development: California and Overseas of America. In addition there is a number of banks, including Chase Manhattan, Bank of America, Barclays, etc. These names were extracted from *Al-Jarida al-Rasmiyya* [The Official Gazette] and *Al-Waqaʿ al-Misriyya* [The Egyptian Chronicle]; several issues over the period 1975–1980.

A politically favored formula is joint ventures between multinationals and public sector companies (see *Al-Ahram,* 17 June 1980). Foreign multinationals often insist on majority equity and hence management. As the report of the Ministry of the Economy mentions, public sector companies are forced to accept in order to escape from controls under which they may be operating. See Ministry of Economy, Foreign Trade and Economic Cooperation (Economic Studies Unit), *Taqrir ʿan siyasat al-istithmar al-jadida...* [Report on New Investment Policies (Law No. 43 for 1974)], (Cairo, December 1979), pp. 40–41.

21. This applies more to the period 1960/61–1964/65 than to the period 1965/66–1969/70. In the second period the economy was strained by the 1967 War and the War of Attrition in 1969.

22. For a survey of the development of the exchange rates and regulations in Egypt since the Second World War see National Bank of Egypt, *Economic Bulletin,* Vol. 30, no. 1 (1977), pp. 11–20.

23. The latter three banks are joint banks.

24. See Central Bank of Egypt, *Annual Report 1976,* Part II (June 1977), pp. 43–47; and Ministry of Economy, *Taqrir ʿan siyasat...,* op.cit., p. 60.

25. In 1978, remittances amounted to some LE1248.8 million, or 40 percent of current receipts in the balance of payments.

26. The famous Ministerial Decree No. 199 for 1977, issued by the Minister of Trade and Supply, set an upper limit of 30 percent on the profit margin for imported items. The merchant lobby has succeeded so far in blocking the Decree.

27. The parallel market involves the buying and selling of foreign exchange against the Pound at a premium; this parallel market institution was created in 1973. In May 1980 a degree of regulation was introduced by requiring own importers to deposit a fraction of the value of the shipment (the fraction varies according to the type of goods, e.g. 20 percent for foodstuffs, 40 percent for intermediate goods and 100 percent for consumer goods). See *Al-Ahram* (20 June 1980).

28. See *Al-Ahram* (15 January 1978). Premier Mamduh Salim announced that the rationale was to make every citizen an owner of the means of production. In fact the measure means just the opposite since some will own and control, while others will neither own nor control.

29. According to Foreign Investment Authority data, the Authority withheld approvals for 36 projects during 1979 with a total capital of LE47.6 million (because of lack of serious intent on the part of the investors); this represented 9.1 percent of capital of all the projects approved during that year.

30. The amount was LE1377 million. See Central Bank of Egypt, *Annual Report 1978,* Part I, Table 20.

31. Total investment in the 1980–1984 Plan is estimated at LE20 billion. See Ministry of Planning, *Egypt's Development Strategy, Economic Management and Growth Objectives*

1980–84. Report submitted to the Consultative Group Meeting, Paris, 28 October 1979, p. 33.

32. I have argued elsewhere that fundamentally it is a process of re-absorbing Egypt into the world capitalist system, following the unsuccessful attempt in the 1950s and 1960s to break away from it and to follow a course of independent development. See Gouda Abdel-Khalek, "Looking Outside or Turning Northwest?", op.cit.

33. Ministry of Economy, *Taqrir ʿan siyasat...*, op.cit., p. 67. Emphasis added.

34. See *Financial Times* (31 July 1978).

35. Ministry of Economy, *op.cit.*, p. 61.

36. See Ministry of Planning, *Egypt's Development Strategy...*, op.cit., p. 33.

37. Central Bank of Egypt, *Annual Report 1978*, p. 4.

38. Ibid., p. 6.

39. The report of the Ministry of Economy referred to above estimates the ratio of the inland non-financial projects geared to the production of luxury goods to the total number of inland non-financial projects. It defines luxury goods to include (a) so-called pleasure items; (b) goods consumed by the top 10 percent of the population, and (c) as excluding goods and services geared for exports such as tourism, and intermediate goods. This is an unduly narrow definition, especially since all goods will be competing for scarce resources that could be used to satisfy basic needs. For example, devoting resources (labor and capital) to building a hotel diverts these scarce resources from the construction of badly needed housing units. It should therefore not be surprising that, according to this definition, only 9 percent of inland non-financial projects which have started production, and 16 percent of total investment in these areas, are geared to the production of luxury goods. Out of a total of 375 projects examined, only 32 projects produce luxury items. The report excludes projects in agriculture, transport, contracting, consultancy, tourism, health, construction material, pharmaceuticals, and spinning and weaving as being non-producers of luxury items. Ibid., pp. 41–42.

Such a conclusion is hard to endorse for a number of reasons. First, it leaves out financial projects which alone account for 46 percent of inland investment. These are involved in the outright draining away of the economic surplus. Secondly, while only some projects in agriculture, industry, transport, pharmaceuticals, spinning and weaving may produce necessary goods, almost all projects in contracting, consultancy, tourism, health and construction material produce luxury goods. Referring to the Data in Table IV, and assuming that 50 percent of the inland projects in industry and agriculture produce necessary goods, one may estimate that 80 percent of inland investment projects produce luxury goods.

40. Figures for investment per employment opportunity for *infitah* are calculated from the General Authority for Investment and Free Zones (GAIFZ), *Statistical Statement of Projects Approved Under Investment Law Until 31/12/79*. Figures for investment per job opportunity for the whole economy are taken from the Central Bank of Egypt, *Annual Report 1978*, op.cit., Tables 20 and 21. See also Ministry of Economy, *Taqrir ʿan siyasat...*, op.cit., p. 22.

41. Calculated from current figures in Central Bank of Egypt, *Annual Report 1978*, Tables 18 and 22.

42. For a detailed analysis of this point see Gouda Abdel-Khalek, "Al-tanmiya wa al-iʿtimad ʿala al-nafs wa al-ʿadala..." [Development, Self-Reliance and Justice] in *Proceedings of the Fourth Conference of Egyptian Economists*, Cairo, May 1979.

43. See *Al-Jarida al-Rasmiyya* and *Al-Waqaʿiʾ*; various issues.

44. See Roger Owen, "Egypt and Europe: From French Expedition to British Occupation" in R. Owen and B. Sutcliffe, eds., *Studies in the Theory of Imperialism* (London: Longmans, 1972). It is significant to note the return of persons like Empin and Adès, whose

families possessed large interests in Egypt until the late fifties. See also the chapter by Galal Amin in the present volume.

45. Cf. Mark C. Cooper, "Liberalization in Egypt 1967-77", unpublished PhD dissertation, Yale University, 1978; referred to in Galal Amin, *Al-Mashriq al-ʿArabi wa al-gharb* [The Arab Mashriq and the West], (Beirut: Centre for Arab Unity Studies, 1979), p. 166. See also Fouad Ajami, "Egypt's Retreat from Economic Nationalism: The 'Open Door' Economy and its Roots and Welfare Consequences" in Robert Tignor and Gouda Abdel-Khalek, eds., *The Political Economy of Income Distribution in Egypt* (New York: Holmes and Meier, forthcoming). Also Nazih Ayubi, "Implementation Capability and Political Feasibility of the 'Open Door' Economic Policy in Egypt" in the present volume.

46. See the analysis of the historical process in Galal Amin, op.cit., especially Chaps. 1 and 4, as well as his chapter in the present volume.

47. The Consultative Group is the name given to the association of lenders to a country, whether they be countries, regional or international organizations. In Egypt's case, the basic members of the group are the United States, Britain, France, West Germany, Italy, Japan, Iran (until 1978), Kuwait (until 1977), Saudi Arabia (until 1977), the Gulf Authority for the Development of Egypt (until 1977), the IMF and the World Bank. Policies and priorities of the borrower are discussed regularly through the annual meetings of the Consultative Group, before any pledges for assistance are made by the lenders.

48. During the period 1974 to 1977, Gross Domestic Product (GDP) in oil and oil products rose by 61 percent per annum, and in transport and communications and storage, by 41 percent per annum. See Central Bank of Egypt, *Annual Report 1978,* Table 18. Over the period 1975 to 1978, remittances rose by 84 percent per annum. See ibid., Table 4 and Central Bank of Egypt, *Annual Report 1977,* Table 23.

49. One-time influential figures such as Abdel-Aziz Hegazi, Aziz Sidki (both former Prime Ministers), Taher Amin (former Minister for Economic Cooperation) and various public sector leaders. See more details in the chapter by Nazih Ayubi in this volume.

50. The most important of these are Law No. 134 for 1971 (for safeguarding the safety of the people); Law No. 32 for 1977 (concerning the security of both the citizen and homeland); Law No. 40 for 1977 (regarding the regulation of political parties); Law No. 33 for 1978 (for protecting the internal front and social peace); the "Law of Shame" of 1980; and the Press Law introduced in 1980.

IX

External Factors in the Reorientation of Egypt's Economic Policy

Galal Ahmad Amin

The purpose of anyone who writes the history of any large epoch must necessarily be to impose a pattern on events, or at least to discover a pattern. A sound general theory, or even an instinctive grasp of probability might be more useful than a mountain of learning... A history constructed imaginatively would never be right about any single event, but it might come nearer to essential truth than a mere compilation of names and dates in which no one statement was demonstrably untrue.[1]

I. INTRODUCTION

In studying the economic, political or cultural development of a country which is truly independent it may be perfectly legitimate to have as one's starting point the nature of the country's natural or human resources, its technological development, the changing balance of power among its own social classes, or even, sometimes, the personal characteristics of its political leadership. The same approach might, however, be seriously misleading when applied to a country which is desperately dominated by another, and in such a case, it may be much more fruitful to have as one's starting point whatever developments that might have occurred within the dominant country itself.

In a country which is economically or politically dominated by another, it may indeed be that its natural or human resources strongly influence the rate and pattern of economic growth. Yet the degree of exploitation of such resources, and sometimes even their sheer discovery, may depend largely on the nature of the economic and political interests of the dominating country. Similarly a change in the balance of power of various social classes in the dominated country may have an important influence on its economic and social system, yet one has seen a number of such countries in which a "closed" economy has been replaced by an "open" economic system without any significant change occurring in the internal balance of the power of the social forces. Economic growth may come to a halt as a result of a coup d'état in which internal social change may have no hand, or as a result of a military defeat from which one or another social group may indeed benefit but which cannot at all be attributed to the actions of any such groups. A group of dominated countries may enter into a series of political or military conflicts which might bring some benefit to the political or social elites in each of them, and which might be accentuated by the personal ambitions or rivalries of their rulers. Yet whatever the number of such benefits or rivalries, it will be insufficient to explain why such countries have failed to achieve a greater degree of cooperation or integration when internal interests, no less powerful and mature, would have benefitted from such cooperation. And finally, the whole cultural climate of a dominated country may quite suddenly change from one of vitality and innovation to one of slavish imitation and utter vulgarity, without any noticeable change in the country's ability to innovate or in the ability of its people to appreciate a higher level of culture.

In this chapter, I have tried to trace the role of external factors and foreign pressures in the development of economic policy in Egypt, drawing an analogy between the rise and fall of Muhammad ʿAli's regime in the first decade of the 19th century and that of Gamal ʿAbd al-Nasir in the middle of the 20th century. Emphasis will be laid on some striking similarities between the two experiences, where a "closed door" economic policy was replaced by a policy of economic liberalization — not as a result of internal developments but mainly because of foreign pressure. The consequences of the collapse of the two experiments will also be seen to have much in common.

What motivated me to make this attempt was the belief that it is impossible to understand what Egypt, and indeed the whole of the Arab world, has passed through over the past two decades without taking into account the changes that occurred in the economies, and in the political relationships, of the big powers, as well as the changes that took place in the Israeli economy. It is my belief that to persist in explaining the important events that occurred in the Arab world — such as the defeat of 1967, the change in the orientation of inter-Arab economic and political relations, or the conclusion of the peace treaty between Egypt and Israel...etc. — as if they were little more than a reflection of political or economic developments occurring within the Arab world or an expression of the independent will of one or another Arab government, would simply result in further mystification and confusion.

II. THE RISE AND FALL OF MUHAMMAD ᶜALI

(1)

Few figures in modern Arab history have attracted as much attention from political and economic historians as that of Muhammad ᶜAli of Egypt. His attempt during the first four decades of the 19th century to undertake an economic revolution based on the establishment of modern industries and the reform of irrigation, taxation and educational systems is very well known, and it is not my intention here to give an account of his achievements. Rather, the question which is raised here is why such a promising attempt could take place during that period but suddenly come to an end towards the end of the 1830s.

Before embarking on this, however, it is worth noting that Muhammad ᶜAli's experience in economic and political reform in Egypt, although the best known, was by no means the only one in the Arab world at that time. Indeed it is interesting to note that during the first four decades of the 19th century there was a serious attempt, in almost every country of the Arab Middle East, at economic or cultural revival; and for almost every one of them there was quite a good chance for success. The rise and fall of most of these movements were, however, closely tied with the rise and fall of Muhammad ᶜAli in Egypt, a situation paralleled in the case of Gamal ᶜAbd al-Nasir as we shall see later in this essay.

For one thing, the reforms of Muhammad ᶜAli were extended to those Arab countries that came under his rule: in Syria between 1831 and 1840 (when his troops were forced to withdraw), and in the Sudan between 1831 and 1849 (the year of his death).

> ...During the ten years of Egyptian rule in Syria, the outdated Pashalik administrative system was abolished and all Syria was put under a civil governor residing in Damascus, a registry system for the preservation of governmental records was established, the administration of justice was improved and the privileges of the rich were abolished making all equal before the law. In the taxation system, Ibrahim [Muhammad ᶜAli's son] abolished the Iltizam and broke the power and monopoly of the local notables. A new personal tax was levied. Military service was made compulsory and no 'badal' [exemption money] from those unwilling to serve was accepted.[2]

In the Sudan, the governors who ruled in Muhammad ᶜAli's name had irrigation canals dug, experimented with new crops and industries, introduced the cultivation of sugar cane and different kinds of fruit, set up water mills to supply cattle with drinking water, eradicated agricultural pests, searched for metal ores and protected trade routes. Muhammad

ʿAli sent them farmers, goldsmiths, masons, carpenters and tanners. Those governors devoted much energy to the development of Khartoum, to the repair of mosques and to the building of new ones, provided a dockyard set up on the Nile, encouraged the townspeople to build permanent houses in place of their leather-made tents, and supplied them with the necessary building materials.[3]

In Lebanon, the reign of Amir Bashir II which lasted for over fifty years (from 1788 until it ended in 1840 with the end of Muhammad ʿAli's rule in Syria) is described by Philip Hitti as

> ... the highest point ever attained by Lebanon in more than three centuries of its feudal career... It was marked by a steady move toward expanding Lebanon, developing it and making it autonomous in defiance or with the consent of the Porte... Lebanese folklore is rich in anecdotes memorializing the emir's administration of justice and measures of security... Narrow roads were widened and new ones built, old bridges were repaired and modern ones built... Conscious of the medical needs of his country he sent five students to the oldest medical school in the area, that of Cairo, founded by his ally Mohammed Ali...[4]

In Baghdad, the same period witnessed fifteen years of the rule of Dawud Pasha (from 1817 to 1832); he introduced reforms in the educational system, opened new schools, set up the first printing press in Iraq, and during his reign "books and writings of all sorts multiplied, while men of learning tried to win his favour by writing books for him."[5] He built up a strong army and reformed its system, and established textile factories to meet the needs of his country. He was reported to have said that "no European rights exist in Baghdad"[6] and to have imposed a new system of protection against British goods as well as a strict criterion for the evaluation of goods of the East India Company that passed through his country. This last measure earned him the Company's anger and this was enough to cause his dismissal by the Porte. A year later, in 1833, the Company's agent in Baghdad wrote

> ...In their misery, the people [here] look to Ibrahim... Merchants at Baghdad...deplored the decision of Palmerston to prevent the addition of the province to what they had already begun to call the Egyptian Caliphate.[7]

In Cyrenaica and the Arabian Peninsula, the same period witnessed the growth of two forceful movements of religious revival, the Sanusiyya and the Wahhabiyya, both of which were movements calling for a return to the fundamental principles of early Islam, for Muslims to be bound solely by the Quʾran and the Sunna, and for the purification of Islam from innovations (*bidaʿ*) that had attached themselves to it during centuries of decline. The two movements met with brilliant success on both the religious and the political levels. With the alliance between the intellectual influence of Muhammad Ibn ʿAbd al-Wahhab and the political power of the Ibn Saʿud dynasty in Nejd, the Wahhabi movement extended its power over most of the Arabian Peninsula, reaching the frontiers of Syria and the outskirts of Baghdad, while the Sanusi "zawiyas" were spreading in Cyrenaica, Egypt, Sudan and the Arabian Peninsula.[8]

It is customary to study each of the movements discussed above as part of the history of this or that particular Arab country, or else to classify the Sanusi and Wahhabi movements as a chapter in the history of Islamic revival and religious reform, thus distinguishing these religious movements from the purely secular movements such as those of Muhammad ʿAli in Egypt, of Amir Bashir in Lebanon, and of Dawud Pasha in Iraq. It is possible of course to find reasonable explanations for the emergence of each of these movements in the internal conditions of each Arab country. But the fact that they all occurred more or less at the same time and all managed, during the early decades of the century, to achieve a considerable measure of success, then subsided afterwards, would strongly suggest the importance of the role of external factors both in their rise and in their subsequent fall.

Indeed it is not difficult to detect the importance of such factors. For on the one hand, the decline of the Ottoman State tempted the governors of Egypt, Baghdad and Lebanon to try and reach for independence, while the weakness of the Porte's hold on the Arabian Peninsula and the Libyan desert contributed to the success of the Wahhabi and Sanusi movements. On the other hand, for virtually the whole period of the first forty years of the century, European economic and political interests in the region did not constitute a sufficient motive for exerting an active military or political pressure. Until 1815 the European powers were preoccupied with the Napoleonic wars, and for two more decades neither Britain nor France felt any pressing need to acquire new markets or new sources of raw materials in the Arab world. As is well known, the predominant interest of Britain during the whole of the 19th century was to safeguard its trade route to India, but until the fourth decade of the century, the sea voyage round the Cape of Good Hope remained the preferred route. The application of steam power to navigation had in fact not yet been made use of on the route between Europe and India, and without steam power, neither the passage to India up the Euphrates, nor the Red Sea route, could rival the voyage round the Cape, with the first being exceedingly slow and the second being closed to navigation for several months of the year.[9]

In explaining the failure of Muhammad ᶜAli's experiment, it has been customary to refer to the high cost of his industries, to the fact that his new textile factories were producing at a cost far above the price of the British cloth that Egypt could import, and that by 1840 his losses had reached such high levels that he would have been forced sooner or later to abandon his attempt at industrializing Egypt. The collapse of his regime in Syria is often attributed to the high burden of his taxes as well as to the strict application of his compulsory military service; his rule of the Sudan is also said to have been unpopular for similar reasons, while his Arab conquests are usually explained by his sheer personal ambition and greed. It is indeed striking how the criticisms directed by Western writers against Muhammad ᶜAli's economic and Arab policies are similar to those directed against Nasir. But high production costs — as compared with the price of imports — have rarely dissuaded countries that are now fully developed from embarking on their own industrial revolutions under heavy protecton, nor has the excessive personal ambition of a great ruler necessarily been detrimental to his country's progress. To explain the failure of Arab reform movements of the last century one has therefore to look for causes that lie outside such internal weaknesses an shortcomings.

(2)

In 1830, the first steamship to cross the Red Sea made its voyage to India. But the use of steam power in navigation along this route required the establishment of coaling stations on the Red Sea, and as Aden was found to be the best natural port in the area it was occupied by Britain in 1839. The new route also required protection against the possible threats of rival European powers, which made it highly desirable for the route to be under Britain's direct control or subject to a power unable to threaten British interests. Since the Ottoman Empire was such a power, the preservation of its integrity continued to be the basis of British policy towards the Arab East for the remainder of the 19th century.

Meanwhile the increasing use of steam power in British industry led to a rapid rise in output and a consequent search for new opportunities for export, while the introduction of steam power in transportation and the invention of the telegraph led to a significant reduction in transport costs. Britain's adoption of the policy of free trade in 1846 was both a response to these developments and a factor in the pressure for enlargement of the export markets.[10] Any system of protection for infant industries such as those set up by Muhammad ᶜAli in Egypt, Syria and Sudan, was regarded as an obstacle in the way of the expansion of British textile exports that had to be eliminated. Restrictions on the movement of European traders between one part of the Ottoman Empire and another were regarded as unnecessary obstacles in the way of free trade, as was any system that reduced the freedom of these traders to establish direct contact with the actual producers or consumers. Muhammad ʿAli's state monopoly was such a system and it too had to be abolished.

By the end of the Napoleonic wars, Britain had become a capital-exporting country.[11] During the 1820s and 1830s, its surplus capital went mainly towards the reconstruction of Europe and towards investment in the plantations and mining activities of the United States and South America, while during the 1840s it was directed towards building railways inside Britain itself. By mid-century, however, British industry's — and particularly the textile industry's — need for new sources of raw materials and for new markets, required an increase in investment to develop the transportation facilities of countries providing such markets and raw materials. Ports had to be built or expanded, roads extended and improved, and railways introduced. British capital had to move outside Europe, into such new areas of investment as the development of wool production in Australia and Argentina, tea plantations in Ceylon, gold mines in South Africa, as well as into the development of transport facilities necessary for such investments.[12] During the second half of the century, Britain led the movement of foreign investment, with its foreign investments increasing at a faster rate than investments inside the country, and with its investments in Europe actually declining in favor of its investments overseas.[13]

It is in the light of these developments occurring outside the Arab world that one should seek an explanation for the events which occurred in the Arab East during the fourth decade of the century. As Lord Palmerston remarked in 1833,

> It would indeed have been an act of great folly to have assisted, without any moral or political obligation, in placing both [overland routes to India, by the Euphrates and by Suez] under Mehemet Ali's command at the very moment that they were coming into high political importance.[14]

In another letter written by Palmerston to his brother in Naples, he referred to Muhammad ʿAli by saying

> ... his real design is to establish an Arabian Kingdom, including all the countries of which Arabic is the language. There might be no harm in such a thing in itself, but as it would necessarily imply the dismemberment of Turkey, we could not agree to it. Besides, Turkey is as good an occupier of the road to India as an active Arabian sovereign would be.[15]

In yet another letter, Palmerston wrote, "...there is no question of fairness to Mehemet [Ali]... a robber is always liable to be made to disgorge."[16]

In Syria, a revolt against the rule of Ibrahim Pasha was instigated by Britain which supplied arms, while a British agent (Richard Wood) was sent, under the cover of learning Arabic, to Lebanon to contact those dissatisfied with the rule of Amir Bashir. In 1840 a revolt forced Amir Bashir to surrender and he was transported to Malta on a British ship. British, Austrian and Ottoman guns bombarded Beirut and Acre, forcing Ibrahim Pasha to withdraw, while their battleships lining the coast off Alexandria forced Muhammad ʿAli to accept the dictates of the great powers, including the implementation of the commercial treaty of 1838 between Britain and the Porte and the abandonment of the monopoly system in Egypt and Syria in 1840 and in the Sudan in 1842.

Had Britain not been satisfied that France would not come to his aid it would probably never have resorted to military action against Muhammad ʿAli. It was something of a gamble, and the British cabinet was split between those supporting military intervention and those opposing it for fear of war with France. To Palmerston, however, it was a risk worth taking. No less than 60,000 French soldiers were involved in the completion of the invasion of Algeria, while the French fleet in the Mediterranean was too weak to stand against the British fleet which was supported by Russia, Austria and Prussia. The King of France and his ministers, as well as the French press, threatened war, but war was not to come. As Louis-Philippe remarked, it was one thing to talk about going to war, but quite another thing actually to do it.[17]

Palmerston claimed that the abolition of the monopoly system would, in the long run, have the effect of increasing the revenues of Egypt and the Ottoman Empire though it might for the moment paralyze Muhammad ʿAli's scheme of finance. Indeed, not only Muhammad ʿAli's financial scheme but all his industrialization efforts were paralyzed, with damaging results for Egypt's development, not only in the short run, but for almost a whole century. A few years after the implementation of the 1838 treaty, "...all that remained of the vast industrial structure, which had cost millions to create, was a quantity of rusting machinery in old, deserted buildings scattered through the country."[18]

Egypt's imports of British textiles increased so rapidly that by 1850 they were three times their level in 1835, while Egyptian exports of raw cotton to Britain increased eightfold between 1835 to 1839, and 1850 to 1852.[19] In Baghdad, Damascus and Aleppo, the number of looms declined sharply as the Syrian and Iraqi weavers sold their looms; they became instead importers of European textiles,[20] while silk fabrics were exported from Lebanon to turn the wheels of textile mills in Lyon. During his visit to Damascus in 1850, Alfred Von Kremer, the Orientalist, wrote

> ...the sole cause of the decline of the once important Damascus silk weaving industry is to be found in the import of British and Swiss-made goods. These goods are a quarter cheaper than the Damascus silks, though far less durable. They are bought by the poorer classes, who as a result of their increasing improverishment, gave up the better and more expensive qualities to purchase the cheaper grade goods.[21]

Foreign investment in Arab countries, from mid-century up to the First World War, took two main forms. One was the direct investment in transportation projects serving the export-import trade, such as the extension of railways, the expansion of ports and the digging of the Suez Canal, as well as direct investment in certain public utility projects such as gas, electricity and the telegraph. The feeble Porte and the local governors were prevailed upon to hand out concessions and to grant monopoly rights for the construction of such projects on highly exploitative terms. It has been said, for example, that when Saʿid Pasha of Egypt was presented by De Lesseps with the concession for establishing the Suez Canal Company

> ... he signed without even reading it and it had certainly not been examined by his judicial and financial advisors. But De Lesseps was his friend and he [Saʿid] was promised 15 percent of the profit.[22]

The other form was the extension of loans to local governors at exorbitant rates of interest, particularly to the successors of Muhammad ʿAli in Egypt and to the Porte. The greater part of these loans was spent on the personal pleasures of the governor and his entourage, or on prestige projects that brought little or no return.

The degree of Western pressure on different parts of the Arab world was proportionate to their relative economic or strategic importance. Thus while Egypt, Syria and Iraq were linked to the Western economy from the mid-19th century, the relatively low importance of the Libyan desert allowed a greater degree of freedom for the growth of the Sanusi movement which was left alone until the Italian occupation of 1911. Similarly, as Britain's interest in exploiting the agricultural resources of Sudan was not aroused until late in the 19th century, an independence movement with a high degree of vitality and power emerged during the second half of the 19th century. With much in common with the Sanusi and Wahhabi movements, the Mahdiyya ruled the Sudan for thirteen years (from 1885 to 1898), uniting most of the country under one state, and enjoying tremendous popularity, not only in Sudan but also in

Egypt, where many Egyptians pinned on it their hopes for deliverance from the British occupation. Again, while the strategic importance of the coastal regions of the Arabian Gulf led Britain to subject them, during the last two decades of the century, one after the other to British protection, the virtual absence of any economic or strategic attraction in the hinterland of Arabia allowed this region to be left alone until its oil was discovered between the two World Wars.

A good indicator of the effects on the Arab world of a century of Arab-Western relations is to see what had happened to the three great Arab reform movements — the Mahdist, the Sanusi and the Wahhabi — by the middle of the 20th century. Britain adopted the youngest son of the Mahdi, using his influence to spread popular feeling against the Ottoman Empire during the First World War. When the War ended with British victory ʿAbd al-Rahman al-Mahdi headed a Sudanese delegation to London to congratulate King George V on his victory and presented the king with his father's sword as a symbol of his loyalty to Britain; in 1926 he was knighted for his efforts. By the mid-fifties, the Saʿudi royal family, whose founders had embraced the teachings of Muhammad Ibn ʿAbd al-Wahhab and supported his cause, was living on money paid to it by ARAMCO, while King Idris al-Sanusi, the grandson of the Grand Sanusi, was living on American and British aid extended in return for the lease of military bases.

III.   THE RISE AND FALL OF GAMAL ʿABD AL-NASIR

(1)

During the ten years from 1955 to 1965 the Arab world witnessed a new and vigorous movement towards economic and political independence which, looked at in retrospect, is strongly reminiscent of the first four decades of the 19th century. But whatever may have been the gains achieved during this period and in spite of all the hopes that these gains may have revived, again one should not ignore the role played by changing economic and strategic conditions in the world at large, conditions that made the emergence of such a movement possible. Indeed, what I would like to argue is that however important the internal political and social conditions may have been within any of the Arab countries in contributing to the emergence of movements such as Nasirism, Arab Nationalism or Arab Socialism, the most important "permissive" conditions for the successes of these movements has to be sought *outside* the Arab world. More specifically, I will argue that during those ten years, several factors contributed to the decline of foreign pressure on the Arab world, and thus allowed several Arab countries to acquire a much greater degree of independence in economic and foreign policies than could have been conceived either before or after that period.

For one thing, it was during those ten years that the Western defence system saw the replacement of the intermediate-range ballistic missile as the main deterrent against the Eastern bloc by the inter-continental ballistic missile and by Polaris-carrying submarines on the high seas; this meant that it was no longer crucial for the Western defence system to draw the Middle East countries into military pacts.[23] Thus, whatever truth there is in the claim that Egypt's attack on the Baghdad Pact was merely the result of American influence on the new regime in Egypt — the Pact being seen by the United States as "too British" — it seems certain that the linking of Iraq, Turkey and Iran to the Atlantic Pact through CENTO was by that time losing much of its importance, as was the linking of other Arab countries to it. Then there was the Eisenhower Doctrine; proclaimed just after the Suez War, it saw the decline in British and French influence in the area as causing a "power vacuum" that needed the United States to fill it. It was attacked by Nasir just as fiercely as was the Baghdad Pact, and was, in fact, no more than a worn-out extension of an outdated policy which was soon left to die in peace. In fact both the Eisenhower Doctrine and the landing of Amercian troops in Lebanon in the summer of 1958 were the last measures of that kind taken by the United States against the Arab nationalist movement until the mid-sixties, and no attempt was made to use Israel to launch an attack on Arab countries until 1967.

Coupled with this decline in the strategic importance of the Arab world from the Western point of view was a decline in its relative economic importance. Although Western Europe continued to rely on Middle Eastern oil, with the receding of the Soviet threat its continued flow seemed more assured than had been the case in the immediate post-war years. At the same time, the oil market was being transformed from a seller's to a buyer's market with the discovery of new sources of production and the difficulty of selling the oil outside Western Europe.

A number of new factors also caused a decline in the relative economic importance of the Third World as a whole in the continued growth of the Western economy. For one thing, the resurgence of the European economy and the establishment of the European Economic Community (EEC), in which the United States itself played a very important role, offered highly attractive opportunities for American exports of goods and capital. If the American economy was to suffer in later years from competition from the EEC, this danger seemed remote at the time, given the obvious supremacy of the American economy and the strength of the dollar. Likewise, the relatively low wage levels and high unemployment rates in the EEC countries as compared with levels in the United States made it considerably more profitable to invest in Western Europe than in America, where the profit rate in the mid-fifties was estimated at about half its level in West Germany.[24]

This increase in the importance of Western Europe for American trade and investment was accompanied by a relative decline in the importance of trade and investment in primary commodities produced by the Third World. This was partly caused by the high growth rates achieved in agricultural production in the industrial countries and their increased levels of protection for their agricultural producers, and partly because of the increasing tendency to replace natural products by synthetic materials. Thus new investment by industrial countries in the Third World tended to decline, and the terms of trade moved against primary products and in favor of manufactures, from 104 in 1955 (1953 = 100) to 88 in 1965. In terms of total world trade, the share of the Third World's exports to the industrial countries declined from 24 percent in 1953 to 18.5 percent in 1965, and the share of the exports of industrial countries to the Third World fell from 22 percent to 19 percent; during the same period the share of the industrial countries' trade among themselves increased from 33 percent to 46 percent.[25]

But what was perhaps the main feature of this period, as far as international relations are concerned, was the changing balance of power between the Western and the Soviet blocs in such a way as to allow the countries of the Third World to play off one superpower against the other without the risk of falling a prey to either of them. And it is with reference to such factors that one should seek an explanation for the fact that during the period from 1955 to 1965, the Third World saw the rise to power of a completely new brand of leaders—of the caliber of Nehru in India, Sukarno in Indonesia, Nasir in Egypt, Ben Bella in Algeria, and Nkrumah in Ghana—who adopted and actually put into effect policies of "positive neutrality" in their foreign relationships, and who advocated "Afro-Asian solidarity".

It was also due largely to these factors that a country such as Egypt was able to obtain a large amount of food aid from the United States as well as substantial aid from the Soviet Union for financing the High Dam and for industrial projects, while preserving a high degree of political independence, a state of affairs which was closed to Egypt before the mid-fifties, and which was again closed to it once that era came to an end. Indeed, without in any way detracting from the importance of the role played by Nasir in Egypt's modern history, one would be at a loss to explain his success in the nationalizing of the Suez Canal Company in 1956 without referring once again to the changing international climate.

With the nationalization of the Suez Canal, Gamal ʿAbd al-Nasir came to be regarded all over the Third World as a symbol of the struggle against foreign domination. With the 1958 revolution in Iraq came the end of Iraq's subordination to the West, and in the same year, a civil war brought an end to Lebanon's pro-Western regime. This was a period that saw the formation of the Organization of Petroleum Exporting Countries (OPEC) in 1959, with the aim of arresting the decline in oil prices, the outbreak of a revolution in Yemen in 1962, and another in Aden against the British occupation. Other Arab governments found themselves forced to introduce reforms which were thought to be necessary to check the advance of nationalist movements and to appease populations whose sympathies were with the newly formed United Arab Republic. In Saudi Arabia, Crown Prince Faisal took power in an attempt to put an end to the follies of the Saudi government and to introduce some long-delayed reforms, while King Hussein of Jordan dismissed the British command of his army and King Idris of Libya asked Britain and the United States to evacuate their military bases in his country.

Again, it was during this period that Egypt, Syria and Iraq raised the banner of socialism, nationalized their industries, promulgated more radical land reforms, adopted comprehensive planning, raised customs tariffs to protect national industries and introduced severe restrictions on the movements of capital and on foreign exchange transactions. Luxury imports were severely cut and dependence on trade with the Western bloc was greatly reduced.

In both Syria and Iraq, neither industrialization nor land reform achieved a high degree of success, mainly because of political instability. The average annual rate of growth of manufacturing did not exceed 4.6 percent in Iraq between 1960 and 1968, and was less than 4.8 percent in Syria from 1956 to 1968, while land redistribution proved extremely slow. Egypt was much more successful in both respects, with the manufacturing growth rate reaching 9.3 percent annually from 1957 to 1967 and the real per capita income growth rate exceeding 3 percent between 1956 and 1965 after it had remained virtually stagnant for almost fifty years.[26] Although land redistribution according to the successive land reform laws did not exceed 12 percent of total cultivated land in Egypt by 1965, these laws undoubtedly brought benefits both to land tenants by making their tenancies more secure, and by fixing a ceiling on agricultural rents, and also to agricultural laborers whose share in total agricultural income showed an increase.

The same period also witnessed what could be regarded as the only serious attempt since the fall of the Ottoman Empire at Arab economic integration. In 1958 Egypt and Syria formed the United Arab Republic, which abolished almost all barriers facing the flow of trade between the two countries. Two five-year development plans for each country were drawn up for the period from 1960 to 1965, and were closely coordinated. As a result, Syria's imports from Egypt multiplied more than five times between 1957–58 and 1960–61 (compared with an increase of 47 percent in her total imports), while exports to Egypt multiplied 2.5 times during the same period (compared with a decline of 33 percent in total Syrian exports).[27] During this period Egypt concluded a large number of trade and payment agreements with most Arab countries, reducing or abolishing customs duties levied on a large number of commodities.[28] Egypt's imports from all Arab countries therefore increased by 25 percent between 1955–56 and 1964–65, raising the share of Egypt's imports from the rest of the Arab world in its total imports from 5.8 percent to 7.9 percent during the same period.[29]

Important agreements aiming at greater economic integration were also concluded among a number of Arab countries, a cause which was fully supported by the United Arab Republic. In 1962 the Council for Arab Economic Unity was established, and in 1964 a decision was taken by Egypt, Syria, Iraq, Jordan and Kuwait to establish the Arab Common Market, with the object of abolishing all trade barriers and customs duties among the member countries. Excluding Kuwait, the four countries confirmed this decision by ratifying the agreement on 1st January 1965, and if the actual implementation of the decision to establish the Arab Common Market was to meet with only a modest degree of success, notwithstanding some increase in the share of inter-Arab trade in total Arab trade,[30] one should not minimize the effect of the political developments in the area after 1965, which contributed to the reversal of the whole trend which we have been describing and to which we shall shortly turn.

But it is interesting to note how this trend towards greater economic and political independence was reflected in the social and cultural climate of the period, again most noticeably in Egypt. A feeling of national pride came gradually to replace that feeling of inferiority towards the foreigner which had accumulated over a century of foreign domination. Egypt's middle class was forced to consume Egyptian products until it came eventually to admit that foreign products were not always superior. Members of this class wore Egyptian instead of British cloth, furnished their houses with Egyptian-made furniture, smoked Egyptian cigarettes and drank home-processed beverages in place of Coca-Cola which disappeared from the market. The involvement of Egyptian women in political and social life increased, while an increasing number of industrial workers dared to hope for much higher levels of consumption and education for their children.

It is by no means surprising that in the field of culture this period was also one of the most fertile in Egypt's modern history. Novelists and short story writers produced what might be considered to be their best works, a new school of poetry appeared, numerous new theaters were opened, Arab classics were republished, and translations and folk arts encouraged, while a new type of singing flourished and enjoyed a great deal of popularity. Egypt's cultural climate at the time was described in 1966 by Dr. Louis Awad:

> ...The strict neutrality observed by the State between the old and the new and vis-à-vis the different schools of art and literature — another evidence of the middle path the Egyptian revolution is determined to take — has given impetus to the vital and left the decaying to its fate. It has released the spontaneous overflow of new modes and sensibilities which, given free play, were able to sweep away the crumbling facades of official culture inherited from the *ancien regime*... This triumph of the new creativity is most demonstrable in the fields of drama, poetry, folklore and the plastic arts...[31]

Commenting on the political developments that occurred in the Arab world during the period from 1958 to 1965, William Quandt, until recently a member of the United States National Security Council, wrote,

> ... These developments were generally accepted in Washington with a degree of calm that would have been unlikely in the previous decade.[32]

We have already alluded to a number of factors that could explain why this was the case. One should perhaps also refer to the service rendered by the Arab nationalist movement to the United States insofar as it helped to speed up the process of liquidating the last bastions of British and French influence in Algeria, Lebanon, Jordan, and Southern Arabia. But whatever may have been the relative importance of each of these external factors, it seems impossible to escape the conclusion that the lack of external pressure during those ten years was of paramount importance in allowing Egypt to take its own decisions, whether in the field of economic policy or in Arab and foreign affairs; and that by the mid-sixties new developments in international relations, in the world economy, and also in Israel, had already made it imperative that this trend in Arab political and economic development should be brought to an end.

(2)

In the early sixties, new developments in the relationship between the two superpowers had a tremendous impact on the political and economic development of the Third World. In 1962 the Cuban missile crisis and the exchange of serious threats of war that followed must have made it clearer than ever to the two superpowers that an end must be put to the possibility of confrontation that could lead to a nuclear war. The two powers came to some kind of understanding, particularly after the assassination of Kennedy late in 1963 and the fall of Krushchev a few months later, to the effect that although each of them could continue to seek greater influence in the countries of the Third World, the other party should refrain from the use of force against such attempts. Each of them could indeed seek new clients, but each should warn its clients not to rely on unlimited support from their patron in their confrontation with clients of the other superpower.

Détente was also motivated by the increase in tension between the Soviet Union and China and by the fact that both the Soviet Union and the United States found détente conducive to the solution of their growing economic problems. With the growing strength of the economy of Western Europe, the EEC was now becoming a much more serious competitor to the American economy, and with the increasing difficulty of marketing American goods in Europe and the rising wage levels in the West, the Third World came to acquire greater importance for American and European exports and investment. Both the United States and Western Europe saw in the markets of Eastern Europe, and particularly of the Soviet Union, the same opportunity as that seen in the Third World for increasing exports and solving the balance of payments problem, with the added advantages of the Soviet Union's vast market, its political stability and the lack of industrial strikes. The Soviet Union, for its part, had started to recognize, under the pressure of the slow growth of its agricultural production and of the economy as a whole, the benefits that could be reaped from importing certain types of Western capital goods and technology, whereby it could modernize some of its industries, raise agricultural productivity, and exploit its rich oil and natural gas resources in Siberia.

Thus, during the United States-Soviet Summit meeting held in Moscow in May 1972, Brezhnev remarked to Nixon, referring to a map showing the rich resources of Siberia, "this is the wealth we are prepared to share with you", while an article in *Pravda* noted that

> ... this advantageous cooperation between Soviet organizations and American firms in developing... [our] natural resources... could, in our opinion, be one of the most promising paths... and could create a lasting and long term basis for expanding Soviet-American trade and economic ties.[33]

In July 1972 the Soviet Union concluded with the United States the biggest single grain trade agreement, a transaction worth $750 million, and opened its doors to the importation of farm machinery and

American chemical plants. By mid-1973, American and West European firms had entered into more than 1,200 agreements for economic cooperation with Eastern Europe.[34] In April 1973, the American Deputy Secretary of State noted that "at a time when we have a trade deficit with most areas of the world, our balance of trade surplus with Eastern Europe is particularly welcome". The new détente, according to the vice-president of the Chase Manhattan Bank, was "born out of necessity", and some people started to speak of a "balance of weakness" instead of a "balance of power".[35]

As a result of détente, countries of the Third World were suddenly deprived of their ability to take a neutral stand vis-à-vis the two super-powers, to remain at an equal (or almost equal) distance from both, to neutralize the pressure exercised by one by falling back on the other's support, or to compensate for a decline in one power's economic aid by getting more from the other. Again, as a result of détente, each of the two superpowers felt more at ease in bringing a Third World country under stricter control without fearing the intervention of the other, and in reducing the "waste" of foreign aid resulting from the readiness of the other power to give aid to the same country.

Looking back at the years following the fall of Kennedy and Krushchev, it does not now seem surprising that this was a period when naked force was used against small countries that not long before had enjoyed a high degree of freedom of movement, and when the intervention of one power was met by no more than empty and futile condemnation from the other. This was also the period which witnessed the fall of one Third World leader after another. In no more than two years, between 1963 and 1965, the regimes of Sukarno in Indonesia, Nkrumah in Ghana, Ben Bella in Algeria and Goulart in Brazil were toppled. Nehru was allowed to leave this world in peace, while Tito, left only with Nasir as a non-aligned leader, began to look by himself for a way for economic cooperation with Western Europe. The Soviet Union's hegemony over Eastern Europe was confirmed with the suppression of rebellious Czechoslovakia in 1968, while its influence increased in Southeast Asia in the wake of the Vietnam war. It also gained new spheres of influence in Angola and Ethiopia. Progressive or semi-progressive regimes in Latin America were replaced, one after the other, by regimes completely loyal to the United States, except for Cuba whose subservience to the Soviet Union gradually increased. In one country of the Third World after another it became evident that nothing less than complete allegiance to one of the two superpowers was possible. Slogans of non-alignment and positive neutrality became things of the past, while each superpower was busy creating the most favorable conditions in those countries that had come under its sway.

It was natural that the method used in implementing this change should differ, according to the special circumstances of each, from one Third World country to another. In the Arab world, an Israeli attack was obviously a convenient tool, but there was also the manipulation of foreign aid, and particularly of food aid, on which several Arab countries had become dependent. The use of both weapons had already begun a few years before the 1967 war. In 1963 the United States supplied Israel with Hawk missiles and took over from West Germany, under Johnson's administration, the supplying of tanks to Israel, then supplied it with Skyhawk aircraft. In November 1966 Israeli forces attacked some Jordanian towns and in April 1967 they were engaged in an air battle with Syria. When the food aid agreement between Egypt and the United States was about to expire in June 1965, the American ambassador in Cairo informed the Egyptian government that "he cannot at present talk about this matter [PL480] at all, because he does not like Egypt's conduct."[36] Although Egypt stopped assisting the rebels in the Congo, this was not sufficient to appease the United States, which extended the food aid agreement only for periods ranging from three to six months and then ended it completely in February 1967. The Soviet Union, on the other hand, was disinclined to increase its aid to Egypt sufficiently to replace American aid unless Egypt became wholly allied to the Soviet Union.[37] Egypt was no longer able to finance its Second Five Year Plan; accordingly it was subjected to continuous change and reformulation and finally abandoned altogether.[38] Egyptian planners then confined themselves to the task of drawing up short-term plans for the allocation of scarce foreign exchange for periods that rarely extended beyond three months. In fact, the First Five Year Plan turned out to have been Egypt's only plan worthy of the name, until in the mid-seventies, the very principle of comprehensive economic planning became a thing of the past.

The big blow came, of course, in June 1967, when Israel attacked Egypt, Syria and Jordan. In describing what went on inside American policy-making circles during the three weeks following Nasir's closing of the Straits of Tiran to Israeli shipping on 22 May 1967, William Quandt remarks that what occurred "is almost impossible to know with certainty. The focus of decision-making rapidly shifted from the expert level of the State Department to the senior levels of State, to the Pentagon and to the President and his close advisers."[39]

The Soviet Union condemned the Israeli attack, but it had already agreed with the United States, on 5 June 1976, (using the Hot Line between the Kremlin and the White House for the first time since its installation) that neither should intervene directly in the war. In the few years following the war, the Soviet Union benefitted from the state of "no war, no peace" by strengthening its position in Egypt and Syria; it also exploited Egypt's desire to wage a war of attrition against Israel in 1969–70 by establishing new military bases in Egypt, using this as a bargaining card in its negotiations with the United States on various political and economic transactions. This was continued even after the events of May 1971 in Egypt, in which Egyptian supporters of the Soviet Union were removed from power. The Soviet Union immediately hastened to conclude a "long term" treaty of "friendship and cooperation" with Egypt with the sole aim of keeping Egypt for as long as possible as a card in its negotiations with the United States. This game did not end until May 1972 when, during the Moscow summit meeting between Brezhnev and Nixon,

> ...the Russians finally confirmed that they regarded their growing détente with the U.S. as more important to them than their military and political commitments to the Arabs and to Egypt in particular.[40]

Thus when the Egyptian government claimed for itself the "honor" of expelling Soviet military experts from the country two months later (18 July 1972) and subsequently the "honor" of unilaterally abrogating the Treaty of Friendship and Cooperation (in March 1976), the Soviet Union was not greatly bothered. Indeed, it finished withdrawing its 20,000 experts before the date that had been fixed, insisted that the withdrawal should be complete including bases and equipment not covered by the Egyptian order, and declared that the experts were back home after "having completed the task assigned to them."[41] What remained to be done was for the Soviet Union to recover the money owed to it by Egypt, and Egypt's requests for a reduction or a rescheduling of this debt were refused; trade agreements concluded with Egypt successively in 1974, 1975 and 1976 had one important common feature in that the value of Egyptian exports to the Soviet Union always exceeded that of Egyptian imports.[42] In June 1974 the American president visited Egypt and was given a conqueror's welcome by the government. He had come to see for himself the country which had recently been added to the American sphere of influence, following almost twenty years of mutiny that had begun in 1955 when the Egyptian government had dared to buy arms from the other camp.

(3)

By the late sixties new symptoms were also starting to appear in the Israeli economy, as the beginning of another stage in Israel's economic history, with new features that distinguish it from two earlier stages, the first of which falls between the establishment of the State in 1948 and the end of the fifties, and the second of which occupies most of the sixties.

During the first period, high priority was given to agriculture, a necessary emphasis because of the rapid increase in the demand for food and clothing resulting from the flow of Jewish immigrants, and one that was made possible by the availability of large areas of land deserted by their Arab owners. High priority was also given to investment in infrastructure projects such as roads, housing, education and health, again in order to absorb the flow of immigrants.

By the end of the fifties however, only limited opportunities remained for further expansion in agriculture, as water for irrigation became more scarce; unemployment declined and the demand for food grew more slowly. Priority was therefore given to industrial growth, supported by the introduction of various protective measures. Thus while the share of agriculture in the total Israeli labor force remained virtually constant between 1955 and 1960, it declined from 17.3 percent to 12.3 percent in the following six years from 1960 to 1966, with the share of industry rising from 23.2 percent to 26.1 percent during the latter period.[43]

In the years following the 1967 war, another important change in the economic structure became noticeable, with the decline in the share of traditional industries such as food, leather, textiles and furniture, in total industrial output, and the rise in the share of metal products, particularly machinery and transport equipment, and of electrical equipment and electronics.

Thus in the early seventies total net investment in metal, electrical and electronic industries constituted about 50 percent of total investments in industry; their output multiplied three times in real terms between 1965 and 1975 and their share in total industrial output rose from 20 percent in 1965 to 30 percent in 1975.[44] Several factors contributed to this development, including the rapid growth in the demand of military industries for these products, the decline in the rate of growth of domestic demand for the products of traditional industries, and the increase in the rate of growth of domestic demand for consumer durables resulting from the rapid increase in average income.

However, this growth in domestic demand—both military and civilian—was soon to reach the limit set by the small size of the Israeli market, and it was necessary for the new industries to look increasingly for export opportunities if their growth was to continue at the same high rates.

Israeli exports of metal products and electrical and electronic equipment did in fact grow rapidly, but it is important to note that only a proportion of total output of these industries was absorbed by exports. Thus, although the exports of metal products multiplied eight times between 1965 and 1974, bringing in $155 million in 1974, this latter value constituted no more than 9.6 percent of the total sales of metal industries, reaching $1,620 million in the same year. Similarly, while the exports of electrical and electronic equipment multiplied more than three times between 1970 and 1974, their total output increased during the same period at nearly the same rate, so that the percentage of exports to total output did not exceed 2.2 percent in 1974.[45] It could therefore be said that although exports of metal, electrical and electronic products did increase rapidly, the rate of increase was not sufficiently high to absorb a good part of the increase in output. This constituted a problem when the domestic market was growing at a low rate.

This view is supported by the figures in the Israeli Plan for these industries; it aims at increasing the output of metal, electrical and electronic industries by 59 percent between 1975 and 1980, and by 61 percent between 1980 and 1985. It also aims at an increase in the exports of these products by 194 percent and 111 percent respectively in these two periods, thus raising their share in total Israeli exports (other than diamonds) to 44 percent in 1985, which is double their share in 1974.[46]

But there is another reason why Israel is in need of a strong push for its exports. Israel's industrial growth has always faced two basic problems: the narrowness of the domestic market and the scarcity of industrial raw materials. The problem of market size was partly solved during the fifties by the large flow of immigrants and in the sixties by import-substitution policies. However, by the end of the sixties, the problem started to be felt acutely as the import-substitution policies approached their limits and as the flow of immigrants started to decline. The problem of the scarcity of industrial raw materials was, in its turn, postponed so long as industrial growth was concentrated in traditional industries relying on agriculture for inputs, but was to be strongly felt as the share of the new industries started to rise. Israel's imports of capital goods increased more rapidly after 1965 at a rate of 13.4 percent annually between 1964/65 and 1969/70 as compared with 10.7 per cent in the previous twelve years (from 1952/53 to 1964/65).[47] Noteworthy also is the increase in the ratio of Israel's import surplus to total resources (i.e. the surplus of imports over exports as a proportion of GNP, plus the surplus of imports over exports) which, after a steady decrease from 40 percent in 1950 to 23 percent in 1965, 15 percent in 1960 and 10 percent in 1966, began to increase after that date to reach 20 percent in 1970, 34 percent in 1972 and 39 percent in 1973.[48]

The realizing of a deficit in the balance of current accounts has therefore been a regular feature of the Israeli economy, not only because of the high level of imports of armaments, but also because of the high import content of both domestic consumption and exports,[49] and in spite of the rapid increase in exports, the deficit went on increasing. Israel continued to rely on the flow of foreign loans, reparations and transfers so that during the twenty years from 1950 to 1970, the average flow of foreign capital to Israel was no less than $500 million per annum. In 1968, however, this flow failed, for the first time in Israel's history, to cover the deficit in the balance of current account. The balance of payments was now realizing a deficit and the foreign currency reserves declined in 1968/69 by $330 million.

Therefore the Israeli economy seemed by the early seventies to have reached a crossroads: it had either to find new openings for exports or to choke. In order to sustain a rapid increase in income it was more dependent than ever on the growth of the new industries, which required a high level of demand if they were to be able to compete with European and American products. The domestic market was, however, too narrow to absorb more than a very modest proportion of total output. At the same time, the high level of average income and the high level of import content of industrial output was bringing an increasing pressure to bear on the balance of current account.

It was, of course, possible to increase exports to existing markets: the EEC and America, as well as some African and Asian countries. It was also possible to try to attract foreign private investments to Israel as a substitute for foreign aid. Israel tried both. With the aim of increasing exports and reducing imports, the Israeli currency was devalued by 20 percent in August 1971, by 43 percent in November 1974 and again by 30 percent in November 1977. The government also took various measures for subsidizing exports which in one year (1973) cost it about one billion Israeli liras. A number of preferential trade agreements were concluded with the EEC and other European countries, and with America and Japan, in order to boost Israeli exports.[50] The Begin government declared the beginning of a "New Economic Policy" whereby a number of measures were taken to encourage the flow of foreign investment; these included the abolishing of foreign exchange control and the promulgating of a new law bestowing various advantages on foreign capital.

However, there are reasons for doubting the adequacy of these measures to solve Israel's export and balance of payments problems. The devaluation of the Israeli lira would undoubtedly lead to an increase in the proceeds of some exports and to some reduction in the imports of consumption goods, but it would also raise the cost of imports of raw materials and other inputs on which Israeli industries, including the export industries, depend heavily. Although the EEC countries and the

United States have until now absorbed the greater part of traditional Israeli exports (diamonds and foodstuffs) it is unlikely that their demand for the products of the new industries would increase particularly rapidly, in view of the tough competition from rival European and American industries and given the size advantage of the latter. The immediate results of the 1975 agreement with the EEC seem to support this view. In an evaluation of these results, published in *Israel Trade and Export Journal,* an Israeli official commented,

> ...we expected that with the coming into effect of the agreement, there would be a substantial increase in our exports to the E.E.C., as compared to other destinations... Unfortunately for us, the figures show that altogether Israel's exports to the E.E.C. have been moderate, that foodstuffs, fresh and processed, still account for 36.5 percent of our exports to the E.E.C. and have even slightly gone up (by 3.4 per cent) and that industrial exports to the E.E.C. (diamonds excluded) accounted for 37 percent of our total exports to E.E.C., a decline from the previous figure of 40 percent... It is now clear that the reduction of tariffs alone will not be sufficient under prevalent conditions in Israel's industry to bring about a sizeable increase in exports. We need more investments and more know-how to bring about a sizeable increase in exports.[51]

As for foreign investment, it seems likely that Israel's success in attracting it would itself depend on its success in opening new markets for its exports and in securing new sources of raw materials and cheap labor. Private foreign investment in Israel has been discouraged not only by the narrowness of its market and the scarcity of raw materials but also by the continued Arab economic boycott and the continued threat of war with Arab countries. More recently, a new factor related to the labor market was added, for although Israel had access to a new source of cheap labor with the occupation of the West Bank and Gaza in 1967, some 30 percent of its labor force was withdrawn from the labor market for military mobilization in 1973. The rate of Jewish migration into Israel also tended to decline in the seventies.[52] The growing scarcity of labor was reflected in a rapid increase in wages, production costs, and in the rate of inflation which ranged between 40 and 50 percent during the period from 1974 to 1977. All this may partly explain the tendency of foreign investment in Israel to decline after 1973.

By the mid-1970s Israeli economic publications were persistently emphasizing the need for raising the rate of growth of exports, which is regarded as an essential condition for solving the balance of payments problem and indeed for maintaining a high rate of growth for the economy as a whole. In an article published in September 1975 it was stated that

... Israel must increase its flagging exports by twice or three times the present level, or face an economy that will be physically destroyed by the size of its gaping trade deficit.[53]

In another article earlier in the same year, published in the same journal, we read that

... Israel is struggling through one of the most difficult economic situations since the establishment of the State. Despite really drastic measures, the economy, and particularly the export sector, has been slow to respond.[54]

Three years previously, David Horowitz had written,

... Investments are now maturing and the domestic market is saturated. Balance of payment difficulties reveal the weakness of an inward economy: it proves too narrow and, if it is to grow, a reorientation becomes imperative. That means exports and penetration into world markets... The country has been undergoing fundamental modifications of structure. Step by step, it is becoming more of a seller's and a producer's environment. The interests of investor, importer and consumer are no longer the exclusive consideration. The reason is fairly obvious. The capital imported in the past was used to enlarge productive capacity. The investments are now maturing, production has effactually expanded and exports have begun to rise steadily. This maturing of earlier capital intake has been accompanied by a growing diversification of export trade. Therefore, the very essence of Israel's economic life and problems is being transformed.[55]

In 1977, Nadav Safran wrote that

... for the U.S., a settlement [of the Arab-Israeli conflict] had become a matter of imperative necessity, for Israel it was still only a desirable consummation. The main thing to the latter was under what terms.[56]

The terms with which Israel was concerned must have been many, but one of the most important was undoubtedly related to the opening of the Egyptian market to Israeli goods. Egypt's market is the largest in the Arab world, and reaching it would allow Israeli industries to increase their scale of operations so that they might be able effectively to compete in the wider markets of the more advanced countries, while Egypt could receive those goods and services which Israel had difficulty in selling to the more developed countries. Reaching the Egyptian market would also increase the attractiveness of Israel for the foreign investor who could now have access to a market wider than that of Israel alone, and would supply a cheap labor force that could compensate for the more costly Israeli labor. Then, if Egypt were to pull out of the Arab economic boycott, it would lose most of its value. The ending of the Arab boycott, or at least the boycott by Egypt, was indeed becoming an urgent demand among foreign investors, and it is wrong to underestimate the harm that it had brought to foreign private interests. It has been estimated that more than seven hundred American companies have suffered from the economic boycott by one or more of the Arab countries. For example, the Coca-Cola Company became subject to the boycott regulations in 1966 as a result of its giving a production licence to an Israeli firm, the French Renault Company was led to abandon plans to establish an assembly plant in Israel, while Air France was denied overflying and landing rights until it had cancelled its contribution to some development projects in Israel.

The relative importance of Israel, as compared with the Arab countries, as an outlet for European and American exports of goods and capital seemed also to be on the decline, with the rapidly growing ability of Israeli industries to satisfy domestic demand and with the big increase in Israel's wage level. We have already referred to the decline in foreign investment in Israel; there was also a decline in Israel's share in total American exports to the Middle East, from 39.5 percent in 1971, to 23.1 percent in 1974, and to 18.4 percent in 1975.[57] But if an expansion in exports and foreign investments in Arab countries required the ending of the Arab boycott, a big flow of foreign investments to Arab countries also required the ending of the state of war. Foreign investors are no less sensitive to political conditions than to wage levels, and no large-scale foreign investments in Egypt were conceivable until the threat of war with Israel was brought to an end.

These are probably some of the reasons which made the settlement of the Arab-Israeli conflict "a matter of imperative necessity" for the United States. But there are others. American economic and military aid to Israel between the establishment of the State and the October War of 1973 exceeded $3 billion. After this war the *annual* average of American aid to Israel jumped to $2 billion while the balance of trade deficit vis-à-vis the United States was rapidly rising. With the deterioration in its own balance of payments, America's aid to Israel must have started to look like an unnecessary burden, and one that was increasingly difficult to justify. It must have seemed strange in the eyes of American policy makers that the United States balance of payments should continue to carry a burden of this size at a time of mounting economic difficulties and on behalf of a country which had reached such a degree of economic maturity and for whom the Arab countries no longer constituted a real threat. The time must indeed have come for bringing to an end—or at least for greatly reducing—this burden, and the best that the United States could give to Israel on launching its new independence must have seemed to be the creation of conditions that would be conducive to the conclusion of a peace treaty between Israel and Egypt, one that would state unequivocally Egypt's commitment to open its doors to Israeli goods.

IV. THE "REOPENING" OF THE EGYPTIAN ECONOMY

In modern Arab history it is rare to find as striking an example of similarity between two historical experiences as that between the conditions that surrounded the fall of Muhammad ᶜAli's experiment in Egypt in the mid-19th century and those surrounding the fall of Nasir's towards the end of the sixties.

In the years following the Suez War of 1956, the Soviet Union regarded Nasir as a friend worthy of support and spoke of him in a manner strongly reminiscent of the manner in which the French government had spoken of Muhammad ᶜAli: in 1833 the French Foreign Ministry, referring to Egypt, wrote,

> ...we rejoice that we have facilitated the birth and development of a power worthy of our collaboration and as interested as we are in the prosperity of the Mediterranean. We shall always be ready to give the Pasha in the future the same evidence of our friendship and goodwill as he has received in the past from the French government.[58]

But when Britain threatened Muhammad ᶜAli with war in order to force him to evacuate Syria and put into effect the terms of the 1838 Treaty, France did no more than advise him to resist without coming to his aid, and threatened war without ever fighting. Similarly, when Israel attacked Egypt, Syria and Jordan in 1967, the Soviet Union did no more than condemn the act, gave Egypt its moral support in the United Nations, but did not fight on the Arab side. The arms lost in the battle were not replaced at the required speed, for which the Soviet Union gave the excuse that the arms requested were not available in sufficient quantities.[59] They were indeed gradually replaced in the following years by new Soviet supplies, but the Soviet Union always made sure that the new weapons would be insufficient to liberate the occupied territories and the Egyptians were made to understand that the war of attrition would not go beyond a certain limit.

Between 1840, when he was forced to accept the Treaty of London and to implement the commercial agreement of 1838, and his death in 1849, all Muhammad ᶜAli's hopes of building an independent economy or of uniting the Arab countries into one strong state had been lost and his resources drained. Similarly, in the few years following 1965, but particularly between the defeat of 1967 and his death in 1970, Nasir's will had already been paralyzed and his resources drained so that, although he continued to rule Egypt, it was virtually impossible for him to pursue his economic, Arab, or foreign policies independently. Egypt was rendered incapable of taking any serious measures for furthering economic development or for supporting the Arab liberalization movement, Arab unity or the liberation movements in other Third World countries. The rate of growth in Egypt declined from the mid-sixties — as it did in Syria and Jordan after 1967 — to more or less the rate of population growth. Military expenditure absorbed excessively high proportions of the resources of the three countries so that each of them had to rely increasingly on the aid of the Arab oil countries. Arab ambitions and aspirations were reduced from those of achieving rapid economic progress, socialism, and Arab unity, to the modest demand of liberating the Arab territories that had been occupied in 1967. An explanation for the defeat was sought in the internal weaknesses of Arab society and the shortcomings of Arab governments, merely because they were so much easier to detect and to believe in, in a climate of complete loss of self-confidence (that was encouraged by the insistence of the foreign media on "Israeli invincibility" and "Arab inefficiency"). It was also difficult for the Arab Left to believe that the leader of the socialist camp on which their hopes had been pinned for decades, could allow his policies to be governed by considerations that had nothing to do with the principles of socialism, if these principles were to lead to positions in direct conflict with the interests of the Soviet State. It was indeed no longer possible to reiterate the slogans of socialism, development, or Arab unity, nor was it possible to ask the people for new sacrifices for any such cause. It had now become imperative to appease the people at home, even at the expense of growth, to appease the aid-giving Arab governments, and to try even to appease the United States, in whose hands the power to end the Israeli occupation or to perpetuate it now seemed to lie.

Under Muhammad ʿAli's successors, the doors were opened for foreign goods and foreign investments while the state relinquished its control of national industry and agriculture. After Nasir's death, a similar direction was taken in Egypt, and in varying degrees in other Arab countries, with the promulgation of laws abolishing restrictions on trade and foreign exchange, and for the promoting of foreign investment. Incentives for foreign investments included the establishment of free zones, the reduction of income taxes, the exemption from customs duties, the abolition of restrictions on profit repatriation, and protection against sequestration and nationalization. The immediate result was that — just as British manufactures had started to flood Arab markets in the mid-19th century thus replacing the products of national industries — American goods began to flow at startling rates into Arab markets in the early seventies but particularly after 1973. American exports to Egypt increased by 78 percent between 1974 and 1976, to Sudan by 66 percent, to Jordan by 122 percent, to North Yemen by 150 percent, and to Syria by 597 percent.[60]

Again, just as Arab countries turned away in the mid-19th century from producing for the home market to production for exports, and as investment turned increasingly towards the export sector and infrastructure, so the economic structure in Egypt, Syria, Jordan, and North Yemen started to change in a similar direction with the beginning of the seventies. Economic activity is now increasingly turning towards production for exports, whether of goods or services, while investments are rapidly turning away from those branches that were geared to the domestic markets towards the production of export items and to infrastructure projects that enhanced the production of the same items. This change of direction is again most obvious in Egypt simply because of the greater contrast between the new economic policies and those that had been pursued in the sixties.

In the light of all this it would indeed be a great folly to think that the fundamental transformation of Egypt's economic policy, which was timidly hinted at after 1967 but boldly implemented in the early seventies, was simply the result of some "clever" ideas that passed through the minds of some Egyptian policy makers as a reaction to an economic deterioration caused by the "closed door" policies of earlier years. Indeed, these "clever" ideas, as well as the economic deterioration, were themselves nothing more than the result of foreign pressure that was determined to bring the "closed door" policy to an end.

NOTES

1. George Orwell, *The Collected Essays, Journals and Letters, Vol. IV 1945–50* (London: Penguin Books, 1971), p. 145.

2. Elias Saba, "Wilayat Suriyya 1876–1909", unpublished PhD thesis, University of Michigan, 1971, pp. 6–7.

3. Richard Hill, *Egypt in the Sudan 1820–1881* (London: Oxford University Press, 1959), pp. 49–62.

4. Philip Hitti, *A Short History of Lebanon* (London: Macmillan, 1965), pp. 184–187.

5. ʿAbd al-Aziz Nawwar, *Dawud pasha, wali baghdad* [Dawud Pasha, Governor of Baghdad], (Cairo: Dar al-Kitab al-ʿArabi, 1968), p. 313.

6. S. H. Longrigg, *Four Centuries of Modern Iraq* (Oxford: Clarendon Press, 1925), pp. 255–56.

7. H. Dodwell, *The Founder of Modern Egypt: A Study of Mohammed Ali* (Cambridge: Cambridge University Press, 1931), p. 126.

8. E. Evans-Pritchard, *The Sanusi of Cyrenaica* (Oxford: Clarendon Press, 1949), p. 8.

He rightly remarks that the Sanusiyya, like many other religious movements in the Muslim world was "an expression of a sense of social and cultural exclusiveness... [they] were all reactions against foreign domination as much as revolts against orthodoxy. The religious deviation was the expression of the intense desire of a people to live according to their own traditions and institutions. Today their desire is expressed in the political language of nationalism. In the past it was expressed in religious movements. Arab nationalism is not a new phenomenon. Only its dress is new."

9. Dodwell, op.cit., p. 136.

10. It is estimated that the share of exports in total British industrial output more than doubled between 1826 and 1836, and between 1884 and 1889. Arthur Lewis, *Economic Survey 1919-39* (London: Allen and Unwin, 1943), p. 74. See also J. B. Condliffe, *The Commerce of Nations* (New York: Norton, 1950), pp. 322–341.

11. France did not participate in direct foreign investment during the second half of the 19th century to the same degree as did Britain, partly because of its slower rate of industrial growth and capital accumulation, and partly because of the prevailing preference among French financiers for fixed income investments. As for the United States and Germany, whatever capital was available was invested domestically.

12. Condliffe, op.cit., pp. 322–341.

13. Ibid.

14. Dodwell, op.cit., p. 134.

15. Dodwell, op.cit., p. 184.

16. Quoted in Afaf L. S. Marsot, in an unpublished manuscript on Muhammad ʿAli and Palmerston.

17. "M. Thiers," said Louis-Philippe, "est furieux contre moi parce que je n'ai pas voulu faire la guerre. Il me dit que j'ai parlé de faire la guerre, mais parler de faire la guerre et faire la guerre sont deux choses bien différentes." Quoted in Afaf Marsot, ibid.

18. G. Kirk, *A Short History of the Middle East* (London: Methuen, 1952), p. 101.

19. Roger Owen, *Cotton and the Egyptian Economy, 1820–1914* (Oxford: Clarendon Press, 1969), p. 82.

20. D. Chevalier, "Western Development in the Eastern Crisis in Mid-Nineteenth Century", in W. Polk and R. Chambers, eds., *The Beginnings of Modernization in the Middle East* (Chicago: Chicago University Press, 1968), p. 218; and Muhammad S. Hassan, *Al-tatawwur al-iqtisadi fi al-iraq* [Economic Development in Iraq...], Vol. I (Sidon: Al-Maktaba al-Asriyya, n.d.), p. 281.

21. Quoted in A. Bonné, *State and Economy in the Middle East* (London: Kegan Paul, 1948), p. 230.

22. Kirk, op.cit., p. 82.

23. N. Safran, "American-Israeli Relations: An Overview", *Middle East Review,* Winter 1977–78, p. 32.

24. Within two years (from 1959 to 1961) United States investment in the EEC countries more than doubled, while American exports to the EEC at the end of the sixties reached three times their level ten years previously. See G. Kolko, *America and the Crisis of World Capitalism* (Boston: Beacon Press, 1974), pp. 86 and 115.

25. D. Brown, "New Trends in Trade and Investment" in B. Chattopadhayay, ed., *Imperialism in the Modern Phase,* Vol. I (New Delhi: People's Publishing House, 1974), p. 71.

26. B. Hansen and G. Marzouk, *Development and Economic Policy in the U.A.R.* (Amsterdam: North Holland Press, 1965), p. 4.

27. A. Musrey, *An Arab Common Market* (New York: Praeger, 1959), pp. 192–3.

28. During the period under consideration, Egypt concluded two trade and payment agreements with Syria (1956 and 1957), one with Lebanon (1956), one with Iraq (1958),

three with Saudi Arabia (1955, 1956 and 1958), two with Libya (1956 and 1960), two with Tunisia (1957 and 1962), two with Morocco (1958 and 1959), two with Sudan (1957 and 1959), and one with Algeria (1963). See ibid., p. 92.

29. Ibid., pp. 194–5.

30. The share of trade among the four member countries which ratified the Arab Common Market Agreement (Egypt, Syria, Iraq and Jordan) in their total exports increased from 3.8 percent in 1964 to 6.2 percent in 1969. UNESCO, *Etude Comparative des Cadres Institutionnels du Commerce Intra-Marché Commun Arabe* (mimeo.), June 1971.

31. Louis Awad, "Intellectual and Cultural Development", in P. J. Vatikiotis, ed., *Egypt Since the Revolution* (London: Allen and Unwin, 1968), pp. 157–59.

32. W. Quandt, *United States Policy in the Middle East: Constraints and Choice* (Santa Monica, Calif: Rand Corporation, 1970), p. 31.

33. Kolko, op.cit., p. 154.

34. R. Barnet and R. Muller, *Global Reach: the Power of the Multinational Corporations* (New York: Simon and Schuster, 1974), p. 89.

35. R. Scalapino, "Reflections on East-West Relations", *Survey,* Summer-Autumn 1976, p. 129.

36. From a speech by Gamal ʿAbd al-Nasir in Port Said on 23 December 1964.

37. See an interesting chapter on the change in Soviet attitude towards Egypt following the fall of Krushchev in Mohammed H. Heikal, *The Sphinx and the Commissar* (New York: Harper and Row, 1978), pp. 148–171.

38. The annual average of economic aid received by Egypt from Western countries and multilateral institutions increased from $50 million in the period from 1955 to 1960, to $200 million between 1961 and 1966, but declined to $16 million from 1967 to 1969.

39. Quandt, op.cit., p. 40.

40. R. Stephens, "The Great Powers and the Middle East", *Journal of Palestine Studies,* Summer 1973, pp. 3–12.

41. Y. Ro'i, *The U.S.S.R. and Egypt in the Wake of Sadat's July Decisions* (Tel Aviv: The Russian and East European Research Center, September 1975), p. 11.

42. Y. Ro'i, "Soviet Economic Presence in Egypt", *The Jerusalem Quarterly,* Spring 1977, pp. 119–20.

43. D. Horowitz, *The Enigma of Economic Growth: A Case Study of Israel* (New York: Praeger, 1972), p. 59.

44. *Israel Export and Trade Journal,* August 1976, p. 7.

45. Ibid., June 1975, p. 5.

46. Ibid., April 1978, p. 15.

47. Horowitz, op.cit., p. 121.

48. Ibid., p. 123; and Charles Issawi, "The Economy of the Middle East and North Africa: An Overview", in A. Udovitch, ed., *The Middle East: Oil, Conflict and Hope* (Lexington, Mass.: Lexington Books, 1976), p. 82.

49. In the late sixties, the import content of the total value of Israeli exports ranged between 40 and 50 percent. L. Preston and K. Nashashibi, *Trade Patterns in the Middle East* (Washington: American Enterprise Institute for Public Policy Research, 1970), p. 49.

50. The most important of these agreements were those of May 1975 with the EEC and of January 1976 with the United States.

51. *Israel Export and Trade Journal,* July 1976, p. 5. Even with regard to agricultural exports, the same journal recently reported that "some disappointments are being experienced in citrus exports to the E.E.C. in view of the relatively small benefits actually attained as a result of the 1975 agreement". One reason given was the increased competition from such countries as Greece, Portugal and Spain. Ibid., February 1978, p. 9.

52. While immigration to Israel led its population to double during the first three years of the establishment of the state, it took another twenty years for the population to double again. In the seventies, the rate of immigration declined rapidly until 1976 when the number of those leaving Israel exceeded the number of immigrants.

53. *Israel Export and Trade Journal,* September 1975, p. 9.

54. Ibid., January 1975, p. 5.

55. Horowitz, op.cit., p. 143.

56. Safran, op.cit., p. 39.

57. F. Gottheil, "United States-Middle East Economic Relations", *Middle East Review,* Summer 1977, p. 59.

58. Kirk, op.cit., p. 76.

59. On the Soviet position with regard to the 1967 war see Heikal, op.cit., pp. 172–189.

60. Special Report on Arab Economic Commerce, *Middle East Economic Digest,* November 1977.

Part Three

The New Arab Political Order

X

The New Arab Political Order: Implications for the 1980s

Ali E. Hillal Dessouki

I. INTRODUCTION

During the last two decades the study of regional political relations has gained increasing significance. The concept of the regional or subordinate system was employed to provide an intermediary level of analysis between the global system and the foreign policy of a particular state or actor. Regional systems are studied in terms of their membership, systemic attributes and level of capabilities, distribution of power within the system, patterns of policies and alliances, sources of cohesion or dissensus, and norms governing the interactions between their members.

The objective of this chapter is to outline and analyze the changes that have taken place in inter-Arab relations in the 1970s, with particular emphasis on the impact of oil and the wealth newly acquired by a small number of Arab states, on these relations. Since it is almost impossible to isolate the impact of one variable (in our case oil) from the more complex matrix of other important economic, social and political developments in the area, our analysis will locate the impact of oil-producing countries within a broader context in which other factors come into play.

The main argument of this essay is that the inter-Arab system is undergoing changes emanating both from within and from without, which can lead to a systemic transformation[1], a change *of* the system and not only *in* it. The change affects the style and substance of inter-Arab politics. The oil wealth has contributed to this transformation both in its normative and structural dimensions.

First of all, oil has created a new cleavage between Arab states based on economic status. It has altered the balance of power in favor of the rich, who are not only subsidizing the poor but also attracting their trained manpower. Saudi Arabia, the leading oil-producing country, perceives itself and is perceived by others as playing an influential role in Arab affairs: in particular the roles of financier, broker and guardian of

Arab solidarity. As will be explained later, oil wealth has also exercised a moderating influence on Arab ideological cleavages, and a more pragmatic problem-solving outlook can be observed in most Arab politics. It has thus reinforced *"raison d'état"* at the level of the ruling elite and what has been described as the "new realism" at the level of the masses.[2] For instance, Arab unity is nowadays perceived by most regimes in terms of solidarity and cooperation, rather than in constitutional political terms.[3]

Another aspect of the impact of oil wealth is that it has made the Arab world, since it contains what is considered the most important strategic commodity for some time to come, more susceptible to foreign penetration and open to global intrusion. The struggle for oil increasingly seems to be a vital issue of the 1980s, as symbolized by super-power moves in Afghanistan and the Gulf region. Geo-political priorities have undergone some changes; it has frequently been argued that the center of gravity in the Arab world has moved from its traditional site, the Fertile Crescent and Egypt, to the Gulf area. Control of oil, the waters of the Gulf and the Strait of Hormuz has acquired added importance. This shift was underlined by the outbreak of war between Iraq and Iran in September 1980. Thus issues of energy and geo-politics have come to reinforce each other, and the search for military bases which recalls the past is being revived by the United States with great enthusiasm in the early 1980s. For some, it follows that the Arab-Israeli conflict has lost its critical significance, given the emergence of more immediate and vital concerns. The problem with this argument is that it poses the relation between the Arab-Israeli conflict and oil-Gulf security as a zero sum game. A better and more meaningful argument is that the tension area has been extended to include the Gulf region. The future availability of Arab and Iranian oil, after the revolution, depends to a large extent on the settlement of the Arab-Israeli conflict.[4] The linkages between the Palestine issue and Gulf security will be examined in the course of the chapter.

The balance of power and the balance of concerns in the Arab world are thus undergoing a process of transformation. What are the reasons and manifestations of this transformation? What kind of regional political order will emerge? This essay will attempt to answer some aspects of these questions, with a particular emphasis on the role of Saudi Arabia and Egyptian-Saudi relations.

II. INTER-ARAB POLITICS: CONVENTIONAL
PATTERNS AND SOURCES OF CHANGE

Inter-Arab relations have been the subject of a host of writings.[5] All agree that inter-Arab relations constitute a system of interactions that cannot be analyzed exclusively as a function of superpower rivalries: this is not to underestimate the role of external factors and client-patron networks, but rather to demonstrate that inter-Arab relations have their own dynamism and vitality. Outside powers set the limits and parameters of the behavior of their allies by a variety of negative and positive enticements. But within these limits, small states enjoy a certain amount of manoeuverability. Further, we know that most states usually act in response to regional rather than global stimuli and that interactions within each region have a certain degree of autonomy and also parochialism, not necessarily related to great-power politics.

There has also been a consensus that inter-Arab politics cannot be understood only in terms of ideological differences in orientation or sympathies. Again this is not to deny the real differences in orientation between Arab regimes, but rather to indicate that political processes are complex phenomena in which personal, ideological and situational variables exercise some influence. It is true that ideological differences are used by ruling elites as a justification for their policies; in fact they are more of a rationale than the real reason. Conflicts between regimes of similar ideological orientations are as recurrent and bitter as those between states with different outlooks. This can perhaps be attributed to the personalized style of policy-making in all Arab states, the pragmatic nature of many Arab "revolutionary" regimes, the different stages of economic and social development of Arab states, and finally the influence of great-power policies.

The features of inter-Arab relations throughout the 1950s and the 1960s can be summarized as follows. First, during the mid-fifties and the rise of Nasir's pan-Arab leadership, inter-Arab relations were characterized by an oscillation from consensus to dissensus; from the maximalist objective of Arab unity, usually defined in constitutional political terms, to the minimalist objective of Arab solidarity and cooperation between Arab states. Using familiar Nasirist terms, inter-Arab relations fluctuated between *wihdat al-hadaf* (unity of objective) which involved a small number of states agreeing on a wide range of substantive issues, and *wihdat al-saff* (unity of ranks) which included all, or the vast majority, of Arab states agreeing on the lowest common denominator.

Secondly, with the exception of the period of ideological polarization from 1961 to 1967, inter-Arab politics were characterized by a flexible system of alliances. Alliances were made in a short period of time and were dissolved with the same ease. The shifting alliances can be understood in the light of unstable political regimes, personalized foreign policies and the influence of external factors.

Thirdly there existed a number of pan-Arab core concerns and issues which were addressed by most Arab regimes and leaders and particularly by those aspiring to perform a leadership role. Chief among these concerns were Arab unity, Palestine, and non-alignment. These core concerns were perceived by Arab politicans as legitimacy resources, and acted upon accordingly. Regimes claim their legitimacy in part by adhering to these concerns and using them to discredit their adversaries internally and externally as being unfaithful to them.

Fourthly, the centrality of Egypt's position was generally accepted as a fact of Arab politics among Arabs and foreigners alike. The Egyptian role was based on a number of factors: a large cohesive population, central location, trained manpower, an advanced educational system and an educated elite, developed political institutions and governmental machinery, and possession of a strong military capability. Thus Cairo was chosen in the 1940s as the site of the headquarters of the League of Arab States, and an Egyptian was to be its Secretary General. Historically, too, Egypt had been in charge of the prestigious task of annually furnishing the cover of the Ka'aba in the Grand Mosque at Mecca. Nasir's charismatic leadership capitalized upon Egypt's traditional position, followed an active Arab policy and embraced the movement of radical Arab nationalism in the 1950s and 1960s. Not unnaturally the Egyptian position was challenged by other aspirant states such as Iraq and Saudi Arabia with varying degrees of success until 1967.

Lastly, inter-Arab politics has been highly penetrated by external influences. The geo-strategic location of the Arab world, its straits and international waterways, its religious and ethnic composition, are all factors that have traditionally invited foreign intervention. In the post World War II era, oil and the Arab-Israeli conflict added to the region's significance and intensified competition over it among the superpowers.

It is against this background that the war of 1967 represents a watershed in the history of Arab regional politics. The multi-faceted impact of the war is beyond the scope of this essay which confines itself to the regional consequences. As a result of the war, Israel occupied new Arab territories three times as large as its own territory. The war shattered the image of the Egyptian army, which brought home to Egypt, perhaps for the first time since 1948, a profound sense of defeat. It was even worse in that the 1948 defeat could be attributed to a corrupt king and an irresponsible political leadership, making it easy to point the finger of blame at those elements and to set the stage for the 1952 army takeover. The war of 1967, on the other hand, involved both Nasir and the Ba'th, who together represented the mainstream of revolutionary Arab politics.

In the three remaining years until his death, Nasir displayed little of the vitality and charm he had shown before. With defeat he was confronted by a dilemma clearly beyond Egypt's military and economic capabilities, that prompted an end to the war in Yemen and confirmed Saudi Arabia as "the unchallenged dominating power in the Peninsula".[6] The Khartoum conference of 1967 signalled Nasir's *compromesso storica* with Saudi Arabia and the beginning of Egypt's economic dependence on oil-producing states. Two years later King Faisal seized upon the occasion of the burning of the al-Aqsa mosque to advance his pan-Islamic message and renew his call for an Islamic summit meeting, which was held in Rabat in September 1969. The conference gave Faisal and other conservative Arab regimes the opportunity to increase their influence at the expense of the radicals.[7]

The politico-military defeat of 1967 put in motion a train of events in the Arab world and the Middle East. The death of Nasir in 1970 created a leadership vacuum and deprived Egypt of a major source of its regional prestige. Nasir's death must have relieved many Arab leaders, who perceived him as a threat even in his moment of weakness, allowed others to pursue more assertively their inter-state quarrels or their aspirations for leadership, and provided foreign powers with a greater chance for intervention in the Arab states.

The emergence of the oil-producing states, especially after 1973, introduced an important new variable in the dynamics of inter-Arab politics. The Gulf area became a new center of political gravity, regional influence and international rivalries. To the various sources of disunity among Arab states was added a new one, that between rich and poor. It affected the institutions of the Arab system, its balance of power, and the norms governing relations among its members. It also changed Arab relations with the outside world by making inter-Arab relations more inviting to external penetration.

III.   INSTITUTIONAL AND NORMATIVE DEVELOPMENTS

The rise of the oil-producing countries resulted in the 1970s in a noticeable growth in inter-Arab regional institutions, particularly economic ones. In January 1979, out of 107 inter-Arab unions, federations, organizations and companies, we find that 44 had been established before 1970 and the other 63 after; that is to say, the growth of inter-Arab institutions in the eight years following 1970 was almost one and a half times the number of those established in the preceding twenty years. In fact the three years from 1974 to 1976, after the oil embargo and the rise of oil prices, witnessed an unprecedented institutional proliferation. Out of the 63 organizations founded after 1970, 41 (64.7 percent) were established in those three years. Tables I and II summarize the growth of inter-Arab institutions.

In addition to quantitative institutional development, one notices the

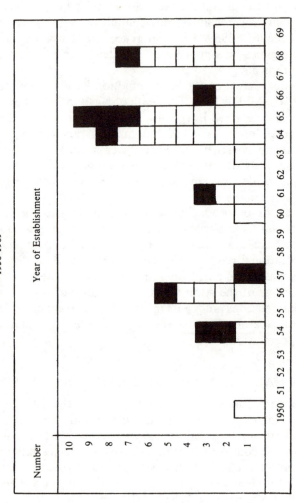

TABLE I
Development of Inter-Arab Institutions
1950-1969

Number

Year of Establishment

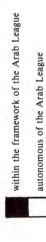

■ within the framework of the Arab League

□ autonomous of the Arab League

SOURCE: Based on a compilation of these institutions in ʿAli E. Hilal and Gamil Matar, *Al-nizam al-iqlimi al-ʿarabi* [The Arab Regional System], (Beirut: Centre for Arab Unity Studies, 1979), pp. 211-217.

TABLE II
Development of Inter-Arab Institutions
1970-1978

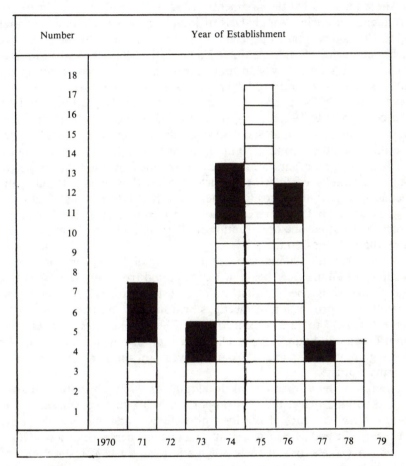

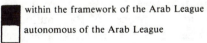 within the framework of the Arab League

autonomous of the Arab League

SOURCE: as for Table I.

increasing role of economic organizations such as joint economic ventures and Arab funds. Before 1970 there were eight inter-Arab economic organizations representing 18 percent of all existing organizations, whereas the percentage jumped to 56 percent of those founded after 1970.

These institutional developments reflect the increasing weight of oil-producing countries. An analysis of joint inter-Arab economic ventures up to 1979 shows that 55 per cent of their capital was contributed by five Arab countries—Saudi Arabia, Kuwait, the United Arab Emirates (UAE), Qatar and Libya. In most cases, the country contributing the most is the host country for the project's headquarters. Another related development is the locale of the new inter-Arab institutions. In 1970 Cairo was host to 29 Arab organizations (65 percent) whereas new ones were moving to Iraq and Saudi Arabia, thus reflecting the added weight acquired by both countries. For instance before 1970 there was not a single inter-Arab organization based in Baghdad. In the following eight years 12 established their headquarters there, thus giving Baghdad the second highest ranking position after Cairo (until the exodus of all Arab organizations in 1979 after the Egyptian-Israeli treaty). Saudi Arabia, which had hosted one organization until 1970, added eight more to occupy the third position.

A third institutional indicator is the location of Arab League meetings. A survey of all meetings held during the period from 1975 to 1978 shows that Cairo maintained its first ranking position, though it deteriorated steadily. The proportion of meetings held in Cairo decreased from 70.5 percent in 1977 to 42.2 percent in 1978. The beneficiaries were Algeria, Iraq, Libya and Saudi Arabia, all of them oil-producing countries. The ranking, however, changed from one year to another with no stable ranking status.[8]

Alongside these institutional developments, slow normative changes started to take place, the most important being the recognition of the *raison d'état* as a fact of life in Arab politics, and which has been described as the end of pan-Arabism[9] and as the emergence of a new logic of inter-Arab relations, namely pragmatic Arabism.[10] This development brought to the fore the tension that always exists in most Arab states between the norm of Arab unity and the process of state-building. The call for Arabism had different consequences; it was a legitimacy resource at the pan-Arab level, but it also helped to undermine the legitimacy of the institutions and symbols of each Arab state. Arabism departs from the one-ness of the Arab nation—that existing political boundaries are artificial importations and that political fragmentation is a colonial legacy. Arabism channelled sentiments of political allegiance from the state to a larger human and social body. Thus, while the ruling elites — even in the most recently independent states of the Gulf — embarked on the traditional exercise of state-building, the norm of Arab unity continued to exist, causing a rift between actual developments and the goals half-heartedly professed by governments. In Egypt the process implied a more inward-looking orientation, and more emphasis on "Egyptian patriotism". In other Arab countries the goal became Arab solidarity and cooperation rather than unity.[11]

Thus the new Arabism which is heavily influenced by oil-producing countries emphasizes Arab solidarity as opposed to unity, and economic cooperation based on mutual interests and maintenance of the political *status quo,* rather than the Nasirist type of nationalism that was closely associated with anti-colonialism, non-alignment, republicanism and socialism. The instruments of the new Arabism are essentially financial and diplomatic. It employs checkbook diplomacy and the power of the purse[12] for the achievement of its goals. A real problem with this brand of Arabism is its technocratic, elitist and status-quo orientation. In contrast to the Nasirist type, it does not involve the mobilization of the masses, and it operates in most instances at the level of governments.

Raison d'état and pragmatic Arabism paved the way for the relaxation of the "Arab cold war" and the increasing "de-ideologization" of inter-Arab relations which was achieved in the Khartoum Conference in 1967 and reinforced at Rabat in 1974. During most of the seventies, the politics of consensus, not confrontation, once again became the order of the day and as a result most Arab states enjoyed high degrees of stability, defined in terms of the survival of regimes. Iraq and Syria, two of the most unstable Arab polities, have been under the same regimes since 1968 and 1970 respectively. Similarly other regimes displayed the same trend, such as Algeria (1965), Sudan (1969), Libya (1969) and, of course, Egypt (1952). The regimes of Algeria, Egypt and Saudi Arabia stood the test of peaceful political succession after the deaths of strong leaders. This tendency can be attributed to a number of factors: a government's more efficient use of instruments of repression and manipulation, the exhaustion of opposition forces, the uses of oil wealth for purposes of appeasement and co-optation, and the existence of a regional and international environment that supports the *status quo.*

Mohamed Heikal was perhaps too affirmative in his contrast between *thawra* and *tharwa.* He argued that in the Arab world, power passed to new men. In the 1950s and 1960s, men who directed the course of events were officers and ideologues. Now they were joined "by a new breed of power brokers, the middlemen, the arms dealers, the wealthy merchants who flitted between East and West, between royal palaces and the offices of oil companies—men like Kamal Adham, Mahdi Tajir, Adnan Khashoggi... Oil fields began to loom far bigger in the public mind than battlefields; *tharwa* [riches] it was said, had begun its takeover from *thawra* [revolution]."[13]

Yet the argument has more than one element of truth. Wealth cut across conservative and revolutionary Arab regimes alike, creating new areas of common interest such as oil prices and foreign aid. Further, the so-called "radical" regimes, such as those of Iraq and Syria, became aware of the value of friendly relations with conservative countries. The Iraqi leadership could reconcile itself in 1975 to a *modus vivendi* with the Shah of Iran according to which the Shah withdrew his support from the Kurds. In 1976 Saddam Hussein visited Saudi Arabia and presented Crown Prince Fahd with a copy of the Qur'an. In 1978 Iraq signed an agreement with Saudi Arabia regulating bilateral security issues, and the two countries worked closely in 1979 in reaction to the Iranian revolution and its impact on the Gulf area. Further evidence for Heikal's argument is an analysis of voting behavior of Arab states in the Economic Council of the Arab League for a five year period from 1973 to 1978, the results of which show no noticeable difference between the so-called radical and conservative rich oil-producing states.[14]

The argument has its failings, however. Oil might have moderated ideological differences, but it did not make them irrelevant. Ideological orientations continue to exist in some oil-rich countries such as Algeria, Iraq and Libya. Nor should we underestimate the destabilizing and revolutionary impact of oil on the social structure in conservative Arab states. A particular case in point is the processes accompanying Saudi Arabia's increasing Arab role. The Saudis have clearly attempted to achieve Arab solidarity through "de-ideologizing" inter-Arab relations. While this is true, it is also true that the more Saudi Arabia has become involved in the complex web of Arab politics, the more radicalized she has become. As one of the most influential Arab states she is called upon to speak on behalf of the Arabs, her advice is sought, and her actions are closely watched by the rest of the Arab world, friends and foes alike. Saudi Arabia can no longer enjoy the luxury of her previous silence or ambivalence.

It is interesting to note that receding ideology has been accompanied by a growing interdependence in certain economic sectors among Arab states.[15] The most striking example of this is the demographic revolution which has moved hundreds of thousands of individuals from Egypt, Jordan, Lebanon, to the oil-producing Gulf states and Libya, a process dealt with by Saad Eddin Ibrahim in Chapter II of this volume. A particular aspect of this situation has been the reluctance of Arab ruling elites during the past decade to use the migration issue as an explicit instrument of foreign policy. For example, when Egypt and Libya were engaged in limited military operations against each other in 1977, the influx of Egyptians into Libya did not stop, and the Egyptian government saw no wisdom in preventing Egyptians from going there. Thus it seems that both sending and receiving states have sufficiently high stakes in the process not to want to subject it to the fluctuations of inter-Arab politics.

The last aspect of the new Arabism is the element of pluralistic leadership. It would seem that the days in which one country could exert its leadership over the Arab world are gone. Nowadays elements of national power are diffused rather than concentrated. Thus it seems that the Arab world has moved into an era of polycentrism, multiplicity of centers of influence, dispersion of capabilities and sharing of power. Egyptian centrality has been weakened and no other state has taken its place. Rather, a new situation has emerged in which elements of power (economic, political, moral-ideological, military...etc.) are distributed between a number of states. What has taken place is not just a change in the balance of power but a more fundamental change in the configuration and nature of state power that raises the question as to what are the elements that constitute state power and enable it to exercise influence over others. It seems that certain elements of power that previously appeared less important—that is, the power of resources or what William Bundy calls "commodity power"[16]—have moved to the center. Another issue is the relation between elements of state power. In contrast to the common belief that these elements tend to be cumulative and to reinforce each other, it seems that elements of power in the case of oil-producing countries are more separable. Saudi Arabia for example has a great deal of financial power, but is heavily lacking in almost all other elements, including the military one.[17]

These developments raise the fundamental issue of the meaning and sources of state power. For a long time, state power was conceived of as a summation of the total mobilized human and material resources of a state, eventually manifested in military capability; the ability to defend one's society has long been considered the ultimate test of state power. The fact that elements of power are separable in the Saudi case should not lead to a rethinking of the concept of power but rather to a questioning of the authenticity and durability of "Saudi power" or "commodity power". Despite its enormous wealth, the ruling elite of Saudi Arabia must feel vulnerable, both demographically and strategically, in relation to other regional states. While it is common—and undeniably true—to talk about Saudi assistance to other Arab countries as giving her political leverage and influence, it is equally possible to look at it as protection money and as a manifestation of vulnerability.[18] It is this feeling of vulnerability and uncertainty which explains Saudi Arabia's tendency to ally herself with one of the traditional powers in the area, Egypt or Iraq in particular.

Finally it goes without saying that the era of oil power will not last indefinitely. However long it may seem to those who live it, it is in fact just "a brief moment in human history".[19] Whether Saudi Arabia and other super-affluent Arab oil-producing countries will capitalize on their "moment of wealth and world attention"[20] and transform their financial wealth into more durable sources of power is yet to be seen. What can be discussed, however, is the changing balance of power in the Arab world and in particular the relationships between Egypt and Saudi Arabia.

IV.   THE CHANGING BALANCE OF POWER: THE EGYPTIAN-SAUDI SYMBIOSIS

As the balance of power shifts throughout the region, the changing roles of Egypt and Saudi Arabia are of particular interest. For many years Egypt saw herself, and was perceived by most other Arabs, as the leading Arab state, *al-shaqiqa al-kubra* (the big sister). The image rested on her advancement in education, social development and industrialization, as well as in military power. Over the years thousands of Egyptian teachers, engineers, doctors and university professors—many sent as a form of aid—served in other Arab countries and contributed positively to their development, while Arab tourists poured into Cairo and Alexandria in large numbers during the summers and Egyptian universities received thousands of Arab students every year. To this must be added Egypt's location, the charismatic leadership of Nasir and her active foreign policy after 1952.

However, during the past decade or so, Egypt's role has gradually declined as a result of a number of political and economic factors including the defeat of 1967, the death of Nasir, and most importantly a severe economic crisis and an increasing economic dependence on the outside world. In the three years from 1973 to 1975 it was reported that Egypt received $2.5 billion in Arab economic assistance.[21] The Saudi newspaper *Al-Riyadh* reported on 23 May 1979 that the total Arab aid to Egypt in the previous six years had been $13 billion, a figure which, according to Saudi governmental sources, did not include finances for Egypt's arms purchases and credit guarantees. The contribution from the Gulf states was $7 billion from Saudi Arabia, $2 billion from Kuwait, $1.9 billion from Qatar and $2.1 billion from the UAE.[22] All these factors placed serious limitations on Egypt's political ambitions and operational capabilities. President Sadat recognized the tradeoffs between economic and political goals in the conduct of foreign policy and was ready to court and praise Saudi Arabia in return for her economic assistance. He assured Saudi leaders about his intentions, coordinated his policies closely with theirs and was open to their advice.

Simultaneously with the waning of Egyptian influence came the ascendancy of the oil-producing countries and in particular Saudi Arabia, whose role reached new heights after 1973.[23] The oil embargo provided Saudi Arabia with the moral legitimacy and political credibility necessary for playing an influential role in the Arab world. To the power of wealth she added the image of political commitment to Arab causes and the desire to employ wealth in the service of these causes.

It is interesting to recall that during most of the fifties and sixties it seemed only a matter of time before the remaining Arab monarchies and traditional kingdoms would disappear under the pressure of revolutionary Arab nationalist movements. Monarchies had already toppled in Egypt, Iraq, Libya and Yemen. But oil, the defeat of 1967 and external support came to the rescue of these regimes, and during the seventies Saudi Arabia emerged as an influential state in inter-Arab politics. This influence rests basically on oil. Saudi Arabia is the world's largest exporter of oil (in 1980 producing 9.5 million barrels a day, about one third of all OPEC production) and has the largest proven oil reserves in the world (27 percent). Further, Saudi Arabia produces far more oil than is needed to cover the country's current and developmental expenditures, which results in a huge surplus of petro-dollars. In 1977 she acquired a seat on the executive board of the International Monetary Fund (IMF) as a *quid pro quo* for becoming the second largest contributor to the IMF's Witteveen Facility.

Thus in the post-1973 years Saudi Arabia, under the leadership of the late King Faisal, came to the fore of inter-Arab relations and started to translate wealth into political influence. The view of Saudi diplomacy as passive has to a great extent become a matter of the past. Examples of the more active Saudi role include her intervention, with Kuwait, to stop the Egyptian-Syrian feud over the second Sinai disengagement agreement, her part in achieving a settlement of the civil war in Lebanon, and her mediation in the Algerian-Moroccan conflict and in the Iraqi-Syrian dispute over the Euphrates waters. The Saudi position on the Camp David accords and the Egyptian-Israeli treaty will be analyzed later.

Saudi Arabia has used wealth as an instrument of her foreign policy. This has taken various shapes — economic assistance in the form of loans and gifts, arms purchasing, direct investment, deposits in banks and personal gifts to ensure the loyalty of leaders and men of influence. For example, she provided money for the confrontation states — Egypt (until 1977), Jordan, Syria and the Palestine Liberation Organization (PLO) — and in the case of Egypt committed herself further, in 1975, to pay for all Egypt's military needs for a period of five years, deposited approximately one billion dollars in the Central Bank of Egypt, and contributed to the establishment of the Gulf Organization for the Development of Egypt (GODE).[24] In return, Saudi Arabia pressed for a reduced Soviet presence in Egypt — both for her own interests and upon the request of the United States — and for more desocialization of the economy.[25]

Other examples abound. Saudi Arabia helped elements hostile to the People's Democratic Republic of Yemen (PDRY) who resided in North Yemen to launch an attack on the radical regime in September 1972. In the same year King Faisal visited five African Muslim countries. When Iraq occupied some Kuwaiti border posts in the spring of 1973, Saudi Arabia sent troops to Kuwait. In 1974 the centuries-long dispute with Abu Dhabi over the Buraimi Oasis was settled and diplomatic recognition was afterwards extended to the United Arab Emirates. Again, when the PDRY initiated an armed attack against North Yemen in February 1979, the Saudi cabinet issued a communiqué which declared that the Yemeni border dispute endangered "not only the security and stability of the Kingdom but also the countries of the Arabian Peninsula". The Saudis asked for American military assistance to North Yemen to enhance her military capability, and the United States rushed $390 million in emergency military aid. Prince ʿAbdallah, leader of the National Guard and Prince Saʿud al-Faisal, Minister of Foreign Affairs, mediated and brought the sides together at a meeting in Kuwait in March 1979.[26]

The ascendancy of the oil-producing countries creates a situation full of ironies and discrepancies. There is a discrepancy between wealth and the ability to protect it. Neither Saudi Arabia nor any other Arab oil-producing Gulf country, with the exception of Iraq, is a military power of significance. This explains the various arms deals that Saudi Arabia has concluded since 1977. Though heavily dependent on the United States as a source of arms and protection, the Saudis have also diversified their sources of armaments. The visit by King Khalid to France in 1978 opened the way for military cooperation, and the French President's visit to Saudi Arabia and the Gulf states in 1980 gave momentum to the process. Another discrepancy is between wealth and the level of social development. With the exception of Iraq and Algeria, wealth has gone to one of the most socially underdeveloped parts of the Arab world; a situation which has led to lavish consumerism and patterns of spending associated with the *nouveaux riches,* including corruption, waste and wanton profligacy. The lavish life-style of an increasing number of Saudis has come into conflict with the regime's moral source of legitimacy, Wahhabism, which insists on simple, austere and non-materialistic conduct.

A third question is the discrepancy between Saudi Arabia's regional role and her capabilities, which can be described as "status inconsistency". Apart from her immense financial wealth, Saudi Arabia does not enjoy other elements of national power. There are a number of structural limitations such as a modest population of seven million (according to the 1974 census)[27] of which over a million are Yemenis and 85 percent are illiterate; a shortage of skilled labor and professionals; and dependence on foreign manpower, of about 1.3 million Arabs and non-Arabs who constitute one half of the labor force. For a while Saudi officials pondered the impact on the stability of the Kingdom of foreign technicians and workers needed to carry out the $142 billion second development plan (1976–1980), not to mention the third five year plan (1980–1985) which will involve the expenditure of another $285 billion.

Saudi Arabia today still has almost all the characteristics of an underdeveloped country, though its GNP per capita reached $4,420 in 1976.[28] Life expectancy is low, infant mortality rates are high and there is massive illiteracy.[29] There is also a lack of sizeable military and industrial power, in contrast to Iraq and Iran, the two other major powers on the Gulf.[30] The country further faces the problems resulting from accelerated social change and the conflict between outmoded political and social structures and the impact of modern technology and education. Sources of change and/or instability are multiple. There is the historical-regional cleavage between Najd and al-Hijaz and the continuing Najdi monopoly of political power. The army has been a source of contention, and there were reports of troubles in the army in June 1969, September 1969, March 1970, October 1974 (the National Guard) and February 1979. A third source is the new professional middle class and its aspiration for more participation and political change in a country which has no constitution, no elections, no labor unions and, of course, no recognized political parties.

Thus, while bringing much needed revenue to Saudi Arabia, the massive oil wealth has also brought conflict and tensions. For a while the local elite thought that wealth and security went hand in hand. In fact money brought new contradictions, the most important being the problems of political stability which were brought into the limelight by the events of the attack on the Kaʿaba in 1979.[31] While it seems erroneous to make a rash analogy between the situation in Iran and in Saudi Arabia (because of the difference in the structure of the royal family, its direct control over governmental affairs, nature of religious organizations and the relation between religious and political authorities), one cannot dismiss a number of similarities in the nature of problems faced by both: over-ambitious development plans, increase in military expenditure, influx of foreigners and growth of new groups seeking political expression. As John Campbell suggests, "the financial rewards of successful revolution are so enormous that the temptation to an ambitious politician or military man may be uncommonly strong."[32]

Finally one feels a sense of uncertainty among the Saudi political elite about its new role. The elite has found itself almost in no time in the midst of the muddied waters of Arab politics with all its problems and its unpredicabilities. One could even argue further that the Saudis started to develop a perception of their role in response to the praise of other countries and requests for aid. In the 1970s leading Arab countries such as Egypt, Iraq and Syria vied for their friendship, bringing home to the Saudis how important their country had become.

During most of the seventies, Egypt and Saudi Arabia came very close to each other, and their relations were described as "special" by President Sadat in 1976.[33] However, the relationship was not without its sources of potential friction. The differences between levels of social and cultural development created a number of problems. Many Egyptian intellectuals felt uneasy about their country's dependence on such a conservative state and the possible social-cultural consequences resulting from it, a state of affairs that has been jokingly described by Nazih Ayubi as the "beduinization" of Egypt.[34] This was evident in Egypt's television industry whose main clients became the Gulf countries. Many television shows and programs contained a message and content that appealed to an audience essentially beyond the frontiers of Egypt. A number of Islamic groups and organizations in Egypt, including al-Azhar, received financial help from Saudi Arabia.

But most important was the feeling among Egyptians, encouraged by the government, that rich Arab states were not giving a sufficient amount of aid to their country. Sadat called for an Arab Marshall Plan to help rebuild the ravaged economy of Egypt, arguing that every drop of blood spilt in Sinai had been translated into an increase in oil prices and that the rich Arab states should therefore come to Egypt's economic aid not only because of a moral obligation to the collective Arab fight against Israel, but also to compensate Egypt for its losses. He continually reminded his audience in the oil-rich states that had it not been for Egypt and the 1973 war, oil prices would still have been under the control of the oil companies.

Thus, up till 1977 and Sadat's visit to Israel, the process of Egypt's declining role and Saudi ascendency appeared as two sides of the same coin. During this period, with America's encouragement and blessing, the Arab world came under the umbrella of a Cairo-Riyadh axis,[35] based on a new equilibrium and an alliance between Saudi money and Egyptian military power and expertise. Egypt needed Saudi financial help, and also needed her diplomatic influence over Kuwait and the UAE for the same purpose. In exchange Faisal needed Sadat to maintain stability (defined as curbing revolutionary or leftist groups) in the Arab East and to continue de-radicalizing Egypt internally as well as moving her externally closer to the United States and Western Europe.

The Saudis are aware of the ambivalence of their role and how unprepared their country is to perform it. It seems in fact that both the Saudi and most other Arab leaders have recognized the necessity of sharing influence. In the period immediately following the 1973 war there was a working alliance between Algeria, Egypt and Saudi Arabia, while in the mid-seventies the triangle involved Egypt, Saudi Arabia and Syria.[36] Both alliances came to an end: the first because of the failure of Egypt and Saudi Arabia to support Algeria in her conflict with Morocco; and the second because of Sadat's visit to Israel in 1977, the Camp David accords in 1978, and the treaty with Israel in 1979. Another relationship developed in 1979–1980 between Saudi Arabi and Iraq, a country long perceived by the Saudis as a threat.

Despite the rupture in relations between Egypt and Saudi Arabia, the interests of the two countries, under their present regimes, converge on a number of issues. Both assume a basically pro-Western and anti-Soviet diplomatic and strategic posture, and the United States has developed a "special relation" with each. The Saudi elite perceives a radicalized or highly unstable Egypt as a threat to its interests and is more likely to bail out Sadat's regime, directly or indirectly.[37] Whether Iraq can partly replace Egypt as far as Saudi Arabia is concerned is yet to be seen. The two countries have common interests in the security of the Gulf and in coordinating their policies towards the new regime in Iran.

Iraq has long been considered a potential regional power. It has most of the elements of leadership, a population base of around 12 million, a diversified economic base, oil wealth (being the second largest exporter and fourth in proven reserves) which brought her per capita GNP to $1,390 in 1976, a sizeable educated elite and an increasing military capability. Iraq's leadership potential has been constantly frustrated, however, by three factors: problems of national integration and in particular the Kurdish issue, her political instability and frequent military coups, and finally the negative image of her politics and the excessive resort to violence (one example being in August 1979 when the regime put on trial a number of high officials on charges of conspiracy; twenty-one were sentenced to death, thirty-three imprisoned and thirteen released).

During the 1970s Iraq made definite progress on the road towards becoming a "regional influential".[38] The Baᶜthist regime has maintained power since 1968, the longest rule by any Iraqi regime since the Second World War. The regime has worked for a resolution of the Kurdish problem, and military operations have virtually ceased since 1975. Border problems were settled with Iran (1975), Kuwait (1976) and Syria (1977) and oil wealth has enabled the rulers to expand their programs of economic development, provide economic assistance to a number of Arab and African countries and build a strong military capability.

Saddam Hussein, Iraq's president since July 1979, has embarked on an image-building campaign internally and externally. Iraqi television and press publicize his frequent tours all over the country and project his image as a man of the people. The Baghdad Arab Summit and Foreign Ministers' conferences of November 1978 and March 1979 placed Iraq at the center of Arab attention and she became the coordinator of anti-Sadat forces. Internationally Iraq chaired the committee that drafted the political declaration of the non-aligned conference in Havana in 1979. Baghdad was chosen as the site of the next conference in 1982, with Hussein to succeed Castro as head of the non-aligned group. These developments have enhanced Iraq's role in inter-Arab relations, and project her in a new and more positive image. However, Iraq's Arab role will largely depend on the result of the war with Iran, and her ability to transform initial military victory into political influence.

V.   REGIONAL AND GLOBAL INTERVENTION

Another significant development of the seventies is the increasing involvement in Arab affairs of non-Arab states in the region, in particular Israel and Iran.[39] The importance of this development lies in the fact that from the mid-fifties, the Arab nationalist movement, as led by Nasir, sought to prevent regional non-Arab states from playing a role in inter-Arab politics, perceiving the non-Arab states as hostile to the aspirations of the Arab nation and surrogates of Western imperialism. In the seventies, the situation altered radically.

A slow and gradual process towards the recognition of Israel was set in motion after 1967. The acceptance of UN Security Council Resolution 242, which involves the acceptance of Israel within "recognized boundaries", by Egypt, Syria (with reservations) and Jordan; the Egyptian and Jordanian answers to Ambassador Jarring's questions (1969) in which both countries registered their readiness to recognize Israel within the 1967 boundaries; Sadat's peace plan (1971) and his frequent references to a Palestinian state in the West Bank and Gaza, alongside Israel, during 1974 to 1976; the Palestinian National Council's resolution of 1975 regarding *al-sulta al-wataniyya* (national authority) which implied Palestinian acceptance of the establishment of a government in the West Bank and Gaza; and the growth of a "moderate" wing within the Palestine Liberation Organization (PLO) that publicly accepted the two-states theory of Palestine and Israel—all these are just some of the manifestations of the change.[40] Sadat's visit to Jerusalem in November 1977 represented a new development, opening the way for an Egyptian-Israeli treaty which has introduced a new variable into regional politics. The treaty isolates Egypt from the Arab world and disarms the latter from its most deterrent military power. It makes the positions of Syria and Jordan more precarious and further limits the options of their leaders. Other than the issues of occupied lands in 1967 and the political rights of the Palestinians, there remains unresolved the more important question of what role Israel will play in the region and how she will affect its balance of power.

Arab responses to Sadat's visit to Israel varied widely. Immediate response from Saudi Arabia was restrained and the government made no official comment; however, the Saudis resented not having been consulted by Sadat.[41] While Saudi Arabia did not share with other Arab states their condemnation of Sadat at this stage, she also failed to support him; thus in a sense giving him the benefit of the doubt.

The Camp David accords, however, provoked a different reaction from Saudi Arabia. Acting with unusual speed and bluntness, the Saudi cabinet rejected the agreements as being an unacceptable formula for a comprehensive peace.[42] The Saudis were critical of the agreements' failure to endorse Arab sovereignty over the West Bank and of the absence of any reference to Jerusalem, and after some hesitation joined other Arab states in approving a number of sanctions against Egypt that included suspension of Egypt's membership in the Arab League, the transfer of the League's headquarters from Cairo, and a boycott of Egyptian firms dealing with Israel.

Saudi Arabia's official position was that Egypt's accord with Israel was not a first step to a comprehensive peace. The treaty removed Egypt, the most powerful Arab state in military terms, from the confrontation with Israel and allowed the latter to dictate its terms over occupied Arab territories. In particular, the Saudis were concerned about the future of Jerusalem. Further, they believed that the treaty reduced the United States' incentive to put pressure on Israel. From their perspective, the

Arabs were left with three negative choices: tolerating continued Israeli occupation, capitulating to Israeli terms, or turning to the Soviet Union for military aid and political support. Saudi Arabia was opposed to any course of action that involved radicalization of the Arab countries, since a more radical Arab world might press Saudi Arabia with the threat of internal instability and subversion with the aim of using the leverage of oil against the United States to bring pressure on Israel. The Saudis knew quite well that the oil fields were vulnerable and could not be protected during a time of war with Israel when the latter would again enjoy American support. The fires of Ras Tanura in 1973 and Abqaiq in 1977 were a reminder that the oil could not be permanently secured against sabotage. Saudi Arabia's special relationship with and her dependency on the United States would become a serious liability in any Arab-Israeli military confrontation, by threatening her legitimacy in the Arab world and making her more vulnerable to attack by radical Arab states and Iran.

The other non-Arab regional state whose role was enhanced during the 1970s was Iran. Under the Shah Iran emerged as a regional military power and assumed the role of the "sole guardian" of the Gulf area through the prudent use of military-diplomatic leverage backed by oil wealth.[43] She became the largest buyer of arms from the United States. Military sales to Iran were valued at $524 million in 1973, $3.91 billion in 1974, $2.6 billion in 1975 and $1.3 billion in 1976 — a total of $8.3 billion in four years. In 1975 Iran bought more arms than all its neighbors put together (Iraq, Afghanistan, Pakistan, India, UAE, Qatar, Saudi Arabia, Oman, Bahrain and Kuwait).[44]

Iran followed a strategy of military build-up, territorial acquisition, active diplomacy and economic enticements. In response to a request from Sultan Qabus she sent troops to suppress the Dhofari armed uprising. In November 1971 she took over Abu Musa and the two Tumb islands which had belonged to the Sharjah and the Ras al-Khaima Emirates respectively. When she objected to the use of the term "Arab Gulf" in the name of a newly-established news agency of the Gulf states, the offending word "Arab" was promptly dropped. Cordial relations were developed with Egypt, Iraq and Syria, and Iranian troops were sent to Lebanon as part of the United Nations peace-keeping forces.

Iran acted as the "protector" of the Gulf and her military presence was felt by all the Arab Gulf states. Of particular importance strategically is the Strait of Hormuz through which oil tankers pass carrying oil to the markets of Western Europe, Japan and the United States. About 90 percent of Japan's oil supply and over 50 percent of imported oil for the United States and Western Europe travels daily through the narrow

Iranian-controlled strait. There has always been a concern about possible military operations such as mining of the strait or something similar to what happened in June 1971 near the Strait of Bab al Mandab when a rocket attack was launched against the *Coral Sea,* a Liberian tanker bound for Israel.[45]

Revolutionary Iran poses a different set of problems for the Arabs. It is generally accepted in the Arab world that the revolution marked a historic turning point and a change in the regional balance of power with far-reaching ramifications for the Gulf countries. Arab reactions ranged from profound apprehension to open elation. Saudi Arabia showed concern over both the nature of the new regime and its policy towards her. In February 1979 Kuwait and Bahrain rushed high officials to Saudi Arabia for consultation. Sadat was openly hostile to the new regime and Iraq activated her conflict with Iran, which led to a prolonged military confrontation in 1980 and 1981. At the other end of the scale the PLO was joyful; the victory of the Iranian revolution was the victory of the Palestinians, stated officials of the PLO. Arab governmental reactions were clearly a reflection less of Islamic concerns than of internal interests.

The Iranian revolution of 1979 also presents a complex array of problems for the Saudi monarchy. The Saudi ruling elite was alarmed by the revolution which they believed the United States could and should have prevented. When the Shah left Iran, the National Guard, Saudi Arabia's tribal army, was deployed around the Eastern province to seal off the oil fields. There was concern about the reactions of foreign workers, with the massive strike of Iranian oil-field workers which had been crucial for the victory of the revolution still in mind. Around 60 percent of the total labor force of the Arab-American Oil Company (ARAMCO) consists of Palestinians or Palestinian-born Jordanians.[46] Another source of concern to the Saudis was the response to the events in Iran of the Shi'ite minority in the Arab world, including some in Saudi Arabia. In December 1979 a group of Shi'ites paraded in the oil towns of the Eastern province waving pictures of Khomeini. Saudi officials were particularly concerned about Iranian-Palestinian cooperation. In February 1979 Yassir Arafat was the first "head of state" to visit Iran after the revolution. From the very beginning the revolutionary regime condemned Israel, supported the Palestinian cause and promised military and economic help.

The real threat posed by Khomeini came, however, from a different source—Islam. Saudi Arabia prides herself on being Islamic to the core. The official Saudi position states that the Qur'an is the moral and legal foundation of the state. A major factor in the legitimization of the royal family is the degree to which Islam is ingrained in Saudi culture and society. The country has no constitution, its laws and the interpretations of legal and moral behavior being supposedly based on the Qur'an. It was exactly this source of legitimization which Khomeini seriously challenged. He denounced the Saudi royal family for their un-Islamic relations with the United States, Israel's main supporter, their monarchical, undemocratic rule which is based on kingship and tribal affiliations, and their lavish lifestyle.

One example of Saudi Arabia's vulnerability to this type of attack occurred in November 1979 when a group of armed elements seized the Grand Mosque in Mecca. The raiders appeared to have mixed religious and socio-political motives and one of them stated that the revolution in Iran represented a new dawn for Islam. There were reports about similar uprisings in various parts of the kindgom other than Mecca, so that the Mecca event was not an isolated act but part of a larger operation, and arrests were made in a number of Saudi cities.

As a response to the events in Iran, the United States dispatched a dozen F15 aircraft to Saudi Arabia in January 1979, as evidence of America's policy of protecting her interests in the region. The American action was partly motivated by Saudi Arabia's expression of concern that the United States was failing to demonstrate its commitment to pro-Western regimes. American officials were particularly concerned over the situation in Saudi Arabia and Stanfield Turner, the then Director of the Central Intelligence Agency (CIA), professed to see some of the same potential for conflict in Saudi Arabia that was tormenting Iran.[47]

The final issue to be discussed in this essay is the intensification of super-power rivalries. In 1979 and 1980 a number of major developments took place in the Arab world and the Middle East: a pro-Soviet coup in Afghanistan leading eventually to the entrance of the Red Army to protect its client regime, just three hundred miles from the Gulf; armed conflict in the Horn of Africa; the murder of the two heads of State in North Yemen and PDRY and armed clashes between the two Yemens; closer relations between the Soviet Union and PDRY that led to a treaty between the two countries; the signing of a friendship treaty between the Soviet Union and Syria; the presence of Cuban military personnel and advisers in PDRY and Libya; establishment of Soviet naval facilities in Ethiopia; political turmoil in the Arab world in response to the Camp David accords; the isolation of Egypt; the dramatic fall of the Shah's regime in Iran; and war between Iran and Iraq. These events led to an American search for military bases and facilities which were set up in Kenya, Somalia, Oman and Egypt, while the United States organized the Rapid Deployment Joint Task Force, a military unit designed for speedy and mobile action in the Gulf area. She started enlarging her naval and air bases in Diego Garcia and in April 1980 the largest American fleet since the Second World War was sent to the Indian Ocean. All of this pinpoints the vital strategic importance of the Gulf area and the approaching struggle over oil, the prize of the 1980s.

During 1979 and 1980, and under the impact of the events in Iran and Afghanistan, American strategic thinking has undergone a major change. For most of the seventies the United States relied on local powers, or what was called the Nixon Doctrine, to defend Western interests. The idea was to build up local police states to act as regional guarantors of the *status quo*. The United States, in theory, had developed a "two pillar" system in the Gulf, according to which arms supplies were provided to Iran and Saudi Arabia. In practice, the United States relied only on Iran to police the area: subsequently it moved to assume a direct military role and maintain a military presence in what is called a "security framework for the region" or the Carter Doctrine.

In this context the position of Saudi Arabia is crucial because of her oil production and reserves and for her role in maintaining Western interests.[48] Saudi Arabia, a country whose name until a few years ago conjured up dramatic fantasies and adventure, has become a "vital interest" for the United States. Over the years the growth of the dependence of Western countries on the Middle East, where 60 percent of oil reserves lie, has meant that the United States has had to be more attentive to the geo-strategic implications of the region. Depending on one's position, Saudi Arabia can be seen to play the role of "moderator" or "spoiler" in OPEC by restraining other members from sharp price increases and by boosting its production to provide more oil supplies and stem price increases. In January 1979 she pushed her production up to 9.5 million barrels a day, one million more than before, to help compensate for the five million barrels of oil lost to the world market by the Iranian shutdown. As a result Saudi Arabia was producing about 20 percent of all the oil consumed by the non-communist countries.

This explains America's policy declarations about its readiness to use force to protect the flow of oil. On 25 February 1979 the Secretaries of Defence and Energy both stated that the United States would defend its vital interests in the Middle East and the Gulf with military force if necessary.[49] The same theme was repeated by President Carter in January 1980 in what came to be known as the Carter Doctrine, referred to above, and a particular reference to Saudi Arabia was made by the then Secretary of State Cyrus Vance in March 1979 when he said that "we should consider the territorial integrity and security of Saudi Arabia a matter of fundamental interest to the United States."[50]

American policy reflects the weight of the interests of the United States in the area. In addition to her traditional interests such as support for Israel, help for pro-Western regimes, containment and combatting of Soviet influence and free passage in international waterways, in the 1970s two vital and immediate interests came to the fore. First there is the oil — its price and transportation — upon which the life of her allies in Western Europe and Japan depends. Second is the recycling of the petro-dollars in the form of the sale of American technology (civilian and military), investment in United States bonds, deposits in banks, and payments for American services.

The Soviet Union has also directed a great deal of attention to the Gulf. With the erosion of Soviet influence in Egypt and the unstable relations with Iraq, the Soviet Union seems to have shifted its emphasis from the centre to the periphery of the Arab Middle East — Ethiopia, the PDRY and Afghanistan — with its eyes on the oil. Some see the Soviets as closing in on the Strait of Hormuz and encircling the oil fields from the northwest across Afghanistan and from the southwest via the Horn of Africa and the PDRY. Whether Soviet moves are part of a "master plan" or not is irrelevant. What seems really important is that the Soviets miss no chances and exploit all opportunities in their favor.

From the Soviet perspective, the United States and Western countries have up till now reaped the fruits of the Middle Eastern oil. The Soviet need of oil has been the subject of different judgements. A maximalist view estimates that the Soviet Union will be a net importer of oil by the mid-eighties, thus leading Moscow to compete with the West for access to the oil of the Gulf. A minimalist position, while not predicting such a need in the near future, would still perceive Soviet interest in Middle Eastern oil to free its own local oil for sale. In fact the Soviet Union started to purchase Algerian oil in 1967, Egyptian oil in 1969 and Iranian oil in 1972.[51] Hence it may develop the role of "strategic middle man" by simultaneously importing oil from friendly Arab states on a barter basis, and, after satisfying its own needs, exporting oil and natural gas from its reservoir of Middle Eastern and local production to Western countries.[52]

VI.   CONCLUSION

The picture that emerges from this analysis is obviously complex and less than optimistic. The objective of constitutional Arab unity is pushed to the back alleys of Arab politics for some time to come. The rise of Saudi Arabia radiates a sense of conservatism and pro-Westernism. Arabism is being overshadowed by an upsurge of political Islam and the quasi-secular revolutionary nationalist option has lost its appeal for the time being. The "Islamic revolution" in Iran undoubtedly contributed a lot to the process, and the appeal and popularity of Ayatollah Khomeini cut across diverse Arab groups, religious and secular alike.

All indications are that the Arab world is undergoing a systemic transformation. It is going through a period of change in its internal relations and balances of power, as well as in its relations with the outside world, while a new power map is emerging under the pressure of regional and external factors. There are a number of conclusions to which our analysis leads, and which seem relevant to the future of the area in the 1980s.

First there is a wide leadership vacuum, created by Egypt's declining role and the recognition of Israel that has resulted in her regional isolation. In the absence of Egypt there does not seem to be any one country or an alliance of two countries capable of leading the Arabs. What is at stake here is not hegemony or imposing one's will upon others, but rather the role of leadership in its broad sense, which goes beyond strategic-military capabilities and involves moral, human and ideological dimensions. It is ironic that Saudi Arabia, the country whose influence has been in the ascendant during the 1970s, is one of the least qualified to perform such a role. The leadership vacuum is evident in the way the Arab states handled Sadat's diplomacy towards Israel and their failure to come up with an alternative.

Secondly, the leadership vacuum is related to an increasing dependence on the West and in particular on the United States. There is a decline of "the will for independence" among most Arab regimes. The ascendancy of oil-producing countries carries with it an unmistakeably pro-Western orientation. Saudi dependence on the West, particularly the United States, is almost total, from food to arms.

Thirdly, there is the issue of the future of Arab nationalism. Inter-Arab relations have in most cases been a sub-system of a larger system, Islamic or Middle Eastern. By the early 1980s there were two Arab actors pushing to open the system to certain non-Arab regional states: Sadat for Israel and the PLO for Iran. These policies, aside from their political ramifications, raise a problem with regard to the notion of Arab nationalism defined even in the loosest terms. Arabism is challenged both by communal religious cleavages and particularistic loyalties and by the resurgence of Islamic groups and the revolutionary appeal of the Iranian revolution.

Finally, there exists a great source of instability in the area. The new Arab order of the seventies is basically created by Arab and foreign governments under the impact of oil and the feelings of frustration resulting from the inability to liberate lands occupied since 1967 or to stop Israel from further annexation moves. Simultaneously there are forces at work in the social base of these societies; alienation from and disbelief in the integrity of rulers, a widening of the social gap between rich and poor within each society and between societies, the rise of political Islam, and an increasing awareness that something must be done. But no country or group has an alternative that is convincing to others, or enough power to change the course of events.

Our present times are in some respects reminiscent of the late 1940s with the unrest and uncertainty that accompanied these years. Are we to witness a new 1952 or to experience a similar type of Nasirist leadership? The answer depends on the interaction between the two images and sets of variables referred to earlier: a new map of relations constructed by Arab governments, and supported from the outside from above; and social forces and ideas operating at the bottom of these societies.

Nothing perhaps reveals the delicate balance and the potential instability of the region more than what has been happening in Lebanon for almost a decade. The Lebanese civil war is a microcosm of Arab contradictions and tensions. It reflects, among other things, the cleavage between the Palestinians and the Arab governments which host them, the politicization of religious sentiments and the gap between rich and poor. The roles played by Iran, Israel, Egypt, Saudi Arabia and Syria represent the new balance of power in the region. Lastly the Lebanese crisis is an index of the new level of foreign intrusion in Arab affairs.

These challenges are not totally new; in fact a number of them are a repetition of such themes as Islamic resurgence and cold war politics. What is perhaps new is the piling up of these issues, their contradictory implications and consequences, and the lack of Arab leadership or strategy to stand up to the challenge.

NOTES

1. The concept of systemic transformation refers to a decisive change in one or more of the system's "defining characteristics" which affects the structure and/or the behavior of the system and is more likely to last. By the defining characteristics is meant "its main actors, the central patterns characterizing their interactions, what is considered to be within and that without the system". Richard L. Merrit, "On the Transformation of Systems", *International Political Science Review,* Vol. 1, no. 1 (1980), p. 14.

2. Saad E. Ibrahim, *Ittijahat al-raʾiy al-ʿam al-ʿarabi nahw masʾalat al-wahda* [Arab Attitudes Towards Unity], (Beirut: Centre for Arab Unity Studies, 1980), pp. 212–214.

3. Throughout the 1970s President Qaddafi of Libya was a solitary voice for Arab unity. It remains to be seen how the Libyan-Syrian unity established in September 1980 will develop.

4. On this link see Rouhallah K. Ramazani, *Beyond the Arab-Israeli Settlement: New Directions for US Policy in the Middle East* (Cambridge: Insititute for Foreign Policy Analysis, 1977).

5. See the bibliography on the subject in Ali E. Hillal and Gamil Matar, *Al-nizam al-iqlimi al-ᶜarabi* [The Arab Regional System], (Beirut: Centre for Arab Unity Studies, 1979), pp. 211–217.

6. Fred Halliday, *Arabia Without Sultans* (London: Penguin, 1974), p. 61.

7. A. M. al-Sindi, "King Faisal and Pan-Islamism", in Willard A. Beling, ed., *King Faisal and the Modernization of Saudi Arabia* (London: Croom Helm, 1980), p. 191.

8. Out of 19 cities in which meetings were held the ranking of the four states during the four years 1975 to 1978 is as follows: Algeria; 1,5,6,2: Iraq; 4,2,3,4: Libya; 2,1,8,5: and Saudi Arabia; 15,5,6,5. Tables are found in Hillal and Matar, *The Arab Regional System*, op.cit., pp. 47–50.

9. *Foreign Affairs,* Vol. 57, no. 1 (October 1978), pp. 355–373.

10. Ijaz Gilani, "Pragmatic Arabism: The Logic of Contemporary Inter-Arab Relations". Unpublished PhD thesis, Department of Political Science, Massachusetts Institute of Technology, 1977.

11. On this theme see Richard H. Pfaff, "The Functions of Arab Nationalism", *Comparative Politics,* Vol. 2, no. 2 (January 1970), pp. 147–168; P. J. Vatikiotis, *Conflict in the Middle East* (London: Allen and Unwin, 1977), pp. 14–36; and Vatikiotis on "Inter Arab Relations" in A. L. Udovitch, ed., *The Middle East: Oil, Conflict and Hope* (Lexington, Mass.: Lexington Books, 1976), pp. 145–179; also Malcolm Kerr, "The Changing Role of Arab Nationalism", *Journal of the Middle East* (Cairo), Vol. 4, (1977) , pp. 1–10.

12. John Campbell, "Oil Power in the Middle East", *Foreign Affairs,* Vol. 56, no. 1 (October 1977), p. 102.

13. Mohamed Heikal, *The Sphinx and the Commissar* (New York: Harper and Row, 1978), pp. 261–262.

14. Gamil Matar, "Al-tajarub al-wahdawiyya al-wazifiyya..." [Experiences of Functional Integration in the Arab League] in *Al-qawmiyya al-ᶜarabiyya fi al-fikr wa al-mumarasa* [Arab Nationalism in Theory and Practice], (Beirut: Centre for Arab Unity Studies, 1980), pp. 492–493.

15. Nazli Choucri, "Labor Transfers in the Arab World: Growing Interdependence in the Construction Sector" (mimeo.), Cambridge, MIT, 1979.

16. William Bundy, "Elements of Power", *Foreign Affairs,* Vol. 56, no. 1 (October 1977), p. 1–2.

17. This discrepancy should not be compared to the situation in either Japan or West Germany since in contrast to their economic might, their limited military capability is related to the post-war settlement.

18. On Saudi vulnerability see Adeed Dawisha, *Saudi Arabia's Search for Security* (Adelphi Papers No. 158), (London: International Institute for Strategic Studies, 1979); and Dale R. Tahtinen, *National Security Challenges to Saudi Arabia* (Washington D.C.: American Enterprise Institute for Public Policy Research, 1978).

19. Campbell, "Oil Power...", op.cit.

20. The statement was made about Iran. See Hudson Research Europe Ltd., *Iran: Oil, Money and the Ambitions of a Nation* (Paris, 1975), p. 30.

21. *Middle East Economic Digest,* 16 January 1976.

22. *Middle East Reporter,* 24 May 1979, p. 8.

23. See the three articles by Mohamed Heikal, entitled "The Saudi Era in Contemporary Arab History" [Arabic] in *Watan* (Kuwait), 20, 21 and 23 May 1977.

24. For a comprehensive review of Saudi economic assistance to Egypt see Jake Wien, *Saudi-Egyptian Relations: The Political and Military Dimensions of Saudi Financial Flows to Egypt* (Santa Monica, Calif.: The Rand Corp., 1980).

25. On the American connection see Edward R. Sheehan, *The Arabs, Israelis and Kissinger* (New York: Thomas Crowell, 1976), p. 65; and *The New York Times* (24 July 1972).

26. John K. Cooley, "Iran, the Palestinians and the Gulf", *Foreign Affairs,* Vol. 57, no. 4 (Summer 1979), pp. 1030–1031. On Saudi Arabia's policy see Sheikh Rustam Ali, *Saudi Arabia and Oil Diplomacy* (New York: Praeger, 1976); ʿAbd al-Ati Muhammad, *Al-diblumasiyya al-saʿudiyya fi al-khalij wa al-jazira al-ʿarabiyya* [Saudi Diplomacy in the Gulf and the Arabian Peninsula], (Cairo: Centre for Political and Strategic Studies, 1979), and the contributions of David Long and Abdullah al-Sindi in W. A. Beling, *King Faisal...,* op.cit., pp. 173–201.

27. See a detailed analysis of Saudi population in ʿUmar A. S. Rajab, "Al-kharita al-sukkaniyya lil mamlaka al-ʿarabiyya al-saʿudiyya" [The Population Map of Saudi Arabia] in *Al-Dara* (Saudi Arabia), Vol. 4, no. 2, (June 1978), pp. 166–223; and Fouad Alfarsy, *Saudi Arabia: A Case Study in Development* (London: Stacey International, 1978), p. 26.

28. The World Bank, *World Bank Atlas,* (Washington D.C., 1978).

29. Ruth L. Sivard, *World Military and Social Expenditures 1978* (Virginia: WMSE Publications, 1978). See also John Waterbury and R. El-Mallakh, *The Middle East in the Coming Decade* (New York: McGraw-Hill, 1978), pp. 30–33; and Hillal and Matar, op.cit., pp. 31, 163–176.

30. Alvin J. Cottrell and Frank Bray, *Military Forces in the Persian Gulf* (Beverly Hills, Calif.: Sage Publications, 1978), pp. 15–47.

31. Arnold Hottinger, "The Rich Arab States in Trouble", *New York Review of Books,* 15 May 1980, pp. 23–24.

32. Campbell, op.cit., p. 104.

33. *Al-Akhbar* (4 August 1976).

34. Nazih N. Ayubi, "Binaʾ al-insan al-misri al-jadid" [Building the New Egyptian Man], symposium at the Centre for Political and Strategic Studies, Cairo, published in *Al-Ahram* (9 October 1976).

35. Some argue that Sadat conceived a strategic alliance between Egypt, Iran and Saudi Arabia. See Sheehan, op.cit., p. 89; and Mohamed Heikal, "Egyptian Foreign Policy", *Foreign Affairs,* Vol. 56, No. 4 (July 1978), p. 726.

36. Fouad Ajami, "Stress in the Arab Triangle", *Foreign Policy,* Vol. 29 (Winter 1977–1978), pp. 90–108.

37. By mid-1980 there were journalistic reports about some improvement in Egyptian-Saudi relations. Sadat and the Egyptian press ceased to attack Saudi Arabia. Unofficial contacts were reported, including an estimated 68,000 Arab tourists in Cairo, almost twice as many as in the previous year, and most of them Saudis. *Time,* 8 August 1980, p. 31; *Newsweek,* 8 August 1980, p. 13.

38. Claudia Wright, "Iraq: New Power in the Middle East", *Foreign Affairs,* Vol. 58, no. 2 (Winter 1979–1980), pp. 257–277.

39. Some observers include Pakistan. See M. G. Weinbaum and G. Sem, "Pakistan Enters the Middle East", *Orbis,* Vol. 22, no. 3 (Fall 1978), pp. 595–612.

40. For further elaboration of this argument see Ali E. Hillal, *Mashruʿat al-dawla al-filistiniyya* [Projects for a Palestinian State], (Cairo: Centre for Political and Strategic Studies, 1978), pp. 89–92.

41. *The New York Times* (6 December 1977).

42. *The Washington Post* (22 September 1978).

43. Sepehr Zabih, "Iran's Policy Toward the Persian Gulf", *International Journal of Middle East Studies,* Vol. 7, no. 3 (July 1976), pp. 351, 358; and Rouhallah K. Ramazani, "Emerging Patterns of Regional Relations in Iranian Foreign Policy", *Orbis,* Vol. 18, no. 4 (Winter 1975), pp. 1043–87. For a critical analysis see Feroz Ahmed, "Iran: Subimperialism in Action", *Pakistan Forum,* Vol. III, nos. 6–7 (1973), pp. 10–20; and Fred Halliday, *Iran: Dictatorship and Development* (London: Penguin, 1979), pp. 260–284.

44. Leslie M. Prayer, "Arms and the Shah", *Foreign Policy,* Vol. 31 (Summer 1978), p. 57; and Alvin J. Cottrell and James E. Dougherty, *Iran's Quest for Security: US Arms Transfers and the Nuclear Option* (Cambridge, Mass.: Institute for Foreign Policy Analysis, 1977).

45. The most comprehensive study of the Strait is R. K. Ramazani, *The Strait of Hormuz* (Leiden: Sijthoff, 1979).

46. Cooley, "Iran, the Palestinians...", op.cit., pp. 1026, 1030–31.

47. *Baltimore Sun* (26 February 1979).

48. Bahgat Korani, "Petro-puissance et Système Mondial: Le Cas de l'Arabie Saoudite", *Etudes Internationales,* Vol. X, no. 4 (Decembre 1979), pp. 797–819.

49. *The New York Times* (26 February 1979).

50. Cooley, op.cit., p. 1032.

51. Arthur J. Klinghoffer, *The Soviet Union and International Oil Politics* (New York: Columbia University Press, 1977), pp. 116–118.

52. Lincoln Landis, *Politics and Oil: Moscow in the Middle East* (New York: Dunellen, 1973), p. 121.

XI
Implementation Capability and Political Feasibility of the Open Door Policy in Egypt

Nazîh N. M. Ayubi

I.   THE EMERGENCE OF INFITAH

The "open door policy" (*infitah*) is not just one among Egypt's public policies; it can indeed be taken to represent the country's master policy, believed by the current leadership to be the most suited for Egypt's developmental needs.

This master policy is also of significance to the whole of the Arab world, for Egypt, in spite of its economic poverty, is a country of tremendous cultural and political influence in the region and is therefore quite often the main "developmental model" for many other Arab countries, some of which have already started to show signs of taking a direction similar to that of contemporary Egypt.

The present chapter is a study of some of the political and administrative dimensions of the open door economic policy in Egypt. It aims at an analysis of the way in which this policy has developed from within the Nasirist experiment and at an examination of the organizational framework within which this master policy is being implemented, with particular emphasis on the way in which capital available to the country is being utilized. The possible outcome of this policy is also briefly considered with a view to evaluating its likely impact on development in particular and on the Egyptian society in general.

It is suggested that Egypt's open door policy represents the outcome of developments on three distinct levels: the domestic, the regional and the international. Domestically it was a result of Nasir's developmental experiment of "socialism without socialists". Nasir's experiment, which relied heavily on the managers and technocrats in a mixed economy that boasted a private as well as a public sector, was bound under the slightest hardship or the slightest temptation to turn its back to its socialist ideals and to witness an eventual *embourgeoisement* of the system, given among other things the higher rewards that managers and technocrats can obtain from private business.

Regionally, the oil boom that took place in many neighboring countries following the war of October 1973 stimulated a growing perception that Egypt might be able to benefit from some of this sudden wealth as a means of solving some of its chronic economic problems. Arab aid as well as growing remittances from Egyptians working in the oil-exporting countries was apparently too strong a temptation for the capital-hungry Egypt to brush aside. And logically, making use of such resources would have required important policy changes on the part of Egypt, involving above all a reconsideration of its radical principles, both as a guiding orientation for its internal development and as a sought-for outlook for the whole region.

Last, and in no way the least, comes the international factor. For Egypt is a strategically important country which, thanks to its situation, is so vital to any dominant super-power of the day that it can hardly be left alone to mind the difficult problems of its own "site" and to look after its eternal dilemma of imbalance between people and resources. The cold war atmosphere that made it possible for some small countries to acquire a certain degree of independence of will and even to play one super-power off against another when it came to matters such as the receipt of aid, was changing in favor of an atmosphere of semi-détente, where the super-powers looked for more certain demarcation lines and became less prepared to take serious risks. This has also happened at a time when Middle Eastern oil has become much more critically vital to the West and when a renewed strategic interest in the Middle East has therefore been taking place. This was accompanied by a growing belief among the Egyptian leadership that the United States held ninety-nine percent of the cards of the game (of the Middle East problem), and it was therefore thought necessary to achieve some sort of rapprochement and coordination with the United States and with international organizations that reflected American ideas and concepts—particularly in economic matters—such as the International Monetary Fund (IMF) and the World Bank. The reintegration of Egypt into the capitalist world market and the Western sphere of influence must also have been the goal of many external quarters, who were no doubt pleased to see this country—of great cultural and geo-political importance in the region—shift to a position of close alliance with the United States of America in particular and with the West in general.

External interest in Egypt is not only stimulated by the country's large size and influential status but also by the fact that it represents a major developmental model that calls the tune in the Arab region. It is not merely a coincidence that when Egypt was embarking on its experiment of developmental nationalism known popularly as "Arab socialism", similar radical orientations were shortly after adopted in many other Arab countries such as Syria, Iraq, Algeria, and then to a lesser extent Libya, the Sudan, and so forth. And it should not now be surprising that as Egypt opts for *infitah*, similar orientations seem to be developing in Syria, Iraq, Algeria, the Sudan, and other Arab countries.

The official presentation of the rationale for the open door policy reflects by itself the importance of these three groups of factors — the domestic, the regional and the international — as it aspires to combine Egyptian human resources with Arab money and Western know-how for the benefit of Egyptian development.

This chapter will concentrate, however, on some aspects of the first of these three factors related to *infitah*, namely the domestic factor. Whatever the regional and international variables might have been, there is no doubt that the internal dynamics of the Egyptian system were already pointing towards new directions. Most obvious of course was the change in political leadership as President Anwar al-Sadat succeeded President Gamal ʿAbd al-Nasir.

It would be a mistake, however, to attribute the transformations in Egyptian society simply to the change in leadership, for the movement of socio-economic events was already indicating a new direction under Nasir himself, starting in particular from the late sixties. And by the beginning of the seventies, the higher officials in Egypt (managerial and technocratic) were on the horns of an ideological and class dilemma. They were on the side of the order which brought them into positions of eminence, and were interested in its survival for the benefits which were to be gained from it. At the same time they were afraid of any radical change towards the uprooting of its shortcomings and towards any real "socialist transformation" since this would reduce their privileges and influence and close the gaps through which they were able illicitly to enrich themselves, thus making them less able to gain materially and to influence politically.[1]

Thus the bureaucratic elite was at the crossroads. The main trend among them continued to favor the public sector which provided them with rewarding and distinguished positions that they were unlikely to have enjoyed in another system. A sizeable and growing group, however, preferred a full return to a capitalist economy, while the middle group desired the best of both worlds, tending to think of their public sector posts as stepping stones to private business. By utilizing capital accumulated from their relatively high incomes, and by benefiting from contacts developed in both the public and the private sectors, they hoped to set up their own businesses at, or even before, retirement (i.e. *pantouflage* in colloquial French) and indeed many of them have done so.

It appears, however, that the results of the October war in 1973 tilted the balance in favor of those who defended a return to private enterprise. Early in 1974 there was some talk in the press about selling the public sector, or at least 49 percent of its shares, to private companies. The prospect of heavy investment in Egypt by the oil-rich Arab states, by the United States and Japan and by European countries, has tempted the technocrats to depart from their previous support of a wide-ranging public sector. In the previous conditions of low capitalist investment, the majority of bureaucrats favored a wide public sector (but preferably devoid of any socialist content and rather similar to the Turkish model) that would enable them to hold relatively privileged positions unattainable elsewhere. Now, however, a larger proportion would opt for an increasingly capitalist system, which they assume will bring them greater gains either as salaried managers or as investing businessmen.

History may thus be repeating itself, in a new cycle or pendulum swing, and in a fashion similar to that which occurred after the collapse of Muhammad ʿAli's monopoly system; except that instead of the emergence, as in the latter case, of government employees as landowners, what would now emerge would be a new business class from within the community of public managers and technocrats.

The emergence from *within* the bureaucracy of an entrepreneurial elite is by no means an unknown practice in other countries, although the scale on which it can occur is likely to distinguish the Egyptian experience. Up to the early seventies, the top bureaucrats, especially those of the technocratic type, represented a privileged elite in the Egyptian society, even though they did not form a ruling or a socio-economic class in any sense; economically they were not the wealthiest group in a society where the national bourgeoisie still played an important role, while politically they remained subservient both to the leader and to the army. What is occurring at present, however, is that the managerial and technocratic elite, together with the middle- and the petit-bourgeoisie, who in the final analysis were the main beneficiaries of most of the changes that took place in the fifties and the sixties, are now in revolt against the very socialist ideas and étatist policies that led to their eminence and their flourishing.

Politically the situation of relative bureaucratic monopoly that existed in the fifties and sixties is now changing under the open door policy, and new groupings and alliances are increasingly being formed outside the public establishment as the society moves from the phase of being a bureaucratic polity to that of being an oligarchic polity.[2]

Interrelationships betwen the public and the private sectors have indeed been actively developing during the last two decades and are now acquiring some new dimensions. The model example in this respect is the case of Engineer ʿUthman Ahmad ʿUthman, whose prominence started under Nasir.[3] Probably among the richest handful of individuals in Egypt, ʿUthman's Arab Contractors Company employs tens of thousands of engineers, technicians, administrators and workers, has branches in several Arab countries, and has since the beginning of the seventies undertaken gigantic projects in Egypt and eight other countries. After the 1973 war, ʿUthman emerged with great political stature as Minister of Reconstruction, while continuing partly to own and personally manage his companies. Now he is officially a Deputy Prime Minister, and is politically very influential. He is member of parliament for Ismaʿiliyya, and is the head of the important engineers' syndicate. He is one of the main confidants of the President and his son is married to Sadat's daughter. When ʿUthman's expanding empire was criticized in 1978, the President went out of his way in his subsequent speech to defend at great length the "patriotic" qualities of Egypt's millionaire, and to confirm that the involvement of public personalities in dubious financial dealings was not as widespread as the press maintained.[4]

This may be an exceptionally striking example, but personal observations confirm that this interchangeability between the public and the private sectors is becoming a familiar pattern. And as, in the process, more and more members of the large community of official-technocrats tie their futures to that of the private sector, it becomes clear that the same people who gained influence under the banners of socialism and the slogans of a meritocracy would turn against the very regime that brought them to eminence, as the elite establishes itself in the society and integrates many of its members with private business and with the more conventional elements of the society.

Given this, it may not be inaccurate to suggest that much about the direction of Egypt's political development will be determined, among other things, by the legal, economic and personal links which are now being established between a public sector that is almost dominated but mostly hated by the technocrats, and a re-emerging private sector (both local and foreign) that can present the technocrats with alternative opportunities for socio-economic advancement. And these linkages have certainly acquired particular importance with the escalation in measures for increased economic liberalization that occurred in Egypt in the seventies. Furthermore, there is much to suggest that most linkages between the public sector and private business since the seventies are leading to the growth of the latter literally at the expense of the former.

It is no secret that ex-army officers and high government officials have been consistently moving into private business since the late sixties and early seventies. One writer could count among the prominent businessmen in 1976 (mainly in the area of commercial agency work, import-export and contracts) two ex-premiers, twenty-two ex-ministers, dozens of ex-chairmen of public enterprises, undersecretaries of state and governors, and he confirms that "most of the 'big deals' are done by these people."[5] In another case, one of the officials of the General Investment Authority was found to hold the following posts in foreign business, in addition to his public post: member of the board of directors of Bank Misr-Iran, member of the board of the Egypt Company for Tourist Development, member of the board of the Egyptian-American Bank, and delegate member of the Abu Dhabi Investment Company.[6] Using the network of contacts and affiliations which they acquire in public office (and sometimes private funds also accumulated directly or indirectly through their official positions), they normally start their own so-called trade agencies, import-export firms, or consultation bureaux.

Quite frequently, and this is particularly alarming, these officials cannot wait until they retire or resign from their jobs, but will start to engage themselves in private business of the same nature (i.e. competing) as that of their public office, sometimes exploiting the facilities and personnel of the public sector for the promotion of their personal projects in Egypt or outside it. Such cases are numerous and I will mention only a few typical practices to illustrate the nature of the phenomenon, chosen from among the cases documented in the confidential reports of the Administrative Control Authority (ACA) during the five-year period from 1972 to 1977.[7]

For example, a number of members and chairmen of boards of directors were found to be carrying out activities which represented a major part of the jurisdiction of the public companies in which they were employed; or they were forming similar firms in Egypt or in other countries that were in direct competition with the activities of the public companies which employed them. Some high personnel were found to be utilizing the means of transport and communication of the public sector as well as its staff—some of whom were given leave of absence for the purpose—in order to promote and market their own private products.

Employees of the public sector often arrange for the public companies to be supplied with equipment and materials by the companies that they privately own and manage (sometimes using the names of their relatives as illusionary owners of these private firms). The prices in such cases are usually higher and the quality lower than could otherwise be obtained on a free and equitable basis. Or else they compete, illegally and unfairly through their own enterprises, with the public companies that employ them in exporting or importing the same goods, sometimes to or from the same countries, and usually gaining more or paying less than the public sector companies would be able to.

Another very important way in which private business exploits the public sector is achieved through arranging for the public sector to act as a marketing agent for certain private companies in relation to the public sector or the government. This gives the appearance of dealings between different units in the public sector (one selling a particular product to the other) while it is in reality a fraudulent practice that always involves exaggerated prices and unwarranted commissions for the intermediary public company and which usually involves, in the process, aspects of bribery and corruption. The ACA has been investigating many cases of this sort. For example (and of these there are many), the Misr Import-Export Company (public sector) was found in 1976 and 1977 to be marketing (for a commisison of 1 to 5 percent) engines, cranes, tractors and vehicles to other public companies, public organizations and also to the Alexandria Governorate, for the benefit of private sector suppliers who were sometimes selling this equipment for up to 400 percent of the normal prices. To add to the exploitation, one private supplier was found to have produced two different sets of pricing documents for his vehicles and equipment: a set with reduced prices for the Customs Department, to avoid having to pay high taxes, and another set with exaggerated prices for the Misr Company which then marketed these items for him with other units of the public sector.

It was the capital accumulation by such people and in such ways that led, among other things, to the movement towards, and eventually the formal adoption of the open door policy in 1974, as embodied in the October Paper of the same year, and more specifically in the Investment Law (No. 43 for 1974, concerning the Investment of Arab and Foreign Funds and the Free Zones).[8]

For a number of years, however, the political explanation given to the *infitah* policy remained rather contradictory. On the one hand, President Anwar al-Sadat had defined the policy's aim as being "to inject the veins of the national economy with more production". Mr. Mamduh Salim, the then Prime Minister, had also said that *infitah* was an economic policy aiming at developing the society through releasing its productive energies, emphasizing that this policy did not deviate from the general philosophy of the system nor from the principles of equal distribution; and that it would not weaken the public sector or reduce the importance of national comprehensive planning. Yet the same person was also to remark that the rule was to allow investment and that specifying any "conditions" would mean restriction, each "restriction" meaning "closing up" — which was not conducive, he maintained, to the achievement of a "free economy".[9] Then a few years later, President Sadat was to make things clearer by assuring the chambers of commerce in August 1979 that private enterprise and capitalist endeavor were "no longer a crime" in Egypt.[10] So it seems that after some years of ambiguity *infitah* has eventually been sanctioned as a policy for total economic liberalization, and not simply as a means of securing increased financial resources for the national economy.

In defending the open door policy, supporters of *infitah* have suggested that concentration on economic and technological dealings with the socialist countries had been harmful for Egypt, in view of the defects of the bilateral trade agreements system (i.e. the importation of unwanted commodities, etc.), and because of what is believed to be the technological underdevelopment of these countries compared with the capitalist West. Others, however, commented that what Egypt needed most for her development may not necessarily be the most modern and ultra-sophisticated of technologies. And several people have complained that, despite the declared slogans of free trade, they have not been allowed to import from or export to markets of the Communist countries which for one reason or another they have found to be more rewarding or convenient.[11]

In their enthusiasm for the open door policy, supporters of *infitah* were inclined to make light of the idea that this policy might eventually act against the full independence of the national economy, or badly damage the national industries or contradict the requirements of national planning. As one member of the parliament put it

> ... there is no need to fear the domination of foreign capital, for the national authority in Egypt is derived from the people and supported by the people... We are not at all apprehensive about foreign economic containment of our economy; every fear at this point may indeed harm the national economy for it would lead to the disinclination of Arab and foreign capital to enter Egypt...[12]

While some critics thought that foreign investments should be encouraged only in certain areas and within certain limits to be decided in view of the goals and activities of the national development plan, others believed that for *infitah* to work, it had to be full and complete. As another member of parliament put it, "...unless the investor feels that he is using his money freely and without restriction, no money will enter this country for investment; the open door has to be total."[13]

In short, therefore, it can be said that the view was growing that the way to surmount any difficulties that *infitah* was facing, or would face, would be to open up even further and create an overall environment of freedom, stability and certainty that would encourage capital to invest. And it was this concept of the totally open door, and not only one that was merely "ajar", to quote a member of parliament, which was eventually to dominate resulting, among other things, in shifting the emphasis of *infitah* from a means of securing increased capital and improved technology for the purpose of invigorating the productive capacity of the economy to a general mood of "commercialism" in the society characterized by an unmistakeable "consumerist" drive.

Supporters of the open door policy were also inclined to belittle the possible social costs of that policy in terms of increasing income differentials and solidifying social stratification. Social justice—as well as increasing revenue for the state—would be guaranteed, it was suggested, through taxation measures. Others, however, have warned that the Egyptian taxation system was far from efficient in mobilizing the economic surplus in general, and that it has always been particularly hard on wage and salary earners while being exceptionally lax with merchants and businessmen. It is very active when it comes to imposing indirect taxes, which normally have a considerable inegalitarian impact on lower income groups, but rather ineffective as regards direct taxation except, of course, for that aimed at the salaried strata.[14]

Now, having very briefly presented some of the socio-political factors that led to the adoption of *infitah* as the master policy in Egypt, we turn to a consideration of just how effective the implementation of that policy has been in practice, and to an examination of the socio-political impact of applying that policy on the Egyptian economy and polity. Although many people did oppose *infitah* in principle, there were certainly a great many who adopted a "wait and see" approach to find out how that policy would fare in practice. And it was only when foreign capital proved to be far less forthcoming than expected, and when application showed how very inefficient the institutions were when it came to the utilization of the capital that did arrive, that more and more people started to question the suitability of this policy for Egypt's present conditions.

And as is the case when studying many other Egyptian problems, one finds that the public bureaucracy is there to take the blame in quite a few respects. The dominant role of the government in the Egyptian political culture is a well-known fact. Therefore to centralize or to de-centralize in Egypt will involve an important role for the state; and it is in the sense of the governing Establishment that we use the term bureaucracy in this respect. Here again we find that the bureaucracy that was so severely criticized for being a hindrance to socialist transformation in the sixties is now standing in many a fashion in the way of capitalist endeavor. So much so, in fact, that some leftist Egyptians have jokingly attached to the Egyptian bureaucracy at present a "historical patriotic" role in preventing—or at least slowing down—the overtaking of the Egyptian economy by world capitalism.

But in evaluating the role of the Egyptian bureaucracy we continue to keep in mind the requirements of Egyptian development. Like most bureaucracies, the Egyptian bureaucracy is slow to learn and to adjust. And hence we observe some of the contradictory aspects that are to be found these days: at a time of de-socialization of the political orientation, the Egyptian bureaucracy seems to have had enough time to learn how to get to grips with the problems of managing public enterprises to the extent that the public sector (looked at from within) does not appear now to be really badly run! It is dealing with new varieties of technology and new types of organization related to *infitah* that seem to be causing the bureaucratic establishment the largest number of problems at present.

Nothing better illustrates the limited effectiveness of the Egyptian bureaucracy than the way in which it processes—or indeed even attracts—foreign capital. At a time when the Egyptian establishment has made it clear that its intention is to encourage foreign capital to come, and has offered it rights and facilities that have been considered excessive by many a patriotic zealot, "bureaucratic complications" remain the basic complaint of most foreign investors and aid donors, and the utilization of capital for any but consumer (and mainly food-related) purposes remains very low indeed.

The present situation is in fact characterized by a weird contradiction whereby there is a reasonable amount of money circulating (from aid as well as from remittances), but there is only a limited capacity to utilize this money for productive purposes that may add to social capital accumulation. It is suggested that this commercialism, whereby money may change hands but little production is carried out, is becoming the dominant economic activity. This will, of course, ease some of the bottlenecks, create an appearance of freedom and prosperity, and help enrich some segments of the society. But we maintain that as real development remains slow, more problems are likely to ensue. The public sector and the national industries are bound to suffer. Corruption would also grow, work ethics would decline, and the precious links between financial reward and productive achievement would become distorted beyond recognition. The lack of productivity combined with rabid commercialism would promote income differentials and a sense of relative deprivation, which would in turn create an atmosphere that is most conducive to socio-political unrest.

The main theme that we are arguing in this chapter is that it is the utilization of money (both in the sense of how it is used and what for), more than the acquisition of money, which determines the developmental path of any society. Egypt is indeed in need of huge amounts of money for its development, yet it is the uses and abuses of that money that matters most; and indeed, we suggest, some utilization of money may be more costly from a socio-political point of view than not having that money at all.

But before we continue any further with our thesis, let us consider first in some detail the way in which Egyptian institutions with their present characteristics, abilities and disabilities, are coping with the requirements of translating the targets of the *infitah* policy into reality in the field of capital utilization.

II. IMPLEMENTING INFITAH: CAPITAL UTILIZATION IN CONTEMPORARY EGYPT

Summarized in one phrase, the open door policy is about the importance of capital for development; or so it has been basically presented and justified. However, the amount of capital that has so far been coming into Egypt has in no way been up to expectations, let alone being sufficient for meeting the country's developmental needs. Three or four years after the October War, Arab aid had already started to dwindle and American aid, which began to come in significant amounts only after 1975, was not yet showing any concrete impact on economic life. Foreign investment was also hesitant in coming, and once it arrived it needed to spend rather a long time in dealings with Egyptian institutions before many of its projects were actually able to start functioning. Some personal Arab money flowed into the country immediately after the October War and tended to be concentrated in the fields of housing and entertainment. Conspicuous residences by the Nile and the Mediterranean, and a taste for cheap theatre and cabaret entertainment, especially around the notorious Pyramids Road, were actively contributing to the rise in housing prices, and showing a negative impact on the arts and on intellectual life in the country in a way that might have threatened a kind of "beduinization of the Egyptian culture".[15] But even this money was soon to decline as the Arabs started to discover equally good places for entertainment and residence outside Egypt (with England, Greece and Spain being the most favored), and as Egypt's separate settlement with Israel led to its alienation from the majority of Arabs.

The purpose of this section is not to examine whether Egypt has, and will have, enough for its economic needs, but rather to consider how it utilizes whatever capital it manages to acquire. We will therefore survey

TABLE I
Egypt's Major Aid Sources, 1978
($ million)

Source	Allocated Aid
United States	970
World Bank	270
I. M. F.	240
Japan	184
Arab States	166
West Germany	163

SOURCE: *Middle East Economic Digest* (5 January 1979), p. 5; (23 February 1979), p. 24.

briefly the various types of capital transfers that Egypt receives, mainly in the form of aid and investment, and analyze how Egypt manages to utilize this capital through her various institutions.

The main hypothesis is that it is not only the availability of capital that matters, but also the ability to absorb this capital and to utilize it at the right time, in the right way, and, of course, for the right purpose.

A. FOREIGN AID FOR EGYPT

How much aid does Egypt receive, and who gives it? This is not an easy question to answer, given the sketchy and often inconsistent nature of the available data, especially that which is provided by the Egyptian authorities. Yet this is very important for understanding a great deal about the actual implementation, as well as the prospective feasibility, of Egypt's current economic policies.

If we consider the situation in 1978, for example (see Table I), we find that Egypt received authorized grants, facilitated loans and standby credits from various sources. However, in the years preceding 1978, Arab grant assistance was of paramount importance in financing the external deficit of Egypt. Arab financial grants to compensate for the loss of revenue from the Suez Canal were a regular feature of Egyptian finance between the two Arab-Israeli wars of 1967 and 1973. Under this arrangement, about $310 million were to be provided to Egypt annually by Saudi Arabia, Kuwait and Libya.

The October War in 1973 and the oil boom that followed it have led to an outstanding multiplication of grant assistance to Egypt, mainly from Arab sources. It increased to $725 million in 1973, reached a peak of $1,264 million in 1974 and $988 million in 1975, and was $625 million in 1976. As Table II indicates, the bulk of these grants was provided by

TABLE II
Grant Assistance to Egypt, 1973-76
($ million)
(military assistance not included)

Country	1973	1974	1975	1976
Saudi Arabia	353	572	373	377
Kuwait	202	288	406	69
Libya	170	—	—	—
Iraq	—	—	43	—
Qatar	—	24	64	25
U.A.E.	—	103	77	150
Other countries*	—	277	25	4
TOTAL	725	1,264	988	625

* may include Arab countries specified above

SOURCE: World Bank *Arab Republic of Egypt: Economic Management in a Period of Transition* (in 6 vols.: Report No. 1815-EGT), Vol. IV, 1978.

Saudi Arabia and Kuwait. Libya was a substantial contributor until 1973 when its political differences with Egypt resulted in a termination of assistance. Other major donors of grant assistance since the October War have been the United Arab Emirates (particularly Abu Dhabi) and Qatar.

Although the post-October 1973 period was characterized by the open door policies, accounts from the period show a negative capital flow into Egypt from both Eastern and Western countries, if one excludes the special loan of $320 million provided by Iran in 1975. This was a result of several factors: the slowing down of assistance from the Socialist countries; heavy repayments due to the same bloc; the long period (between 1967 and 1973) when almost no new commitments of medium and long-term assistance were made which led to no disbursements in 1974 and 1975; the accumulation in repayments due to Western countries in the period under review; and the difficulty of prompt disbursement of the new Western commitments of 1974 and 1975.[16]

The deterioration in Egypt's economic relations with the Soviet Union is reflected in the slowing down of disbursements under Economic Technical Cooperation Agreements, the almost complete withholding of supplier's credits and the heavy repayments on these two accounts. As a result, net capital movements from the Soviet Union to Egypt changed from a positive inflow of about $38 million in 1972 to net outflows of

TABLE III
Net Capital Movements: Egypt and the USSR, 1972-76
($ million)

Category	1972	1973	1974	1975	1976
Balance on Economic and Technical Agreement Accounts	50	63	− 183	141	− 175
Balance on Suppliers' Credit Accounts	− 12	− 53	− 45	− 26	27
Overall Balance	38	10	− 228	− 67	− 148

SOURCE: As for Table II.

about $228 million in 1974, about $67 million in 1975, and about $148 million in 1976 (as Table III shows).

Western economic assistance (particularly from the United States) and aid from multi-lateral organizations reached significant proportions in 1975 and 1976 in terms of commitments, but disbursements continued to be slow (except for the program aid component of United States assistance), as Table IV illustrates.

In the meantime, Arab deposits with the Central Bank of Egypt in 1975 were, in conjunction with Arab grants, the most important aspect of Egypt's capital accounts. These deposits consisted of $600 million of deposits by Saudi Arabia, $600 million by Kuwait, $150 million by the United Arab Emirates, and $50 million by Qatar. A further $180 million of cash loans were also guaranteed by Arab governments. During 1976 deposits from Kuwait amounted to $200 million, from Qatar $25 million, and from the UAE to $50 million. By 1979, Arab deposits in Egyptian banks were estimated by independent sources at over one billion dollars from Kuwait, $900 million from Saudi Arabia, and $350 million from the UAE, and the total of Arab deposits was estimated at some $4 billion.

Given Egypt's chronic problems of finance and liquidity, the massive aid flows from Arab countries were still insufficient to cover the external deficit in 1973, 1974 and again in 1976. Egypt accordingly resorted to short-term borrowing in the form of banking facilities — $36 million (net) in 1973, $583 million (net) in 1974, and $227 million (net in 1976 — a self-perpetuating practice that carries with it problems of great magnitude.[17]

TABLE IV
Medium and Long Term Loans: Commitments From Western Countries,
Iran and Multilateral Institutions*, 1973-76
($ million)

Countries/Institutions	1973	1974	1975	1976
World Bank	. .	85.0	77.0	157.0
I D A	74.9	55.0	55.0	40.0
Denmark	. .	9.0	. .	6.6
France	. .	40.0	81.4	113.0
West Germany	59.1	83.1	99.8	91.4
Japan	11.3	22.7	178.6	39.2
Netherlands	. .	. .	4.4	17.4
United Kingdom	24.5	. .	. .	. .
United States	. .	. .	401.0	694.0
Iran	. .	. .	320.0	. .

* excludes Suppliers' Credits

SOURCE: As for Table II.

Who Gives What?

Let us now look at the main type of aid offered by every donor country or group of countries.

American aid to Egypt is of basically two types: aid offered under PL480 which tends to be used for the importation of foods and commodities and to a lesser extent the payment of salaries and benefits; and aid supplied by the United States Agency for International Development (AID), of which a fair proportion goes to industrial investment, technical assistance, and rural development. The amounts of these two types of aid as of January 1978 are given in the following table (Table V).

From December 1975 to June 1979, seven agreements were signed with the United States involving loans to the value of $215.9 million, to be used for industrial investment and development. A large number of industrial enterprises have already begun to, or will eventually benefit from such loans, especially in the area of foods, textiles and metallurgical and engineering industries.[18]

West European loans have been allocated to a whole variety of projects in the area of iron and steel, machinery, chemicals, dairies, cement, textiles, fertilizers, aluminium, sugar, television sets, food processing and many others.

TABLE V
US Economic Aid to Egypt, 1975-77
($ million: US fiscal years)

	1975		1976		1977		1978	
	Committed	Spent	Committed	Spent	Committed	Spent	Committed	Spent
A I D	261.3	174.9	794.9	120.8	700.0	108.0	1756.2	403.7
PL 480	109.3	109.3	186.5	186.5	209.6	193.1	505.4	488.9
TOTAL	370.6	284.2	981.4	307.8	909.6	301.1	2261.6	893.1

SOURCE: *Middle East Economic Digest*, "Egypt: Special Report", May 1978, p. 4.

In addition to aid donated by states, among which the United States is by far the most prominent, Egypt also receives financial aid from international as well as from Arab financing institutions: the following table (Table VI) shows the total amount of aid obtained from each of these sources until September 1978 in most cases, or until June 1979 in some cases.

Let us first consider the uses for which aid from the international financing agencies was allocated. Most of the loans and facilities of the International Monetary Fund (IMF) were used for covering the deficit in the country's economy and for supporting its liquidity. The World Bank (IBRD) on the other hand has allocated money ($ million) for the following purposes: re-opening the Suez canal ($50m); imports from agriculture and industry ($35m); the expansion of the Tora Cement Factory ($40m); development of Egyptian railways ($37m); development of Alexandria Port ($45m); a second project for Covered Drainage in Upper Egypt ($10m); textile development projects ($52m); the Alexandria Water Utility ($56m); development projects for vegetables and fruit ($50m); industrial imports ($70m); a second project for Delta Drainage ($39m); electrification of the countryside ($48m); Iron and Steel Development ($2.5m); widening of the Suez Canal ($100m); the Industrial Development Bank ($40m).

The International Development Agency (IDA), affiliated to the World Bank, has also allocated funds ($ million) for the following purposes: the Delta Covered Drainage Scheme ($26m); development of Egyptian Railways ($30m); Covered Drainage Project for Upper Egypt ($36m); the Industrial Development Bank ($15m); development of ginning works ($18.5m); housing ($5m); the Talkha Urea Fertilizers Plant ($20m); industrial and agricultural imports ($35m); development of communica-

TABLE VI
Financial Aid to Egypt from International
and Arab Funds, 1978-79
($ million)

International Financing Agencies	
I M F (1 September 1978)	2.023.0
World Bank (30 June 1979)	1.184.0
I D A (1 September 1978)	433.5
TOTAL	3.640.5
Arab Financing Funds	(30 June 1979)
The Arab Development Fund	230.6
The Kuwaiti Fund	217.9
The Saudi Fund	214.2
The Abu Dhabi Fund	99.0
The African Development Bank	32.8
The OPEC Fund	23.2
The Arab Monetary Fund	17.7
The Islamic Development Bank	12.0
The Arab Libyan Bank	10.1
TOTAL	834.2
GRAND TOTAL	4.474.7

SOURCE: Ministry of the Economy and Economic Cooperation, 1978 and 1979, (internal memoranda).

tions systems ($30m); a second project for the Industrial Development Bank ($25m); a second project for drainage in Upper Egypt ($40m); education and training ($25m); a second drainage project for the Delta ($27m); drinking water studies ($2m); a second communications project ($53m); agricultural development ($32m); settlement and construction ($14m); a second education and training project ($40m); and the Abu Tartur Phosphates project ($11m).

Aid provided by Arab financing and development funds (which, it should be remembered, does not include government grants and loans), was also put to a variety of development purposes, such as the re-opening of the Suez Canal, the development of a number of plants for fertilizers, cement, natural gas, and so on, as well as the improvement of the water, electricity and sewerage systems.

B. FOREIGN INVESTMENT IN EGYPT

Let us now examine Arab and foreign investments in Egypt that were pursued under the new investment laws of the open door policy. Until the end of 1978, 591 projects were approved by the General Authority for Investment and Free Zones (GAIFZ), involving total capital commitments amounting to LE1664 million, of which 41 percent was in Egyptian currency and 59 percent was in foreign currencies. Investment expenditures involved in these projects amounts to LE3045 million, of which 34 percent are in local currency and 66 percent in foreign currencies. Of the capital of all projects approved, 65 percent goes to the projects in the distribution and services sectors (20 percent for distribution and 45 percent for services). Indeed, tourism, housing, banking and investment companies are together responsible for as much as 55 percent of the total investment. On the other hand, only 35 percent of the capital is allocated for commodity sectors, with agriculture receiving a very low 6 percent of the total.[19]

If we rank the investment activities in descending order according to the amount of capital allocated for each area of activity, the following ranking, as illustrated in Table VII, is obtained. It is important however, to observe that of the total production of all projects which are already functioning, banks are responsible for as much as 78 percent of the total value. Metallurgic industries represent 6 percent of the value of total production, chemical industries 4 percent, and housing 2 percent.[20] From this we can realize the dominant impact of banking activities on the output side of *infitah* investments. It should also be remembered at this point that as much as 72 percent of the capital of such banks is foreign (Table VII) — indeed banking witnesses the highest ratio of foreign-to-Egyptian capital among all branches of projects approved after *infitah*. It is no wonder therefore that the rapid and disproportionate expansion of foreign banking activities in Egypt since the open door policy has, given the vital role banks play in any national economy, aroused doubts and suspicions among a sizeable number of observers.

Another benefit attributed to *infitah* investments involves the employment opportunities that they may represent. About 13,500 Egyptians were employed in the functioning *infitah* projects by the end of 1978. The average annual wage of the Egyptian employee in the functioning approved projects was estimated at LE826.00, compared to an average of LE243.00 in the projects listed in the national development plan. The Egyptian employed in an *infitah* company receives therefore on average 340 percent of the average wage received by an Egyptian working in the public or private sectors. Within these averages there are, of course, very

TABLE VII
Ranking of Foreign Investment Activities Approved Until 31 December 1978

Rank	Sector/Activity	% Capital to Total Investments	% Local Capital	% Foreign Capital
First	Tourism	22%	48%	52%
2nd	Housing	13%	53%	47%
3rd	Investment Companies	11%	32%	68%
4th	Education, Training & Services	8%	2%	98%
5th	Banking	8%	28%	72%
6th	Agriculture & Husbandry	6%	51%	49%
7th	Weaving & Textiles	9%	59%	41%
8th	Engineering Industries	5%	40%	60%
9th	Building Materials (cement, bricks, tiles, etc.)	5%	73%	37%
10th	Chemical Industries	5%	30%	70%
11th	Health & Hospitals	2%	43%	57%
12th	Contracting & Consultation	2%	34%	66%
13th	Transport & Communication	2%	12%	88%
14th	Metallic Industries	2%	38%	62%
15th	Food Industry	2%	56%	44%
16th	Medical Industries	1%	40%	60%

SOURCE: GAIFZ, *Taqrir ʿan mashruʿat al-istithmar...* [Report on Investment Projects up to 31 December 1978], (Cairo, 1979), pp. 8-15.

important differences depending, among other things, on the sector in which the worker is employed. So, while the yearly average income of the Egyptian working in the construction sector is LE2833.00 and of the Egyptian working in the banking sector is LE2048.00, the average wage of an Egyptian employed in the food industry is a miserable LE54.00 a year. As for productivity, it was claimed that the average production of the Egyptian worker in *infitah* companies is equivalent to 821.7 percent of the average productivity of the Egyptian worker in the economy at large,[21] but no indication was given as to how this productivity was measured in the two cases.

Who Invests in What?

The question now concerns the areas of investment that tend to be favored by investors from particular countries or groups of countries.[22]

Arab capital, which amounted to LE270 million by the end of 1978, represented 16 percent of the total value of investments. It tended to concentrate on the following fields, in descending order: investment companies (28.5 percent of Arab capital); housing (16 percent); chemical industries (9 percent); banking (8.5 percent); tourism (8 percent); engineering industries (6 percent). Over 40 percent of all capital invested in metallurgic industries and of all investments in investment companies was provided by Arab sources.

American capital committed until the end of 1978 amounted to LE168.6 million, representing about 10 percent of total investment. American capital was directed, in descending order, to the following areas: education, training and services (72 percent of total American investments); banking (7 percent); agriculture and husbandry (6 percent); engineering industries (3 percent); weaving and textile industries (3 percent). American capital represented as much as 92 percent of all capital allocated for education, training and services. In general the number of scholarships and fellowships offered for students and scholars has greatly increased over the last few years, and technical assistance to educational institutions has also grown, especially in the area of equipment (laboratories, books, etc.), and to a lesser extent, in the area of personnel. More specifically, the AID has financed projects for technology transfer, technical feasibility studies, and programs for manpower development, and has also offered a grant to the Egyptian Academy for Scientific Research and Technology to help with research into some of the practical problems that inhibit economic and social improvement in the country.

West European (EEC) countries committed LE100 million until the end of 1978, representing 6 percent of the total investments. Of the funds allocated, the following areas have benefitted, in descending order: engineering industries (24 percent of all West European capital); tourism (20 percent); banks (13 percent); investment companies (6 percent); and chemical industries (6 percent). European capital represented as much as 66 percent of all funds allocated to petroleum industries.

Other countries not included in any of the previous categories (of which Japan and Greece are particularly important) had, until the end of 1978, committed LE223 million, representing 13 percent of all investments. The main areas here were tourism (67 percent of capital committed by these countries); weaving and textile industries (10 percent); banking (3.5 percent); construction materials (3.5 percent); and health services (0.5 percent).

It may be worth reiterating at the end of this section that Egyptian capital indeed accounted for LE905 million of the total LE1664 million (i.e. 55 percent) that was committed for *infitah* investments until the end of 1978. About 40 percent of all Egyptian capital went to commodity sectors and nearly another 40 percent went to services sectors. The Egyptian public sector provides LE445 million (i.e. 49 percent of all Egyptian capital), with building materials, agriculture and husbandry, metallic industries, weaving and textiles, and housing being the main areas of concentration. The Egyptian private sector, on the other hand, had contributed LE460 million, which were allocated as follows: services (48 percent of all capital committed); medical and chemical industries, woodwork and carpentry and contractors' activities (37 percent); and distributional activities (15 percent). All in all, therefore, foreign investments have not been lured to the Egyptian economy to the same extent that was once expected.

C. CAPITAL UTILIZATION IN EGYPT

Egyptian officials have for a long time maintained that the main bottleneck for Egyptian development was that of finance; above everything else, they held, Egypt needed huge quantities of liquid, preferably foreign capital. Nobody can, of course, doubt that Egypt is short of money and that significant funds are required for most of its developmental projects; what has to be emphasized, however, is that money alone does not do everything and that indeed money may not be the most difficult of Egypt's problems.

Between the point at which financial resources are earmarked for a particular project, and the stage at which we arrive at a working production or service enterprise, there is a considerable time span with many processes and procedures involved. This is partly related to the absorptive capacity of a particular recipient economy or sector, and to the capability of a particular country to ingest capital and utilize it in the most effective way.

In addition to the size of the market, the constraints here are normally related to institutions and to personnel. The Middle East offers some interesting contrasts here; whereas the absorptive capacity of a country like the United Arab Emirates, for example, is constrained—in a basically quantitative way—by the country's smallness as well as by its lack of qualified personnel and adequate institutions. Egypt's capacity for the utilization of capital seems to be constrained, in a more complex way, by the cumbersome and yet decaying state of its institutional networks and by the inflated and yet distorted nature of its manpower structure.

The Utilization of Financial Aid

A consideration of loans made available to the Egyptian public sector for the purposes of industrial development will show that, with the exception of loans from the socialist countries, only a proportion of the funds allocated was ever utilized. It can be seen from Table VIII that it is only the loans offered by the socialist countries that were fully utilized.[23]

TABLE VIII
Distribution of Loans for Industrial Investment from 1958 to March 1979

	Value of Loans (in LE millions)	Value Utilized (in LE millions)	% of Utilization
Eastern Bloc	300	300	100%
Western European countries	186	104	56%
U. S. A.	154	7	4.5%
TOTAL	826	505	61%

SOURCE: The General Industrialization Authority, *Taqrir an mutaba at al-qurud...* [Report on the Follow-up of Foreign Loans for the Industrial Investment Sector Until 31 July 1979], internal memorandum (Cairo, 1979).

These loans were normally offered under comprehensive agreements that involved the scheduled transfer of machinery, technology and training in return sometimes for a proportion of the prospective production. They were usually incorporated in the development plan and were therefore tied to other projects and subject to a fair degree of control and follow-up. About half only of the loans offered by Western European countries or international agencies were utilized, probably because of the lack of adequate feasibility studies and project planning, or because of shortages in matching local funds or required materials and equipment. These criteria and many more must also be responsible for the exceptionally low utilization of American capital made available for Egypt's industrialization. In this particular case, the time-lag factor is also important, given that the main bulk of American aid did not start to flow before 1975.

However, before analyzing more thoroughly the possible reasons for this phenomenon, let us first look at a more detailed table of industrial loans to Egypt that shows not only the utilization of capital from every Western country separately, but also the utilizaton of capital emanating from international agencies and Arab funds (Table IX).

In analyzing the data, one is struck by the fact that it is only Arab loans that are utilized to a reasonable extent (74 percent). In fact, if one excludes the loan earmarked by the Arab Fund for Social and Economic Development for the improvement of the textile factories of Kafr al-Dawwar and Al-Bida (dated 31 December 1976), then the rate of utilization of Arab funds is practically 100 percent, with the Urea Fertilizer Project in Talkha being the main absorber of seven different loans in 1974 and 1976 (from the Arab Fund for Social and Economic Develop-

TABLE IX
Absorption of Foreign Loans in Industrial Development From April 1969 to July 1979*
(LE Million)

	Allocated	Expended	%
W. European Countries			
W. Germany	147,0	67,0	45.5%
France	40,4	25,6	63.3%
Britain	16,0	5,5	34.3%
Denmark	15,4	9,3	60.3%
Spain	10,0	10,0	100.0%
Holland	4,0	0,3	7.5%
Italy	1,0	—	—
TOTAL	232,4	117,7	50.6%
U. S. A.	215,9	13,6	6.2%
International Agencies	133,64	35,7	26.7%
Arab Monetary Funds	134,13	99,83	74.4%
GRAND TOTAL	716.07	266.83	37.2%

*Socialist countries excluded; Japan not available

SOURCE: As for Table VIII.

ment, the Kuwait Fund for Arab Economic Development, the Abu Dhabi Fund for Arab Economic Development, and the Libyan Arab Bank). The main reason for this effective utilization is probably the freedom given to the recipient in choosing the suppliers, the machinery and the technology involved in each project, which provides a significant element of flexibility and promptness.

This observation can, in fact, be generalized concerning most Arab loans made available to Egypt for a whole variety of purposes, and, as can be seen from Table X, Arab aid was on the whole fairly promptly utilized. This table illustrates the value and utilization of Arab financial flows to Egypt (excluding government to government grants) up to the end of September 1976.

Egypt's utilization of Arab capital can be even more prompt when the

TABLE X
Utilization of Arab Aid to Egypt Until 30 September 1978

Source	Total Loan	Amount Utilized	%
The Arab Development Fund	LE 230.6m	LE 181.8m	78.8%
The Kuwaiti Fund	217.7	206.4	94.8%
The Saudi Fund	213.6	192.0	89.8%
The Abu Dhabi Fund	99.0	98.2	99.1%
The African Development Bank	24.0	18.0	75.0%
The OPEC Fund	23.2	15.6	67.2%
The Arab Monetary Fund	17.7	17.7	100.0%
The Islamic Development Bank	12.0	12.0	100.0%
The Libyan Arab Bank	10.1	10.1	100.0%

SOURCE: Ministry of the Economy and Economic Cooperation, 1978, 1979, (internal memoranda).

liquid flow could be used for consumption rather than for production purposes. The case of the Gulf Authority (or Organization) for the Development of Egypt, is very much to the point here. This organization was formed in 1976, its initial capital of $2 billion being provided by Saudi Arabia (40 percent), Kuwait (35 percent), the United Arab Emirates (15 percent) and Qatar (10 percent). The purpose was basically to help in establishing industrial and agricultural investment projects and in financing imports for the productive sectors of the economy. A secondary purpose was to help in solving Egypt's liquidity problem and in supporting its balance of payments.

In exactly a year and a half (from December 1976 to May 1977) Egypt had exhausted the entire capital of the Gulf Authority in obtaining loans and credit facilities from Chase Manhattan and other banks to pay back debts and to meet the deficit in its balance of payments.[24] The officials of the Gulf Authority were naturally displeased that none of the Authority's capital was used for any productive investment, and their governments were not to renew the Authority's capital after it had been exhausted.

If we now turn to a consideration of the rate of utilization of American loans, one is struck in particular by the exceptionally low rate (5 to 6 percent) of utilization of American aid made available for industrial investment (as shown in Tables VIII and IX). This could be partly attributed to the relatively recent start of American financial flows (around 1975) compared, say, to those from the East or, for that matter, from the Western European countries. For in July 1979, and after more than three years of allocating the Loan No. 30 (on 22 May 1976), only 20 percent of

TABLE XI
US Capital Transfers to Egypt, 1975-1977
($ million: US Fiscal Years)

	Allocated	Expended	%
A I D	1,756.2	403.7	22.98
PL 480	505.4	488.9	96.73
TOTAL	2,261.6	893.1	39.48

SOURCE: *Middle East Economic Digest*, "Egypt: Special Report" (May 1978), p. 41.

its value was spent, and further, after three years also of the allocating of Loan No. 33 (on 4 July 1976), as little as 4.6 percent of its value was spent. Not a single dollar from the loans allocated from the beginning of 1977 had been utilized by the end of July 1979.[25] And of course it is still too early to judge how much of (and when) the balance of this aid will eventually end up being utilized.

The reason for this, apart from the time-lag factor, is probably connected with a combination of two main factors: the relative novelty of American technology, and the relative inflexibility of the Egyptian bureaucracy.[26] The files of the General Industrialization Authority do indicate that on occasions modifications were required in equipment or supporting products, or that other instruments were needed, or that certain items were submitted for tender, or that some items were found not to be needed, or that reallocation of funds was being requested, etc. And all this, of course, indicates problems of adjustment with regard to technology and organization.

Egypt does not seem to have the same degree of difficulty, however, in utilizing aid offered under Public Law 480, which normally takes the form of foods, commodities and liquid payments. A comparison between the utilization of AID funds and the absorption of PL480 funds made available to Egypt during three recent years (see Table XI) can be useful in illustrating this point.

It can be seen clearly enough that several adjustments will be required at both ends of the process — that of the donor as well as that of the recipient — before American loans for industrial development can be more promptly utilized and more effectively absorbed by the Egyptian economy, and that this applies most particularly to aid given for the purpose of industrial development.

The Utilization of Investment Capital

If we now turn to a consideration of the ways in which investment capital is utilized in Egypt, we find that foreign and joint venture projects approved by the General Authority for Investment and the Free Zones and carried out under the encouraging laws of *infitah* do not really fare much better in terms of implementation capability. Details of projects approved and/or executed under the new investment Law No. 43 for 1974 up until the end of 1978 are presented in the following table (Table XII).

From this table it can be seen that implementation is definitely lagging behind the approval of projects. Of all the projects approved, only 32 percent had started operation by the end of 1978. Their investment spending represented only 16 percent of the total for all the approved projects, they employed only 11 percent of the manpower that was supposed to be employed by the approved firms, and the wages actually paid represented only 10 percent of the target wage bill of the projects. A sizeable number of projects, however, were reported to be "in process" or "under construction". These represented by the end of 1978: 44 percent of the capital committed, 68 percent of the employment conceived, and 62 percent of the wages planned.[27]

The number of projects in operation as well as those under construction by the end of 1978 represented 76 percent of all approved projects (450 out of 591) and their total capital amounted to LE1160 million (or about 70 percent of all capital involved in the approved projects) – of this capital, 44 percent was to be in the local currency and 56 percent was to be in foreign currencies.

The delays in implementation can be attributed to a number of factors, among which problems of dealing with the Egyptian bureaucracy are quite prominent. Investors have frequently complained that, to start with, the General Authority for Investment and Free Zones takes quite a long time to study projects before making a decision to approve or to reject a project. GAIFZ maintains that of all applications for projects submitted until the end of 1978, 75 percent were eventually approved. They also claim that on average 10 percent of proposals submitted are normally studied in one month, 55 percent are studied in two to three months, 30 percent in four to five months, and 4 percent required six months or more to study.

The difficulty, it should be remembered, is that GAIFZ does not decide by itself on projects, and does not perform all the procedures on its own. Quite often it would be necessary to consult the General Industrialization Authority or a ministry or public organization that is particularly concerned, and to coordinate with a large number of government authorities. This usually takes time as does the process of obtaining information on the financial and economic status of new investors. Nor should one forget, of course, that the investors may not provide in the first place all the information that Egyptian authorities may require, or that they may decide to change or modify some aspects of their proposals at one point or another.[28] This would usually start a new series of complications and delays, which will undoubtedly increase the investor's annoyance with the bureaucracy even further. Such complications seem to happen more frequently in the case of Arab investments, where the rigidity of the Egyptian bureaucracy combined with the relative inexperience of the Arab investor tend, outside the conventional areas of real estate, to reduce considerably the rates of capital absorption and utilization.[29]

The Egyptian bureaucracy is without doubt riddled with a large number of serious pathologies, and the investor does have his share of the burden of putting up with them.[30] What strikes the investor first in any contact he may have to make with some governmental authority or other is usually the very appearance of the Egyptian bureaucracy. For government buildings are almost invariably in a state of physical decay, with the interiors often dim, dusty and decrepit. Office rooms are small, hot and crowded, and there are rarely enough desks to accommodate the numerous employees who are supposed to work there.

Even the casual passer-by cannot fail to observe that the Egyptian bureaucracy is incredibly over-staffed, and the figures would confirm this impression. The public bureaucracy (i.e. the civil service and the public sector excluding enterprise workers) employed in 1978 over 1,900,000 people. If state companies are added, the public Establishment was employing about 3,200,000 officials and workers.[31] Further, the public bureaucracy continues to receive the bulk of the country's university and college graduates, and appoints annually around one hundred thousand graduates at a basic cost of LE35 million each year.[32] Fortunately (or unfortunately!) a large number of these employees will be "on their way" to the office, or "getting ready" to leave and many will not have come to the office at all. It has been conservatively estimated, for example, that 50,000 working hours are lost every day in the Transport sector, 45,000 daily within the Ministry of Industry, 40,000 in the Legal Department and the Courts, 35,000 in the Ministry of Irrigation, and 24,000 in the Ministry of Education. On the whole only 15 percent of all Egyptian employees always went on time to their offices and most of these were in the security, order and command departments such as the Ministry of Defence, Ministry of the Interior, the Presidency and the Cabinet secretariat. Elsewhere the average Egyptian civil servant was

TABLE XII
Foreign and Joint Venture Projects up to 31 December 1978
(Value in L. E. 1000)

| Projects* | Number | Approved Capital | | | Total Investment |
		Local C.	Foreign C.	Total	
1. Investment Companies	49	58316	125710	184026	194526
2. Banks and Banking Institutions	37	35758	93709	129467	129467
3. Touristic Projects	86	177163	189225	366388	570282
4. Housing Projects	35	115183	100723	215906	243248
5. Transportation Projects	10	3387	23102	26489	60706
6. Health Projects	13	15301	19707	35008	51519
7. Agricultural Projects	33˙	53919	52303	106222	251219
8. Contracting Projects	57	10226	18497	28723	56759
9. Education, Training and Services Projects	19	2361	128454	130815	139061
10. Textile Projects	33	61912	43197	105109	586097
11. Food and Beverages Projects	32	14292	10782	25074	67271
12. Chemical Projects	70	24530	56709	81239	112434
13. Wood Products Projects	11	3609	5597	9206	16246
14. Engineering Projects	40	34924	52771	87695	282108
15. Building Materials Projects	27	53679	31731	85410	221739
16. Metallurgical Projects	21	10653	18141	28794	36208
17. Pharmaceutical Projects	9	3831	6062	9893	16731
18. Mining Projects	5	2287	2986	5273	6094
19. Petroleum Projects	4	774	2510	3284	3284
Total	591	682105	981916	1664021	3045002

* Do not include either the public or the private free zone projects in Cairo, Alexandria, Suez or Port Said.

SOURCE: GAIFZ, *Facts and Figures IV*, Dec. 1978.

estimated to work solidly for a period of between 20 minutes and two hours each day. Lost (or wasted) working hours were estimated at 2.5 million hours in the ministries and departments, and about 1.5 million hours in companies and corporations, with a total cost of over LE5 million every month.[33]

Many of the employees who *are* in their offices will be eating *fūl* or *falafel* sandwiches, reading the newspapers, exchanging jokes and gossip, drinking tea, or having their shoes shined. If women, they may be knitting, crocheting or cross-stitching. A general atmosphere of disorganization will be unmistakeable and it would not be out of the ordinary, for example, to find a document of the Plan, the Budget, or the

TABLE XII *continued*

| | In Production Capital | | | | | Under Execution Capital | | | |
No.	Local C.	Foreign C.	Total	Total Investment	No.	Local C.	Foreign C.	Total	Total Investment
12	16642	36558	53200	53200	22	37257	51219	88476	98976
29	28688	61779	90467	90467	5	3500	28500	32000	32000
22	18740	39103	57843	83768	48	56254	124005	180259	327313
4	91107	33239	12436	124346	22	20242	48496	68738	82572
3	1803	4862	6665	7665	4	1551	2934	4485	26852
−	−	−	−	−	11	14686	19160	33846	50147
7	10910	4804	15714	36731	17	37872	37508	75380	165026
19	3139	5121	8260	10416	23	3997	8234	12231	32842
7	774	1169	1943	2331	5	790	2462	3252	3252
15	1204	3882	5086	6091	15	60325	38719	99044	575983
6	1137	2802	3939	5451	17	7376	4537	11913	25639
36	7956	16740	24696	26519	23	8020	21632	29652	49957
3	254	387	641	713	5	2305	3810	6115	12179
10	1728	3178	4906	5175	12	6188	6871	13054	20024
2	295	459	754	754	16	47736	17360	65096	199838
10	5760	10169	15929	19137	8	4462	7105	11567	15672
1	72	168	240	240	4	540	2543	3083	5779
1	1277	1728	3005	3005	2	410	434	844	1329
4	774	2510	3284	3284	−	−	−	−	−
191	192260	228658	420918	479293	259	313511	425529	739040	1725380

Legal Code being used as a cushion for a wobbly chair. Other documents, files and folders may be found under desks, behind doors, outside on balconies and sometimes even in water closets!

The appearance of the Egyptian bureaucracy cannot therefore give any impression other than one of extremely poor performance. But just how efficient or inefficient the bureaucracy is — especially regarding the civil service — is a very difficult matter to measure, and is made particularly ambiguous since less than half of all the administrative units have any performance standards set for them. Then only in 54 percent of these latter units are the available standards considered appropriate for measuring performance in these departments and organizations, and only in 33 percent of the cases does the information obtained through these performance standards have any impact on the evaluation and rewarding of employees.[34]

One of the aspects the investor will notice quite quickly about the performance of the Egyptian bureaucracy will be the frequency of changes in the laws, structures and leaderships, which make organizational instability a real problem (for example the average period of position tenure for an Egyptian minister is a year and a half; barely sufficient to enable him to familiarize himself with the tasks of his post).[35] Excessive compartmentalism and lack of coordination will also be obvious. Then, on all levels of the bureaucracy, the investor cannot but feel the impact of the idolization of papers and documents, signatures and seals, and the complexity, repetition, and overlapping of a large number of formalities and procedures, which of course inevitably lead to various bottlenecks and delays.[36] The excessive number of approvals and controls is a particular source of complaint from investors and entrepreneurs, both foreign and domestic. And foreign investors do complain particularly that while they are normally asked again and again to supply detailed information about their projects, they get very little themselves when they ask government agencies for data that might be necessary or useful for the initiation or promotion of their projects.

Once a project is approved — against all these odds — the more complicated task of putting it into practice starts. Dozens of procedures are of course required, and it is interesting to note that GAIFZ, in an attempt to minimize the agony of the investors in dealing with the Egyptian bureaucracy has reproduced a bureaucracy in miniature within its own headquarters, in the hope that this would save the businessmen from having to go themselves to the departments concerned. So, in addition to a general Investors' Service Bureau, there is also in the same building as GAIFZ a taxation unit, a registraion and documentation branch, a work permits office, a business registration office, and a passport and immigration office. GAIFZ has also permanent representatives on its premises from the Department of Customs and from the General Industrialization Authority, who are authorized to take decisions concerning a number of issues without referring back to their headquarters.

Such measures may, of course, reduce some of the initial agonies of the investor in having to struggle with Cairo's hectic traffic in getting from one inaccessible administration to another unyielding department; but he will soon discover that dealing with the bureaucracy is an everyday necessity (for approvals, permits, licences, authorizations, notifications, endorsements, signatures, seals, stamps and the lot!). For Egypt might have deserted its socialist ideals and the role of the state in Egypt may be declining in all economic and social fields, but the control functions of the bureaucracy are far from being noticeably reduced, and the open door policy remains in more than one respect an expresssion of what one may call "controlled commercialism". This kind of control is made possible, among other things, by the familial character of much of the emerging business, and facilitated by the previous bureaucratic (military or technocratic) contacts of many of the emerging entrepreneurs. The result is that although the market is free in theory, the granting of licences, approvals, permits and so on may depend to a large extent on a person's family and/or bureaucratic connections. Some foreign investors have already sensed this phenomenon and have learned how to come to terms with it.

Another reason which is usually presented by the investor to explain the delayed start or the complete halting of many projects after they have been approved is the poor state of the infrastructural facilities and services in Egypt. To be sure there was a marked decline in the real value of investment expenditure in the country from 1966 to 1973 in electricity, construction and housing. Power failure has indeed become a serious problem for many industries from the mid-seventies, and the obtaining of premises for industry and business is normally very difficult and in most cases extremely costly. Although roads are not really bad, other modes of transport have been seriously neglected. There are indeed indications that there exists some excess capacity in the road sub-sector (which now carries more than 80 percent of total freight tonnage), compared to severe under-capacity in all other sub-sectors. The complex organizational responsibility for management and development in the various sectors is partly to blame: for example the responsibility for the transport sector is divided among five ministries and thirty public companies, a situation that is not exactly conducive to a well-coordinated national policy in this very vital field.

Somehow related to this is the problem of Cairo traffic, which is now having a serious impact on the conduct of business in and around this large and dominant capital city. City streets are very inadequate, given that most often pedestrians too are obliged to walk in the roadways, the footpaths being occupied by vendors, workshops, cafes, cars, donkeys, sheep and a great variety of other things. The limited, narrow and collapsing streets of Cairo now carry something like a third of a million motorized vehicles and probably up to 22 thousand horse and donkey driven carts. Getting from one point to another in Greater Cairo through the confusion and the traffic jams may take up to two hours. Many new flyovers and bridges have been constructed in the last few years in an attempt to ease the problems of congestion, yet Cairo streets remain something of a nightmare, not only for the ordinary citizen but also for the businessman, Egyptian and foreigner alike.

Also deficient since the late sixties is the capacity of the Port of Alexandria, the main port for the whole country. The limited physical capacity combined with the multiplicity of authorities functioning in the port and the lack of coordination among them, has often caused serious congestion, with average waiting time for general cargo ships reaching 6.2 days in 1975. The impact of this on many new projects has been quite serious at times.

The inadequacy of the state-operated telecommunications system is also a significant constraint on many economic activities. The postal service is far from reliable, especially for internal mail. As a result, many firms have adopted a system of running their own messenger services within Cairo. On the other hand, telephone availability has declined to 56 percent in 1976 and the official number of waiting applicants surpassed 268,000 (i.e. more than 75 percent of the existing number of connections). Actual unsatisfied demand is likely to be higher, and an ordinary applicant in Cairo may have to wait as long as fifteen years or more. Given that approximately 95 percent of all calls during business hours in Cairo and Alexandria are business-related, one can see the economically harmful impact of this phenomenon. The almost total impossibility of acquiring a telephone since *infitah* has led to many corrupt practices within the telecommunications organization (including the payment of an LE3000 bribe for a telephone and one of LE5000 for a telex); these have sometimes involved individuals as high up the ladder as the Deputy Chairman of the Organization.[37]

The condition of the infrastructure was showing signs of beginning to improve towards the end of the seventies (as we will see in some detail later) but the situation is by no means adequate or satisfactory.

In the meantime, the organizations involved in attracting and handling foreign investments continue to do their best within the existing circumstances. GAIFZ did in fact announce that from 1978, detailed studies of required or desirable projects would be submitted to interested investors and would be advertized on the international capital market. This signifies that the authority wants to take the initiative rather than always to remain on the receiving end.[38] A proposal was also presented by the Central Agency for Organization and Administration (CAOA) in 1979 to reduce the number of stages required for the approval of foreign investments from twenty to thirteen. And other proposals have been put forward for providing data and information to investors, for ensuring cooperation from other departments and agencies, and for the provision of trained manpower for the new projects. Many investors do indeed find that in Egypt there is too much, but also too little bureaucracy. The state organizations seem to be immediately present and noticeably active when it comes to things like checks and controls, but their presence and activity seem to diminish considerably when it comes to things such as the provision of infrastructural facilities or useful information systems and feasibility studies. And in helping the investors, GAIFZ cannot by itself do the whole job and much concerning the attracting and channelling of capital into Egypt will always depend on broader economic and political considerations and not simply on the managerial efficiency of an organization's personnel.

One can therefore conclude from this analysis that Egypt's absorptive capacity for available funds may be constrained and that its ability to attract investments and utilize capital for developmental purposes is quite restricted. This is due, as we have seen, to various structural problems, which are the source rather than the result of Egypt's liquidity problem. Egypt's development difficulties will not therefore be solved simply by pumping in more and more money. A more complicated process that aims at improving the capabilities of its institutions and personnel will be needed and efforts will have to be exerted to ensure that money is utilized in the right way for the right purposes.

And it is indeed the uses to which the money is put which will determine in the final analysis the benefits and the costs, and therefore the prospects, of the open door policy as a developmental strategy for Egypt.

III. POLITICAL FEASIBILITY OF INFITAH: BENEFITS, COSTS AND PROSPECTS

To draw a balance sheet of *infitah* at this stage of its evolution would be almost impossible, given the brief life that this master policy has so far had. The evaluation of performance will therefore still need to be combined with a study of the feasibility of that policy. In analyzing the outcome produced so far, a rudimentary cost-benefit presentation can be suggested, but this should always be combined with an element of analysis of the political feasibility of this policy in terms of its likely political risks and its chances of failure or success.

A. THE BENEFITS OF INFITAH

Taken in its broadest sense, *infitah* has not been without benefit if one is to take into account as a whole package all the related and contemporaneous developments that accompanied it. We now look briefly at some of the benefits brought about directly, or indirectly, by *infitah*.

Relaxation of Political Controls

First of all, economic liberalization was accompanied by a certain degree of political liberalization. It is of course possible to argue that economic and political liberalization do not necessarily have to go hand in hand, especially in countries of the Third World; indeed that the cases of economic liberty accompanied by political repression are more the rule than the exception in less-developed countries. It is also true that the present regime in Egypt is not a fully democratic one, that it has gone back on many liberal steps (especially regarding political parties), and that the ultimate power in it is very personalized indeed.

Yet one must admit that contemporary Egypt is by no means a police state, that the use of naked force for the oppression of individuals is very rarely used, if at all. This may not necessarily last, especially as the scope of what the regime can offer to its people narrows further and further. But this should not overshadow the fact that the regime has not used open oppression to force the basic policy reversals that it has achieved during the last decade. This becomes all the more significant when it is compared with other cases where reversal of a radical socio-economic orientation was intended and where this has usually been accompanied by a considerable amount of violence (e.g. Ghana, Indonesia, Chile, etc.).

Detention without trial is quite limited, and even though critical opposition parties have been pushed out of the political arena (e.g. the new *Wafd* party) or else deprived of many rights of association and publication (e.g. the *Tajammuᶜ* "Progressive" party), political parties as such have not completely disappeared. Indeed there are many signs to the contrary. The alternative opposition party (*al-ᶜAmal*) created by the regime to offer only mild (and preferably only decorative) criticism was soon to turn its official organ into a major platform for independent opinion, that even dared to criticize vigorously some of the president's favorite projects such as the Law of Shame (*al-ᶜAib*) that would have seriously curbed personal freedom had it been passed in its original form, or the extension of a branch of the Nile to Israel, which is not only symbolically hurtful to the feelings of Egyptians (who almost idolize their river) but also existentially dangerous, given Egypt's vital and growing need for water.[39] It seems also that against all odds, the left (*Tajammuᶜ*) party has managed over the past few years to multiply its membership in a very impressive way.[40]

It is of course possible to argue that such developments have taken place in spite of the government, or to point to the very sophisticated and expensive security arrangements (including para-military forces) developed by the government since 1977, or to refer to the prevailing feeling that the conduct of the last parliamentary elections in 1979 was far from being fair. It remains true, however, that in a comparative perspective Egypt does not seem to represent a viciously oppressive police state. And although the correlation is by no means inevitable, it would be possible to argue that the existing personal and political freedoms, however limited they may be, are not completely unrelated to the policy of economic liberalization that Egypt has developed.

Increase in Financial Flows

In the economic field, supporters of *infitah* are not completely without something to boast about either. They can point to the annual growth rate in Egypt's GNP in the late seventies of about 9 percent (according to official sources), which is quite a handsome rate.[41] More careful analysts will show that most of this growth is due to types of invisible trade that do not reflect a real growth in the productive capacity of the country: remittances from Egyptians working abroad, dues from the Suez Canal and earnings from Egypt's small but growing oil industry.[42] But supporters of *infitah* could still argue that these were precisely some of the blessings of the open door policy, although the argument may become more complex and contrived at this point. It is possible to see how the open market for Egyptian labor in Arabia and the Gulf might have encouraged in some way the move towards *infitah;* yet large labor migration from a planned economy is not completely impossible, Yugoslavia being a case in point. It is also possible to attribute the re-opening of the Suez Canal in some roundabout sort of way to *infitah,* and to suggest that the settlement with Israel is but one aspect of the whole package of liberalization, peace, and pro-Westernism. This argument is persuasive, but there is little concrete evidence to prove that things which have taken place concurrently were necessarily causally correlated. Nor is it inevitable that a capitalist Egypt has to be friendly with Israel: Lebanon and Jordan, both frontline countries, follow an open door policy of sorts without having to exchange ambassadors with Israel.

Last but not least, it would be possible to relate the increase in revenues from oil not only to having regained the Sinai oilfields (through settlement with Israel), but also to improved relations with the United States. Egypt is one of the earliest Middle Eastern countries to have discovered oil in its territory, yet Egypt continues to be a very minor producer of petroleum, in spite of its being surrounded on either side by Saudi Arabia and Libya, both of whom are very rich in that valuable mineral. Popular political myth has it that it was Egypt's independent policies (especially under Nasir) that made international oil companies, with their important American dimension, somewhat reluctant to develop Egypt's petroleum resources, even though the country, according to popular belief, is "floating on a lake of oil".

Be that as it may, the increase in revenues from these three sources (remittances, the Suez Canal and petroleum), to which one may also add tourism, has taken place under President Sadat, and some official correlation has been imparted to them: thus to relate them all to a package that some may want to call *infitah* is not completely illogical.[43] Returns from oil and the Suez Canal go to the state, and their effective utilization will therefore depend on government policies. Returns from tourism, on the other hand, have a tendency not to trickle down to the ultimate benefit of large segments of the society (indeed there are indications that the long-term economic and social costs of tourism may well outweigh the initial gains). We are therefore left with remittances from Egyptians working abroad, the most recent but yet the largest single source of foreign currency for the Egyptian economy.

It is a little too early to predict how Egyptians will spend the money obtained abroad. Personal observation indicates that at present a great deal of it goes towards buying cars and consumer durables. Since most of these items are imported, the final impact of such expenditure cannot be expected to benefit to any great degree the productive forces within Egypt itself. A considerable proportion of the money obtained abroad is also allocated for construction activities and to a lesser extent for buying furniture and household effects. The influx of capital into building operations may eventually have a positive stimulating effect on many other sectors of the economy, although this (together with migration) has had the immediate result of creating a shortage in many crafts and occupations. Some money also goes to things like running a taxi service or operating a grocery shop, a fashion boutique, or a store for appliances. None of these activities is productive in the strict sense, yet they can trigger off the activities of a whole variety of professions and vocations to support them (e.g. mechanics, electricians, decorators, etc.). More important probably is the availability in the society of money, the source of which is *not* the state. This, together with the impact of inflation and the temptation of the available "good things", has encouraged many people to have more than one job and also to engage in traditionally less prestigious jobs (for the middle clases) such as taxi driving or grocery selling. This is producing a drive away from dependence on the government and is creating a sense of mobility which may eventually help in stimulating personal initiative in the country and in reviving the economy in more than one way.

Supporters of *infitah* can also point to other useful outcomes of that policy on the micro-economic level and in the field of management.

Through flexible import policies and higher financial liquidity, shortages and bottlenecks have eased in a number of intermediary goods and items, that used to represent a chronic problem for many industries and crafts in the sixties and early seventies, and which led to the deterioration in the quality of many products, sometimes for the lack merely of small "nuts and bolts". This is not only confined to the private sector. Many public companies have benefited too, as they were permitted to keep a larger proportion of their returns and to diversify their sources of supply (to include not only the Egyptian private sector but also direct importation from overseas). Indeed, as we have seen before, Egyptian official sources claim a marked improvement in the financial status of many public sector companies as a result of *infitah*.

Shortages and bottlenecks in many consumer goods, especially those for the use of the middle and upper classes, have also eased considerably. Cairo and Alexandria indeed look quite prosperous and colorful, with clothes and goods of all sorts, and delicacies from all over the world filling the shop windows and the pavements.

Improvement in the Infrastructure

Not only are the streets of Egypt's two main cities filled with more goods of all descriptions, but since 1978 or so the streets themselves have shown signs of improvement. Cairo streets had reached a ludicrous state of disrepair in the seventies, lacking pavements, filled with potholes, with poor lighting, and frequently covered with leaking sewage. This represented one aspect of the decline in facilities and services within the infrastructure which was discussed in the previous section. Many of the main streets have recently started to improve as, it seems, have telephones and to some extent traffic flows in the central city areas.

Since 1977 the government has been paying particular attention to the extension and modernization of the telephone network, with the help of a number of European companies. The first five year phase of this program is to cost about LE700 million. Some signs of improvement have already started to appear, but the end result of these projects cannot yet be evaluated.

The attention paid by the authorities of late to roads, telephones and the like is, in fact, indicative of the emphasis that the government is placing on improving the country's infrastructure as yet another means of encouraging investments. The government had in fact allocated as much as 45 percent of all public investments in the 1978–1982 Five Year Plan to the various infrastructure facilities and services (about 9 per cent for power, 27 percent for transport and telecommunications, and the rest for housing and construction). This is probably an excessive proportion but it certainly goes where it is needed.[44] What is more, this shift in emphasis is likely to continue in the future, as the public bureaucracy will be called upon to raise its spending on the infrastructure and to reduce its direct involvement in the area of economic enterprise. What is happening may, therefore, not simply be a temporary change in the investment programs but rather a reconsideration of the whole role of the executive branch in the economic life of the country, including in particular the entrepreneurial role of the government as represented by its ownership and its management of the public sector.

This takes us to a consideration of some of the economic and social costs of *infitah*.

B. THE COSTS OF INFITAH

There can be no doubt that the implementation of *infitah* does indeed involve a number of costs and risks in the economic as well as in the socio-political fields, and a small number of these will now be briefly considered.

Deterioration of the Public Sector and of Domestic Industry

The role of the public sector in the Egyptian economy represents an emotionally charged issue. It must be noted, however, that much of the criticism directed at the efficiency of the Egyptian public sector is politically motivated and often has as its real target for criticism either Nasir or his socio-economic policies, or both. We therefore agree that "the notion that the public sector has been inefficient and has failed to fulfil the targets set for it by the state is a misleading generalization which conceals exceedingly divergent performance among the different industrial sectors and *within* each of these sectors. To ignore the many positive achievements is witness to a simplistic attitude and will defeat any attempts at reform."[45]

We argue in this section that, all things considered, many of the public sector industries have not been doing badly at all, and that the decline that many of these enterprises are going through as a result of *infitah* should therefore be counted among the costs of implementing this policy. We will look briefly therefore at the performance in the last two decades of the public sector, before considering the harm done to it and to the national industries in general through the implementation of certain aspects of the open door policy.

It is known that a number of international cost comparisons of some of Egypt's industries — for example, cement, fertilizers and rubber tires — have shown the country to be at an advantage (for a variety of factors) compared with a number of European countries, and that labor productivity is also seen to be high in some other Egyptian industries like phosphates and nitrates. Other public sector organizations, in non-industrial fields, such as the Suez Canal Authority and the Petroleum Organization, were also judged by many experts to be quite efficient and successful.

An evaluation has been attempted of the performance of public sector industries based on a measurement of three criteria: domestic value added at international prices (DVA); the social rate of return on invest-ment (SRR); and effective rate of protection (ERP).[46] The author of this study found accordingly that several of the newly established industries as well as some of the more traditional ones have fared reasonably well, given the under-utilization of capacity, the difficulties caused by the Egyptian pricing system, and of course the socially justifiable but finan-cially burdensome overstaffing of the enterprises.[47] The pharmaceutical sector is one of the main examples of outstanding success, when judged by international price standards. Even Egypt's automobile industry which is frequently cited as an example of bad project planning cannot be considered inefficient, and appears to have reasonable potential for competitiveness if it were to operate at full capacity.

According to government sources, public sector industrial companies incurring losses in 1976–77 numbered 22, with total losses amounting to LE19.3 million, while profit-making enterprises numbered 125 with total profits amounting to LE168.9 million. Furthermore the value of public sector production had risen from LE583 million in 1971 to LE786 million in 1977, and its contribution to GNP had risen from 22 percent at the beginning of the seventies to 26 percent in 1977.[48]

It is also possible to argue that it was poor feasibility studies and inade-quate project evaluation, as well as a variety of legal and financial con-straints that were mainly responsible for the inadequate performance of some of the losing public industrial enterprises, and the Helwan Iron and Steel Complex is an important example here. But even in the cases where the technology was seriously deficient, as in the case of the Abu Zaʿbal Chemicals Complex, the management showed many aspects of flexibility and ingenuity, thus rescuing the project from becoming a total failure.[49]

Furthermore, the project has shown a remarkable ability not only to sustain and provide the basic needs of Egypt during the harsh inter-war period from 1967 to 1973 (an aspect that President Sadat has repeatedly alluded to), but also to respond to the economic and political challenges of these agonizing years by considerably raising its standards of efficien-cy.

In another good study, the author considers the levels of efficiency of both labor and capital as well as the economies (output increments) in-curred by the public and the private industries in Egypt.[50] In the period from 1963 to 1967, it was found that the public sector had two cases of two factor plus efficiency, one case of two factor efficiency, three of one factor efficiency and 13 cases of various inefficiencies. In the period 1967 to 1971 the number of inefficiencies declined to eight only. The following branches of industry were judged by a specialist to have had in the period 1967 to 1971 the following patterns of efficiency: two factor efficiency with economy—tobacco, furniture, paper, printing, transport equipment, electric machinery; two factor efficiency—rubber; one factor efficiency—metallurgic and non-metallurgic industries. Among those branches in the public sector which moved from the inefficient to the efficient categories, two were due to a change in the output/capital ratio, two were due to a change in the output/labor ratio, and four were due to changes in both. Overall, however, labor productivity advanced much more sharply than capital productivity, and in the public sector the output/labor ratio was increasing in 10 cases in the period 1963 to 1967, and in 16 cases from 1967 to 1971.

There has undoubtedly been even greater improvement in the private sector but this should in no way belittle the degree to which the nationalized industry has managed to reform itself after the 1967 war. After all, the efficiency criteria that have been invoked since 1967 have been very private sector oriented; for these were the criteria chosen by the regime at the time in pursuit of political support.[51] It should also be noted that in the post-1967 war period, 14 out of 17 cases of efficiency in the private sector were with capital growing, whereas in the public sector there were only 5 out of 11 cases, and this is particularly revealing since the public sector was undergoing a severe resources squeeze at that time.[52] If this rise in efficiency was later on to mean very little, as the drop in investment continued and the capital stock of the public sector was continuously being cut down, this can hardly be the fault of the public sector's managers and workers alone. Problems were being stored up for the public sector, and as very little repair or renewal was taking place the public sector factories were actually starting "to eat of themselves" as the popular expression suggested.

What is still more particularly alarming is the financial squeeze and technical negligence that led to the unnecessary decline of a number of Egypt's traditionally successful industries. The textile industry, for example, was allowed to drop from a two factor efficiency industry in 1963-1967, to a two factor inefficiency industry in 1967-1971. The food industry was also allowed to drop from a two factor plus efficiency level in 1963-1967 to a one factor inefficiency in 1967-1971.

It should not be understood from this, however, that these two traditional industries with declining efficiency represent necessarily a financial burden for the state. Quite the contrary—the industries of textiles and food have achieved relatively higher percentages of *profits* than the rest of the industries with, for example, a financial rate of return of 12.8 percent for the year 1977. And once we take into consideration the social rate of return it will be established even further that some of the public sector industries criticized on a purely financial basis may be found to be of great significance both economically and politically. For example, some fertilizer and food companies were being criticized for their low financial performance in 1977, while their real economic contribution for the country is significantly high. One hears complaints in government circles of having to subsidize the fertilizers company (which received an explicit subsidy of LE900,000 in 1977) when it is in fact saving the country $26 million. Because of their limited financial success, this and other industries of similar national importance "will receive insufficient funds for expansion in spite of high social rate of return, negative rate of effective protection, and low implicit exchange rate (DRC/$)."[53]

The reality of the matter is that, in spite of all the odds and constraints against it, the public industrial sector is neither universally inefficient nor hopelessly unable to reform itself, as many of its political antagonists would have us believe. There are indeed many drawbacks and weaknesses in the public sector as it stands today, but given the amount of financial and human investment put into the public enterprises, it would be a great social loss to permit the Egyptian public sector to decay and disintegrate.

What the Egyptian public sector needs is treatment, not execution; and one does sometimes feel that many of the champions of the open door policy are more interested in killing the public sector than they are in developing the Egyptian economy. Given that its performance is not so poor, it would make sense to ensure that the application of the policy would benefit rather than harm the public sector. Was not this, after all, one of the main arguments given in support of *infitah* during its initial stages—that it would invigorate Egyptian industry by infusing more capital and better technology into it?

There is no denying that the Egyptian public sector is in need of serious reform, yet it should be emphasized that many of the remedies suggested for the public sector within the framework of *infitah* may, if care is not taken, undermine its whole functioning; for there are limits to the degree to which public enterprises can be treated as ordinary capitalist corporations that are not significantly different from private enterprises.

Many suggest, for example, that freedom of management is the key to the solution of most of its problems. Yet it is possible to see that such a principle may not work very efficiently, especially in a less advanced society where favoritism may play an important part in social relations. The abolition in December 1975 of most public holding organizations (*muʾassasat*) has certainly led to many confusions and to the lack of control and coordination. Practice has already shown, more specifically, that the application of Law No. 48 for 1978, which involved a liberal widening of the freedoms and rights of the boards of directors of public companies (especially in changing the organizational structures of their companies) has led to some serious abuses, particularly in the area of personnel recruitment and salary adjustment.[54] It was reported that this had led to several cases of unjustified exchange of favors and unwarranted inflation of posts and salaries at the higher echelons, while management ability to deal with negligence and poor performance at the lower levels was still restricted by its inability or by its reluctance so far to dispense with surplus or else "inefficient" manpower. As things stand now, public enterprises (as distinct from the civil service) are not subjected to the same degree of pressure to accept new recruits who are not needed, and employment tends now on the whole to be done on the initiative of every firm according to the methods they find appropriate.

Excessive administrative autonomy may also lead to unnecessary competition between certain public companies, and may generally stand in the way of attempts at rationalizing and coordinating the activities of the public sector in accordance with the national plan's requirements. Nor is financial independence a pure blessing for although it may encourage certain companies to increase their profits by allowing them to retain a larger proportion of their returns for the purpose of re-investment and for other purposes of capital liquidity, it would certainly deprive the state budget of resources that it would otherwise have obtained, and may also in all probability act disfavorably against firms which are involved in essentially non-profitmaking fields. However, what hurts many public enterprises most at the present time is the fact that price controls do not apply to all economic activities, and firms very often find that they are required to keep the prices of their products at a certain level while the components of those products may only be obtainable at market prices. This problem was eased somewhat in 1979 when many sectors were allowed to price their products according to market considerations but many other side problems are still being encountered by the public companies in the area of pricing policies.

In any case, what is clear is that *infitah* has not neatly and automatically solved all the problems of the public sector in the same manner that many managers had rather naively expected. What has happened, most often, is a rearrangement of the order of these problems. And this can be detected from the results of empirical studies conducted in 1978 with the financial and personnel managers of seventy-four public companies functioning in a wide and reasonably representative variety of fields.[55] These studies indicate that whereas production was the main problem area for most public sector companies before *infitah*, the main problem areas now are both finance and personnel, and the main problem area that is expected to be paramount in five years' time is definitely that of personnel.

The exodus of desirable personnel from the public sector to *infitah* companies, especially joint venture ones, has already started, and the manpower categories which suffered the main draining were skilled and technical labor as well as middle management (over 10.5 percent in each case). Higher management lost over 9 percent of its employees and lower management lost nearly 9 percent; clerical and minor administrative personnel lost nearly 7 percent of employees. The lowest rates of quitting were among the non-skilled workers and the newly appointed university graduates. The managers were also clear in predicting an escalating rate of exodus to the private sector in the five coming years and beyond. They also felt on the whole that *infitah* has complicated personnel problems for the public sector in general and they thought that new policies for manpower planning, management development and technical training were accordingly needed.

It can generally be seen therefore that the open door policy—at least to judge by the managers' experience—has not proved so far to be very useful in solving the problem it was meant most to solve in the public sector (which is the problem of financing) and that it has in fact led to matters of personnel, whose abundance has long been taken for granted, becoming a problem of increasingly serious dimensions. It is clear that the most desirable personnel are departing from the public sector in large numbers, leaving behind only the least qualified and the least trained of all employees.

Infitah is not a panacaea; furthermore, it can hurt precisely where it may have been expected to cure. To utilize *infitah* for renovating and invigorating Egyptian industry makes sense: to allow it to strangle the Egyptian public sector out of spite or in the name of some mysterious economic liberalism would be a disastrous policy indeed.[56] And one cannot help feeling that the type of *infitah* which is sweeping the country nowadays is not only unjustifiably biased against the public sector but also predominantly mercantile and basically anti-industrial. Together with a number of other groups, the Egyptian Federation of Industries, which represents about five thousand firms in the private as well as in the public sector, has indeed made it clear that Egyptian industry is being subjected to unfair, and on the whole harmful competition from foreign capital. *Infitah* projects are given several tax exemptions and privileges that local projects do not enjoy. Furthermore, no restrictions whatsoever are put on the import, through the "own-currency importation" system or through other arrangements, of finished goods that compete with local products.[57] This danger is also reinforced by a fair amount of smuggling in of products, individually by what are known as "the suitcase merchants", and more widely through the newly established free zones that have turned into little more than a staging post for foreign manufactured goods to slip into the country.

The industrialists have also complained of the fact that customs dues on imported intermediary goods required by the national industries were in many case higher than customs levied on the same items if they were imported ready-made. This of course acts unfairly against the locally-produced goods. Furthermore, certain sectors of the economy (such as transportation, construction and tourism) are allowed to import duty-free items, which often end up being cheaper than their locally-produced equivalent since the intermediary items for these latter are not exempt from customs dues. Other treasury tariffs are also levied on locally manufactured items (for example textiles, electrical appliances, formica, etc.) with no equivalent taxation on the imported items. On top of all that, the policy of allowing public sector firms to import whatever they need, even if an equivalent product is locally manufactured, will only make things worse for Egyptian industries.

As a result of these policies, all of which act unfavorably against Egyptian manufacture, the Federation of Industries has complained that local products are stagnating in the market and that Egyptian firms in consequence have had to incur higher costs or else to stop production completely.[58] And such is the nature of the impact of sweeping commercialism on Egyptian industry, for the building of which Egyptians have sacrificed so much.

Corruption and the Decline in Work Ethics

Corruption, believed to have grown considerably under *infitah*, is a problem that affects negatively the performance of the civil service and the public sector alike. It is also acquiring new social dimensions that are almost certain, in our view, to have devastating long-term effects on developmental prospects.

Of course corruption, broadly defined as the illegitimate utilization of public office for unjustified private gain, is not confined just to Egypt, and indeed Egypt may not be among the very worst cases in this respect. Yet the problem has recently reached dimensions that make it a serious administrative and political problem, with grave effects on the processes of development in particular. Corruption now is petty and grand; it permeates all echelons of the bureaucracy, and it involves all the known varieties; bribery, nepotism, favoritism, forgery, embezzlement, smuggling, illegal exchange of favors, the devious allocation of permits and licences, and several other forms.

Since the beginning of the seventies, the scale of corruption in the financial and economic fields, which have the most immediate impact on development has — by all accounts — greatly increased, especially in the areas of customs, taxes, import and export, real estate, credit, supplies, and many others. The phenomenon of "commissions" and "percentages" (rake-offs and kickbacks) has also become very widespread. There is as well a popular belief that the shortages in certain locally produced commodities in the market (such as soap, cigarettes, etc.) are caused intentionally by the "dirty hands" of importers in collaboration with officials. Some officials also contribute to creating black markets or semi-monopolistic situations for the benefit of certain merchants. And there is of course the increasingly recurring phenomenon of theft and embezzlement often followed these days by an almost ritualistic fire at the end of the financial year to cover up all the traces. As one member of parliament commented in 1978, "Cairo alone has witnessed 2704 'fires' in 1977, of which 227 'fires' occurred in the public sector and government establishments, and most of these took place in the period from November to March which is the period between stock-taking and preparing the budget."[59]

The under-secretary of the Ministry of Finance had admitted that the financial year 1978, for example, had seen large and unprecedented embezzlements. Other agencies such as the State Security Investigations, the Public Socialist Prosecutor, the Central Auditing Agency and most particularly the Administrative Control Authority (which was, ironically, dismantled in June 1980) have also repeatedly revealed countless cases of fraud and misconduct reaching serious criminal levels among public officials. But the practice of preferring simply to remove such high officials from their posts rather than trying to punish them as well has not been conducive to the prompt eradication of corruption.[60] In fact if the official is well-connected and the charges of corruption are undeniable, then he may be removed from his post only to be given another, sometimes better one! The machinery dealing with cases of illegal earnings is however very lax indeed. For example, the Illicit Gains Administration which examines 400,000 files of public officials every year (every official has to submit a detailed statement of his financial status at least once every five years) caught in 1978 only 66 cases of illegal gain that were transferred to the courts — and this was judged by the of-

TABLE XIII
Perceptions of Bribery Among Public Officials

Prevalence of Bribery	Number of Respondents	%
"Internal" bribery	5	2.6
"External" bribery	143	75.9
Internal and External	29	15.3
Not indicated	12	6.3
TOTAL	189	100.00

SOURCE: National Centre for Social and Criminological Research, Symposium on Deviance in the Public Service, (Cairo, 3-5 March 1979) -- see footnote 63 *supra*.

ficials as reflecting a very slow and imperfect performance on the part of this important Administration.[61]

The scope of corruption in recent years has indeed become quite alarming, involving as it does such top public personalities as the Deputy Prime Minister, the President of the Higher Council for Islamic Affairs, the Minister of the Economy, the Minister of Civil Aviation, the Minister of Electricity, the Chairman of EgyptAir, the Chairman of the Water Board, and many other highly placed officials.[62] There is also a pervasive view among officials that bribery is quite extensive on all levels within public organizations and more particularly in dealings with the clientele and the public. For example, a study of 189 officials from the government, the public and the cooperative sectors[63] indicated the following perceptions (Table XIII).

Documents of the Public Security Department also reveal some very interesting, if incomplete, facts concerning crimes related to public funds. Such crimes represent a high percentage of all registered crimes, especially in the urban provinces that have most of the important centers of administration, business and trade. In 1975 for example, such crimes represented the following percentages of all crimes: in Cairo, bribery 12 percent, embezzlement 7.7 percent; in Alexandria, embezzlement 25 percent, forgery 6.3 percent, bribery 3.5 percent; in Suez, bribery 23.5 percent, embezzlement 15.4 percent; and in Port Said, bribery 20 percent.[64] Three years later, recorded cases of corruption-related crimes in the major commercial and administrative cities of Egypt (as illustrated in Table XIV) represented a high proportion of all registered crimes in these cities. A special report concerning the year 1978 submitted by the Security Department to the Minister of the Interior indicated a very serious rise

TABLE XIV
Corruption-Related Crimes in Major Urban Centers, 1977
(as percentages of all crimes)

Major Urban Centers	Bribery	Embezzlement	Forgery of Documents & Banknotes	Arson	TOTAL
Cairo	7.0	6.6	4.6	2.9	21.2
Alexandria	2.9	22.7	7.3 + 0.7	1.8	35.4
Port Said	16.2	–	8.1 + 2.7	–	27.0
Ismailia	17.2	6.9	6.9	3.5	34.5
Suez	27.3	9.1	–	–	36.4

SOURCE: Ministry of the Interior, *The Public Security Report*, 1977, passim.

in crimes of arson (whose corrupt significance we have already explained), and a considerable rise in crimes of forgery of travel documents (for working in Arab countries).[65]

The reasons for corruption in Egypt are multiple and many of them have nothing to do with *infitah*.[66] First of all the civic culture is still generally weak and primordial, and informal organizations are very influential. Particularly important among these are the extended family (*ʿāʾila*), the village kinship (*baladiyyat*), the "old boy network" (*dufʿa*), and the socio-functional clique (*shilla*).[67] Added to this is a long history of poverty, combined with certain aspects of parasitism by many groups (e.g. the desert nomads, the Mamluks and Ottomans, Europeans and Levantines of the Capitulations, etc.). And of course there are many technical and administrative factors that can encourage corrupt behavior, such as excessive routine, loopholes in legislation, deficiencies in organization, disparity between authority and responsibility, and inefficient control devices.[68]

There can be little doubt, however, that corruption has grown in scope and magnitude since the adoption of the open door policy. As people see more big money circulating, and as the salaried people in particular find it increasingly difficult to make ends meet, the temptation of corruption becomes more powerful. Inflation, of which a large proportion is imported as a result of *infitah,* hits particularly hard the salaried groups of employees and workers in the government and the public sector who may find in corrupt practices a way of overcoming some of their growing financial difficulties. The dominant mercantile types of activities that have prospered under *infitah,* with their emphasis on import-export, agency work and brokerage, also give the ordinary citizen an impression

TABLE XV
Perceptions of Reasons for Bribery

Reasons	Number	%
"Growing burdens of living"	112	59.3
"Looseness"	110	58.0
Limited income	29	15.3
Poor morals	26	13.8
Limited control	16	8.5
Bureaucratic "routine"	6	3.2
Not indicated	37	19.6
TOTAL	189	100.0

SOURCE: As for Table XIII.

of a lot of easy money circulating about, and the indulgent consumerism to which much of this money is directed is not particularly conducive to making the citizen think of abstention or self-control.

In addition to all this there is the mania, not unrelated to *infitah,* for wanting to go to an Arab country, as this is found to be one of the few possible ways to "make it" for an ordinary Egyptian. A whole cancerous network dealing in (real and false) work permits, entry visas, travel documents and the like has developed in several parts of the country. Given, among other things, the extremely rigid and very restrictive nature of the Egyptian bureaucracy, nepotism, bribery and forgery may represent possible ways for getting round the unyielding bureaucracies of Egypt as well as those of the receiving countries.[69]

The motivations for corruption are of course partly economic and partly social and psychological, and the following table (Table XV) shows, for example, the views of 189 officials on bribery, and is very illuminating as to the importance of various factors in causing people to indulge in corruption in this particular form.

It can be seen from this table that the main factors considered responsible for the spread of corruption were "growing burdens of living" and "looseness". It is interesting to note here how these two factors differ from the more static and formalistic, but yet similar, factors of "poor morals" on the one hand, and "lack of control" on the other. Corruption is more clearly motivated by a sense of relative deprivation and a sense of loose conduct in the society at large, and both of these have grown greater since *infitah.*

Under such circumstances, corruption seems to have increased remarkably, and what is particularly alarming is that corruption is becoming less and less condemned socially as a form of behavior — people are increasingly accepting it as a normal practice. Indeed the government itself seems indirectly to be condoning corruption. A Prime Minister declared officially (in March 1975) that commissions were all right, provided that a portion of them was handed over to the government, and it is common practice now to exempt embezzlers from all criminal interrogation and responsibility if they agree to restore to the government a portion of the money they have stolen! I have therefore warned on one occasion that instead of merely confronting a phenomenon of the "corruption of administration", the danger is that the country may be moving towards a situation of the "administration of corruption".[70]

It is of course sometimes argued that corruption may not necessarily be harmful to the conduct of business: indeed some have argued the case for "economic development through corruption". Corruption may, among other things, reduce uncertainty among businessmen and ease the complications of increasing investments, of which there are, of course, many in a country like Egypt. It is also further argued that corruption can be politically functional in integrating elites in the society as it helps to absorb the rising groups within the establishment and to unite the wealthy strata with the influential strata, therefore helping to consolidate political stability. Indeed it can be seen that a similar process to this is taking place in today's Egypt. Given such considerations, it has been suggested that one of the results of governmental efforts to reduce corruption in countries such as Egypt was to produce additional obstacles to economic development, and that therefore, in terms of economic growth, "the only thing worse than a society with a rigid, over-centralized, dishonest bureaucracy is one with a rigid, over-centralized, honest bureaucracy."[71]

There is no denying that this argument has its attractions. However, one can hardly fail to see its weaknesses. Indeed, if we consider *infitah* as a panacaea, then corruption may be quite functional in making the job of many investors much easier through various acts that aim at "greasing the sluggish bureaucratic machine". But if one is more concerned about development (which is not, of course, simply growth) and not merely about the success of *infitah* as a policy, then one may be inclined to look at things in a different light. What is probably more dangerous than anything else is the likely spread in the society, as a result of the institutionalization of corruption, of values unfavorable to honesty and integrity, and above all the eventual destruction of the precious link between work and achievement on the one hand, and compensation and reward on the other, which can be most socially harmful for all developmental prospects in the long run. This takes us to the problem of work ethics in contemporary Egypt.

Related partly to corruption and more generally to commercialism is the marked decline in work ethics that one cannot fail to discern everywhere in the country these days, not least represented by the frequent absence from, or late arrival to their places of work of employees and laborers. An aspect of what the Egyptians call "looseness" (*tasayyub*) does in fact permeate most facets of Egyptian life at present, and can be symbolically noticed in cases as varied as the traffic system (for the regulations of which there is near total disregard) or theatrical performances (which witness some of the most noisy and inconsiderate behavior).

The decline in the personal and social value attached to productive work is a function of a variety of factors. But the main reason is probably people's perception that if money can come more easily and more abundantly in some other way, why toil and struggle simply to make ends meet? There are several possible ways of making relatively "good" or "fast" money in Egypt today, none of them particularly conducive to the spread of serious and productive work ethics. One way, of course, would be to indulge in some of the corrupt activities to which we have already referred. Another is to try to go to another country, Arab or otherwise; at least a million Egyptians are now working in Arab oil-producing countries where they make, on average, twenty times as much money as they would make in Egypt. "Getting there" is everybody's dream, and what is more significant is that getting there is basically a matter of luck which has very little to do with a person's productivity at work. So why work for little at home, and why struggle to improve your performance if getting out would save you the agony and provide you with more? To leave is becoming an obsession for many groups, including those who have not yet graduated.[72] Nor does the "going" necessarily have to be to an Arab country: for example, there are already tens of thousands of Egyptians working in London, Milan and Piraeus. Emigration to the New World is also a very attractive idea for many.[73]

Much harm is done to the country by the loss of some of the most needed elements of its labor force.[74] According to the Ministry of Manpower and Training, as many as 1,890,000 Egyptians were working abroad in 1978. Supply of manpower in Egypt is estimated at about 12 million, of which only about 4.5 million belong to the urban sector. About a million and a half of those latter are unemployed; assuming, not unjustifiably, that most migrants to Arab countries are recruited from among the urban labor force already in actual employment, there is sufficient reason to believe that the massive migration of Egyptian workers is leaving behind a much larger "vacuum" than is often assumed.[75]

Although the economy tends to lose through emigration the most needed elements of its labor force the level of unemployment remains quite high, even by official estimates of the Ministry of Manpower (11.8 percent in 1979). According to two experts this may indicate an unusually limited occupational mobility in Egypt.[76] Their hypothesis may be exaggerated and their data may not be up-to-date (they still tell us, for example, that in 1979 the number of Egyptians working abroad is 600,000, which was indeed the figure in 1976: the number has been increasing by at least 250,000 annually since then). But the description remains accurate—that Egypt has suffered from sudden and prolonged shortages in the numbers of technicians and craftsmen both among the formally and the informally qualified. Another profession which also suffered as a result of mass emigration to Arab countries is that of the teachers and educators (over 23,000 school teachers were officially seconded by the Ministry of Education to work in Arab and African countries in 1979 alone: the number of teachers and educators working by personal contract is certainly much larger). And these happened to be among the most needed occupations, required by Egypt for its own economic development. The quality of work in these and other fields in Egypt has therefore deteriorated quite rapidly, as no systematic training arrangements are promptly introduced to develop skilled personnel to fill the gaps.[77]

The Rise of Commercialism

The harm done to the country through the loss to its economy of some of the most vital and essential elements of the labor force tends to be multiplied socially as such people return to Egypt, especially from oil-producing countries, laden with money, of which they indeed bring a lot! (Workers' remittances from abroad now form the top single source of foreign currency for the country). Suffice it to say that according to the Ministry of the Economy, the equivalent of about LE 1 billion in foreign currencies were leaked into the Egyptian black market in 1979 by Egyptians working abroad, to be utilized in "own currency" import operations.

The first type of harm they cause is through competing with their larger financial resources over the limited facilities available, especially in the area of housing. This, among other things, leads to simply unbelievable rates of inflation in the price of accomodation. The "key money" paid to acquire the lease of a small unfurnished apartment in

Cairo is now in the order of thousands, in a country where the salary of a young university graduate is about LE300 a year, and where the per capita income is only LE180 annually. Related to this is also pressure on building land. Here the prices rise every summer as Egyptians working abroad come to spend the summer months at home, bringing with them large amounts of money. The infusion of such huge sums for the purchase of land all the year round has also generally pushed the prices very high. For example, a square meter of land on the Nile Corniche had increased in price from LE400 in January 1976 to LE1,500 in January 1978, i.e. by 270 percent in just two years.[78]

The second way in which this money can be said to be socially harmful is that it is to a large extent spent on conspicuous luxury consumption, thus creating a bad demonstration effect as well as a marked duality between the "haves" and the "have-nots". For one thing, people returning to Egypt for their summer holidays bring with them more than 50,000 new cars every summer. Thousands of other cars are also brought in unaccompanied every year, in addition to tens of thousands of electrical appliances, mostly of foreign manufacture. The sale of exotic foods and drinks also continues and this is popularly known as the *infitah* of imported ice cream, caviar and whiskey.

Thirdly, returning workers do not go back to productive work when they return to Egypt, but prefer to indulge in various mercantile activities, many of which are of a rather parasitic nature. Thus a carpenter or a mechanic who would make a reasonable amount of money in an oil-exporting country would not return to his original craft once back in Cairo but would usually prefer to engage his money in some commercial activity, such as those to which reference has already been made.

It is now obvious to many that Egypt's *nouveaux riches* are joining the *pantouflage* bureaucrats in spreading a type of economic life that is based on finance and trade but very little real production. The market is indeed flooded with all varieties of commodities and goods, without much regard for the possible negative effects or impact on the local industries. The main drive is mercantile and more specifically consumerist in orientation, and the ideal was very eloquently expressed by the Minister of Trade, Zakariyya T. ʿAbd al-Fattah, when he said that

> ...twenty years ago Cairo was abundant in everything; it was the city of good taste and new fashion, and the meeting place for all the chic classes. I want it now to be a prosperous city whose markets are full of everything to be found in the civilized capitals of the world.[79]

This pattern of development *à la libanaise,* or through mercantile activities, can hardly be a suitable pattern for a country like Egypt with a much larger population possessing less of a commercial tradition; not that the shattered Lebanon is a very alluring example to want to follow. What is taking place is merely commerce, and often "dirty" commerce at that. Dog and cat food is sold for human consumption, poisonous potato chips (Bozo!), decaying tomato puree, tins of "corned beef" filled with minced-up hoofs, heads and intestines... these are some types of foodstuffs that the new mercantile class is importing for the Egyptians, according to reports of the Ministry of Supplies.[80]

The field of housing and property development has also witnessed in particular the activities of many crooks and shady types, of which one of the most daring cases was that of the so-called "Maspero Towers".[81] A large number of fake companies for selling non-existent land or houses at huge prices was also uncovered by the government.[82]

This cheap commercialism seems to permeate more and more aspects of Egyptian work and life, including education. One of the examples for this, which has acquired serious dimensions in recent years, is the spreading of very expensive, sometimes almost obligatory, private tutoring by public school teachers for their pupils, a phenomenon that has recently spread even to the universities (involving for one thing the smuggling of corpses to private houses for the tutoring of medical students).[83] Even an illusionary Organization for International Freedom was said to have been formed (capital $500 million) as an Egyptian-Saudi-American company for publishing, information, and the "combatting of communism" and was busy collecting contributions for those purposes.[84]

Not that all these crooks are local. The Pyramid Plateau fiasco, for example, has shown very clearly how very dubious foreign personalities and companies could make huge fortunes by selling to the Egyptians and Arabs the site of their own pyramids, while promising them one of the most appalling projects for the vulgarization of culture and archeology that has ever been dreamt of: the Great Pyramids of Giza complete with night clubs, golf courses, luxury hotels and, as a concession to the "Egyptian-ness" of the site, a huge artificial *ankh*-shaped swimming pool![85]

It is indeed a very suspect business atmosphere, very much reminiscent of what happened in Egypt over a century ago in the aftermath of the collapse of Muhammad ʿAli's development experiment and under the rule of the Khedive Ismaʿil, when the country was the destination of every capricious speculator from Europe and the Mediterranean who wanted to make a quick and easy gain.[86] The Egyptian market is indeed being laid open to the products of an enormous number of foreign companies, and according to the Ministry of Commerce there were as many as 3,600 foreign companies operating in Egypt through agents, at the end of April 1978.[87]

Yet another aspect of the growing commercialism — this time in a more specifically economic sense—is represented by the fact that the present Egyptian society is not only over-banked but also that very little of the banking activity goes towards the financing of industry or other particularly productive areas. The Central Bank of Egypt had indeed reported that until the second half of 1978

> ...the role of the banks which were formed to benefit from the Investment Law is almost confined...to competing with public sector banks in attracting local savings, without in return directing these savings for domestic usages; on the contrary, the accumulation of these savings with banks abroad has been on the increase...[88]

Only 21.5 percent (in 1977) and 26.4 percent (in 1978) of the banks' resources were allocated to domestic investments and credits, whereas the overseas debt of these banks had represented 44.1 percent of these resources in 1977 and 34.6 percent of the resources in 1978. But again of all the loans and credits extended by the foreign banks, as much as 75 percent has gone towards short-term financing of commerce and services, as distinct from the more productive commodity sectors.[89]

Commercialism is indeed growing so powerful that it is harming the interests of all other groups except the merchants, with the consumer, of course, being among the first of the groups to suffer. Fervently supportive of *infitah*, the merchants are actively developing their collective strength through, among other things, the chambers of commerce.[90] The merchants, estimated by their Federation to be about two million in number, have also already shown that they are able to challenge the authority of the government when it comes to defending their newly acquired gains. A decree restricting the importation of some eighty items without the prior approval of the Ministry of Trade (because of the likely negative effects on national industries) was reversed in 1977 under pressure from the merchants' lobby.[91]

Another of the occasions in which the chambers of commerce have actually shown their teeth in defending the merchants' interests is related to the controversial Decree No. 119 for 1977 for the specification of certain percentages of profit for imported goods. This decree was issued in January 1977, to be applied from May of the same year, setting an upper limit of 30 percent on the net profit on imported items. The General Federation of Egyptian Chambers of Commerce asked more than once for a postponement of its application. When the Federation managed, with great difficulty and costly manoeuvering, to persuade its members to accept a decision regulating the profits there was a serious split among the member Chambers and among the regional branches (*shu'ab*) concerning the actual application of this decision. This meant in practice that the maximum percentage rule was, to all intents and purposes, never enforced.[92] Particular resistance had been put up by certain groups, such as the merchants dealing in machinery, equipment, and stationery. The merchant pressure group has thus succeeded in preventing the application of the decree, manifesting on the one hand its newly promoted political power, while at the same time acting against the claimed objective of strengthening the Egyptian pound. Nor is the merchants' preference (sometimes insistence) that the customers should pay in foreign currency particularly conducive to the improvement in the value or prestige of the national currency of the land.

It has also to be remembered that the organizational vitality of the federation has recently been enhanced by the rise of many new faces to the leadership of various of the Chambers of Commerce, notably that of Cairo (where over half the leadership is reported to be "new faces") in the elections of summer 1979. These new men are to a large extent the product of *infitah* and its era of spiralling commercial activity, and they are more than likely to have sharper teeth than the generation which preceded them.

The rapid commercialism that these merchants, together with other members of the emerging lumpen-bourgeoisie, seem to be intent on forcing on the society, indeed threatens to produce some distorting and possibly very dangerous transformations in the country's social map. And it is the costs and risks involved in such transformations that will be discussed in the following section of this study.

C. SOCIO-POLITICAL PROSPECTS OF INFITAH

A re-forming of the class structure is already taking place in Egypt today. The most novel development is that of the "commercialization" of a number of social groups as illustrated by the tendency of technocrats and officials on the one hand, and skilled workers on the other, to turn to mercantile activities. This is accompanied by an important element of integration between the three distinguished classes of three different generations: the semi-aristocracy of the *ancien régime,* the military-technocratic elite of the Nasirist period (especially its *pantouflage* elements), and the commercial *nouveaux riches* of *infitah.* A newly converging upper class is already closing the ranks in contemporary Egyptian society, and laying the ground for a socio-economic basis of political support for the system.

But at the same time that this process of integration is taking place at the top, there is an element of disintegration at the bottom and the middle. At the bottom the workers (especially those of the public sector) stand to lose the most. It should be remembered here that workers were

among the classes that benefited most under the Nasirist policies of industrial expansion, full employment and social welfare. Politically they
had also achieved a "historic" gain as a minimum of 50 percent representation was guaranteed for workers and peasants in all political institutions (especially the Arab Socialist Union and the National
Assembly—now the People's Assembly). Admittedly they have not yet
lost this symbolically significant achievement, although the attempts to
make it more accurately and concretely significant have now been
discontinued.[93] The workers were therefore quite critical of the reconsideration in 1974 of the whole concept behind the Arab Socialist Union
(ASU) and the move towards a system of multi-partism and political
pluralism, in case this might rob them completely of their revolutionary
gains. The workers were also quite apprehensive about what the open
door policy might involve in terms of reducing the numbers of workers in
certain firms, especially given the talk in the mid-seventies about selling
some of the public sector companies. There were in fact reports of some
violent resistance when a number of workers of some military factories
were threatened with losing their jobs as the ownership of these factories
had been transferred to Arab joint ventures.[94]

The situation seems under control as the government tightens its grip
over the workers' unions and with the head of the General Federation for
Egyptian Trades Unions acting also as the Minister of Manpower. But it
is not easy to forget that most large demonstrations that have been
witnessed in the country since 1968 have started among the public sector
workers, and that the workers as a group still harbor some significant
Nasirist sympathies. However, nobody can easily predict how the
workers will react as the implementation of *infitah* makes more of an impact on their work and their lives.

The combination of rapid inflation and stagnant wages is bound to
hurt and the workers are also likely to be dissatisfied with the loss of
several privileges and sharing in profits, as well as the loss of the right for
guaranteed employment and for job security. Joint venture projects are
normally of the capital-intensive type and will not therefore offer work
opportunities in significant numbers (although of course their workers
are likely to receive higher wages than those obtainable within national
industries). These foreign projects are not, on the other hand, bound by
Egyptian labor legislation, and even some Egyptian corporations (such
as banks) have started to depart from the practice of employee representation on their boards of directors. All in all, therefore, there can be little
doubt that the workers as a class will stand to lose under *infitah*.
Unemployment will in all probability continue to rise in a country with
rapid population growth and receding industrial development. Inflation

(a great part of it is imported with *infitah*) will also go on rising beyond tolerable limits.

In fact the conditions of life of most ordinary people will in all probability continue to deteriorate, especially among the urbanites with their higher expectations and therefore sharper sense of relative deprivation. After the industrial worker or small official has got over the excitement of buying for his family once a year a luxurious mixture of nuts imported from every country on earth, what good would it do him if every day he would find the shops full of Parisian perfumes and no cheap washing soap, full of fancy imported cheeses and no cooking oil? And what a ludicrous thing in the country of abundant fresh limes and delicious grilled kebabs to find at the top of the list of foreign *infitah* enterprises a project for "Seven-Up" beverages and another for "Wimpy-burgers". This process, described by some as the "Cocacola-ization" of Egypt cannot help eventually but produce its inevitable results, in terms of deprivation and alienation, as "modernization" continues to be irrelevant to the real social and cultural needs of the majority of the population. And the growing inequality that can be seen in many economic and social fields can, of course, only make things worse.[95]

These kinds of problems will hit the salaried classes most, starting with the workers and potential workers, but then extending to the middle classes of officials and technocrats (especially in the public sector) — and this applies to the existing as well as to the potential ones (i.e. the recent university graduates). Unemployment of the educated is indeed a politically dangerous problem, especially in the light of the political and educational developments that took place during the past decade. From the time of the 1952 Revolution to the end of the sixties Egypt produced some 250,000 graduates. They were all employed, admittedly with some over-staffing, in the expanding public bureaucracy and industry. From the end of the sixties to the end of the seventies, the country produced over half a million new graduates just at a time when industrial and organizational activities were declining as a result of the changing role of the state. In fact Egypt produced, during the seventies alone, some 565,000 graduates, almost double the number that the country had produced in its whole history up to the end of the sixties (about 300,000). The state is therefore finding it extremely hard to have these graduates employed. As it is, graduates are not normally given jobs until two or three years after their graduation and these are often organizationally unnecessary and professionally unsatisfying jobs at that. Indeed the government is seriously considering leaving the whole process to market forces, which is bound of course to turn the issue into a more politically heated one altogether.[96]

As a result of the problems of the workers and the graduates, as well as those of the urban lumpen proletariat, and the growing sense of deprivation and alienation, the cities are quite likely to turn into very suitable beds for socio-political unrest that could erupt into violence at the slightest provocation. Two types of political violence have already illustrated the uneasiness of the situation. The first presented itself in the sweeping "food riots" of January 1977 which took place in most Egyptian cities and which were dominated to a large extent by the urban lumpen proletariat. And the second is the much smaller but more determined acts of violence initiated by the "neo-fundamentalist" Islamic groups (of which at least three were uncovered by the government in 1974, 1977 and 1980), which tend to be concentrated among the educated youth of lower middle class background and of recent migration to the cities.[97]

Perhaps the most risky thing for the regime, from a political point of view, would be the alienation of the salaried middle classes under the impact of unemployment of the educated and high inflation rates combined with rigidly fixed salaries. For it would be very dangerous indeed for any regime to lose the support of the classes that it claims to serve most. After all it was the dissatisfaction of the middle class that led more than anything else to the 1978–79 revolution in Iran, and indeed the situation in Egypt is even more problematic than it was in Pahlavi Iran, for the Shah did not have at hand such an insurmountable dilemma as the Arab-Israeli problem and in contrast he had also the additional advantage of being able, through handouts from the huge oil revenues, to appease most members of the middle classes, at least financially. This cannot be reproduced in Egypt where most members of the middle classes are indeed becoming economically miserable.

The regime now seems to be very well aware of the potential dangers involved in the situation, and since the riots of 1977, which were put down only by the intervention (for the first time since the early fifties) of the armed forces, tight security measures have been taken, especially in the cities. The presence of police, security and para-military forces is very quickly felt in the cities and no secret is made of their political role.[98] There are also several measures for the economic appeasement of the city dwellers under the banner of "food security", including the treatment of the transport of certain items of food and clothing beyond the main cities as a major crime.[99] *Infitah* might therefore have made Egypt's foreign trade more "free" in a manner of speaking, but there can be little doubt that political life remains less liberal and that the system is still based on bureaucratic control and on social discipline "enforced by the president through the security apparatus and ultimately the army."[100]

Security measures are barely sufficient by themselves, however. Some promises, including those related to "the blessings of *infitah*" will have to be at least partially kept; and even though some people have undoubtedly benefited, the blessings of *infitah* remain for the majority of Egyptians more of a promise that has not yet been fulfilled.

NOTES

1. Cf. Nazih N. M. Ayubi, *Bureaucracy and Politics in Contemporary Egypt* (London; Ithaca Press, 1980), Chaps. 5 and 6.

2. For details see Ayubi, ibid., Chaps. 3 and 6 and references therein.

3. ꜥUthman Ahmad ꜥUthman's career as an entrepreneur had actually started even before the 1952 Revolution. He and other members of the ꜥUthman family were the main shareholders of the Engineering Company for Industries and Contracts, and were also prominent shareholders in other companies such as the Nasr Company for Pencils and Graphite Products. Cf. Mahmud Murad, *Man kana yahkum misr* [Who Was Ruling Egypt?], (Cairo: Madbuli, 1975), pp. 76, 119. According to the Nationalization Laws of 1961, his contracting companies were to be half-owned by the government but he remained constantly as the chairman of the board of directors, and used the companies greatly to expand his activities in the sixties and seventies.

4. See for example President Sadat's tough speech of May 1978 in which he condemned all critical views and said that inequality and corruption were not as rampant as the critics had claimed. *Al-Ahram* (15 May 1978).

5. ꜥAdil Husain, "Irhamuna min hadha al-infitah al-tijari" [Relieve Us From this Commercial 'Opening'!], *Al-Taliꜥa*, Vol. 12, no. 10 (October 1976), p. 47.

6. *Al-Ahram al-Iqtisadi,* no. 544 (15 April 1978), p. 17.

7. For this and for several other cases see Administrative Control Authority (ACA), *Awjuh al-qusur wꜥal-khalal fi al-jihaz al-idari li al-dawla* [Shortcomings and Deficiencies in the State Administrative Machinery], (Cairo, 1977), Vol. I, pp. 169ff, and Vol. II, Part I, pp. 16ff and 84–88. See also *Al-Ahram al-Iqtisadi,* no. 569 (1 May 1979), pp. 6–7.

8. For other aspects of *infitah* see John Waterbury, *Egypt: Burdens of the Past, Options for the Future* (Bloomington: Indiana University Press, 1978) and the chapter by Gouda Abdel-Khalek in the present volume.

9. For a good analysis of these announcements and of the legal and economic changes that accompanied them see Fuꜥad Mursi, *Hadha al-infitah al-iqtisadi* [This Economic 'Opening'!], (Cairo: Dar al-Thaqafa al-Jadida, 1976).

10. *Al-Akhbar* (19 August 1979). The constitutional amendment characterizing the country's system as a "social-democratic" one was approved by popular referendum on 22 May 1980. See for details *Al-Mustaqbal,* Vol. 4, no. 194 (November 1980), pp. 25–27.

11. In August 1976 the Ministry of Commerce instructed that no importation was allowed of any goods (except for white cheese, with special permission) from Communist countries. *Al-Jumhuriyya* (5 August 1976). This policy has hit a great many importers who could have secured many goods from the socialist countries at better prices. As a consequence of the resulting revocation of most bilateral trade agreements with these countries their imports from Egypt have also declined sharply, with serious harm to many small Egyptian industries, especially in the fields of furniture, leather and knitted goods. *Al-Ahram al-Iqtisadi,* no. 543 (1 April 1978).

12. People's Assembly, *Mahdar al-ijtimaꜥ*...[Deliberations on the Law for the Invest-

ment of Arab and Foreign Capital and Free Zones], Minutes of the First Session. (Cairo, 21 May 1974), p. 100.

13. People's Assembly, *Deliberations...*, ibid., Minutes of the Second Session. (Cairo, 22 May 1974), p. 123.

14. Tax revenue in 1978 for example amounted to LE1717 million, of which LE1147 million were indirect taxes and only LE570 million were direct taxes.For details see: Qutb Ibrahim-Muhammad, *Al-muwazana al-ʿamma li al-dawla* [The General State Budget], (Cairo: Al-Haiʾat al-Kitab, 1978), pp. 247–279.

15. This is the term I coined and used in the symposium on "Binaʾ al-insan al-misri al-jadid" [Building the New Egyptian Man] reported in *Al-Ahram* (9 October 1976). On the flow of actual and possible Arab money into Egypt, see in general: T. ʿAbd Al-ʿAlim Taha, *Al-fawaʾid al-bitruliyya al-ʿarabiyya wa imkaniyyat tadaffuqiha ila misr* [Arab Petroleum Surplus Funds and the Possibility of their Flow to Egypt], (Cairo: Centre for Political and Strategic Studies, 1977). Even at this highest point Arab funds flowing to Egypt were deemed by the Egyptians to be far too meager, not only in light of their belief that they were at least partly responsible for the oil boom through their fighting of the war of October 1973, but also given the magnitude of the oil money surplus and taking into account the large amount of that surplus channelled into Western markets or wasted on unnecessary arms and on conspicuous projects. See on this point: Mohamed El Beheiry, "Egypt and OPEC" in R. A. Stone, ed., *OPEC and the Middle East* (New York: Praeger, 1977), pp. 207–8

16. For these and other estimates of the World Bank quoted in this chapter see: *Arab Republic of Egypt: Economic Management in a Period of Transition* (6 vols.), World Bank Report No. 1815-EGT; Vol. IV, 1978, pp. 47–56 et passim.

17. A major proportion of the loans offered, for example, by the Gulf Fund for the Development of Egypt was to be used for the servicing and repayment of Egyptian debts to various, including Arab, financiers.

18. American development aid during the latter half of 1979 and the earlier part of 1980 was estimated at about $100 million a month. In the 1977 fiscal year, 49 percent of all American economic aid went towards commodity import programmes, 20 percent for PL 480, 25 percent for capital projects and 6 percent for technical assistance. Until 1977 food and raw materials represented the main part of American aid but the emphasis was shifted from 1978 towards rural development, education, health and social services, as well as investment projects. Cf. Agency for International Development, *Development in Egypt: A Report on United States Economic Assistance* (Cairo: 1978), p. 8ff.

19. GAIFZ, *Taqrir ʿan mashruʿat al-istithmar* [Report on Investment Projects Until 31 December 1978], (Cairo, 1979), p. 16ff.

20. Ibid., p. 42.

21. Ibid., pp. 38–41.

22. Ibid., pp. 49–65.

23. The General Industrialization Authority (GIA), *Taqrir ʿan mutabaʿat al-qurud...* [Report on the Follow-up of Foreign Loans for the Industrial Investment Sector Until 31 July 1979], internal memorandum (Cairo, 1979).

24. Samira Bahr, "Misr wa haiʾat al-tamwil al-ʿarabiyya" [Egypt and Arab Financing Agencies], *Al-Siyasa al-Dawliyya,* no. 54 (October 1978), pp. 108–9.

25. GIA, op.cit., pp. 36–42.

26. The controversial case of the Ward buses that were running in Egypt in the second half of the seventies is symbolically significant. These incredibly noisy buses have also been short-lived and have given rise to two different stories, partly presented in the Egyptian and the American press: the Egyptians maintained that the buses were not made to the required Egyptian specifications and compared their performance unfavorably to that of the other

makes of buses running in Cairo. The American suppliers, on the other hand, claimed that it was bad running conditions and poor maintenance standards that led to their almost total collapse. *Time* (28 July 1980) summarized the case as follows: "Many of the 1,600 buses the U.S. provided for Egypt's chaotic transport system two years ago have broken down, either through bad maintenance or over-loading; some arrived in Egypt without mufflers or produced a grating roar that Cairenes cynically refer to as 'the Voice of America'."

27. GAIFZ, op.cit., p. 29ff.

28. Ibid., pp. 100–105.

29. See on this subject in general, Hikmat al-Nashashibi, *Istithmar al-arsida al-ᶜarabiyya* [Investment of Arab Funds], (Kuwait: Dar al-Shayiᶜ, 1978), especially Chapter 8, "Absorptive Capacity of the Arab Economy".

30. For more details on some of the recent problems of the Egyptian bureaucracy see: Nazih N. M. Ayubi, "Bureaucratic Inflation and Administrative Inefficiency: The Deadlock in Egyptian Administration", forthcoming in *Middle Eastern Studies*.

31. Data from the Central Agency for Organization and Administration (CAOA) and the Ministry of Finance, 1978.

32. Cf. *Al-Jumhuriyya* (19 January 1978) and (7 March 1978).

33. See on this subject Malak Girgis, *Saikulujiyyat al-shakhsiyya al-misriyya wa muᶜawwiqat al-tanmiyya* [Psychology of the Egyptian Personality and Constraints to Development], (Cairo: Rose al-Yusuf, 1974), pp. 55–59.

34. Fathi Muharram, "Bahth maidani fi istikhdamat al-quwa al-bashariyya" [An Empirical Research on the Utilization of Manpower], *Administrative Leaders' Programmes* (Cairo, 21–26 October 1978).

35. Generally speaking, programs for structural reorganization were implemented more easily than other programs for administrative reform, at a rate of about 90 percent or so. See CAOA, *Al-taqrir al-sanawi...* [The Annual Report 1976], (Cairo: Al-Matabiᶜ al-Amiriyya, 1977), pp. 26–29.

36. For details see Nazih Ayubi, *Al-thawra al-idariyya wa azmat al-islah fi misr* [The 'Administrative Revolution' and the Crisis of Reform in Egypt], (Cairo: Centre for Political and Strategic Studies, 1977), especially Chap. 1.

37. Cf. *Akhbar al-Yaum* (2 June 1979) and *Al-Ahram* (4 June 1979).

38. GAIFZ, op.cit., pp. 107–111.

39. See for example *Al-Shaᶜb* (8 January 1980) and (27 May 1980).

40. According to a leftist source, the membership of the Nationalist Progressive Unionist Party had grown, in spite of official harrassment, from 128 in April 1976 to 150,000 in April 1980. *Al-Yasar al-ᶜArabi* (May 1980).

41. See for example the interview with the Egyptian Minister of the Economy in *Al-Sharq al-Awsat* (27 September 1979), p. 13.

42. Remittances from Egyptian workers abroad accounted for some $2.5 billion in 1980. Revenues from exporting petroleum for 1980 were also expected to reach nearly $2 billion, while attempts are being made to raise revenues from the Suez Canal to nearly $1 billion by 1981–82. All in all, foreign exchange earnings have grown from $2.7 billion in 1975 to about $7 billion in 1979. Compare: The Economist Intelligence Unit, *Quarterly Economic Review of Egypt*, I, 1979, pp. 2–3.

43. The settlement with Israel has indeed been justified to the public in basically domestic terms — that the relaxation of military efforts will help development and result in prosperity. The excessive emphasis given to this argument is of course potentially dangerous from a political point of view, given that economic improvement for the masses did not immediately follow, and will not necessarily follow, the settlement: if anything,

allocations for military expenditure for 1980 had actually increased—by 10 percent.

44. The government had allocated as much as 45 percent of the Five Year Development Plan 1978–82 to various infrastructure sub-sectors, which is rather excessive though understandable. The 1980–84 Plan allocates about 6 billion pounds, or nearly one third of all investments, to expenditure on the infrastructure.

45. Heba A. Handoussa, "The Public Sector in Egyptian Industry 1952–1977" in Société Egyptienne d'Economie Politique..., *Al-Iqtisad al-Misri fi rub* qarn... [The Egyptian Economy in Quarter of a Century, 1952–1977] ed. Ismaᶜil Sabri ᶜAbdallah et al., (Cairo: Haiᵖat al-Kitab, 1977), pp. 497–518.

46. Ibid., p. 516ff.

47. The most comprehensive study of employment in the public sector indicates that in 1975 it employed over 868,000 perople of whom about 573,000 were working in 170 industrial companies, about 26,000 in 160 service companies, and about 29,000 in 25 agricultural companies. Institute of National Planning, *Bahth hasr wa taqdir al-ihtiyajat min al-ᶜamala bi al-qitaᶜ al-ᶜam* [Employment in the Public Sector: the Present Situation and the Expected Needs], ed. Md. ᶜAbd al-Fattah Munji. (Cairo: INP, 1975), p. 13ff.

48. Quoted in *Al-Ahram* (16 May 1978).

49. Handoussa, op.cit., p. 506.

50. Mark Cooper, "Egyptian State Capitalism in Crisis: Economic Policies and Political Interests 1967–1971", *International Journal of Middle East Studies,* Vol. 10, no. 4 (November 1979), pp. 481–516.

51. Ibid., p. 515.

52. Ibid., p. 506ff.

53. Heba A. Handoussa, "Time for Reform: Egypt's Public Sector Industry" in Herbert M. Thompson, ed., *Studies in Egyptian Political Economy,* The Cairo Papers in Social Science, Vol. 2, Monograph 3 (March 1979), pp. 107–122.

54. *Al-Mudir al-ᶜArabi,* no. 65 (October 1978), p. 44.

55. Fuᵖad Abu-Ismaᶜil, "Bahth maidani ᶜan idarat al-afrad wa al-idara al-maliyya bi sharikat al-qitaᶜ al-ᶜam fi zil siyasat al-infitah" [Empirical Research on Personnel Administration and Financial Administration in Public Sector Companies under the Open Door Policy], *Administrative Leaders' Programmes* (Cairo, 12–23 May 1979).

56. ᶜAli al-Gritly, *Khamsa wa ᶜishrun ᶜaman: dirasa tahliliyya li al-siyasat al-iqtisadiyya fi misr* [An Analytical Study of Economic Policies in Egypt in Twenty-five Years], (Cairo: Haiᵖat al-Kitab, 1977), especially pp. 301–306.

57. See on the Federation's membership, The Egyptian Federation of Industries, *Al-kitab al-sanawi...* [The 1977 Yearbook], (Cairo, 1978), pp. 1–2; for its reporting of industrial projects under *infitah,* ibid., pp. 47–55. The traditional textile industry, as well as some other industries such as generators, tractors, television sets, medicines, steel pipes, plastics, paper, etc., have been badly hit as a result of the new importation policies. Cf. ACA, *Awjuh al-qusur...,* op.cit., Vol. I, pp. 223–331. In fact, given that over half the imports coming to the free zones are textiles, it is no wonder that the unmarketed products of Egyptian textile factories were estimated at over LE400 million in 1978. *Al-Ahram al-Iqtisadi,* no. 556 (15 October 1978), p. 10. It was probably in the light of such difficulties in the marketing of locally produced textiles that the controversial project for the ᶜAmiriyya Textiles Complex was dropped (though not without much argument).

58. Egyptian Federation of Industries, *Ahamm al-muᶜawwiqat allati tuwajih qitaᶜ al-sinaᶜa* [The Main Constraints Facing the Industrial Sector], memorandum from the Chairman's Bureau, 1979, pp. 1–7.

59. Quoted in *Al-Ahram* (21 March 1978).

60. The case of Ashraf Marwan is indicative of this practice. This fast-rising person was

removed by presidential decree in October 1978 from his post as the Egyptian appointee for the Chairmanship of the Arab Industrialization Organization. The following day, however, Marwan was being appointed by another presidential decree as an ambassador of the "distinguished order" (*min al-daraja al-mumtaza*) at the Ministry of Foreign Affairs. *Al-Akhbar* (10 October 1978) and *Al-Jumhuriyya* (11 October 1978).

61. *Al-Jumhuriyya* (8 February 1979).

62. See among many others the cases documented in *Al-Ahram* (21 March 1978) and (21 November 1978); *Al-Akhbar* (1 December 1978) and (11 December 1978).

63. Ibrahim Abul-Ghar, "Inhiraf al-wazifa al-ᶜamma fi al-mujtamaᶜ al-misri" [Deviance of Public Officials in the Egyptian Society] in National Centre for Social and Criminological Research (NCSCR), *Symposium on Deviance in the Public Service* (Cairo, 3–5 March 1979), p. 15ff.

64. Ministry of the Interior, *Taqrir al-ᵓamn al-ᶜam...* [The Public Security Report for 1975], (Cairo, 1976), passim.

65. Public Security Reports [in Arabic], 1977 and 1978. In spite of their benefits, public security reports are disappointing in studying corruption since the majority of bribery cases go unreported. Furthermore the majority of corruption cases that are reported are the ones related to minor officials; so we are asked to believe that in 1977, for example, 78 percent of all people involved in embezzlement and 75 percent of all people involved in bribery were minor officials with no formal education! (The 1977 *Report,* p.13).

66. See for details: Nazih Ayubi, "Fasad al-idara fi misr..." [The Corruption of Administration in Egypt: Its Aspects, Causes and Costs], *Symposium on Deviance in the Public Service,* (Cairo, 3–5 March 1979), pp. 4–12.

67. Compare Robert D. Springborg, "The Ties that Bind: Political Association and Policy Making in Egypt", unpublished PhD dissertation, (Stanford University, 1974).

68. Ahmad Rashid, *Al-fasad al-idari* [Administrative Corruption], (Cairo: Al-Shaᶜb, 1975), pp.24–28.

69. Just to illustrate the magnitude of the phenomenon it may suffice to say that one careful check of the travel documents on one aeroplane carrying Egyptians to Saudi Arabia under the pretence of wanting to do their ᶜumra (an off-season pilgrimage) resulted in the finding of no less than twenty forged passports among the passengers. *Al-Akhbar* (12 September 1977).

70. Ayubi, "The Corruption of Administration...", op.cit., p. 12.

71. Samuel Huntington, *Political Order in Changing Societies* (New Haven, Conn.: Yale University Press, 1969), p. 69.

72. Cf. ᶜAdil Husain, "Al-mal al-nafti ᶜaᵓiq li al-tawhid" [Petro-dollars as a Constraint to Arab Unity], *Al-Mustaqbal al-ᶜArabi,* Vol. II, no. 5 (1979), pp. 26–30. Even preparatory school pupils have been made aware of this possibility: the general examination in Arabic for the preparatory school certificate in 1977 asked the pupils to write their composition on the subject of the joys of a person who could obtain work in an Arab country, thus managing to accumulate money and return home to start a new life. Cf. *Al-Ahram* (18 May 1977).

73. Another amusing story might be illustrative here. The marriage advertisements page of a weekly magazine carried in 1977 an unusual notice concerning the interest in marriage of an Egyptian girl with residence rights in Canada. Within a few days, the girl (who promised her prospective husband the right of residence in Canada too) had received thousands of applications from men wishing to marry her—the largest number of applicants ever to have responded to this service. See *Rose al-Yusuf,* No. 2551 (2 May 1977).

74. See Ibrahim Saᶜd al-Din, "Al-athar al-salbiyya li al-furuq al-dakhliyya bain al-aqtar al-ᶜarabiyya..." [Negative Effects of Income Disparities Between Arab Countries on Development in the Lower Income Countries], in Société Egyptienne d'Economie Politi-

que..., *Istratijiyyat al-tanmiyya fi misr* [Development Strategy in Egypt], ed. Ismaᶜil-Sabri ᶜAbdallah et al., (Cairo: Haiᵖat al-Kitab, 1978), pp. 107-125.

75. See for these estimates Central Agency for Public Mobilization and Statistics (CAP-MAS), *Statistical Yearbook 1978* [Arabic]; Ministry of Information, *The Arab Republic of Egypt Yearbook 1977* [Arabic]; Ministry of Planning, *Report on the Labor Force of Egypt in 1976* [Arabic]; Khalil Barsum, *Mashakil takhtit al-quwa al-ᶜamila* [Problems of Manpower Planning], (Cairo: Kitab al-ᶜAmal, 1979), pp. 13, 16, 18, 44-47; *Al-Ahram* (18 September 1978); *Al-Akhbar* (1 May 1979); *Al-ᶜUmmal* (7 January 1980).

76. J. S. Birks and C. A. Sinclair, "Egypt: A Frustrated Labor Exporter?", *Middle East Journal,* Vol. 33, no. 3 (Summer 1979), pp. 288-303.

77. As a result it is not surprising nowadays in Egypt to see mechanics, carpenters, electricians, and so on, who are barely into their early teens, or to see women working on a large scale for the first time as construction laborers.

78. The best socio-political treatment of the housing problem is in Milad Hanna, *Uridu maskanan...* [I Need a Home: A Problem That *Has* a Solution] (Cairo: Rose al-Yusuf, 1978).

79. Quoted in *Al-Taliᶜa,* Vol. 11, no. 2 (February 1976), p. 59.

80. See for example *Al-Musawwar,* No. 2746 (27 May 1977); *Al-Jumhuriyya* (20 April 1978).

81. See *Al-Ahram* (3 March 1978) and (3, 5, 6, and 11 April 1978).

82. See the many cases reported in *Akhbar al-Yaum* (7, 14 and 21 July 1979).

83. Administrative Control Authority, *Awjuh al-qusur...,* op.cit., Vol. II, Part 1, pp. 231-2.

84. Cf. *Al-Jumhuriyya* (13 July 1978).

85. For technical details see the articles by Neamat Fouad and Ahmad Gamiᶜ in C. Nelson and K. Koch, eds., *Law and Social Change in Contemporary Egypt,* The Cairo Papers in Social Science, Vol. 2, Monograph 4 (April 1979), pp. 135-175.

86. See the fascinating and, despite its historic nature, currently relevant book: David Landes, *Bankers and Pashas* (London: Heinemann, 1958), and consult more specifically: Roger Owen, "Egypt and Europe: From French Expedition to British Occupation", in R. Owen and B. Sutcliffe, eds., *Studies in the Theory of Imperialism* (London: Longmans, 1972), pp. 195-209.

87. *Al-Jumhuriyya* (14 May 1978).

88. GAIFZ, "Dirasa li wadᶜ al-bunuk..." [A Study on the Position of Banks Created Under the Investment Law], *Conference of the Commerce Syndicate on the Open Door Economic Policy,* (Cairo, March 1979), p. 5.

89. Muhammad Saqr, "Al-istithmar al-ajnabi..." [The Role of Foreign Investment in Meeting Production Requirements in Egypt], *Conference of the Egyptian Society for Financial Management on Problems of Production and Development* (Cairo, January 1980), pp. 8-18.

90. Heads of all Egyptian chambers of commerce, plus the secretary-general of the Cairo chamber and the Alexandria chamber, in addition to six members appointed by the Minister of Commerce, form the main body of the General Federation of Egyptian Chambers of Commerce. Cf. The General Federation of Egyptian Chambers of Commerce, *Al-qadaya wa al-tashriᶜat al-munazzima li al-ghurfa al-tijariyya* [Cases and Legislations Regulating the Chambers], (Cairo, c. 1978), pp. 26-28.

91. *Al-Ahram al-Iqtisadi,* no. 545 (15 April 1978), p. 21.

92. For details see General Federation of Egyptian Chambers of Commerce, *Al-Nashra al-Iqtisadiyya,* no. 8 (December 1977), pp. 119-120; no. 10 (February 1978), p.116.

93. The formal definition of a worker issued in 1962 was far too loose, based as it was on eligibility to join Workers' unions or being a self-employed craftsman. Many higher technocrats could therefore occupy several representative seats under the banner of "worker". In 1968 the definition was narrowed to some extent by adding some new criteria and specifying that a worker should not enjoy the right of joining a professional syndicate (which excluded virtually everybody with a university degree). See Al-Akhbar Research Division, *Man huwa al-ʿamil wa man huwa al-fallah?* [Who is a Worker and Who is a Peasant?], (Cairo: Akhbar al-Yaum Est., 1968). But the definition remained rather loose, permitting, for example, bank managers and business executives with no university degrees to classify themselves as workers. One of the demands of the workers for a number of years had therefore been for a more realistic specification of the political category of "worker" and this was among the main points they raised when the issue of political parties and the Arab Socialist Union was being publicly discussed in 1974. See *Akhbar al-Yaum* (21 September 1974).

94. Four public factories of a military or semi-military nature represented Egypt's contribution to assets of the Arab Industrialization Organization, whose activities were being reconsidered as a result of Egypt's separate settlement with Israel. See Muhammad Anis, "Al-haiʾa al-ʿarabiyya li al-tasniʿ... [The Arab Industrialization Organization and Challenges for Arab Security], *Al-Siyasa al-Dawliyya,* no. 56 (April 1979).

95. Cf. Saad E. Ibrahim, "Social Mobility and Income Distribution", mimeo, November 1979, (forthcoming in R. Tignor et al., eds., *The Political Economy of Income Distribution in Egypt*).

96. For details see Nazih Ayubi, *Siyasat al-taʿlim fi misr* [The Policy of Education in Egypt: A Political Study], (Cairo: The Centre for Political and Strategic Studies, 1978), especially Chaps. 3 and 4; and CAPMAS, *The Statistical Yearbook,* various issues.

97. Nazih N. M. Ayubi, "The Political Revival of Islam: The Case of Egypt", *International Journal of Middle East Studies,* Vol. 12, no. 4 (December 1980).

98. As the Minister of the Interior, Muhammad Nabawi Ismaʿil, explained, "the police will not hesitate to confront most firmly the hostile minority which is trying to act against the national regime and against the national goals." *Al-Akhbar* (29 June 1979).

99. It is rather curious that in the oldest unitary state on earth, the transport of items like flour, maize, sugar, beans, rice, tea, oil, soap, and cigarettes between various provinces of the country should be labelled illegal and prevented by the police, and that its cases should be brought to the state security court. See for example *Al-Jumhuriyya* (6 May 1978); *Al-Ahkbar* (11 May 1978).

100. Raymond W. Baker, *Egypt's Uncertain Revolution Under Nasser and Sadat* (Cambridge, Mass.: Harvard University Press, 1978), p. 244.

XII
Oil, Arms, and Regional Diplomacy: Strategic Dimensions of the Saudi-Egyptian Relationship

Paul Jabber

INTRODUCTION

A common thread running through many contributions to this volume is the centrality of the special relationship between Egypt and Saudi Arabia in the contemporary Arab political system. This relationship emerged in the early seventies, and is the most salient expression of the major power realignment that occurred within the inter-Arab regional balance in the wake of the war of June 1967. Such realignment resulted principally from Nasirist Egypt's eclipse as the predominant Arab actor and ideological pacesetter, combined with the rapid increase in the financial wealth and political influence of the conservative oil-rich states.

A major purpose of this chapter is to analyze the evolution, objectives, and future of the Saudi-Egyptian relationship, with particular emphasis on its politico-military aspects. Another is to highlight the effect that the economic costs of the Arab-Israeli arms race had on Cairo's policies.

Despite the thorough militarization of the Middle Eastern international system over the past quarter-century, much political and economic analysis of Arab internal and regional affairs continues to pay scant, if any, serious attention to the impact that military-related factors, broadly defined, must perforce have on the perceptions, policy alternatives, behavior and overall decisional context of Arab political leadership, as well as on the performance of those economic systems over which they preside. Particularly absent is a sensitivity to the fairly narrow range of policy options truly available to decision-makers of states where heavy military commitments have for a long time far outstripped domestic capabilities. This is primarily the case of Egypt, and of Syria to a somewhat lesser extent. Whether in assessments of past behavior, critiques of current policy, or forecasts of future developments, it is remarkable how often analysts implicitly assume that a leadership such as Egypt's in the seventies or the eighties has in hand a veritable menu of choices from which it can pick at will: confrontation or cooperation with the conservative-monarchist camp; peace or war with Israel; a closed or an open economy; dependence or autonomy in its economic ties with the rest of the world; Arab bloc leadership and pan-Arabist fervor, or an "Egypt first" application to consolidating the state as the *ultima ratio.*

In endeavoring to interpret the major aspects of Egypt's foreign and security policies under President Anwar al-Sadat, the analysis that follows will suggest that in fact no such menu was available. The alliance with the Arab conservatives, the economic liberalization, and peace with Israel, were policies driven by far more compelling imperatives than Sadat's policy preferences. Indeed, while timing, tactics and detail might have varied, in their fundamental parameters these policies would have been espoused by any other likely alternative leadership, including that of Gamal ʿAbd al-Nasir, had his death not intervened. The analysis will seek to trace their linkages to the unfolding Arab-Israeli arms race, patterns of weapons acquisition by the major regional powers, and the economic consequences of heavy military spending. Saudi policy objectives and security concerns will be reviewed, and the probable course of Saudi-Egyptian relations for the balance of the decade will be outlined, within the context of increasing superpower — particularly American — involvement and commitments in the Middle East.

I. THE BURDEN OF MILITARY SPENDING

The Arab world has enjoyed over the past decade the rather mixed but not altogether unwelcome blessings of abundant oil-generated wealth. It has also shouldered the heavy burden of military spending on an extraordinary scale. In 1977, a typical year, eleven countries worldwide spent more than 10 percent of their Gross National Product (GNP) on defense. Six of them were Arab—Egypt, Syria, Iraq, Saudi Arabia, the United Arab Emirates, and Oman. An additional two were also in the Middle East—Israel and Iran.[1]

Not only does this region collectively boast the highest per capita rates of military spending on earth, but it has also witnessed five major Arab-Israeli wars since 1948[2] and seven substantial inter-Arab armed conflicts over the past twenty years.[3] Furthermore, internal insurgencies—such as the extended Kurdish uprising in Iraq—and the activities of transnational guerilla movements—particularly the many Palestinian organizations—have added heavily to the incidence of armed conflict within it.

The numerous military balances (Arab-Israeli, Arab-Iranian, several Arab-Arab) that in interlocking fashion frame the power relationships within the area have had a pre-eminent influence on the shaping of the new regional order in the seventies. Their impact far outweighed pan-nationalist or other ideological considerations in guiding ruling-elite behavior. Several major shifts in long-term trends affecting the central Arab-Israeli arms race — occurring within a context of continued dominance by Israel in sheer armed power, with the emergence of Iran as an assertive and strongly armed aspirant to hegemony over the Gulf and its ocean reaches, and with the heightened possibility of extra-regional military intervention in oil-bearing areas — all contributed to an acute sense of basic strategic insecurity among Arab oil-rich governments. Strenuous efforts to build up local defense capabilities were launched, but these were, and will continue to be, obviously constrained by severe manpower limitations, both in quantity and quality. Perhaps more significant was the endeavor, led by Saudi Arabia, to bolster Egypt's military capabilities from 1975 onwards, in an apparent decision to place strong reliance on Egyptian military strength as an additional defensive asset for the protection of the Arabian Peninsula's oil producers.

The Arab countries to which particular attention is devoted in this chapter have, on the average, devoted extremely large percentages of their national resources to defense. As may be seen from Table I they have spent in various years from one sixth to one third of their GNP on the military sector. The economic drain represented by these figures is aggravated by the fact that a large percentage of these outlays goes to the purchase of weaponry from foreign producers and represents a net loss, given the lack of substantial domestic weapons-manufacturing capacity.

In some instances, the extent of the military burden is the result of discretionary choice, of selecting one among several rather painless options created by the availability of resources and an absence of urgent limiting commitments, obligations and needs. Among these fortunate few, Saudi Arabia stands out, both because of the sheer size of its military outlays in absolute terms (US$21 billion in constant 1977 dollars in 1975–1977), and as a paragon of a state whose choices were minimally affected by economic constraints. The flow of petrodollars enabled the Saudis to quintuple their military spending between 1970 and 1975, while simultaneously amassing the second largest monetary reserves globally, and becoming the second largest world contributor of foreign aid. Seldom in history has a government enjoyed as much economic flexibility and freedom of decision in setting national policies across the whole spectrum of domestic and foreign affairs as has Riyadh recently ex-

TABLE I

Military Expenditures and Gross National Product of Selected Arab States
(in US $ billions)

		1970	1971	1972	1973	1974	1975	1976	1977	1978	1979
Egypt	MILEX	1.3	1.5	1.5	2.8	4.1	6.1	4.9	4.4	2.8	2.2
	GNP	6.7	7.1	7.6	8.9	9.5[a]	11.7	12.9	13.3	n.a.	16.5
	%	18.9	21.1	19.9	31.0	42.8	52.4	37.0	32.8	n.a.	13.1
Syria	MILEX	.2	.2	.3	.4	.5	.7	1.0	1.1	1.1	2.0
	GNP	1.5	1.5	2.1	2.5	2.9	4.7	6.1	7.1	n.a.	9.2
	%	11.9	11.8	12.1	16.0	15.7	15.1	16.3	15.0	n.a.	22.1
Jordan	MILEX	.1	.1	.1	.1	.1	.2	.2	.2	.3	.4
	GNP	.7	.6	.7	.9	1.0	1.3	1.3	1.8	n.a.	2.7
	%	14.8	14.8	16.0	16.4	14.2	12.2	12.9	10.9	n.a.	14.2
Iraq	MILEX	.3	.2	.5	.8	1.6[a]	1.6[a]	1.4	1.7	2.0	2.7
	GNP	3.8	3.7	6.6	9.2	10.2[a]	13.4	14.2	16.3	15.5	21.4
	%	7.7	6.5	7.2	9.8	15.7	11.8	9.6	10.2	13.0	12.5
Saudi Arabia	MILEX	.4	.4	.9	1.5	1.8	6.8	9.0	7.5	13.2	14.2
	GNP	4.0	4.3	5.2	8.3	24.8	37.2	51.1	55.8	87.8	94.6
	%	9.8	8.9	18.1	18.3	7.3	18.0	17.7	13.5	15.0	15.0

a/ author's estimate

SOURCE: International Institute for Strategic Studies, *The Military Balance* (London, annual).

perienced. Indeed, military expansion was viewed not as a "burden" but as a natural and positive development of previously neglected capabilities to go hand in hand with the country's growing regional influence and international stature, and to enhance the local protection of its all-important national resource.

For some other Arab states, almost the exact opposite conditions prevailed. In their case, low and insufficient national income combined with insistently urgent and ineluctably growing domestic demands to provide powerful incentives for reducing military expenditures. Yet the high, almost ruinous rates of defense spending characteristic of the 1970s were the inescapable legacy of choices made decades earlier, of long-standing decisions and policies—both foreign and domestic—whose outcomes had so structured the national condition as to leave little if any room for substantial downward alterations.

Egypt presents the classic case. When the "age of plenty" began, with the Teheran round of oil-price renegotiations in early 1971,[4] Egypt found itself locked into a set of circumstances that left no margin for selectivity in the apportionment of governmental resources and that seriously limited its ability to draw on the new wealth of the oil-producing Arabs to reinvigorate its economic life. It was a leading participant in the most virulent conventional arms race worldwide, with important national territory under foreign occupation, a stalemated confrontation with a militarily superior opponent, its major source of foreign-exchange earnings (the Suez Canal) closed, and a bloated military establishment acting as an employer of last resort for hundreds of thousands of men who otherwise would find no gainful occupation in a stagnant economy. In its international relations, Egypt found itself closely tied to the Soviet bloc, both its exclusive source of major weaponry and its most important trading partner. Intermittent large-scale warfare with Israel, the heavy presence of Soviet troops and advisory personnel, and ruptured diplomatic and other relations with the United States and Great Britain strongly inhibited the flow of investment capital from abroad, already discouraged by the restrictions typical of a centrally planned economy, the overwhelming preponderance of the public sector, the severe limits on capital transfers abroad, a history of punitive politically motivated nationalizations, and the excesses of a pervasive make-work bureaucracy. A radical improvement in structural economic conditions—achievable in the best of cases only in the longer term—and/or a no less fundamental overhaul of foreign policy orientations and commitments appeared necessary before a significant reduction in the ratio of military expenditures to national income could be had.

In the Middle East, the gap between modest national resources on the one hand and ambitious foreign policies requiring heavy military outlays on the other has been of yawning magnitude for several decades. It is often remarked that, with the exception of Iraq and Algeria, by some ironic twist of fate those Arab countries that enjoy the most plentiful oil resources are also those that have the smallest populations, the most undeveloped institutional, manpower and other infrastructural assets, and the least pressing needs. Seldom noted is the fact that a similar negative correlation can be posited between oil wealth and participation in military conflicts. Before the supply of surplus petrodollars became a torrent in 1974, the highest rates of military spending were incurred by "front-line" states actively involved in the Arab-Israeli conflict. In Egypt and Syria, oil revenues were until recently minimal or non-existent. Moreover, scarce natural resources, economic mis-management, political instability, and runaway population growth further affected these states in varying degrees and different combinations to turn them after the 1950s into deficit economies perennially dependent on infusions of foreign aid to keep barely afloat.

By contrast, all Arab states in the immediate outer ring surrounding the Palestine conflict zone — with the single exception of the Sudan to the far south — were reaping the easy harvest of ample wealth from black gold. While the "poor", front-line states bore the brunt of the armed conflict with Israel, the participation of the wealthy second tier was both limited and spasmodic.

By the early seventies, Egypt and Syria were devoting the maximum effort of which they were financially capable to the military confrontation with the Jewish state, yet Israel was clearly winning the arms race. This was apparent both in terms of the absolute amounts of money that each side was able to devote to the arms race (see Table II), and in the quantitative arms balance. Furthermore, the qualitative edge in battle performance that Israel had clearly demonstrated in the 1967 war, particularly in the air, appeared undiminished, judging from the course of the 1969–70 War of Attrition on the Suez Canal front.

In the three years preceding the 1973 war, Israel out-spent all three Arab front-line states combined, climaxing an upward trend that had climbed steadily since 1961.[5] Its ability to do so was a function primarily of its much higher rate of economic growth — helped by heavy infusions of foreign aid — from the mid-1950s, which averaged around 12 percent annually in the years from 1954 to 1972, as compared with less than 5 percent for Egypt, and only slightly more for Syria.[6] A most significant advantage that these figures do not reveal is that Israel was able to concentrate its efforts and planning exclusively on meeting the challenge along its borders, while its major Arab adversary extended its own

TABLE II
Military Expenditures of Front-Line States, 1951-1979

Annual Averages (in US $ millions)

	1951-1960	1961-1970	1971-1973	1974-1976	1977-1979
Egypt	191.6	649.7	1921.3	5011.0	3116.6
Syria	45.5	121.8	276.6	720.3	1408.3
Jordan	36.8	75.7	118.0	150.6	295.3
total Arab	273.9	847.2	2315.9	5881.9	4820.2
Israel	143.6	531.2	2357.3	4053.0	4134.7

SOURCES: For the years 1951-1960, Y. Evron, "Arms Races in the Middle East and some Arms Control Measures Related to Them", in Gabriel Sheffer, ed., *Dynamics of a Conflict* (New York: Humanities Press, 1975), tables 2-6; International Institute for Strategic Studies, *The Military Balance.*

military commitments to other regional concerns as well. The most important of these was Egypt's involvement during the period 1962 to 1967 in the Yemen war, which at different stages involved between 20,000 and 70,000 expeditionary forces and required the creation of two new divisions, as well as the mobilization of reserves. Not only did the Yemen diversion contribute to Egypt's collapse in the June war in 1967. It also sapped the country's economy to the tune of $120 million annually,[7] or about 25 percent of total yearly average defense spending from 1963 to 1966.

Finally Israel had access to superior weaponry from external sources. While Egypt and Syria had to rely primarily on Soviet armaments from 1955 onwards, Israel obtained its major weapons systems principally from France in the period from 1955 to 1966, and from the United States following the June war.

In looking at motivations for heavy military spending in the Arab states, the confrontation with Israel looms particularly large, but is only one among several factors. Since the emergence of the present state system in the region, Egypt and Syria — both intellectual birthplaces of the Arab national movement — no less than Iraq have been rival aspirants to Arab bloc leadership, competing claimants as standard-bearers of Arab nationalism, and aggressive activists in the constant interplay of Arab politics. Geographical proximity to disputed territories in Palestine, nationalist commitment and hegemonial aspirations have thus combined to encourage political leaderships to amass armed power. Since these leaderships have predominantly emerged from the military ranks through coups and revolutions, and have continued to anchor their political base in the military institutions whence they sprang, it was to be expected that military strength would always be a matter of high priority for them in any case. Added to this was the desire to build up army morale after years of purposeful neglect on the part of former colonial masters, as was the case in both Syria and Egypt, and the need to assure regime security in an environment rife with political and economic instability, border disputes, and strong continued concern over the regional designs of major foreign powers.

Given this mix of motives, it is very likely that regional military expenditure levels would have been high even if the conflict over Palestine had taken a less violent course early on. By the same token, it is highly probable that these levels will remain higher than in all other world regions (5.7 percent of GNP was the world average in 1977) even if a comprehensive Arab-Israeli settlement is achieved. Nonetheless, the arms race with Israel had an enormous expansionary impact on the defense burden of Egypt in particular, and Syria since 1967. The extent of this impact is impossible to determine with any accuracy, but it might be in the order of 5 percent of GNP since 1955 in the Egyptian case, increasing to 10 percent in the period 1968 to 1976.

EFFECTS OF THE OCTOBER 1973 WAR

Egypt and Syria launched the October 1973 war to break a diplomatic stalemate that followed years of futile efforts by Cairo to induce an active American role in eliciting Israeli withdrawals. It was an all-out effort, but one with limited military objectives and a strictly political purpose: to force into being the requisite conditions for diplomatic movement by frightening the United States into action, shaking Israel out of its complacency, and restoring a psychological equilibrium to the Arab-Israeli power balance without which necessary concessions by both sides would have been unfeasible. "...[If] we could recapture even 4 inches of Sinai territory," stated Sadat in discussing the "strategic basis" for his war decision, "and establish ourselves there so firmly that no power on earth could dislodge us, then the whole situation would change—east, west, all over. First to go would be the humiliation we had endured since the 1967 defeat..."[8]

From a strictly military perspective, the war was an extremely risky gamble, a desperate throw of the iron dice. Egypt expected to sustain 10,000 casualties in the crossing of the Canal, and was willing to hazard the destruction of an army reconstructed after a gargantuan national effort to reestablish a mere foothold on Sinai. But it was also a case of "now or never". The Egyptian economy's ability to sustain the military effort was at a breaking point. The year 1972–73 represented a peak in the national defense effort that a stagnating economy would simply have been unable to repeat or even approximate in subsequent years. Escalating domestic needs, a dwindling foreign aid input basically limited to a post-1967 subsidy from the oil-rich states that only partially covered revenue losses resulting from the Suez Canal closure, and uncertain relations with the major superpower patron following the expulsion of Soviet personnel in July 1972, had brought the country to the verge of bankruptcy. As Sadat explained to his National Security Council on 30 September 1973, in justifying his decision to go to war;

> ...Let me tell you that our economy has fallen below zero. We have commitments (to the banks, and so on) which we should but cannot meet by the end of the year. In three months' time, by, say, 1974, we shan't have enough bread in the pantry! I cannot ask the Arabs for a single dollar more; they say they have been paying us the aid in lieu of the lost Canal revenue, although we didn't, or wouldn't, fight.[9]

As Nasir did in May-June 1967, Sadat resorted in October 1973 to military confrontation to break out of a political dead-end *and* alleviate impending economic penury. By exercising leadership on the battlefield on behalf of the key pan-Arab cause, Egypt could then lay claim to a bigger share of the growing wealth of the Arab rear, which otherwise would remain beyond reach. "As soon as the battle of October 6 was over," Sadat would add in a 1974 interview, "our Arab brethren came to our aid with $500 million...and this sum would never have come had we not taken effective action as regards the battle."[10]

But whereas Nasir's 1967 gamble failed,* Sadat's succeeded. This was due primarily to the achievement of a remarkable degree of strategic and tactical surprise, the effective implementation of a two-front war plan, the improved performance of Arab armies, and the ramifications of the effective use of the "oil weapon" by the Organization of Arab Petroleum Exporting Countries (OAPEC).

To offset Israeli military superiority, Egypt and Syria relied primarily on surprise and mass. These two factors were in evidence not only in the execution of the offensives that began on both fronts on 6 October, but also in the unexpectedly heavy use of anti-tank and anti-air precision-

---

*In 1967, there had been no intention or readiness to engage in full-scale war. With almost half of Egypt's effective military strength still committed in Yemen, Cairo's purpose was a deterrent one: to dissuade the Israelis from carrying out a threatened invasion of Syria.

guided weapons. In the opening days of the war, the Arab armies demonstrated skill in the use of sophisticated equipment, and the ability to conduct largescale combined-arms operations. Their success in this first phase would eventually enable them to fulfill most of their limited war objectives, although from a purely military standpoint the net results of the conflict clearly favored the Israelis.

The war of course had a tremendously significant side-effect, the triggering in its second week of a concerted reduction in oil exports by Arab petroleum producers, and an outright embargo against the United States and a number of small Western countries considered overly friendly to the Israeli side. The resultant supply squeeze soon created market circumstances that would enable OPEC to quadruple oil prices in the course of the next few months. There ensued a transfer of financial resources from the industrial world to the oil producers within a span of a few years of probably unprecedented proportions in international economic history, with Middle Eastern producers—led by Saudi Arabia, the single largest world wide exporter of crude—as the principal beneficiaries. Table III depicts this momentous development in stark figures: current account balances of OPEC rose from a total of $5.2 billion in 1973 to $63.4 billion one year later, and a cumulative total of $255.3 billion by the end of 1979. Its political, economic and social impact on Middle Eastern states is well documented in other parts of this study.

Among the oil-poor, no country would be as affected as Egypt by the new wealth. Sadat may have looked forward to a substantial augmentation of the $300 million annual subsidy by Saudi Arabia and Kuwait in his pre-war thinking. His secret trip to Riyadh in August 1973 was followed by the announcement of Saudi credits of up to $1 billion.[11] But not in his wildest dreams could any Egyptian planner have foreseen the impact the October conflict would have on international oil prices and the abundance of aid that would flow into the country from the Arabian peninsula states in the wake of the 1973 war. By the end of 1978, this aid would amount to some $15 billion, by conservative estimates. Many additional billions would also become available from non-Arab governments and international financial institutions.[12] By decade's end, however, it was clear that one effect this bounty had failed to produce was the creation of a sound basis for Egypt's economic regeneration.

Several reasons for this failure are explored in other contributions.[13] Some are of such structural character that one may well wonder whether any realistic level of resource availability would have been sufficient. In any case, on the assumption that availability of financial resources is a relevant variable and allocation strategies do make a difference in the Egyptian situation, a major contributing factor in the country's inability

TABLE III

Current Account Balances of OPEC Member Countries, 1973-1979

(Including Official Transfers; Millions $ U.S.)

	1973	1974	1975	1976	1977	1978	1979E
Algeria	-445	158	-1,662	-885	-2,325	-3,539	-2,740
Ecuador	6	37	-219	-6	-341	-150	-50
Gabon	-36	209	58	27	42	200	620
Indonesia	-475	597	-1,109	-908	-50	1,249	1,025
Iran	155	12,267	4,708	4,713	5,082	1,900	4,500
Iraq	800	2,618	2,705	3,500	3,000	3,200	10,900
Kuwait	1,540	7,360	5,891	6,949	4,766	6,167	11,850
Libya	67	1,831	-68	2,437	2,906	1,025	3,980
Nigeria	26	4,945	63	-299	-1,357	-3,782	4,440
Qatar	250	1,400	860	870	490	840	1,700
Saudi Arabia	2,204	23,007	13,931	13,791	12,791	-58	10,400
United Arab Emirates	300	3,140	2,270	2,670	990	925	2,550
Venezuela	861	5,810	2,306	967	-2,050	-4,484	-1,610
TOTAL	5,253	63,379	29,734	33,834	23,944	995	48,135

Note: Figures in italics represent estimates   E-Estimate

SOURCE: Security Pacific National Bank, Los Angeles, California

to improve its long-term economic prospects was the persistence of extremely high levels of defense spending.

REGIONAL MILITARY SPENDING AFTER THE 1973 WAR

In absolute terms, the Arab-Israeli arms race continued to spiral upwards at a vertiginous rate following the October war. Some of the increased spending went to defray the very high costs of the war, but much of it was attributable to the ambiguous military results and the strategic consequences of the Arabs having taken the initiative.

After a quarter of a century of diplomatic immobility, political stalemate and periodic warfare, the Arab-Israeli confrontation moved into a new stage of active diplomacy, as the United States, for the first time, became committed to a sustained effort to defuse the conflict. On the other hand, the overall Arab-Israeli confrontation paradoxically became *less* stable. As a direct result of the 1973 war, the deterrent effect of Israeli superiority lost much of its credibility. The Egyptian and Syrian armies had fought well and regained their prestige and self-confidence. The Arabs' resort to arms had yielded political and diplomatic dividends, and even resulted in the recovery of some occupied territory, which could tempt them to follow the same path again. For the Israelis, allowing the enemy to strike first had proved extremely costly, which could be expected to result in a return to a preventive or pre-emptive war posture.

It is this strategic instability, in addition to the escalating costs of sophisticated military hardware, that accounts for the much higher military outlays of the major parties (excluding Jordan) since 1973, despite the accent on diplomatic solutions. On the Israeli side, the substantial margin of military superiority that existed on the eve of 6 October 1973, was proven inadequate for deterrence. On the Arab side, despite the success of their surprise attack and their improved battlefield performance, the Egyptian and Syrian forces could not register a military victory. A virtually irresistible incentive existed for all parties to seek substantial increases in their military power. As Table IV indicates, the arms race continued through the 1970s, with Egypt's role declining from 1977 on but with Syria taking up the slack and emerging by the end of the decade as Israel's main Arab competitor. For both Syria and Israel, the drastic rise in military spending from 1973 on has been reflected in an even more drastic decline in both countries' growth rate in recent years. Throughout much of this period, Israel registered almost no growth, and negative growth in 1976–77, while Syria's rate plummetted from an average of 8 per cent from 1970 to 1976, to under 3 per cent in 1977–79.[14]

The two major Arab oil producers, Iraq and Saudi Arabia, continued

TABLE IV

Comparative Increments of Military Power in Israel and Selected Arab States, 1974-1980

	Combat Aircraft				Tanks				Active Military Personnel (thousands)			
	1974	1976	1978	1980	1974	1976	1978	1980	1974	1976	1978	1980
Egypt	672	688	612	668	2000	1975	1680	1680	323	342	395	367
Syria	440	440	392	395	1670	2400	2600	3170	137	227	227	247
Jordan	50	66	76	58	490	490	500	609	75	68	68	67
Iraq	218	299	339	482	1390	1390	1900	2750	112	158	212	242
S. Arabia	90	97	171	136	115	385	325	412	43	47	47	47
Israel	466	543	543	565	1900	2765	3065	3375	145	158	164	170*

* Total mobilizable personnel within 24 hours is about 400,000

SOURCE: International Institute for Strategic Studies, *The Military Balance.*

to devote high proportions of their GNP to defense, despite the vast increases in their national income since 1973, Iraq because her leadership perceives a number of security threats from many directions, internal and foreign, and Saudi Arabia because of a largescale effort to develop a diversified, modern and well-stocked military establishment practically from scratch. The defense outlays of both these countries historically have been less directly affected by developments on the Arab-Israeli front than those of the more immediate participants. Since the mid-seventies, this has been changing. Were a stable Arab-Israeli peace to materialize, the military budgets of front-line states would reflect larger proportional decreases than those of Saudi Arabia and Iraq. If it does not, the latter will probably become more centrally involved in the Arab-Israeli race.

Already in the October 1973 war, both countries were participants in the hostilities, unlike any previous rounds (except in 1948-49). The Saudis, in particular, have since 1973 gained a more salient role as purchasers of arms for the front-line states, are building military bases and other installations in the northwest quarter of their territory, close to the battlegrounds of Sinai, and are gradually acquiring a large arsenal that may make it politically very difficult for them to stand aloof in any future generalized Arab-Israeli war. For their part, the Iraqis have expanded their weapons inventories and mobility capabilities—including, most significantly, tank transporters—to a degree that would enable them to contribute very sizeable forces quickly to battlefields on Israel's eastern front. Division-sized armored forces and air power from forward Iraqi bases could reach the front in the early stages of any future war.

In Egypt, the increased military burden was cushioned by the heavy influx of Arab aid following the war, and a reduction in weapons imports forced by the growing breach with the USSR. Nonetheless, the military share of the national effort grew steadily in both absolute and relative terms, peaking in 1975-1976 at an estimated 44 per cent of GNP.

This was an extraordinary level of expenditures for any country, but particularly so for one with an annual population growth of 2.5 per cent (which, if sustained, would double the population in 28 years), and a stagnating economy. That it was at all feasible was due, as in the parallel Israeli case, to the inflow of external resources.

From 1973 to 1976, Egypt received some $5,122 million in bilateral financial aid from four Arab oil-rich states, Saudi Arabia, Kuwait, the United Arab Emirates, and Qatar.[15] An additional estimated $400 million were provided by multilateral Arab funds, such as the Arab Fund for Economic and Social Development, and the Islamic Development Bank. The United States contributed $1,637 million, while the Interna-

TABLE V
Egypt: Military Expenditures and Manpower, 1972-1979

	1972	1973	1974	1975	1976	1977	1978	1979
Defense Expenditures (US$m.)	1,512	2,727	4,071	6,103	4,859	4,365	2,810	2,168
Military Manpower (thou.)	325	323	323	323	342	345	395	395

SOURCE: International Institute for Strategic Studies, *The Military Balance.*

tional Monetary Fund, other international institutions and several OECD states, provided some $1,096 million.[16] Thus, over a period of four years, Egypt received about $8,248 million in foreign aid. This amount which is almost equivalent to its entire Gross National Product in 1973, reflects published statistics only on aid actually disbursed to the Egyptians, and undoubtedly underestimates the volume of funds that in fact entered the economy. It does not include, for instance, the substantial amounts provided as military assistance by Arab oil producers, for which no reliable, cumulative figures exist in the public domain, but which have been estimated at $1,000 million annually by some sources.[17] With all this external assistance factored in, a conservative calculus would find Egypt devoting some 30 per cent of all resources available to it to defense spending, at mid-decade.

In the 1977–78 period that preceded the general cut-off in diplomatic and economic relations between Egypt and the Arab World, precipitated by Sadat's unilateral overtures to Israel, the major item of Arab aid was the $1,975 million in budgetary support provided to Cairo by GODE, the Gulf Organization for the Development of Egypt.[18] Bilateral Arab assistance fell sharply from 1976 on, as donors became disenchanted with the seeming inability of the Egyptian bureaucracy to use available resources effectively, and increasing signs of mismanagement and illicit diversion of aid funds. The slack was taken up by Western aid sources, the United States in particular. American economic aid, funneled mainly through the Agency for International Development (AID), mounted from $370.5 million in 1975 to $950 million in 1979. Military assistance did not begin until 1976, when the approval by Congress of the sale of six C-130 transport aircraft opened the door to expanded weapons transfers. Thereafter, it increased at a rapid rate, rising from $68.5 million in 1976 to an estimated $1,500 million in 1980. Made available in the form of

long-term loans with concessional features—albeit at hefty market interest rates—these funds have enabled Egypt to purchase a full panoply
of heavy armaments, including some of the most sophisticated, late-
model equipment in US stocks. These acquisitions, on which more
below, will permit the country to effect a substantial transition to an all-
Western army and air force by the late 1980s, although overall inventories will be lower than those in existence a decade earlier.

Prior to 1979, however, only voluminous assistance from the oil-rich
Arabs permitted Egypt to continue to hold its end of the arms race. The
bulk of this aid was provided by Saudi Arabia. Under King Faisal to his
death in March 1975, and subsequently under his successor, Khalid, the
Saudis sought to supplement their own domestic defense efforts with the
bolstering of Egyptian military capabilities and economic stability. This
they did, once it became clear from 1971 on that the Sadat regime was
making a clear break with Nasirist policies, and steering Egypt along new
paths that coincided with long-standing tenets of Saudi foreign policy.

II. THE CAIRO-RIYADH AXIS

The essence of the "special relationship" between Egypt and Saudi
Arabia, which had its gestation at the Khartoum Arab summit of August
1967, gradually developed in the interwar period from 1967 to 1973, and
which reached full maturity following the October conflict, has consisted in
a trade-off of mutual expectations between Cairo and Riyadh. As the
Middle East entered the petrodollar era, an Egypt under relentlessly increasing economic strain henceforth expected substantial and continuing
access to the growing riches of the oil states. In exchange, a Saudi regime
acutely conscious of its multifaceted vulnerability, and for years under
ideological, political and even military attack by the "radical-
revolutionary" camp now looked forward to, indeed demanded, relief
from such pressures. It expected from Cairo, the erstwhile leader of the
adversary camp, abandonment of revolutionary confrontation, supra-
national appeals, unduly close ties to the Communist world, the promotion of socialism within the Arab world, and other such policies and
practices subversive of the *status quo*.

Sadat was happy to oblige. In inter-Arab affairs, he had sought from
the outset to normalize Egypt's relations with the other Arab states,
eschewing pan-nationalist rhetoric, and reasserting Egypt's own distinct
identity. The steady support King Faisal had given Egypt in the wake of
the June war, despite the bitter confrontation with Nasir in Yemen that
preceded the 1967 debacle, had made a lasting impression on Sadat, who
often contrasted it with the fickle friendship of those revolutionary

regimes his predecessor had cultivated. His disappointment with the Soviet Union—both as a reliable arms supplier and as an effective ally against the Israeli-American coalition—and his crucial decision to reorient Egypt toward the West in 1972–73 erased all major areas of disagreement between Riyadh and Cairo.

In looking to its security, Riyadh has traditionally relied on shrewd diplomacy and the power of the purse to complement its meager military strength. In true balance-of-power fashion, it has periodically shifted its inter-Arab alignments, with an eye both to avoiding isolation for itself, and promoting whenever possible a rough equilibrium of power and influence among contending regional blocs that would safeguard the status quo. In the 1940s and 1950s, wary of Hashemite revanchist ambitions that might be harbored by the Iraqi and Jordanian monarchies, Saudi Arabia sought refuge in a close alignment with Egypt, and in support for the Arab League. The 1958 anti-royalist coup in Baghdad put a sudden end to any Hashemite hopes of pan-Arab leadership, but it also deprived the monarchist camp of its most powerful member and, together with the formation of the United Arab Republic, underlined the emergence of Nasir's Egypt as a dynamic revolutionary force with broad ideological appeal and the potential to destabilize governments throughout the region. The 1960s subsequently witnessed an active Saudi effort to rally the conservative Arab forces under its leadership as a counterweight to the Cairo-led "revolutionary" camp, culminating in the long and bloody Yemen conflict.

The 1967 War and its aftermath marked the decline of the Nasirist tide in regional affairs and a general relaxation of inter-Arab tensions ensued, as ranks were closed in face of the Israeli victory. Propelled in part by their fear of Iraqi militancy—as Baghdad came under firm Baʿthi control from 1968 on—and the spreading revolutionary influence of Palestinian activism, the Saudis quickly reverted to a policy of cooperation with a dramatically weakened Egypt, which was transformed into a virtual alliance once Sadat assumed power.

The most tangible instrumentality of the evolving Saudi-Egyptian relationship was military-related assistance, both through armaments procurement—by way of direct transfers, subsidies, intermediary purchases, and joint production efforts—and through indirect budgetary support. Some of this aid was provided as part of a multi-Arab effort to share the costs of the confrontation with Israel among the oil-rich states and the frontline combatants, but the bulk was made through direct bilateral channels. Furthermore, while no official statements explicitly attested to the fact, it is clear that the two countries were moving toward a military security partnership of potentially far-reaching consequences.

The formation of the Arab Military Industries Organization (AMIO) in 1975 was intended to promote not only the mating of Gulf money with Egyptian production capabilities, but also the emergence of coordinated military planning, force complementarity, and — most significantly — shared Saudi-Egyptian military combat structures. A prime example was the set of agreements reached in late 1975 between Great Britain, Egypt and Saudi Arabia involving the sale of 200 Anglo-French Jaguar strike fighters. With Saudi financing, the initial 30 to 60 aircraft were to be supplied by Britain, with the balance to be built in Egypt under licence. A joint Saudi-Egyptian Jaguar force would provide the core for a new air defense system for Saudi Arabia, which would be developed by the British and include the Rapier SAM system.[19]

By the Summer of 1977, despite some irritants, most indicators pointed to a close, stable, smoothly functioning relationship. There were grumblings, which at times found a rather caustic outlet in Cairo's media, about insufficient aid from "the oil profiteers in the rear" to those who had "shed their lifeblood at the frontlines for the common Arab cause." There was resistance to rising Saudi demands for controls over how the funds provided should be spent. The ostentatious and inflationary spending habits of Gulf nationals in Egypt's cities provided additional grounds for friction. Nonetheless, the many common political and strategic interests that had come to bind the two countries remained in full force. The international diplomatic environment — dominated by US President Carter's push for comprehensive Arab-Israeli negotiations and US recognition of Palestinian national rights during his first year in office — suggested that their joint pro-Western approach was at long last beginning to bear fruit. Bilateral affairs continued to be characterized by large and long-term commitments by Riyadh to aiding the Egyptian economy, including an undertaking to finance Egypt's rearmament efforts for the next five years from 1977 to 1982.

Shortly thereafter, however, the "special relationship" was dealt a jolting blow, from which, as of this writing (Summer 1980) it has yet to recover. In November 1977, Sadat launched his unilateral peace initiative by suddenly journeying to Jerusalem, and in the following months clearly signalled his determination to take Egypt out of the conflict with Israel, even if Arab demands regarding Palestinian interests and Jerusalem were not met. While Riyadh sought to restrain the violent Arab reaction that followed, it eventually joined most of the Arab world in breaking official diplomatic and political relations with Cairo, once the Israel-Egypt peace treaty was signed in March 1979. Moreover, contrary to Egyptian and US expectations, the Saudi leadership also fell in line with the economic boycott declared by the Arab League, and suspended all aid programs. Several major arms purchases for Egypt already concluded were cancelled, most notably a $525 million deal for US supply of fifty F-5E jet fighters. The most significant example of Saudi displeasure with Sadat came in May 1979, when AMIO was ordered to be liquidated, thus dismantling a whole array of ongoing projects that involved Saudi Arabia's own defense effort.

A number of factors account for the Saudis' behavior. In common with many other Arabs, they were outraged by Sadat's bestowal of legitimacy and recognition on an Israel that had shown no signs of moderating its intransigence, shocked by his willingness to act outside the Arab consensus, and finally angered by his acceptance of a separate peace and normalization of relations with the Jewish state without having secured meaningful concessions beyond a conditional return of the Sinai. More immediately, their role as protectors of Islam's holy places, and self-perception as titular leaders of the Islamic community could not be squared with any acquiescence in a course of action that left Israel in more secure control of Jerusalem than ever before. Having supported and bankrolled the Sadat regime since its inception, and served as middlemen in its growing military and political ties with the West, a half-hearted response would have been interpreted as collusion. This could be doubly damaging to Saudi prestige and security in a climate of rising Islamic militance, further fanned in Saudi Arabia's immediate neighborhood by the Iranian revolution. No less significant a factor was the chagrin of the Kingdom's leadership at Sadat's unwillingness to take Saudi interests into account on this issue. In this respect, they were particularly offended by Sadat's persistence in going through with the peace agreement despite discreet but strong and repeated Saudi counsel to the contrary. "He was taking us too much for granted", was a complaint often voiced by high-level officials. The United States stood accused of similar neglect, and Riyadh's punishment of Egypt was directed as much at Washington as it was at Cairo.[20]

The damage to Saudi-Egyptian relations inflicted by Sadat's peace diplomacy was undoubtedly severe. Disagreement over this issue, however, has not nullified the convergence of interests that exists on other fronts, nor, by the same token, did it invalidate Saudi Arabia's stake in the survival of the Sadat regime and its other policies, both regional and domestic. On the contrary, events in Iran since 1978, the growing Iraqi assertiveness in Arab and especially in Gulf affairs, and the entrenchment of Soviet control in South Yemen can only make the future need for an Egyptian backstop even more compelling in Saudi eyes.

In recognition of this reality, while governmental ties were severed, private economic dealings were allowed to continue. No sanctions were taken against Egyptian workers in the Kingdom, nor were their remittances home interfered with, despite the hold Egypt placed on Saudi government assets in its banks. Tourism in Egypt by Saudi nationals was curtailed during the summer of 1979, but was edging back to normal one year later. While the highly visible F-5E fighter deal was cancelled, the purchase of $100 million worth of jeeps and trucks from the United States was financed by the Saudis in June 1979.[21] The step-up in US aid that accompanied the peace process gave Riyadh confidence that Egypt's immediate needs would be met for the period ahead.

Despite the 1979 breach, the same strategic conditions that brought the two countries together in the 1970s make a re-emergence of the Cairo-Riyadh axis in the decade ahead more likely than not. In Egypt's case, the unresolved Arab-Israeli crisis, the intrinsic momentum of military competition even in stable environments, the high levels of military expenditure throughout the region, the growing presence and visibility of Superpower forces in the region, the important role played by the armed forces in Egyptian politics and society, are all factors which clearly portend an abiding commitment by its leaders to military strength. The viability of such policies, however, may be critically dependent on a renewal of large-scale financial assistance by the oil-rich states of the Peninsula.

From a Saudi perspective, Egyptian military strength, constrained by a weak domestic economic base and conditioned by its direct and necessary reliance on Saudi/American financing and Western technology, continues to offer the most attractive option open to Riyadh for external assistance in meeting its principal security requirements. The military buildup and vigorous "riyal diplomacy" after 1973 were a response to a heightened sense of vulnerability shared by the ruling family and the country's technocratic elite, for which two long-term developments were primarily responsible.

One was the Kingdom's emergence as the *de facto* leader of OPEC and key petroleum exporter in the non-Communist world. Coupled with the fact that access to Gulf oil has become so vital to the industrial world that the most extreme measures might be used to secure it, this turned the Saudi government into a global actor and also a target of intense pressures.

The other was the growing Soviet military presence in the immediate vicinity of the Arabian Peninsula, aggravated by the heavy penetration of the military and bureaucracy in neighboring South Yemen by Cuban and East German personnel, and rendered more menacing by Riyadh's longstanding hostility to and suspiciousness of the USSR. While Saudi officials did not expect an outright Soviet military offensive in the area, they made no secret of their concern over Moscow's use of regional surrogates to undermine Middle East stability.

These trends show no signs of abating in the foreseeable future, nor can Saudi Arabia expect to rely on its own power to meet the challenges they pose. The significant strategic threats it faces in the 1980s relate, not to regime survival in the face of domestic upheaval or revolution — which, as Saudi decisionmakers themselves believe, and the analysis below indicates, is highly unlikely — but to the maintenance of a stable *status quo* on the Peninsula, and in adjacent areas such as the Horn of Africa.

SAUDI SECURITY IN THE 1980S

Speculation abounds in much contemporary analysis regarding the potential for instability within Saudi Arabia, and the danger of military coup or revolution in this wealthiest of Middle Eastern states, and the most vital for the security of the industrial world. Particularly in the wake of the Shah's overthrow in Iran, general concern has been voiced over the prospects for survival of the Saudi monarchy.[22]

For the balance of this decade, such fears are unjustified, and they are likely to prove similarly unfounded beyond 1990 as well. Essentially, four types of destabilizing events could hypothetically happen: a palace coup, or forced change of leadership within the royal family; a military coup d'état; a popular uprising or revolution; and an internal breakup of the country, or regional secession. The only contingency with a small but significant probability of occurring over the next several years is that of a forced leadership change at the top, within the ruling family, as an outgrowth of rivalry for supreme power among a number of potential successors to the current monarch, Khalid, or his appointed heir to the throne, Fahd.

Were this to occur, however, it is most unlikely that the process would be allowed to become conflictive enough to threaten the survival of the regime. While for a brief period there may be instability and uncertainty at the top, as the struggle for power unfolds, the consequences of such strife for the country's foreign policy, relations with neighboring states, and the internal workings of the society will be marginal.

Beyond this contingency, predictions of regime-threatening levels of internal instability in Saudi Arabia for the foreseeable future are for the most part based on faulty extrapolation from conditions that affect other oil-producing states along the periphery of the Arabian Peninsula, or on superficial knowledge of particular Saudi circumstances. In fact it is no exaggeration to state that among all Arab governments, indeed all

Middle Eastern governments, the Saudi regime is the least threatened and the most secure at the helm. Furthermore, in absolute rather than relative terms, it is difficult to make a persuasive case for any projection of significant, regime-threatening levels of domestic strife in the Kingdom.

The ruling Saudi family enjoys unquestioned political legitimacy. Although its system of governance is decidedly authoritarian, this quality is tempered by complex and effective procedures for consultation among the political, religious and tribal elite, the "paternalistic" nature of Saudi rule, and careful adherence to deeply ingrained and longstanding rules of custom. Moreover, authoritarian leadership leavened by consultation with the "elders" of the society has been the traditional pattern of political rule throughout the region, and as such remains perfectly acceptable to the overwhelming majority of Saudis, most of whom (65 percent) continue to live within traditional tribal structures organized around the principle of kinship.

The legitimacy and prestige of the House of Saʿud itself constitutes one of the strongest ties binding the country together. This standing is based not only on the family's preeminent *tribal* leadership role in much of the Peninsula for over two centuries, but also on its sponsorship of Wahhabism upon the emergence of this fundamentalist Islamic doctrine in the mid-eighteenth century, and its retention of the movement's *religious* leadership ever since. The puritanical zeal of ʿAbd al-Aziz Ibn Saʿud and his religious authority were among the most effective tools he used in uniting the bulk of the region under his rule in the first quarter of this century, culminating with the formation of the Kingdom of Saudi Arabia in 1932. Thus, the House of Saʿud today combines in its hands the reins both of tribal/political and of religious authority, a formidable combination in a society that remains deeply traditional in outlook and allegiances.

The stability of the present system rests on several additional, no less firm foundations. The royal family's huge membership appears to be sufficiently cohesive, and it occupies the upper levels of power in key sectors of the governmental structure, whether in the armed forces, bureaucracy or economy. This not only militates against the emergence of rival power centers, and allows the leadership substantial direct control over the day-to-day management of the country; it also enables the regime to be more responsive in a preemptive mode to new pressures and demands than most traditional authoritarian political systems are wont to be. Also the enormous financial resources available from oil exports, combined with the country's relatively small population and an enlightened approach to wealth distribution, have produced ample opportunities for upward mobility by the small emerging "modern" elite of secularly educated,

Western-trained Saudis who would otherwise provide a potential nucleus for revolutionary, system-threatening political or violent activities under the banner of social and economic reform.

The armed forces, which in many less developed countries have provided the main vehicle for destabilizing political challenge to incumbent regimes, are in the Saudi case most unlikely to play an independent political role for the foreseeable future. Geography and organizational structure are the two major impediments. Geographically, the vast distances separating the county's major strategic assets and the limited communications and transportation network available make a military coup extremely difficult to accomplish successfully.[23]

The structure of the Saudi armed forces has been deliberately shaped with an eye to minimizing internal military threats to Saudi authority. The conventional army (Saudi Arabian Land Forces, or SALF), numbers some 45,000 troops and is entrusted with the primary mission of territorial defense against external aggression. In organization, command structure, and armaments it is completely separate from and counterbalanced by the National Guard (SANG). The SANG, with 35,000 personnel, has as its main mission the maintenance of internal security, including the suppresion of insurgencies and other large-scale civil disturbances. While recruitment for the army is country-wide, with universal conscription now planned as a major source of new manpower, National Guard elements are overwhelmingly recruited among the tribes of the Najd region, whence the House of Saʿud sprang and birthplace of Wahhabism. Indeed, the SANG itself is organized on a tribal basis, and its loyalty to the regime is considered extremely high.

Deployment of these two major components of the country's military institution reinforces their organizational separateness and the decentralized nature of the system. The army is largely deployed in the northwestern sector around Tabuk, covering the approaches to Israel and Jordan, and in the southwest protecting the borders with North and South Yemen, while the National Guard is mainly deployed in the northeast, protecting the oil producing areas. In both forces, senior commanders are all either members of the royal family or of the "nobility", scions of families often connected to the Saʿuds by multiple marriage ties and of unquestioned loyalty to the regime. Significantly, in the Air Force, a service where a few rebellious units, though not able to mount a coup by themselves, could hypothetically pose a grave physical threat to members of the ruling elite, a substantial proportion of pilots and senior officers are members of the royal family.

Finally, the major social fissures that present serious potential threats to internal stability in many other smaller states on the periphery of the

Arabian peninsula either do not exist in Saudi Arabia or are present in a much less acute form. One is the Sunni-Shi^{c}i split, which has always been politically significant and has gained further import throughout the Gulf following the Iranian revolution. This split does not affect the Saudi kingdom, whose ethnically homogeneous population is overwhelmingly Sunni (90 percent). The other is the large-scale presence of foreign labor, often on a permanent residency basis, which in some neighboring states — Kuwait, Qatar and the United Arab Emirates — makes up the majority of the country's population. Although Saudi Arabia has imported foreign labor at a rather furious pace since 1973 in response to the needs of an economy undergoing speedy growth in every sector, foreigners do not make up more than 15 to 20 percent of the total population. Even if present rates of economic expansion are maintained through the eighties, which is unlikely, estimates are that in ten years foreign labor will make up only one third of the total Saudi labor force.[24] Moreover, the bulk of non-Saudi labor is blue-collar Yemeni, a politically unsophisticated and relatively undemanding group.

In short, for the medium term future, significant challenges to the security and stability of Saudi Arabia may be posed by external opponents, but are most unlikely to originate from within the country.

Against external threats, many factors that have worked to enhance domestic security, such as large territory, small population, and public resistance to social change, become distinct liabilities. Despite the gigantic outlays for defense of the past decade, and the acquisition of sophisticated military technology, the Kingdom remains unable to field armed forces of sufficient size, proficiency, and experience to provide an effective, dependable shield against potential aggressors. Almost all neighboring countries that might conceivably entertain future designs against Saudi territorial integrity or threaten damage to its oil industry, including Israel, Iraq, and Iran, have far larger military establishments. Even small South Yemen, which has had a history of constant border tension and political hostility with the Saudis since its independence in 1967, boasts land and air forces that match the Kingdom's closely in overall numbers and would hold a quantitative edge in any probable local theater of confrontation in the Peninsula's southwestern quadrant.

Egyptian military power can serve several important Saudi strategic purposes: (a) despite the 1979 Treaty, by its mere existence it would continue to serve as a deterrent to and check on Israeli ambitions and behavior toward the eastern Arab states; (b) in inter-Arab affairs, it would counterbalance the growing might of Iraq, which undisguisedly covets a strongman role in the Gulf, has not flinched in the past from heavy-handed pressure on its southern neighbors, and clearly is well equipped to exercise a leading regional role in coming decades; (c) it would stiffen the resistance of the conservative pro-Western Arab camp—which includes Morocco, Tunisia and Jordan in addition to the small oil sheikhdoms and would, without Egypt, lack a single member with armed forces of regional significance—against pressures from the militant Arab states; (d) it would provide a tested mobile capability for rapid armed support of friendly regimes, both in the Middle East and in surrounding regions, that face internal insurgencies or Soviet-supported subversion.

Not coincidentally, the structure and equipment of the Egyptian armed forces in recent years have been evolving toward an enhanced capability for speedy deployment abroad, as weapons procurement has shifted almost exclusively to US suppliers.

EGYPT'S ARMED FORCES SINCE THE 1973 WAR

Egypt's military establishment went through two clearly distinct phases from 1973 to 1980. The first phase, lasting from the close of the October war to the onset of Sadat's peace offensive in the fall of 1977, was characterized by continued heavy reliance on weaponry from the Soviet bloc, strenuous efforts to maintain a high state of combat readiness, despite equipment shortages and obsolescence, and a continued focus in deployment and doctrine on Israel as the primary adversary. Although a substantial proportion of war losses, particularly ground weapons, were replaced by the Soviets in the immediate aftermath of the conflict, by mid-1974 the arms flow from Moscow had slowed down considerably. Henceforth, as Cairo's diplomatic relations with Washington flourished, culminating in the second Sinai disengagement accord with Israel signed in September 1975, only selected spare parts, some ground transport units, a number of helicopters, and some surface-to-air missile batteries were supplied. The sole major direct transfer to have occurred from late 1974 to the total breach in 1978 reportedly was of 50 refurbished and re-engined MiG-21 interceptors, delivered in 1977. Additional Eastern-bloc equipment, including essential spare parts, was procured from Algeria, Yugoslavia, Syria, North Korea and China. In partial compensation for the shortage in advanced weaponry, and to maintain a degree of military pressure on Israel, the number of men under arms was increased. The Egyptian army's ability to engage Israel in large scale war remained in serious doubt, however, despite the enormous defense outlays.

Efforts toward weapons diversification began during this period, with the placing of orders in Britain for Sea King antisubmarine-warfare helicopters and Swingfire air-to-surface missiles, among other weapons; the purchase of 44 Mirage F-1 fighters and 53 Gazelle helicopters from

France, and of the C-130 transports from the United States. They were made possible both by the new pro-Western orientation of the Sadat regime, and the availability of funding through Saudi and some Kuwaiti aid. The French purchases were financed through a direct payment by the Saudis to France. Saudi Arabia also financed the helicopter purchase from Britain, to the tune of $70 million.[25] The military impact of these transactions would not make itself felt, however, until deliveries and integration were substantially accomplished several years later.

The Sadat visit to Jerusalem inaugurated a new stage marked primarily by a clear-cut end to the uneasy military relationship with the USSR, large increases in US aid, and a gradual—and partial—shift in deployments and orientation away from the Israeli front. Cairo's denunciation of its Friendship Treaty with the Soviets in May 1976 was followed in November 1977 by a suspension of military debt repayments to Moscow, resulting in a total severance of the twenty-two year old military relationship between the two countries. Egypt now had left itself no choice but to attempt a long-term fundamental shift of its entire armed forces from Soviet to Western equipment. Given the size of the military establishment, relatively unfettered access to US suppliers was essential. Washington's traditional reluctance to provide weaponry that might be used against Israel dissolved rather quickly in the face of Sadat's determined wooing of American public opinion, the obvious sincerity of his efforts to achieve a permanent peaceful settlement, and his now frequent lambasting of Soviet regional designs.

In May 1978, while Cairo and Jerusalem engaged in serious peace talks with US participation, the Carter Administration approved the sale of fifty F-5E fighter aircraft to Egypt. This transaction, which the Saudis pledged to finance, would fall through in 1979, a victim of the political rift between the two Arab states. The signing of the peace agreement with Israel, however, brought with it over $1,500 million in US military credits, pledged as part of the peace package for disbursement through 1981. The cancelled F-5E deal was replaced by the transfer of 35 of the more advanced and far more powerful F-4E Phantom fighter-bombers. In addition, 800 M-113 armored personnel carriers and twelve batteries of defensive Improved Hawk surface-to-air missiles were procured.

THE NEW STRATEGIC ENVIRONMENT

The 1979 invasion of Afghanistan by the Soviet Union provided the context for a further jump in US weapons supply to Egypt. Coming only months after the overthrow of the Pahlavi regime in Iran, Moscow's action brought the Red Army within easy tactical striking range of the Gulf, fanning Western concern over the future security of access to its

TABLE VI
United States Assistance to Egypt, FY1975 - FY1979
(in US $ millions)

	1975	1976	1977	1978	1979
Foreign Military Sales Agreements	–	68.4	1.7	937.3	623.1
Economic Assistance Obligated	370.5	984.6	892.3	943.0	950.0
total	370.5	1053.0	904.0	1880.3	1573.1

SOURCES: For FMS agreements, US Congress, House, Committee on Appropriations, *Foreign Assistance and Related Programs: Appropriations for 1981, Hearings, Part 4*, 96th Cong. 2d Sess. (April 1980), p. 139. For economic aid, US Agency for International Development (A.I.D.) statistical sheets.

vital petroleum resources. Suspicions of aggressive Soviet intent in the region had already been exacerbated by the increased presence of military elements from the Soviet bloc in Libya, South Yemen, Ethiopia and the Indian Ocean since the mid-1970s, and the stockpiling by Libya of advanced heavy weaponry far in excess of its absorptive capabilities. These moves accompanied a continued Soviet drive to achieve potential superiority over the Western Alliance in strategic weaponry, and the attainment by the Soviet Navy of an effective global reach on the high seas. This further disquieted an American administration that had come to office committed to downplay the role of force in the conduct of foreign affairs, and which now stood accused by domestic opponents of neglecting its national-defense responsibilities. In the wake of the Shah's quick fall and the resurgence of anti-foreign religious fundamentalism throughout the Muslim world, Middle Eastern governments—including those of Saudi Arabia and the Gulf Emirates—that had traditionally relied on the United States to help counter Soviet pressures as well as threats emanating from regional neighbors, also questioned whether the rewards of a close relationship with the United States were not outweighed by its liabilities.

As the United States moved to shore up its military position in Southwest Asia, enunciating through the "Carter Doctrine" its determination to use armed power if necessary to maintain unimpeded access to oil, it negotiated with Oman, Somalia and Saudi Arabia for the use of military facilities. Sadat's Egypt, however, loomed as the only major

Arab or Muslim state in the region capable of providing a local military and political foundation for the reinforcement of Western security interests.[26] The upgrading of Egypt's armed forces now became a matter of shared interest, and no longer a price to be rather begrudgingly paid for Sadat's signature on the Camp David accords. In January 1980, Egypt was offered additional credits of $1,150 million for FYs 1981 and 1982, and in following months was offered the purchase of 40 F-16 fighters, 244 M-60 battle tanks, 550 additional armored personnel carriers, one more I-Hawk SAM battery, and an assortment of communications equipment, spare parts, ammunition, battlefield engineering units, and maintenance training arrangements.[27]

The scope of Egyptian-American military cooperation has grown well beyond mere weapons transfers. Three activities in particular illustrate the extent to which the relationship has matured in the relatively brief period of three years. In the fall of 1979, following the withdrawal by Saudi Arabia, the UAE and Qatar of their financial support for the Arab Military Industries Organization the United States stepped in with technical assistance and hardware to modernize Egypt's military plants. AMIO had been formed in April 1975 as a joint venture intended to concretize inter-Arab cooperation through a combination of funding from the oil-rich states with Egyptian skilled manpower and installations already extant in a modest industrial military capability developed in the early 1960s under Nasir.[28] In early 1980, as the Soviet intervention in Afghanistan unfolded, advanced US electronic intelligence and battlefield control aircraft, AWACS, operated from Egyptian airfields, and Cairo offered its military facilities for the use of American personnel.[29] Later in the year, lengthy joint exercises and training were conducted in Egypt by F-4E Phantom air units of the two countries, in a familiarization exercise that laid the groundwork for the rapid deployment of US military forces to Egypt in future Middle East contingencies.[30]

Underlying these growing ties was a convergence of strategic perceptions by the American and Egyptian leaderships, and substantial agreement on Egypt's regional role in the 1980s. Both governments identified Soviet expansionism as the major external threat, and the militarily weak and politically vulnerable oil-producing countries of the Arabian Peninsula and the Gulf as Moscow's principal targets. While the possibility of a direct Soviet attack could not be dismissed — particularly after Afghanistan — internal subversion and across-the-border offensives by regional allies or client states were far more likely contingencies. The activities of Moscow's closest associate in the Arab World, the People's Democratic Republic of Yemen, over the past decade appeared paradigmatic. Sanaa's support of an extended insurrection in Dhofar against the Sultan of Oman by the Marxist PFLOAG (Popular Front for the Liberation of Oman and the Gulf), and its invasion of North Yemen in February 1979, both posed serious challenges to the political *status quo* in the oil regions.

Closer to home, Sadat also perceived a range of threats against Egypt — all abetted by Soviet arms and encouragement as well — whether in the unionist zeal and personal animosity of Libya's Qaddafi, the "Rejectionist Front" opposition to his independent policy toward Israel, or Ethiopia's grievances against the Sudan, the latter a part of Egypt's self-proclaimed southern Nilotic security zone. Needless to say, for Washington the stability of the Sadat regime was also a primary concern, for on it rested all hopes of continued movement toward a resolution of the Arab-Israeli dispute.

To the Cairo leadership, all these contingencies posit the requirement of an Egyptian military role. Beyond those circumstances where the state's territorial security may be immediately at stake, the sending of expeditionary forces to other countries in the Middle East or Africa may serve a variety of Egyptian interests. Among them is the assertion of the country's historical claims as leader and "protector" of the Arab bloc; avoidance of encirclement by ideological opponents, particularly if they are closely tied to the USSR; and defense of conservative, oil-rich rulers, who are far more generous providers of economic aid than any likely successor revolutionary leadership. A no less important motivator is the need to provide a mission and strategic justification for the continued maintenance of a large military establishment, inescapably mandated by the preeminent political power wielded by the armed forces.

Egypt's willingness to act beyond its borders was well received by an American administration that had just lost in Iran the mainstay of its regional defense structure for Southwest Asia, and faced an increasingly bold Soviet adversary. In fact, Egypt is far better suited to the part of regional watchdog and potential interventionary force than the Shah ever could have been. Its traditional stature within the Arab world and the legitimating agency of pan-Arabism provide Egypt with ample opportunities, and foils, for the exercise of a regional policing function denied any non-Arab Power. Thus, while Egyptian Defense Minister General Kamal Hassan ʿAli commented that, in the wake of peace with Israel, "it is time to look around us", and outlined plans for converting the military into a smaller, yet more advanced, more mobile force that "would be able to defend its own territory and also any other Arab country when this support is needed and...asked for."[31] US Assistant Secretary of State for the Near East Harold Saunders justified arms sales to Egypt in rather similar terms. In addition to national defense, he said in Congressional testimony on the FY1981 aid program, "...we do feel there may be occasions when the Egyptian forces may be useful in one place or another—not on a large scale but rather particular units in a situation, for instance, playing a role in Zaire, or closer by, in Oman or in Yemen, if there was a conflict in those areas."[32]

Egypt's plans for military modernization in the 1980s do not, however, call for spending levels of the ruinous magnitude that characterized the previous decade. Absolute amounts devoted to defense will rise, due both to the high price-tags of Western weaponry and continuously escalating manpower costs in the open, high-inflation economy produced by Sadat's post-1975 liberalization policies. But the relative military burden, which had been reduced to some 25 percent of GNP by the latter part of the 1970s, is likely to stabilize around 20 percent if projected reductions of one-third in the number of men under arms are carried out in the next few years, and if the 8 to 9 percent economic growth rate attained in 1978–80 can be sustained.

III. CONCLUSION

The extreme economic difficulties under which Egypt has labored, compounded over the past twenty years by heavy military expenditures and runaway population growth, have practically dictated a permanent condition of, at best, precarious political stability, ever poised on the verge of collapse. The homogeneity and cohesiveness of Egyptian society are steadying factors, as is the pervasive and millenial bureaucratization of state institutions and the traditional political apathy of the bulk of the population. By the early 1970s, as we have seen, the country's fundamental policy choices had become severely circumscribed, with the defense burden fast reaching intolerable levels. Cairo's two major policy departures under Sadat, the determined effort to reach a peaceful settlement with Israel and the Open Door economic policy, were in large measure dictated by the objective conditions facing the country, and did not flow simply from the personalist predilections or caprices of the man at the top.

High popular expectations of reaping the economic benefits of peace account for much of the general public's acquiescence in Sadat's bold and extremely risky unilateral initiative, expectations that the regime itself persistently encouraged. Despite opposition from some imporant segments of public opinion, the President's prestige and authority were strengthened by his peace diplomacy. The stability of the regime was not threatened even when the signing of the 1979 Peace treaty resulted in

Egypt's denunciation by the bulk of the Arab world and its subjection to unaccustomed political ostracism and economic boycott by the Arab League.

The realization that tangible economic rewards cannot reasonably be instantaneous, and the highly popular spectacle of Israeli withdrawal from Sinai were important factors. But these are wasting assets. The major political challenge facing the Egyptian leadership in the 1980s is (a) to bring forth the promised economic revival for the sake of which it repudiated long-standing central tenets of Egyptian Arab and foreign policy, while (b) maintaining for the country the international leadership role it has historically played and which all its elite strata — military, political, commercial, intellectual — aspire to and demand. The interventionary capability for "regional police" action that Egyptian planners are seeking with US assistance is undoubtedly expected by Cairo to provide it with the instruments for retaining regional leverage and a voice in vital strategic and political affairs of Africa and the Middle East, at a cost that the country can afford.

Whether Egypt can have both guns and butter in the 1980s and beyond is likely to depend in substantial measure on its evolving relationship with Saudi Arabia, just as Saudi diplomatic and financial support for Sadat's foreign and domestic policies after the October War were essential to their fruition. The special Saudi-Egyptian relationship forged in the 1970s was supported by strong common interests of enduring substance. Because of its strategic centrality to how ruling groups in both countries perceive the threats and opportunities that lie ahead, the Cairo-Riyadh axis will, despite temporary setbacks and unavoidable frictions, probably reemerge in the 1980s as a balance wheel of the inter-Arab regional system.

NOTES

1. US Arms Control and Disarmament Agency, *World Military Expenditures and Arms Transfers, 1968–1977* (Washington D.C.: GPO, October 1979), p. 4.

2. Palestine War (1948–49), Suez War (1956), Six Day War (1967), War of Attrition (1969–70), and the October War (1973).

3. Algeria-Morocco (1962–63), Yemen War (1962–67), Jordan-Syria (1970), Oman-South Yemen (1972–75), Egypt-Libya (1977), Morocco-Sahara (1977-), North Yemen-South Yemen (1979). Only conflicts having a substantial inter-state component are listed.

4. An excellent account of the international oil revolution brought about by the behavior of the Organization of Petroleum Exporting Countries (OPEC) in the first half of the 1970s is in D. Rustow and J. F. Mugno, *OPEC: Success and Prospects* (New York: New York University Press, 1976).

5. For a good analysis of the dynamics of the Arab-Israeli arms race up to the June 1967 war see Nadav Safran, *From War to War: The Arab-Israeli Confrontation, 1948–1967* (New York: Pegasus, 1968), especially Chapter IV.

6. Robert Mabro and Samir Radwan, *The Industrialization of Egypt, 1939–1973* (London: Oxford University Press, 1976), p. 43.

7. Mohamed Heikal, *The Sphinx and the Commissar* (New York: Harper and Row, 1978), p. 148.

8. Anwar El-Sadat, *In Search of Identity: An Autobiography* (New York: Harper and Row, 1977), p. 244.

9. Ibid., p. 245.

10. *Al-Ahram* (9 October 1974).

11. Colin Legum, ed., *Middle East Contemporary Survey, 1976–1977* (New York: Holmes and Meier, 1978), p. 471.

12. A breakdown of available statistics is included in the following section of the present chapter.

13. See in particular the contribution of Nazih N. M. Ayubi in this volume; also the chapter by Malcolm Kerr.

14. Legum, ibid., p. 470; International Monetary Fund, "Recent Developments Stimulate Hopes for Renewal of Rapid Growth in Syria", *IMF Survey* (Washington D.C., June 1979), pp. 182–185.

15. United Nations Conference on Trade and Development (UNCTAD), "Financial Solidarity for Development; Efforts and Institutions of the Members of OPEC", January 1979. Statistics detailed in Jake Wien, *Saudi-Egyptian Relations: The Political and Military Dimensions of Saudi Financial Flows to Egypt* (Santa Monica, Calif.: The Rand Corporation, P-6327, 1980), p. 48.

16. Ibid., pp. 36–37, 75–76.

17. Abstracted from Haim Barkai, "Egypt's Economic Constraints", *The Jerusalem Quarterly*, 14 (Winter 1980), table 3. Barkai seriously underestimates Arab aid to Egypt during 1973–76 in this study.

18. Interview with Dr. Abdul Aziz Aldukheil, Chairman of GODE and former Saudi Deputy Minister of Finance, Riyadh, June 1980. Saudi Arabia, Kuwait, Qatar and the United Arab Emirates formed GODE in early 1976, with a capitalization of $2 billion. Its operations were frozen following the signing of the Israel-Egypt peace treaty in March 1979.

19. Herbert Coleman, "Britain, Egypt Negotiate Sale of 200 Jaguar Strike Fighters", *Aviation Week and Space Technology* (17 November 1975), p. 22.

20. The analysis of Saudi perspectives and policy in this section is based in part on several lengthy interviews with cabinet and sub-cabinet level officials, conducted in Riyadh and Jeddah by the author in June 1980.

21. Testimony of Erich von Marbod, Acting Director, Defense Security Assistance Agency, in US Congress, House Committee on Appropriations, *Foreign Assistance and Related Programs: Appropriations for 1981, Hearings Part 4,* 96th Congress, 2nd Session, April 1980, p. 168.

22. For example, see the final scenario in Malcolm Kerr's chapter in this volume.

23. As Holden correctly states, "Saudi Arabia... is ill-adapted to revolutionary coups... With a population less than half the size of London's scattered over an area as big as Western Europe, a successful coup would be difficult to accomplish even with an efficient central administration to direct it and a large and coherent army to enforce it. Saudi Arabia, in spite of its recent changes, has neither. Its civil power is still split into thirds, be-

tween the royal seat in Riyadh, the Foreign Ministry, diplomatic missions and commercial houses in Jeddah, and the vital oilfields in Dhahran." David Holden, *Farewell to Arabia* (London; Faber and Faber, 1966), p. 138.

24. For example, for estimates up to 1985 see Arthur Smithies, *The Economic Potential of the Arab Countries* (Santa Monica, Calif.: The Rand Corporation, R-2250-NA, 1978), pp. 37, 45, 46. In 1975 the total Saudi labor force (excluding Yemenis) was 1.6 million, of whom 1.286 were Saudi and 0.314 were foreign.

25. A useful list of weapons purchases by Egypt and Saudi Arabia from West European suppliers from 1973 to 1977 is included as an appendix to Robert L. Pfaltzgraff, Jr., "Resources Constraints and Arms Transfers: Implications for NATO and European Security", pp. 178–212, in Uri Ra'anan, Robert Pfaltzgraff, Jr. and Geoffrey Kemp, *Arms Transfers to the Third World: the Military Buildup in Less Industrial Countries* (Boulder, Colo.: Westview Press, 1978).

26. For an analysis of the "Carter Doctrine" and its limited relevance to American political and security problems in the Middle East, see Paul Jabber, "U.S. Interests and Regional Security in the Middle East", *Daedalus,* Vol. 109, no. 4 (Fall 1980).

27. US Congress, House, *Foreign Assistance...,* p. 158; "U.S. to Offer Egypt F-16s and Tanks", *Aviation Week and Space Technology* (28 January 1980), p. 22; *Wall Street Journal* (26 March 1980), p. 7.

28. A good detailed discussion of AMIO's activities and plans during the period 1975 to 1979 can be found in Wien, op.cit., pp. 58–71. See also *Middle East Economic Digest* (1 June 1979), p. 8.

29. *Washington Post* (9 January 1980).

30. David R. Griffiths, "F-4Es Deploying to Egypt for Training", *Aviation Week and Space Technology* (23 June 1980).

31. *An-Nahar Arab Report and Memo,* Vol. 2, no. 8 (February 1978), pp. 2–3.

32. Saunders' testimony, US Senate, Committee on Foreign Relations, *FY 1981 Foreign Assistance Legislation, Hearings,* 96th Congress, 2nd Session, March 1980, p. 252. Also *Boston Globe* (23 November 1979), p. 21.

33. Saunders' testimony, ibid., p. 248.

XIII
Egypt and the Arabs in the Future: Some Scenarios

Malcolm H. Kerr

The purpose of this chapter is to speculate about Egypt's prospects during the 1980s in the light of specific political circumstances that may arise within Egypt itself and in the Arab world.

As with all futuristic speculation, there are many elements of arbitrariness in this; the range of hypothetical cases is limited, the interconnection of variables is incomplete, and the subconscious temptation to focus on the immediate future rather than on the long term is difficult to avoid. By the time these lines are published, several changes in the Middle East may well already have invalidated some of our assumptions.

Still, it seems important to try to look ahead. Egypt is the largest and in some ways the most advanced Arab state, yet the danger she faces of sliding into ever-deepening mass poverty is the most alarming and poignant among all the countries of the region. This is because of her size, and also because, as a nation that has known strength, prestige, and bright promise in the past, a collapse of her hopes could leave such an explosive legacy of frustration and bitterness. It would also be a particularly alarming indicator of long-term Third World trends, inasmuch as in the past several decades Egypt has been conspicuous as a participant in international development councils, as a recipient of international aid and investment, and as an experimenter with distinctive national development policy approaches. Especially tragic would be the realization that despite the accumulation of fabulous oil wealth in the hands of the Arab family to which Egypt belongs, the opportunity for her economic salvation had somehow been missed.

The scenarios that follow are not so tidy and conclusive as to represent simple recipes for success and failure. They each lead to multiple paths, and the outcomes that we forecast for them are more political than economic in nature. While—as we shall explain—we do not believe that

President Sadat's economic policies are destined to be very successful in the long run, we do not assume that a return to the socialist formula of the 1960s, or anything else likely to be adopted, would necessarily be better. Much would depend in any case on the domestic and international political environment in which any economic strategy was carried out.

We have selected and arranged our scenarios as follows. Scenarios I, II and III represent the alternative forms of regime that we consider most plausible in Egypt in the coming decade: a continuation of the present Sadat regime; a revival of Nasirism, broadly defined; and an Islamic fundamentalist revolution, dedicated to a combination of principles borrowed from Khomeini and Mao. The prospects for each of these are discussed primarily within the domestic Egyptian context, and to some extent within an international context assuming the continuation of the *status quo* elsewhere in the Arab world.

In the remaining two scenarios we discuss the possibility of certain changes in the regional environment and speculate about their impact on Egypt. Scenario IV assumes an Islamic fundamentalist revolution in Saudi Arabia and the Gulf; Scenario V assumes an Iraqi-dominated union or combination of the Fertile Crescent states. How may we expect each of these development to affect the competition for power in Egypt among the alternative types of regime described in the first three scenarios, and the policy options open to them? In each of Scenarios IV and V we propose more than one answer, depending on alternative sets of secondary circumstances. Thus no precise set of developments in these scenarios is assumed, but rather general events with variable implications. This being the case, the scenarios do not lead to single, cut-and-dried outcomes.

We shall omit from our speculations one scenario whose potential importance cannot be denied: the "doomsday" case of a war in the Gulf that drastically reduces oil production or drastically alters the arrangements by which the oil is sold. These developments would have critical consequences for neighboring states such as Egypt, because of the elimination of the market for their labor and for many other reasons. (Meanwhile the value of Egypt's own modest oil exports would skyrocket). But the doomsday scenario involves so many worldwide as well as local ramifications that it is a better subject for a whole book, not necessarily written by a Middle East scholar.

Two brief observations are worth making before we ignore the prospect of "doomsday" altogether, however. The first is that with the passage of time, the likelihood increases that it could be precipitated by one of several garden-variety local events: another Arab-Israeli war, a revolution in Saudi Arabia, an Iraqi invasion of Kuwait, etc. Such events could trigger an international crisis, great-power intervention, sabotage, and large-scale destruction.

The second observation is that however such a crisis might end and oil production resume, we cannot necessarily assume that large surplus revenues would once again accrue to the local governments. If, for example, the underpopulated states of the Arabian Peninsula were occupied by foreign armies, there is little reason to suppose that these Humpty-Dumpties would be put back together. Who would want to re-invent Qatar or Abu Dhabi, or even Saudi Arabia, if they no longer existed? And who can say what income the renewed production might generate, or whose it would be to spend? Egyptian labor migration, and the flow of Gulf aid and investment to Egypt, would no longer be in question if the petro-dollars were not there any more. Egypt would have to find a political formula for a life of extreme austerity, such as the Khomeini-Mao approach described below in Scenario III.

In short, while we are not prepared to consider the "doomsday" scenario in any depth, we must bear in mind that the chances of its arising are not negligible, and that the financial consequences for many parties, including Egypt, could be of critical importance.

SCENARIO I: CONTINUATION OF THE SADAT REGIME

In this scenario we assume that the Sadat regime continues in power, either under President Sadat himself or under a constitutional successor who represents the same general interests and policies. We shall briefly review some features of the political system under this regime, and their implications for Egypt's development prospects.

Having grown directly out of the Nasir regime and claiming for itself the same revolutionary legacy, the Sadat regime has come to represent the antithesis of many Nasirist principles. Sadat's Egypt has been led mostly by men who first rose to prominence under Nasir, and the center-piece of Sadat's domestic policy—the "open door", or *infitah*—evidently answers to the interest of a class of people whom the Nasirist system, in spite of itself, somehow permitted to prosper. The new class of private entrepreneurs has emerged from the interstices of the mixed economy of the 1960s.[1]

Despite the announced philosophy of *infitah* which preaches the liberation of private domestic as well as foreign investment potential for the development of productive enterprise, the areas of activity into which the new class has in fact moved—real estate, tourist services, luxury imports, etc. — are ones that do little to build up the productive capacities of the country. Nor do the foreign investors with whom the domestic interests associate themselves have a different tendency.[2] As long as *infitah* continues, however, these activities should continue to be profitable for the individuals involved, and thus they will constitute an important interest group well placed to press for the prolongation of the policy even if it is not paying off for the nation as a whole, and to convince the government that the present state of affairs is actually quite satisfactory.

Superficially at least, such an argument is not hard to make. The rate of growth in the GNP (around 9 percent in 1980) and the improvement in the balance of payments, the ever-growing revenues from American aid, oil, the Suez Canal, tourism and the remittances of Egyptians working in the Gulf, the appearance of the new prosperity in central Cairo with its construction boom, the October bridge and the traffic flyovers, the imported goods for sale and the slightly improved telephone system — all of this suggests at face value that things are getting better, as in some respects of course they are. But it encourages the government to settle for overall improvements in the national accounts, to ignore problems of productivity and income distribution, and — in the assurance that more windfall revenues are always on the horizon — to adopt a rather casual attitude towards the intractable problems of basic reform. One analyst has compared this attitude to that of the governments of the oil-rich states: despite Egypt's poverty she is run like a *rentier* state, always relying on windfalls, with the difference that her windfalls always come from outside the country rather than from inside.[3]

In some ways a situation of this sort is reminiscent of that of Lebanon before the civil war; in others, it is more like Iran before the revolution. The comparison with Lebanon stems from the inordinate emphasis on commercial activities as the backbone of the economy: importing and retailing of consumer goods, banking, business services, real estate, and tourism. In addition there is, as in Lebanon, the low priority attached by the government to the level or the quality of social services, and the reliance on private education, private medical care, etc., by those who can afford it. There is the same lack of attention to the needs of rural areas and provincial towns (despite President Sadat's fondness for alluding to the cultural values of rural life). There is the same effort by the regime to cultivate the good will and protection of the Western powers, as well as the tolerance of militant states in the region, by building up the country's reputation as an international commercial entrepôt, political sanctuary, playground, and all-round facility.

There are, of course, many differences between Lebanon and Egypt which preclude a really systematic effort by the Egyptian government to seek to adopt the Lebanese role, although it does appear to pursue it, however unconsciously, to an unhealthy degree. The most obvious difference is that Lebanon's ability to play the role in the past depended vitally on the fact that, like Switzerland, she was a neutral country within the region with a small, compromise-minded population of diverse communities, background and political orientation, and without external ambitions; thus she was more easily accepted by the others as a common convenience. For Egypt, with the largest population, industrial base and military forces in the Arab world, the Lebanese role is incompatible with her national stature and strategic interests.

On the domestic economic and social levels there are other differences that have received perhaps less recognition from the government. The traditional Arab-Islamic culture of the great majority of Egyptians does not make them plausible candidates to acquire, or to encourage in their midst, the cosmopolitan, mercantile, polyglot personality of Levantinism. Furthermore, the purveying of commercial services to the region brought considerable prosperity to Lebanon, but it cannot sustain an economy of the scale of Egypt's. Even in Lebanon it eventually failed to serve the larger community well: the poorer communities, excluded from participation, came to pose a social and political challenge to the system as they camped in the "belt of misery" on the outskirts of Beirut. So also in Egypt, where a much smaller proportion of the population can hope to benefit from the new commercialism, the accentuation of social inequality may eventually erode the political passivity of the country's great mass of urban migrants.

The comparison with Iran is a rather different one. It stems first of all from the phenomenon of rapid and poorly controlled growth, coming largely from sources of income accruing to the government rather than to private individuals (in Egypt's case, revenues from oil, the Suez Canal and foreign aid), which the government at least ostensibly tries to direct towards investment in industry, agriculture and infrastructure. It does so, however, in an improvised manner and in cooperation with a new class of entrepreneurs largely of the regime's own making: favored individuals and foreign interests who learn to capitalize on their connections with those in power and, of course, to cut them in on the deal. The reason the planning is so poor in such a system is that the rationalization of a modernizing, industrializing economy is not the controlling consideration: rather it is the appearance of great progress and activity, represented simply by a rapid rise in GNP, the prosperity of a growing new upper class, and the very visible integration of the country into the world economy. Again, as in the Lebanese case, a high rate of inflation and an increasing degree of inequality between social classes are obvious consequences, with the added feature in the Iranian model of the almost forceful disruption of the life patterns of certain traditional groups (merchants, artisans and peasants).

These economic features of the Iranian model have certain political accompaniments. The bureaucracy is more than ever a dumping ground for unusable high school and university graduates, but presiding over it is a new class of technocrats who, in turn, are politically subservient to the political leadership. There is a built-in ambivalence between the bureaucracy and the technocracy: together they nominally represent the interest of management and supervision of a growing modern economy, but with the emphasis on appearance rather than reality, on private deals rather than national development, it is always easy for both bureaucrats and technocrats to be bypassed by those above them. Of course, the bureaucracy-technocracy syndrome was already a phenomenon in the socialist Egypt of Nasir but with the difference that in those days, for the political leadership and for many individuals employed with the apparatus, concrete national purposes really were important.

Another feature of the Iranian model is militarization. Egypt had already been militarized under Nasir and, according to various presidential declarations, was supposed to undergo a measure of demilitarization after the peace treaty with Israel. In the following year both the rhetoric and the military budget shifted, and it became clear that the importance of the armed forces was destined to grow rather than to shrink. This is because the attention devoted to these forces was not a function of national defence needs but of the political preoccupations of the regime: close relations with the new weapons supplier, the United States; the adoption of a forceful posture towards certain neighbors (Libya and Ethiopia); and, presumably, a desire to cultivate the loyalty of the generals and colonels on whom the life of the regime depends.

Finally the Iranian model presents the figure of the patrimonial leader, with striking implications for Egypt. The patrimonial leader holds the system together through a network of personal loyalties centered on himself, with the object of building up patronage, power and control. The dispensing of favors, the manipulation of clients, the rotation of office-holders, the keeping of one's own counsel on vital matters, the primary reliance on confidants whose membership in the inner circle is unrelated to any official status, the cultivation of a whole mythology of omnipotence, omniscience, benevolence, unaminous popularity — all these are essential ingredients of the cult of patrimonialism.

The patrimonial syndrome is traditionally associated with hereditary monarchy but it is by no means limited to it. More important, the syndrome is associated with a static society and static economic resources, more successfully than with a situation of flux and rapid change. When the resources to be passed around are limited, then everything has its steady value, and the personalities to be manipulated are more or less stable as well, so that the game is more easily controlled. The introduction of sweeping and unfamiliar changes, as in the Iranian case in the 1960s and 1970s or, to some extent, in the Egyptian case today, threatens to throw the game into confusion by inserting the element of uncertainty. It is thus not surprising that the demise of Shah Muhammad Reza Pahlavi, some 37 years after he ascended the throne, came not very long after the sudden rise of oil prices had pumped additional billions of dollars into his nation's economic and social bloodstream. For the patrimonial form of leadership fits poorly with rapid economic change and with demands for planning, rationalization, delegation of authority, and transformation of social and political relationships. No doubt, after the Shah's fall, when he spent a few weeks in Morocco, he was in a position to compare interesting notes with King Hassan II, still on *his* throne and still presiding over a comparatively stagnant economy.

Of course, Egypt is different in many ways from Iran, and President Sadat is different from the Shah. Sadat in some ways maintains a more realistic human touch with his populace and with the outside world; he visits his village, he attends the mosque, he wears a safari suit, he gives extemporaneous speeches to his people on television. His economy has not exactly been inundated with wealth *à l'iranienne*. His people are generally better educated and his government better institutionalized than those of the Shah, and he treats them accordingly with more respect. He does not rule by terror. His religious establishment is cooperative, and lays no claim in the Shi'ite fashion either to martyrdom or to theocratic primacy.

Yet these differences, important as they are, are balanced by major similarities: the one-man rule, the manufacturing of unanimous support, the promise of great days, the reliance on an inner circle and the manipulation of the regular state administration, the shuffling of cabinet ministers in and out of office, the impatience with detail, and the preference for grand schemes, the hobnobbing with world leaders, the attention to uniforms and ceremonies, all the while preaching nostalgia for the village life of simplicity—all this adds up to a picture quite close to that of the Shah. Add to this the rapid changes in the Egyptian economy, in which fortunes are being made, inflation is rampant and in which some traditional livelihoods and values are being abruptly undermined, plus the sudden and unrestrained Americanization of everything in Egyptian life from foreign policy to consumption habits, and one can hardly grant President Sadat the right to complacency.

Overall, then, Egypt under Sadat appears in the long run to be headed for an accumulation of social strains and tensions. On the economic front the prospects are for several years of continued very rapid growth, followed by a levelling-off and the risk of stagnation in the longer run if the rapid-growth sectors of the economy should exhaust their potential for further expansion. These sectors include the Suez Canal, oil production, tourism, remittances, and the construction boom. There is a limit to how much further growth can be counted on in these sectors; and in the longer run, sustained advances in the economy must be fuelled by the expansion of agriculture and industry, sectors which the open door economic policy purports to encourage (though with negligible results during the first half dozen years).

With the onset of the Egyptian-Israeli peace and the passage of time, and as international business confidence in Egypt builds up, it may be that the flood of foreign investment in industry and agriculture for which *infitah* was designed will finally materialize. And under the impact of this competition, perhaps the public sector industries will streamline themselves. Together with the continuing general growth of the economy, these developments may serve to absorb Egypt's under-employed manpower in a productive fashion. Unfortunately, however, we see little reason to hope for anything of the kind.

What then might Egypt look like by the year 2000, assuming the survival of the present regime under Sadat or a natural successor? With a population of 62 million[4] and a per capita income, at 1980 prices, of $500-$600 (up from the 1980 level of $350), a population in the greater Cairo area of 20 million, a booming tourist industry, a continuing but moderately reduced exportation of manpower to the Gulf, an export-oriented agriculture, a chronically ailing public sector industrial network, a business community of many thousands of Westerners, a large and prosperous complex of international banking and commercial interests, and — last but not least — a tough-minded authoritarian system of rule on the model of Chile or Brazil, Egypt will enter the next century. Central Cairo will wear the new look of the future, its skyline dominated by hotels and office buildings, the streets and sidewalks well-paved, and the donkey carts banned from public thoroughfares, while surrounding the city will be one of the world's largest and most miserable slums in which the real Egypt is tucked away from the world's view.

This scenario may not survive until the year 2000, for the beneficiaries of such a system may find their position undermined as time passes. According to the Lebanese mercantile model, the problem is the lack of real productivity in the system, the lack of central direction, and the inequality between classes; however, the system might survive for many years, and it may require an external catalyst (in Lebanon the Palestinian problem) to bring on a crisis. According to the Iranian patrimonial model, on the other hand, the problem is mass alienation from social dislocations and repression. To the extent that Egypt follows in the footsteps of either or both of these models, the future does not bode very well in the long run. The gaps between rich and poor may become too glaring, the challenge to traditional values too degrading, the costs of propping up the level of living of the upper classes too exorbitant, and the tools of repression too inadequate. Even if the system survives into the 21st century, it is unlikely to dazzle the Arab world as a showcase of success.

SCENARIO II: REPLACEMENT OF SADAT BY A NASIRIST REGIME

The two groups in Egypt that would appear to have the greatest chance to succeed the present regime in power are the Nasirists and the Islamic fundamentalists. We use these labels in a very general way and do not refer to any particular formal organization or any well-defined ideologies, but only to tendencies. While there are obvious ideological differences between the two groups, whether this matters very much depends on which brand of fundamentalists we are talking about (see below).

Let us imagine a return of something called Nasirism to rule in Egypt. We can suppose that few or none of the leading personalities of the old Nasir regime would re-emerge, although some second-echelon figures might do so. The important point is that the new leaders—military or civilian—would invoke Nasir's name and legacy, seek to reactivate his principles, and accuse the Sadat regime of having betrayed the revolution. They would be critical of *infitah,* of the Egyptian-Israeli peace treaty, of the break in relations with the Arab world and of the switch of partnership from Moscow to Washington. They would seek to revive the importance of centralized state planning of the economy, the primacy of the public sector, and the control of foreign trade and currency exchange. They would take a reserved view of many aspects of foreign and Arab business operations in Egypt. At least in principle, they would attach greater importance to problems of income distribution, and less to sheer growth in GNP.

Certainly at the outset, and perhaps for a good many years thereafter, a new regime with this orientation would face grave difficulties in implementing its principles; and the magnitude of these difficulties raises the fundamental question of whether in fact Egypt really possesses any meaningful freedom of choice in charting her future course, or whether she has been locked by circumstances and by the implications of her past decisions, into her present set of policies. On the other hand, some of the obstacles to changing her policies depend on the assumption that nothing changes *elsewhere* in the region—an assumption that might be erroneous.

The first obstacle to change arises from Israel and the peace treaty. To denounce the treaty outright would be tantamount to a declaration of war, probably triggering an immediate Israeli attempt to reoccupy the Sinai Peninsula or to punish Egypt militarily in some other severe way. But even lesser moves on Egypt's part, such as the denunciation of the Camp David formula for Palestinian autonomy or the partial curtailment of diplomatic or commercial relations would, if they came on the heels of a forcible change of government in Egypt, be likely to escalate progressively towards a similar outcome.

The second obstacle is the United States government, which has worked long and hard since 1973 for the liberalization of Egypt's economy, her orientation towards the West, and close dependence on America for aid, investment, and mediation with agencies like the World Bank and the International Monetary Fund. Of course this encouragement is geared towards Egyptian foreign as well as economic policy. Thus any Egyptian move away from Israel or towards the Arab militants or the Soviet Union would jeopardize the continuation of American aid and helpfulness. However much it may have entered the conventional wisdom in Washington that John Foster Dulles was wrong in 1956 to withdraw the offer of a loan to Egypt to build the High Dam because he did not like Nasir's foreign policy, it is more than likely that such an action would be repeated today, for the present aid is closely tied to American expectations of Egyptian policies, if not exactly to an American identification with the person of Sadat.

The third obstacle is Saudi Arabia, whose present leaders do not wish for regional upheavals, new rounds of fighting with Israel, confrontations with the United States, new opportunities for the Soviet Union, or the reversion of so important a country as Egypt to socialist economics. They would fear a return to the period of confrontation between Cairo and Riyadh before 1967, with the danger of Egyptian-led subversion campaigns against them; and they would try to use the power of the purse to dissuade any new Egyptian government in advance from taking undesired steps.

Fourth and last, there are obstacles within Egypt itself. We can imagine a change of regime coming in response to a wave of public dissatisfaction with certain features of the liberal economic policy, and yet there would be important immediate penalties to be paid if the policy were substantially curtailed: the drying up of foreign investment in those fields in which it currently does exist, the stoppage of remittances from Egyptian expatriates reluctant to send their money into an uncertain atmosphere, the flight of hard currency, a chilling effect on domestic investment...etc. Legal guarantees against nationalization and taxation of foreign business would in any case minimize the possibilities for government action against them.

To carry through its ideological policy preferences, even slowly, a Nasirist government would have to rely on far-reaching commitments of support from the more radical oil states and from the Soviet Union. It is doubtful whether Libya, which has sharply reduced her oil production for the sake of conservation, or Iraq, which has very large internal needs and has suffered serious war losses, would be ready to underwrite the Egyptian economy sufficiently; while the conservative Gulf states would only make contributions to the extent that Egypt undertook to avoid a return to the old economics or diplomacy of Nasir. As for the Soviet Union, it must worry a great deal about both the financial and strategic implications of re-acquiring its erstwhile Egyptian client with its enormous needs, its unpaid military debts from the 1960s and 1970s, and the risks it would bring of renewed conflict in the Middle East.

In short, any group of Nasirists replacing Sadat in power would find itself under powerful constraints and pressures to go very slowly in making policy changes, even to the point perhaps of negating the very purposes for which power was seized in the first place. To be sure, this may sound much like what many people said of the limited options of Egypt's Free Officers after 1952, which Nasir proved wrong within five years. A significant difference between then and now is that then, although Egypt was a poor country, she was far more self-sufficient economically, possessed large sterling credits, and did not depend in the short run on large financial transfusions to pay for current consumption. Today a great deal in Egypt's economic life has come to depend on her credit standing, as she struggles to service her debt and to cover her perennial balance of payments deficit, and this is a powerful lever for any creditor to exercise against her.

Under these considerations, it might be expected that the advent of a Nasirist government would produce only limited and gradual changes in Egypt's internal and external policies and in her development strategy, concentrating perhaps on larger investment in the public sector and in agriculture, a relative slowing down in the encouraging of foreign enterprise, and some effort to curb luxury imports. The development of relations with Israel would slow down, without actually being rolled back; the other Arab states would be assured that Egypt planned quietly to keep relations with Israel at a bare minimum level compatible with treaty obligations. Relations with the United States would inevitably cool off to some extent, with the Egyptian side seeking to avoid major provocations that might lead Washington to stop the aid program. Relations with the Soviet Union would no doubt improve, but without any dramatic agreements or gestures.

All these elements of a cautious posture would serve to enable the Nasirist regime to bide its time while consolidating Egypt's renewed control of the Sinai and waiting for changes in the regimes of the Gulf states and/or Saudi Arabia, changes that might liberate Egypt from her financial bondage to the West and enable a more frankly Nasirist approach to various problems to emerge: notably, an end to the open door policy and a full-fledged reversion to the principles of Arab socialism. Some such changes will be discussed in subsequent scenarios.

While awaiting such a breakthrough and playing the cautious game we have described, Egypt could not expect to prosper much; her economy would be falling between two stools, with the confidence of private investors shaken and the enthusiasm of the American government cooled, but without the resources available for the massive investment in agriculture and industry within a socialist or state-capitalist framework that is needed.

However, several developments could rapidly bring considerable sums of new revenue into the hands of a Nasirist government and transform its prospects. Large oil deposits might be discovered in Egypt; she might unite with Qaddafi's Libya and, under present oil prices, easily cream $5 or $6 billion dollars annually off Libya's oil revenues, or there might be a change of regime in Saudi Arabia or another of the Gulf states bringing a sympathetic leadership to power and causing a similar volume of aid to flow. What would a Nasirist government do with an extra $5 billion a year?

In fact it is not difficult to spend $5 billion in Egypt. Half of it might be needed to compensate for the loss of other revenues as the government began to do the things it had been afraid to do earlier: American aid, foreign investment, and tourism might all decline or disappear. The remaining $2.5 billion could be entirely used up by raising the present miserable wages of Egypt's 3.5 million public employees by $60 a month — roughly a 100 percent increase, yet not unreasonable. Substantial sums could disappear into an enlarged military budget or an inefficient but conspicuous industrial scheme. The point is simply that with heavy pressures to spend, there is no great cause for confidence that the expenditures actually decided upon will be productive ones.

Still, when all is said and done, the hallmark of the Nasirist legacy of economic policy is central planning of public investment priorities, which suggests some likelihood that experts would be listened to and a serious effort made to locate suitable ways to spend the money. Reorganizing and re-equipping the public sector industries, many of which were starved for investment capital at their inception in the 1960s, would be another. From the viewpoint of the Nasirists, a return to power with better finances than in the 1960s would represent a chance to complete — and to vindicate — the experiment in national planning that was aborted in 1965 when Egypt ran out of money and had to cancel her second five-year plan. From the viewpoint of the critics, there is the danger that the Nasirists would be no more conscious than before of the principle of cost-effectiveness, and that a renewed experiment, however well financed, would eventually accumulate the same errors of inefficiency and wastefulness all over again.

SCENARIO III: REPLACEMENT OF SADAT BY A MUSLIM FUNDAMENTALIST REGIME

In order to differentiate clearly between alternative scenarios, we shall speak here of fundamentalists of the most militant and radical kind: devoted revolutionary zealots, not simply conservative reformers. The shades of difference between the two are many, as they are also between fundamentalists and Nasirists, or between Nasirists and Marxists. The more moderate brand of fundamentalism overlaps considerably with Nasirism, with little besides the symbolic issue of secularism, past memories of political strife and, perhaps, the question of orientation to the Soviet Union to divide them. Both are movements of populist reformism, opposed to a free-wheeling capitalism, attached to Egypt's Arab and Islamic affiliations and to the principle of neutralism in world affairs.

On the other hand the more extreme variety of fundamentalism, comparable to that of the Ayatollahs in Iran, does present a distinctly different policy alternative and therefore deserves to be explored. On the international level, the advent of such a movement to power in Egypt could quickly lead the country into all sorts of trouble: an Israeli reconquest of the Sinai, the closing of the Suez Canal, a break with the United States. Such a regime could be expected to ally itself closely with Qaddafi's Libya (despite its probable disapproval of some of his arbitrary innovations in religious doctrine) and to work for the overthrow of the present regime in Saudi Arabia. Most interesting of all for our purposes, however, it might seek to impose severe austerity inside Egypt, and reject the conventional models—whether Marxist or liberal—of capital-intensive, high-technology forms of development.

Admittedly, the Khomeini model seems implausible for Egypt, a country traditionally too exposed to the currents of the outside world to turn very easily to isolationist practices. As already mentioned, there is the growing reliance on food imports and on foreign credit; in addition, it is an important consideration that for geographical and political reasons, outside powers are unlikely to leave Egypt alone. And the Egyptian educated and commercial classes thrive on external contact. The restrictions on such contact during the years under Nasir—imposed mostly for reasons of austerity—were always the object of widespread disaffection, and their lifting brought Sadat considerable support. Moreover, the imposition of strict, militant religious discipline on a relaxed society like that of Egypt cannot be done easily.

Still, a Khomeinist Egypt is particularly interesting to imagine, because of the prospect it offers of putting into practice some of the principles that some critics of both Nasir and Sadat have long held to be the only ones that really offer Egypt much hope for the future; autarky, import substitution, rural development along radically collectivist lines, cottage industry, labor-intensive technology, austerity, egalitarianism, and decentralization.[5] In short, it is really the Chinese or Maoist model, with the difference merely that Islam rather than Marxism-Leninism supplies the ideological symbols. A very active and authoritative functional equivalent of the Chinese Communist Party, combining religious devotions with political work, would be an essential part of the picture.

How would such a regime fare? Could it survive for long? What would be its long-range requirements for success? It is important to recognize that despite the ideals of self-reliance and isolation, Egypt under a militant Islamic regime would certainly not exist in an international vacuum. While working towards greater agricultural self-sufficiency, she would need to continue to finance food imports; while turning towards agriculture and light industry, she would have to find a more profitable way of operating an existing network of publicly-owned heavy industries designed for export. And she must pay her debts—or at least some of them.

All these needs point to the importance of a suitable financial patron willing to invest in Egypt's revolutionary Islamic experiment: perhaps Libya, perhaps one of the states of the Arabian Peninsula after a change of regime there. In theory the investment should be modest compared to what either Sadat or the Nasirists would require, given the projected de-emphasis on heavy industry and other capital-intensive projects, but it would still be substantial, perhaps of the order of $2 billion a year, and it could only be secured by taking some chances with a foreign policy that would risk costing a lot of money and embroiling Egypt in unwanted conflicts. In Chinese fashion, a Maoist/Khomeinist Egypt might prefer to turn its back on foreign enemies, i.e. Israel and the United States, and merely abuse them verbally; if the Sinai were reoccupied by Israel, it could be written off for decades like Taiwan, not forgotten but practically ignored, while the country concentrated on its internal problems. The Palestinian problem likewise would remain on the shelf. But what financial backer of Maoist Egypt would accept such a policy? The Soviet Union? Iraq? Libya? A revolutionary Saudi Arabia? It hardly seems plausible.

Thus the first problem in conceiving a prolonged Maoist experiment in Egypt, paradoxically enough, is the lack of resources for a more modest and isolated way of life. Those in the world who put money into Egypt demand from her one kind or another of international activity that will serve their interests. Who will invest in her withdrawal from the world?

We come to the second problem when we imagine a Maoist Egypt meeting her financial needs through some sort of dramatic windfall, like the one discussed above that might bail out a Nasirist regime (large oil discoveries, union with Libya, etc.). The extra $5 billion per year about which we speculated, in the hands of a Maoist leadership, would risk having a corrupting effect and transforming the system into a Nasirist one, through the temptation to invest in expensive industrial or military projects and to concentrate authority in the hands of a centralized bureaucracy.

The emphasis in the Maoist model on rural development and decentralization flies in the face of certain established Egyptian political and cultural values. Bureaucratic centralism is a political tradition in Egypt since ancient times; it has a material basis in the "hydraulic society" of Wittfogel.[6] There have been periodic calls for administrative decentralization in recent decades, but the primacy of the capital city and its ministerial bureaux over local officials in the provinces keeps reasserting itself.

Furthermore, Egypt has the rest of the world for company in its general urban bias. Government benefits, public and private investments, the outlook of the average educated person, all tend to reflect the assumption that it is the welfare and productivity of urban rather than rural inhabitants that needs to be encouraged.[7] Whatever excellent arguments may be made against perpetuating this bias, it has the weight of Egyptian history and of worldwide prejudice behind it.

SCENARIO IV: IRAQI HEGEMONY IN THE
                         FERTILE CRESCENT

Regardless of its immediate outcome, the 1980 Iraqi-Iranian war has served as a reminder of the growing potential of Iraq for a leading regional role, comparable to that played by Egypt during the period under Nasir. Just as Nasirist Egypt's bid for hegemony stirred up the Arab pot, exciting the nationalist enthusiasm of the masses but arousing the fears and suspicions of other Arab regimes, so Baᶜthist Iraq may well do the same in the coming years. For Egypt, however, the emergence of a new "Arab Prussia" also would carry the unwelcome message that Egypt's own regional role was in inexorable decline. We shall try to discern in what tangible ways the mounting influence of Iraq could affect Egypt, and what Egyptian responses might be expected.

Iraq's own development potential has long appeared in theory to be considerable because of her multiplicity of resources: an agriculture generated by two river valleys, an industrial base, a relatively large population (12 million) including a skilled work force, an established educational system, a bureaucracy, an army, a development-minded government, and enormous oil reserves: in short, all the assets of Nasir's Egypt plus the financial resources that Egypt has lacked. With these advantages, how could Iraq miss? How could she fail to capture the leadership of the Arab nationalist movement?

Despite the persistence of this question over many years, Iraq has somehow continued to miss, thanks in part to chronic social divisions and political instability. Still, one imagines, these problems may be overcome by a period of effective leadership and material progress, and sooner or later Iraq will achieve her promise. Furthermore, beyond her own potential, there are much more dramatic possibilities implicit in any union or stable and close cooperation that might be formed between Iraq and her Fertile Crescent neighbors, Syria, Jordan, Lebanon, the Palestinians: altogether another 18 million people including much of the Arab world's intellectual and professional elite, plus an impressive increment of agricultural, industrial, and military resources and strategically vital territory. Despite the recurrent feuds among the governments of these countries, especially between Iraq and Syria, there remains the intriguing consideration that an electrifying transformation of the situation, leading to a grand unification of the Fertile Crescent under Iraqi leadership, may be but a coup d'état away.

For an added bit of spice, let us add that such a powerful new entity, in some circumstances, might easily manage to implement the longstanding Iraqi claim to sovereignty over Kuwait. The absorption of the latter would render the new state not only large and well-endowed but very rich indeed. However, this additional element is not essential to the scenario.

Many problems could forestall or disrupt a Fertile Crescent union. The Iraqis might find the Syrians indigestible, as the Egyptians did during their 1958–1961 union with Syria. The Lebanese problem—since 1976 a headache for Damascus—might prove too difficult to deal with. Israel might see fit to forestall the whole experiment in unity with a devastating pre-emptive attack on the Syrian and Iraqi air forces. Jordan's King Hussein might attempt to sabotage the union from within; the Saudi monarchy might do so from without. In general, the Iraqi leaders might spoil their own chances by pressing for the union and for domination of the remaining Arab world too recklessly.

But let us imagine otherwise. Given enough determination and enough care, the Iraqis would work with the utmost caution to protect the legitimacy of their actions, to reassure the great powers, and to avoid unnecessary provocations to all concerned. Should they succeed, they would emerge as a distinctly more powerful entity than was Nasir's Egypt at its peak, by reason of their financial self-sufficiency and their status as an oil producer. Even a bilateral Iraqi-Syrian or Iraqi-Jordanian union, without additional partners, would still represent a potent combination, capable of heavily affecting the inter-Arab balance of power and influence.

Leaving aside the possibility of war with Israel, two alternative political outcomes in the Arab world seem particularly plausible. In the first of these, despite its initial cautiousness, the new Fertile Crescent union would emerge—somewhat like Nasir's Egypt at its high point—as the champion of revolution in the Arab world and as a fairly close partner or client of the Soviet Union. Egypt, still under the Sadat regime or something resembling it, would respond by establishing a strong conservative alliance with Saudi Arabia, the remaining Gulf monarchies, and the United States, dedicated to holding the line against any further progress of the "Soviet-dominated" revolutionary movement. This revival of the pre-Camp David Cairo-Riyadh axis would rest on precise understandings: Egypt would make gestures of suspending the "normalization" of her relations with Israel and the negotiations over the status of the occupied Palestinian territories, leaving the United States to persuade Israel to accept this; Egyptian air and ground forces, with American support, would be provided for the defense of Saudi Arabia; and Saudi Arabia would respond by committing massive economic assistance to Egypt.

According to this logic, the interest of the Saudi government in strengthening Egypt would be directly in proportion to the magnitude of the radical challenge from Iraq. An Iraqi-dominated union including

Syria, Jordan and Kuwait, could persuade the Saudis of the need not just to lend Egypt a measure of tactical encouragement, but to make a lasting strategic investment in reviving Egypt's economic and political strength so as to make her an effective counterweight to the threat from the north. Such a decision might not necessarily aim particularly to save the Sadat regime so much as to bolster Egypt as a state, on the premise that geo-political realities would drive almost any Egyptian regime of the day to stand with Riyadh against Baghdad. But of course the practical effect of this revitalized Saudi-Egyptian alliance would be to strengthen all the tendencies which Sadat has represented, and which Riyadh has consistently approved: social conservatism, free enterprise and the Open Door, cultivation of an Egyptian deterrent force, and reliance on the United States.

Of course, all the blessings of Saudi Arabia and the United States combined could not guarantee the survival of Sadat or his policies in Egypt. There is no little risk in letting oneself become the chosen pillar of the defence of Western interests against a dynamic populist movement, as the fate of Nuri Said and of the Shah of Iran suggests. The more reliance is placed on the Sadat regime in such a role, the less capable it may be of performing it. Furthermore, as we have already indicated earlier in our comparison of Sadat's style of governance with that of the Shah, the Iranian case also suggests that the influx of additional billions of dollars—in the form of Saudi assistance in this case—may actually undermine rather than strenghten the authority of the regime.

However, this is highly speculative. What seems more conclusive is that a militant, expansionist, Soviet-oriented Iraqi regime would tend to drive Sadat's Egypt and Saudi Arabia together, with American encouragement.

The alternative outcome proceeds from the assumption that the Iraqi-led union would remain subdued in its aims and style, and would, as a matter of caution, seek to cultivate amicable relations with both Saudi Arabia and the United States. Kuwait would be scrupuloulsy left alone; diplomatic relations with Washington, broken by Iraq since 1967, would be restored. Trade with Western Europe would flourish. The Soviet Union would be kept at arm's length. These moves would be designed to reduce the risk of an Israeli attack and to head off a Saudi-Egyptian counter-alliance. On the contrary, Baghdad would seek to collaborate with Riyadh in formulating a common policy towards Egypt, designed to persuade her to minimize her relationship with Israel and to adopt a passive role in Arab affairs, and, in return, to offer her the chance to inherit the previous role of Lebanon in the Arab world. Egypt would be tolerated as a haven for political exiles and cultural expression, and as a center for international business, and she would continue to be encouraged to supply the oil states with manpower and miscellaneous services and supplies.

Thus, according to such a bargain, as the "new Lebanon" of the Middle East Egypt would be reduced to serving as a regional facility, tolerated on condition that she swing no political weight of her own. Not only is this role inadequate for Egypt on the domestic level as we have already noted, but it would not provide a sufficient political incentive for other states to respect Egyptian interests. American aid would dwindle away, Israel would be tempted to reoccupy Sharm el Sheikh and the Sinai oilfields. Holding no great importance for anyone, Egypt would face a long-term decline in her material fortunes and in her political and social morale.

This turn of events would present a natural situation for revolutionary change, whether of the Islamic or the Nasirist variety. An Islamic fundamentalist regime in Egypt, faced with the challenge of Iraqi (or joint Iraqi-Saudi) hegemony in the eastern Arab world, would have little choice but to turn to Libya for support, a prospect that raises interesting possibilities of Libyan-Egyptian partnership, or even full union, dominated in all likelihood by the personality of Muammar Qaddafi. Here perhaps would be an opportunity for the Mao-Khomeini ethic of autarky, decentralization and austerity to be put to the test, provided Qaddafi's priorities did not interfere. Some of Qaddafi's more heretical ideas about Islam might not win the approval of the Egyptian militants, but when the chips were down they might well decide that he was their best bet. Whether the Egyptian Army command would tolerate a partnership with Qaddafi's Libya is also an open question. As we have indicated earlier, the Islamic fundamentalist form of government is not one that appears likely to last for long in Egypt, without evolving into something else.

A Nasirist regime installed in Egypt under the circumstances of this scenario would be another matter. A striking consideration is that, compared to the Nasirist regime in Scenario II in which no changes in Egypt's external environment were assumed, this regime would have a wider range of policy choices before it because of the ambiguous posture of the Iraqi bid for Arab leadership, compromised by its overtures to the Saudis and the Americans.

In this situation, we certainly do not assume that a Nasirist group seizing power in Egypt would proceed to join hands with the men in Baghdad out of some presumed ideological affinity. Initial gestures of this sort might be made, but they would be unlikely to prosper, any more than did the initial contacts between the United Arab Republic of Nasir and the Iraqi revolutionary regime of ʿAbd al-Karim Qasim in 1958, or those between Nasir and the Syrian and Iraqi Baʿthists in 1963. Geopolitical rivalry and the competition for Arab nationalist leadership—a role that Egyptian Nasirists would instinctively claim by inheritance but which few persons in the Fertile Crescent countries would see fit any longer to accord to Egypt—would rise quickly to the surface.

In these fluid circumstances, it would be open to the Nasirists to take their position as far to the left of the Iraqis and as close to the Soviet Union as they wished, and to revert to most of the socialist economic policies of the 1960s. Prudence might induce them to proceed gradually in this, but the point is that with the Arab world and the West having too little to offer them, with *infitah* at a dead end, and with the Soviet Union in need of more reliable Arab friends than the Iraqis had proved to be, the temptation for Egyptian Nasirists to return to the policies they have always fundamentally believed in would be very great. It would be essential for them, however, to avoid such direct provocations of Iraq, Saudi Arabia and the other oil states as would jeopardize the status of Egyptian workers there. This should not be difficult: the Nasirists' concern would be to set their own policies for Egypt, and to protect their position in the Arab world, not necessarily to return to the contentiousness of inter-Arab relations at the height of the era of Nasir. Meanwhile, a limited rapprochement with Libya might be worked out, bringing with it some financial assistance—enough, perhaps, to offset the loss of American aid.

SCENARIO V: AN ISLAMIC REVOLUTION IN
SAUDI ARABIA AND THE GULF

The prospect that Saudi Arabia may one day go the way of Iran is one that has attracted considerable speculation ever since the departure of the Shah. The catalogue of similarities and differences is widely familiar: in both cases a royal family rules autocratically over a traditional Muslim society undergoing rapid and disruptive change, under the impetus of very large oil revenues and with the highly visible presence of thousands of Westerners; on the other hand, in Saudi Arabia the royal family is more socially integrated, its religious legitimacy is greater, its political repression is less harsh, its population is smaller and more dispersed, and its dispensing of wealth throughout the society is more effective. So the parallel is far from complete, and the likelihood of the Iranian revolution being repeated across the Gulf is far from predictable.

Professor Jabber may well prove to be right in insisting, in his chapter in this volume, that the overthrow of the Saudi regime is not a realistic prospect in the 1980s. Still, two considerations make such a scenario quite a plausible one in my opinion. First, it is obvious that the changes in the social and cultural life of Saudi Arabia wrought by the sudden circulation of wealth have brought with them a great deal of strain, for they do not accord well with the traditional values of the society, nor with the highly personalized and authoritarian methods of family rule customarily exercised by the Saudi dynasty. Consequently some impetus for revolutionary change is being generated.

Secondly, it is quite obvious that in Saudi Arabia, unlike some other countries of the region, the attachment to traditional symbols and values remains very strong, even among the most educated classes. No pre-revolutionary or post-revolutionary regime can afford to disregard them. If they are the basis of the orthodox legitimacy invoked by the Saʿud family, they are also the inevitable cutting edge of radical protest by those who see the virtues of traditional life being corrupted by money, greed, luxury, sloth, waste, sex and alcohol. While some Saudis may dream of revolution for the sake of political parties, co-education, and the disbanding of the religious police, it is surely a much greater number who are restless because the present regime is giving Wahhabism a bad name.

Thus a Saudi Arabian version of the Iranian revolution (and with it, similar revolutions in the neighboring Gulf principalities) is not an altogether unlikely prospect. Like Iran under Ayatollah Khomeini, it could enter upon a course of virulent xenophobia and of punitive hostility to everything associated with the old regime. Alternatively, in a much milder form, the revolution could even be led by conservative princes of the royal family itself, seeking to preserve the monarchy, and work simply to reform the Kingdom and its overexposure to the external world. If the revolution is restricted to that extent, however, it loses most of its relevance for regional and international politics and is hardly worth our considering. Therefore we shall focus on something closer to the Iranian model.

Like Khomeini's Iran, such a revolutionary regime would be likely to see the Egypt of Sadat as a carbon copy of much of what it was reacting against at home, and thus as a prime target for its wrath. There are three ways in which it could strike out against Egypt.

First, it could dismiss Egyptian workers—easily a large number or perhaps virtually all of them. To some extent this would follow naturally from a revolutionary decision to cut back sharply on the pace of domestic development expenditures; even a simple palace-led campaign of conservative reform would be likely to take some steps in this direction, if not so drastically. In addition, however, the action would be a frankly punitive blow aimed at the Egyptian regime in retribution for Camp David and other sins.

But would this not be "irrational"? Would it not be damaging for Saudi Arabia suddenly to deprive itself of hundreds of thousands of school-teachers, economists, clerks, engineers, mechanics and road-builders? Of course it would: that is what would make the action revolutionary, and that is why the Arab states objecting to Egypt's peace treaty with Israel failed to expel Egyptian labor previously. Some of them, after all, worried about what might happen in Egypt if Sadat were to fall. This time, the Islamic revolutionaries would be determined to produce results; and, as they would very well know, a massive cutoff of labor migration would be an intolerable blow for Egyptian society and for the government.

Secondly, the Saudi revolutionaries could mount a strong campaign of criticism against the Sadat regime and work to stimulate Islamic fundamentalist subversive activity inside Egypt, hammering on the theme that the regime and its policies offer no sense of moral direction or public purpose and that they represent the same ills as those that prompted the revolution in Saudi Arabia. The returning flood of discharged workers and the financial disaster that they represented would no doubt underline the message, and would also probably offer an opportunity to infiltrate numerous revolutionary activists into Egypt.

Thirdly, the Saudi revolutionaries would adopt a posture of extreme hostility to the United States and to Israel, in the Iranian manner, and of close comradeship with the Palestine Liberation Organization, Syria and Libya. These steps would be designed to put Egypt's relationship with Israel under added pressure and perhaps to encourage an Israeli-Syrian war, on the theory (long familiar in some radical circles) that escalation of the Arab-Israeli struggle would accelerate the process of radicalization of Arab politics and the international isolation of Israel. Certainly such escalation would severely jeopardize the security of the Sadat regime.

How would Egyptian society respond to such a campaign? It cannot be denied that, coming from Saudi Arabia as well as from Libya and Iran, it would constitute a powerful force. In particular, the dismissal of Egyptian workers and the realization that the Saudi financial pipeline was closed off would add up to a tremendous blow at public morale in Egypt, probably enough to destroy the credit of the regime.

If other Arab states were to follow the lead and also send Egyptian workers home forthwith, the overall result would be catastrophic. With a total of at least 1.5 million Egyptian workers deprived of livelihood, not only would the effect on Egypt's balance of payments be devastating but so too would the social effect inside Egypt. The workers include people at all levels of Egyptian society, representing—on account of their earnings in the oil countries—the most privileged 10 to 15 percent of the national work force. Not only would Egyptians at present employed abroad be affected, but so too would an indeterminate number of others who had hoped to follow them one day.

Thus the crisis would be at once on the level of national finance and on the levels of social welfare and public psychology. At best, phased in over a period of several years, such an action would progressively introduce depression and discontent into Egypt that would be very difficult for the government to cope with; carried out all at once, it would create a first-class disaster. It could well trigger an armed assault by Egypt on one or another of her neighbors, once again with little regard for "rationality", such as an armed invasion of Libya or a bombing run over Saudi oil installations; but sooner or later it would be likely to lead to revolution inside Egypt.

But what kind of revolution? It is easy on the face of it to imagine that because of the dire character of the challenge—a Khomeinist Saudi Arabia and a mortal challenge to Egypt's national livelihood—the Egyptian response should somehow be on a similar primordial level, that is, an Islamic fundamentalist explosion matching that of the Saudis, which would introduce the austere autarkic regime of Scenario III. This is assuredly within the range of possibilities, but we should not lightly assume it. There are many countervailing forces in Egyptian society always on hand to suppress or to pre-empt outbursts of popular feeling: the armed forces, the police, the bureaucracy, the secularist professional classes, the national political culture that values moderation, order and control. These elements are deeply rooted in Egypt, as they have not been in Iran or in Saudi Arabia.

Therefore, whether for the sake of restoring an atmosphere of purpose to governmental policy, or simply of forestalling a takeover by "irrational" elements, a military coup similar to that of 1952 may be the most realistic response to the crisis for us to anticipate. As in 1952, a high degree of subsurface turbulence, on the part of social groups much more disaffected with the regime than those who wound up seizing power, would be obscured from the world's view by a pre-emptive coup. A series of pragmatic moves designed to nip in the bud the expulsion of Egyptian labor from various Arab countries might begin with emergency appeals to Iraq, Algeria, Syria, Libya, and possibly the Gulf states themselves, and then continue with a sustained effort to cultivate Iraqi friendship and to capitalize on a secular nationalist alternative to religious fundamentalism. In time, the new Egyptian regime would try to develop its own program of reforms, its own progressive ethos, and an organized popular following. These, of course, are the ingredients of Nasirism, and it is in a new Nasirist era that Egypt might eventually find herself.

NOTES

1. Not surprisingly, Marxist discussion of the open door policy and the revival of capitalism in Egypt sees this class as a consequence of the inadequacies of Nasirist socialism, which because of its incompleteness was aborted after the 1967 war. See Fuʾad Mursi, *Hadha al-infitah al-iqtisadi* [This Economic 'Opening'!], (Cairo: Dar al-Thaqafa al-Jadida, 1976), Chap. 4. See also Gouda Abdel Khalek, "Aham dalalat al-infitah..." [The Most Important Implications of Infitah with Regard to the Structural Transformations in the Egyptian Economy, 1971–1977] in Société Egyptienne d'Economie Politique, de Statistique et de Législation, *Al-Iqtisad al-Misri fi rubᶜ qarn...* [The Egyptian Economy in Quarter of a Century, 1952–1977: Papers and Discussions of the Third Conference of Egyptian Economists], ed. by Ismaᶜil Sabriᶜ Abdallah et al. (Cairo: Haiʾat al-Kitab, 1977), p. 366.

2. For a negative assessment of foreign investment potential in the Egyptian economy under the open door policy see ᶜAli Al-Gritli, *Khamsa wa ᶜishrun ᶜaman: dirasa tahliliyya li al-siyasat al-iqtisadiyya fi misr* [An Analytical Study of Economic Policies in Egypt in Twenty-five Years], (Cairo: Haiʾat al-Kitab, 1977), p. 288.

3. Marie-Christiane Aulas, "La provocante 'modernisation' de l'économie égyptienne", *Le Monde Diplomatique,* March 1979, pp. 6–7.

4. A middle range estimate based on a 1968 National Planning Institute study; other alternative estimates were 55 million and 71 million. John Waterbury, "The Wages of Dependency", in A. L. Udovitch, ed., *The Middle East: Oil, Conflict and Hope* (Lexington, Mass.: Lexington Books, 1976), p. 298.

5. The widespread acceptance of high technology as the sacrosanct basis of development in Egypt and in Third World countries generally is sharply criticized, and a Chinese type of model advocated, by Saad Eddin Ibrahim, "Nahwa nazariyya sosiolojiyya li al-tanmiya fi al-ᶜalam al-thalith", in Société Egyptienne d'Economie Politique..., *Istratijiyyat al-tanmiya fi misr* [Development Strategy in Egypt], ed., Ismaᶜil Sabri ᶜAbdallah et al., (Cairo: Haiʾat al-Kitab, 1978), pp. 53–81. See also the chapter by Ismaᶜil Sabri ᶜAbdallah, "Istratijiyyat al-tiknulujiya" [Technology Strategies] in *The Egyptian Economy in Quarter of a Century...,* op.cit., pp. 227–250. The Maoist argument in favor of appropriate technology in Egypt was introduced as early as 1964 against the Nasir regime by Hassan Riad (pseud.), *L'Egypte nassérienne* (Paris: Ed. de Minuit, 1964).

6. See Nazih N. M. Ayubi, *Bureaucracy and Politics in Contemporary Egypt* (London: Ithaca Press, 1980).

7. See Michael Lipton, *Why Poor People Stay Poor: Urban Bias in World Development* (Cambridge: Harvard University Press, 1979).

Index

The Contributors

MALCOLM H. KERR is Professor of Political Science at the University of California, Los Angeles. From 1979 to 1981 he was Director of the University of California Study Center at the American University in Cairo.

EL SAYED YASSIN has been the Director of the Centre for Political and Strategic Studies, Al-Ahram Foundation, Cairo, since 1975. From 1957 to 1975 he served as research fellow in the National Centre for Social and Criminological Research in Cairo.

SAAD EDDIN IBRAHIM is Professor of Sociology at the American University in Cairo, and Head of the Arab Affairs Unit at the Centre for Political and Strategic Studies in Cairo. In 1980 he was a Visiting Professor and Research Sociologist at the University of California, Los Angeles.

GEORGES SABAGH is Professor of Sociology at the University of California, Los Angeles.

ESSAM MONTASSER is Director of the United Nations African Institute for Economic Development and Planning in Dakar, Senegal. From 1978 to 1980 he was Visiting Associate Professor of Economics at the American University in Cairo.

JESWALD W. SALACUSE is Dean and Professor of Law, School of Law, Southern Methodist University, Dallas, Texas.

HAZEM EL-BEBLAWI is Director of the Economics Department of the Industrial Bank of Kuwait, on leave from the University of Alexandria where he is Professor of Economics. He was Lecturer and Research Economist at the University of California, Los Angeles in 1979.

NAIEM A. SHERBINY is an economist and ISMAIL SERAGELDIN is a planner with the World Bank in Washington, D.C.

GOUDA ABDEL-KHALEK is Associate Professor of Economics at Cairo University. From 1980 to 1981 he was deputy leader of the IBRD Core Planning Team at the Kuwait Ministry of Planning.

GALAL AHMAD AMIN is Professor of Economics at the American University in Cairo. Until 1978 he was with the Kuwait Fund for Arab Economic Development, and was a Visiting Professor and Research Economist at the University of California, Los Angeles in 1978–79.

ALI E. HILLAL DESSOUKI is Associate Professor of Political Science at Cairo University, and Head of the Political Systems Unit at the Centre for Political and Strategic Studies in Cairo. He was a Visiting Associate Professor and Research Political Scientist at the University of California, Los Angeles, in 1980.

NAZÎH N. M. AYUBI has been Visiting Associate Professor of Political Science at the University of California, Los Angeles, since 1979. He has taught at Cairo University and at the American University in Cairo, and has also been a Fellow at the Centre for Political and Strategic Studies, Cairo.

PAUL JABBER is Associate Professor of Political Science at the University of California, Los Angeles.